Florida
ALMANAC
2012
Edited by Bernie McGovern

PELICAN PUBLISHING COMPANY
Gretna 2012

First published 1983 by
Pelican Publishing Company, Inc., as the "Fifth Edition"
Fifth edition: 1983-84
Sixth edition: 1986-87
Seventh edition: 1988-89
Eighth edition: 1990-91
Ninth edition: 1992-93
Tenth edition: 1995-96
Eleventh edition: 1997-98
Twelfth edition: 1998-99
Thirteenth edition: 1999-2000
Fourteenth edition: 2000-2001
Fifteenth edition: 2002-2003
Sixteenth edition: 2004-2005
Seventeenth edition: 2007-2008
Eighteenth edition: 2012

ISSN: 0361-9796
ISBN: 978-1-58980-846-1
e-book ISBN: 978-1-45561-553-7
*The 2012 edition has been updated
by the editors of Pelican Publishing Company, Inc.,
and any errors made by them
are their responsibility.*

Printed in the United States of America

Published by Pelican Publishing Company, Inc.
1000 Burmaster Street, Gretna, Louisiana 70053

CONTENTS

PREFACE

The *Florida Almanac,* now in its eighteenth edition, was first produced in 1972 in response to a newspaper editor's complaint about the lack of one source for information on the state. Subsequent editions have grown to reflect Florida's increasing population, laws, university enrollments, sports activities, zip codes, and landmarks.

Over the years this almanac has become the most widely used and quoted reference book about the state. It is now an essential part of any family, academic, corporate, and political reference shelf.

The *Florida Almanac* also is much used in the North by people planning to relocate to the state. They are eager to learn all about their exciting future home.

We thank the many people whose interest in the state has prompted them to purchase each of the previous seventeen editions so that they may stay on top of new developments. To those of you who are reading the *Florida Almanac* for the first time, we can promise that you will find much useful and fascinating information contained in these pages.

The Editors

INTRODUCTION

THE SUNSHINE STATE

Florida is a peninsula of superlatives, geographically and socially. For example:

• Florida is the youngest part of the continental United States—the nation's last landmass, say geologists, to emerge from the ocean.

• With 54 inches annually, Florida is second only to Louisiana in rainfall, yet it is in the same latitudinal belt as the great Sahara and Arabian deserts.

• The state has more than 700 springs, including 33 first-magnitude springs, which are defined as discharging at least 100 cubic feet of water per second. The springs give Florida the highest concentration of underground fresh water in the world.

• Within the state's boundaries are 7,800 lakes, the largest being the 448,000-acre Lake Okeechobee, the nation's second largest freshwater lake wholly within the U.S.

• Florida's southern tip is only 1,700 miles from the Equator, yet two-thirds of the nation's population is within a two-day drive of the state.

• The state's 58,560 square miles make it larger than England and Wales combined, and if the Continental Shelf around Florida were raised by just 500 feet, Florida would double in size.

• Because Jacksonville is directly south of Cleveland and Pensacola directly south of Chicago, Florida is more a Midwestern than an Eastern state, yet all but a portion of the Panhandle is in the Eastern Time Zone.

• The state misses being within the Tropic Zone by less than 100 miles.

• Florida lightning packs more punch than lightning anywhere else, a robust bolt sending out an average current of 45,000 amps, enough to momentarily supply the electrical needs of 300 homes.

• Cities in the Panhandle may record two dozen days a year of below-freezing temperatures, but, 800 miles to the south, the Miami airport has recorded only four winter seasons of freezing temperatures since 1952.

• Florida is the nation's fourth most populous state, with an estimated 17.8 million people, yet nearly half of the state is covered with uninhabited forests.

• Regions such as Tampa/St. Petersburg have an unusually high number of days with thunderstorms, more than 100, yet St. Petersburg, between 1967 and 1969, registered a record 768 consecutive days of sunshine.

• Florida, over the centuries, has belonged to five different nations—Spain, England, France, the Confederacy, and the United States.

• Eight Indian tribes—the Timucuan, Tocobaga, Apalachee, Tequesta, Calusa, Ais, Seminole and Miccosukee—have called Florida their home.

• The state has 34 major rivers, including the famous Suwannee and the unusual north-flowing St. Johns.

• More available groundwater flows beneath Florida than under any other state, all of it stored in major aquifers.

• Florida beaches, if arranged to lie in a straight line, would extend 1,800 miles.

• Since 1955, nearly two-thirds of Florida's new residents have moved to the state from New York, Ohio, New Jersey, Pennsylvania, Illinois, Michigan, and Georgia.

Undeniably, Florida stands out among North American locales as uniquely blessed with natural resources, a sensational climate, and a rich history. Such amenities, no doubt, explain why the state's growth seemed to know no bounds. For the decade, Florida kept growing, its population increasing 17.6 percent. But in 2009, the unthinkable happened. With the collapse of the national, and the state, economy, Florida's growth came to a screeching halt. Indeed, Florida lost population for the first time since 1946, losing 26 residents a day, net. In 2010, however, the streak began again, although amounting to just 54 net new residents each day. It was a far cry from the more than 1,100 people who became Floridians every day in 2007 but it was a start.

CLIMATE AND WEATHER

Florida's official nickname, the "Sunshine State," reflects the economic importance of climate to its visitors and residents. Often called Florida's most important natural resource, the climate is usually pleasant and uniform. General climatic conditions range from a zone of transition between temperate and sub-tropical conditions in the extreme northern interior to the tropical climate found in the Florida Keys. The chief factors affecting the state's climate are latitude, proximity to the currents of the Atlantic Ocean and the Gulf of Mexico, and numerous inland lakes.

Summers throughout the state are long, warm, and relatively humid. Winters, although punctuated with periodic invasions of cool to occasionally cold air, are mild due to the southerly latitude (between 24° 20' and 31°N) and relatively warm adjacent seawaters.

Coastal areas in all sections of Florida average slightly warmer temperatures in winter and cooler ones in summer than do inland points at the same latitude. The Gulf Stream, which flows around the western tip of Cuba through the Florida Straits and northward around the lower east coast, exerts a warming influence to the southern east coast because of the prevailing easterly winds in that area.

TEMPERATURE

In winter, southern Florida is one of the warmest places on the United States mainland. Summers generally are hot throughout the state, although sea breezes tend to modify the climate along the coastal areas. Even though southern Florida is 400 miles closer to the tropics than northern Florida, it has fewer hot days each summer because of the sea breezes. Summer heat is tempered in all areas by frequent afternoon or early evening thunderstorms. These showers, which occur on the average of about half of the summer days, are accompanied frequently by a rapid 10- to 20-degree drop in temperature, resulting in comfortable weather for the remainder of the day.

Because most of the large-scale wind patterns affecting Florida have passed over water surfaces, hot drying winds seldom occur.

AVERAGE ANNUAL TEMPERATURES FOR SELECTED LOCATIONS		
Location	Minimum	Maximum
Daytona Beach	61	80
Fort Lauderdale	67	84
Fort Myers	64	84
Gainesville	58	82
Jacksonville	59	79
Key West	73	83
Lakeland	64	82
Melbourne	63	81
Miami	69	83
Naples	64	85
Ocala	59	83
Orlando	62	83
Pensacola	59	77
St. Petersburg	66	82
Sarasota	62	83
Tallahassee	56	79
Tampa	63	82
West Palm Beach	67	83

The highest recorded temperature was 109 degrees at Monticello, in North Florida, on June 29, 1931. The lowest recorded temperature was 2 degrees below zero, 30 miles away at Tallahassee on February 13, 1899.

In Florida, more people die from excessive heat than from lightning. Medical experts explain that the human body temperature rises dangerously when hot days combine with high relative humidity because perspiration cannot evaporate and cool the body.

A National Weather Service Heat Index chart defines how hot the weather is on a given day. The chart combines Fahrenheit air temperature and relative humidity.

HEAT INDEX CHART

Percentage of Relative Humidity

		30	35	40	45	50	55	60	65	70	75	80	85	90	95

APPARENT TEMPERATURE

		30	35	40	45	50	55	60	65	70	75	80	85	90	95
T															
E	115	135	143	151											
M	110	123	130	137	143	150									
P	105	113	118	123	129	135	142	149							
E	100	104	107	110	115	120	126	132	138	144					
R	95	96	98	101	104	107	110	114	119	124	130	136			
A	90	90	91	93	95	96	98	100	102	106	109	113	117	122	
T	85	84	85	86	87	88	89	90	91	93	95	97	99	102	105
U	80	78	79	79	80	81	81	82	83	85	86	86	87	88	89
R	75	73	73	74	74	75	75	76	76	77	77	78	78	79	79
E	70	67	67	68	68	69	69	70	70	70	70	71	71	71	71

The chart's apparent temperatures are readings in shady, light-wind conditions. For full sunshine, calculate a 15-degree increase.

Elderly persons and small children, or persons who are on certain medications, overweight, or have an alcohol habit are particularly vulnerable to heat stress.

Symptoms and treatment of various levels of heat stress are:

Sunburn—Skin redness, swelling, pain, blisters, fever, and headaches. Ointments help mild cases; more severe sunburns should receive medical help.

Cramping—Occurs in legs and occasionally in the abdomen. Gentle massage may help, as do sips of mild salt water (teaspoon of salt to 8 oz. of water). If persistent, see a doctor.

Heat Exhaustion—Marked by profuse sweating, weak pulse, and severe fatigue. Skin may appear pale and feel cold and clammy. Fainting and vomiting signal greater severity. Person should be moved to cool location, preferably air-conditioned, where cool compresses should be applied. Continuing symptoms require medical attention.

Sunstroke—High (106°) temperature, rapid and strong pulse, and hot, dry skin. Once a victim is moved to a cool location, medical help should be summoned while cool, wet compresses are applied. This condition can be fatal.

FROST

Although average minimum temperatures during the coolest months range from the middle 40s in the north to the middle 50s in the south, no place on the mainland is entirely safe from frost or freezing. With few exceptions, these cold waves seldom last more than two or three consecutive days. It is rare for temperatures to remain below freezing throughout the day anywhere in the state. On the first night of a cold wave there usually is considerable wind which, because of the continual mixing of the air, prevents marked temperature differences between high and low ground. By the second night, winds usually have subsided and radiational cooling under clear skies accelerates the temperature drop after sundown.

Some winters, often several in succession, pass without widespread freezing in the southern areas. The most distressing winters to the agriculture industry are those with more than one severe cold wave, interspersed with periods of relative warmth. The later freezes almost always find vegetation in a tender stage of new growth.

Noteworthy cold spells of the 20th century were in January 1905, December 1906, December 1909, February 1917, January 1928, December 1934, January 1940, February 1947, the winter of 1957-58, December 1962, January 1977, January 1981, January 1982, Christmas 1983, January 1985, and Christmas 1989. It was the 1962 freeze that killed many tropical palms and Australian pines throughout the central part of the state, but the most severe freezes recorded in the state were those of 1894, 1895, 1899, 1983, 1985, and 1989.

One of the longest and most widespread freezes occurred at Christmas in 1989. Freezing temperatures penetrated as far south as Miami. Falling snow and sleet on Dec. 23 forced the closing of icy interstate highways and airports in most of north and central Florida. The freezing temperatures and fallen snow lingered through Dec. 25, causing power outages statewide.

HUMIDITY AND FOG

Florida's humid climate is attributed to the fact that no point in the state is more than 60 miles from salt water and no more than 345 feet above sea level.

Humidity is the degree of wetness or dryness of the air and is measured by a percentage ratio called "relative humidity." This is a ratio of the amount of moisture and temperature at a given spot to the maximum amount (99 percent) of moisture that could be contained by the same air at the same spot. The warmer the air becomes, the more moisture it can hold. Therefore a person can feel stickier on a warm day with 80 percent humidity than on a cold day with the same humidity.

The climate of Florida is humid. Inland areas with greater temperature extremes enjoy slightly lower relative humidity, especially during hot weather. On the average, variations in relative humidity from one place to another are small.

Heavy fog is usually confined to the night and early morning hours when the humidity range is about 85 to 95 percent. Fog is more prevalent in the late fall, winter, and early spring months. It occurs, on the average, about 35 to 40 days per year over the extreme northern portion; 25 to 30 days per year in the central portion; and less than 10 days per year in the extreme southern areas. Fog usually dissipates soon after sunrise. Heavy daytime fog is seldom observed in the state.

AIR QUALITY

Florida is one of just three states, and the only highly urbanized state, east of the Mississippi that meets all National Ambient Air Quality Standards established by the U.S. Environmental Protection Agency. On a typical Florida day, the Air Quality Index throughout the state, including its major metropolitan areas, stands at "Good," the highest ranking on the federal scale. Three areas of Florida–Cape Coral-Fort Myers on the West Coast, Port St. Lucie-Fort Pierce on the East Coast, and Tallahassee in North Florida–are considered to be among those places having the nation's cleanest air.

PREVAILING WINDS

Prevailing winds over the southern peninsula are southeast and east. Over the remainder of the state, wind directions are influenced locally by convectional forces inland and the sea breeze, from the west in the morning, the east in the afternoon. Consequently, prevailing directions are somewhat erratic but, in general, follow a pattern of northerly in winter and southerly in summer. March and April are, on average, the windiest months. High local winds of short duration occur occasionally with thunderstorms in summer and with cold fronts moving across the state in other seasons. Average annual wind speed in Florida is 8.3 miles per hour.

RAINFALL

The state's rainfall is varied both in annual amount and in seasonal distribution. Individual rainfall measuring stations have annual averages from about 50 to 65 inches. In the Florida Keys, annual averages are only about 40 inches. The main areas of high annual rainfall are in the extreme northwestern counties and at the southeastern end of the peninsula. Many localities have received more than 100 inches in a calendar year. In contrast, most localities received less than 40 inches in a calendar year.

Although the state average rainfall is 53 inches (averaging 150 billion gallons of water daily), evaporation reduces the "available" rainfall amount to about 40 inches annually.

In the summer "rainy season," there is close to a 50-50 chance some rain will fall on a given day. During the remainder of the year, the chances are much less, some rain being likely on one or two days per week. The seasonal distribution changes somewhat from north to south. In the northwestern counties or Panhandle, there are two wet periods: late winter or early spring, and again during summer, and one pronounced low point, October-November. A secondary low point occurs in April and May. On the peninsula, the most striking features of the seasonal distribution are the dominance of summer rainfall (generally more than half the average annual total falls in the four-month period June through September) and the rather abrupt start and end of the summer "rainy season."

Most localities have at some time experienced two-hour rainfalls in excess of three inches, and 24-hour amounts of near or greater than 10 inches.

The chart shows the wind chill factor for exposed skin, your face, for example, on a brisk, windy day. To read the chart, find the air temperature on the top line, then locate the wind speed in the column on the left. Follow the wind speed line over to the temperature column and read the approximate chill on your bare skin.

WIND CHILL

Temperature (Fahrenheit)

		5	40	35	30	25	20	15	10	5	0	-5
W	10	36	31	25	19	17	7	1	-5	-11	-15
I	15	32	25	19	13	6	0	-7	-13	-19	-26
N	20	30	24	17	11	4	-2	-9	-15	-22	-29
D	25	29	23	16	9	3	-4	-11	-17	-24	-31
	30	28	22	15	8	1	-5	-12	-19	-26	-33
M	35	28	21	14	7	0	-7	-14	-21	-27	-34
P	40	27	29	13	6	-1	-8	-15	-22	-29	-36
H	45	26	19	12	5	-2	-9	-16	-23	-30	-37
	50	26	19	12	4	-3	-10	-17	-24	-31	-38
	55	25	18	11	4	-3	-11	-18	-25	-32	-39
	60	25	17	10	3	-4	-11	-19	-26	-33	-40

AVERAGE ANNUAL RAINFALL
Record 24-Hour Rainfalls

Year	Location	Amount (inches)
1941	Trenton	30
1950	Yankeetown	38.7
1950	Cedar Key	34
1969	Fernandina Beach	22
1980	Key West	23.3

The above totals, with the exception of the Fernandina Beach figure, occurred in connection with a tropical disturbance or hurricane. Maximum daily rainfall has been reported in all months except December, but more than 60 percent of extreme rainfall has occurred in September and October.

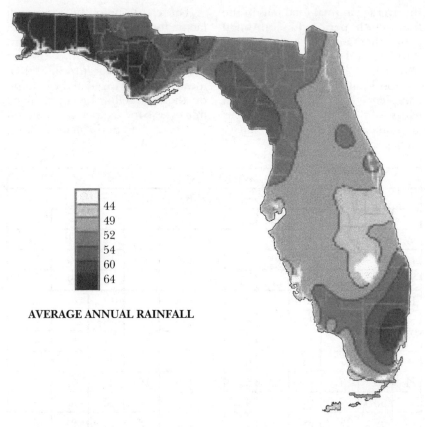

| 44 |
| 49 |
| 52 |
| 54 |
| 60 |
| 64 |

AVERAGE ANNUAL RAINFALL

THUNDERSTORMS

Florida is the thunderstorm capital of the nation. A study by the National Oceanic and Atmospheric Administration shows Fort Myers averages 100 days with lightning annually, the Tampa Bay area, 90, and Miami, 76. The so-called "lightning belt" in Florida is an area from between Orlando and Tampa south along the west coast to Fort Myers and east to Lake Okeechobee. One study revealed 120 days of thunderstorms occurred in one year within a 50-mile radius of Tampa.

Few of the state's thunderstorms last more than two hours. They are attributed to hot, wet air close to the ground combined with an unstable atmosphere. An average lightning bolt lasts just a thousandth of a second and packs around 30,000 degrees Fahrenheit in a one-inch channel that can deliver a shock in the 6,000-25,000-amp range. But Florida's lightning frequently packs a walloping 45,000 amperes. Researchers believe Florida lightning is particularly powerful because it is born of tall, more highly charged storm-cloud formations.

The state has the nation's worst record of deaths by lightning, with storms occurring nearly every day from June to September, usually in the afternoon. Since 1960, lightning has killed an annual average of 10 and injured 45 in Florida. Lightning is the leading weather cause of death in Florida, responsible for more than half of all such fatalities.

Florida Lightning Deaths	
Location	Percentage
In an open field	27%
Under a tree	13%
On water	25%
Using heavy equipment	6%
On a golf course	3%
Unknown or unreported	25%

Lightning injuries to trees appear to be governed by the voltage of the charge, the moisture content of the tree, and the species of the tree. "Hot" bolts—those with temperatures above 25,000 degrees—will make an entire tree burst into flames; "cold" lightning can make a tree explode, as it strikes at 20,000 miles per second. Tall trees or those growing alone in open areas, and trees with roots in moist soils or those growing along water, are most likely to be struck.

Some species are more resistant to lightning strikes than others. Commonly hit are oak, pine, and maple. Experts point out that trees high in oil, such as birch and beech, are poor conductors of electricity, but oaks and pines have high starch contents, making them good conductors. Deep-rooted and decaying trees also appear more susceptible to lightning. Some trees are known to have been hit by lightning up to seven times.

Experts suggest the following precautions be taken during a thunderstorm:

1. Avoid using electrical appliances, especially the telephone. Lightning can strike telephone lines and utility poles and the current may be carried through the wires.

2. Avoid water—whether it's in the shower, at the beach, or out on a boat. Water conducts electricity and lightning tends to strike the highest point on a plain. Your boat or your body could be the highest point on a level area. If you are out on your boat, take extra precautions and head for a protected shoreline or marina if possible.

3. If outside, especially on a golf course or other open area such as a ball field, seek shelter anywhere but under trees. These are primary lightning targets. If no shelter is available, lie low in the deepest ground depression around.

4. Never hold onto any lightning attractants such as golf clubs, metal tennis rackets, or fishing poles. Avoid proximity to other electrical conductors such as wire fences, clotheslines, or metal pipes.

5. If riding in a car, stay inside but avoid touching any metal parts.

6. A tingling sensation or your hair standing out from your head may indicate a bolt is close to striking nearby. Drop to the ground and lie flat.

7. Be aware of the lightning season—July to August is the peak period—and schedule outdoor activities for times other than the mid-afternoon, when most thunderstorms occur.

8. In the event someone is struck by lightning, cardiopulmonary resuscitation must be administered immediately.

FROST LINES

Average dates of first and last killing frosts in Florida.

SNOW

Snowfall in Florida is rare. The greatest recorded snowfalls in Florida occurred on the same date, February 13, in 1899 and 1958. In 1899, four inches were measured at Lake Butler in Union County, and one-half inch at Bartow in Polk County. In 1958, most of Florida west of the Suwannee River received two to three inches of snow while areas east of the river and north of about Latitude 30 degrees measured one to two inches. Three inches measured at Tallahassee in February 1958 is the greatest ever recorded there since records began in 1886.

It's doubtful, however, that Florida ever experienced as wide-ranging a snowfall as occurred in the winter of 1977. Recorded as the most consistently cold January on record, the first month of that year saw the appearance of snow all the way from the Georgia border into Miami. Traces were measured in Broward and Miami-Dade counties, in Palm Beach, and in Miami Beach for the first time. A half-inch was measured in the Tampa Bay area, and an inch in St. Augustine and parts of Volusia County. Snow and sleet fell on three different days during that month in 1977 in Jacksonville. And in Fort Myers, recordkeepers recorded snowflakes during that spell for only the fourth time in its history. Pensacola also measured an inch, and Orlando reported snow on two consecutive days. Florida's most recent snowfall came with sleet to Northeast and Central Florida, the Jacksonville and Orlando areas, on January 9, 2010.

DROUGHT

Drought is a prolonged period of below normal or expected precipitation. The annual cycle of temperature and rainfall leads to seasonal droughts in many areas of the state. Drought conditions in south Florida occur every year that winter rainfall is even slightly below normal. In north Florida, a seasonal drought occurs most often in fall and spring.

A study of several regions of the state from 1980 to 1982, when compared against a 30-year mean (1951-1980), revealed a decline in rainfall for the Pensacola, Tallahassee, Jacksonville, and Lake Okeechobee areas. By contrast, that same study revealed a rise in rainfall for the Fort Myers and West Palm Beach areas.

The most severe lack of rainfall was recorded for the Pensacola area during the years 1889-94, when three consecutive years recorded less than 45 inches of rainfall. Florida's latest drought began in 1998, with the year 2000 being the state's driest on record. The return of El Nino rains in 2002 brought rainfall, rivers, aquifers, and lakes back to normal, or near normal, levels.

EARTHQUAKES

Florida is relatively free of earthquakes, thanks to the limestone base that supports the land and tends to act as a shock absorber for any subterranean shifting that might occur.

Nevertheless more than 30 earthquakes have been recorded in the state although most have been attributed to disruptions of the earth far from the peninsula. The earliest recorded earthquake occurred on May 8, 1781, when a tremor described as severe hit a military installation at Pensacola. No one was injured but a home was leveled. The event followed what was described as a minor tremor the year before. A more widespread event occurred on January 12, 1879, when two severe shocks, each lasting approximately 30 seconds, rocked most of the peninsula and caused some structure damage in Tallahassee, Jacksonville, St. Augustine, Daytona, Tampa and Fort Myers, and all areas in between. It is now believed to have been centered near Palatka, making it the only earthquake to originate in the state although in 1935 two short tremors, the second lasting 15 seconds, sent Palatka residents fleeing from their homes. Two other verified tremors, according to University of Florida seismologists, occurred in 1973 and 1975 in the Daytona and Sanford areas when the earth's crust made a minor adjustment.

Notable earthquakes felt in Florida but not centered in the state include a two-day 1880 quake in Cuba, which rocked Key West and the famous 1886 Charleston, South Carolina, event, which was felt on the Northeast Florida coast. In 2006, a 5.8 quake centered 250 miles south of Apalachicola and 250 miles west of Anna Maria in the Gulf of Mexico was recorded and felt but raised little general notice.

Florida has no active faults, no emerging volcanoes, and no growing mountain ranges, which are the geological prerequisites to most major earthquake activity.

TORNADOES

April, May, and June are considered peak periods for tornadoes. Florida, with 20 twisters a year, ranks eighth in the nation's annual numbers of tornadoes. Fortunately, many of Florida's tornadoes are the weaker, waterspout type of storm. The more severe tornadoes, associated with a squall line, occur mainly in Florida's Panhandle during February and March.

Tornadoes can surpass hurricanes in deadly force. The counterclockwise, upward movement of air within the twister causes rapid expansion, cooling, and condensation, which contribute to the formation of the dark cloud of the tornado funnel. A tornado is seen most often in muggy, oppressive weather when large thunderstorms are apparent. Rain, hail, and flashes of lightning may precede the storm. Inside the funnel, air pressure is so low it can cause structures to explode. Destructive paths of tornadoes average about a quarter-mile wide and 16 miles long, although many in Florida are shorter. Tornadoes travel from southwest to northeast.

If tornado conditions are present, weather forecasters will issue warnings or watches on emergency broadcasting stations. A "tornado watch" means tornadoes and severe thunderstorms are possible in the area; a "tornado warning" means a tornado has been detected in the area.

Hurricanes also generate tornadoes. 2004's Hurricane Ivan, for instance, spawned more than 90 verifiable tornadoes that may, or may not, have accounted for five deaths in the panhandle.

Tornado Categories

Tornadoes in the United States are measured on the Enhanced Fujita Scale, the EF Scale, replacing the Fujita Scale in 2007. The EF Scale better aligns tornado wind speeds with associated damage.

Category	Wind Speed Mph	Relative Frequency	Potential Damage
EF-0	65-85	53.50%	Minor
EF-1	86-110	31.60%	Moderate
EF-2	111-135	10.70%	Considerable
EF-3	136-165	3.40%	Severe
EF-4	166-200	0.70%	Extreme
EF-5	More than 200	less than 0.1%	Total

The first use of the new system came on February 2, 2007, in Florida when a super cell produced three tornadoes beginning shortly after 3 a.m. that cut a 70-mile swath across Central Florida's Sumter, Lake, and Volusia counties. The siege, lasting more than an hour, killed 21, destroyed more than 500 structures, and damaged 1,500 others. The event was rated EF-3 or "Severe."

Fortunately, most Florida tornadoes are recorded as doing no more than minor or moderate damage. Over water, a tornado takes the form of a waterspout. It is safe boating practice to stay away from any thunderstorm cell, especially any so-called "anvil-shaped" clouds whose level bases can form the deadly swirling winds.

If a tornado is spotted, move away from it. Persons in open country should seek a depression and hide inside it. In a house, residents are advised to open windows to help balance the air pressure and then move to a secure location such as a bathroom or another room centrally situated within the house.

Florida Tornado Deaths		
1882	Gadsden-Baker Counties	6
1892	Orange County	1
1901	Miami	1
1909	Polk County	1
1917	Hillsborough County	1
1925	Miami	5
1926	Palm Beach County	1
1928	Lake County	1
1929	Duval County	1
1932	Escambia County	1
1934	Escambia-Alachua Counties	2
1936	Washington County	7
1939	Jacksonville	4
1941	Marion County	1
1945	Leon County	1
1947	Franklin County	2
1948	Gadsden County	2
1951	Franklin County	3
1954	St. Lucie County	2
1958	Palm Beach County	1
1959	Orange County	1
1960	Lee County	1
1962	Okaloosa-Santa Rosa Counties	18
1966	Tampa-Lakeland-Davenport	11
1967	Okaloosa-Bay Counties	2
1968	Charlotte and Collier Counties	4
1972	Okeechobee-Hendry and Jackson Counties	8
1973	Okaloosa County	1

Florida Tornado Deaths		
1974	Gadsden County	1
1975	Bay and Marion Counties	2
1976	Pinellas County	1
1977	Putnam County	1
1978	Pinellas County	3
1979	Polk County	1
1980	Broward County	1
1982	Hendry and Okeechobee Counties	2
1983	Highlands and Citrus Counties	4
1985	Venice	2
1986	Hillsborough County	1
1987	Mount Dora	1
1988	Madison County	1
1989	Franklin County	3
1992	Pinellas County	4
1993	Levy and Alachua-Lake Counties	5
1994	Brevard County	1
1995	Marion, Okaloosa, and Gadsden Counties	3
1996	Putnam and Okeechobee Counties	2
1997	Hillsborough County	1
1998	Winter Garden-Kissimmee-Daytona	42
2003	Miami	1
2004	Bay, Santa Rosa, and Calhoun Counties	7
2007	Sumter, Lake, and Volusia Counties	21
2008	Columbia County	1

HURRICANES

Florida and other Gulf and Atlantic coastal states lie in the general path of tropical hurricanes. Most of these vicious storms spawn in the Caribbean Sea or in an area east of the Lesser Antilles in the Atlantic Ocean.

Florida's vulnerability varies with the progress of the hurricane season. August and early September tropical storms normally approach the state from the east or southeast, but as the season progresses into late September and October, the region of maximum hurricane activity concerning Florida shifts to the western Caribbean. Most storms that move into Florida approach from the south or southwest, entering the Keys, the Miami area, or along the west coast.

Caused by wind rushing toward a low-pressure area, hurricanes take the form of huge doughnuts. In the Northern Hemisphere, high winds revolve counterclockwise around a calm center or "eye." The movement is clockwise in the Southern Hemisphere.

The lowest sea level pressure ever recorded in an Atlantic storm was 882 mb, recorded by Hurricane Wilma on Oct. 19, 2005. It broke the record of 1988's Hurricane Gilbert that stood at 888 mb. Wilma formed as a tropical depression October 15 southwest of Jamaica. It became a tropical storm two days later and was named Wilma, the first storm to reach "W" since alphabetized names for storms was introduced in 1950. Moving slowly northwest, it became the 12th hurricane of the season on Oct. 18. It began that day as a tropical storm, but in the afternoon, the storm's pressure began to drop at an unprecedented rate, diving 90 mb in 24 hours. In the same period it went from a storm to not just a hurricane but a Category 5 hurricane with sustained winds climbing in the same period from 70 mph to 185 mph. Its intensity was underscored by the size of its eye, which shrank to less than two miles in diameter, one of the smallest eyes ever recorded. It was on that day, Oct. 19, that the pressure fell to the record low. Winds slackened slightly late that night, reducing it to a Category 4 storm. But even in that category, Wilma remained unprecedented, the first Category 4 storm with a pressure below 900 mb. As a 4 or a 5, Wilma was the most intense hurricane in recorded history. Wilma made landfall Oct. 21 on the resort coast of Mexico's Yucatan Peninsula with winds of 150 mph. Some areas endured hurricane winds for more than 24 hours. On Oct. 23, Wilma exited the Yucatan and entered the Gulf of Mexico as a Category 2 storm. But it reintensified to a 3, veered east, and made landfall again in Southwest Florida the following day, flooding the Naples metropolitan area, severely damaging the Everglades, and, undeterred, slamming its now 35-mile wide eye into the Miami-Ft. Lauderdale-Palm Beach metropolitan area causing heavy damage throughout. Its storm surge also flooded Key West and the keys. It entered the Atlantic, reintensified to a Category 3 over the Gulf Stream, and hit the Bahamas. Ten days after it began, Wilma gradually weakened and was classified as extratropical. Still, south of Nova Scotia, its winds howled at hurricane force. Hurricane Gilbert, now the second most intense storm, also hit the Yucatan but spared Florida. The third most intense storm didn't. The infamous "Labor Day" hurricane hit the Florida Keys in September 1935. One of the few remaining weather records of the storm was its pressure, 892 mb. All other measuring equipment was literally blown away before the peak of the storm, a feat estimated to require winds of 200 to 250 mph.

Ranging from 60 to 1,000 miles in diameter, a hurricane is defined by winds of more than 74 mph, accompanied by heavy rains, extremely large waves, and dangerously high tides. Immediately outside the eye, winds may surge as high as 125 to 150 mph or more, blowing rain in horizontal sheets. The storm itself has forward movement and can travel very slowly or at speeds of more than 60 mph.

Once a hurricane is formed, it poses a multiple threat to people and property in its path. Wind, rain, waves, and storm surge are its four most destructive forces. Any one of these forces is capable of causing severe damage.

Hurricane rains often come as a blessing to parched lands, but they may also come too fast and cause wholesale flooding and destruction. The average hurricane will drop some six inches of water over a given area. The extremes of this average range from practically no rain to downpours measured in feet.

After an average of eight to 10 days of blowing, the normal hurricane dies by either running too far from the tropical latitudes of its birth, or by advancing over land. Uneven land masses hinder the free flow of winds and fail to offer the supply of moisture the storm needs to keep going. Many hurricanes lose their punch while still at sea and hit land classified only as tropical storms (winds under 74 mph).

The Most Intense Hurricanes		
1. Wilma	2005	882 mb
2. Gilbert	1988	888 mb
3. "Labor Day"	1935	892 mb
4. Rita	2005	895 mb
5. Allen	1980	899 mb
6. Katrina	2005	902 mb
7. Camille	1969	905 mb
7. Mitch (tie)	1998	905 mb
9. Dean	2007	906 mb
10. Ivan	2004	910 mb

How to Estimate Wind Speeds (mph)		
Calm	under 1	Smoke rises straight up, nothing moves
Light air	1-3	Smoke drifts, leaves barely move
Light breeze	4-7	Wind is felt on face
Gentle breeze	8-12	Wind extends light flags
Moderate	13-18	Small breeze, branches move
Fresh breeze	19-24	Small trees move, small crests on waves
Strong breeze	25-31	Large branches move, twigs break, moss falls, wires hum
Moderate gale	32-38	Large trees move, difficulty walking
Fresh gale	39-46	Small and weakened limbs fall,
Strong gale	47-54	Slight structural damage
Whole gale	55-63	Small trees uprooted, much damage
Storm	64-74	More damage
Hurricane	75+	Severe, life-threatening damage

Hurricanes form over all tropical oceans except the South Atlantic and the eastern South Pacific.

The Gulf of Mexico and the Atlantic Ocean produce an average of 10 hurricanes annually. As few as two, and as many as 15, have been recorded in individual years.

In 1898, during the term of President McKinley, the United States established meteorological stations in the West Indies to keep watch on low pressure areas and establish a warning system for the U.S. mainland. Today the National Hurricane Center is located in Miami and, aided by reports from ships at sea, hurricane reconnaissance aircraft, radar detection equipment, and satellite reports, weathermen follow each tropical disturbance closely. The hurricane season runs from June 1 to November 30, but late hurricanes have occurred. Hurricane Alice, for example, formed off the Windward Islands in January 1955.

STORM TERMS USED BY THE NATIONAL WEATHER SERVICE

Advisory—A method for disseminating hurricane and storm data to the public every six hours.

Special Advisory—A warning given anytime there is a significant change in weather conditions or change in warnings.

Intermediate Advisory—A method of updating regular advisory information every two to three hours as necessary.

Gale Warning—Wind speeds of 39 to 54 mph expected.

Storm Warning—Wind speeds of 55 to 74 mph expected.

Tropical Disturbance—An unsettled area of thunderstorms moving in the tropics.

Tropical Depression—A low-pressure area with rotary circulation of clouds and winds up to 38 mph.

Tropical Storm—Counterclockwise cloud circulation with winds from 39 mph to 73 mph. At this time the storm is assigned a name.

Hurricane Watch—A hurricane may threaten the area.

Hurricane Warning—A hurricane is expected to strike the area within 24 hours or less.

Hurricane—A tropical storm that reaches winds of 74 mph.

Storm Surge—Domes of water caused when strong and swirling winds combine with low atmospheric pressure to cause sea level to rise. There are higher than normal waves on the top of the storm surge, but they do not constitute "tidal waves."

HURRICANE CATEGORIES

Hurricane intensity is measured in one of five categories, each determined by the maximum velocity of the winds leading the frontal system. Categories change frequently as wind speeds increase or die down, and forecasters refer to hurricanes as being upgraded or downgraded from one category to another. The categories are as follows:

Category 1	74-95 mph
Category 2	96-110 mph
Category 3	111-130 mph
Category 4	131-155 mph
Category 5	over 155 mph

HURRICANE RISKS

Risk of being in the path of a hurricane varies according to location. Areas marked:

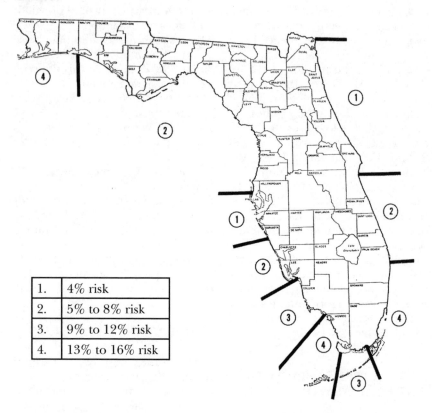

1.	4% risk
2.	5% to 8% risk
3.	9% to 12% risk
4.	13% to 16% risk

Worst Florida Hurricanes

A study of the entry points and direction of the motion of hurricanes passing over Florida between 1885 and 1980 reveals some regions are more susceptible to hurricanes than others. South Florida and the Panhandle are the most susceptible.

1559: Aug. 19—The first recorded Florida hurricane drove five Spanish ships ashore in Pensacola harbor.

1846: Oct. 11—An intense hurricane hit the keys and flooded Key West, perhaps the richest city in America at the time, with five feet of water. Fort Taylor was destroyed.

1848: Sept 25—Unnamed hurricane entered at the Tampa Bay area and destroyed Fort Brooke.

1886: July 19—The third hurricane in one month crossed Florida and cut a swath of destruction from Cedar Key to Jacksonville.

1896: Sept. 22-Oct. 1—Entered at Cedar Key, moving northeastward to Pennsylvania. Claimed more than 100 lives and damage to Florida estimated at $7 million.

1919: Sept. 2-14—Classified as

one of the great storms of the century. The Florida Keys were severely damaged before the storm died in the Gulf of Mexico.

1921: Oct. 21-31—One of the most severe storms to strike the central west coast. Entered at Tarpon Springs and slowly passed into the Atlantic between St. Augustine and Daytona Beach. Adequate warnings kept loss of life to eight persons; damage estimates ranged from $2 to $10 million.

1926: Sept. 6-22—Miami, in the storm's direct path, received the worst damage in the city's history. Three miles of dike along Lake Okeechobee failed to stand against floodwaters of 10-12 feet at Moore Haven and up to 5 feet at Clewiston. More than 250 persons were drowned near Clewiston and more than 130 at Moore Haven. Property damage was estimated, statewide, at between $27 and $37 million.

1928: Sept. 16—Struck Palm Beach with gusts up to 130 mph. It moved inland over an earthen dike, pushing a wall of water over settlements at Belle Glade, Pahokee, South Bay, Pelican Bay, Canal Point, and surrounding areas. The staggering loss of life is newly estimated at more than 2,500 persons.

1935: Aug. 31-Sept. 8—The "Labor Day Hurricane" that is still considered the most severe in terms of wind velocity, central pressure, and resulting storm tides. It passed over the Keys, leveled Islamorada and moved up the Gulf to reenter at Cedar Key. The storm killed 405.

1944: Oct. 13-21—Made landfall near Sarasota, followed a northeasterly course to the Atlantic south of Jacksonville, and reentered Georgia. This large hurricane extended 200 miles to the east and 100 miles to the west of its eye. Eighteen died and damages were among the highest ever recorded with crop losses alone estimated at $63 million.

1960: Aug. 29-Sept. 13—Hurricane Donna is rated as second in intensity to the Labor Day Hurricane, with winds gusting to 175 mph. Total damage estimate was more than $140 million, including $60 million to the state's citrus crop. Twelve persons were killed, 144 hospitalized and another 1,000 injured.

1964: Aug. 25-29—Hurricane Cleo directly struck Miami and then cut a path up the east coast of Florida and into the south Atlantic states. This storm left an estimated $128 million damage in its wake.

1965: Sept. 8-15—Hurricane Betsy entered through the Keys and Miami and exited into the Gulf heading northwest. Before dying in Louisiana, Betsy killed 74 persons.

1966: June 9—Hurricane Alma hit the eastern Florida panhandle, the earliest landfall on the U.S. mainland on record.

1975: Sept. 23—Hurricane Eloise hit Florida's Panhandle with winds up to 135 mph. Only one death was attributed to the storm, but property damage between Panama City and Fort Walton totaled about $100 million and 17,000 residents in the area were left homeless.

1985: Hurricane Elena formed Aug. 29 in the Caribbean, moved around in the Gulf, and battered the state's west coast from St. Petersburg to Pensacola, forcing the evacuation of 1.2 million people and causing $1 billion in damage. The year's final storm, Kate, hit Florida's Panhandle and killed four persons.

1992: August 24—Only one hurricane made landfall in the contiguous U.S.—but it was Hurricane Andrew. After nearly two decades of research, Andrew has been reclassified as a Category 5 storm, the most severe. Andrew proved to be unprecedented in its economic devastation along a route from the northwestern Bahamas, across the southern Florida peninsula, to south-central Louisiana. With damage in the U.S. estimated at $30 billion, Andrew at the time was the most expensive natural disaster in U.S. history. It caused 26 deaths in and around Miami and left 250,000 people homeless. Maximum sustained surface wind speed when it hit Florida near Homestead is now estimated at more than 165 miles per hour with peak gusts of more than 200 mph.

1995: October 4—Hurricane Opal crashed into the Florida panhandle near Ft. Walton Beach with sustained winds of 125 mph and gusts of 145. It tore a swatch through 120 miles of beaches and brought havoc to Pensacola, causing $1.5 billion in damage. It was the third most destructive storm in the state's history.

Hurricanes in Recent Years

2002: For the third year in a row, Florida escaped hurricanes. Only two tropical storms, Hanna and Edouard, had an impact on the state. Three Floridians died while swimming in proximity to Hanna; it is believed they were drowned by riptides caused by the storm. Tropical Storm Edouard formed in the Atlantic on September 1 and came ashore just north of Daytona Beach less than a week later. It

promptly declined to a tropical depression and dumped rain across the peninsula before dissipating in the Gulf of Mexico. Despite the fatalities, Hanna, which formed in the Gulf a week after Edouard, died there and never hit Florida. The state's general good fortune was chalked up to the return of El Nino, the warming of the Pacific that historically has suppressed tropical activity in the Atlantic. Later in the year, El Nino was credited with providing much of Florida with heavier-than-usual, but not tropical, rainfall.

2003: Despite being one of the longest and busiest hurricane seasons on record, Florida suffered hardly at all. There were 16 named storms including seven hurricanes in a season that stretched from April through December, but only one storm reached the state. Tropical Storm Henri formed in the eastern Gulf of Mexico on Sept. 3 but was already downgraded to a tropical depression when it crossed the coast near Clearwater three days later. It delivered gusty winds and localized heavy rains to Central Florida before exiting north of Daytona Beach and dissipating Sept. 8. Its primary effect was to add to what was already one of the state's wettest years.

2004: No living Floridian had ever experienced such a hurricane season. There were 15 tropical storms and nine hurricanes including six classified as major. An unprecedented four hurricanes affected Florida, destroying 20 percent of the state's homes and killing 117 people in two months. All five of the season's storms to make landfall in the U.S. made it in Florida. The state's season opened with Tropical Storm Bonnie, which formed Aug. 9 in the southern Gulf of Mexico and headed north. It hit the panhandle Aug. 12 with rain and sustained winds of 50 mph. The next day, Hurricane Charlie hit Florida. Charley also formed on Aug. 9, off Trinidad and Tobago, before moving west across the Caribbean Sea. It reached hurricane strength on Aug. 11 just south of Jamaica and turned in a northerly direction. Continuing into the Gulf of Mexico, Charley became a Category 4 storm with winds of 145 mph and a projected path toward Tampa Bay. An estimated 800,000 evacuated that sea level metropolitan area for inland Orlando. Traveling up the peninsula coast, Charley ticked a degree to the east and slammed instead into Punta Gorda and Port Charlotte. Maintaining hurricane strength, Charlie traveled north-northeast up the center of the peninsula, causing heavy damage to the towns in its path including Arcadia and Winter Haven before hitting Orlando, swelled with evacuees from the state's west coast. It remained a hurricane as it exited on the east coast. It was the strongest and most costly storm to hit Florida since 1992's Hurricane Andrew, causing approximately $14 million in damage. Hurricane Francis formed Aug. 25 as a tropical storm in the eastern Atlantic and reached hurricane force the next day as it moved westward. By Sept. 4, it lay off Palm Beach, battering the coastline before coming ashore as a Category 2 the next day at Sewell's Point with winds of 105 mph. It, too, passed over Winter Haven on its way to the Gulf of Mexico. But it wasn't through. Downgraded to a tropical storm with winds of 65 mph, it hit St. Marks in Florida's big bend on

Sept. 6. Less than two weeks later, the eye of Hurricane Ivan hit Gulf Shores, Alabama, Sept. 16 as a Category 3 storm, its northeast brunt clobbering Pensacola and breaking Interstate 10's spans across Escambia Bay. Working around the clock, engineers reopened the bridges to two-way traffic in 17 days. As a tropical storm, Ivan formed on Sept. 3 and became a hurricane Sept. 5 and within another day developed into a Category 4, a major storm. On Sept. 9 it reached Category 5 strength and with winds of 150 mph, it devastated the Cayman Islands Sept. 11. It passed between Yucatan and Cuba into the Gulf of Mexico two days later, moving north-northwest but slowly weakening to a Category 3 before coming ashore with its center at Gulf Shores. Its rainfall added to major flooding caused by previous storms in the Southeast. But Ivan wasn't through. It left the U.S. mainland off the Delmarva Peninsula three days later as nothing more than a low-pressure area. It looped to the south and crossed Florida again Sept. 21. In the gulf, it regained its tropical storm status and came ashore at the extreme southwestern tip of Louisiana three days later. It dissipated over eastern Texas the next day. Hurricane Jeanne formed as a tropical storm Sept. 14 as it moved across the Leeward Islands. It dumped a deluge of rain on Puerto Rico and Hispanola. It reached hurricane strength briefly while approaching Hispaniola, but that island's mountains knocked it back down to a tropical storm. It regained hurricane strength on the 20th and reached the Category 2 level as it looped in the Atlantic before heading toward Abaco and Grand

Bahama which it hit as a Category 3 on Sept. 25. The next day, 20 days after Frances, Hurricane Jeanne came ashore at Sewall's Point, the first time in recorded history that two hurricanes made landfall at the same location. It, too, crossed the state and became the third hurricane of the season to pass directly over Winter Haven. The names of all four Florida hurricanes—Charley, Frances, Jeanne, and Ivan—were retired.

2005: And it just kept coming. It was a record-setting hurricane season. There were 27 named storms, six more than the previous record of 21 set in 1933. Of those 27 storms, 15 became hurricanes, three more than the previous record of 12 in 1969. And three Category 5 Hurricanes hit the U.S., three more than the previous record two set in both 1960 and 1961. Seven tropical storms formed before August 1, two more than the previous record of five in 1997. There were more records still to be set. In Florida the season opened on June 9 with the first storm of the season. Tropical Storm Arlene formed June 8 in the southwest Caribbean Sea and moved north, crossing western Cuba. On June 11, just short of hurricane status, it hit the Florida panhandle causing only moderate damage but killing one. Hurricane Dennis formed as a tropical depression July 4 and became the season's first major hurricane and the strongest Atlantic hurricane to form before August in recorded history. Unlike the season's previous three storms, it developed in the southwest Caribbean. Almost immediately it hit the island of Grenada and was upgraded to tropical storm status as it moved west-northwest. It

became a hurricane July 6 and on the 7th it had achieved Category 4 strength. Passing between Haiti and Jamaica the storm battered both before making landfall in Cuba. It lost strength over the island's mountains but reemerging over water it reintensified at an astonishing rate. On July 9, Dennis was again a Category 4 storm registering record intensity for a July storm and heading for Florida's panhandle. Fortunately, and as had the previous year's Hurricane Ivan, it deintensified, dropping to Category 3 just before making landfall at Santa Rosa Island July 10. Despite losing steam, the storm claimed 42 lives and caused $2.23 billion damage in the panhandle. It finally disappeared three days later in Illinois. Tropical Depression 10 came off Africa August 13 and almost immediately fell apart. Its remnants drifted northwest and virtually disappeared. But just enough remained to be folded into another minor system off the Leeward Islands. Together they became Tropical Storm 12. And that became Hurricane Katrina. As nothing more than disturbed weather, it hovered over the Bahamas and became a tropical depression on August 23, a tropical storm the following day, and a hurricane August 2, making landfall in south Florida and sweeping across the state the same day. In the Gulf it rapidly intensified to Category 5 and headed for the northern Gulf Coast where it slammed into Louisiana and Mississippi as the worst natural disaster in American history. Almost lost in the statistics of the storm was the fact that in its few short hours over Florida, Katrina killed 13. Hurricane Ophelia settled in off

Florida's east coast on September 8, three days after forming as a tropical depression over the Bahamas. It lingered off Jacksonville for two days, its high surf killing one and causing coastal erosion before moving on to North Carolina. On September 18, Rita formed as a tropical depression over the Turks and Caicos Islands. Two days later, it passed south of the Florida Keys as a Category 2 hurricane and intensified into a Category 5 in the Gulf of Mexico before heading into history and toward Louisiana and Texas as Katrina's little sister. Tropical Storm Tammy sprang as a surprise from virtually nothing to a full-fledged tropical storm October 5 north of the Bahamas and made landfall at Mayport that night. It did little damage in Florida but brought heavy rains to Georgia and the Carolinas before being considered as the major cause of the year's record flooding in the northeast U.S. No storm gave more warning or was the subject of more precise forecasting than Hurricane Wilma. It formed as a tropical depression October 15 southwest of Jamaica. Two days later it was a tropical storm. On October 18, the storm developed a very small but well-defined eye and began intensifying. It reached Category 5 strength the next day. The intensification from tropical storm to Category 5 hurricane happened in 24 hours, making it the fastest developing storm in the history of Atlantic hurricanes and the second fastest in world history. Wilma slowed and weakened as it approached Mexico but still hit Cozumel and Cancun as a Category 4 hurricane October 22. As predicted, when it reentered the Gulf of Mexico, it moved

northeast, straight for Naples which it hit October 24 as a Category 3. It flooded Everglades City, hammered the Everglades, and hit the Greater Miami-Fort Lauderdale area as it speeded into the Atlantic. Despite its international ferocity, most of its fatalities occurred in Florida where 35 died. It also did $16.8 billion of damage in the state, making it the third-costliest hurricane to ever hit the United States. It also indicated that all of the upgrades, preparations, and precautions the state had taken in the wake of 1992's Hurricane Andrew and the on-slaught of 2004 were not enough. Despite new codes, commercial buildings, especially high-rises, in the South Florida metro, fared poorly in the storm. And too much of the Broward and Miami-Dade population did, too. Despite all the storms, all the warnings, and all the experience, after Wilma completely unprepared crowds gathered for such essentials as water, ice, food, and gasoline. While they received aid, they got little sympathy. At this point and for the first time, the national weather service ran out of names. But there was more to come for the record. Tropical Storm Alpha formed on October 22 and merged with Wilma. Hurricane Beta formed October 26, Tropical Storm Gamma on November 15, Tropical Storm Delta on November 23. Hurricane Epsilon reached that status on December 2, two days after the end of the "official" hurricane season. And equally undeterred by the calendar, Tropical Storm Zeta formed December 30. It ended the 2005 season when it dissipated January 6, 2006 as the longest-running January tropical storm ever in the Atlantic. None of the

Greek-alphabet storms affected the state.

2006: Despite expert predictions that Florida faced its third consecutive devastating hurricane season, it proved to be the quietest in a decade. There were only nine named storms and only two made it to Florida, both as shadows of recent storms. Alberto formed as a depression south of the western tip of Cuba to kick off the season June 10. It became a tropical storm the next day. Entering the Gulf of Mexico, Alberto made landfall at Apalachicola June 13, never having attained hurricane status. Although it did little damage, as the first storm of the season it was not a good omen, and the state prepared for the worst. It didn't happen. Ernesto, the first hurricane of the season, formed August 24 southeast of Martinique and moved west. It achieved tropical storm status on the 25th and strengthened briefly to a minimum hurricane on August 27 off the coast of Haiti. But it faltered back to being a tropical storm when it made its first landfall August 28 at Guantanamo Bay. Torn by the mountains of Cuba, Ernesto remained a tropical storm when it drenched the Keys on its way to making landfall with just 45 mph winds at Plantation Key south of Miami on August 30. It moved up the peninsula before exiting into the Atlantic at Cape Canaveral. The season's seven other storms came nowhere near the state.

2007: Although a heavy hurricane season was predicted, Florida hardly had one at all. The season such as it was started early with Subtropical Storm Andrea forming May 9, 150 miles off Daytona Beach, but it dissipated two days later without making landfall.

On June 1, the first day of the "official" hurricane season, Tropical Storm Barry formed in the southeast Gulf of Mexico. It weakened just before making landfall as a tropical depression at Tampa Bay the next day. Although a surfer died, the storm provided the benefit of heavy rain around the state, extinguishing numerous wildfires. And that was that.

2008: It was another busy hurricane system but not for Florida. Tropical Storm Fay was the only storm to reach the state, but it was one of the most interesting storms in Florida's hurricane history. It formed Aug. 15 in the Caribbean after spreading heavy rains as a tropical depression. It continued as a rainmaker across Hispanola and Cuba before making landfall at Key West Aug. 18. Traveling north-northwest, it again made landfall at Cape Romano on the Gulf coast near Naples Aug. 19. Crossing the peninsula it intensified to its strongest level, just short of hurricane status, it exited Florida into the Atlantic near Melbourne only to return with its third landfall Aug. 21 at Flagler Beach. It crossed North Florida to reenter the Gulf and made its fourth landfall at Carrabelle, east of the Apalachicola River on Aug. 23. It traveled along the panhandle coast brushing Panama City but not making another landfall in the state. Five died in the storm-generated tornadoes and floods and the entire state was declared a disaster area. Hurricane Ike was one of the largest storms in recorded history and the third most costly storm in U.S. annals but it skirted Florida, delivering rain to the evacuated Florida Keys Sept. 7 when the storm hit Cuba and to

Pensacola as the 900-square-mile-storm barreled toward Galveston, Texas, which it hit September 13.

2009: It was the quietest Atlantic hurricane season in more than a decade and Florida was again visited by only one tropical storm. Tropical Storm Claudette came off Africa August 7 as a tropical wave and doggedly made its way across the Atlantic and into the Caribbean despite El Nino-inspired wind-sheer that kept it from developing into anything stronger than traveling rainy days. But as it passed over the Florida Keys on Aug. 15, it began developing an identity. In the Gulf of Mexico off Charlotte Harbor the next day, it organized into a tropical depression and hours later became T.S. Claudette. Then it shot to the northwest and the Panhandle to make landfall at Santa Rosa Island after midnight the morning of Aug. 17, it quickly dissipated over Alabama, having killed two people offshore.

2010: It was the third busiest hurricane season in more than 150 years, but for Florida, it was the year of the remnant. There were 19 named storms including 12 hurricanes, five of them major. Most storms turned north into the Atlantic or west to bother Central America and the Yucatan. Tropical Storm Bonnie formed in the Bahamas but dropped back to a depression as it crossed south Florida July 22, bringing rain to Miami and Fort Myers. It regained tropical storm status in the Gulf of Mexico but there was little concern for Florida as Bonnie headed toward the site of the Gulf Oil Spill where, again weakened, it halted clean-up efforts for several days. Tropical Depression No. 5 formed Aug. 11 in the northeastern Gulf,

and because of its characteristics, a tropical storm warning was hoisted for Destin on the Panhandle. But it never happened. Destin was unbothered and the remnant moved west along the coast to bring rain to the Mississippi and Louisiana coast. It drifted back east and sitting off Panama City, was predicted to intensity and promptly fizzled. Still, after a week and a half in the Gulf, it had brought heavy rain and flood warnings not just to the coast but also to much of the South. A month later, Hurricane Matthew hit the Yucatan. But more importantly, it spawned Tropical Storm Nicole. Whether Nicole was a separate storm cloaked by Matthew or an unprecedented breakaway portion of that hurricane, has not been determined. Nicole turned from the western Caribbean toward Florida. But in the pattern of the season, it declined to a tropical depression in the Florida Straights. It brought rain to Key West and then Miami. Off Fort Lauderdale, the remnant of Nicole pick up a trough and ran up the east coast to join another low. Although never tropical again, Nicole nonetheless brought torrents of rain to and from the Carolinas through New England causing widespread flooding. Its cloud cover stretched from New Brunswick, Canada, down the Atlantic to Puerto Rico. When Hurricane Paula menaced Cuba Oct. 13, a tropical storm watch went up in Key West but was taken down the next day. It was the fifth consecutive year hurricanes spared the state.

HURRICANE SURVIVAL GUIDE

Aiming at apparent and recurring apathy toward hurricanes by

Floridians, state emergency managers issued a blunt and dire warning: **"The first 72 are up to you."** Their message is clear. In the face of a storm calamity, those affected cannot reasonably expect emergency services to come to their aid for a full three days after the event.

As recent hurricane history should have taught all, hurricanes are literally deadly and awesome in their destructive power.

A review of Florida hurricanes reveals many don't just affect the coasts. They move inland along the Panhandle; they cross the peninsula at varying speeds and varying angles after crossing the coasts on the Gulf or the Atlantic Ocean. Either with storm surges or deluges of rain, hurricanes flood rivers, lakes, creeks, and streams and fill wetlands. Since 1970, freshwater flooding from rainfall has claimed more lives than any other hurricane-related phenomenon.

More than half of all hurricanes that make landfall in the United States do so in Florida, and all hurricanes each season are capable of hitting the state.

Long Before the Storm

Before a hurricane is on the horizon, even before the hurricane season "officially" begins on June 1, it is time to get your emergency preparedness in order.

A priority: buy insurance. In Florida, agents cannot write homeowners insurance when a hurricane watch or warning is in effect and flood insurance requires a 30-day waiting period. Review the policies you have and know what they cover. Inventory your possessions, making a list of everything you own, with receipts, date of purchase, model numbers, costs—whatever will support your eventual claim, should the need arise.

Have a plan and heed the warnings.

Get and store: nails, plywood, duct tape, and sheets of clear plastic. Opaque plastic not only covers roof damage, it masks it as well. Install new high tech storm shutters.

Get prescriptions filled.

Learn where your gas, water, and electrical shutoffs to your home are located and how to operate them.

Inspect your trees and shrubs and trim as necessary to minimize overhang damage. But do not do it in the face of a storm. It only increases the supply of flying debris. There will be no trash pickups during a hurricane and, depending on damage, some period after a storm.

Delegate responsibilities among family members and establish a communication plan. Organize, evaluate, and maintain your emergency supplies. Experts recommend emergency supplies sufficient to meet your needs for at least two weeks.

Emergency Kit

That two-week supply should include:

First-aid materials
Portable radios, and TVs,
    flashlights, clocks—all with extra
    batteries
Portable, battery-powered lanterns,
    extra batteries
Infant requirements, including
    baby food, formula, disposable
    diapers
Extra clothing
Pillows, blankets, sleeping bags

Essential needs, such as eyeglasses, toiletries

A manual can opener (the most frequently forgotten item)

Other tools that are battery- or hand-operated

An ice chest and ice

Quiet games, books, playing cards

A fire extinguisher

Mosquito repellent

Disposable plates, glass, utensils

Straight bleach

Trash bags

Water-storage containers

Potable water, three gallons per person

Fuel cans and fuel (gasoline)

Sterno, firewood

Propane

Charcoal

Special dietary foods

Peanut butter and unrefrigerated jelly

Powdered or shelf-pack milk

More bottled water

Canned meats, fruits, vegetables, soups, puddings, milk

Dried fruit

Powdered or individually packaged drinks

Instant coffee and tea

Disposable washcloths and paper towels

Crackers, cereal, cookies, snacks

Condiments

Pet food

A full tank of gasoline

In addition, you should be prepared to have and to keep on your person:

Driver's license or other valid photo ID

Cash: Have enough money on hand to meet your needs for two weeks on your own and don't forget your credit, debit, and ATM cards, and keep them safe! While useless during a power outage, they will be among your most valuable possessions when power is restored, and the consequences of lost or stolen cards could match other storm damages. If you or members of your family routinely wear "medic alert" or similar information jewelry, don't forget it.

Prepare and secure a waterproof container or a resealable plastic bag, or both, containing:

All medicines and prescription medicines in their original containers

Important papers, including insurance policies; inventory; additional valid identification; health records; birth, marriage, and death certificates; social security cards; passports; car titles; and property deeds. If you're eligible for government benefits (food stamps, unemployment compensation, etc.), safeguard your card or other documentation that indicates you're eligible. There is often unemployment following a hurricane. Have a pay stub or other documentation to file for unemployment benefits. Noncitizens should keep safe their passport, visa, or green cards.

If important or valuable items cannot be easily and safely stored at home or transported, make arrangements to transfer them to a more secure place.

If you are responsible for others, especially the elderly, follow the same procedures on their behalf as you do for yourself. In addition, keep a checklist of their prescription medications and other special needs. If any person within your responsibility needs special consideration in evacuation, because of age, physical disability, or medical concerns, register with county Civil Defense or Office of Emergency

Management well in advance of an approaching storm. Many counties have established shelters especially for those with special needs. Floridians receiving home-health care or who depend on electrical life-support equipment should make emergency arrangements with a hospital.

Plan for the care and well-being of pets. Most shelters will not accept them, nor will many hotels or motels. While some veterinarians and kennels will board pets during emergencies, most have limited space and give priority to regular clients.

Evacuation

If many emergency items and preparations seem similar to those taken for a trip, it's because a trip is what you may be taking. Increasingly, evacuation, including massive movements of millions of people, is the focus of the state's preparatory options.

A voluntary evacuation order is just that. It is voluntary. It is also prudent.

A mandatory evacuation order is also just that.

Residents of high-rise buildings and mobile homes can expect mandatory evacuation orders, as can residents of coastal communities, especially beach communities. In a mandatory evacuation, while emergency officers may advise you, even plead with you, they will not drag you from your home, but neither will they come back and get you, not because they don't want to but because they will be unable to.

Know where you're going. Decide—do not guess—where you will go if you evacuate voluntarily or are subject to a mandatory evacuation.

Make at least preliminary arrangements for an evacuation destination, and plan your evacuation route and alternative evacuation routes. Evacuation routes are marked on Florida's roads and highways. The best and safest route, however, will be determined by the path of the storm. Study evacuation maps. Traffic may be rerouted. Know your alternatives. Family and friends or accommodations outside the path of the storm are the best destinations.

Mandatory evacuation may be called at night. "Stay tuned" and know your alternatives. For reasons ranging from agriculture, through tourism, to hurricanes, the state's media industry is hypersensitive to weather and has made a massive investment in ensuring they remain operational in the worse conditions. Many operate weather services that match or exceed those operated by government.

Although Emergency Service officials will do what they can, governments actually make only two decisions at the approach of a storm: to order evacuations and to open public shelters.

If you take pets with you, make sure your dog is collared with proper identification tags, including address and phone number, and take any appropriate paperwork. Keep your dog on a sturdy leash. Small dogs, cats, birds, snakes, and pocket pets should be in carrying containers, along with all necessities.

But you cannot take pets to most public shelters. Neither can you arrive at any public shelter with alcoholic beverages, weapons, valuables, or food other than special dietary needs. You will need your own bedding at a shelter. Pack your toothbrush and paste, soap, and washcloth.

Those fortunate enough to find a public shelter that does accept pets must have a proper identity collar and rabies tag license, vaccination paperwork, carrier or cage, leash, and an ample supply of pet food.

While planning for evacuation is necessary, know that the more elaborate or necessary your plan is, the more time it will take to accomplish it. If you have to move or otherwise secure a boat or a travel trailer, or aid a relative, the more time it will take to accomplish a safe evacuation.

If you have a working fireplace, cover the chimney. The force of torrential rains can force flooding right down the flu.

If you evacuate, turn everything off. Unplug everything.

Before the Storm

If you must ride out a hurricane at home, don't be fooled by calm, clear, mild weather prior to a storm. Stay alert and protect your home and your family as best you can. In addition to taking your planned emergency precautions, pick up outdoors around the house: garbage cans, garden tools, patio furniture, etc.—anything that can become a weapon in the wind. A 74-miles-per-hour wind, the minimum hurricane strength, has the ability to drive a 2 x 4 lumber

through a reinforced concrete wall 4 inches thick.

Prepare a safe room, which can be an interior room, a large closet, or a windowless hallway. Equip it with mattresses or seat cushions to protect during the height of a storm. Garages, spacious rooms, areas with windows, sliding glass doors, and other entrances are considered unsafe in a storm. (Upper stories are, too, but offer some refuge from flooding.)

Close your house up as tightly as possible. Opening a window to reduce air pressure is a myth. The house will not explode if sealed, and wind entering through a window can do great damage.

Know what's in your refrigerator and freezer. Power is likely to be lost at any point during a hurricane and could remain off for a considerable time afterward. You'll want to open those refrigerated cabinets as infrequently as possible.

Prepare to store water. Clean bathtubs before filling with water. Do not use this water for drinking, but you don't want additional contaminates such as soap scum, even for washing or flushing.

Your realistic drinking-water needs are one gallon per person, per day. Don't ration water. If you run out, you can find or make more. Boiling water (a rolling boil for 10 minutes) is the safest way to create clean drinking water. (It will taste a lot better after cooling if poured back and forth between two clean containers.)

GENERATOR SAFETY

The hurricane season of 2004 and 2005, with power outages affecting millions of people for long periods of time, vastly increased the popularity and use of gasoline-powered portable generators for the home. But at least 12 people were killed and hundreds made seriously ill during the period by carbon monoxide emitted by generators.

Carbon monoxide is a colorless, odorless, and poisonous gas that generators send into the atmosphere at a faster and higher rate than other sources including natural gas, LP gas, oil, kerosene, coal, wood, charcoal, and even automobiles.

Virtually all such incidents stemmed from the placement of the generators in poorly ventilated areas, including many that seem obvious. Aftermath studies also indicated that few new generator owners bothered to carefully read the operating instructions, safety precautions, and warnings accompanying the product.

People placing and operating generators in their garages with doors closed or open, placing them right inside or outside open windows, or placing them indoors within their enclosed homes, accounted for nearly all the deaths and illnesses.

Compounding the problem is that carbon monoxide poisoning is difficult to diagnose. Its common symptoms are nonspecific and similar to those of the flu, including headache, dizziness, weakness, nausea, chest pain, and confusion. State healthcare workers have been advised to consider such common symptoms as a sign of carbon monoxide poisoning following power outages.

People operating generators, especially those using the machines for the first time, are advised to:

Read and follow the manufacturer's guidelines listed in the owner's manual for correct operating procedures and power output capabilities.

Never attempt to run more appliances than a generator can handle. Use a generator only on appliances most critical to need.

Never connect a generator directly to a home's wiring.

Never run a generator inside the home, including the garage.

Always run a generator in a well-ventilated area AWAY from the home.

Always use heavy-duty, indoor/outdoor rated extension cords to connect a generator to appliances.

Always turn off all electrical appliances connected to the generator before turning off the generator.

Never attempt to refuel a generator while it is running.

Always let a generator cool down before attempting to refuel it.

With the advent of "sealed" climate-controlled homes, carbon monoxide detectors have become popular. Similar to smoke alarms, the detectors can provide a warning but cannot mitigate the problem.

During the Storm

Remain indoors but stay away from windows and doors. Monitor rising water. Have a supply of cement blocks to raise furniture if necessary. If possible, move to second floor or attic if your home begins to flood. Have an ax up there to cut through the roof if necessary. Just because you're not on a beach doesn't mean a storm surge can't get you. A wind-driven dome of water to the right of the center of a hurricane can reach 25 to 30 feet and can travel inland for miles.

If the center, or "eye," of the storm passes directly over your home, stay put. There will be a lull in the wind. Make only emergency repairs if necessary, and make them as quickly as possible. The wind can return suddenly, from the opposite direction and at greater force.

Despite the natural tendency, don't "watch the storm." Use the safe room.

After the Storm

Notify your relatives of your safety and whereabouts, and seek medical care at hospitals for persons injured during the storm. Call the local Red Cross or similar agencies if you have immediate or special needs after a storm.

If you've evacuated, be patient. Access to affected areas will be controlled, and if you've evacuated, you won't be allowed to reenter such areas until search, rescue, and safety operations are completed. Even then, access may be restricted, and you'll have to show identification and proof that you live in the affected area. Stay out of other closed areas as well.

If you've never left the area and conditions are still difficult, begin with your necessities. Eat your perishable foods first. In a well-filled, well-insulated freezer, food will be frozen at the middle, and safe to eat, for at least three days. Try to eat at least one well-balanced meal each day and take in enough calories to do any necessary work.

For emergency cooking, use a fireplace. Use charcoal grills or camp stoves outdoors only. Although canned food may be eaten right from the can, you can heat canned foods over candle warmers or Sterno in a sauce pan, chafing dish or fondue pot. (If you heat a can, open it and remove the label first.) Beware of spoiled food and throw away any food touched by floodwater. Before eating or drinking, wash your hands with soap and boiled or treated water. After a storm, the threat of disease is everywhere.

Use extreme caution entering a building that may have been damaged, especially your home. Don't touch loose, dangling, or damaged wires; report them to emergency services. Check for leaking gas lines by smell only. If gas leaks are detected inside the home, open the windows and doors and leave. If a propane tank has been in any way affected by the storm, don't use it; call the fire department to remove it. Make fire prevention a priority. Likely low-water pressure will make firefighting difficult.

If you are able, make temporary repairs to correct safety hazards and minimize additional damage. Hire only licensed contractors to do major repairs. If flooded, don't turn on any electricity until an electrician checks site. Report broken sewer and water lines. Assess and photograph damage to your home and its contents.

Beware of snakes, insects, and animals driven to higher ground by the storm, and be very cautious of stray animals. Think twice before allowing children or pets outdoors. Secure food sources and remove all animal carcasses to avoid attracting rats. Wear insect repellent throughout the ordeal.

Drive, if you must, cautiously. Debris-littered streets can be slick and dangerous. Road washouts can be common after a hurricane; never drive in water of unknown depth.

If flood has caused damage, disinfect and dry buildings and all items in them. Clean and disinfect anywhere and anything that has been touched by flood. If something cannot be disinfected, throw it away.

Don't Bother

There are many things done by people facing a hurricane that do no good at all. Among the worthless exercises: Crisscrossing windows with masking or duct tape; parking the car inside the garage with the front touching the garage door; drilling holes in the center of plywood panels covering windows; opening windows on the side of the house facing the wind; opening windows on the side of the house not facing the wind; protecting windows only on the windward side; doing nothing.

Hurricane Names

Early Spanish explorers named the severe storms they experienced after certain saints on whose special days the hurricanes first appeared. Much later, these storms were identified by latitude and longitude. The next method of identification was use of phonetic alphabet letters: Able for A (the first hurricane), Baker for B, and so on.

By 1953, the weather bureau began naming the storms with female names, still following the alphabet. Origin of naming storms after females is obscure, but some say it is based on the World War II

Retired Hurricane Names	
1954: Carol, Hazel	1983: Alicia
1955: Janet, Connie, Diane, Ione	1985: Elena, Gloria
1957: Audrey	1988: Gilbert, Joan
1960: Donna	1989: Hugo
1961: Carla, Hattie	1990: Diana, Klaus
1963: Flora	1991: Bob
1964: Cleo, Dora, Hilda	1992: Andrew
1965: Betsy	1995: Luis, Marilyn, Opal, Roxanne
1966: Inez	1996: Cesar, Fran, Hortense
1967: Beaulah	1998: Georges, Mitch
1968: Edna	1999: Floyd, Lenny
1969: Camille	2000: Keith
1970: Celia	2001: Allison, Iris, Michelle
1972: Agnes	2002: Isidore, Lili
1974: Carmen, Fifi	2003: Fabian, Isabel, Juan
1975: Eloise	2004: Charley, Frances, Ivan, Jeanne
1977: Anita	2005: Dennis, Katrina, Rita, Stan, Wilma
1979: David, Frederick	2007: Dean, Felix, Notel
1980: Allen	2008: Gustav, Ike, Paloma

servicemen's practice of naming Pacific storms after their wives or sweethearts. Protests from women became so strong by 1978 that the following year every other storm was given a male name.

Names of minor hurricanes may be reused a good number of years later, but to avoid confusion, the National Hurricane Center has a policy of permanently retiring the name of any storm that takes a heavy toll in lives and/or property.

2012 Hurricane Names
Alberto, Beryl, Chris, Debby, Ernesto, Florence, Gordon, Helene, Isaac, Joyce, Kirk, Leslie, Michael, Nadine, Oscar, Patty, Rafael, Sandy, Tony, Valerie, William.

2013 Hurricane Names
Andrea, Barry, Chantal, Dorian, Erin, Fernand, Gabrielle, Humberto, Ingrid, Jerry, Karen, Lorenzo, Melissa, Nestor, Olga, Pablo, Rebekah, Sebastien, Tanya, Van, Wendy.

The Busiest Months
Despite their association with summer, tropical storms and hurricanes occur most frequently in September and October in Florida.

The "hurricane season" is from June 1 through November 30.

The monthly breakdown of such storms that have affected Florida from 1885 through 2010 follows.

June	28
July	16
August	43
September	70
October	63
November	9

HOT, HOT, HOT

The highest temperature ever recorded in Florida was 109, on June 29, 1931, at Monticello.

GEOGRAPHY

PHYSICAL FEATURES

Florida has an area of 58,560 square miles of which 4,308 square miles are water. The 22nd state in size, its geographic center is 12 miles northwest of Brooksville, in Hernando County.

Because of Florida's peninsular shape, no part of the state is more than 60 miles from salt water.

The state's highest point, 345 feet, is in the Panhandle, in northern Walton County. Its lowest point is sea level. Landform regions have been divided into four sections, but the division between each is hazy. The regions are as follows:

1. Northwest Plateau and the Tallahassee Hills. This original flat upland is dissected by many streams. In some places nothing is left of the plateau.

2. Central Highlands. At most places flat and at others hilly, this landform is studded by lakes and sinkholes. The four ridges that border this area are thought to be ancient beach ridges.

3. Coastal Lowlands. Generally quite flat and covered with flatwoods.

4. Southern Lowlands. Of the Everglades type, a swamp-sink flatland. Former beach ridges paralleling the coast are quite common for many miles inland.

GEOLOGICAL FORMATIONS

The first critical observations on the geology of Florida were made in 1846 in the vicinity of Tampa. The years since then have been fruitful in the field of Florida geology.

Subsurface formations have been explored by many deep borings, made chiefly in the search for petroleum.

Floridian Plateau is the name applied to the great projection of the continent of North America that separates the deep water of the Atlantic Ocean from the deep water of the Gulf of Mexico. This definition includes not only the state of Florida but also an equally great or greater area that lies submerged beneath water less than 300 feet deep. The plateau terminates at the Florida Keys, where the southern end drops off steeply into the Straits of Florida.

The Floridian Plateau apparently has always formed part of the continental mass, as distinguished from the deep sea. Its earliest history indicates links with the Caribbean islands. This can be seen in the shape and direction of the peninsula today. The geological story of Florida is complex, but for sake of simplicity it can be broken down into six periods:

1. Mountains. Hundreds of millions of years ago, south Florida was an arc of volcanic mountains. These ancient precambrian formations were then buried. In Highlands County they are now 13,000 feet below the surface. *(Paleozoic)*

2. Limestone. Limestone sediment was deposited on the plain caused by erosion of the ancient mountains. Their weight caused further sinking of the land, and over a period of about a hundred million years, thousands of feet of limestone was formed. *(Mesozoic and Early Tertiary)*

3. Marls and Phosphate. The limestone layers arched and Florida rose above the ocean waters. Erosion leveled this plain and it submerged slightly, forming marshes and lagoons. *(Late Tertiary)*

4. Ice Age. When the ice sheet covered much of Canada and the northern United States, Florida became cool and rainy. Because so much of the earth's supply of water was piled up in glaciers, the sea level around the world lowered, leaving much of the Continental Shelf (now covered by the Gulf of Mexico) exposed, and Florida became twice the size it is today. Many animals—bears, wolves, saber-toothed tigers, mastodons, and other prehistoric creatures—roamed over this large land mass. *(Pleistocene)*

5. Terraces. During the melting and reforming of the northern ice sheet, the sea level rose and fell, cutting bluffs and terraces into the land. The climate was drier than before and winds built dunes on many of the newly-formed terraces. *(Pleistocene and Holocene)*

6. Florida Today. The land is still being worn away by rain, rivers, waves, and wind. Underground water dissolves the limestone and forms caves and sinkholes. The land continues to change with the east coast building up and the west coast sinking.

SINKHOLES

Geologists classify sinkholes into two types: solution sinkholes and collapse sinkholes. Both occur as a result of natural erosion of the state's underlying bed of limestone. *Solution sinkholes* occur most often where overlying soil touches limestone. As the limestone underpinning erodes, the surface soil begins sinking gradually, the terrain often forming a bowl-shaped depression. A pond or marsh may form in the resultant bowl. *Collapse sinkholes* are usually more violent and occur when an underground cavern can no longer support the ground above it and a hole suddenly opens.

Groundwater plays a vital role in all sinkhole development. During periods of prolonged drought, for instance, a low water level in the supporting limestone may prompt a collapse of land triggered by a loss of buoyancy, gravity, and water pressure. Similarly, sinkholes may occur after heavy rains, causing groundwater circulation in underground limestone caverns to become active and exert pressure on weak joints and cracks.

The area in Florida least likely to suffer sinkholes is south Florida, from slightly north of the Lake Okeechobee area south to the Keys. In this region, artesian pressures are at or above land surface while limestone formations are deep. But any area of Florida is capable of producing sinkholes, for the depressions form wherever the roof of an underground cavern is unstable. Excessive pumping of water during a drought, outside stresses such as heavy traffic, or an increase in heavy buildings can trigger the collapse of an area's limestone support system.

New sinkholes are reported at a rate of 300 to 400 each year in Florida, but most, perhaps 4,000 annually, go unnoticed. Many are less than 20 feet wide and occur in isolated areas. The largest sinkhole recorded in Florida occurred in

1981 at Winter Park. It reached a width of 300 feet and a depth of 100 feet, swallowing a house, six vehicles, part of a swimming pool, and portions of two streets. Damage totaled $4 million. Only one death has been attributed to a sinkhole. In 1959 a well driller was buried when the ground caved in under him near Keystone Heights.

Currently there are no means by which sinkhole development can be predicted. Many Florida homeowners buy "sinkhole insurance," but it is not necessary or recommended in all areas of the state.

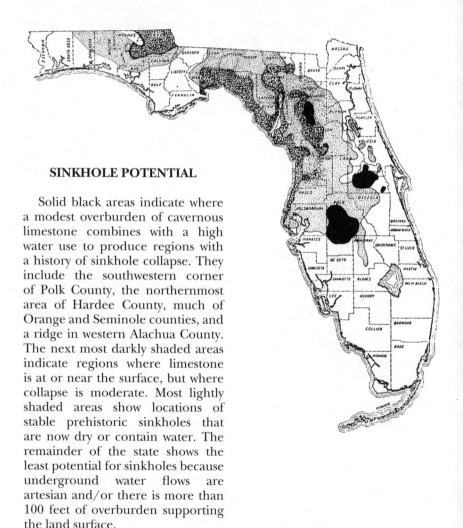

SINKHOLE POTENTIAL

Solid black areas indicate where a modest overburden of cavernous limestone combines with a high water use to produce regions with a history of sinkhole collapse. They include the southwestern corner of Polk County, the northernmost area of Hardee County, much of Orange and Seminole counties, and a ridge in western Alachua County. The next most darkly shaded areas indicate regions where limestone is at or near the surface, but where collapse is moderate. Most lightly shaded areas show locations of stable prehistoric sinkholes that are now dry or contain water. The remainder of the state shows the least potential for sinkholes because underground water flows are artesian and/or there is more than 100 feet of overburden supporting the land surface.

ANATOMY OF A SINKHOLE

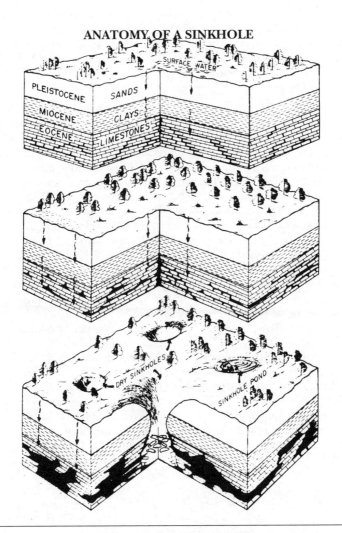

THE DEVIL'S MILLHOPPER

Florida's oldest sinkhole, a tourist attraction, is the Devil's Millhopper in northwest Gainesville. Geologists estimate the sink was formed nearly 20,000 years ago. It is 117 feet deep, its sides covered from top to bottom by vegetation. The sink got its name after fossilized bones and teeth were found in the bottom and visitors termed the hole the lair of the devil. Once owned by the University of Florida, the sink and surrounding 63 acres were deeded in the 1970s to the state. To accommodate visitors, the state in 1976 built a 221-step wooden stairway from top to bottom. The Devil's Millhopper is a state park and a State Geological Site, one of two in Florida. Windley Key Fossil Reef Geological State Park is the other. Windley Key, near Islamorada, is where Key Largo limestone was quarried to build Henry Flagler's Overseas Railroad and mined to produce exquisite Keystone jewelry. The park features 8-foot-high quarry walls clearly showing cross-sections of the ancient coral.

CAVES

With all the sinks and limestone in Florida, there is only one large cave—Florida Caverns. This cave is three miles north of Marianna in the Panhandle section.

Smaller caves exist near Brooksville, Ocala, and Gainesville. Bat Cave east of Gainesville, Devil's Head east of Lake City, and Natural Bridge Cave in Jackson County are three of the better known small caves.

SOILS

Florida soils are generally sandy with underlying clay or limestone layers. With the exception of those areas with a high water table, drainage in such soils is good.

Leaching is a problem in sandy soils and soil nutrients must be replaced by the use of fertilizer or cover crops. Sandy soils also tend toward acidity and liming may be necessary for certain crops. Peat is sometimes added to soils low in humus.

The Florida farmer finds that even on mediocre soils, the combination of good till and the Florida climate makes agriculture one of the state's most prosperous industries.

In general, there are eight soil types in Florida:

1. Western Highlands Ultisols— Level to sloping loamy and sandy soils, with loamy subsoils that are well drained. Used for field crops, pastures, and forestry.

2. Western Highlands Untisols— Nearly level to sloping thick sands that drain excessively. Field crops, pastures, and forestry are primary uses.

3. Central Ridge Entisols—Nearly level to sloping thick sands used for field crops, watermelons, and citrus in the south.

4. Central Ridge Alfisols and Ultisols—Gently sloping, well-drained sand with loamy subsoils underlain by phosphatic limestone. Used primarily for field crops, tobacco, vegetables, pastures, and citrus in the south.

5. Flatwoods Spodosols—Nearly level and somewhat poorly drained sandy soils with dark, sandy subsoil layers. Mostly used for pastures, vegetables, flowers, forest products, and citrus. Is the predominate soil type in Florida, but is considered only good to poor for homesites.

6. Soils of Organic Origin—Level, very poorly drained organic soils underlain by marl or limestone. Primarily used for sugarcane, vegetables, pastures, and sod. Located primarily south of Lake Okeechobee and classified as very poor for homesites and urban development.

7. Soils of Recent Limestone Origin—Level, very poorly drained marly, sandy soils underlain by limestone. Used for winter vegetables. Found primarily in southernmost reaches of state and classified as poor for homesites and urban development.

8. Miscellaneous Coastal—Beaches, tidal marshes, and swamps. Dominated by sloping sandy beaches and sand dunes. Primarily used for recreation and wildlife.

Highly variable as homesites and for urban development.

BEACHES AND COASTLINE

Sand beaches account for 825 miles of the state's Atlantic Ocean and Gulf of Mexico coastlines. These beaches continue to be listed by tourists as a major reason for vacationing in Florida.

Unfortunately, more than half of the state's beaches are experiencing erosion, with 399 miles listed as being at the "critical" stage, an increase over past years. While popularly attributed to coastal development, state environmentalists chalk it up to the pounding of hurricanes, tropical, and other storms, especially the violent weather of the past mid-decade.

Erosion is dubbed "critical" if it threatens upland development, recreational interests, wildlife habitat, or cultural resources. Of the 399 miles, 205 are on the Atlantic, 183 on the Gulf, and 11 are in the Keys.

Some Florida beaches are estimated to annually lose as much as 28 feet of sand to erosion, although the sea action usually rewards other beaches with as much as 16 feet of new sand annually. Publicly funded renourishment of beaches costs $1 million per mile.

For decades, the state has experimented with various types of barriers to prevent beach erosion. Tried have been permeable groins, wooden piers, concrete walls, and jetties, but none have shown marked success. The result is that many eroded beaches, particularly those used for recreation, have had to be replenished with sand dredged from off shore.

But Florida's beaches continue to be rated some of the most attractive in the nation. A ranking of the nation's beaches by Florida International University coastal researcher Dr. Stephen Leatherman consistently has Florida beaches in the top ten. In both 2010 and 2009, "Dr. Beach" ranked Siesta Beach at Sarasota second on the list, up from third the year before, while Cape Florida State Park at Key Biscayne annually makes the top ten. No Panhandle beaches were considered in 2010 because of the Gulf oil spill.

Other beaches around the nation have gotten a chance to shine, too, because so many Florida beaches have been named the "Best Beach" in the annual assessment and been retired from the list. Thusly honored through the years have been Bahia Honda State Recreation Area; Big Pine Key; Caladesi Island State Park, off Dunedin; Fort DeSoto Park, St. Petersburg; Grayton Beach State Recreation Area, at Santa Rosa Beach; St. Andrews State Recreation Area, Panama City; and St. Joseph Peninsula State Park, at Port St. Joe.

SAND

Florida's Panhandle has the whitest beaches in the world. They are made of sand that is 99.4 percent pure crystal which traveled from the area of what is now the Appalachian Mountains to the shores of the Gulf of Mexico at the conclusion of the Ice Age. The stretch of gulf front running from approximately Pensacola to Panama City has become known as the Emerald Coast because of the bright green color of the water over the glistening white sand.

Central Florida Gulf beaches are composed of a combination of calcium carbonate from crushed sea animals, and quartz. Beaches along the Atlantic coast are formed by heavy deposits of crushed shell and are noted for their large grains.

South Florida sand is a mixture of quartz and crushed coral.

AQUIFERS

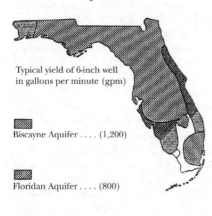

Typical yield of 6-inch well in gallons per minute (gpm)

Biscayne Aquifer . . . . (1,200)

Floridan Aquifer . . . . (800)

Other aquifers . . . . (300 gpm)

PRINCIPAL SOURCES OF GROUNDWATER

Studies reveal that Florida has more available groundwater than any other state. This is because nearly all of the state sits atop groundwater reservoirs called aquifers. These aquifers are of two types—*artesian* and *nonartesian*.

An *artesian* aquifer is one that contains water under sufficient pressure to rise above the top of the containing ground formation.

A *nonartesian* aquifer is one that contains water that is not confined so that the upper water surface (water table) is free to rise and fall.

Six primary aquifers have been identified in Florida with the state's principal groundwater source being the artesian Floridan Aquifer. It supplies most of the state's water users. Five other more superficial or intermediate aquifers overlie the Floridan Aquifer.

FLORIDAN AQUIFER is dubbed Florida's "rain barrel" by hydrologists. This aquifer measures more than 100,000 square miles. It stretches into southernmost Alabama, southern and eastern Georgia, and into South Carolina. Only in the westernmost part of the Panhandle and the southern regions of the state is the Floridan Aquifer's importance supplanted by other aquifers. And along much of the Atlantic and Gulf coastal areas, the aquifer contains highly mineralized or brackish water.

The Floridan Aquifer includes the Lake City, Avon Park, and Ocala Limestones, all of the Eocene Age; the Suwannee Limestone of the Oligocene Age; and the Tampa Limestone and permeable parts of the Hawthorn Formation of the Miocene Age. In some areas the Floridan Aquifer is exposed at the surface, but over much of the state it lies beneath several hundred feet of sediments.

Well yields in the Floridan Aquifer average about 1,500 gallons per minute and range from several hundred gallons per minute to more than 10,000 gallons per minute, depending mainly on well size, depth, and location.

Natural recharge of the state's primary aquifer is divided by hydrologists into four categories:

1. Areas of generally no recharge under natural conditions, which includes about 45 percent of the state. This occurs because the level to which water will rise in a tight well casing is actually above the land surface and thus classified as an artesian flow area.

2. Areas of very low recharge. These are areas where the aquifer's confining beds are relatively impermeable and often more than 25 feet thick. Recharge occurs at rates of less than two inches per year.

3. Areas of very low to moderate recharge of from two to ten inches annually. Low to moderate recharge occurs because both the water table and the level to which water will rise in a tightly-encased well are at or near land surface.

4. Areas of high recharge, which includes about 15 percent of the state. This occurs primarily in well-drained upland areas—porous sand ridges such as are found in western Alachua and Marion counties, nearly all of Gilchrist and Suwannee counties, and portions of Orange and Lake counties. These areas recharge at a rate estimated at between 10 and 20 inches per year.

Additional high recharge of the Floridan Aquifer takes place in areas where drainage occurs through sinkholes, such as in portions of Pasco, Polk, and Hernando counties.

BISCAYNE AQUIFER is a non-artesian aquifer that underlies about 3,200 miles of Miami-Dade, Broward, and Palm Beach counties. It is the sole source of water for these heavily populated areas. A highly permeable, wedge-shaped formation that ranges from 100 to 250 feet thick along the coast, the aquifer thins considerably from southeastern Palm Beach County to where it nears the Big Cypress Swamp in the state's southern interior.

This aquifer is recharged primarily by rainwater and from the canal system that extends outward from Lake Okeechobee. Because of its permeability, the Biscayne Aquifer is especially prone to outside contamination. And because it comes in direct contact with the ocean, the aquifer is susceptible to saltwater intrusion.

CHOKOLOSKEE AQUIFER is situated in southwestern Florida. This aquifer is recharged largely by local rainfall. It underlies about 3,000 miles of the Big Cypress Swamp and the coastal regions of Collier, Lee, and Monroe counties, where it is the prime source of water. The extreme eastern and southern reaches of this aquifer are most permeable. Urban development and agricultural use is rapidly depleting freshwater in this aquifer and increasing the intrusion of salt water.

HAWTHORN FORMATION AND TAMPA LIMESTONE are primary water sources for those southwestern Florida stretches that lie outside of the Chokoloskee Aquifer. It is not in direct contact with the Floridan Aquifer and supplies only about 2 percent of the publicly used water in Florida.

SAND AND GRAVEL AQUIFER lies beneath approximately 2,400 square miles at the tip of the state's Panhandle, principally in Escambia and the western half of Santa Rosa counties. It is also a secondary water source of Okaloosa and Walton counties. Wedge-shaped, with thicknesses up to 700 feet, this formation is primarily recharged by local rainfall.

UNDIFFERENTIATED AQUIFERS are a collection of unspecified water sources that include beds of sand, shell, sandstone, dolomite, claylike sands, and limestone. These important water containers span Florida's east coast from Duval County south to portions of Palm Beach County, and inland to Hendry, Glades, Collier, and Monroe counties, and on the west coast to parts of Lee, Charlotte, and Sarasota counties. The undifferentiated aquifers are estimated by hydrologists to supply about 7 percent of the water for public use.

FUTURE WATER SUPPLY

Although Florida sits atop the nation's largest pool of fresh water, it has been long plagued by water shortage and distribution problems caused by its long population boom and poor allocation of resources. But better water management, public conservation, the wide introduction of reclaimed water systems, added desalination plants, and the wider use of reservoirs and other ground preserves in this century have improved the situation.

Floridians now count their daily use of fresh water in millions of gallons rather than billions and per capita use of fresh water has dropped more than 70 percent to 138 gallons per day.

The state's fresh water comes from its aquifers via wells, and from surface sources including lakes, rivers, canals, and springs.

One of the greatest uses of fresh water in the past has been for the watering of residential lawns, golf courses, and other green space. But with reclaimed water systems, that use of fresh water has dropped to just 10 percent of daily usage. Reclaimed water systems in cities around the state now provide 90 percent of such water use, putting 660 million gallons a day on the state's grass. Some reclaimed water is pumped back into the aquifers for natural cleaning and systems today do not deliver potable water. Florida is the national leader in reclaimed water use.

The public is the greatest user of fresh ground water, consuming 52 percent of it each day. Agriculture is the second largest consumer at 31 percent. But agriculture is the largest consumer of surface water, taking 56 percent, while the public consumes just 13 percent. Power generation accounts for less than 1 percent of daily ground water consumption, but 13 percent of the daily surface water draw. Nearly all water used in power generation is saline.

While a lull in the state's growth has given the state more opportunity to continue improvement of its water development, preservation, and delivery systems, a water event during the 2010 cold snap demonstrated how fragile the system can be. In an effort to save winter crops, farmers in West Central Florida pumped one billion gallons from the aquifer in just a few days. The result was almost immediate with surround wells going dry and both major and minor sinkholes opening up throughout the area. In the past, nature would have been allowed to take its course. Nevertheless, projects already are under way to vastly increase the number of retention ponds throughout the affected area to provide high volume water in the next such emergency.

WETLANDS

Wetlands is a generic term used to describe any of many different ecosystems that are periodically inundated by fresh or salt water. These would be swamps, marshes, bogs, and overflowed lands.

In Florida, wetlands are categorized as cypress ponds, prairies, floodplains, river swamps, forested freshwater wetlands such as hammocks, freshwater marshes, wet prairies, salt marshes, and mangrove swamps. These soggy areas are crucial habitats for fish and wildlife food sources, nurseries, and breeding areas. It is estimated that 20 percent of all the state's endangered plants and animals depend on wetlands for survival.

In addition, wetlands play a major role in improving water quality by trapping nutrients, toxins, and disease-producing microorganisms. Other wetland functions include erosion protection, flood runoff, and storage.

With 11 million acres, Florida has the nation's largest area of wetlands save for Alaska. But since 1975, the state has lost 200,000 wetland acres, including 84,000 acres since 1990 when federal policy requiring replacement of lost wetlands went into effect. Most such replacement efforts have failed.

Types of wetlands include:

HAMMOCKS, a word of Indian derivation that approximates the meaning of "jungle." The essential characteristic of a hammock is its thick tangle of vegetation. Two kinds of hammocks exist in Florida: high (light soil) and low (heavy soil). Both are extremely fertile. The largest bodies of rich hammock lands are to be found in Levy, Alachua, Marion, Hernando, and Sumter counties. Gulf Hammock in Levy and adjoining counties comprises perhaps the largest body of rich land in the state. Leon, Gadsden, Jefferson, Madison, and Jackson counties also have large areas of high, rolling hammock lands.

Trees in low hammocks are predominately cypress. Live oaks, hickory, magnolia, and other hardwoods grow in the high hammock areas.

CYPRESS STRANDS, best known of which are the Fakahatchee Strand and Corkscrew Swamp, both in south Florida. With their canopies of cypress, some more than 100 feet tall, the strands harbor a rich range of plant life including orchids, bromeliads, vines, and ferns. Strands are prime breeding sites for birds and mammals.

FRESHWATER MARSH, of which the vast Everglades is Florida's primary example. It is unique in the world. As home to alligators and other animals such as the rare Florida Panther, such wetlands maintain a complex cycle of water, grasses, and fire—all necessary to retain ecological balance. Hardy grasses form muck, which supports other plant life. As water tables fluctuate naturally, these grasses grow wet or dry.

During dry seasons, organic matter decomposes. When wet, the decomposed matter releases nutrients. Gradually the grass humus expands, held in check only by naturally-occurring fires. Artificial manipulation of water levels through use of canals and drainage systems greatly interferes with the critical natural flow of freshwater marshes.

MANGROVE SWAMPS, where mangrove plants thrive in salt water and serve as protective breeding habitats for fish and shellfish. The plants prevent soil erosion. In Florida, several varieties of mangroves grow along the east coast from Daytona Beach south, around the state's tip, and up the west coast to the Cedar Key area. Red and the black mangrove grow in and at salt water. The white mangrove and the related buttonwood grow near the shore. Once viewed as a developer's headache, many of the state's mangrove swamps have been routinely removed. In recent years the value of mangrove areas has become known and they are protected by law

ESTUARIES abound in Florida and are perhaps the state's most productive ecosystems. They form when freshwater and seawater combine, and are characterized by tidal fluctuations. While spring and other freshwater gets progressively saltier as it flows in rivers and streams toward the Gulf and Mexico and the Atlantic Ocean, they bring inland nutrients that allow plants to thrive in saline zones along

the coasts. These plants set off a chain of nature. Fish, spiny lobster, shrimp, oysters, clams, indeed fully 70 percent of Florida's important recreation and commercial sealife, spend a portion of their lives in the estuary environment. Estuaries also provide breeding and nesting areas for a large assortment of coastal and migratory birds including endangered species. Sea grasses, salt marshes, and mangroves provide species cover and aid greatly in preserving the coastlines. Urban and agricultural development, ill-advised public projects involving flood control, canalization, and a wide variety of dredging programs have done great harm to many of the state's estuaries over the years, including some that are unlikely to recover. But Florida's Water Management Districts and other state agencies have planned or embarked on further alteration programs, carefully monitored and intended to undo the damage.

FORESTS

At one time Florida was nearly 90 percent forest. Very little of this virgin forest is left because lumbering was one of the state's earliest industries. Almost all of today's pine is second or third growth, but whether pine or otherwise, nearly half of Florida remains in forest land.

Florida's mixed vegetation reflects the state's location on the border of the tropics. Soils, drainage, and latitude are the primary controls over what trees may be growing where. Nearly half of the species of trees native to the United States are found in Florida, but the palmetto and the pitch pine are the only trees found on both the southern and northern borders of the state.

LAKES

Name of Lake	Size (Acres)
Alachua County	
Ledwith Lake	1,785
Levy Lake	4,556
Little Lochloosa Lake	2,642
Lochloosa Lake	5,705
Lake Newnan	7,427
Orange Lake	12,706
Paynes Prairie Lake	4,292
Baker County	
Ocean Pond	1,774
Bay County	
Deerpoint Lake	5,000
Bradford County	
Lake Sampson	2,042
Little Santa Fe	1,135
Santa Fe Lake	4,721
Brevard County	
Lake Poinsett	4,334
Lake Washington	4,362
Lake Winder	1,496
South Lake	1,101
Broward County	
Conservation Area 2 lake	134,400
Conservation Area 3 lake	585,280
Citrus County	
Tsala Apopka Lake	19,111
Clay County	
Doctors Lake	3,397
Kingsley Lake	1,652
Lake Geneva	1,630
Sand Hill Lake	1,263
Collier County	
Lake Trafford	1,494
Flagler County	
Lake Disston	1,844
Gadsden County	
Lake Talquin	8,850
Gulf County	
Dead Lake	3,655
Lake Wimico	4,055
Highlands County	
Lake Istokpoga	27,692
Lake Jackson	3,412
Lake Josephine	1,236
Lake June-in-Winter	3,504
Lake Placid	3,320
Indian River County	
Blue Cypress Lake	6,555

Jackson County	
Jim Woodruff Reservoir	37,500
Ocheesee Pond	2,225
Jefferson County	
Lake Miccosukee	6,226
Lake County	
Lake Beauclair	1,111
Lake Dora	4,475
Lake Dorr	1,533
Lake Eustis	7,806
Lake Griffin	16,505
Lake Harris	13,788
Lake Louisa	3,634
Lake Minnehaha	2,261
Lake Minneola	1,888
Lake Norris	1,131
Lake Yale	4,042
Little Lake Harris	2,739
Okahumpka Swamp	3,226
Leon County	
Lake Iamonia	5,757
Lake Jackson	4,004
Levy County	
Lake Rousseau	3,657
Madison County	
Hixtown Swamp	9,776
Marion County	
Lake Kerr	2,830
Lake Weir	5,685
Sellers Lake	1,050
Orange County	
Bay Lake	1,060
Big Sand Lake	
Johns Lake	2,417
Lake Apopka	30,671
Lake Butler	1,665
Lake Conway	1,075
Lake Hart	1,850
Lake Mary Jane	1,158
Lake Tibet	1,198
Osceola County	
Alligator Lake	3,406
Cat Lake	2,080
Cypress Lake	4,097
East Lake Tohopekaliga	11,968
Econlockhatchee River Swamp	4,108
Lake Conlin	6,281
Lake Gentry	1,791

Lake Hatchineha	6,665
Lake Jackson	1,020
Lake Kissimmee	34,948
Lake Marian	5,739
Lake Tohopekaliga	18,810
(Unnamed Lake)	3,778
Palm Beach County	
Conservation Area 1 Lake	141,440
Lake Okeechobee	448,000
Pinellas County	
Lake Tarpon	2,534
Polk County	
Ariana Lake	1,026
Crooked Lake	5,538
Lake Arbuckie	3,828
Lake Buffum	1,543
Lake Clinch	1,207
Lake Eloise	1,160
Lake Hamilton	2,162
Lake Hancock	4,519
Lake Livingston	1,203
Lake Marion	2,990
Lake Mattie	1,078
Lake Parker	2,272
Lake Pierce	3,729
Lake Rosalie	4,597
Lake Weohyakapka	7,532
Reedy Lake	3,486
Tiger Lake	2,200
Putnam County	
Crescent Lake	15,960
Levy's Prairie	1,938
Little Lake George	1,416
Seminole County	
Lake Jessup	10,011
Puzzle Lake	1,300
Sumter County	
Lake Panasoffkee	4,460
Volusia County	
Gopher Slough	1,088
Lake Ashby	1,030
Lake Dexter	1,902
Lake George	46,000
Lake Harney	6,058
Lake Monroe	9,406
Lake Woodruff	2,200
Washington County	
The Deadening Lakes	2,538

Florida has about 7,800 lakes, many of which are still unnamed. They range in area from mere one-acre ponds to mighty Lake Okeechobee, which measures 448,000 acres.

Nearly all of Florida's lakes are natural, having originated either as sinkholes, as sea-bottom depressions, or as erosion points of rivers. More than one-third of the state's lakes are to be found in just four of the 67 counties—Lake, Orange, Osceola, and Polk. The previous chart lists Florida lakes of 1,000 acres or more in size.

SPRINGS

The stratified components of Florida's peninsula—mainly basal rock, limestone, and clays—and the unique limestone cap thousands of feet deep that extends over most of the state, provide Florida with a steady flow of fresh water. Tens of thousands of years ago, when the peninsula emerged from the sea for the last time, these rocks and the sandy soil trapped the salt water. But centuries of heavy rains forced the salt below sea level and today Florida's heavy annual rainfall floats on top of this ancient sea-water with little mixing. The groundwater collects in the porous limestone layer, forming a statewide underground reservoir. These reservoirs are called aquifers and they underlie almost all of Florida.

Many of Florida's lakes and springs are supplied by these aquifers. There are two kinds of springs—the *seepage spring*, which is formed when the ground surface dips below the water table, and the *artesian spring*, which receives its water through deep fissures or well-like channels that may run 100 feet or more below the surface. The water is forced up into these springs by the tremendous pressures of its accumulated weight in the aquifers below. When this outlet is near the top, the water in the spring bubbles on the surface. Outlets deep below are not reflected on the surface, but the water gushes out, unseen, with tremendous force, at the opening.

Some of Florida's lakes are simply sinks and are directly affected by the amount of rainfall. During dry seasons, the "lake" becomes a pond, a mud bed, or it may dry up completely. These disappearing lakes are common throughout the state. Some lake basins were formed by the sea in low places that were formerly ocean floors, some are fed by artesian springs, while still others are created when the wind cuts through the sand to make a sea level channel to a depression.

There are more than 700 known springs in Florida and they are found in 46 of the 67 counties. Thirty-three of that total are classified as *first magnitude* springs. In a first magnitude spring, water flows at a rate of at least 100 cubic feet per second. More than a dozen springs are to be found offshore along Florida's coast. These *submarine* springs simply emerge below sea level and if large enough will create a boil that can be seen at the water's surface. Several submarine springs have been identified in the Atlantic Ocean off Crescent Beach. Six are in the Gulf near Wakulla, four lie near Pasco County, and one is adjacent to Lee County.

So-called *pseudo-springs* are not true springs, but are actually flows from artesian wells of depths of

1,000 or more feet. There are seven pseudo-springs, all in south Florida. They are Carlsbad Spa Villas in Broward County, Hot Springs in Charlotte County, Hurricane Lodge and the Mineral Springs in Miami-Dade County, Shangri-La Motel Health Resort and Warm Spring Spa in Lee County, and Pennecamp in Monroe County.

The following are major springs by county:

Alachua County
Glen Springs
Hornsby Spring
Magnesia Spring
Poe Spring

Bay County
Gainer Springs
Pitts Spring

Bradford County
Helbronn Spring

Calhoun County
Abes Spring

Citrus County
Blue Spring
Chassahowitska Springs
Kings Bay Group
Homosassa Springs
Ruth Spring

Clay County
Green Cove Spring
Wadesboro Spring

Columbia County
Bell Springs
Columbia Spring
Ichetucknee Spring
Santa Fe River Rise
Tree House Spring

Dixie County
Copper Spring
Little Copper Spring
Guaranto Spring
McCrabb Spring

Escambia County
Mystic Springs

Gadsden Count
Chattahoochee Spring
Glen Julia Springs

Gilchrist County
Bell Springs
Blue Springs
Devil's Ear Spring
Ginnie Springs
Hart Springs
Lumber Camp Springs
Otter Springs
Rock Bluff Springs
Siphon Creek Rise
Sun Springs
Townsend Spring

Gulf County
Dalkeith Springs

Hamilton County
Alapaha Rise
Holton Creek Rise
Morgan Spring
White Springs

Hernando County
Bobhill Springs
Little Springs
Salt Spring
Weeki Wachee Spring

Hillsborough County
Buckhorn Spring
Eureka Springs
Lettuce Lake Spring
Lithia Springs
Six Mile Creek Spring
Sulphur Springs

Holmes County
Jackson Spring
Ponce de Leon Springs
Vortex Blue Spring

Jackson County
Black Spring
Blue Spring
Blue Hole Spring
Bosel Spring

Daniel Springs
Double Spring
Gadsen Spring
Hays Spring
Mill Pond Spring
Springboard Spring
Sand Bag Spring
Waddells Mill Pond
Spring

Jefferson County
Wacissa Springs Group:
Big Spring
Gerner Springs
Blue Spring
Buzzard Log Springs
Minnow Spring
Cassidy Spring
Springs No.1 and 2
Thomas Spring
Log Springs
Allen Spring
Horsehead Spring

Lafayette County
Allen Mill Pond Spring
Blue Spring
Convict Spring
Fletcher Spring
Mearson Spring
Owens Spring
Perry Spring
Ruth Spring
Steinhatchee Spring
Troy Springs
Turtle Spring

Lake County
Alexander Spring
Apopka Spring
Blue Spring
Bugg Spring
Camp La No Che Spring
Holiday Springs
Messant Spring
Seminole Springs

Leon County
Horn Spring
Natural Bridge Spring
Rhodes Spring
St. Marks River Rise

Levy County
Blue Springs
Fanning Springs
Manatee Springs
Wekiva Springs

Liberty County
White Springs

Madison County
Blue Spring
Pettis Spring
Suwanacoochee Spring

Marion County
Juniper Springs
Orange Springs
Rainbow Springs Group
Salt Springs
Silver Springs
Silver Glen Springs
Fern Hammock Springs
Wilson Head Spring

Nassau County
Su-No Wa Spring

Orange County
Rock Springs
Wekiva Springs
Witherington Spring

Pasco County
Crystal Springs
Horseshoe Spring
Magnolia Springs
Salt Springs

Pinellas County
Health Spring

Putnam County
Beacher Springs
Mud Spring
Nashua Spring
Satsuma Spring
Forest Spring
Welaka Spring
Whitewater Springs

Santa Rosa County
Chumuckla Springs

Sarasota County
Little Salt Spring
Warm Mineral Springs

Seminole County
Clifton Spring
Elder Spring
Heath Spring
Lake Jessup Spring
Miami Springs
Palm Springs
Sanlando Springs
Starbuck Spring

Sumter County
Fenny Springs
Gum Springs

Suwannee County
Bonnett Spring
Branford Springs
Charles Springs
Ellaville Spring
Falmouth Spring
Little River Springs
Peacock Springs
Royal Spring
Running Springs
Suwannee Springs

Thomas Spring
Tilford Spring

Taylor County
Carlton Spring
Ewing Spring
Hampton Springs
Iron Spring
Nutall Rise
Steinhatchee River Rise
Waldo Springs

Union County
Worthington Springs

Volusia County
Blue Spring
Gemini Springs
Green Springs
Ponce de Leon Springs
Seminole Springs

Wakulla County
Grays Rise
Indian Springs
Kini Spring
Newport Springs
Panama Mineral Springs
River Sink Spring
Spring Creek Springs
Group
Wakulla Springs

Walton County
Euchee Springs
Morrison Spring

Washington County
Beckton Springs
Blue Spring
Cypress Spring
Blue Springs
Williford Springs

LOCATION OF SPRINGS

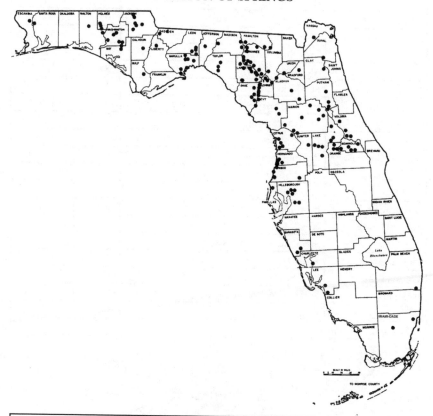

FIRST MAGNITUDE SPRINGS				
		Avg. Flow Cubic Ft. Per Second	Temp. °F	Discharge Cubic Ft. Per Second
Citrus County	Chassahawitska Springs	139	74	32-197
	Kings Bay Group	975	75	*
	Homosassa Spring	191	74	186-197
Columbia County	Columbia Spring	–	95	39
	Ichetucknee Springs	191	74	186-165
	Santa Fe River Rise	–	75	75
	Tea House Spring	202	74	39-406
Gilchrist County	Devil's Ear Spring	–	76	207
	Siphon Creek Rise	–	75	120
Hamilton County	Alapaha Rise	608	66	508-699
	Holton Creek Rise	288	72	69-482
Hernando County	Weeki Wachee Spring	176	73	101-275

Jackson County	Blue Spring	190	71	56-287
Jefferson County	Wacissa Springs Group	262	70	264-605
Lafayette County	Blue Spring	69	73	46-93
	Troy Springs	153	73	149-205
Lake County	Alexander Spring	118	78	74-162
Leon County	St. Marks River Rise	452	71	310-950
Levy County	Fanning Springs	98	75	52-139
	Manatee Springs	178	76	110-238
Madison County	Blue Spring	103	72	71-141
Marion County	Rainbow Springs Group	763	76	487-1,230
	Silver Springs	820	73	539-1,290
	Silver Glen Springs	112	76	90-129
Suwannee County	Falmouth Spring	135	72	60-220
Taylor County	Nutall Rise	360	73	360
	Steinhatchee River Rise	350	72	350
Union County	Santa Fe Spring	99	75	48-150
Volusia County	Blue Spring	121	76	63-214
Wakulla County	Spring Creek Springs Group	1,154	72	307-2,000
	Wakulla Springs	6880	70	25-1,910

Tidal-affected discharge

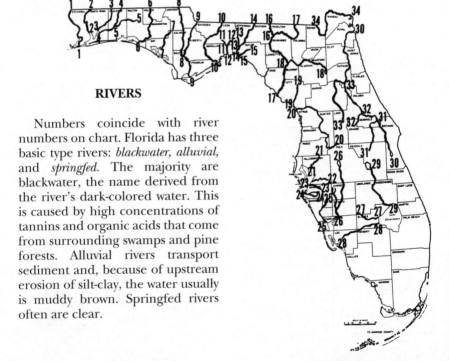

RIVERS

Numbers coincide with river numbers on chart. Florida has three basic type rivers: *blackwater, alluvial,* and *springfed.* The majority are blackwater, the name derived from the river's dark-colored water. This is caused by high concentrations of tannins and organic acids that come from surrounding swamps and pine forests. Alluvial rivers transport sediment and, because of upstream erosion of silt-clay, the water usually is muddy brown. Springfed rivers often are clear.

Map No.	River	Length in Miles	Drainage Area in Sq. Miles	Type
22	Alafia	25	335	Blackwater
9	Apalachicola	94*	17,200	Alluvial
14	Aucilla	60*	747	Blackwater/Springfed
3	Blackwater	49*	860	Blackwater
28	Caloosahatchee**	75	1,378	Blackwater
8	Chipola	89	781	Springfed
6	Choctawhatchee	100*	4,676	Alluvial
7	Econfina Creek	36	435	Blackwater
15	Econfina	43	239	Blackwater
31	Econlockhathcee	36	129	Blackwater
2	Escambia	54*	4,233	Alluvial
27	Fisheating Creek	51	436	Blackwater
21	Hillsborough	56	690	Blackwater
29	Kissimmee	134***	2,945	Blackwater
23	Little Manatee	38	222	Blackwater
24	Manatee	35	357	Blackwater
25	Myakka	68	235	Blackwater
10	Ochlockonee	102*	1,720	Alluvial
33	Oklawaha	79	2,970	Blackwater/Springfed
26	Peace	106	1,367	Blackwater
1	Perdido	58*	925	Blackwater
30	St. Johns	273	8,840	Mixed type with springs
12	St. Marks	36	535	Springfed
34	St. Mary's	127	1,480	Springfed
18	Santa Fe	76	1,520	Springfed
5	Shoal	37	499	Blackwater
17	Suwannee	177*	9,630	Blackwater/Springfed
19	Waccasassa	29	610	Blackwater
13	Wacissa	12	99	Springfed
11	Wakulla	10	0	Springfed
32	Wekiva	14	189	Springfed
16	Withlacoochee (N)	23*	2,120	Blackwater/Springfed
20	Withlacoochee (S)	86	1,710	Blackwater/Springfed
4	Yellow	61*	1,365	Blackwater

*Distances from mouth to Florida state line.
**The Caloosahatchee is classified a canal because of its locks.
***Before river was rechanneled. The Kissimmee is being restored to its original state with scheduled completion in 2015.

THE GREEN SWAMP

One of the last remaining wilderness areas of Florida is the Green Swamp, 850 square miles of wet marshland, sand hills, thick forests, rivers, and lakes in the center of the state. The swamp is bounded by Brooksville, Clermont, Haines City, Lakeland, and Zephyrhills. It is of unique hydrologic significance and the headwaters of four major Florida rivers—the Hillsborough, Oklawaha, Peace, and Withlacoochee. From the swamp's surface water runoff and its base flow comes the initial flow of the four rivers. In addition, the huge Lake Okeechobee and the Everglades are dependent on the Green Swamp through the Kissimmee River system.

Beneath the swamp is one of Florida's greatest water sources. Its underground streams supply 70 percent of all the water used in the state and about 90 percent of the water supply for central Florida. Most importantly, the highest groundwater altitude in Florida is within the Green Swamp, a factor that creates pressure on groundwaters to flow into low pressure metropolitan areas in all four directions. Without this constant pressure from the swamp, salt water would force its way into the underground caverns or aquifers that hold so much of the state's freshwater.

Much of the Green Swamp region has been set aside for natural water storage, with other portions opened up for recreation. The state owns 172,988 of the swamp's 560,000 acres.

Besides the Green Swamp's vast underground water reservoir, its visible features also are of immense importance to many Floridians. The region is the habitat of an enormous variety of plants and animals, some of which depend completely on wetlands.

MILES OF FRESH WATER

Florida has 3 million acres of freshwater lakes and 12,000 miles of streams and rivers. From those waters, over 250 different species of freshwater fishes have been collected.

BEST WATER

The natural quality of groundwater in Florida varies widely and depends on the aquifer, location, and depth at which the water is obtained. The best quality of groundwater is found in northwestern Florida.

MINERALS

Floridians have been digging in the dirt since their earliest days. Native Americans mined limestone to get chert for weapons and tools and dug clay for cooking and storage ware. The Spaniards quarried coquina limestone to build forts and homes. But it wasn't until the late 19th century that Florida emerged as a major mining and mineral center with the discovery of phosphate.

Phosphate: The first proven sample of phosphate rock came from a well in Alachua County in 1880, just 30 years after the recognition of phosphorus as a necessary nutrient for crops and animals. More deposits were found in Clay, Gadsden, Wakulla, and Charlotte counties. Pick and shovel mining began in 1889 in Marion County and mining has been continuous in the state since. But in none of those places is phosphate plentiful. The development of the dragline and the discovery of "Bone Valley" and another large deposit in North Florida's Hamilton County boomed the industry. Bone Valley, named for its unending fossil finds, is a mineral rich area including Polk, Hillsborough, Manatee, and Hardee counties. Although heavily mined for half a century, Bone Valley is still highly productive. But the longterm future of phosphate is expected to drift south down the Peace River.

And there will be a future. As recently as the last decade, it was estimated that phosphate reserves in Florida would last for 25 years at current rates of production. However, research and new technology being brought to bear in the industry indicate that Florida may have as much as a 300-year supply of the valuable rock still in the ground. Florida supplies 75 percent of the nation's and 25 percent of the world's phosphate, most of it shipped in bulk through the nearby port and transportation hub of Tampa. Phosphate mining companies own or hold mineral rights to nearly 475,000 acres of Florida land.

Phosphate is a natural chemical compound containing phosphorus and oxygen. It is found in phosphate rock, usually in combination with calcium and magnesium. It is also found in bone ash and vegetable mold, all created by Florida's ever-changing landscape through the millennia. Phosphate requires heavy industrial milling before it becomes a usable product. The principal products are diammonium phosphate (DAP), monoammonium phosphate (MAP), fertilizers, and SMAP animal feed supplements. Approximately 90 percent of the product becomes fertilizer, 5 percent animal feed.

Companies involved in the process also produce sulfuric acid, triple superphosphate, ammoniated phosphate, recovered fluoride products, and other related items. They produce phosphoric acid for their own process uses. Phosphate by-products for consumers include vitamins, soft drinks, toothpaste, light bulbs, film, bone china, flame-resistant fabrics, and optical glass.

Phosphate mining and production has long required vast amounts of water, but today mining and production use of water has declined 75 percent from its peak and more than 90 percent of water used for both is recycled.

In 2009, phosphate mining companies paid $38 million in severance taxes to the state. The first $10 million of each year's tax payment goes to buy environmentally endangered land while 40 percent of the remainder goes into the state's general fund. Approximately 10 percent of the revenue goes to reclaim land mined before 1975. The mining companies are required to reclaim land mined since then. Reclamation projects have surpassed in quality the requirements set by the state. In addition to land deemed suitable for park and recreational use and donated to the public, companies have restored mine sites to levels where they can be used for residential, commercial, industrial, and agricultural use. Nearly 70 percent of all used phosphate lands have been reclaimed. Another 10 percent of the severance tax is returned to the affected counties. Several counties, eyeing recent increases in the market value of phosphate, are agitating for a greater share. Remaining revenues are parceled out to various industry- and area-related projects. In addition to severance taxes, phosphate companies pay and convey sales taxes to the state and pay property taxes to the counties.

The companies closely hold revenues and production data. Economic reports from outside the industry peg phosphate exports at $3.9 billion in 2008. The industry provides approximately 67,000 jobs at well above average market wages and has an estimated $6.7 billion economic impact on its areas of operation.

Limestone: Limestone accounts for most of the crushed stone mined in Florida, followed by shell. The highest quality limestone goes into portland and masonry cement. Portland value was $557 million in 2007, while masonry was valued at $86 million. Florida is the nation's leading producer of masonry cement. Also going into the crushed stone market are dolomite and sandstone. Crushed stone is used primary as road base. In 2007, Florida accounted for 96 million metric tons of crushed stone with a value of $1.1 billion. Lime production and revenues are proprietary.

Clays: Three types of clay are mined in Florida, Fuller's Earth, Kaolin, and Common. Fuller's Earth, noted for its absorbency and having many uses, is mined primarily in Gadsden County. It is narrowly defined by the state to protect it from inferior product and production and revenue aspects are privy by law. Mined Kaolin, used in the manufacture of paper and refractories had a value of $2.7 million in 2007. Common clay is a minor mining interest but, mixed with other material, is used in bricks, cement, and lightweight aggregates.

Peat: Given Florida geological history, it is not surprising that Florida is the nation's leading peat producer. The industry, centered in North Central Florida, is estimated to generate $10 million annually.

Heavy Minerals: Ilmenite, rutile, leucoxene, zircon, and titanium are among the heavy minerals gleaned from Florida sands and stones. The first three are basic ingredients for titanium dioxide pigments used in paints, varnish and lacquers, plastics, and paper. Florida is the only state to produce rutile. Heavy mineral operations are concentrated in Northeast Florida.

Oil and Gas: For as long as geologists have searched for phosphate, they've searched for oil and gas in the belief that the state had to be an extension of Gulf Coast oil country. They found it in 1970 in the northwestern panhandle and in southwest Florida. Today there are 11 oil fields, but they are still grouped as Jay and Sunniland after the sites of the first successful finds. The Jay field is in Santa Rosa and Escambia counties. Sunniland is in Collier, Miami-Dade, Hendry, and Lee counties. They were both considered minor fields with Jay peaking in 1981 and Sunniland in the year it came in. Both have declined ever since as have other wells in their areas. The refinery at Jay is now closed.

RARE MINERAL

Florida is home to a world's record deposit of one of the rarest minerals, fulgurite, a glassy tube formed below ground when the ground is hit by lightning. The bolt melts sand, which when cooled forms tubes surrounding the lightning's path. University of Florida scientists carefully unearthed a two-branch fulgurite on the grounds of Camp Blanding in 1997. One branch was 17 feet long, the other 16. Having recovered it in one piece, Florida claimed the world's record. The previous record was held by a one-prong fulgurite measuring 13 feet.

FLORIDA HISTORY

EXPLORATION AND COLONIZATION

Scholars estimate the first human inhabitants of Florida arrived about 12,000 BC. Little is known of these early Indian settlers because there are no surviving written records until the arrival of Juan Ponce de Leon in 1513. Between March 27 and April 2 of that year the Spanish explorer sighted the Florida coast and made landfall in the vicinity of present day St. Augustine.

It is believed that other Spaniards, and perhaps Englishmen, explored the coastal waters between 1487 and 1513, but crudely drawn maps from that era are not conclusive.

The name Florida is credited to Ponce de Leon, who selected it because of the "many cool woodlands" he saw and because the discovery was made during the Spanish Feast of the Flowers.

In 1521, Ponce de Leon returned to establish a plantation colony for Spain. The settlement was short-lived, but it marked Europe's first attempt to colonize the New World. Nearly two decades later, Spanish explorer Hernando de Soto landed at Tampa Bay, traveling up the peninsula to winter at Tallahassee before moving on to the Mississippi River, which he is credited with discovering and where he died.

While in Florida, De Soto found Juan Ortiz, a Spanish soldier who had accompanied intermediate explorer Panfilo de Narvaez and had been held captive by Indians. Ortiz's knowledge of his Indian captors enabled scribes accompanying the De Soto expedition to elaborate on their Florida adventures. Their notes would provide future historians with their first knowledge of the land's native inhabitants of that era.

Early Spanish explorers and would-be colonizers found neither the gold nor glory they were seeking in Florida, but their efforts were not entirely wasted. The strategic geographical importance of the Florida peninsula in the Spanish dreams of empire gained military and political recognition. Conquests in Central and South America were bringing big dividends of silver, gold, and jewels into the mother country's treasury. To carry the loot to King Philip II, the Spanish treasure fleet sailed from Mexico and other points along the Caribbean coast, following the Gulf Stream along Florida's southern and eastern coasts. But pirates were often waiting for the heavily laden vessels to sail into the Florida straits. Between buccaneers and hurricanes, many of the Spanish galleons learned that the Florida Keys opened the door to Davy Jones' Locker.

Another attempt at colonization in Florida had been undertaken by Spanish explorer Tristan de Luna in 1559. He established a settlement on Pensacola Bay that year, but it was abandoned two years later when a storm wrecked most of his fleet.

Florida's geographical advantages became apparent to France so that in 1562 Jean Ribaut was dispatched to establish a colony for religious freedom from which Frenchmen could prey on the Spanish plate fleet. Two years later, Rene de Goulaine de Laudoniere built Fort Caroline near the mouth of the St. Johns River, known to the French as the River of May.

The intrusion threw the Spanish court into a royal temper. King Philip promptly commissioned Pedro Menendez de Aviles, captain-general of the armed fleet, to rout the French and set up a haven for shipwrecked sailors. In August 1565, Menendez sailed into a harbor he called San Augustin and the following month he established the first permanent settlement in what is now the United States.

Menendez and his troops succeeded in wiping out the French through a series of massacres typical of the period. The French-built Fort Caroline was renamed San Mateo and converted into a Spanish outpost after its capture.

While European armies battled for physical possession of Florida, European missionaries battled for the souls of the natives. Unfortunately, the Indians could not, or chose not to, distinguish a clergyman from a soldier. The first priest known to die for his faith in Florida was Frey Luis Cancer de Barbasto, a Dominican missionary killed by Indians near Tampa Bay in 1549. Despite discouraging losses, efforts to convert the Indians to Christianity were in full swing by 1566. Jesuit and Franciscan friars had hoisted the fallen banner and humbly ministered to their half-heathen, half-Christian flocks.

Meanwhile, in Europe, the French were fuming over the loss of Fort Caroline and Dominque de Gourgues was ordered to lead an expedition to avenge the massacres. He successfully executed both his orders and the Spanish garrison of San Mateo before returning to France.

Spain's loss of the outpost failed to halt its advance in the New World. It established a colonial pattern of forts and missions from Florida to Rappahannock, Virginia. As her power in the New World grew, however, her prestige among her peers was dwindling. In 1586, Sir Francis Drake sacked and burned the Spanish settlement of St. Augustine, and two years later English sailors routed the proud Spanish Armada, paving the way for more British encroachments upon Spanish territory.

WIDENING HORIZONS, 1600-1800

Despite these losses, Spain remained entrenched in the southeastern portion of North America, prompting the English to concentrate their settlements on the upper eastern seaboard. The English settled Jamestown in 1607, followed by the Pilgrim landing at Plymouth Rock in 1620. In succeeding decades, the English moved steadily southward, pushing the northern border of Spanish Florida closer to the present-day state line. By 1670, the British had moved into South Carolina, making nearby Spanish outposts easy prey for marauding English colonists.

By the end of the 17th century Spain found her position threatened on all sides. The English were moving down from the north and the French were moving along the Gulf coast from the west. Fortifications were built at Pensacola to guard against French encroachment.

England wanted Florida to round out her seaboard colonies, so in 1702 Gov. James Moore of South Carolina set sail with that objective in mind. His forces staged a two-month siege of St. Augustine during which the town was captured, but the Spanish held the well-fortified Castillo de San Marcos. After a futile bombardment of the Castillo's impenetrable walls, Moore's fleet withdrew.

To the west, in 1719, the French captured Pensacola from the Spanish. But the English threat soon united Spain and France and the colony was returned to the Spanish. During this period, the French occupied the Gulf coast west of Pensacola.

Meanwhile, British Gen. James Oglethorpe founded the colony of Georgia in 1732. For eight years it was the buffer between the British-owned Carolinas and Spanish-owned Florida, but in 1740 Oglethorpe struck. He seized outlying Spanish forts and bombarded Castillo de San Marcos. For 27 days the siege continued, but lack of water and provisions, coupled with the July sun and hordes of insects, forced him to withdraw.

Unable to successfully penetrate Florida from the north, the English tried another strategy. During the Seven Years' War (1756-63) England captured Havana, Cuba. To get Cuba back, England forced Spain to relinquish Florida.

England found Florida mostly wilderness. St. Augustine was a city of only 900 houses, and Pensacola in the 18th century had grown little beyond its original settlement. The English did acquire a fort, San Marcos de Apalache, near the St. Marks River, but the peninsula was largely unexplored.

The new government made elaborate plans to attract settlers. To govern the territory, England divided Florida into two provinces, east Florida with the capital at St. Augustine, and west Florida with Pensacola as its capital. A plantation economy was established and the first Florida exports began to trickle across the Atlantic. For the first time Florida was experiencing a measure of economic and political security.

Elsewhere on the continent, conditions were far from peaceful. British rule was new in Florida and accepted by the settlers who remained, but the citizens of the northern colonies were moving to free themselves from the stranglehold of King George III of England. Throughout the Revolutionary War, Florida remained loyal to the Crown and became a haven for several thousand wealthy Tories. The newcomers established plantations in east Florida and soon assumed a position of leadership in the territory's affairs. But British ownership was not to last long.

In 1783, Spain evened a 20-year score by capturing the British-owned Bahamas. To regain the islands, England returned Florida to Spain.

The last significant event of the 18th century for Florida was the Pinckney Treaty between the United States and Spain in 1795. It set the northern boundary of Florida at the 31st parallel.

THE AMERICANIZATION OF FLORIDA, 1800-1865

Spain's second attempt to gain a foothold in North America was doomed from the start. British plantation owners left when the Union Jack was lowered, and Florida began leaning toward annexation by the United States. In Europe, Napoleon was threatening the already-weakened mother country. Finally, in 1819, Spain and the U.S. began negotiations to transfer the Spanish colony to the United States of America. Two years later, the Stars and Stripes became the fourth national flag to fly over Florida.

At the time, Florida had some 4,300 inhabitants, nearly all clustered along the coasts at Pensacola, St. Marks, Key West, St. Augustine, and Fernandina Beach. Two or three hundred more settlements were scattered throughout north Florida. The rest of the land belonged to the Indians. Virtually all of the former Spanish colonists had emigrated and the cultural patterns of the settlements were becoming Americanized.

With the lure of virgin land as bait for new residents, Florida's provisional governor, Andrew Jackson, set out to remove the Indians to the central part of the peninsula. As this was accomplished, settlers began to immigrate from both the United States and the Bahamas. In 1822, when the area gained official territorial status, Florida began to grow. A capital site was selected in 1824 and a year later the new town, Tallahassee, was settled by immigrants from Georgia, Virginia, and North Carolina. By 1830 the population of the new territory had reached 35,000.

As in the west, Florida's Indian problems mounted as more and more white settlers moved in. An 1832 pact with the Seminole tribe, which had drifted into Florida some 80 years earlier, seemed to solve the problem when the Indians agreed to migrate west of the Mississippi River. Despite the truce, however,

a group of warriors led by Chief Osceola was tired of being forced to vacate their own land. They rebelled in 1835. Indian war parties attacked Fort King near Ocala and ambushed two companies of U.S. troops near Bushnell. The latter encounter is remembered as the Dade Massacre.

The Second Seminole War (1835-42) was costly to both sides. The ranks of the Indians were decimated and they, in turn, killed about 2,500 soldiers and an unknown number of settlers. In the end, 3,824 Indians and Negroes were relocated in Arkansas. Several hundred Seminoles remained hidden in the Everglades. Osceola, who had entered an American camp under a flag of truce, was imprisoned and died in a military jail.

The war over, Florida concentrated on its preparations for statehood. The Tallahassee to St. Marks and the St. Joseph-Lake Wimico railroads had been completed, and the agricultural pattern of the plantation system was established. With the Indian situation resolved, the territory boomed. By the time Florida attained statehood in 1845 the population had grown to 65,500. Most of the leaders who were to fashion the state's future were southern plantation owners.

In 1855 the General Assembly passed the first Internal Improvement Act, which used swamp, overflow, and other land ceded to the state by the federal government to stimulate an intrastate system of railroads and canals. Interest in cross-state canals as a system of transportation had been generated 25 years earlier and the idea still appeals to some Floridians today.

As the slavery issue assumed national proportions, a new national political party arose to challenge the Democrats, but it gained little support in Florida. As the Whig Party disintegrated, southerners moved into the Democratic camp, leaving the strength of the newly organized Republican Party to the northern states. With the election of Republican Abraham Lincoln as president in 1860, the Florida Legislature rushed through an act for a constitutional convention to meet at Tallahassee and appropriated $100,000 for state troops. The census that year listed Florida's population as 140,000, of which nearly 45 percent was black.

Florida withdrew from the Union on Jan. 10, 1861, and the War Between the States began in April. During the next four years, Florida furnished 15,000 troops for the Confederate Army, a Florida militia, plus salt, beef, bacon, and cotton to the Southern army. Another 1,290 Floridians served in the Union forces. Supply lines from Florida to the Confederate forces further north were saved when Confederates defeated a Union force at Olustee in north central Florida. And during the final months of the war, home guards and cadets saved Tallahassee from capture by turning back invading Union forces at the Battle of Natural Bridge. Thus, Tallahassee was the only Confederate capital east of the Mississippi River to escape capture.

At war's end, Federal troops entered Tallahassee on May 10, 1865. Ten days later the American flag again flew over the Florida Capitol. A Florida constitutional convention convened Oct. 25, 1865, to annul the Ordinance of Secession and declare that slavery no longer existed. Nonetheless, a Floridian's right to vote remained restricted to "free white male persons of 21 years or more, but none others."

RECONSTRUCTION
1865-1900

The conclusion of the war left the Republicans in power in both the northern and southern states. Florida became part of the Third Military District under a military governor and the state was ordered to draft a new constitution. The 1868 document granted equal suffrage to all races, initiated a uniform system of free schools, provided for an enlightened criminal code, and furnished a measure of protection for workers. It also ended military rule. The civil government was formally reinstated on July 4, 1868, but the state's political destiny remained in the hands of newcomers and newly enfranchised voters.

Eight years later, Florida's electoral votes were the decisive factor in placing Republican Rutherford B. Hayes in the White House, but the Democrats regained control of enough state offices to end carpetbag rule when federal troops were withdrawn in 1877.

While the state struggled to adjust politically, the people were learning to live without the slaves who had constituted a large part of the wealth and labor economy of the plantation system. Many former planters tried to reestablish their position by hiring former slaves, but the old holdings gradually gave way to small tracts worked by tenant farmers.

While once-prosperous coastal towns and railroads were bankrupt, other industries were born and flourished in the post-war economy. Among them were timber, shipping, and cattle. In addition, cigar makers emigrated from Cuba to Key West and then to Tampa. Key West also lost its grip on the sponge fisheries when a group of Greek divers settled at Tarpon Springs. Mining became an important industry with the discovery of phosphate in the Peace River Valley in 1881.

An infant citrus industry began spreading throughout the state, but severe freezes in 1894 and 1895 killed or damaged most of the groves. Many north Florida growers were forced to take up other occupations. The freeze loss provided an incentive for remaining Florida citrus growers to develop better and hardier strains. Their success eventually projected the state into the nation's top citrus producer.

As the economic welfare of Floridians increased, the state's natural blessings were attracting a growing number of tourists and sportsmen, many of whom remained to contribute to the peninsula's rapid growth. Florida's population more than doubled between 1870 and 1890, and by 1900 had passed the half-million mark.

The Reconstruction constitution forced upon the State Legislature in 1868 was replaced by a more democratic document adopted in 1885. It made cabinet and supreme court posts and most county offices elective. It created the State Board of Education and authorized the establishment of Normal schools. The 1885 constitution remained the basis of Florida government for 84 years.

THE 20TH CENTURY

Despite its rapid population increase in the final decades of the 19th century, Florida could not begin to develop its vast resources without an intrastate transportation system. So large land grants were given to men like Henry Plant, who promptly built 600 miles of railroad track, opening the southwestern portion of the state, and to Henry Flagler, who laid lines extending the length of the state's east coast and into the Florida Keys. But neither man limited his interest to railroads; each built luxury hotels to accommodate the influx of tourists his railroad would carry, thus contributing to the phenomenal growth of the state's tourism industry.

By 1917, the state was ready to embark on a major road-building program to supplement the railroads. In 1924, Connors Highway connected West Palm Beach and Okeechobee City, where the new highway met the road to Tampa. Four years later the Tamiami Trail cut through the lower Everglades to join the booming west and lower east coasts. Railroads, too, pushed on during this period with lines being built around both sides of Lake Okeechobee. The expanding transportation system, together with the availability of automobiles, fostered the great Florida land boom of the 1920s.

The boom's opening shot was an advertising campaign that brought thousands of land speculators to the state. It was fired in 1919 by Carl Fisher of Miami Beach. He had dredged enough sand from the bottom of Biscayne Bay to turn a mangrove swamp into an inviting seashore. He then set out to sell it to the American public as the rising national economy was giving them more spare time and extra cash.

As word of the fabulous land and unbelievable bargains spread northward, a restless Yankee population swarmed into Florida to buy, to speculate, and to settle. By the summer of 1925 land fever had become epidemic and Florida had become a coast-to-coast real estate office. Men became millionaires in a matter of weeks or months, but the wealth was all on paper—titles, mortgages, options, and promissory notes. When the bona fide buyers with cash in the bank gave out, the boom collapsed like the bubble it was.

In its wake came the Great Depression that followed the stock market crash of 1929. During the 1930s, Florida's progressive pace stabilized, concentrating on scientific and technological advances to cure old ills rather than to undertake new projects. When World War II broke out, the state became a military training camp and an embarkation center for men and supplies. Many servicemen who were stationed in Florida at some time during their tour of duty returned with their families when the war was over.

In recent years the peninsula that was a pawn in the battles between the most powerful nations of Europe for three centuries has become one of the nation's fastest growing states. According to the 2000 census, Florida ranked fourth among states in population. Native industries continue to play an important role in the world market, and the state has become the nation's leader in space exploration and research. Meanwhile, the famous Florida climate and wide range of attractions continue to make the state one of the most popular resort destinations in North America.

CHRONOLOGY

10,000-8,000 b.c.—First human inhabitants migrate to the Florida peninsula from southern Georgia.

8,000 b.c.-1500 a.d.—Aboriginal Indian tribes settle in small communities. Tribes from the north are joined by migrating natives of Cuba and Mexico bringing variations in ethnic culture.

1500—European seamen explore coastal waters and islands surrounding Florida.

1513—Juan Ponce de Leon becomes the first known explorer to disembark on Florida soil, probably somewhere between present-day St. Augustine and Jacksonville.

1516-42—Expeditions by Spanish explorers Miruelo (Pensacola), Pineda (Gulf coast), Ponce de Leon (Charlotte Harbor), Narvaez (Gulf coast north of Tampa Bay), and De Soto (march from central west coast through interior to Mississippi River).

1539—Hernando de Soto and his company celebrate the nation's first Christmas at Tallahassee.

1549—Dominican priest Frey Luis Cancer de Barbasto first churchman to die for his faith in Florida.

1559—De Luna expedition attempts settlement at Pensacola.

1564—Rene de Laudoniere of France builds Fort Caroline near the mouth of the St. Johns River and establishes Huguenot colony.

1565—Pedro Menendez de Aviles

lands at what becomes St. Augustine, captures Fort Caroline to the north and slaughters the surviving French after their counter-attacking fleet is destroyed by the storm. The nation's first Thanksgiving celebration and accompanying feast is held with the Spaniards providing garbanzo beans, olive oil, bread, pork, and wine while the Timucuan Indians, from the nearby village of Seloy, provide oysters, clams, and other local delicacies.

1568—De Gourgues avenges the French massacre at Fort Caroline.

1586—British adventurer Sir Francis Drake razes St. Augustine.

1600—The 17th century becomes noted for the spread of Spanish colonization throughout Florida and up the eastern seaboard, the rise of English interest in the strategic value of the Florida peninsula, and Indian rebellions leading to the construction of some of the state's earliest fort settlements.

1679—Spanish construct the first Fort St. Marks (San Marcos de Apalache) at the junction of the St. Marks and Wakulla rivers.

1698—Pensacola founded by the Spaniard Arriola.

1702—British Gov. James Moore of South Carolina lays unsuccessful siege on St. Augustine.

1719—Pensacola captured by the French, recaptured by the Spanish, then recaptured by the French.

1723—Pensacola restored to Spain by alliance pact with France.

1740—Georgia founder and British Gen. James Oglethorpe's siege of St. Augustine is unsuccessful.

1743—Oglethorpe continues raids into Florida.

1756—Start of Seven Years' War between Spain and England during which British capture Havana, Cuba.

1763—Spain relinquishes Florida to England to ransom Havana. Population declines.

1763-76—British establish plantation colonies in Florida.

1776-80—Florida remains loyal to England during American Revolution and provides a haven for Tories.

1783—England returns Florida to Spain in exchange for the Bahamas and Gibraltar. British loyalists emigrate.

1785-95—Spanish-American border disputes precipitate Spain's subsequent withdrawal from Florida.

1795—Spain relinquishes its claim to the northern part of West Florida.

1800—Spain cedes Louisiana to France.

1803—Louisiana Purchase. U.S. claims West Florida.

1810—Rebellion in West Florida following Napoleon's brother Joseph assuming the Spanish throne. Republic of West Florida proclaimed.

1813—Gen. Andrew Jackson drives British out of Pensacola.

1818—Brief First Seminole War centers around Gen. Jackson's invasion of Spanish Florida.

1819—Negotiations with Spain to transfer Florida to U.S. begin.

1821—U.S. acquires Florida, Andrew Jackson provisional governor.

1822—Congressional Act providing for a Florida governor and a 13-member legislature signed into law by President Monroe. William P. DuVal becomes first territorial governor.

1823—Tallahassee, a traditional meeting place, selected as site of new capital because of its location midway between Pensacola and St. Augustine.

1824—First Legislature meets in log cabin near site of present Capitol.

1830—Beginning of first land boom, with settlers arriving by steamboat. In one decade, Florida's population increases from 15,000 to 34,730.

1835—Dade Massacre marks beginning of Second Seminole War.

1836—Florida's first railroads begin operation.

1837—Osceola captured. Battle of Okeechobee on Christmas Day is last major engagement of the Second Seminole War.

1838-39—Convention at St. Joseph drafts constitution in anticipation of statehood. Construction of Capitol begins.

1840—Population: 54,477.

1841—Yellow fever epidemic.

1842—U.S. declares Second Seminole War ended; 3,824 Indians and blacks relocated in Arkansas. Some 300 Seminoles remain in Florida and are assigned to reservations.

1845—Statehood. First governor William D. Moseley; first congressman, David Yulee. Census lists 66,500 Floridians.

1849-50—Coastline surveyed. Sections and townships laid out by General Land Office. Population 88,000.

1851—Dr. John Gorrie of Apalachicola patents artificial ice maker.

1855—General Assembly establishes first Internal Improvement Fund of $1 million.

1860—Following election of President Lincoln, Florida Legislature convenes to enact a constitutional convention and appropriate $100,000 for state troops. First east-west railroad completed between Fernandina and Cedar Key. Population: 140,424.

1861—Florida secedes from the Union (Jan. 10). State forces seize Fort Clinch, Fort Marion (Castillo de San Marcos), Fort Barrancas, Fort McRee, the Pensacola Navy Yard, and the arsenal at Chattahoochee.

1861-65—Florida furnishes salt, beef, and bacon for the Confederate Army, as well as 15,000 volunteer soldiers, 5,000 of whom are killed or die of wounds or disease.

1865—War Between the States ends with Union victory. Slavery abolished, and Florida put under military rule.

1868—New state constitution drafted and accepted by the U.S. government. Civil government resumes and Harrison Reed elected governor. Equal suffrage granted to races. Free school system established.

1870—Population: 187,748.

1873—Despite Depression, 50,000 tourists visit Silver Springs.

1876—Democrats regain control of state offices. Internal Improvement Fund bankrupt.

1877—Federal troops withdraw, ending carpetbag rule.

1877-81—Term of Gov. G. F. Drew ends Reconstruction. Population: 196,493.

1881—Philadelphia industrialist Hamilton Disston buys 4 million acres of Everglades to free Internal Improvement Fund of debt and opens way for development of south Florida. Phosphate discovered in Peace River Valley.

1883-85—Era of railroads. Henry B. Plant opens the west coast; Henry M. Flagler penetrates the east coast. Both men build luxury hotels to accommodate their rail passengers.

1885—Constitutional Convention. Cabinet posts, Supreme Court seats, and most county offices made elective. Normal schools established.

1888—Phosphate mining begins. Yellow fever epidemic leads to creation of State Board of Health.

1889—Poll tax introduced to hamper black voting.

1890—Population: 391,422.

1891—Railway mileage increases from 500 miles in 1884 to 2,560.

1894-95—Citrus boom in north central Florida hit by frosts; industry moves southward.

1897—State Railroad Commission established.

1898—Spanish-American War. Army camps set up in Miami, Tampa, and Jacksonville. Thousands of soldiers returning to northern homes advertise Florida.

1900—Population: 528,542.

1901—Primary election law replaces convention system of nominating candidates for public office.

1904—Flagler begins rail line to Key West.

1905—Buckman Act consolidates universities into University of Florida in Gainesville, Florida State College for Women in Tallahassee, and Florida Agricultural and Mechanical College in Tallahassee (for blacks). Everglades Drainage District created.

1908—Ocala and Choctawhatchee National Forests established.

1910—Population: 752,619.

1912—First train into Key West.

1913—First Corrupt Practices law enacted. Maximum allowable expenditure for candidates seeking the governorship or a U.S. Senate seat set at $4,000.

1914—World's first scheduled airline service starts between St. Petersburg and Tampa. Naval air station built at Pensacola.

1915—State takes first steps to assume responsibility for highway system. Carl Fisher dredges Biscayne Bay.

1917-18—First World War. Florida used for training camps and shipbuilding; 42,000 Floridians serve in Armed Forces.

1920—Population: 968,470.

1922—First state radio broadcasting station, WDAE, Tampa.

1923—Use of state convicts in private enterprise abolished. Eradication of tick fever in cattle begins.

1926—Hurricane swamps Miami and Lake Okeechobee. The Florida Boom bursts, presaging the Great Depression.

1927—Sugarcane plantations at Clewiston begin on large scale.

1928—Tamiami Trail opens from Tampa to Miami. Heavy loss of life at Okeechobee in wake of hurricane.

1929—Key West-Havana air service marks start of Pan American's Latin American routes. President Coolidge dedicates Bok Tower.

1930—Population: 1,468,211.

1931—Using part of gasoline tax, Legislature secures bonds for roads and bridges. Pari-mutuel wagering at dog and horse tracks legalized.

1933—Chicago mayor Anton J. Cermak fatally wounded in Miami during attempt on Franklin D. Roosevelt's life. Beer sales legalized.

1935—Overseas railroad converted to highway. Fred and Ma Barker slain by federal agents in Oklawaha.

1937—Poll tax abolished.

1939—Highway Patrol created.

1940—Parole Commission created

by Legislature. Florida plays host to 2.5 million tourists. Population: 1,897,414.

1941—World War II begins. Florida used for training camps and recuperation centers, plus shipbuilding and tooling industries; 250,000 Floridians serve in Armed Forces.

1942—Constitutional amendment pledges 2 cents of gas tax for 50 years to retire county road and bridge bonds.

1943—Cigarette tax enacted to replace revenue lost on wartime horse and dog racing.

1945—Florida celebrates 100 years of statehood. Sin tax increased to provide more money for state institutions and schools.

1947—The Minimum Foundation Program, for the support of schools, is enacted. Two state universities, FSU and UF, become coeducational. President Truman dedicates Everglades National Park.

1949—Sales tax initiated during special Legislative session. Fence Law enacted to keep livestock off roads. Jim Woodruff Dam construction begins.

1950—Frozen citrus concentrate becomes major industry. Population: 2,771,305.

1954—Sunshine Skyway toll bridge (15.2 miles) across the mouth of Tampa Bay connects St. Petersburg with Manatee County.

1955—Construction on Florida Turnpike begins.

1958—First satellite *(Explorer I)* placed in orbit from Cape Canaveral. First domestic jet airline passenger service in the U.S. inaugurated by National Airlines between New York and Miami.

1959—Fidel Castro assumes power in Cuba, starting massive immigration of Cubans to Florida.

1960—Population: 4,951,580.

1961—Cmdr. Alan B. Shepherd, Jr. completes first U.S. manned suborbital space flight from Cape Canaveral.

1962—Lt. Col. John H. Glenn becomes first American in orbit, circling earth three times in Mercury capsule *Friendship 7.*

1963—Maj. Leroy Gordon Cooper orbits earth 22 times in final and longest flight of Project Mercury. State constitution amended to authorize sale of state bonds for building programs at colleges and vocational schools, and for conservation. Governor and cabinet elections changed to nonpresidential years. Cape Canaveral's name changed to Cape Kennedy by presidential decree.

1964—Florida Atlantic University in Boca Raton and University of West Florida in Pensacola established.

1965—Maj. Edward H. White becomes first American to walk in space. University Board of Regents established. American Football League franchise awarded to Miami Dolphins.

1966—First soft landing on surface of moon by an unmanned spacecraft launched from Cape Kennedy. Claude R. Kirk becomes first Republican governor since 1877. Announcement of Walt Disney World to be built near Orlando.

1967—Three U.S. astronauts killed in fire aboard *Apollo I* on Cape Kennedy grounds. Federal Court rulings set boundaries of legislative districts, new elections ordered.

1968—Constitution revised for first time since 1885. Republicans at Miami Beach nominate Richard M. Nixon. Teachers lose statewide walkout for a school budget increase.

1969—Crew of *Apollo II* first humans to walk on the moon. Florida schools integrated.

1970—Major oil spill in Tampa Bay becomes a prime campaign issue. Reubin Askew elected governor. Population: 6,789,437.

1971—Corporate profits tax enacted. Raiford State Prison scene of state's worst prison riot. Disney World opens at Orlando.

1972—Federal panel declares Florida's voter residency requirements unconstitutional. State is among first to hold its presidential primary and Independent George Wallace is top vote getter. Democrats nominate George McGovern and Republicans President Nixon during their national conventions in Miami Beach.

1973—Florida recognizes 18 as the legal age. Skylab missions rocket nine men into space, last of the manned space flights prior to space shuttle vehicles. The undefeated Miami Dolphins win Super Bowl VII.

1974—Energy crisis and gas shortages prompt lower maximum speed limit to 55. Daylight saving time is enacted to conserve energy. Red Tide hits Florida's west coast causing millions of dollars of damage in fish kills. Tampa gets National Football League franchise Gov. Askew reelected. Dolphins win second straight Super Bowl.

1975—January jobless rate hits 25-year high of 8.3 percent, by November peaks at 13 percent. South Vietnam refugees arrive at Eglin Air Force Base, number 10,000 by midyear. Gov. Askew chooses a black U.S. Magistrate, Joseph Hatchett, for Supreme Court vacancy.

1976—U.S. Supreme Court upholds Florida's death penalty.

Construction of new state Capitol under way; controversy over razing of old Capitol results in its preservation. New pro football team Tampa Bay Buccaneers fumble way through first season, losing all 14 league games.

1977—Equal Rights Amendment rejected. Sunshine Amendment requiring many state and county officeholders to disclose their financial statements takes effect.

1978—A club-wielding attacker creeps into FSU sorority house and kills two coeds; police arrest Theodore Bundy. Democrat Bob Graham elected governor.

1979—State Supreme Court decides interest rates on home mortgages may climb above 10 percent without violating state usury laws. John Arthur Spinkelink becomes 197th person executed in Florida electric chair. Miami jury finds Theodore Bundy guilty, sentenced to death.

1980—Coast Guard buoy tender *Blackthorn*, with 50 men aboard, collides with 605-foot oil tanker *Capricorn* in Tampa Bay, killing 23 Coast Guardsmen. Bundy convicted of another murder. Freighter *Summit Venture* strikes Sunshine Skyway bridge across Tampa Bay, collapsing southbound span and killing 35. Four ex-Miami policemen acquitted in death of black insurance executive, spawning three days of rioting. National Guard sent in, 16 persons killed, 370 injured. Mass exodus of refugees from Cuba; 140,000 enter south Florida during the year. Population: 9,739,992.

1981—With a 41 percent increase in population since 1970, the state earns four new congressional seats. Severe January cold ruins nearly 20 percent of citrus crop. Space shuttle

Columbia launched on maiden voyage, becoming first reusable spacecraft. Boatload of Haitian refugees founders near Hillsboro Beach, 33 drown.

1982—Hard January freezes prompt governor to declare emergency in citrus industry. Sales tax increased to 5 percent. The legislature goes to single member districts.

1983—Federal judge upholds state's literacy test for high school graduation. Gerald Stano admits killing eight Florida women, is sentenced to death. Record Christmas freeze statewide. Police shooting of a black man sets off three days of rioting in Miami.

1984—Governor says 1983 Christmas freezes damaged 30 percent of crops in half the state's counties; loss set at $1 billion Miami opens $1 billion Metro rail system. University of Florida football team wins SEC title for first time, ruled ineligible for Sugar Bowl because of NCAA violations. Infestation of citrus canker spreads through state groves. Three Pensacola abortion clinics bombed.

1985—Temperatures hover below freezing for 36 hours in most widespread January cold spell in century. Legislature raises drinking age back to 21. Forest fires destroy 150,000 acres, 200 homes, mostly in Flagler and Volusia counties. Rosemary Barkett becomes first woman appointed to Florida Supreme Court. Florida Gators stripped of SEC title for NCAA violations.

1986—Seven astronauts killed at Cape Canaveral when *Challenger* space shuttle explodes after launch; all manned space missions cancelled. Legislature approves Sunday pari-mutuel racing. Gov.

Bob Graham elected U.S. senator replacing Paula Hawkins. Tampa Republican Bob Martinez elected governor.

1987—Lt. Gov. Wayne Mixson sworn in as governor for three days to fill office between Senator Graham's Jan. 3 move to Washington and Governor-elect Martinez's inauguration on Jan. 6. Miami and Orlando awarded pro basketball franchises. $770 million tax hike, largest in state's history. State allows 65 mph speed on 60 percent of Florida's interstate system. New state lottery game okayed by governor. Pope John Paul II visits Miami. Lawton Chiles announces he will not seek reelection to U.S. Senate.

1988—Sales tax increased from 5 to 6 percent. *Jacksonville Journal* and *Miami News* newspapers fold. Shuttle *Discovery* launched, first since *Challenger* disaster. Connie Mack wins Chiles' U.S. Senate seat. New NBA franchise team Miami Heat wins first game after 17 defeats.

1989—Three days of rioting in Miami's black neighborhoods leaves three dead. Serial killer Ted Bundy, 42, executed after 10-year legal battle. University of Florida basketball team wins SEC for first time. U.S. Rep. Claude Pepper dies at 88. Brutal murder of Bradley McGee, 2, by stepfather prompts reform of child abuse cases handled by the state. Former University of Florida quarterback and Heisman Trophy winner Steve Spurrier named as new UF football coach. State's worst drought in 27 years brings mandatory water restrictions to south Florida. Devastating Christmas cold front brings state to a standstill.

1990—Captured Panama president Manuel Noriega brought to Miami for trial on drug charges. Flooding Panhandle rivers force evacuation of 2,000 homes. Owners/players contract dispute delays spring training baseball season. St. Petersburg's Suncoast Dome opens. Jacksonville gunman James Pough, 42, kills 10 people in loan-office rampage, the worst mass murder by a single gunman in Florida history. Roswell Gilbert, 81-year-old inmate convicted of mercy killing his ailing wife in 1985, is released from prison. Five college students in Gainesville brutally murdered by unknown attacker. Iraq's invasion of Kuwait results in massive state National Guard and Army Reserve unit callup. Nation's thrift scandal begins toppling savings and loan associations including Miami's giant CenTrust. Florida State University, an independent in college sports, joins Atlantic Coast Conference. Florida Supreme Court upholds right-to-die case. Lotto awards record $106 million jackpot. State gasoline prices soar to seven-year high. Former U.S. senator Lawton Chiles soundly defeats Republican incumbent Bob Martinez in gubernatorial race. Fall encephalitis outbreak in 27 counties causes 10 deaths among 213 cases. Outgoing Gov. Martinez named nation's drug czar. Tampa awarded National Hockey League franchise. Population: 12,937,926, up 34 percent from 1980.

1991—Miami-based Eastern Airlines closes. Former U.S. Sen. George Smathers donates record $20 million to University of Florida library system. Legislature approves $29.3 billion state budget, including $164 million in new taxes. Queen Elizabeth II visits, confers honorary knighthood on Tampa resident Gen. Norman Schwarzkopf. Miami awarded new National League baseball franchise.

1992—Panama's Noriega convicted in Miami federal court on drug conspiracy charges. State Senator Ander Crenshaw, Jacksonville, becomes first Republican senate president in 118 years. Term limits instituted for state elected officials. Orlando judge grants 12-year-old a divorce from his parents. Hurricane Andrew slams into southeast Florida.

1993—March "no-name" storm spawns at least 50 tornadoes throughout state. Tides and high winds cause 51 deaths and $620 million in damages in 21 counties. Jacksonville wins National Football League franchise. Miami state attorney Janet Reno becomes U.S. attorney general. Seminole Indian Bingo Hall in Tampa opens 24-hour poker parlor, first in state. Three-ship collision in Gulf off St. Petersburg spills 328,000 gallons of oil that pollutes 16 miles of beaches. Pro-life protestor Michael Griffin fatally shoots Dr. David Gunn at Pensacola abortion clinic.

1994—Republicans win the Florida Senate for the first time since Reconstruction. Florida State University wins football national championship. Danny Rolling convicted of 1990 murders of five Gainesville college students and sentenced to death. Florida legislature approves compensation for 1923 massacre of six black residents and razing of Rosewood. World Cup Soccer games held in Orlando's Citrus Bowl. Dr. John Britton and volunteer escort shot to death by Paul Hill at Pensacola abortion clinic.

1995—Gov. Lawton Chiles sues tobacco industry to recover $1.2

billion Florida spent in treating smoking-related illness among its Medicaid population. Disney World and rival Universal Studios announce expansions. St. Petersburg awarded an American League baseball team. Malcolm Glazer buys the Tampa Bay Buccaneers NFL franchise and demands a new stadium from local government under the threat of moving the team.

1996—Cuban MiG fighter jets down two unarmed civilian planes, killing four and spurring passage of the Helms-Burton Law toughening the U.S. economic boycott of Cuba. ValuJet Flight bursts into flame and goes down in the Everglades, killing 110. It disappeared beneath the swamp. The U.S. Supreme Court overturns the federal Indian Gaming Act of 1988 saying the Seminole Nation of Florida could not sue the State of Florida for refusing to negotiate on the issue of gambling. Separately, it tells Florida to redraw its Third Congressional District, claiming it was racially gerrymandered. The state did and incumbent Corrine Browne was reelected. Florida mandates the re-inoculation of all students. Floridians vote for Democrat Bill Clinton for president but give Republicans a majority in the Florida House for the first time in 122 years. GOP also retains control of the Senate. Tampa voters approved a half-cent sales tax increase to boost schools and public safety and, not incidentally, build a new football stadium. The NFL rewards Florida with nearly back-to-back Super Bowls to the state with Miami's new stadium hosting the 1999 game and Tampa's the 2001 outing. Citing mismanagement and corruption, the state declares a "financial emergency" in Miami and

steps in with a powerful panel of oversight experts after investigators found the city on the verge of bankruptcy.

1997—Low-stakes poker rooms at the state's pari-mutuel facilities legalized. Tobacco companies agreed to a settlement requiring them to pay the state $13 billion and drastically reduce their merchandising in the state. Mediterranean fruit flies and the equally feared citrus canker bacteria strike Central Florida citrus groves; at the same time, southern pine beetles attacked the Ocala National Forest and other north Florida woodlands. The U.S. Supreme Court upholds the boundaries of a State Senate District allowing it to weave through urban areas in three Tampa Bay counties. The World Series-winning Florida Marlins baseball team is put up for sale. A judge declared "Ol' Sparky," the state's electric chair, to be functioning in good order and to not constitute cruel and unusual punishment. Sentinel chickens alerted health officials to the return of mosquito-borne St. Louis encephalitis in central Florida. In what was described as the largest bank merger in American history, NationsBank of Charlotte, N.C., purchased Barnett Banks of Florida for $14.6 billion to create the third largest U.S. bank. The Jacksonville Port Authority was fined by the federal government for dealing directly with Cuba. Miami survived an attempt to abolish it when an overwhelming 85 percent of voters elected to keep the 101-year-old city intact. Schools sent thousands of middle-school students home and told them not to return until they complied with stringent new inoculation rules. University of

Florida football coach Steve Spurrier, already the highest paid coach in college football, agreed to a $1 million raise. Forty-year-old University of South Florida fielded its first football team and won its first game 80-3 over Kentucky Wesleyan. Possession of tobacco products by a minor became a crime. The tobacco industry settled for $349 million the first-ever class-action "second-hand smoke" suit.

1998—The year was one of one natural disaster after another: record tornadoes, unprecedented forest fires, recurring blights, and the return of hurricanes. The worst tornado storm in the history of Florida killed 42 people and injured more than 250 in March. Medflies invaded citrus and vegetables. The value of citrus groves continued a decade-long decline. Lightning over a drought stricken northeast Florida brought devastating forest and grass fires. The entire population of Flagler County and most of the populations of Brevard and Volusia Counties were evacuated when three separate fires moved toward combining into a massive firestorm. The fires, which raged in every Florida county except Monroe, destroyed nearly a half-million acres. More than 200 buildings were destroyed. No one was killed in the fires but more than 100 were injured. Property damage was more than $392 million. Despite disaster, Florida drew a record 48 million visitors during the year. Jeb Bush, who narrowly lost the governorship to Lawton Chiles eight years before, won a landslide victory for the office over Lt. Gov. Buddy MacKay, giving the Republicans the governor's office and both houses of the legislature for the first time since Reconstruction. MacKay, however, did become governor for 23 days when Chiles died in December. Floridians, who have historically declined to change their constitution via popular vote, swept a dozen amendments on the ballot into the basic charter and fundamentally changed both Florida's unique form of government by eliminating half the statewide elected Cabinet offices and its traditional politics by opening its primaries. Judi Buenoano was executed 27 years after killing her husband, the first women to be executed by the state in 150 years. Freddie Lee Pitts and Wilbert Lee, two Floridians who spent 12 years in prison after twice being wrongfully convicted of murder, were awarded $500,000 each plus legal expenses authorized by the Legislature. They were pardoned by Gov. Reubin Askew in 1975. Adam Herbert became the first African-American to be named chancellor of the state university system. Joe Carollo convinced an appeals court that massive absentee voter fraud robbed him of the office he should have won outright in 1997 and took the reins as mayor of Miami, ousting former mayor Xavier Suarez. There was no evidence linking Suarez to the fraud. The Tampa Jai-Alai fronton closed after 45 years. St. Petersburg's Sunken Gardens attraction was put on the sales block. Walt Disney World opened its fourth theme park and became the largest employer of staff in one place with 50,000 workers. Rival Universal Studios, meanwhile, readied its $1 billion Islands of Adventure park, with plans for two more Orlando parks early in the next century. Pepsi entered the juice market against

Coca-Cola's Minute Maid brand by purchasing Bradenton's Tropicana from Seagram's. America's first orbiting astronaut, John Glenn, 77, returned to space aboard the shuttle *Discovery*. A nine-year-old boy was taken by a shark off Vero Beach, the first shark death in Florida waters in a decade. Despite warnings, rip tides off Daytona Beach forced lifeguards to rescue 421 swimmers in two days. The state received a $4.1 million grant through the National Oceanographic and Atmospheric Administration to find a way to predict the appearance of red tide. Scientists could not explain the appearance of a band of cold water off the Panhandle coast in mid-summer that produced fish kills. Pensacola launched a yearlong celebration of its founding 440 years ago and its refounding 300 years ago. Marjory Stoneman Douglas, 108-year-old grande dame of conservation died at her Miami home. The FBI arrested eight men and two women in Miami on charges of spying for Cuba, the first breaking of a Cuban spy ring. The U.S. Coast Guard declared virtually all of peninsula Florida's coast a "security zone" requiring all boats of less than 150 ft. in length to get a permit to make trips to Cuba. In baseball, the Tampa Bay Devil Rays began play in the American League, while in the National League, the Florida Marlins went from first to worst after trading away most of the members of its winning team. Jacksonville University opened its inaugural football season.

1999—The first week of the year greeted Floridians with the coldest weather in three years with a hard freeze into Central Florida. Jeb Bush was sworn in as only the third Republican governor of the 20th Century and the first with a Republican legislature since Reconstruction. It passed a $48.9 billion dollar budget including a billion dollar tax cut. Republicans honored late Democratic Governor Lawton Chiles by establishing a $1.7 billion healthcare endowment, based on the $13-billion tobacco company settlement personally negotiated by Chiles. Florida's radical new education voucher plan was inaugurated, grading schools and allowing children in failing schools to take state money with them if they wished to change schools, public or private. Two Pensacola schools were judged to have failed but less than 100 children choose to take the vouchers and make a move. Taking advantage of another option offered by the legislature, two entire school districts, Hillsborough and Volusia, became the nation's first "charter school districts," allowing them to operate outside the traditional norms. Polk County mandated a strict school uniform policy for elementary and middle school students with no option for parents. In an effort to hire more minority teachers, Palm Beach County schools recruited six new teachers from Spain. The Florida Supreme Court upheld a 1992 amendment vote on limit terms. Forty percent of the legislature was not allowed on the ballot for re-election in 2000. Popular Republican U.S. Senator Connie Mack declined to seek another term. Florida's most famous piece of furniture, 76-year-old "Old Sparky," the electric chair, was retired. The concept was not. "New Sparky" was bigger and sturdier to accommodate larger death-row inmates and said to be "more comfortable." One woman and 237 men sat in the old fatal seat. First to die on the new furniture was 344-pound Allen Lee Davis. His nosebleed on execution set off a new "cruel and unusual" debate. The state Supreme Court ruled, again, the method constitutional. By fall, seven death row inmates had died during the year, but only Davis died by execution. Five died of natural causes, one in an altercation with guards. The high court granted a new trial to a man convicted of a murder-for-hire scheme and told prosecutors it was tired of having to grant new trials or overturning convictions because of "egregious and inexcusable prosecutorial misconduct." Attractions offered discount deals to Canadians similar to those made to Florida residents when the annual migration of "Snowbirds" was crimped by a weak Canadian economy. St. Joe Co. of Jacksonville, the state's largest private landowner said it would sell 800,000 of its 1 million acres of timberland in northwest Florida. Carolina Power & Light of Raleigh bought Florida Progress, parent company of Florida Power, the state's second largest and most expensive electric utility. A bacterial meningitis outbreak centered in Palatka felled nine and killed one. St. Petersburg's Derby Lane canceled races for the first time in its 74-year history after six greyhounds died of a virus infection popularly called kennel cough. Unable to stop the spread of dreaded citrus canker in south Florida, where it had killed more than 100,000 trees, the state proposed a $165-million fight against it, including building a mile-wide "firebreak" in Broward County from the Atlantic to the Everglades. Georgia is famous for its Okefenokee Swamp, but when it went up in flames, it was in the little known Florida portion of the great wilderness. 53,000 acres burned away, 50,000 of them in Florida. With rainfall measuring less than half that of the previous year, devastating forest fires returned to the state for the second consecutive year. Harsh weather, drought, and wildfires had a negative effect on the state's considerable and illegal marijuana crop, forcing more planters indoors. Miami-Dade and Pinellas counties led the state in homegrown crops. Red Tide appeared simultaneously off all three Florida coasts for the first time on record. Two swarms of African bees were destroyed in bait hives at the Jacksonville port, marking the first time they made it ashore. American crocodiles were nesting in Biscayne Bay north of Homestead for the first time in a century. Monroe County Sheriff Rick Roth accepted a $25 million check from the U.S. Customs Service, his department's share of the $50 million seized from a drug dealer, the largest currency seizure in Customs' history. The reward was the highest ever paid to a local agency by the federal government. Broward County joined Monroe County in offering health benefits for "domestic partners." Officials okayed a plan to build the world's second largest desalinization plant on Tampa Bay. Miami-Dade voters crushed a measure to raise the sales tax in the county to 7.5 percent. St. Petersburg purchased the venerable Sunken Gardens attraction near downtown and designated it a botanical garden. A corporation, SabreTech Inc., was charged with

110 counts of third-degree murder and second-degree manslaughter murder in the 1996 ValueJet crash in the Everglades. First Lady Columba Bush was stopped by customs officials at Atlanta's airport and fined for failure to declare $19,000 worth of Paris clothes and jewelry. She said she was afraid her husband would be angry at the extent of her shopping spree. Florida State University replaced the University of Florida as the nation's top party school according to the annual Princeton Review rankings. Florida placed second. Officials were not amused. Tallahassee's Lake Jackson disappeared one night—again. The 4,000-acre lake drained down a sinkhole as it has before on what scientists believe is a 25-year cycle. Citrus land value rose for the first time in a decade with orange groves reaching $7,000 per acre. Southeast Asian green mussels invaded Tampa Bay. Sheep were imported into Okeechobee County to combat kudzu. Alligators, feeding on the sheep, put an end to the project. Two fishermen plucked a shipwrecked young boy from the waters off Florida. His name was Elian Gonzalez.

THE 21ST CENTURY
The Hanging Chad

In 2000, for the second time in its history, the state found itself selecting the next president of the United States in a most controversial election. The controversy began before the polls closed when elderly Palm Beach County Democratic voters were contacted by a Texas phone bank with the suggestion that they were "confused" by the local ballot, which may have caused them to vote for someone other than Democratic candidate Albert Gore. That suggestion set off a flurry of phoned complaints to election officials, who noted that there was no way to determine whether a voter had made the desired choice or not and that all voters had up to three opportunities to vote exactly as they wished before leaving their polling place. With a close vote in the contest between Gore and Republican candidate George W. Bush, recounts—mandatory where the vote was very close, requested where it was not—got under way. Bush won the original count in the state and the recount. But Gore proponents protested the recount in those counties using the "punch card" ballot, including Palm Beach, which gave rise to the now famous and concurrent "hanging chad" complaint. Hand recounts, but only in selected precincts in selected counties, began. Secretary of State Katherine Harris, the state's highest election official—and honorary chairman of the Florida Bush campaign—warned affected counties to get on with it and that the law required her to have a final return by a date certain in order to certify the winning electors to the Electoral College. Results in the nation indicated the Florida electors would determine the presidency.

Meanwhile, the Gore Campaign went to courts around the state to force additional recounts and to disallow absentee ballots—most from overseas military personnel who were presumed to have voted for the Republican candidate. Appearing primarily before Democratic circuit judges, the Gore Campaign met the Bush Campaign and lost. But they found a friendlier forum in the Florida Supreme Court, which ordered Harris to extend the certification deadline to allow for continued recounts. The Bush Campaign went to federal court and the U.S. Supreme Court ordered the State Supreme Court to "reconsider" its decision. Meanwhile, the Republican-controlled legislature—already angry at the Supreme Court on other issues—asserted its right to name electors in the midst of controversy. The Florida Supreme Court reconsidered its decision but did not change it. The Bush Campaign returned to the U.S. Supreme Court. Florida Attorney General—and honorary chairman of the Florida Gore campaign—Bob Butterworth, defended the state supreme court action. The High Court, ruling on two constitutional issues, voted 7-2 and 5-4 against the Florida Supreme Court, set aside its ruling, and cleared the way for Harris to certify the result. Florida electors cast the state's 25 Electoral votes for Bush, who won the presidency 271-269. Although the controversy continued, Bush had won the original state count and all of the official recounts. Independent post-election recounts, conducted primarily by the media, also indicated Bush had won by margins ranging from 500 to 1,500 votes among the 5,963,110 cast by Floridians. Prior to Election Day, Florida Republicans spent more than $33 million and Democrats more than $30 million, smashing their combined spending record of $34.7 million on the 1998 elections.

2000—Also that year, a Central American weevil, believed to have entered the state in a shipment of plants a decade ago, was found feasting on many of Florida's bromeliads including several endangered species. Another imported weevil munched citrus trees, infesting 10 percent of the state's citrus acreage. Sentinel chickens were set out to monitor the newly introduced West Nile encephalitis virus. The legislature killed auto emissions testing in the six metropolitan counties where they had been required. Motorcyclists over the age of 21 were freed from helmet requirements if they carried at least $10,000 in personal injury insurance. Finding a $13 billion surplus in the state pension plan, the legislature restored pension benefits that had been temporarily lowered for public safety workers.

The legislature put another billion dollars into the state's portion of public school funding but raised tuition at universities and community colleges by 5 percent. It required new homes to have added protection against hurricanes. A mandatory penalty, "10-20-Life," for the use of a gun in the commission of a crime, was instituted. Performing the medical procedure known as partial birth abortion became a felony. The legislature began dismantling the Department of Labor and Employment Security. It also passed the One Florida program, overhauling affirmative action in state contracts. Mothers became allowed to abandon their newborns at hospitals or fire stations without penalty. Tax dollars were put into five spring training facilities in return for baseball's commitment to stay at those sites for at least 15 years. The last of the surplus of the huge but abandoned Naval Training Center at Orlando went up for auction. Historic Cecil Field at Jacksonville closed. Terry Melvin Simms became the first Florida inmate to be executed by lethal injection. Five more followed. To the shock of state officials, voters approved a constitutional amendment requiring the state to begin building a high-speed rail system by 2003. Voters rejected proposals to end the election of circuit and county judges. Both Congress and the state legislature signed off on a plan to share the cost of both restoring the Everglades and ensuring a water supply for South Florida at a cost of $7.8 billion. Much of the state continued to endure the third year of drought with water levels in lakes, streams, and the aquifer falling to the lowest levels in recorded history. Ten staff members of a New Port Richey nursing home saw their Lotto ticket come in to the tune of $81.6 million, the biggest single winning ticket in Florida lottery history. Litigation flew around Florida's school voucher program. No public schools "failed" in 2000 and the two that had received an "F" the year before jumped to an "A." The state kept the standard test program, used to determine school performance, in place. A less-noted voucher program was expanded to include all handicapped children. U.S. District Court discrimination oversight of Pinellas County Schools and Hillsborough County Schools ended. The legislature approved a new medical school for Florida State University, and new law schools for Florida International University and Florida A&M University. The

legislature approved a restructuring of education throughout the state that included the elimination of the university system governing Board of Regents. It also decreed that enrollment at elementary schools built after 2002 be capped at 500 pupils, new middle schools at 700, and new high schools at 900. Florida's schools were among the largest in the nation. Judy Genshaft was named president of the University of South Florida. Former Miami Dolphins quarterback Don Strock was named coach of the new Florida International University football program. The Governor signed a bill awarding high school diplomas to all honorably discharged Floridians who dropped out of high school to fight World War II. Daytona Beach halted nearly a century of tradition by banning vehicles from the beach in high-concentration tourist areas. However, 16 miles of the famous 23-mile-long beach remained open to traffic. Thadeus Kubinski jumped off his dock as he always did for his daily swim in Boca Ceiga Bay. But on this day, he was immediately hit by a 9-foot bull shark that ripped through his torso. He was dead when paramedics pulled him from the water. After months of litigation, an armed federal force, under orders of U.S. Attorney General and former Miami prosecutor Janet Reno, staged a pre-dawn raid on the home of Elian Gonzalez's uncle and seized the boy at gunpoint. He was returned to Cuba. Population: 15,982,378, a 23.5 percent increase over 1990.

2001—The 9-11 attack on New York's World Trade Center and the Pentagon in Washington had a devastating impact on Florida. Residents and officials were stunned to learn that 14 of the 19 terrorists involved in the skyjack attacks, which killed thousands, lived in Florida, did their flight training in Florida and carried Florida driver's licenses or official photo identification cars. The state was rocked again eight days later, when the first anthrax attack arrived in the mail at the offices of American Media in Boca Raton. One editor at the national tabloid newspaper company died, another was seriously ill, and a half-dozen more were infected. The building was sealed off and eventually abandoned. Anthrax was also found at the Boca Raton post office. The state's giant tourist industry virtually disappeared, and it wasn't alone. Other industries in the state suffered similarly, to the extent that Florida firms received more federal "economic injury" grants in the wake of the terrorist attacks than any other area outside metropolitan New York and Washington. Meanwhile, a collection of mobile homes became established on the parking lots of the Central and the Special Operations Commands at Tampa's MacDill Air Force Base, the nucleus of a "coalition village," housing and headquartering allies in the shortly to be launched fight against terrorism. In the wake of the 2000 election uproar, the Florida Legislature banned punch-card ballots, set statewide standards for recounts, and for the first time, allocated money to counties to install optical scanner or touch-screen voting machines. It reapportioned the state to add two new Congress seats and had all new legislative districts, save one, approved by the Justice Department. Legislators passed a $48-billion budget, renewed the popular nine-day back-to-school-sales-

tax holiday, and raised both per pupil spending and tuition at state universities. Acting on the 1998 constitutional amendment diluting the Cabinet system, the legislature gave the governor vast new power in the naming of judges. Having eliminated the Board of Regents, the legislature also created a State Board of Education to run all levels in the state, gave each state university its own board of trustees, and gave the governor appointment power to name all members of the new education panels. Also in education, the legislature split top-caliber New College away from the University of South Florida as the state's 11th state university, gave USF's St. Petersburg and Sarasota campuses a measure of independence, and gave St. Petersburg Junior College, the state's oldest, the right to grant four-year degrees. The trauma-filled death of NASCAR's Dale Earnhardt at February's Daytona 500 race put a crack in Florida's Sunshine Law. The legislature exempted autopsy photos from the public records law, requiring a judicial ruling before such photos can be released to the public. The legislature banned capital punishment for mentally retarded killers but also voted to place the practice of capital punishment into the constitution via amendment on the 2002 ballot. The legislature removed more than 16,000 workers from civil service protections and made poor performance a just cause for dismissal. Chicken pox immunization became mandatory for all students entering school or day care. Orange and Alachua counties' Online High School drew public, private, and home students from throughout the state to the virtual place where they could gain additional credits while attending their local school or complete a three-year early graduation program. With much of Florida in the fourth year of severe drought, wildfires again scorched the landscape, often shutting down major roads, including the state's network of interstate highways. An arid section of Lake Okeechobee caught fire, the Green Swamp was hit regularly, and a fire in the Morley Swamp, south of Mayo, became one of the largest in state history, burning for weeks and scorching more than 60,000 acres. The state purchased 57,379 acres of the Pinhook Swamp, creating a wildlife corridor connecting the Okefenokee National Wildlife Refuge with the Osceola National Forest. The Cabinet created the nation's largest no-fishing zone in the Dry Tortugas portion of the Florida Keys National Marine Sanctuary. Wildlife officials began dumping 250 tons of fossilized oyster shells on the western shore of Pelican Island National Wildlife Refuge near Sebastian Inlet, in hope of preventing further erosion. Established by President Theodore Roosevelt as the first such refuge, the bird-hosting island has shrunk from more than five acres to less than two. President George W. Bush named Cuban-born Orange County Commission Chairman Mel Martinez to the Cabinet as Secretary of Housing and Urban Development. Unable as Texas governor to lure Florida Parks Director Fran Mainella there for its chief parks post, the president named her head of the National Park Service. Commissioner of Agriculture Bob Crawford stepped down to become head of the Florida Citrus Commission. Overrun by thousands of city-protected feral chickens, Key West launched "Operation Chicken Snatch," rounding them up and shipping them off to Pinellas County's Suncoast Seabird Sanctuary for redistribution around the state. The Southwest Florida Water Management District purchased Weeki Wachee Spring from the City of St. Petersburg for $16.5 million. The State Supreme Court ruled that public land used for private businesses, sports stadiums for instance, were subject to property taxes even when owned by the public. Joseph Celestin was elected mayor of North Miami, becoming the first Haitian-American to lead a Florida city. The Seminole Tribal Council unanimously suspended chairman James E. Billie after 21 years amidst a federal investigation of his administration and the filing of a sexual harassment suit against him. King Juan Carlos and Queen Sofia paid the Spanish monarchy's first visit ever to its former domain. Alan Diaz, freelancing for the Associated Press, won the Pulitzer Prize for his dramatic photo of a federal agent in riot gear and pointing an assault weapon, flushing Elian Gonzalez from a closet in his uncle's home. The *Miami Herald* also won a Pulitzer for its coverage of the pre-dawn raid that seized the young Cuban refugee. A fourth federal prison was planned for Sumter County's 1,400-acre, three-prison facility, making it the largest Federal corrections complex in the nation. Threatened by Major League Baseball with the loss of the Florida Marlins, the Tampa Bay Devil Rays, or both, state attorney general Bob Butterworth tossed a high and inside subpoena at the leagues, seeking the financial records of both teams. Talk of cutting the teams subsided. Under pressure from developers, the value of general agricultural land rose, but the value of citrus land fell 10 percent. Drop was blamed on declining prices for citrus products. Orange groves still brought more than $6,000 per acre, while grapefruit groves were down below $4,500 per acre. Florida disbarred nationally famous lawyer F. Lee Bailey. The state supreme court ruled he mishandled a client's stock worth nearly $6 million, pocketed $3.5 million of it, and used a portion of that money to defend O. J. Simpson in California. The collapse of Enron Corporation cost the state employee pension fund an estimated $200 million, and the state got in line to file suit. The state held nine million shares of the company's stock. The loss accounted for just three-tenths of pension plan's $100 billion. Four years after hitting the tobacco industry with a $13-billion judgment for the state's health costs and in turn, banning tobacco stocks from the state's investment portfolio, the State Board of Administration voted unanimously to again invest in the stock of cigarette makers. Failure to participate in the market of tobacco stocks cost the state an estimated $300 million since 1997. The board, which oversees the state's trust funds, including its retirement fund, cited its fiduciary responsibilities under the law. Before divesting, the state held $835 million worth of tobacco stocks, making it one of the industry's largest shareholders. Five Cuban nationals were convicted of conspiring to commit espionage. Retired Army Reserve Col. George Trofimoff, 74, of Melbourne, was convicted of espionage, the highest-ranking military officer in U.S.

history to be so judged. Dempsey Barron, a legendary Panhandle legislator who shaped Florida politics for three decades and who survived being struck by lightning three different times, died at 79. A sibling compromise between President Bush and Governor Bush allowed additional drilling for oil in the Gulf of Mexico but kept new activity no less than 100 miles from Florida's shore. Mosquitos brought the feared West Nile Virus into the Florida Panhandle.

2002—Despite election reforms, it happened again. Polls opened late in Broward and Dade counties for the first Democratic gubernatorial primary, pitting former U.S. Attorney General Janet Reno against political newcomer Bill McBride. Poll workers were said to be ill trained in both counties, new touchscreen voting machines didn't work, and voters received incorrect ballots and inaccurate registration information. Gov. Jeb Bush ordered polls to stay open an extra two hours throughout the state to make up for the late start in the two counties, and they did, except in those two counties where many precincts closed early when poll workers quit. In addition, thousands of votes were not counted until a week after the election, at least those that could be found. Brunt of the criticism fell on Broward Supervisor of Elections Miriam Oliphant, but the Republican governor declined to remove the Democratic supervisor, who broke no law. He told local officials to work it out themselves, which they did by getting Oliphant to agree to have nothing to do with conducting elections. Reno conceded to McBride, despite the close and controversial vote. Bush then defeated McBride in a landslide to become the first Republican governor ever reelected. Bush and McBride raised $19.2 million for their election bid, a record for the governor's race. Former secretary of state and attorney general Jim Smith, who led the Florida Election Reform Task Force following the traumatic 2000 election, was named by the governor to replace Secretary of State Katherine Harris when she resigned, belatedly, to run for Congress. The state office became appointive in 2003. Before she resigned, however, her office told candidates the wrong qualifying fee, requiring virtually all to send additional money before the deadline, two days later. But a FedEx plane carrying candidate checks and revised paperwork to meet the deadline crashed and burned in Tallahassee. No one was injured, but the additional payments were a total loss. The governor stepped in to extend the deadline. Then Harris announced her resignation, retroactively. She said she erred when she qualified for Congress by failing to resign because, she believed, her elective office was being abolished. Democrats brought suit in her congressional district, seeking to have her stricken from the ballot. Republicans mulled a similar suit against Atty. Gen. Bob Butterworth, seeking a seat in the Florida Senate, who resigned his state office nine days later than required. Both Harris and Butterworth became nationally famous during the 2000 election aftermath. Harris was the titular head of the Bush campaign for president in Florida while Butterworth held the same post for Albert Gore. No suit was filed against Butterworth, while the suit against Harris was dismissed. Harris went on to win her seat handily. But, surprisingly, Butterworth, one of the state's most popular officeholders, long considered a potential governor, did not. He was later named a senior judge in his home county, Broward, and dean of the Barry College Law School. Florida voters approved a constitutional amendment mandating smaller class sizes, despite its estimated $27.5 billion price tag. They also passed a measure offering voluntary prekindergarten to all four-year-olds. The governor named Raoul Cantero III of Miami to the Florida Supreme Court, the first Hispanic named to the court. Past House Speaker T. K. Wetherell was named president of Florida State University; Fred Gainous, president of Florida A&M University; John Cavanaugh, president of the University of West Florida. Florida coach Steve Spurrier stunned fans by abruptly resigning from his estimated $2.1 million post to join the Washington Redskins. Florida International University won its inaugural football game. Florida Atlantic University won a berth in the NCAA Basketball Tournament for the first time. Ted Williams died, and his body was frozen while a bitter family dispute played out in court, which ruled he could remain frozen. The legislature passed a $50.4 billion budget, did a massive rewrite of the state education code and laid out the duties of the newly created Cabinet office of chief financial officer. The legislature allowed homeowners to fly the flag in a respectful manner, regardless of any rules or requirements of homeowner and condominium associations; made drag racing a crime rather than a traffic offense; required drivers convicted of DUI twice to install Breathalyzer starters on their cars; approved bonds of up to $100 million a year to buy land for Everglades restoration; provided extra money for improved security for Florida's 14 seaports; and denied public access to blueprints of government buildings. College tuition was raised 5 percent. Companies begin receiving a dollar-for-dollar tax break for donating a maximum of $5 million to scholarships for low-income children to attend private school. More than 300 of the 8,900 public-school students who became eligible for vouchers to attend private or an alternative public school notified the state they would take them. All Florida students with disabilities remained eligible for vouchers, and more than 4,000 used them. Florida, in the wake of 9-11, required foreign nationals wishing to renew their driver's licenses to do so in person. The Iraq war call-up of the Florida National Guard and Reservists was the largest since World War II. A 15-year-old boy wrote a suicide note sympathetic to terrorists, buzzed MacDill Air Force Base, and then flew into a 42-story bank building in downtown Tampa. He was killed, but no one else was hurt. Allen Morris, the retired and venerated clerk of the house, died at 92. Morris, a distinguished journalist and historian, was the author of the *Florida Handbook,* considered the bible of state government. Atty. Jim Shore, blind and the first Seminole admitted to the Florida Bar, survived being gunned down in his Hollywood home by unknown assailants. Shore was instrumental in the removal of tribal chairman

James Billie from office and was cooperating with officials in a federal investigation of Billie's administration. But the case against his key aides on embezzlement and other charges collapsed with Billie's undisputed testimony that he authorized the dispersal of the $2.77 million in question under the chairman's discretionary powers. As elsewhere, the Catholic Church saw priests, including the bishop of Palm Beach, ousted and arrested in child sexual-abuse charges. Five-year-old Rilya Wilson was discovered missing for nearly a year and half before the Department of Children and Families acknowledged they had no idea where she was. Polk County suffered the nation's worst outbreak of hepatitis A. Three died and hundreds were seriously ill. An Ocala man became the first in the state to die from West Nile virus. Poisonous lionfish, native to the seas off Australia and Malaysia, took up station in deep water off Florida's east coast. Experts had no idea how the fish, in large numbers, got there, but conjecture pointed to a combination of Hurricane Andrew and the state's tropical-fish industry. Divers were considered most at risk. Lee County banned the taking of any shell containing a live creature. "Shelling" is a major draw of the county's Sanibel and Captiva islands, but the ban extends to any and all of the county's coasts. The city of Tampa limited lawns to just 50 percent of new residential and commercial yards in an effort to cut water use. It rained "the way it used to," with record downfalls that raised the hope that the state's two-decade drought might be ending.

2003—Sixteen minutes from touchdown at Cape Canaveral, the space shuttle *Columbia* disintegrated on reentry over Texas. Seven astronauts were killed. Wreckage, strewn over Louisiana, Texas, and points west, was brought to the Cape for investigation. The new Cabinet, chaired by the governor and consisting of three executive officers, the attorney general, the secretary of agriculture, and the chief financial officer, met for the first time and did very little. An old law required five votes for Cabinet action, something the now four-member panel could not muster. Legislative action was required to fix it. Newly elected second-term Lt. Gov. Frank Brogan resigned to become president of Florida Atlantic University. The governor named two-time Senate president Toni Jennings to succeed him. She was the first woman to hold the post. A state senate committee met in secret for the first time in two decades, to discuss the state's version of homeland security. The legislature modified the Sunshine Law after 9-11. The new board of governors to oversee the state's public universities, approved by voters via amendment and advocated by Sen. Bob Graham to undo Governor Bush's reforms, met and delegated major decisions back to the individual universities, where the governor had placed them. Advocates of the new board hoped it would replicate the Board of Regents, which controlled the entire university system before Bush eliminated it. The new board also left it to the board of education, created in Bush's first term, to make decisions for the system as whole as well as oversee education in the state, beginning with kindergarten. Legislation gave military reservists and guardsman financial protection while on active duty, including the right to cancel leases. It again cancelled Florida's traditional runoff "second primary" for the 2004 election process. Republicans supported the measure; Democrats opposed it. But the state's Supervisors of Elections supported it, complaining they did not have enough time to prepare for a runoff. The legislature cut $40 million from the university system, made no provision for an anticipated 22,000 new university students, and authorized an 8.5 percent tuition increase. Twenty-three percent of the state's public school third-graders, 43,000, flunked the reading section of the Florida Comprehensive Assessment Test. For them, the choice was summer school or being left back. Approximately 13,000 high school seniors flunked the state's graduation test, despite six chances to pass it. The number of schools earning an "A" from the state jumped by a third, but nine schools, five in Miami, received their second consecutive "F," making their students eligible for vouchers that enable them to attend any school of their choice. More than 600 did. After three special sessions, the legislature passed a cap on "pain and suffering" awards in malpractice cases. Cracking down on insurance fraud and abuse, Florida "sunset" no-fault auto insurance by 2007. Florida banned the sale of diet supplements to all under the age of 18. The Florida indoor workplace smoking ban went into effect. The governor signed a new Everglades Restoration bill, delaying the cleanup of the great swamp and threatening federal funding for the

$8-billion project. Upon signing the bill, Bush asked the legislature to revise it, which it did, setting a delay in the completion of the overall project for seven years but avoiding a financial crisis The Florida Supreme Court struck down a law calling for parental notification when a minor seeks an abortion. University of South Florida's tenured Assoc. Prof. Sami Al-Arian was arrested in the predawn hours and charged in a 50-count, 121-page indictment in Tampa with being the worldwide financial chief of the Palestinian Islamic Jihad and the head of its North American operations. Seven others also were arrested and charged after an eight-year investigation broken open by the Patriot Act, which allowed police and intelligence agencies to work together. The Seminole Tribal Council made it official, ousting suspended chairman James Billie after more than two decades. Cattleman Mitchell Cypress was elected chairman. Cypress Gardens at Winter Haven, recognized as the state's first theme park and lauded for virtually creating the modern tourism industry, closed after a 67-year run. The city of Weeki Wachee and all of its nine citizens took over operation of the famous living mermaid attraction. The state's jobless rate of 5.3 percent was lower than the national average, and Florida led the states in job creation, with more than 89,000 new positions. School districts estimated they'd be 20,000 teachers short for the fall term: 7,000 to meet the demands of the class-size amendment, 13,000 to accommodate new growth. It took 27 years for the Tampa Bay Buccaneers to go from worst to first in the NFL, but the much-maligned team won Super Bowl XXXVII over the Oakland Raiders 48-21. The Florida Marlins went from worst to first in one season, winning baseball's World Series in six games. Ave Maria University, the first new U.S. Catholic institution of higher learning in four decades, opened at Naples. Mosquito-borne West Nile virus—and malaria—returned to the state. Riptides off the Panhandle coast drowned 18 people in four months, including eight on one day. A March squall line swept the peninsula and spawned at least 6 tornadoes, killing one and injuring 12 in Miami. And the rains kept coming, with many areas of the state reaching their annual norms by August, without resorting to hurricanes. Orange County became the state's fourth to make its entire system a charter school district. Enrollment in Florida's Prepaid College Plan jumped to new heights as other states announced cutbacks in similar programs. Governor Bush announced the creation of the nation's first entirely faith-based prison at Lawtey Correctional Institution. A Florida appeals court ruled Coastal Petroleum Company could not collect damages for the state's refusal to allow it to drill off its coasts, despite the company's holding leases off St. George Island since 1941. Walt Disney World opened the state's largest hotel, a 2,880-room facility. Defense became Florida's third largest industry, extending to all of the state's 67 counties and accounting for nearly 10 percent of the state's gross product. Miami-Dade voters created two new cities, Miami Gardens and Doral.

2004—Voters rejected the high-speed bullet train between Tampa and Orlando they had approved in 2000. Following the 2000 election's "hanging chad" flap, in the 2004 presidential election more than half of Florida's voters used touch screen voting machines in the state's 15 largest counties. Voters in the 52 other counties used paper optical scanning ballots. Susan Benton of Highlands County became Florida's first elected female sheriff. Morris Young was elected sheriff of Gadsden County, the first black to be elected to the office in Florida's only majority black county since Reconstruction. Former U.S. Cabinet member Mel Martinez of Orlando was elected to the Senate, replacing the retiring Bob Graham. Republican Congressman Porter Goss of Sanibel was named director of the CIA. The state budget was $58 billion. Taxes weren't raised but fees were. The Hurricane Catastrophe Fund was increased from $11 billion to $15 billion, which raised the maximum post-hurricane assessment on homeowners' policyholders. Condominium owners won the right to rent their units to others without the approval of their associations. A new driver license rule required those 80 or older to pass a vision test for renewal. Miss Florida, Shauna Pender, suffered near fatal injuries on her way to an appearance when her limo was destroyed by an 18-wheeler. Alfred Pugh, the last known combat-wounded U.S. veteran of World War I, died just 10 days short of his 109th birthday. Cypress Gardens completed a 19-month, $45-million refurbishment and reopened. A "second story" addition to Tampa's Crosstown Expressway sank into what proved to be fill. A spate of violent and fatal attacks on young girls led to a state and then nationwide crackdown on sexual predators. The number of "snowbirds," part-time winter residents, reached 920,000. Disney closed its Orlando animation studio founded in 1989 at Disney World as it shifted from hand-drawn animated films to computer-generated movies. The Tampa Bay Lightning won hockey's Stanley Cup. Governor Jeb Bush easily defeated Tampa attorney Bill McBride to win a second term.

2005—Florida continued to lead the nation in job growth with unemployment staying at least one percent below the national average, falling to 3.3 percent. Brevard, Lee, and Collier counties led the nation in job creation. Terri Schiavo died 13 days after her feeding tube was removed after a seven-year court battle and being in a vegetative state for 15 years. Her situation pitted right-to-life against right-to-die advocates from the local to the federal level and thwarted state and congressional legislative efforts to keep her alive. A federal jury cleared accused terrorist Sami Al-Arian on eight charges but deadlocked on other charges. He was not released. Three men on Florida's death row were saved from death by the U.S. Supreme Court ruling barring the execution of criminals who committed their crimes as juveniles. A "Stand Your Ground" law allowed Floridians who were threatened anyplace they might lawfully be to use a firearm to protect themselves. Previously they were required to attempt flight before legitimately defending themselves. More than 350,000 Floridians held "concealed carry" permits. The legislature passed a $63.1 billion budget including tax cuts of $225 million. It permanently eliminated runoff elections, the "second primary." With an eye on past controversy, it set up a statewide voter registration list. After decades of complaints, it became illegal to drive in the left-hand lane of a multi-lane highway except to pass. Oceanographers announced the discovery of the deepest coral reef in the United States, 190 to 328 feet below the Gulf of Mexico, 40 miles west of the Dry Tortugas. NASA flew its first shuttle mission since the *Columbia* disaster. *Discovery* went to the International Space Station. An additional estimated 150,000 agricultural acres were believed lost to development during the year. Citrus acres went for $9,800 per acre, improved pastures for $6,400, and unimproved for $3,800. Florida's World War II Memorial was dedicated in Tallahassee. Tourism reached a record 85.3 million, including a 7.5 percent increase during hurricane season.

2006—Millions of Floridians faced severe financial hardship and the potential loss of their homes stemming from unprecedented increases in property insurance, escalating property values, and the reluctance of local governments to cut property tax rates. The legislature put $715 million toward the $1.7 billion deficit being run by Citizens Insurance, the state's insurer of last resort, lessening the assessment being paid by all Florida homeowners. Porter Goss resigned as CIA director. Rep. Mark Foley resigned from Congress in disgrace amid allegations of inappropriate behavior involving congressional pages. Eyeing issues ranging from national security to identify theft, the legislature continued to roll back provisions of Florida's open-records law. It eliminated the Florida intangible tax. The state budget was set at $71.3 billion. Despite state objections, Broward voters approved slot machines in their county. The state then set a tax rate of 50 percent on the gambling machines. The University of South Florida's St. Petersburg branch became the state's first branch campus to be accredited as an independent entity. Florida high school students became required to declare a major and a minor, similar to college students. Polk County opened the state's first public military high school. Governor Bush ordered out the National Guard to aid local peninsula communities in fighting wildfires blazing coast to coast during the spring dry season. The Herbert Hoover Dike around Lake Okeechobee was discovered to have serious weaknesses caused by hurricanes and other heavy rains over the years, and massive evacuation planning began in the bordering counties. The slash and burn fight against citrus canker was abandoned after the destruction of more than 60,000 acres of grove. 2005's Hurricane Wilma, especially, spread the tree-killing disease to another 200,000 acres. The federal Department of Agriculture banned fresh citrus fruit exports to six other citrus-producing states. Another tree-destroying blight, bug-borne "greening," also spread through groves. But the reduced and battered citrus crop brought record prices. Biomedical researches discovered another new coral reef nearly 3,000 feet down in the Florida Straits. Citing rampant fraud, the governor vetoed a bill continuing no-fault auto insurance. The death of a

14-year-old in custody prompted the state to cut off funding for various county-run "boot camp" juvenile facilities around the state. Penalties for social or political protesting at military funerals were increased. The line of succession for governor became codified with the lieutenant governor first, the attorney general second, and the chief financial officer third. Airboats were required to have mufflers for the first time. The "shooter voter" law required stores selling hunting, fishing, or trapping licenses to have voter registration forms for customers. The state purchased the 74,000-acre Babcock Ranch in Southwest Florida for $310 million. The ranch hosts a growing population of Florida panther and black bear. The Florida Supreme Court threw out as excessive the largest punitive judgment in history, $145 billion, against the tobacco industry. Three sinkholes opened beneath and drained Lakeland's Lake Scott, damaging homes on its shores. Florida became the first state to put all of its emergency responders on the same communications system. After alligators killed three people in three different areas of the state and with the gator population estimated to be more than a million, the state issued a record number of alligator hunting permits and extended the season by more than a month. The University of Florida won the NCAA national basketball championship. The University of Tampa won the NCAA Division II national baseball championship, for the fourth time. The NCAA put the troubled Florida A&M on four years of probation for 196 admitted rules violations in all 15 men's and women's sports from 1998 through 2005.

It exonerated fired football coach Billy Joe. Crossbow hunters, long lumped with archers, got their own hunting season. The ban on ticket scalping was lifted. The *National Inquirer* moved back to Boca Raton. It had moved to New York after a 2001 anthrax attack on its building, which killed one. Lee County vowed to wipe out its 10,000-strong alien spiny-tailed black iguana population on Boca Grande before they spread to the mainland. The Goliath grouper was reported recovered from overfishing to an extent that it has been removed from the federal list of species of concern. It is still illegal to catch the giants, which can measure 8 feet, weigh more than 800 pounds, and live for 35 years. The historic Marineland oceanarium reopened to large crowds with a new centerpiece, its 1.3 million-gallon Dolphin Conservation Center. The reopened Cypress Gardens attraction, having been hit directly by three hurricanes, filed for bankruptcy protection while continuing to operate and even expand. Tornadoes swept across Central Florida on Christmas day, producing no deaths but heavy damage. Embry-Riddle Aeronautical University, well prepared for a hurricane, lost 50 of its 65 planes. The Seminole Tribe of Florida purchased the Hard Rock Café enterprise from Britain's Rank Group for $965 million. The tribe, which operated two Hard Rock label resort casinos and five other casinos in Florida, gained 68 additional Hard Rock operations in the U.S., Canada, Europe, Australia, and Puerto Rico. The Seminoles were the nation's first in Indian casino gambling and advised other tribes as they entered the field, which now generates more than $22 billion in annual revenues. Charlie Crist was elected governor.

2007—In a harbinger of things to come, the state's cities, counties and school districts staged a run on the State Board of Administration when they discovered the board held $2.2 billion of debt newly classified as junk along with $700 million in defaulted debt. The board, consisting of the governor, the attorney general and the chief financial officer, manages short-term investments for the entities as well as the state. The downgrade represented 4 percent of the fund with another 7 percent coming under scrutiny. The investments involved sub-prime debt. Local governments and school boards pulled $10 billion out of the investment pool, approximately more than 30 percent of its assets, in a matter of weeks until the state shut down withdrawals. The pool was the largest in the country. Home foreclosures in Florida rose to the second highest in the nation, up more than 200 percent over the year before. Tourism dipped nearly 2 percent, the first yearly decline since the 2001 terrorist attacks roiled the travel industry. The drop came amid record gas prices and a slowing economy. The state's population growth dropped by half compared to the decade's previous years and to its lowest level in three decades. Florida's public employee retirement fund divested nearly $1.3 billion invested with 21 companies doing business in Iran or Sudan. Tornadoes ripped across Central Florida killing 20 and damaging or destroying more than 1,200 homes including brand new up-to-the-latest-codes structures. The U.S. Department of Agriculture declared

58 Florida counties as primary natural disaster areas because of the continued drought. Because contiguous counties can also apply for natural disaster benefits, it meant all of the state's 67 counties were covered. The drought cost Florida agricultural producers $100 million a month in losses. The legislature in special session "solved" the property insurance crisis with caps, a ban on cancellations and other mandates but not to anyone's satisfaction. Rates dipped but only slightly. No fix for soaring property taxes came out of the regular legislative session. Minorities made up 35.7 percent of the student population at Florida's public universities. Florida Virtual School celebrated its 10th anniversary, having grown from a small pilot project to a public school that put Florida at the forefront of online learning. Enrollment went from 75 students at inception to more than 54,000 from around the state and beyond. Mulberry-based Land South Holdings bought the oldest theme park in the state, Cypress Gardens, for $16.8 million at a bankruptcy auction in Georgia. Becoming the third owner in a dozen years. Dr. Robert Cade, 80, who as the University of Florida's first professor of kidney medicine invented Gatorade to combat dehydration of the Gator football team, died. Five Florida universities placed their football teams in bowl games: Florida, FSU, USF, UCF and FAU, while FIU won its very first football game after 23 straight losses. Gator QB Tim Tebow won the Heisman Trophy, the first sophomore to do so. The University of Tampa repeated as Division II baseball national champions. Boating deaths jumped 10 percent

in Florida, marking the 16th year in 20 that the Sunshine State has led the nation in fatalities. Statewide, the leading cause of death continued to be drowning. Comparing Floridians' love for manatees to their love for Santa Claus, state wildlife commissioners indefinitely postponed a decision to take the animals off the endangered species list. Killer bees became established in the state's wild hives. A burglary suspect fleeing Miccosukee Tribal police jumped into a lake past signs warning "Danger, Live Alligators" and was killed.

2008—An early January cold snap brought the coldest weather in five years to the peninsula. It snowed at Daytona Beach and dropped temperatures into the 30s as far south as the Keys. The State Board of Administration did not have the proper federal credentials to purchase nearly one of every three securities analyzed in a legislative audit. The finding opened the possibility to pursue refunds of some of the $1.2 billion in local taxes the board invested in mortgage-backed securities that were downgraded within days of the purchase. The board, which manages 34 public funds including the state pension system, saw its assets fall to $62 billion, a third of its former value. Another mortgage-backed securities fund holding $187 million belonging to more than a dozen small Florida cities, collapsed. The program was sponsored by the cities' lobbying organization, the Florida League of Cities. But the league made good on the participants' investments. Cities that had invested outside the league program took loses. Unemployment jumped to a 15-year high at 7.3 percent The state made an upfront payment of $227 million from its hurricane reserves to Warren Buffet's Berkshire Hathaway company in return for a guarantee to purchase $4 billion in Florida bonds in the wake of a future storm, making the state liable for property claims. The state's prison system reached more than 97 percent capacity and growing as the system balked at a legislature request to trim 10 percent from its proposed $3.2 billion budget. Florida Power & Light won state approval to build the state's first new nuclear plants in more than two decades. Beekeepers fought to maintain and restore their hives as a mysterious malady continued to kill the nation's honeybees. The state's bees create Florida's $11.3 million annual honey crop. The state's first confirmed human death by killer bees came in Okeechobee County. Florida expanded its concealed carry law by establishing a "take your gun to work" law. Florida public schools lost nearly 37,000 more students after losing 10,000 the year before, a result of the state's decline in population growth. Declines came in 48 of the state's 67 counties. Enrollment peaked in 2005-2006 at 2.6 million students. It was the third straight year of falling enrollment. The University of Central Florida offered all 40 entering students at its new medical school a full ride: full scholarships worth $160,000, including $20,000 for tuition and $20,000 for living expenses per year. Three of the state's largest universities raised their tuition up to 15 percent while other state universities raised their tuitions at least 6 percent. All the universities announced intentions to cut programs, faculty, staff and enrollments. The Southern Association of Colleges and Schools found that Florida A&M, the nation's largest historically black university, had fixed the financial management and leadership problems that had it on the verge of losing accreditation. For the third consecutive year, Miami was deemed the worst U.S. city for road rage, but there were no homicides in Miami during October, the first month without the violent crime since 1996. Gen. David Petraeus reported as head of U. S. Central Command at Tampa. Rock pioneer Bo Diddley, 79, died at home near Gainesville. Peggy Quince was named Chief Justice of the Supreme Court, the first black woman to head any branch of state government. Charles Canady was named to the Florida Supreme Court, the first of four appointments expected to fundamentally change the court which ruled for Al Gore in the 2000 election and which remained the last vestige of Democratic Party power in the state government. The court ruled the governor did not have the authority to sign a casino gambling deal with the Seminole Tribe of Florida. The average age at death of Seminoles dropped 12 years to 48. Drugs and alcohol were blamed for the decline measured over the last decade. Average life expectancy for Floridians is 73. The Seminoles' new individual wealth, at $120,000 a year, also was seen as a contributing factor. Going from worst to first, the Tampa Bay Rays won the American League pennant. Mold, mildew, odor and decaying wiring drove people from their homes in Manatee County's sprawling Lakewood Ranch community as Chinese drywall rotted in place. After similar scattered and isolated outbreaks over the previous three years, primarily in south Florida, massive lawsuits blossomed.

2009—Florida's population declined for the first time since 1946. The state ordered Broward County to stop building new schools since it could no longer fill the schools it had. Unemployment rose to 10.2 percent, the highest since 1975. Florida lost $1 billion in the Lehman Brothers bankruptcy. More than a half-million homes went into foreclosure, among the highest totals in the nation. Property values continued to plummet followed by property taxes. More than half of all Florida homeowners were believed "underwater," owing more than their homes were worth. Thirteen banks failed. However, financial rating agencies removed the state from their "watch list" and confirmed its solid bond rating after the legislature passed a $66.5 billion budget that included cuts and new revenues from taxes and fees including a $1 per pack tax on cigarettes. Pensacola celebrated its 450th anniversary with 450 celebratory events. The U.S. Supreme Court let stand a lower court ruling confirming Florida and Alabama's claim to the waters of Georgia's Lake Lanier, Atlanta's primary drinking water source. Anheuser-Busch InBev sold Orlando-based Busch Entertainment to the international Blackstone Group for an estimated $2.7 billion. The entertainment company operates Sea World in Orlando and Busch Gardens in Tampa. Blackstone already owned a 50 percent stake in Universal Orlando. Struggling Cypress Gardens, the state's first theme park, reopened, again, and closed, again. Gov. Crist named long-time aide George LeMiuex to the U.S. Senate, replacing Mel Martinez who resigned. The state lost 17,900 buildings, or at least state officials couldn't find them after being ordered to create an inventory of state-owned property. Wendy B. Lilly became the ninth president and first woman to head Stetson University. The Powerball Lottery moved to Florida after 20 years in Iowa as part of the deal to bring the state into the multi-state game. The Florida Gators won their third national football championship crown. Legendary FSU football coach Bobby Bowden retired. The University of Central Florida won the Conference-USA title. The Florida Grapefruit League had an economic impact of $752 million, drawing 1.6 million fans to games over a 39-day season.

2010—The state, especially its agriculture, endured its longest cold snap in 60 years with temperatures throughout the state near, at, or below freezing. While citrus survived with minimal damage, most of the state's winter vegetable crop, the nation's staple, was destroyed. The cold lasted 12 days. Most of Florida was declared an agricultural disaster area. The coldest winter was followed by the hottest summer. Twenty-nine more banks failed. The colossal home foreclosure rate continued to soar. State unemployment reached 12.3 percent, the highest ever recorded with more than 1.26 million out of work. More than one in eight Floridians went on food stamps. Thousands of NASA and other space workers faced unemployment as the Obama Administration changed the agency's missions and direction. The state pension fund went deeper into the red. April's Gulf Oil Disaster pushed oil onto Panhandle beaches in June. Tourism suffered millions in loses on all its coasts on the perception of oil. Cholera, believed to have been imported from Haiti, broke out in Miami. Dengue Fever broke out in Key West, the first locally acquired case in the state since 1934. The Florida National Guard sent off 2,500 to Iraq, its largest deployment since World War II. The state was the only one to see a decline in its illegal alien population. The legislature finally had its say and way on the Seminole Tribe casino gambling issue, making a $1.58 billion five-year gambling pact with the tribe. Florida got federal grants to start building a high-speed rail line between Tampa and Orlando, a project the state's voters first approved, then rejected. The decade-long effort to restore the Everglades ended in a whimper when the state's plan to buy 187,000 acres from U.S. Sugar for $1.75 billion retreated to a purchase of 26,800 acres for $197 million. Jacksonville's veteran Cecil Field got its federal spaceport license to go along with a private $16 billion contract to deliver supplies to the International Space Station. Merlin Entertainment took over the chronically troubled Cypress Gardens theme park site with plans to open the world's fifth Legoland with an investment of $300 million. George Steinbrenner, 80, controversial, hard-nosed New York Yankees owner and softhearted Florida philanthropist died. Legendary band director Dr. William Foster died at 91. Foster created the Florida A&M Marching

100 Band, whose energetic high-stepping style, mass field dancing, exuberant half-time pageants and use of pop music is imitated by high school and college bands throughout the country. It got tougher to graduate from high school with new requirements in math and science and the creation of an exit exam. Florida and FSU cracked down on high schools using themes similar to the Gators and 'Noles, even those using the popular logos and colors, etc., for decades. State universities raised their tuitions by 15 percent with some raising student fees as well. UCF won the Conference USA football championship again. It and four other teams got bowl bids. Republicans choose Tampa for their 2012 National Convention. Florida led a 20-state coalition challenging the constitutionality of the federal health care law. After record campaign spending, the entire State Cabinet was replaced for the first time in the state's history. Republican Rick Scott was elected Governor. Gov. Charlie Christ, after pulling out of the Republican U.S. Senate primary after polls showed him losing to former state House speaker Marco Rubio, ran without party affiliation against Rubio and still lost. The year ended as it began, with record cold. Population: 18,801,310.

THE SEMINOLES

In 1750, Creek Chief Secoffee led his people into Florida from Georgia. They had broken with their old nation in the north, formed a strong confederation, and were now known as Seminoles, or "runaway." Also part of the Seminole Nation were the last of the old, aborigine tribes such as the Yamasee (driven from the Carolinas) and the Oconee, who migrated from the Apalachicola region.

In the early 1700s, Creek Indians sided with the British against the Spanish and launched raids from Georgia into Florida as far south as the Everglades. When the British replaced the Spanish in Florida, the Indians welcomed their British friends and together they formed a unified confederation.

This was not to last, however, and in 1783, when the Spanish regained possession of Florida, the Indians once again were fighting with whites. Some of the friction resulted from runaway slaves who were given refuge by the Indians; other unrest was caused by the Indians' British friends.

In late 1817, at the start of what is known as the First Seminole War, the U.S. government ordered the army's Andrew Jackson to take personal charge of the campaign against the Indians, their British allies, and the Spanish. Jackson promised President Monroe to have the job done within 60 days.

By April 1818, Jackson had traveled to Apalachicola and St. Marks and then marched eastward toward the Suwannee River. At the settlement of Old Town (on U.S. 19 today, near Chiefland), Jackson court martialed two Britishers for aiding the Indians—Robert Ambrister, who was shot, and Alexander Arbuthnot, who was hanged.

Jackson soon headed back toward Pensacola, where he arrived in May 1818 to occupy the city and take over Fort Barrancas. But upon arrival he learned that the executions of Ambrister and Arbuthnot had led to demands by Britain for an apology. Congress debated the matter for nearly a month, but never voted to censure Jackson, who enjoyed the support of Secretary of State John Quincy Adams.

Within three years, Florida was transferred from Spain to the United States and by 1822, with Florida a newly designated U.S. territory, Andrew Jackson became its first governor. But friction between white settlers and the Seminoles continued and in 1823 an Indian conference convened in December at Moultrie Creek near St. Augustine, during which an Indian treaty was negotiated. It set aside lands north of Charlotte Harbor and south of Ocala exclusively for Seminole Indians. The Indians, in exchange for giving up the lands to the north that they held and a promise to not provide refuge for runaway slaves, also gained tools, livestock, cash, and a year's ration of meat, corn, and salt.

The Treaty of Moultrie Creek was only a year old when President Monroe began speaking out against Indians in every part of the country, urging their removal to reservations. Meanwhile, in Florida, the Seminoles were having difficulties with the terms of the Moultrie Creek treaty. They did not like the treaty-prescribed land, which had been stricken by a drought. And they continued to harbor runaway slaves, or so white slave owners contended. As U.S. policy toward Indians everywhere became more strident, federal representatives in 1827 tried to interest the Seminoles into moving from Florida, to lands further west.

James Gadsden, a government representative, called a meeting of the Seminole Indians at Paynes Landing on the Oklawaha River and convinced seven chiefs to sign away the benefits of the earlier Treaty of Moultrie Creek. During the meeting, the Indians agreed, wittingly or not, to accept $13,000 apiece and to move west by November 1833. But two chiefs later charged that they had not signed the agreement and they considered the Treaty of Moultrie Creek still in effect. Nevertheless, the U.S. government insisted the Seminoles be prepared to move west by January 1836.

The Indians were not cooperative, however, and for several reasons. Whites murdered Indian chief Charley Emathla, blaming the slaying on Chief Osceola, and U.S. soldiers had captured Osceola's wife, contending she was a fugitive slave. Foreseeing another war, other chiefs and their families fled to U.S. forts for protection, an influx that created further uneasiness among white settlers.

In 1835, the expected Second Seminole War broke out and it was to last for seven years. Seminole factions began attacking a number of sites, including the Simmons plantation in Micanopy, plantations in Matanzas, and settlement buildings in New Smyrna. Then, in December 1835, Indians ambushed Gen. Wiley Thompson and a lieutenant outside of Fort King at Ocala. That same day, an Indian ambush caught Maj. Francis Dade and two companies of soldiers at Bushnell as they were marching from Fort Brooke in Tampa to Fort King. Major Dade was killed by the first shot and a total of 103 soldiers died. The event became known among whites as the Dade Massacre.

News of Dade's fate prompted activation and enlargement of Florida's militia. In January 1836 the U.S. government sent 14 companies of soldiers under the leadership of Gen. Winfield Scott to join the territory's militia. Much of the Indian militancy occurred until 1837 under the leadership of Osceola, who is quoted as having said, "Your men will fight and so will we, until the last drop of Seminole blood has moistened the dust of his hunting ground."

But in 1837, Osceola and another leader, Coacoochee, agreed to arbitrate the hostilities. As the two rode into St. Augustine under a flag of truce sent to Osceola by Gen. Thomas Jesup, Jesup ordered the pair captured and they were taken to St. Augustine's Fort Marion (Castillo de San Marcos). Coacoochee escaped, but later Osceola died.

During the next year, U.S. troops pushed the Indians further south and in December of that year a major skirmish provided then-Col. Zachary Taylor with the only major U.S. victory against the Indians. Taylor's victory triggered the shipment of nearly 3,000 Seminoles out of Florida to areas west of the Mississippi River. Isolated Indian raids continued until November 1841, when Coacoochee, the most powerful Indian leader since Osceola, finally gave up. In 1842 the Second Seminole War was declared over.

The 300 or so Seminoles who did not move west fled into the Everglades. In 1851, they regrouped under another chief, Billy Bowlegs. He had gone to Washington and

New York that year to listen to rationales by white leaders for total Indian emigration. But he returned unpersuaded, and in 1855 a group of his followers attacked a group of white surveyors. Further Indian raids were made on settlers and forts in the Sarasota area, in Hillsborough County, and at Fort Meade. Skirmishes continued through 1857 in what became known as Bowlegs' War or the Third Seminole War. But in 1858 Bowlegs surrendered, and the U.S. government quickly deported him from Florida via steamer from Egmont Key. His followers fled into the Big Cypress area and to the Everglades in south Florida.

Succeeding generations of Seminoles, now nearly 3,000 in number, still live there today, under a truce signed with the U.S. government in 1934. They have divided into two groups, the "Reservation Seminoles," who live on or near four federal reservations; one in Big Cypress in Hendry County south of Lake Okeechobee, another in Brighton in Glades County northwest of Lake Okeechobee, one near Hollywood in Broward County north of Miami, and a fourth, small reservation outside Tampa in Hillsborough County. A second and smaller group, the "Trail Seminoles," better known as the Miccosukee, numbers 350 and lives on four small reservations west of Miami. They are recognized as a separate tribe. The Indians and the white populace in Florida no longer war against each other, but disputes continue, often over the Indians' sovereign status. These days, however, both sides turn their conflicts over to attorneys.

OSCEOLA

The American Indian Osceola is one of Florida's most enchanting historical figures, romanticized to near legend. Osceola's origins remain murky. By some accounts he was born "Billy Powell" near Tuskegee, Ala., in about 1804. His father, William Powell, was an English Indian trader from Virginia. Osceola's part Creek mother is listed as Polly Copinger Powell.

Diaries and other reports describe Osceola as 5 feet, 10 inches tall, thin, with reddish-brown hair. He probably was left-handed.

In about 1813 Polly and son Billy moved to Florida, possibly because of increasing Indian and government conflicts. Sometime after 1818, Billy Powell became "As-se-he-ho-lar" ("Ussa Yaholo" or "Asi yaholo"), which was Anglicized as "Osceola." The name translates to "black drink" or the "black drink singer," reportedly because Osceola not only tolerated quantities of "asi," a ceremonial holly brew, but robustly hollered "yaholo," a traditional post-drink whoop.

During the 1820s, white settlers immigrated to Florida and Indian raids escalated. Osceola was an influential leader among Creeks and Seminoles, but never was a chief.

Precisely what moved Osceola to militancy may never be known. One source says Osceola became enraged over mistreatment of his wife, Morning Dew, by Indian Agent Wiley Thompson. This is unsubstantiated by more modern historians.

But enmity did exist between Osceola and Thompson. In June 1835, Thompson pushed Osceola to sign a treaty that would remove Florida Indians from their lands. Military journals report that Osceola insulted, and perhaps threatened, Agent Thompson.

Thompson had Osceola arrested, but freed him after he signed the treaty. The following November Osceola was implicated in the murder of Indian Charley Emathla, a white sympathizer. One month later, an Osceola-led raid on Fort King left Agent Thompson dead.

Indian attacks continued until October 1837, when Osceola was duped into a peace parley at Fort Peyton, near St. Augustine. Instead of negotiating, Gen. Thomas Jesup arrested Osceola.

On Dec. 31, 1837, an ill and weary Osceola was transferred from St. Augustine's Fort Marion (Castillo de San Marcos) to Fort Moultrie in Charleston (S.C.) harbor. Despite his failing health, Osceola was noted as being popular and good-natured. On Jan. 30, 1838, he died at age 34 from quinsy, an acute throat infection.

Two more events occurred before Osceola was buried. One, a death cast was made of his upper body. And, second, Fort Moultrie surgeon Frederick Weedon removed Osceola's head and kept it at his home until it became part of a New York Medical College-Museum collection.

Legend has attributed the beheading of Osceola to retribution—that Dr. Weedon's wife, Mary Thompson Weedon, was related to the slain Indian Agent Thompson. But historians find no link between Mary Weedon and Agent Thompson.

In 1967, vandalism forced the National Park Service to dig up Osceola's grave. A headless skeleton, verified as Osceola's, was found in the grave. Archaeologist John Griffin, who examined Osceola's body at that time, said the head was likely removed for scientific study. He said, "Craniology or phrenology were popular studies at the time of Osceola's death."

No one knows what happened to Osceola's head. The New York collection burned in 1865 and no records have been found that verify the head was actually with the burnt collection.

Weedon's diary says Osceola's deathbed request was to be buried in Florida. Several failed attempts have been made since 1930 to bring his body to Florida. But because Osceola was in federal custody at the time he died, the National Park Service has chosen to retain this famous Floridian in South Carolina.

MINORCANS AT NEW SMRYNA

The Minorcans have a special place in Florida's history. Recruited from the British-ruled Spanish island of Minorca and from Greece and Italy, the Minorcans arrived at Andrew Turnbull's New Smyrna to establish the most famous of the British plantations in Florida.

Turnbull brought 300 families, more than 1,400 people, to grow indigo as cash crop and Mediterranean food crops to support themselves and for export.

The population consisted of 1,100 Minorcans, 200 Greeks, and 110 Italians, and their arrival marked the largest mass immigration to North America to that time. It more than doubled Florida's known population.

But New Smyrna did not thrive. The Minorcans found on arrival that instead of 20,000 verdant acres ready for planting, the land consisted mainly of mangrove swamp that had to be cleared. An estimated 450 people died the first year at New Smyrna from hardship, disease, and starvation. Another 450 died in the decade that followed.

Although New Smyrna was the most profitable indigo plantation ever established in North America, it still did not meet economic expectations. Mandated food crops regularly failed, even though the Minorcans were the most experienced farmers to ever till Florida land on a large scale.

In addition, while the Minorcans arrived as indentured servants, they found themselves quickly reduced to slavery by Turnbull's overseers.

The Minorcans rebelled against Turnbull their very first year at New Smyrna. The insurrection was quelled by British troops from St. Augustine. But when the plantation collapsed in 1777, most of the plantation's remaining population fled there.

New Smyrna was such a disaster that the British governor, Col. Patrick Tonyn, reversed policy, releasing the Minorcans from their indenture and ignoring their faith. The Minorcans were overwhelmingly Catholic and their presence both at New Smyrna and then as refugees in St. Augustine was a breach of British colonial law.

The Minorcans remained a readily identifiable community through the 1870s, and their descendants and heritage are still centered at St. Augustine.

MILLIONS FORGOTTEN

Over the years hundreds of Floridians die leaving millions of dollars in money, jewelry, coins, and other valuables in their homes or safe deposit boxes with no heirs to claim them. As a result, in 1961, the Florida Disposition of Unclaimed Property Act was enacted. It requires banks, thrifts, insurance companies, fiduciaries, governmental units, and various businesses and trustees to report any abandoned property to the state comptroller. This abandoned property is held by Florida and out-of-state corporations for seven years, and by financial institutions for 10 years, per the state law. Meanwhile, the comptroller's office is required to make an effort to find the owners or heirs by listing the names of the owners of any unclaimed property, money, and deposits in legal advertisements in Florida newspapers. The ads run twice a month each January. Because of the ads, 40 percent of the abandoned valuables are claimed by rightful parties. The balance is turned over to the state school fund. Contents of safe deposit boxes are handled differently; if the owner or heirs do not claim the box within seven years, the contents are sold at public auction and the proceeds given to the school fund.

FLORIDA'S WILD WEST

A little-known aspect of Florida life in the 1800s is its similarity to the Wild West. De Soto County was on a par with Dodge City as the site of frequent cattle wars, rustling, and hangings.

LIGHTNING CAPITAL

Florida receives 35.4 lightning flashes per square kilometer per year, according to NASA, making it the lightning capital of the New World but not the whole world. Based on satellite sensor recordings, that distinction belongs to the African nation of Rwanda, which records an annual 82.7 per kilometer.

RECORD WEATHER

Florida has the sunniest winter climate in the eastern U.S. The state has the highest average January temperature in the nation. It is also the waterspout, thunderstorm, and lightning capital of the nation. The state also has one of the lowest occurrences of hay fever pollen in the country.

ARCHAEOLOGY

Human hunter-gatherers are believed to have entered Florida 14,000 years ago, following now-extinct large game onto a cool and dry land mass twice as large as the Florida of today that emerged from the sea at the height of the Ice Age. Human beings kept coming. How many is open to conjecture but more than 1,500 paleoindian sites are known in modern Florida with perhaps an equal number buried beneath the sea on what is today the continental shelf. With the end of the Ice Age, rising water left the current peninsula, and the state's climate gradually began to change to what it is today. Ancient humans left a lot behind. If it was left behind on what is now state-owned land or sovereign submerged bottoms, it belongs to the state. But all archeological sites are protected by law. Minor sites on private land or public land must be explored, catalogued, and even removed before old land can be put to new uses. Major sites on private land often devolve to the state or other public or private protective entities either directly or indirectly via goodwill or incentives.

RECENT FINDS

An ancient bone etched with a clear image of a walking mammoth or mastodon was unearthed by an amateur fossil hunter at Vero Beach. The find, according to University of Florida experts, demonstrates clearly that humans coexisted with prehistoric animals more than 12,000 to 14,000 years ago. It also newly shows that man inhabited Florida at someplace other than Little Salt Springs on the other coast during the Pleistocene epoch. Nothing similar has ever been found and authenticated in the New World. It's described as "the oldest, most spectacular and rare work of art in the Americas." The bone, brown and mineral hardened, is slightly more than a foot long and was part of a larger bone belonging to a mastodon, a mammoth or giant ground sloth, animals extinct in Florida for 10,000 years. It was carved with either an animal tooth or a very sharp tool when the bone was still fresh, shortly after the animal was killed or died. The four-inch etching shows an elephant-like animal with some perspective, with one rear leg in front of the other, along with a dangling trunk. Veteran fossil enthusiast James Kennedy found the bone on the north side of his hometown. The exact site of the find has not been disclosed. He put it in a box with other items and four years later took a hard look at it. Having found and donated numerous items to the University of Florida through the years, Kennedy sent the bone to the university for authentication, setting off a flurry of excitement in the field. Thus far, all tests have confirmed its legitimacy, as have evidence submitted to experts around the world. The find has given impetus to efforts to redig an area where a century ago prehistoric bones and human remains, including the controversial "Vero Man," were discovered. The site is soon to be obliterated by the expansion of the Vero Beach Water plant.

Buried for an estimated 1,000 years in the muck of Weedon Island in Tampa Bay, a 45-foot-long vessel worked its way to the surface in 2008, the first pre-Columbian seagoing canoe discovered in Florida. It was carved out of a single pine tree and experts believe it was used for trade with people along the Gulf Coast and beyond. The wood has been dated to 890. The canoe is believed to be a legacy of the Weedon Island culture whose influence has been found as far away as Georgia. The canoe is *in situ* and its exact location has not been disclosed.

Ancient mounds containing human teeth, bone fragments, and tools, some up to 5,000 years old, have been found at the headwaters of the St. Johns River in west Brevard County near Melbourne. The site is in the Three Forks Marsh Conservation Area. The find put on hold the $15 million Lake Lawton federal project since the mounds are on the 7,000 acres set to be flooded for the lake. The mounds are approximately 100 feet long and 6 feet high. Officials said they would negotiate with the Seminole and Miccosukee nations on how to proceed.

The large footprint of a 17th-century church along with other artifacts has been found near the Ocklawaha River. The mission church is believed to have been founded in 1627 to serve the Timucuan tribe and is likely to have operated until 1656 when the Timucuan rebelled. All that remains of the site are small object fragments and discolored earth indicating where building features were located. Although most Timucuans were Catholics, the group along the Ocklawaha were not, despite having a mission in their midst for three decades.

Unearthed on prime real estate on the downtown Miami waterfront in 1999, the "Tequesta Stone Circle" continues to be the archeological site that keeps on giving. The site, Brickell Point where the Miami River meets Biscayne Bay, is believed to have been a pre-Columbian religious ceremonial site or the beginnings of the Port of Miami, a center of trade between the Tequesta Indians and the native inhabitants not only of the Bahamas but beyond, deep into the Caribbean. The two-acre center plot is still being explored, researched, and protected by the state in cooperation with Miami-Dade County. In the meantime, burial grounds have been discovered beyond the site. Evidence indicates that the circle was a center starting around 750 BC and continuing sporadically into the 17th century AD.

Archeologists participating in attempts to undo the damage of 20th-century canal works west of Lake Okeechobee discovered an ancient canal running parallel to today's canalized Caloosahatchee River to the gulf. The old canal is believed to have been dug 2,000 years ago by a long-gone Indian civilization named after the river, because nothing else is known of them. Engineers have called the ancient canal a marvel of construction. It is seven miles long, 20 feet wide, and six feet deep. It is believed the old dig was created for the same reason as the current canal, to provide a clear waterway from the lake to the Gulf of Mexico, a way around what was the natural river's rapids. Numerous other ancient and sophisticated canal works have been found around the lake and are believed to be from the same period. It is likely they were dug for the same reason as the modern canal works around the lake: drainage.

Also found in the area but believed to be from a later date, about 700 AD, is a huge man-made depression, a pond also believed to have been dug for drainage.

The state operates several state parks as archeological preserves. Most current interest rests on Letchworth Mounds Archeological State Park, home to four mounds including one that, at 300 feet wide and 46 feet high, is the largest in Florida. Some believe that the site dates to the Weedon Island Period, between 300 and 1000 AD. The Weedon Island Preserve, definitely from that period, is administered by Pinellas County. Many counties control and administer archeological sites.

Both the state and counties hold some archeological sites in secret, primarily to thwart scavengers and thieves.

When portions of the bottom of Lake Okeechobee where exposed to the sun by Florida's long-running drought in 2007, archaeologists discovered the remains of several men and their hand-carved boats, believed to be from the early 16th century. Nothing has been moved from the Palm Beach County site, which archaeologists hope will again be covered with water. Although accessible only after a long trek through waist-deep mud, the site is under guard. Disturbing an archaeological site in Florida is a first-degree misdemeanor punishable by a year in jail. Digging at such a site is a third-degree felony punishable by three years in jail.

During the 2000 drought, water levels in north central Florida fell in many lakes, including Newman's Lake just east of Gainesville, which dried up. Local residents found the remains of numerous 19th- and 20th-century skiffs, but archeologists found among the modern crafts the remains of much older canoes. They numbered 86, the largest concentration of ancient canoes ever discovered in the United States. More than half the canoes have tested to be between 3,000 and 5,000 years old. While a very important find, they have not set the record. The oldest canoes were found buried at DeLeon Springs in Volusia County, and date to 6,000 years. Ancient canoes have been found in more than 200 sites in the state.

Aided by divers and trainers from the Florida Aquarium, University of Miami diving archaeologists began bringing up artifacts estimated to be at least 10,000 years old from a ledge 90 feet below the surface of Little Salt Spring at Northport in Sarasota County. The spring, with little dissolved oxygen, has acted as a preservative for artifacts thousands of years old. A square-meter area on the ledge was excavated. Little Salt Spring is one of the most important archeological sites in the nation. It was discovered as an archeological site in the late 1950s and donated to the University of Miami in 1982. The spring is a 240-foot deep hourglass. Explorations in the 1970s produced signs of life at the springs dating back more than 12,000 years. The university has been actively excavating the site since 1992. In 2005, divers brought up remains from burial sites 30 feet below today's waterline. Less than 10 percent of the spring has been explored.

Another extraordinarily important find came in 1983 in a bog near Titusville called the Windover Site. Preserved in the bog were skulls and skeletons believed to be at least 8,000 years old. Among its many surprising revelations: the Florida Indians of 6,000 b.c. were much like the Florida Indians of 1500 a.d. in appearance, stature, and lifestyle.

Meanwhile in St. Augustine:

Aviles Street in St. Augustine is the oldest continuously occupied residential street in the United States, perhaps 100 years older than Philadelphia's Elfreth's Alley, which has long claimed the antiquity honor. Archaeologists exploring the lower level of the avenue aired in 2010 the discovery of pottery shards from the early 1600s. The street also may predate that. Beneath the pottery level, experts found blackened earth that they speculated might stem from Sir Francis Drake's burning of the city to the ground in 1586.

City archaeologists digging at the Plaza de la Constitucion discovered it isn't quite there, as authorized by the King of Spain in 1598. The city's earliest plaza had to meet the stringent guidelines of the day for an official open meeting space and either it did not or it is not located exactly as expected. The plaza is believed to be the nation's first and oldest gathering spot and the first site of its first bullfight. A dig was begun when the city needed to run new electrical conduits through the site. The surprise came when a house was discovered on what should have been an open space for more than 400 years. In addition, another house was discovered below, and there may be as many as three more constructions beneath that. The city is believed to have been destroyed three times in the last quarter-century of the 1500s, by

Indian attack, by Sir Francis Drake and by a hurricane. The discovery indicates the plaza was smaller and did not sit exactly on the site as originally believed. While there are many documents pertaining to the plaza, there are no maps or sketches. The nature of the plaza is believed to have changed with the coming of the Americans, who, over time, converted the great open space into a tree-shaded, grassy common.

A routine archaeological review prior to putting a fence around St. Augustine's Cathedral School led to the discovery of a boys' school established by the Spanish to overcome the influence of the occupying English. The find is described as the "best evidence of public education in colonial Florida." The two-story school, free to all school-age boys—but not girls—in the city, operated from 1786 through 1820. When the Spanish returned to Florida, they found that most young residents, especially the Minorcans, spoke Greek, Italian, and English but not Spanish.

A slender wood stick with one knobbed end, stored in a preservation solution in a plastic container at St. Augustine's Government House, has been determined to be a *molinillo,* a whisk used in the preparation of a chocolate drink. It indicates knowledge and use of chocolate in the nation's oldest city, dating back to the 1500s, shortly after Spanish explorers determined that Columbus' view of the cocoa bean as worthless was incorrect.

Catholic documents, many more than 400 years old, are among thousands of artifacts detailing the lives of Spanish soldiers, settlers, missionaries, and merchants who populated what is now the nation's oldest city, St. Augustine. They stem from a time when the church was the sole keeper of records. The Florida archives have been scattered hither and yon, most lost for hundreds of years. When rediscovered, most were worse the wear from neglectful storage. They have been gathered together and placed in a new fireproof, waterproof, climate-controlled building at the Roman Catholic Diocese of St. Augustine. The earliest documents detail the births, confirmations, marriages, and deaths of the Spanish residents in St. Augustine from 1594 to 1763, when the British took over Florida. Records for the city's first 29 years are believed to have been destroyed in Sir Francis Drake's raid on the city, which he burned to the ground. When the Spanish evacuated Florida, 15 volumes of records were taken and stored in a crypt at the Havana Cathedral. Fourteen of the volumes were recovered in 1871, and the 15th was found in 1938. Many 20th-century records were discovered in two old homes scheduled for demolition. Others were found in an attic at the University of Notre Dame, where they were shipped for safety as the then-modern records during World War II. Most of the records were tracked down by University of Florida history professor emeritus Michael Gannon who begin searching for the documents more than a half-century ago. Items in the collection include a still-legible marriage certificate dating from 1594 and other records and even a piece of the coffin of Pedro Menendez de Aviles, founder of the city.

A Timucuan village predating the arrival of the Spanish by two to four centuries was unearthed in St. Augustine. The site is on a two-acre city lot that had been vacant for more than 400 years and was being cleared for new home development. Archaeologists said it was the most significant find for this period at the nation's oldest city. The site contains remnants of Timucuan structures as well as cooking and trash pits. When the Spanish arrived, the Timucuan nation stretched in a swath coast to coast from Tampa Bay to what is now Brunswick, Georgia.

Off Shore

Navy construction crews discovered a Spanish ship that was buried for centuries under sand at Pensacola Naval Air Station. The crew was prepping the site for a new swim-rescue school to replace the one destroyed by Hurricane Ivan. The ship, believed built around 1600, was the first in Florida found beneath dry land. The Navy planned to enclose the exposed portion of the wreck and move its construction elsewhere.

There are more than 150 shipwrecks off Pensacola of which two have been fully explored. One of those is believed to have gone down in 1559, the year of Florida's first recorded hurricane.

It is believed that as many as 1,800 ships lay beneath the waters of Florida, and few archeological finds stir the imagination as much as shipwrecks. And little wonder; ten galleons of Spain's 1715 Silver Armada are known to be on the bottom between Fort Pierce and Sebastian Inlet. More than 20 vessels of Spain's 1733 treasure fleet went down in a hurricane while sailing up the Florida Keys. A seven-vessel French treasure flotilla went down off New Smyrna. Ships laden with riches are known to have gone down all along the state's entire Gulf of Mexico coastline.

Rumored treasure, including buried pirate gold, also fires the imagination. And treasure has indeed been found. Tides have placed ancient gold coins on Florida's beaches, even depositing a $50,000 gold necklace on an Atlantic beach.

Salvagers raised 18 tons of relics and treasure in 1959. A commercial treasure hunting company found $5 million in gold and silver from a Spanish flotilla wreck site off Cape Canaveral over a period of years during the 1960s.

The discovery of the legendary *Atochoa* and its sister ship, *La Margarita,* off Key West in the late 1970s and early 1980s, yielded more than $100 million. So the hunt continues.

About That Treasure Trove

Hard pressed by 2010's budget woes, one Florida legislator thought the way out might include selling off the state's vast treasure trove of, well, treasure. But the problem is that the state's vast hoard of booty doesn't exist. Florida chief archaeologist Ryan Wheeler called the stockpile a myth and said that there is no "secret treasure room" stacked with gold. The state has an estimated $17 million in salvaged gold and indeed some of it is in secure storage. But "most of our really exciting stuff is on loan to museums," around the state, Wheeler said. The state typically receives 20 percent as its share salvaged from its seas.

The Treasure Coast

A portion of the Atlantic Coast of Florida is called "the Treasure Coast" because of the amount of treasure ships believed sunk off its shore. A Spanish treasure fleet of 11 vessels sank off the coast of what is now Martin, St. Lucie, and Indian River counties during a hurricane in 1715. As many as 40 other shipwrecks from a variety of nations going back to the 16th century have also been scouted off the same coast. The most recent find from the treasure fleet in the area includes a gold-trimmed portrait necklace, gold and silver coinage, and numerous artifacts found off Indian River Shores. They were located in just 10 feet of water.

EARLY INDIANS

Archaeologists estimate that by the time the first white explorations occurred in Florida there were at least six basic Indian groups or subgroups on the peninsula. Population figures for these early people vary widely. The least number estimated is 10,000; missionaries with explorers wrote of between 16,000 and 34,000. Modern scholars tend toward higher numbers, possibly as high as nearly a million. This high number is disputed, however, by some archaeologists who claim the physical evidence from Indian sites does not indicate such a vast population.

The major Indian groups known to have inhabited Florida include

TIMUCUANS lived throughout the north- and west-central regions, from Tampa Bay across to Cape Canaveral, up through Ocala, Gainesville, and Jacksonville, and in the Suwannee River valley region west to the Aucilla River. They were reported by Spanish explorers to be strong, handsome people of some height. Other explorers labeled the Timucuans as stubborn, perhaps because they resented the Spanish use of them as cargo bearers, a task considered women's work by the Indians. In addition, religious missionaries outlawed such Timucuan enjoyments as ball games and dancing and had declared the traditional medicine men off limits.

TOCOBAGA may have been a branch of the Timucua who lived from about Tarpon Springs south to Sarasota. Some confusion exists because at least one explorer claimed the Tocobaga lived along north Florida's Wacissa River. This is disputed by modern anthropologists who maintain this more northerly group was a small band of about 300 Tocopaca, not Tocobaga, who lived in the St. Marks River area.

APALACHEE occupied the region from the Aucilla River west to the Ochlockonee River, north into Georgia and south to the Gulf of Mexico. Today's Tallahassee was center of the Apalachee territory.

Historians report that it was rumors of Apalachee gold that lured Spanish explorers Narvaez in 1528 and De Soto in 1539. The natives these explorers met were prosperous and ferocious. In fact, the Spanish had been warned not to venture into Apalachee lands for the northern tribe quartered and burned intruders. As for the rumored riches, it is likely the metal the Apalachee possessed was copper, not gold. In 1647, the Apalachee warred against the Spanish, killing three friars and the Spanish governor's lieutenant and his family. The reason for the revolt appears to have been the Indians' fear of ever-growing numbers of Spanish intruders and their missions. Several non-Apalachee Indian groups lived within Apalachee territory, including the Tama, Yamasee, Capara, and Chine.

TEQUESTA lived in the region from today's Pompano Beach to Cape Sable, where it is thought they mingled with the Calusa. Evidence suggests the Tequesta ate the usual berries, sea grapes, palm nuts, and prickly pears but also fed on manatees, deer, and land and sea turtles. Although the Tequesta were considered less warlike than other Indians, they were hostile to whites and took a heavy toll on any shipwreck survivors they encountered. Indians from this region are thought to have made dugout canoe trips to Cuba.

CALUSA occupied territory ranging from Tampa Bay and Charlotte Harbor south to Cape Sable and likely into the Lake Okeechobee area. Archaeological evidence suggests the Calusa were non-agricultural and, as mariners, dined principally on fish and shellfish. Like the Tequesta, the Calusa traveled to Cuba and Hispanola. This Indian group also is known by the names of Calos or Carlos.

AIS lived along coastal areas in the region of the Indian River, Cape Canaveral, and St. Lucie River. A branch of this tribe has been cited as the rescuers of Quaker Jonathan

Dickinson when his ship wrecked off Hobe Sound in East Florida. Despite the rescue, Dickinson later recounted in his book, *God's Protecting Providence,* that the Indians stripped Dickinson's party of men, women, and children of their clothing. After months of wilderness hardships, they made their way to St. Augustine.

The original tribes gradually faded away. Many Indians died initially from Old World diseases contracted during first contact and again later with colonization. But assimilation took the greatest toll on an identifiable Indian population. Beyond St. Augustine, settled and organized Florida over 300 years of Spanish influence became a Mestizo society growing ever more European with each generation. Much of that society emigrated when faced with 20 years of British rule. The rest left en masse, primarily for Cuba, when the U.S. took possession.

FOLKLORE

Florida abounds with folklore because of four basic heritages— "Crackers," Blacks, Latins, and Indians. "Crackers" were the original white settlers, thought to have come from Alabama and Georgia. Two theories persist about the origin of the word. One is that the term is a shortened version of "corn cracker"; the other, more popular theory, suggests that the term is derived from "whip cracker." Early Floridians drove cattle with bullwhips that could be heard cracking for long distances. Cracking of whips was not only useful for moving herds or for driving teams of oxen and mules hauling timbers, but was also an enjoyable pastime at which settlers became proficient.

Much "cracker" folklore has been lost but, like many other peoples, their fishing, hunting, planting, and doctoring were conducted on the basis of superstition. Fence posts, for example, were never set in moonlight.

Likewise, Florida Indians created elaborate ceremonies to bring them good luck and good times. Building a canoe, for example, was a hallowed event. As for weather, Seminoles still believe they can forecast hurricanes by studying sawgrass blooms.

Blacks brought voodoo to the mainland from the Bahamas and West Indies, and today voodoo rituals are still practiced nearly everywhere in Florida. Among the Latins in Tampa, a widely popular cone of incense would be burned to reveal, in its ashes, a number that foretold the current bolita winner. Bolita (little ball), introduced to Tampa by Cubans, was a lottery that spawned superstitions, including interpretations of dreams and the symbolism of numbers.

Folklore also involved medicinal beliefs. Below are Florida folk medicines, some with a possible scientific basis:

Common Name	Use
Onion	antiseptic
Virginia snake root	stimulant or tonic, for headache and ring-worm
Cabbage	for carbuncles

Buttonwood	for fever
Jerusalem oak	anthelmintic
Stargrass	laxative and emetic
Gopher or fever grass	for fever
Dog fennel	diaphoretic
Black walnut	for ground itch
Low bush myrtle	incites coughing
Catnip	for colic
Pine tree	antiseptic
Wild cherry	cough syrup
Black root	Indian purgative
Red oak	for diarrhea
Post oak	Indian poultice
Sumac	Indian poultice
Trumpet plant	for smallpox
Sassafras	a tonic
Queen's delight	emetic, purgative
Deer tongue	diaphoretic
Prickly ash	for syphilis

COWBOY TRIBUTE

Morgan Bonapart "Bone" Mizell remains one of Florida's most famous cowboys. Born in 1863 near Horse Creek in what was then Manatee County (now De Soto County), Bone became renowned for his wit and mischievous pranks. Celebrated cowboy artist Frederick Remington portrayed Bone in the painting *A Cracker Cowboy*. After a lifetime of owning and working cattle, Bone died in 1921 in a train depot at Fort Ogden, Florida. He is buried in Joshua Creek Cemetery near Arcadia, and a historical marker at Zolfo Springs' Pioneer Park was erected in 1974 to honor him.

MOST SOUTHERN STATE

Florida's northernmost point lies more than 100 miles south of California's southern border, and the southern tip of Florida is 1,700 miles from the equator, closer than any other part of the continental U.S.

— NATIONAL MONUMENTS AND MEMORIALS —

CASTILLO DE SAN MARCOS NATIONAL MONUMENT, in St. Augustine, encompasses the oldest masonry fort existing in the U.S., dating from the Spanish colonial period. The Castillo is a symmetrically shaped, four-sided structure surrounded by a moat 40 feet wide. Entrance into the fort is by drawbridge. The outer walls are 16 feet thick at the base and taper to nine feet at the top. They are constructed of coquina blocks cemented together by oyster lime mortar. Beautifully arched casements and interesting cornices testify to the workmanship and imagination of the Spanish builders. The fort contains guardrooms, a jail, living quarters for the garrison, storerooms, and a chapel. Nearly all the rooms open onto a 10,000 sq. ft. court.

Impregnable San Marcos was constructed because of international rivalry over Florida. Spain claimed the area both by papal grant and the discoveries (1513) of Juan Ponce de Leon in his quest for land to compensate his loss of the Puerto Rico governorship. St. Augustine was founded in 1565 as a military outpost to strengthen the Spanish claim to Florida and to protect Spain's trade route from the rich Caribbean areas to the mother country. It was first attacked by the French and later by British freebooters. With the founding of Charleston in 1670 and the menace of English colonists only 200 miles away, the Spanish began construction on the present stone fort at the north entrance to St. Augustine harbor in 1672. The massive fort was intended to replace the last of nine successive wooden forts on the site. Its baptism

by fire came in 1702 when South Carolinians unsuccessfully besieged it. Continued attacks by the English colonists to the north ended in 1740 when General Oglethorpe of Georgia failed to capture the fort after a 38-day siege. However, in 1763, England secured Florida by terms of the Treaty of Paris and occupied the Castillo from July 21, 1763, to July 12, 1784.

After 21 years of British occupation, Florida was returned to Spain in exchange for the Bahama Islands. Florida remained a Spanish colony until 1821, when the U.S. acquired the territory by treaty and the payment of $5 million to American citizens for claims against Spain. Under the U.S. government, the Castillo was renamed Fort Marion in honor of Francis Marion, the Revolutionary War hero.

The fort became a U.S. military prison during the Second Seminole War. Among the prisoners were Osceola, the famous Indian leader, and Coacoochee, who made a spectacular escape through the bars of the casement. Except for a short Confederate occupation, the fort was periodically again used as a prison in 1875-77, 1886-87, and in 1898.

Castillo de San Marcos was declared a national monument in October 1924. Though the fort has lost its military usefulness, the powder magazine (dubbed the dungeon by the public), the shot furnace, the guardrooms, and the chapel are of continuing interest. From the massive walls a visitor can see the old City Gate and the narrow streets of the quaint city that it protected for 149 years.

DE SOTO NATIONAL MEMO-RIAL is five miles west of Bradenton, along the shores of the Manatee River where it enters Tampa Bay. It is a large stone monument and park commemorating Hernando de Soto's landing on the Florida west coast and his captaining of the first major exploration of the southern U.S. (1539-43).

Columbus had given Spain an early claim to the New World and its wealth, and her warriors penetrated the newfound continent with amazing rapidity. Hardy and courageous men, loyal to King and Church, they built some 200 towns in America long before the first English colony was attempted in North Carolina.

De Soto was a typical Spanish conquistadore. Charles V appointed him governor of Cuba and Adelantado (leader) to "conquer, pacify and populate" the North American continent. He landed with his army at Tampa Bay, on the west coast, assigned 100 men to guard the camp, and sent ships back to Cuba for supplies. On July 15, 1539, he began the 4,000-mile northward march through unknown lands and forests. The expedition of about 1,000 men was plagued by heat, hunger, and hostile Indians but along the way De Soto seized village chieftains and forced them to supply food, carriers, and guides.

De Soto spent his first winter near the present site of Tallahassee. Setting forth in the spring of 1540, his army marched to the Savannah River, reached the Xuala region of western South Carolina, then moved up in North Carolina and across the Great Smoky Mountains to Tennessee. Finding no treasure, the weary men turned south, marching into Alabama. Here, powerful Tascalusa, Lord of the Mobile Indians, hid his anger when the Spanish seized him and agreed to furnish 400 carriers as soon as the army reached Mabila. But instead of carriers, warriors greeted De Soto and a fierce battle ensued. The Spanish suffered crippling losses in men, horses, and supplies.

De Soto had planned to go south to the Gulf of Mexico and meet his supply ships but, fearing that many of his men would desert to the ships, he turned his army north again and continued his exploration.

Hoping to find the rumored wealth of Pachaha Province, the expedition crossed the Mississippi River on hastily constructed barges and pushed into Arkansas. But De Soto found no gold so he turned west, then south, to winter on the west bank of the Ouachita River. Discouraged and ill, De Soto returned to the Mississippi River in the spring, planning to settle at a seaport and refit for a westward advance. But he died on May 21, 1542 and was buried in the Mississippi. Remnants of his expedition eventually reached Cuba by way of Mexico under the leadership of Luis de Moscoso. The De Soto National Memorial, established in 1949, embraces 25 acres on the Manatee River shore.

FORT CAROLINE NATIONAL MEMORIAL, 10 miles east of Jacksonville, is a 119-acre park on the St. Johns River. It was established in 1953 to commemorate an attempt by the French to settle in Florida. Here the French and Spaniards vied for supremacy at the beginning of the first century of American colonization.

As part of his plan to strengthen

France by uniting Catholic and Huguenot against the traditional Spanish enemy, Admiral Gaspard de Coligny sought to establish French bases in North America. In the 1560s he sent out an expedition under Jean Ribault, a man of exceptional experience and ability. The expedition touched along the St. Johns River near Mayport, then sailed north to leave a small garrison at Port Royal, South Carolina. But civil war in France prevented reinforcement and, after much suffering, the garrison survivors built a crude craft and returned home.

That same decade the French made a second attempt to settle Florida's east coast, under the leadership of Rene de Laudoniere. Three vessels set out from Havre de Grace conveying some 300 people to the new land. Of this number, 110 were sailors, 120 were soldiers, and the rest artisans, servants, and a few women—but no farmers. As a colony site, the French chose a broad, flat knoll on the shore about five miles upstream from the mouth of the St. Johns River. With the help of Timucuan Indians under Chief Saturiba, the colonists built a triangular fort of earth and wood. They named it Fort Caroline, in honor of King Charles IX.

Greed, mutiny, and famine combined to destroy the efforts of French colonization. And finding neither gold nor silver mines in Florida, a number of the men became impatient with wilderness life. After stealing three vessels, they set forth to prey upon the ships carrying treasure from Mexico and the Indies to Spain.

Before being captured by the Spaniards, the mutineers had seized four ships and plundered a Cuban town. During the same period, the winter of 1564-65, the settlers remaining at Fort Caroline nearly died of starvation. In desperation, they decided to repair a vessel and return to France. As the mutineers had proven, the French colony at Fort Caroline was a threat to Spanish commerce and a possible base for an attack on the Indies. While the French rulers claimed the settlement was in French territory, the Spaniards considered it a pirate's nest on Spanish land. Spain's King Philip II decided to commission Pedro Menendez de Aviles to "explore and colonize Florida" and sent an armada to drive out "settlers and corsairs" of all nations not subject to Spain. But another fleet was already on the high seas. Frenchman Jean Ribault had left France with reinforcements for the settlers and arrived at Fort Caroline just as the colonists were about to sail back to France.

Five days later, part of the Spanish fleet reached the St. Johns River and found the French united. The Spanish fleet offered battle, which the French declined. So the Spanish retreated to the St. Augustine harbor to await the remainder of their forces.

As the Spanish unloaded stores and supplies, the French fleet drew up for a fight. But a low tide prevented the French from entering the harbor to get at the Spaniards. Before the tide turned, a storm blew up and drove the French fleet ashore in the Matanzas Inlet area just south of St. Augustine.

With the French ships being driven ashore by a gale, Menendez decided to march overland and swept down on unguarded Fort Caroline.

After capturing it, he marched back south and successfully attacked the survivors of the shipwrecked French fleet (see Fort Matanzas).

Occupying Fort Caroline, the Spanish changed its name to San Mateo. But in 1568, the French, seeking revenge, landed a force north of the St. Johns River commanded by Dominique de Gourgues. Gourgues, enlisting the Indians as allies, wiped out the Spanish garrison at the fort and burned much of it.

The actual site of Fort Caroline no longer exists because its meadow and part of the bluff washed away after the river channel was deepened in the years following 1880. In addition to the park, the memorial includes a visitors' center with a museum in which is shown a replica of Fort Caroline.

FORT MATANZAS NATIONAL MONUMENT, on Rattlesnake Island, is 14 miles south of St. Augustine across the Matanzas River, opposite the southern tip of Anastasia Island. The fort, of coquina blocks cemented together with oyster lime mortar, has two main levels. The garrison climbed a removable ladder to enter the fortification at the first level—a gun deck some 16 feet above the ground. The second level is a 30-foot two-story tower extending the length of one side and containing a small powder magazine and two guardrooms. Drinking water was stored in a cistern in the lower level. The monument covers an area of 298 acres, and includes Rattlesnake Island and the southern tip of Anastasia Island. It is typical of north Florida dune country with a heavy low growth of scrub and palmetto.

Near Fort Matanzas a decisive episode in the Franco-Spanish struggle for Florida occurred in 1565. A fleet of three hundred Huguenots, under the leadership of Jean Ribault, unsuccessfully attacked the area's Spanish soldiers centered around the new settlement of St. Augustine. A storm blew the fleet ashore south of that area and the crew was hunted down by Pedro Menendez de Aviles, the founder of St. Augustine. Menendez killed all but a few of the 300 shipwrecked survivors. Thus, Matanzas, which means "slaughter" in English, received its name.

The value of the Matanzas site as a warning outpost was proved early when runners raced from the tip of the island to St. Augustine in 1683 with word of the approach of pirate bands set on sacking the city. And during a 1740 attack on the St. Augustine area, the Matanzas Inlet proved to be an invaluable lifeline for provisions from Havana for the garrison at nearby Castillo de San Marcos. Realizing the importance of continued control of the inlet, the Spanish built the present-day Fort Matanzas in 1742, but under great difficulty. Long pilings had to be driven into the mud to support the stones that had been transported by boat from the King's Quarry on Anastasia Island. The English finally gained control of Fort Matanzas, along with the rest of Florida, by the Treaty of 1763, only to trade it all back to Spain for the Bahama Islands in 1784. By the time Florida was ceded to the U.S. by Spain in 1821, the interior of Fort Matanzas was mostly ruins.

The Fort Matanzas area was designated a national monument in 1924 and put under the supervision of the National Park Service. The service stabilized the fort and constructed a headquarters building on Anastasia Island and landing wharves on the river.

FORTS AND BATTLEFIELDS

From the period of Spanish exploration to the end of Reconstruction following the War Between the States, Florida's history can be traced through its military installations.

To conquer the Florida frontier, Spain depended in part on Christianity but it soon learned it had to back up its missions with fortified outposts. Encroaching on the peninsula were the British and the French. To thwart their invasion, Spain chose to construct a super fort. It became the famous Castillo de San Marcos at St. Augustine. So well did it do its job that it preserved Spanish authority long after Spain's boundaries in Florida had dwindled and its inner outposts had fallen to the enemy.

Remnants of the first period of Christian Florida consist primarily of 300-year-old skeletons of former fortresses built by the English, the French, and the Spanish as each attempted to establish a foothold in Florida. In addition to major military centers, many small outposts stretched across north Florida and along the coasts. Most of these left only a name in a government report carefully preserved in the national archives.

A second outcropping of military posts began during the first Seminole War and continued through the Billy Bowlegs War of the early 1850s. The First Seminole War—as some historians call Gen.

Andrew Jackson's campaign of 1817-18—was more of an American attempt to crush Europeans, notably the British, than it was to quell an Indian uprising. It was fought against Indians (who had been planning for years to rebel), runaway slaves, and the English army, which encouraged and supplied the insurgents.

The second and major Seminole War lasted from 1835 to 1842 and ended in a stalemate. It was almost over on Christmas Day 1837 when Col. Zachary Taylor's army defeated a large Seminole force at the Battle of Okeechobee. The Florida frontier was relatively quiet for almost two years when Gen. Alexander Macomb, commander-in-chief of the U.S. Army, led the assembled chiefs to believe the land to which they were to be deported would be a permanent home instead of the temporary quarters he planned.

News of the betrayal reached the Seminole villages in south central Florida and the reaction was immediate and final. A trading post being built on the Caloosahatchee River was attacked and 17 dragoons were killed and scalped. This led to the reactivation of many forts and supply posts and to Taylor's promptly establishing 53 new outposts in the trouble zones. Only a few of these frontier military posts can be considered forts under the true definition. Most were stockades or blockhouses manned by 20 or 30 soldiers, in many instances Florida volunteers, who didn't consider the army a full-time job.

Nonetheless, the development of Florida can be traced to and from these small safety islands. Many present cities and towns grew up around a minor military post and some still bear the name of the army officer who built or commanded the fort. Listed are some of the more familiar military sites that played a role in Florida's history.

CASTILLO DE SAN MARCOS (See National Monuments and Memorials.)

FORT BARRANCAS, at Pensacola Harbor, was built by the U.S. between 1839 and 1845. A bricked tunnel connects it with Batteria de San Antonio, which was built in 1797 on the approximate site of two earlier wooden forts, one constructed by D'Arriola in 1698, the other by the British about 1771.

FORT BROOKE, Tampa, was a pioneer log outpost built in 1823. It was named for its first commander, Col. George Brooke, and played a strategic role in the early part of the Second Seminole War. The base also served as an embarkation point for Indians being shipped out of the state. As the fighting shifted to southern Florida, the center of military activity was transferred to Fort Myers.

FORT CAROLINE at St. John's Bluff was built by French explorer Laudoniere in 1564. More than two centuries later, the English established a settlement near the bluff and named it St. John's Town. It provided a Tory refuge during the final months of the Revolutionary War, then declined during the second period of Spanish rule. By 1817 most of its 300 buildings had disappeared and the fort had washed into the river. (See National Monuments and Memorials.)

FORT CLINCH, on Amelia Island, was begun in 1847 and completed in 1851. It was garrisoned by both Confederate and Union forces during the War Between the States, then by U.S. troops for six years during Reconstruction. The fort, named in honor of Gen. D. L. Clinch, who captured Fort Gadsden and later helped conclude the Seminole War, was reactivated briefly during the Spanish-American War in 1898. The site is a state park.

FORT DADE AND BATTLEFIELD, off U.S. 301 at Bushnell, was the site of the first major battle of the Second Seminole War. In December 1835 Maj. Francis L. Dade and a detachment of several officers and 102 men left Fort Brooke (Tampa) for Fort King (Ocala). On the morning of the 28th, the company was marching along the Withlacoochee River near the present town of Bushnell when it was ambushed by a Seminole war party led by Chiefs Alligator, Juniper, and Micanope. The major and 106 of his men were killed. Of an estimated 180 warriors, three were killed and five wounded.

FORT DE SOTO, at the mouth of Tampa Bay, was built on Mullet Key in 1898 and armed with eight 12-inch mortars that never fired a shot at an enemy. As early as 1849, the key, along with nearby Egmont and Passage keys, were recommended by Col. Robert E. Lee, later of Confederate Army fame, as a coastal defense in Florida. During the War Between the States, federal forces were stationed on Mullet Key as a blockade headquarters for the area and a haven for Union sympathizers. The fort as built at the turn of the century remains. During both World Wars, the federal government made use of the fort and Mullet Key; during World War I it was activated as a Coast Artillery Training Center, and in World War II it was used as an Army Air Corps Gunnery and Bombing Training Center. It now is part of a vast park.

FORT GADSDEN, also known as Fort Blount, was at Buck's Siding in the Panhandle area and built in 1814 by Indians and runaway slaves, with considerable help from the British. In July 1816, U.S. forces attacked the outpost and on the fourth day of battle a hot cannonball landed in the powder magazine and blew up the fort. Only 60 of its 334 occupants escaped instant death, many of the casualties being women and children. Two of the three white men who escaped injury were executed by command of Gen. Andrew Jackson.

FORT GEORGE ISLAND, near the mouth of the St. Johns River, was originally a Spanish outpost and mission. It was subsequently the object of attack by the French, the British, and the soon-to-be Americans.

FORT KING, at Ocala, was established as an Indian trading post in 1825. Two years later the post was garrisoned with troops and renamed Fort King. The site, which lies about two miles east of the present city of Ocala, was the scene of the ambush of Gen. Wiley Thompson and his aide in December 1835. The event, together with the simultaneous Dade Massacre, started the Second Seminole War.

FORT LAUDERDALE, on the approximate site of the present-day city, was a stockade built at New River by Maj. William Lauderdale in 1838. Originally one of many outposts built along military paths during the Seminole wars, the fort and vicinity was settled in 1895 and grew into one of the most popular playgrounds on the east coast.

FORT MATANZAS (See National Monuments and Memorials.)

FORT McREE was built shortly after Fort Pickens, to protect the opposite side of the Pensacola channel. Ruins of its original brick foundation are still visible at low tide. The present channel flows across the old parade grounds.

FORT PICKENS, on the western tip of Santa Rosa Island, once guarded the eastern entrance to Pensacola Harbor. The pentagonal structure was completed in 1834 and at one time was the third largest fort in the U.S. Apache Chief Geronimo and his followers were imprisoned here in 1886.

FORT ST. MARKS, at St. Marks, was built in 1739, the fourth fort to be constructed on the apex of a peninsula formed by the junction of the St. Marks and the Wakulla rivers. The Spanish were the first to fortify the site in 1677. Subsequently, the fort was destroyed (once by pirates), rebuilt, and occupied by British, Indian, and American garrisons.

MARIANNA BATTLEFIELD, near Marianna, now displays a monument in its Confederate Park to commemorate the defense of the town by a force composed largely of boys, wounded soldiers, and old men on Sept. 27, 1864. Sixty of the Home Guards were killed or wounded and another 100 captured by Union forces.

NATURAL BRIDGE BATTLE-FIELD is one of two celebrated Confederate battle sites in Florida. In March 1865, Union forces planned to capture Fort St. Marks, then move into Tallahassee, the state's capital. But due to a combination of Confederate resistance and shoals, the federal assault failed. When the landing force could not cross the bridge at Newport, it tried again at

Natural Bridge. The only defense the state could muster consisted of a few Confederate regulars, the Home Guard, cadets from West Florida Seminary (now Florida State University), and a few children and old men. Good planning stopped the Union troops and Tallahassee became the only Southern capital east of the Mississippi to escape federal conquest. This, the last battle in Florida of the War Between the States, is commemorated by a monument, battlefield markers, and a display of old Confederate earthworks.

OKEECHOBEE BATTLEFIELD was the scene of the final major engagement of the Second Seminole War. On Christmas Day 1837, Col. Zachary Taylor and 1,067 regulars defeated a Seminole force estimated at 400 men. The encounter took place along the northeastern shore of the famous inland lake. The price of the American victory was 26 dead and 112 wounded. The Seminole toll was 11 dead, 14 wounded.

OLUSTEE BATTLEFIELD is on U.S. 90 between Olustee and Sanderson. Florida escaped most of the physical devastation suffered by the Confederacy, but the state did play a significant role as the breadbasket of the Southern armies. To cut this breadline, the Union army marched toward the peninsula's rich agricultural area in February 1864. On Feb. 20, Confederate troops defeated Union forces at Ocean Pond near Olustee, thus saving Florida's interior lines of supply and confining Union soldiers to the coast. The battle between the evenly matched forces (North, 5,000 officers and men; South, 5,200 officers and men) lasted six hours. It cost the

North 203 killed, 1,152 wounded and 506 missing; the South suffered 93 dead, 847 wounded and six missing.

WITHLACOOCHEE BATTLEFIELDS were the site of several decisive battles of the Seminole War, all along the Withlacoochee River. Three days after the Dade Massacre in December 1835, Gen. D. L. Clinch, with 280 regular soldiers and 500 militia, was attacked by a Seminole war party at the river just north of the junction of the present day Marion, Sumter, and Citrus counties. The Indians were repulsed but not defeated.

When news of the fighting reached Army officials, Gen. Edmund Gaines and 700 troops were diverted from New Orleans to defend Fort Brooke in Tampa. Gen. Winfield Scott was given command of the armies dispatched to rout the Seminoles. Both generals battled Osceola's forces in the tri-county corner, General Gaines in February 1836 and General Scott the following month. But neither army was able to pursue its quarry into the dense swamps and hammocks of central Florida. By using the guerrilla warfare tactics that enabled inferior American forces to sap the strength of the English during the Revolutionary War, the Seminoles were able to stall their inevitable defeat for seven years.

The only other significant encounter in the area occurred in November 1836 when Gen. Richard K. Call attacked an Indian encampment in the Big Wahoo Swamp a few miles northeast of the Dade Battlefield. Reinforced by 1,200 troops, the Florida forces chased the Seminoles until the soldiers were "waist deep" in the swamp and could no longer follow.

FORTIFIED OUTPOSTS

FORT ALABAMA was the site of the outpost on the Hillsborough River between Tampa and Zephyrhills that supported old Fort Brooke. It was built in 1836 on the site of Burnt Bridge, the bridge crossed by Major Dade and his men on their way to the Dade Massacre. The bridge was burned by Indians, then rebuilt and burned twice more before it was abandoned.

FORT ANN was a Second Seminole War outpost near present day Titusville.

FORT ANNUTTGELIEA was an outpost established in 1840 to protect Hernando County settlers in event of an Indian attack.

FORT ARMSTRONG was a stockade built in 1836 on the site of the Dade Battlefield.

FORT ARBUCKLE, built in 1850, was part of the ring of civilian and military posts created to protect settlers in the interior sections of southwestern Florida.

FORT BLOUNT was a stockade built by settlers in the Bartow area during the Second Seminole War.

FORT CASEY was built in 1850 on an elevated key in Charlotte Harbor. It was distinguished by two coconut trees visible at a great distance.

FORT CENTER was a crude, wooden fort near the western extremity of Lake Okeechobee used during the Seminole conflicts.

FORT CHRISTMAS, on the St. Johns River, 80 miles north of the Okeechobee Battleground, was constructed beginning on Christmas Day 1837.

FORT CHOKONIKLA, built in 1849, was part of a network of stockades constructed to protect inland settlers between Fort Myers and Fort Meade during Indian uprisings.

FORT CROSS was built in 1838 as a fortified outpost west of the upper reaches of the Withlacoochee River near Brooksville.

FORT CUMMINGS was a military post 16 miles southwest of Davenport in Polk County, built in 1839.

FORT DALLAS, erected on the Miami River in 1836, was used to guard against the Everglades Seminoles for almost two decades. The city of Miami grew from its site.

FORT DEFIANCE was a small outpost near Micanopy, used briefly during the summer of 1836.

FORT DENAUD, an outpost up the Caloosahatchee River from Fort Myers and built in 1837, was reactivated during the latter part of the Second Seminole War.

FORT DIEGO was one of several outlying outposts of Castillo de San Marcos on the St. Johns River. It was captured by General Oglethorpe of Georgia during his assault on St. Augustine in 1740.

FORT DRANE, between Tallahassee and the Withlacoochee River, was built on the plantation of Gen. D. L. Clinch following the Dade Massacre. It served as a district headquarters and was the scene of numerous Indian battles before being abandoned in 1836.

FORT DRUM, near LaBelle, was abandoned before the Billy Bowlegs War and later burned by Indians.

FORT DULANY was a supply

depot near the mouth of the Caloosahatchee River in Lee County. It was built in 1837 as part of the network of outposts necessitated by the Second Seminole War.

FORT FANNIN on the Suwannee River was established in 1838. Numerous arrowheads and shark-tooth fishhooks found on a nearby bluff indicate it was once an Indian village.

FORT FOSTER was the name given to the rebuilt Fort Alabama.

FORT FRASER, near Lake Hancock in Polk County, was built in 1837 to provide protection for nearby settlers.

FORT GARDINER on the Kissimmee River near the northern shores of Lake Okeechobee was built by Col. Zachary Taylor in December 1837 as a base from which to fight the Indians gathering at the lake.

FORT GATLIN, in present-day Orlando, was established in 1837 and named in honor of Dr. John S. Gatlin, a U.S. Army physician who died in the Dade Massacre.

FORT GREEN was one of several outposts along the Peace River during the Billy Bowlegs War. The Hardee County settlement that grew up around it bears its name.

FORT HARLEE, a temporary outpost, was near Waldo on the Santa Fe River.

FORT HARTSUFF was part of an outpost network between Fort Myers and Fort Meade for the defense of area settlers from Indian attacks. It was named after Lt. George L. Hartsuff, a topographical engineer, and is the site of present-day Wauchula.

FORT HARVIE was the original name of the outpost that became Fort Myers. It was built in 1841 and abandoned a year later.

FORT HEILEMAN was a principal depot for the U.S. Army in the late 1830s. It was at the fork of the north and south branches of Black Creek at Garey's Ferry (now Middleburg).

FORT HOOKER was another of the Peace River fortifications built during the Second Seminole War. It was 16 miles north of Fort Meade and garrisoned by Florida Volunteers.

FORT JUNIPER was on the site now occupied by the Juniper Lighthouse. A stockade built in 1838 by Hobe Sound settlers, its records reveal 678 Indians and Negroes were imprisoned at the fort before it was abandoned in 1842.

FORT KEAIS was part of the southwestern interior chain activated during the resumption of hostilities in the Second Seminole War. It was in the Big Cypress south of Fort Denaud.

FORT KISSIMMEE was a stockade built near a trouble spot during the Billy Bowlegs War.

FORT LANE was a militia center built in 1837, 10 miles south of Fort Mellon.

FORT LLOYD was an outpost northeast of the site of the Battle of Okeechobee.

FORT MAITLAND, built in 1838, was named for Capt. William S. Maitland. The city of Maitland was built on its site.

FORT MARION was the American name for Castillo de San Marcos. (See National Monuments and Memorials.)

FORT MASON was a stockade built in 1837 on the shores of Lake Eustis.

FORT McCOY was an outpost 20 miles northeast of Ocala.

FORT MEADE, built on the Peace River during the Second Seminole War, was named for Lt. George Meade, who later gained fame at the Battle of Gettysburg.

FORT MELLON is marked today by a stone monument in Sanford. Built in 1837, it became a trading post called Mellonville.

FORT MITCHELL was a two-story blockhouse east of Ocala built in 1814 to protect a rebel "American" settlement defying Spanish rule. It was named for Gov. David Mitchell of Georgia.

FORT MOSE, an outlying outpost for Castillo de San Marcos, was captured by Gen. Oglethorpe during his 1740 siege of St. Augustine. It was retaken by the Spanish, and was manned by runaway slaves from plantations in the British Carolinas.

FORT MYAKKA was built in 1849 to protect settlers from Indian forays.

FORT MYERS was built in 1850 on the site of the old Fort Harvie, which had been a temporary post during the Second Seminole War. It was named by Gen. David Twiggs in honor of his future son-in-law, Gen. Abraham C. Myers.

FORT OGDEN was an old Indian fort built in 1841, now the site of the town by the same name.

FORT PEYTON was a fort and blockhouse built near Moultrie in 1836. In 1837, Osceola, the great Seminole leader, was en route to the fort under the Indian equivalent of a flag of truce when he was captured. A marker about a mile from the post preserves the site of his betrayal.

FORT PICOLATA, a small fort on the St. Johns River, was captured by Gen. Oglethorpe en route to St. Augustine. Retaken by the Spanish, the fort was rebuilt with two swivel guns. In 1765 it was selected for the festive meeting between East Florida governor James Grant and the Indians to set Indian boundaries.

FORT PIERCE, erected between 1838 and 1842, served as an U.S. Army headquarters and was named in honor of Lt. Col. Benjamin Pierce, a brother of President Franklin Pierce.

FORT POINSETT, on Cape Sable was built in 1836 to protect the southern coast.

FORT ST. ANDREWS was an English outpost built on Cumberland Island during Gen. Oglethorpe's encroachments on Spanish territory in 1734.

FORT ST. FRANCIS DE PUPA, near Green Cove Springs, suffered the same misfortunes as its sister outpost, Fort Picolata. Built by the Spanish in 1737, Fort St. Francis was destroyed by the British forces of Gen. Oglethorpe in 1740, then rebuilt by the Spanish. The original wooden structures of both St. Francis and Picolata were replaced with two-story coquina buildings with two swivel guns mounted on the roof. During the 1760s, the two forts were garrisoned by British soldiers whose primary job was to keep the Indians on the west side of the St. Johns River.

FORT SAN LUCIA was in the vicinity of Jensen Beach and built by the Spanish in 1568. Indians killed so many of the Spaniards that the surviving soldiers mutinied and retreated into St. Augustine.

FORT SAN NICHOLAS is now only a gray stone marker about three miles east of U.S. 1 in Jacksonville. The site of the fort, built by the

Spanish Gov. Don Manuel de Monteano about 1740, lies 1,500 feet north of the St. Johns River.

FORT SCOTT was built in 1816 at the junction of the Flint, Chattahoochee, and Apalachicola rivers to store supplies brought in from New Orleans and to provide defense against Indian and black tribal members.

FORT SIMMONS, built in 1841, superseded Fort Denaud on the Caloosahatchee River and was situated about five miles below the previous fort so as to bypass a sandbar that prevented the passage of steamboats.

FORT STARKE was established in 1840 at the mouth of the Manatee River as part of an outpost network guarding against Seminoles.

FORT SULLIVAN was another Seminole War stockade, built in 1839, 11 miles east of Lake Thonotosassa in Hillsborough County.

FORT TAYLOR served as a way station for travelers. It was a military camp built during the 1880s about 25 miles north of Tampa on the road to Brooksville.

FORT T.B. ADAMS was a supply depot on the north bank of the Caloosahatchee River across from Fort Denaud.

FORT THOMPSON was a Seminole War fort and supply depot on the Caloosahatchee River that was reactivated during the Billy Bowlegs War. After the War Between the States, the area was settled by Capt. F. A. Hendry, who became a successful rancher and for whom the county is named.

FORT WACAHOOTA, a Seminole War outpost, originally had been the site of the Mission Francisco de Potato. The fort was established in the 17th century but no trace of either the fort or the mission remains.

FORT WALTON, on the site of present-day Fort Walton, was built during the Seminole War and was used by the Confederate Army during the War Between the States.

FORT WEADMAN was an outpost eight miles west of St. Augustine.

FORT WILLIAM was an English stockade built on Cumberland Island during Gen. Oglethorpe's raids of the mid-1700s.

NATIONAL LANDMARKS AND THE NATIONAL REGISTER OF HISTORIC PLACES
(By County)

LANDMARKS

Landmark sites in Florida generally contain a single historical feature directly associated with its subject. Most have been designated landmarks by act of Congress.

Alachua
Marjorie Kinnan Rawlings House & Farm Yard

Brevard
Cape Canaveral Air Force Station
Windover Archaeological Siter

Citrus
Crystal River Site

Duval
Maple Leaf (shipwreck)

Escambia
Fort San Carlos de Barrancas
Pensacola Naval Air Station Historic District
Plaza Ferdinand VII

Franklin
British Fort

Hillsborough
El Centro Espanol de Tampa
Tampa Bay Hotel
Ybor City Historic District

Indian River
Pelican Island National Wildlife Refuge

Leon
San Luis de Talimali Mission

Marion
Fort King Site

Miami-Dade
Presidential Railway Car
Ferdinand Magellan United States Car No. 1
Freedom Tower
Miami Biltmore Hotel & Country Club
The Miami Circle at Brickell Point Site
Viscaya

Monroe
Ernest Hemingway House
Fort Zachary Taylor
USCG Cutter *Ingham*
Mud Lake Canal

Okaloosa
Fort Walton Mound
Governor Stone (schooner)

Okeechobee
Okeechobee Battlefield

Palm Beach
Mar-a-lago
Whitehall/Henry M. Flagler House

Pinellas
Safety Harbor Site

Polk
Bok Tower Gardens

St. Lucie
Zora Neal Hurston House

St. Johns
Cathedral of St. Augustine
Fort Mose Site
Gonzalez-Alvarez House
Hotel Ponce de Leon
Llambias House

St. Augustine Town Plan Historic
  District

Sumter
  Dade Battlefield

Volusia
  Mary McLeod Bethune Home
  Ponce de Leon Inlet Light
    Station

Wakulla
  Fort San Marcos de Apalachee

REGISTER OF HISTORIC
PLACES

The National Register of Historic Places is an official list of historically significant sites and property throughout the country that is compiled by the National Park Service. Listed are districts, sites, buildings, structures, and objects that have been identified and documented as being significant to American history, architecture, archaeology, engineering, and culture.

Alachua County
  Alachua Downtown Historic
    District
  Anderson Hall
  Bailey House
  Baird Hardware Co. Warehouse
  Boulware Springs Waterworks
  Bryan Hall
  Buckman Hall
  Cox Furniture Store and
    Warehouse
  Dixie Hotel
  Dudley Farm
  Epworth Hall
  Evinston Store and Post Office
  Flint Hall

Floyd Hall
High Springs Historic District
Hotel Thomas
Kanapaha (Haile Plantation)
Lake Pithlachocco Canoe Site
Liberty Hill Schoolhouse
Library East
Masonic Temple
Matheson House
McKenzie House
Melrose Historic District
Micanopy Historic District
N.E. Gainesville Residential
  District
Neilson House
Newberry Historic District
Newell Hall
Newnansville Town Site
Old P. K. Yonge School
  (Norman Hall)
Old WRUF Radio Station
Peabody Hall
Pleasant Street Historic District
Rochelle School
Rolfs Hall
S.E. Gainesville Residential
  District
Shady Grove Primitive Baptist
  Church
Star Garage
Thomas Hall
Univ. of Fla. Campus Historical
  District
U.S. Post Office, Gainesville
Waldo Historic District
Winecoff House
Women's Gym

Baker County
  Burnsed Blockhouse
  Glen Saint Mary Nursery Co.
  Old Baker County Courthouse
  Olustee Battlefield

Bay County
  Latimer Cabin
  McKenzie House
  St. Andrew's School
  Sapp House

Sherman Arcade
SS *Tarpon*
Schmidt-Godert Farm
Vamar (shipwreck site)

Bradford County
Call Street Historic District
Old Bradford County
  Courthouse
Women's Club of Starke

Brevard County
Alladin Theater
Barton Avenue Residential
  District
Cape Canaveral
  AF Station Launch District
  Central Instrumentation
  Facility
  Crawlerway
  Headquarters Building
  Launch Complex 39
  Launch Complex 39-A
  Launch Complex 39-B
  Launch Control Center
  Press Site Clock and Flag Pole
  Vehicle Assembly Building
  Missile Crawler Transporter
  Facilities
  NASA John F. Kennedy Space
  Center
  Operations and Checkout
  Bldg
City Point Community Church
Community Chapel of
  Melbourne Beach
Duda Ranch Mound
Fla. Power & Light Co. Ice Plant
Gleason House
Hill House
Hotel Mims
Indian Fields
Jorgenson's General Store
J.R. Field Homestead
Judge Robbins House
La Grange Church and
  Cemetery
Melbourne Beach Pier

Moccasin Island
Old Haulover Canal
Persimmon Mound
Porcher House
Pritchard House
Rockredge Drive Residential
  District
Spell House
Rossetter House
St. Gabriel's Episcopal Church
St. Joseph's Catholic Church
St. Luke's Episcopal Church
Titusville Commercial District
Valencia Subdivision Residential
  District
Wager House
Whaley Citrus Packing House

Broward County
Bonnet House
Bryan Building
Butler House
Cap's Place
Croissant Park Administration
  Bldg.
Davie School
Deerfield School
Deerfield Beach School
Dillard High School
Gilliam House
Hammerstein House
Hillsboro Inlet Light Station
Hollywood Boulevard Historic
  Business District
Hollywood Garden Club
Hollywood Woman's Club
King House
Link Trainer Building
Lock 1, North New River Canal
New River Inn
Nyberg-Swanson House
Oakland Park Elementary
  School
St. Anthony School
Sample Estate-McDougald
  Houses
Seaboard Airline RR Station

Southside School
Stranahan House
SS *Copenhagen* (shipwreck)
Williams House
Young Home

Calhoun County
Cayson Mound and Village
Old County Courthouse

Charlotte County
Big Mound Key
Charlotte High School
El Jobean Hotel
El Jobean Post Office and
    General Store
Freeman House
Icing Station at Bull Bay
Mott-Willis Store
Old First National Bank of Punta
    Gorda
Punta Gorda Atlantic Coast Line
    Depot
Punta Gorda Ice Plant
Punta Gorda Residential District
Punta Gorda Woman's Club
Smith Building
Villa Bianca
West Coast Fish Company Cabin
Willis Fish Cabin

Citrus County
Crystal River Old City Hall
Floral City Historic District
Fort Cooper
Hernando Elementary School
Mullet Key
Old Citrus County Courthouse
Old Hernando Elementary
    School
Yulee Sugar Mill Ruins

Clay County
Bubba Midden
Budington House
Chalker House
Clark-Chalker House
Clarke Estate

Clay County Courthouse
Frisbee House
Green Cove Springs Historic
    District
Green House
Haskell-Long House
Helffrich House
Joseph Green House
Memorial Home Historic District
Methodist Episcopal Church
Middleburg Historic District
Orange Park Negro School
Orange Park School
Princess Mound
River Road Historic District
St. Margaret's Episcopal Church
    and Cemetery
St. Mary's Episcopal Church
Westcott House
Winterbourne House

Collier County
Bank of the Everglades
Bay City Walking Dredge
Burns Lake Site
C. J. Ostl Site
Everglades Laundry
Halfway Creek Midden
Hinson Mounds
Horr House
Keewaydin Club
Monroe Station
Naples Historic District
Palm Cottage
Parker House
Platt Island
Plaza Site
Roberts Ranch
Seaboard Coast Line RR Depot
Smallwood Store
Sugar Pot Site
Turner River Site

Columbia County
Columbia County High School
Duncan House
Falling Creek Methodist Church
    and Cemetery

Fort White School Historic
District
Goodbread-Black Farm Historic
District
Henderson House
Archaeological Site
Hotel Blanche
Horr House
Lake City Archaeology Site
Lake City Historic Commercial
District
Lake Isabella Historic
Residential District
Sikes House

DeSoto County
Arcadia Historic District

Dixie County
City of Hawkinsville (shipwreck)
Garden Patch Archaeological
Site

Duval County
310 West Church Street
Apartments
3325 Via De La Reina
3335 Via De La Reina
3500 Via De La Reina
3609 Via De La Reina
3685 Via De La Reina
3703 Via De La Reina
3764 Ponce De Leon Avenue
7144 Madrid Avenue
7207 Ventura Avenue
7217 Ventura Avenue
7227 San Pedro
7245 San Jose Boulevard
7246 St. Augustine Road
7246 San Carlos
7249 San Pedro
7288 San Jose Boulevard
7306 St. Augustine Road
7317 San Jose Boulevard
7330 Ventura Avenue
7356 San Jose Boulevard
7400 San Jose Boulevard
Atlantic National Bank Annex

Avondale Historic District
Bethel Baptist Institutional
Church
Brewster Hospital
Broward House
Buckman and Ulmer Building
Carling Hotel
Casa Marina Hotel
Catherine Street Fire Station
Centennial Hall–Edward Waters
College
Church of the Immaculate
Conception
Dyal-Upchurch Building
El Modelo Block
Elks Club Building
Epping Forest
Florida Baptist Building
Florida Theater
Fort Caroline National Memorial
Grand Site
Grover-Stewart Drug Company
Building
Jacksonville Free Public Library
Jacksonville Terminal Complex
Kingsley Plantation House
Klutho House
Knight Building
Lane-Towers House
La Villa Boarding Houses
Lewis Mausoleum
Little Theater
Lynch Building
Mandarin Store and Post Office
Masonic Temple
Mission of San Juan del Puerto
Archaeological site
Morocco Temple
Mount Zion AME Church
Old Ortega Historic District
Old St. Luke's Hospital
Plaza Hotel
Porter House
Red Bank Plantation
Ribault Inn Club
Riverside Baptist Church
Riverside Historic District
St. Andrews Episcopal Church

St. George Episcopal Church
St. James Building
St. John's Lighthouse
Sammis House
San Jose Administration
 Building
San Jose Country Club
San Jose Estates Gatehouse
San Jose Hotel
South Atlantic Investment
 Corporation Building
South Jacksonville Grammar
 School
Springfield Historic District
Stanton School
Timucuan Ecological and
 Historic Preserve
Title and Trust Company of
 Florida Building
The Village Store
Woman's Club of Jacksonville
Yellow Bluff Fort
Young Men's Hebrew
 Association

Escambia County
Alger-Sullivan Lumber Co.
 Residential District
American National Bank
 Building
Barrancas National Cemetery
Buccaneer (schooner)
Crystal Ice Co. Building
Dorr House
Edmunds Apartment House
Emanuel Point (shipwreck site)
First Christian Church
Fort Barrancas Historic District
Fort George
Fort Pickens
Hickory Ridge Cemetery
 Archeological Site
James House
Jones House
Julee Cottage
King-Hooton House
Lavalle House
L & N Passenger Station

North Hill Preservation District
Old Christ Church
Pensacola Athletic Club
Pensacola Historic District
Pensacola Hospital
Pensacola Hospital/Sacred
 Heart Hospital
Pensacola Lighthouse and
 Keepers Quarters
Perdido Key Historic District
Saenger Theatre
St. Joseph's Church Complex
St. Michael's Creole Benevolent
 Society
San Carlos Hotel
Thiesen Building
U.S. Customs House and Post
 Office
USS *Massachusetts BB2*
 (shipwreck)

Flagler County
Bulow Plantation Ruins
Bunnell State Bank Building
Cherokee Grove
Dixie Highway Old Brick Road
Mala Compra Plantation
Marine Studios

Franklin County
Apalachicola Historic District
Cape St. George Light
Crooked River Lighthouse
Fort Gadsden Historic Memorial
Pierce Mounds and Middens
Porter's Bar
Raney House
Trinity Episcopal Church
Yent Mound

Gadsden County
Chattahoochee Landing Site
Davis House
Dezell House
Gregory, Willoughby House
Judge White House
Love House
Martin House

McFarlin House
Nicholson Farmhouse
Old Philadelphia Presbyterian
　　Church
Planter's Exchange
Quincy Historic District
Quincy Library/Academy
Quincy Woman's Club
Shelfer House
Stockton-Curry House
U.S. Arsenal Officer's Quarters
Willoughby House

Glades County
Moore Haven Downtown
　　Historic District
Moore Haven Residential
　　Historic District

Gulf County
Cape San Blas Light and
　　Keeper's Quarters
Centennial Building
Port Theater
St. Joseph Catholic Mission

Hamilton County
John's House
Old Hamilton County Jail
Spring House
United Methodist Church
White Springs Historical District

Hardee County
Carlton Estate
Paynes Creek Massacre–Fort
　　Chokonikla

Hendry County
Caldwell Home Place
Clewiston Inn
Clewistown Historic Schools
Dixie Crystal Theater
Downtown Labelle Historical
　　District
Duff House
Executive House
Forrey Building and Annex

Old Hendry County Court
　　House
Hendry House
Scharnberg House

Hernando County
Chinsegut Mill Manor House
Jennings House
May-Stringer House
Russell House
Saxon House
South Brooksville Avenue
　　Historic District

Highlands County
Avon Park Historic District
Central Station
Haines House
Hainz House
Harder Hall
Highlands County Courthouse
Kennilworth Lodge
Lake Placid A.C.L. RR Depot
Old Pinecrest Hotel
Seaboard Airline Depot, Old
　　Sebring
Sebring Downtown Historic District
Sebring House
Vinson House

Hillsborough County
36 Aegean Avenue
36 Columbia Drive
53 Aegean Avenue
59 Aegean Avenue
84 Adalia Avenue
97 Adriatic Avenue
100 W Davis Blvd.
116 W Davis Blvd.
124 Baltic Circle
125 Baltic Circle
131 Baltic Circle
131 W Davis Blvd.
132 Baltic Circle
161 Bosporus Avenue
190 Bosporus Avenue
200 Corsica Avenue
202 Blanca Avenue

220 Blanca Avenue
301 Caspian Street
418 Blanca Avenue
1415 N. Frankland St.
Anderson-Frank House
Bay Isle Commercial Building
Bing Rooming House
Centro Asturiano
Chapin House
Circulo Cubano de Tampa
Cockroach Key
Curtis House
Dickman House
Downtown Plant City
  Commercial District
Downtown Plant City Historic
  Residential District
Egmont Key
El Centro Español of West
  Tampa
El Pasaje Hotel/Cherokee Club
Episcopal House of Prayer
Floridan Hotel
Fort Foster
Gardner House
Glover School
Guida House
Hampton Terrace Historic
  District
Hayden Estate
Hillsboro State Bank Building
Hutchinson House
Hyde Park Historic District
J.J. Newberry Building
Johnson-Wolff House
Kress Co. Building
LeClaire Apartments
Leiman House
Levick House
Masonic Temple #25
Meacham Elementary School
Miller House/Ruskin Woman's
  Club
Moseley Homestead
North Franklin St. Historic
  District
North Plant City Residential
  District

Old Federal Building/U.S.
  Courthouse/Postal Station
Old Lutz Elementary School
Old People's Home
Old School House
Old Tampa Children's Home
Palace of Florence Apartments
Palmerin Hotel
Plant City High School
Plant City Union Depot
Robles House
Roosevelt Elementary School
Seminole Heights Historic
  District
Spanish Apartments
SS *American Victory*
Standard Oil Service Station
Stovall House
Taliaferro/Ward House
Tampa City Hall
Tampa Free Public Library
Tampa Heights Historic District
Tampania House
Tampa Theatre
Turkey Creek High School
Union Depot Hotel
Union RR Station
Upper Tampa Bay
  Archaeological District
West Tampa Historic District
Ybor Factory Building

Holmes County
Keith Cabin

Indian River County
Driftwood Inn
Fell Library
Fellsmore Public School
First Methodist Episcopal
  Church
Gregory House
Hallstrom House
Hausmann Estate
Indian River Courthouse
Jungle Trail
Lawson House
Maher Building

McKee Jungle Gardens
Old Palmetto Hotel
Old Town Sebastian Historic
   District East
Old Town Sebastian Historic
   District West
Pueblo Arcade
Royal Park Arcade
Sebastian Grammar and Junior
   High School
Smith Fish Co.
Spanish Fleet Survivors and
   Salvors Camp
Vero Beach Community
   Building
Vero Beach Diesal Power Plant
Vero Beach Women's Club
Vero RR Station
Vero Theater

Jackson County
Ely-Criglar House
Erwin House
Great Oaks/Bryan Mansion
Marianna Historic District
Norton House
Pender's Store
Russ House
St. Luke Baptist Church
Waddell's Mill Pond Site
West House

Jefferson County
Bethel School
Denham-Lacy House
Dennis-Coxetter House
Lloyd-Bond House
Lloyd Historic District
Lloyd RR Depot
Lloyd's Women's Club
Lyndhurst Plantation
May House/Rosewood
   Plantation
Monticello High School
Monticello Historic District
Palmer House
Palmer-Perkins House
Perkins Opera House

San Joseph de Ocuya Mission
   Site
San Juan de Aspalaga Mission
   Site
San Miguel de Asile Mission
   Site
Turnbull-Ritter House
Wirick-Simmons House

Lake County
Bowers Bluff Middens Site
Campbell House
Clermont Woman's Club
Clifford House
Donnelly House
Duncan House
Edge House
Eustis Commercial Historic
   District
Ferran Park/Alice McClelland
   Memorial Bandshell
Harper House
Holy Trinity Episcopal Church
Howey House
Kimball Island Midden Site
Lake County Courthouse
Lakeside Inn
Lee School
Methodist Episcopal Church
   South
Mote-Morris House
Mount Dora A.C.L. RR Station
Norton House
Pendelton House
Phares House
Purdy Villa
Taylor House
Woman's Club of Eustis

Lee County
Alderman House
Alva Consolidated Schools
Boca Grande Community Center
Boca Grande Lighthouse
Boca Grande Quarantine Station
Bonita Springs School
Buckingham School
Casa Rio

Charlotte Harbor and Northern
RR Depot
Demere Key
Dunbar School
Edison Park Elementary School
English School
Fish Cabin at White Rock
Shoals
Fort Myers Beach School
Fort Myers Downtown
Commercial District
Galt Island Archeological Site
Heitman House
Hendrickson Fish Cabin at
Captiva Rocks
Henry Ford Estate
Ice House at Captiva Rocks
Ice House at Point Blanco
Jewett-Thompson House
Josslyn Island Site
Journey's End
Koreshan Unity Settlement
Larsen Fish Cabin at Captiva
Rocks
Lee County Courthouse
Leneer Fish Cabin at Captiva
Rocks
Mound Key Site
Murphy-Burroughs House
Norton Fish Cabin at Captiva
Rocks
Olga School
Pardo Shellworks Site
Pineland Site
Punta Gorda Fish Company
Cabin
Punta Gorda Fish Company Ice
House
Sanibel Colored School
Sanibel Lighthouse and Keeper's
Quarters
Terry Park Ballfield
Thomas Edison Winter Estate
Tice Grammar School
Useppa Island Site
Whidden Fish Cabin at Captiva
Rocks
Whidden's Marina

Leon County
Averitt-Winchester House
Bannerman Plantation
Bellevue
Blackwood-Harwood Plantations
Cemetery
Bradley's County Store Complex
Brokaw-McDougall House
Calhoun Street Historic District
Carnegie Library
Caroline Brevard Grammar
School
Cascades Park
Chaires Community Historic
District
Coles Farmhouse
The Columns
Covington House
Escambe Site
Exchange Bank Building
FAMU Historial District
First Presbyterian Church
Fort Braden School
Freight Depot
Gallies Hall & Buildings
George Lewis II House
Goodwood
Governor's Mansion
Gov. John Martin House
Greenwood Cemetery
The Grove (Governor Call
House)
Hotel Floridan
Johnson-Caldwell House
Johnson-Carter House
Killearn Plantation
Archeological and Historic
District
Lake Jackson Mounds
Leon High School
Lewis House
Lichgate on High Road
Los Robles Gate
Magnolia Heights Historic
District
Masonic-Odd Fellows Hall
Miccosukee United Methodist
Church

Natural Bridge Battlefield
Old City Waterworks
Old Florida State Capitol
Park Avenue Historic District
Pisgah United Methodist Church
Riley House
Roberts Farm Historic and
　　Archeological District
Rollins House
Ruge Hall
St. Johns Episcopal Church
San Pedro y San Pablo de Patale
Smoky Hollow Historic District
Strickland-Herold House
Tallahassee Historic Districts
Tall Timbers Plantation District
Tookes House
Union Bank
Van Brunt House
Walker Library
Williams House
Wingterle House
Woman's Club of Tallahassee

Levy County
Cedar Keys Historic Site
Citizens Bank
Island Hotel

Liberty County
Gregory House/Torreya State
　　Park
Otis Hare Site
Rowlett's Millsite
Yon Mound and Village

Madison County
Bishop-Andrews Hotel
Dial-Goza House
Dr. Smith House
First Baptist Church
Jordan-Beggs House
St. Mary's Episcopal Church
Wardlaw-Smith House

Manatee County
Austin House
Beasley House

Braden Castle Park District
Bradenton Carnegie Library
Cortez Historic District
De Soto National Memorial
Gamble Mansion
Jordan House
Kreissle Forge
Madira Bickel Mounds
Midway Subdivision Historic
　　District
Old Manatee County
　　Courthouse
Original Manatee County
　　Courthouse
Palmetto Historic District
Portavant Mound Site
Reasoner House
Regina (shipwreck)
Reid-Woods House
Richardson House
Seagate (Crosley House)
Shaw's Point Archeological
　　District
Stevens-Gilchrist House
Souder House
Terra Ceia Village Improvement
　　Association Hall
Villa Serena Apartments
Whitfield Estates/Broughton
　　Street and Lantana Historic
　　Districts
Woman's Club of Palmetto

Marion County
Armstrong House
Ayer Houses
Belleview School
Citra Methodist Episcopal
　　Church-South
Coca-Cola Bottling Plant
Dunnellon Boomtown Historic
　　District
East Hall
Ferguson House
Gen. Bullock House
Josselyn House
Kerr City Historic District
Lake Lillian Neighborhood

Historic District
Lake Weir Yacht Club
Marion Hotel
McIntosh Historic District
Mount Zion AME Church
Ocala Historic Commercial
District
Ocala Historic District
Ocala Union Station
Old Fessenden Academy
Historic District
Orange Springs Methodist
Episcopal Church and
Cemetery
Pat's Island Community Site
Randall House
Ritz Apartments
Smith House
Townsend House
Tuscawilla Park Historic District
West Ocala Historic District

Martin County
Burn Brae Plantation Houses
Georges Valentine (shipwreck)
House of Refuge at Gilbert's Bar
Lyric Theater
Mount Elizabeth Archeological
Site
Old Martin County Courthouse
Olympia School
Seminole Inn
Stuart Wellcome Arch
Trapper Nelson Zoo Historic
District
Tuckahoe Building

Miami-Dade County
107 NE 96th Street
121 NE 100th Street
145 NE 95th Street
253 NE 99th Street
257 NE 91st Street
262 NE 96th Street
273 NE 98th Street
276 NE 98th Street
284 NE 96th Street
287 NE 96th Street

310 NE 99th Street
353 NE 91st Street
357 NE 92nd Street
361 NE 97th Street
379 NE 94th Street
384 NE 94th Street
389 NE 99th Street
431 NE 94th Street
477 NE 92nd Street
540 NE 96th Street
553 NE 101st Street
561 NE 101st Street
577 NE 96th Street
1291 NE 102nd Street
10108 NE 1st Avenue
Adams House
Algonquin Apartments
Anderson General Merchandise
Store
Anhinga Trail
Arch Creek Historic and
Archaeological Site
Atlantic Gas Station
Baird House
Barracks and Mess, Dinner Key
U.S. Coast Guard Station
Bay Shore Historic District
Beth Jacob Social Hall
Boca Chita Key Historic District
Bow Library
Brickell Mausoleum
Brickell Point Site
Burkhart House
Bush Apartments
Cadillac Hotel
Cape Florida Lighthouse
Central Baptist Church
Chaille Block
Charles Deering Estate
Citizens Bank
City National Bank Building
City of Miami Cemetery
Clune Building
Coco Plum Woman's Club
Congress Building
Coral Gables City Hall
Coral Gables Congregational
Church

Coral Gables Elementary School
Coral Gables House
Coral Gables Police and Fire
    Station
Coral Gables Woman's Club
Cravero House
Crouse House
Curtiss House
Curtiss House/The Alamo
Curtiss House/Gregory House
Dade County Courthouse
Dorsey House
Douglas Entrance
Downtown Miami Commercial
    Historic Districts
Dr. James Jackson's Office
DuPont Building
Ebenezer Methodist Church
El Jardin
Entrance to Central Miami
Etheredge House
Faust House
Fire Station #2
Fire Station #4
First Church of Christ, Scientist
First Coconut Grove School House
First Presbyterian Church
Fla. East Coast RR Locomotive #153
Florida Pioneer Museum
Freedom Tower
Fuchs Bakery
Gesu Church
Grand Concourse Apartments
Greater Bethel AME Church
Greenwald Steam Engine #1058
Griffiths House
Hahn Building
Haislip House
Half Moon (shipwreck)
Halissee Hall
Hanger at Dinner Key, U.S.
    Coast Guard
Heermance House
Helms House
Helm Stores and Apartments
Hequembourg House
Hervey Allen Study
Hialeah Park Race Track

Hialeah Park Race Track District
Hialeah SAL RR Station
Higgins Duplex
Homestead (Cooper) Public School
Homstead Town Hall
Hotel Country Club
Huntington Building
Hurt Building
Ingraham Building
J & S Building
Kampong Estate
Kentucky Home
King Truck Factory and
    Showroom
Lindeman-Johnson House
Long House
Lummus Park Historic Districts
Lyric Theater
MacFarlane Homestead Historic
    District
Martina Apartments
McMinn-Horne House
Meyer-Kiser Building
Miami Beach Architectural
    District
Miami City Hospital (Bldg. 1)
Miami Edison High School
Miami Senior High School
Miami Women's Club
Millard-McCarty House
Miramar Public School
Monroe Lake Archeological
    District
Mt. Zion Baptist Church
Munroe House
Nike Missile Site HM-69
Ocean Spray Hotel
Offshore Reefs Archaeological
    District
Old Spanish Monastery
Old U.S. Post Office and
    Courthouse
Olympia Theatre
Opa-Locka Bank
Opa-Locka Co. Administration
    Building
Opa-Locka Fire and Police
    Station

Opa-Locka RR Station
Osceola Apartment Hotel
Palm Cottage
Pan American Seaplane Base
Plymouth Congregational
  Church
Priscilla Apartments
Ransom School
Rock Gate
Root Building
St. John's Baptist Church
Sears, Roebuck and Co.
  Department Store
Security Building
Shark River Slough
  Archeological District
Shoreland Arcade
Shrine Building
Silver Palm School House
South River Drive Historic
  District
Southside School
S & S Sandwich Shop
Stiltsville District
Stiltsville Historic District
Sweeting Homestead
Taber Duplex
Temple Israel
Tinsman House
Tooker House
Trapp Homestead
Trinity Episcopal Cathedral
U.S. Coast Guard Air Station
  Hanger at Dinner Key
U.S. Post Office and Courthouse,
  Miami
Venetian Causeway
Venetian Pool
Virginia Key Beach Park
Walgreen's Drugstore
Warner House
Wheeler House
Women's Club of Coconut
  Grove

Monroe County
Adderley House
African Queen

Augustias (shipwreck site)
The Armory
Baldwin House
Bear Lake Archeological District
Cane Patch
Carysfort Lighthouse
Dry Tortugas National Park
Florida Keys Memoria
El Gallo Indiano (shipwreck site)
El Infante (shipwreck site)
El Rubi (shipwreck site)
Ft. Jefferson National
  Monument
Gato House
HA 19 (Japanese midget
  submarine)
Herrera (shipwreck site)
Indian Key
John Pennekamp Coral Reef
  State Park and Reserve
Key West Historic District
LaBranche Fishing Camp
Lignumvitae Key Archaeological
  and Historical District
Little White House
Martello Gallery
Mud Lake Canal
Old Post Office and
  Customshouse
Overseas Highway and Railway
  Bridges
Pigeon Key Historic District
Popula
Porter House
Rock Mound Site
Rookery Mound
Sand Key Lighthouse
San Felipe (shipwreck site)
San Francisco (shipwreck site)
San Jose (shipwreck site)
San Pedro (shipwreck site)
Sloppy Joe's Bar
Suelo de Arizon (shipwreck site)
Sugarloaf Bat Tower
Ten Thousand Islands
  Archeological District
Thompson Fish House
Tres Puentes (shipwreck site)

U.S. Coast Guard Headquarters
U.S. Naval Station Historic
District

Nassau County
Amelia Island Lighthouse
American Beach Historic
District
Bailey House
Ervin's Rest
Fairbanks House
Fernandina Beach Historic
District
Fort Clinch
Hippard House
Merrick-Simmons House
Mount Olive Missionary Baptist
Church
Original Fernandina Historic
Site
Palmer House
"Tabby" House/Lewis House

Okaloosa County
Camp Pinchot Historic District
Crestview Commercial Historic
District
Eglin Field Historic District
Gulfview Hotel Historic District
McKinley Climatic Lab
Valparaiso Inn
WWII JB-2 Launch Site
WWII JB-2 Mobile Launch Site

Okeechobee County
Freedman-Raulerson House

Orange County
1890 Windermera School
All Saints Episcopal Church
Annie Russell Theater
Apopka Seaboard Air Line
Railway Depot
Brewer House
Bridges House
Carroll Building
Comstock-Harris House
Eatonville Historic District

First Church of Christ Scientist
Griffin Park Historic District
Huttig Estate
Knowles Memorial Chapel
Lake Eola Heights Historic
District
Maitland Art Center
Mitchill-Tibbetts House
Mizell-Leu House Historic
District
Newell House
Ocoee Christian Church
Old Orlando RR Depot
Polasek House and Studio
Palm Cottage Gardens
Palmer Building
The Parsonage
Phillips House
Polasek House and Studio
Rogers Building
Ryan & Co. Lumber Yard
Tilden House
Tinker Building
Tinker Field
Twin Mounds Archaeological
District
Waite-Davis House
Waterhouse House
Wells'built Hotel
Windemere Town Hall
Winter Garden Downtown
Historic District
Winter Garden Historic
Residential District
Winter Park Country Club
Winter Park Woman's Club
Withers-Maguire House

Osceola County
Colonial Estate
Desert Inn
First United Methodist Church
Grand Army of the Republic
Hall
Kissimmee Historic District
Old Holy Redeemer Catholic
Church
Osceola County Courthouse

Palm Beach County
1240 Coconut Road
Administration Building
Aiken House
American National Bank
Big Mound City
Bingham-Blossom House
Boca Raton Fire Engine No. *1*
Boca Raton Old City Hall
Boynton School
Boynton Woman's Club
Breakers Hotel Complex
Brelsford House/The Banyans
Central Park Historic District
Clematis Street Historic
   Commercial District
College Park Historic District
Comeau Building
Comeau House
Delray Beach SAL Railroad
   Station
Delray Beach Schools
Dixie Court Hotel
Eastover
El Cid Historic District
Evans House
Ferndix Building
First Church of Christ Scientist
Flamingo Park Historic
   Residential District
Florida East Coast Passenger
   Station
Grandview Heights Historic
   District
Guaranty Building
Gulf Stream Hotel
Hatch's Department Store
Hibiscus Apartments
Historic Old Town Commercial
   District
Holy Trinity Episcopal Church
Hurricane of 1928 African-
   American Mass Burial Site
Jupiter Inlet Historic and
   Archaeological Site
Jupiter Inlet Lighthouse
Kelsey City City Hall
Lavender House

Loftus (shipwreck)
Mango Promenade Historic
   District
Mickens House
Milton-Myers American Legion
   Post
Northwest Historic District
Northwood Historic District
Norton House
Old Lake Worth City Hall
Old Lucerne Historic Residential
   District
Old Palm Beach Jr. College
   Building
Osborne School
Pahokee High School
Palm Beach Daily News Building
Palm Beach Mercantile
   Company
Palm Beach Town Hall
Palm Beach Winter Club
Paramount Theatre Building
Pine Ridge Hospital
Professional Building
Rice House
SAL Dining Car *6113*
SAL Lounge Car *6603*
Seaboard Airline RR Station
Seaboard Coastline RR
   Passenger Station
Sundy House
U.S. Post Office
Van Valkenburg House
Via Mizner
Vineta Hotel
Warden House
West Palm Beach National
   Guard Armory
West Palm Beach Stub Canal
   and Turning Basin

Pasco County
Anderson House
Baker House
Church Street Historic District
Dade City Depot
Dade City Woman's Club
Hacienda Hotel

Jeffries House
Pasco Court House
St. Leo Abbey Historic District
Zephyrhills Downtown Historic
  District

Pinellas County
Alexander Hotel
Anclote Key Lighthouse
Andrews Memorial Chapel
Arcade Hotel
Arfaras Sponge Packing House
Bay Pines site
Belleview Biltmore Hotel
Boone House
Casa Coe da Sol
Casa de Muchas Flores
Central High School
Cleveland Street Post Office
Cretekos (sponge-diving boat)
Dennis Hotel
Domestic Science and Manual
  Training School
Don Ce Sar Hotel
Douglas House
Downtown St. Petersburg
  Historic District
Duchess (sponge-hooking boat)
Ducros House
First Methodist Church
Fort De Soto Batteries
Green-Richman Arcade
Harbor Oaks Residential District
Ingleside Building
Johnson Building
Jungle Prade Site
Kenwood Historic District
Kress and Co. Building
Meres Sponge Packing House
Mt. Olive AME Church
Northshore Historic District
Old Bellair Town Hall
Old Pinellas County Courthouse
Old Tarpon Springs City Hall
Old Tarpon Springs High
  School
Pass-A-Grille Historic District
Potter House

Roebling Estate
Roser Park Historic District
Round Lake Historic District
Safford House
St. Nicholas III (boat)
St. Nicholas VI (boat)
St. Petersburg Lawn Bowling
  Club
St. Petersburg Public Library
St. Petersburg Woman's Club
Sanitary Public Market Building
Snell Arcade/Rutland Building
South Ward School
Studebaker Building
Symi (sponge-diving boat)
Tarpon Springs Historic District
Tarpon Springs Sponge
  Exchange
U.S. Open Air Post Office
Veillard House
Vinoy Park Hotel
Weedon Island site
Williams House

Polk County
Aburndale Citrus Growers
  Association Packinghouse
Atlantic Coastline RR Depot
Babson Park Women's Club
Bartow Downtown Commercial
  District
Baynard House
Beacon Hill/Alta Vista
  Residential District
Biltmore-Cumberland Historic
  District
Brown House
Bullard House
Casa de Josefina
Central Avenue School
Central Grammar School
Chalet Suzanne
Christ Episcopal Church
Church of the Holy Spirit
Cleveland Court School
Cox Grammar School
Davenport Historic District
Dixieland Historic District

Dixie Walesbilt Hotel
Downtown Haines City
  Commercial District
Downtown Winter Haven
  Historic District
Dundee ACL R.R. Depot
East Lake Morton Residential
  District
El Retiro
First Baptist Church
Florida Southern College
Fort Meade Historic District
Haines City National Guard
  Armory
Henley Field Ball Park
Holland House/The Gables
Interlaken Historical Residential
  District
Jenks House
Johnson House
Lake Hunter Terrace Historic
  District
Lake Mirror Promenade
Lake of the Hills Community
  Club
Lake Wales City Hall
Lake Wales Commercial District
Lake Wales Historic Residential
  District
Mountain Lake Colony House
Mountain Lake Estates Historic
  District
Munn Park Historic District
North Ave. Historic District
Northeast Bartow Residential
  District
Oak Hill Cemetery
Oates Building
Old Frostproof High school
Old Lakeland High School
Old Polk County Courthouse
Polk Hotel
Polk Theater and Office
  Building
Pope Ave. Historic District
Roosevelt School
St. Mark's Episcopal Church
South Bartow Residential District

South Florida Military College
South Lake Morton Historic
  District
Swearingen House
Thompson Cigar Factory
Tillman House
Winston School
Winter Haven Heights Historic
  Residential District
Woman's Club of Winter Haven

Putnam County
Bostwick School
Bronson-Mulholland House
Central Academy
Crescent City Historic District
Hubbard House
Interlachen Hall
Mellrose Historic District
Melrose Women's Club
Mount Royal
Old ACL Union Depot
Palatka North Historic District
Palatka Ravine Gardens Historic
  District
Palatka South Historic District
St. Marks Episcopal Church
Tenney House and Groveland
  Hotel

St. Johns County
Abbott Tract Historic District
Alcazar Hotel
Avero House
Bridge of Lions
Castillo de San Marcos National
  Monument
Fish Island site
Fort Matanzas National
  Monument
Grace United Methodist Church
Hastings High School
Homeland School
Lincolnville Historic District
Lindsley House
Lopez House
Markland
Model Land Co. Historic District

Old St. Johns County Jail
O'Reilly House
Record Building
Rodriquez-Avero-Sanchez House
St. Augustine Alligator Farm
  Historic District
St. Augustine Civic Center
St. Augustine Lighthouse
Sanchez Homestead
Sanchez Powder House
Second Fort Mose Site
Shell Bluff Landing
Solla-Carcaba Cigar Factory
Spanish Coquina Quarries
Villa Zorayda
Walker Home
Ximenez-Fatio House

St. Lucie County
Arcade Building
Casa Caprona
Cresthaven
Fort Pierce Old City Hall
Fort Pierre Old Post Office
Fort Pierce Site
Frere House
Hammond House
Immokolee Building
Moores Creek Bridge
Old St. Anastasia School
St. Lucie High School
St. Lucie Village Historic District
Sunrise Theater
Urca de Lima (shipwreck)

Santa Rosa County
Arcadia Sawmill and Cotton Mill
Bagdad Village Historic District
Bethune Blackwater (schooner)
Big Heart West
Butcherpen Mound
Exchange Hotel
First American Road
Florida State Road #1
Louisville & Nashville Depot
Milton Historic District
Mt. Pilgrim African Baptist
  Church

Naval Live Oaks Cemetery
Naval Live Oaks Historic District
Naval Live Oaks Restoration
Ollinger-Cobb House
St. Mary's Episcopal Church and
  Rectory
Third Gulf Breeze
Thomas Creek Archaeological
  District

Sarasota County
507 Jackson Drive
710 Armada Road South
American National Bank
  Building
Appleby Building
Armada Road Multi-family
  District
Atlantic Coastline Passenger
  Depot
Bacheller-Brewer Model Home
  Estate
Bacon & Tomlin, Inc.
Bay Haven Hotel-Ringling
  School of Art
Bay Haven School
Bee Ridge Woman's Club
Bickel House
Binz House
Bisham-Wilson Historic District
Blackburn Point Bridge
Blalock House
Bryson-Crane House
Burns Court Historic District
Burns House
Caples'-Ringlings' Estates
  Historic District
Casa del Mar
Central-Coconut Historic District
City Electric Light and Power
  Plant
City Waterworks
Corrigan House
Crisp Building
Cunliff Residence
DeCanizares House
DeMarcay Hotel
Dr. Kennedy House

Eagle Point Historic District
Earle House
Edgewood Historic District
Edwards Theatre
El Patio Apartments
El Vernona Apartments
El Vernona Hotel
Field Estate
Frances-Carlton Apartments
Gillespie House
Halton House
Harding Circle Historic District/
St. Armands Circle
Hermitage-Whitney Historic
District
Hiss House
Hotel Venice
Iwersen Block
Johnson Chapel Missionary
Baptist Church
Johnson-Schoolcrafy Building
Keith Estate
Kress Building
Leech House
Lemon Bay Woman's Club
Levillain-Letton House
Little Salt Springs
Municipal Auditorium
Myakka School House
Nolan City of Sarasota Plan
Osprey Archaeological and
Historic Site
Osprey School
Out of Door School
Overtown Historic District
Payne Mansion
Purdy House
Reagin House
Reid House
Rigby's La Plaza Historic District
Rosemary Cemetery
Roth Cigar Factory
Sanderling Beach Club
Sarasota County Courthouse
Sarasota Herald Building
Sarasota High School
Sarasota Times Building
Sarasota Woman's Club

Schueler House
South Side School
Southwick-Harmon House
Thoms House
Triangle Inn
U.S. Post Office-Federal
Building
Valencia Hotel and Arcade
Venezia Park Historic District
Venice RR Depot
Warm Mineral Springs
Whitfield Estate
William House
Wilson House
Worth's Block

Seminole County
Bradlee-McIntyre House
Brown-King House
Estes Celery Co. Pre-cooler
Historic District
Lake Mary Chamber of
Commerce Building
Longwood Historic District
Longwood Hotel
Nelson and Co. Historic District
Old Fernald-Laughton Memorial
Hospital
Ritz Theater
St. James AME Church
Sanford Commercial District
Sanford Grammar School
Sanford Residential District
Seminole County Home
Wheeler-Evans House

Sumter County
Thomas R. Pierce House

Suwannee County
Allison House
Blackwell House
Dr. Price House
Hull-Hawkins House
Old Live Oak City Hall
Suwannee County Courthouse
Union Depot & ACL Freight
Station

Taylor County
Old Perry Post Office
Taylor County Jail

Union County
King House
Lake Butler Woman's Club
Townsend Building
Townsend House

Volusia County
The Abbey
All Saints Episcopal Church
Anderson Lodge
Anderson-Price Memorial
  Library
Barberville Central High School
Bethune-Cookman College
Blodgett House
The Casements
Casements Annex
Cat Hammock Site
Chief Master at Arms House
City Island
City Island Ballpark
Clements House
Coronado Historical District
Cypress St. Elementary School
Daytona Beach Bandshell and
  Oceanfront Park Complex
Daytona Beach Surfside Historic
  District
DeBary Hall
DeLand Hall
DeLeon Springs Colored School
Dickenson Memorial Library
Dix House
The Doldrums
Donnelly House
Downtown DeLand Historic
  District
Dunlawton Ave. Historical
  District
Dunlawton Plantation/Sugar
  Mill Bar
El Pino Parque Historic District
El Real Retiro
French House

Gamble Place Historic District
Grace Episcopal Church and
  Hall
Halifax Drive Historical District
The Hammocks
Haynes House
Holly Hill Municipal Building
Kilkoff House
Kling House
Kress Building
Lake Helen Historic District
Lippincott Mansion
Merchants Bank
Moulton-Wells House
Mount Taylor
New Smyrna Beach Historic
  District
New Smyrna Sugar Mill Ruins
Nocoroco (Tomoka State Park)
North Mosquito Lagoon
  Archeological District
Old Daytona Beach *News-Journal*
  Building
Old DeLand Memorial Hospital
Olds Hall
Orange City Colored School
Orange City Historic District
Orange City Town Hall
Ormond Garage
Ormond Hotel
Ormond Yacht Club
The Porches
Port Orange Depot
Rogers House
Ross Hammock Site
Rowallan Building
Seabreeze Historic District
Seminole Rest
Seybold Bakery
South Beach Street Historic
  District
Southern Cassadaga Spiritualist
  Camp Historic District
South Peninsula Historic District
Southwest Daytona Beach Black
  Heritage District
Spruce Creek Mound Complex
Stetson Mansion

Stetson University Campus
    Historic District
Stevens House
Stocton-Lindquist House
Strawn Historic Agricultural
    District
Strawn Historic Citrus Packing
    House District
Strawn Historic Sawmill District
Talahloka Building
Tarragona Tower
Thurman House
Thursby House
Tourist Church
Turtle Mound
U.S. Post Office
West DeLand Residential District
White Hall
Women's Club of New Smyrna
Young Memorial Library

Wakulla County
Bird Hammock

Old Sopchoppy High School
Old Sopchoppy High School Gym
Old Wakulla County Courthouse
St. Marks Lighthouse
Wakulla Springs Archaeological
    and Historic District

Walton County
Biddle House
Chautauqua Hall of
    Brotherhood
DeFuniak Springs Historic
    District
Governor Stone (schooner)
Operation Crossbow Site
Sun Bright/Catts House

Washington County
Chipley City Hall
Moss Hill Church
South Third Street Historic
    District
Woman's Club of Chipley

COUNTIES

When it was still a territory, Florida consisted of two counties—Escambia and St. Johns. Over the years the two counties divided into additional counties so that by 1925 the state reached its present political division of 67 counties. In the 19th century, most of the state's population was in its northern regions. Urbanization of the state first took hold in the southeast, around Miami, after World War I. That Gold Coast area remains the largest metropolitan region, but in recent years giant population centers have grown around Orlando in the central portion of the state, in the Tampa Bay area on the Gulf Coast, and in Jacksonville in the northeast region. Fewest residents per acre in Florida are in the state's north central and northwest sections. Growth over the past decade was more evenly distributed throughout the state than previously with the fastest growth registered by Wakulla County in the Panhandle, Flagler on the upper Atlantic Coast, Sumter in Central Florida, and Collier on the lower Gulf Coast. With an estimated 17.8 million people in the state in 2005, up from 15.98 million in the 2000 census, Florida is the nation's fourth most populous state.

All Florida is divided into two time zones. The Apalachicola River marks the boundary between the Eastern and Central time zones in the state. Most of North Florida and the entire peninsula are on Eastern time while all west of the river are on Central time. Counties in the Central Time Zone are Jackson, Calhoun, Gulf, Holmes, Washington, Bay, Walton, Okaloosa, Santa Rosa, and Escambia.

ORIGIN OF COUNTY NAMES

Alachua—Indian term meaning "grassy."

Baker—for Judge James M. Baker.

Bay—from St. Andrew's Bay.

Bradford—for Capt. Richard Bradford, first Florida officer killed during the War Between the States.

Brevard—for Dr. Theodore W. Brevard, author of the North Carolina Declaration of Independence.

Broward—for Gov. Napoleon B. Broward.

Calhoun—for U.S. Sen. John C. Calhoun.

Charlotte—for the harbor.

Citrus—for the state's citrus industry.

Clay—for statesman Henry Clay.

Collier—for landowner Barron G. Collier.

Columbia—for Christopher Columbus.

DeSoto—for Spanish explorer Hernando de Soto.

Dixie—for the popular term applied to the South.

Duval—for Gov. William P. DuVal.

Escambia—Indian term meaning "barter."

Flagler—for state developer Henry Flagler.

Franklin—for Benjamin Franklin.

Gadsden—for James Gadsden, aide to Gen. Andrew Jackson.

Gilchrist—for Gov. Albert H. Gilchrist.

Glades—for Everglades.

Gulf—for the Gulf of Mexico.

Hamilton—for Alexander Hamilton.

Hardee—for Gov. Cary A. Hardee.

Hendry—for early resident Capt. Francis A. Hendry.

Central Time   **Eastern Time**

Hernando—for explorer Hernando de Soto.

Highlands—for geography of the county.

Hillsborough—for English Earl of Hillsborough.

Holmes—for an early resident.

Indian River—for Indian River.

Jackson—for Gen. and Pres. Andrew Jackson, first American Governor of Florida.

Jefferson—for Pres. Thomas Jefferson.

Lafayette—for the Marquis de Lafayette.

Lake—for the many lakes in the county.

Lee—for Gen. Robert E. Lee.

Leon—for explorer Ponce de Leon.

Levy—for David Levy Yulee, state's first U.S. senator.

Liberty—for the right of U.S. citizens.

Madison—for Pres. James Madison.

Manatee—for marine mammal.

Marion—for Gen. Francis Marion of the Revolutionary War.

Martin—for Gov. John W. Martin.

Miami-Dade—for its principal city and for Maj. Francis L. Dade, killed in Second Seminole War.

Monroe—for Pres. James Monroe.

Nassau—for German Duchy of Nassau.

Okaloosa—Indian word for "black water."

Okeechobee—for Lake Okeechobee, Indian word for "big water."

Orange—in honor of citrus crop.

Osceola—for Seminole Indian leader.

Palm Beach—for palms on beaches.

Pasco—for U.S. Sen. Samuel Pasco.

Pinellas—Spanish for "Point of Pines."

Polk—for Pres. James Polk.

Putnam—for Benjamin Alexander Putnam, adjutant to Gen. Zachary Taylor in Second Seminole War.

St. Johns—from St. Johns River, called by Spanish explorers "San Juan Baptista."

St. Lucie—for Catholic Church saint.

Santa Rosa—for Catholic Church saint.

Sarasota—Indian word referring to "Point of Rocks" on Gulf.

Seminole—for the Indian tribe of that name.

Sumter—for Gen. Thomas Sumter of the Revolutionary War.

Suwannee—Indian word meaning "echo."

Taylor—for Gen. Zachary Taylor.

Union—for unity.

Volusia—for settler named Volus.

Wakulla—Indian word for spring meaning "mystery."

Walton—for a prominent Georgia colonel.

Washington—for Pres. George Washington.

FORMATION OF COUNTIES

Gen. Andrew Jackson, while serving as military governor of Florida, divided the peninsula into counties by an ordinance which read, in part:

"All the country lying between the Perdido and Suwaney rivers, with all islands therein, shall form one county to be called Escambia.

"All the country lying east of the river Suwaney, and every part of the ceded territories not designated as belonging to the former county, shall form a county to be called St. Johns."

The ordinance establishing the first counties was dated July 21, 1821. One year later the territorial council, forerunner of the present state legislature, began dividing the original two counties and adding more. From that time until 1925 seldom did a session of the legislature or, before statehood, the council, pass without at least one new county being added.

Date of formation in the following chart is the date of final action by the council or legislature in approving the county. Where the same date is indicated, order was determined by the order listed in the law.

Rank	County	County Seat	Date Formed
1	Escambia	Pensacola	July 21, 1821
2	St. Johns	St. Augustine	July 21, 1821
3	Jackson	Marianna	Aug. 12, 1822
4	Duval	Jacksonville	Aug. 12, 1822
5	Gadsden	Quincy	June 24, 1823
6	Monroe	Key West	July 3, 1823
7	Leon	Tallahassee	Dec. 29, 1824

8	Walton	DeFuniak Springs	Dec. 29, 1824
9	Alachua	Gainesville	Dec. 29, 1824
10	Nassau	Fernandina Beach	Dec. 29, 1824
11	Orange	Orlando	Dec. 29, 1824
12	Washington	Chipley	Dec. 9, 1825
13	Jefferson	Monticello	Jan. 20, 1827
14	Madison	Madison	Dec. 26, 1827
15	Hamilton	Jasper	Dec. 26, 1827
16	Columbia	Lake City	Feb. 4, 1832
17	Franklin	Apalachicola	Feb. 8, 1832
18	Hillsborough	Tampa	Jan. 25, 1834
19	Miami-Dade	Miami	Feb. 4, 1836
20	Calhoun	Blountstown	Jan. 26, 1838
21	Santa Rosa	Milton	Feb. 18, 1842
22	Hernando	Brooksville	Feb. 24, 1843
23	Wakulla	Crawfordville	Mar. 11, 1843
24	Marion	Ocala	Mar. 14, 1844
25	Brevard	Titusville	Mar. 14, 1844
26	Levy	Bronson	Mar. 10, 1845
27	Holmes	Bonifay	Jan. 8, 1848
28	Putnam	Palatka	Jan. 13, 1849
29	Sumter	Bushnell	Jan. 8, 1853
30	Volusia	DeLand	Dec. 29, 1854
31	Manatee	Bradenton	Jan. 9, 1855
32	Liberty	Bristol	Dec. 15, 1856
33	Lafayette	Mayo	Dec. 23, 1856
34	Taylor	Perry	Dec. 23, 1856
35	Suwannee	Live Oak	Dec. 21, 1858
36	Bradford	Starke	Dec. 31, 1858
37	Clay	Green Cove Springs	Dec. 31, 1858
38	Baker	Macclenny	Feb. 8, 1861
39	Polk	Bartow	Feb. 8, 1861
40	Osceola	Kissimmee	May 12, 1887

41	Lee	Fort Myers	May 13, 1887
42	De Soto	Arcadia	May 19, 1887
43	Lake	Tavares	May 27, 1887
44	Citrus	Inverness	June 2, 1887
45	Pasco	Dade City	June 2, 1887
46	St. Lucie	Fort Pierce	May 24, 1905
47	Palm Beach	West Palm Beach	Apr. 30, 1909
48	Pinellas	Clearwater	May 23, 1911
49	Bay	Panama City	Apr. 24, 1913
50	Seminole	Sanford	Apr. 25, 1913
51	Broward	Fort Lauderdale	Apr. 30, 1915
52	Okaloosa	Crestview	June 13, 1915
53	Flagler	Bunnell	Apr. 28, 1917
54	Okeechobee	Okeechobee	May 8, 1917
55	Hardee	Wauchula	Apr. 23, 1921
56	Highlands	Sebring	Apr. 23, 1921
57	Charlotte	Punta Gorda	Apr. 23, 1921
58	Glades	Moore Haven	Apr. 23, 1921
59	Dixie	Cross City	Apr. 25, 1921
60	Sarasota	Sarasota	May 14, 1921
61	Union	Lake Butler	May 20, 1921
62	Collier	East Naples	May 8, 1923
63	Hendry	La Belle	May 11, 1923
64	Martin	Stuart	May 30, 1925
65	Indian River	Vero Beach	May 30, 1925
66	Gulf	Port St. Joe	June 6, 1925
67	Gilchrist	Trenton	Dec. 4, 1925

ANNUAL PRICE LEVEL INDEX
(2009)

The Florida Price Level Index measures the cost of living in each county compared to a statewide average. It is compiled each year by the Department of Education and is computed by pricing 117 items that consumers normally use. These items fall into five categories—food, transportation, housing, clothing and recreation, and health and personal services. The "index" column following indicates how much above or below the state average (100) it costs to maintain a fixed, specified standard of living in each county. The column marked "rank" compares a county's cost of living with the other 66 counties.

For example, Collier County is the most expensive county in which to live; its 107.37 index says the cost of living in Collier County is 7.37 percentage points higher than the state average. The purpose of the index is to establish a differential formula for state contributions to its school systems. Each county is a unified school district.

County	Index	Rank	County	Index	Rank
Alachua	95.9	34	Hendry	100.85	11
Baker	97.48	28	Hernando	96.92	30
Bay	93.79	47	Highlands	95.39	38T
Bradford	96.91	31	Hillsborough	101.57	7
Brevard	100	15	Holmes	89.81	61
Broward	103.15	3	Indian River	100.45	12
Calhoun	89.66	62	Jackson	89.87	60
Charlotte	97.25	29	Jefferson	90.97	56
Citrus	93.86	45	Lafayette	89.62	63
Clay	99.54	18	Lake	97.51	27
Collier	107.37	1	Lee	102.83	4
Columbia	93.88	44	Leon	93.68	48
DeSoto	97.91	26	Levy	92.58	50
Dixie	90.63	57	Liberty	88.78	65
Duval	101.9	6	Madison	88.23	57
Escambia	94.56	42	Manatee	100.19	13
Flagler	94.44	43	Marion	94.71	41
Franklin	88.36	66	Martin	99.88	16
Gadsden	92.29	52	Miami-Dade	101.18	9
Gilchrist	92.73	49	Monroe	102.15	5
Glades	99.11	20	Nassau	99.13	19
Gulf	90.34	58	Okaloosa	96.16	33
Hamilton	91.54	53	Okeechobee	96.88	32
Hardee	95.53	37	Orange	101	10

County	Index	Rank
Osceola	98.66	22
Palm Beach	105.23	2
Pasco	98.86	21
Pinellas	100.05	14
Polk	98.07	25
Putnam	95.74	36
St. Johns	98.48	24
St. Lucie	98.56	23
Santa Rosa	92.44	51
Sarasota	101.21	8

County	Index	Rank
Seminole	99.81	17
Sumter	95.34	40
Suwannee	91.48	54
Taylor	89.23	64
Union	95.83	35
Volusia	95.39	38T
Wakulla	91.27	55
Walton	93.84	46
Washington	89.68	59
(T) Tie		

COUNTY PROFILES

ALACHUA

Area: 961 square miles
Approx. elev: 165 ft.
Avg. temps: 57 Jan.
           81 Aug.
Avg. annual rain: 50 in.
1990 pop: 181,596
2000 pop: 217,955
2009 est. pop: 243,574

In the north central section of the state, Alachua County is most noted as the site of the state's major higher education facility, the University of Florida. Education is the county's foremost "industry," with its students comprising nearly half the population of the county's major city, Gainesville.

Biggest private sector employers are hospitals, although numerous technological firms have settled in the area because of the university's presence. Major transportation into the county is via I-75, U.S. 301 and the Gainesville Regional Airport.

Besides Gainesville, the county seat, incorporated areas include Alachua, Archer, Hawthorne, High Springs, LaCrosse, Micanopy, Newberry, and Waldo. One of the county's most scenic unincorporated areas is the settlement of Cross Creek, the home of Marjorie Kinnan Rawlings.

Alachua is particularly endowed with natural beauty. Sprinkled liberally through the rolling, heavily treed landscape are springs, rivers, nature walks, a major botanical garden, a vast prairie, and archaeological sites.

BAKER

Area: 588 square miles
Approx. elev: 129 ft.
Avg. temps: 55 Jan.
           81 Aug.
Avg. annual rain: 49.27 in.
1990 pop: 18,486
2000 pop: 22,259
2009 est. pop: 26,336

On the Florida-Georgia border, Baker County is primarily an agricultural county. The Battle of Olustee, one of the state's most important battles during the War Between the States, was fought in the county. Numerous small streams flow through Baker, providing excellent fishing, as does the bordering St. Mary's River. Quail, deer, and turkey also are found in its vast forests.

The Osceola National Forest dominates nearly one-half of the lightly populated county's area. In addition, a large portion of Baker's northern region is composed of valuable Okefenoke wetlands, much of which have been and are being purchased by the state to prevent their development.

Agricultural products are its residents' primary source of income. Major transportation into the county is I-10. It is served by Jacksonville International Airport in adjacent Duval County.

Incorporated places include Macclenny, the county seat, and Glen Saint Mary.

BAY

Area: 861 square miles
Approx. elev: 21 ft.
Avg. temps: 53 Jan.
             81 Aug.
Avg. annual rain: 57.86 in.
1990 pop: 126,994
2000 pop: 148,217
2009 est. pop: 164,767

In the middle of the state's Panhandle, on the Gulf of Mexico, Bay County is a favorite tourist site because of its outstanding beaches. Most of its population clusters around its spacious bays— St. Andrew, West Bay, North Bay, and East Bay—and St. Andrew Sound. Long, narrow barrier islands shield the mainland from the Gulf. Adjoining the county's major populated center, Panama City, is Tyndall Air Force Base.

During World War II, Panama City was a major shipbuilding center. Today, the county still depends for much of its employment and economic resources on nearby military activities. As a result, many retired military persons have chosen the area for their retirement.

Bay County also entertains large tourist populations because of its miles of beaches (known as the Miracle Strip). St. Andrew's State Recreation Area in Bay County is one of the state's 158 parks and among its most visited.

Major private employers include hospitals and paper and chemical manufacturers. Transportation into the county is via I-10 and the Florida Northwest Beaches International Airport.

Largest incorporated places are Panama City, the county seat, and Callaway, Lynn Haven, Springfield, and Parker.

BRADFORD

Area: 305 square miles
Approx. elev: 150-180 ft.
Avg. temps: 60 Jan.
             81 Aug.
Avg. annual rain: 49.40 in.
1990 pop: 22,515
2000 pop: 26,088
2009 est. pop: 29,235

The state's second smallest, Bradford County is a land-bound region in northeast Florida in which truck crops, tobacco, timber, and livestock play an important economic role. Largest private employers include manufacturers of mineral sand, work clothing, and wood products. U.S. 301 is the county's main artery. The nearest airport is 24 miles distant, the Gainesville Regional Airport.

A primary asset of Bradford County is its location, a pleasant hour's drive from the recreation, historical sites, and shopping amenities in Jacksonville, St. Augustine, and Gainesville.

Largest incorporated places are Starke, the county seat, and Lawtey, Hampton, and Brooker.

BREVARD

Area: 1,310 square miles
Approx. elev: 6-26 ft.
Avg. temps: 62 Jan.
      81.5 Aug.
Avg. annual rain: 50.74 in.
1990 pop: 398,978
2000 pop: 476,230
2009 est. pop: 536,357

The U.S. space program is the focal point of Brevard County, which is in the central part of the peninsula fronting on the Atlantic Ocean. Long and narrow, Brevard is 72 miles from north to south, but only 20 miles wide. Cape Canaveral is within its borders.

Brevard's economic health for decades has been tied to the U.S. space program, but annually more of its future is being oriented toward its massive coastline, which is attracting increasing numbers of new residents.

Most of its population is along the Indian River, a major state waterway on the western shore of the Kennedy Space Center complex.

Largest employers are electronics and aerospace manufacturers. Transportation into the county includes I-95 and Melbourne Regional Airport.

Largest incorporated places are Melbourne, Palm Bay, Cocoa, Rockledge, and Titusville, the county seat.

BROWARD

Area: 1,220 square miles
Approx. elev: 8 ft.
Avg. temps: 69 Jan.
      82 Aug.
Avg. annual rain: 65.19 in.
1990 pop: 1,255,488
2000 pop: 1,623,018
2009 est. pop: 1,766,476

Part of the Gold Coast, Broward County's vast metropolitan area runs up its eastern shore on the Atlantic Ocean. The majority of the county's square miles, however, are inland, in the eastern portion of the unpopulated Everglades.

Despite this marked contrast between eastern and western Broward that results in much of the county being sparsely populated, Broward has more than 1,300 people per square mile. That ranks it as the second most populated and second most densely populated of the 67 counties.

Major private employers are in financial services, communications, and computer technology. Transportation routes into Broward include I-75 (Alligator Alley), I-95, and Florida's Turnpike, plus air service at Fort Lauderdale/Hollywood International Airport.

Largest incorporated places are Fort Lauderdale, the county seat, and Hollywood, Pompano Beach, Coral Springs, and Plantation.

CALHOUN

Area: 567 square miles
Approx. elev: 51 ft.
Avg. temps: 53 Jan.
         81.5 Aug.
Avg. annual rain: 58.94 in.
1990 pop: 11,011
2000 pop: 13,017
2009 est. pop: 13,821

A rural county with few people, Calhoun County is tucked in the Panhandle a short distance from the Gulf of Mexico and the Georgia and Alabama state lines. It is primarily forests and wetlands, and largely undeveloped, although it is home to a variety of small industries including trucking, flowers, clothing, and wood products.

Two of Calhoun's greatest assets are rivers—the mighty Apalachicola, which outlines the county's eastern border, and the Chipola, which bisects the county. Both provide abundant recreational activities.

Transportation needs are served by I-10 and the Tallahassee Regional Airport, located 50 miles to the east.

Largest incorporated places are Blountstown, the county seat, and Altha.

CHARLOTTE

Area: 832 square miles
Approx. elev: 3 ft.
Avg. temps: 64 Jan.
         82 Aug.
Avg. annual rain: 52.55 in.
1990 pop: 110,975
2000 pop: 141,627
2009 est. pop: 158,952

On the southwest coast, fronting on the Gulf of Mexico, Charlotte County is only 17 miles from north to south, but has approximately 120 miles of shoreline.

Both the Myakka and Peace rivers flow through it and into expansive Charlotte Harbor, on whose shores sits Punta Gorda, the county seat. West of the harbor is a fast-developing peninsula protected from Gulf storms by numerous barrier islands, including Gasparilla. Nearby Lemon Bay, Placida Harbor, and Gasparilla Sound are excellent fishing grounds.

Health-care facilities are among the largest private employers in the county. Major transportation routes into the county are I-75 and U.S. 41. Air service is at the Southwest Florida International Airport 25 miles to the south in adjacent Lee County.

Largest populated centers are Punta Gorda and Port Charlotte.

CITRUS

Area: 661 square miles
Approx. elev: 45 ft.
Avg. temps: 58 Jan.
         81 Aug.
Avg. annual rain: 51.20 in.
1990 pop: 93,515
2000 pop: 118,085
2009 est. pop: 140,357

New residents and tourists are attracted to Citrus County, a region with its western boundary on the Gulf of Mexico and its eastern area dominated by the Withlacoochee State Forest and Tsala Apopka Lake.

The largest private employer is a nuclear power plant, but others include health care facilities and retailers. I-75 and U.S. 41 are major motor routes into the county.

Nearest major airport is Tampa International 65 miles to the south.

Recreation opportunities abound in Citrus County, which has dozens of freshwater lakes, rivers, springs, wildlife refuges, and parks. The county is most famous for its many manatees, which have made the county's Crystal River one of their favorite eating and mating grounds.

Largest incorporated places are Inverness, the county seat, and Crystal River.

CLAY

Area: 644 square miles
Approx. elev: 25-150 ft.
Avg. temps: 55 Jan.
            81 Aug.
Avg. annual rain: 53.42 in.
1990 pop: 105,986
2000 pop: 140,814
2009 est. pop: 186,756

Its eastern border fronting on the St. Johns River, Clay County is a neighbor of, and a bedroom community for, sprawling Duval County to its north and St. Johns County to its east. Its population has more than doubled in 20 years.

The U.S. Army has a large facility, Camp Blanding, in the western area of Clay. Private employment is in industries producing concrete and asphalt, lumber and wood chips, minerals, and dairying. Routes with spurs into the county include I-95, I-10, and U.S. 17. Jacksonville International Airport, 33 miles to the north, is the nearest major air facility.

Numerous sulphur springs near the St. Johns River have been thought to have medicinal benefits and, say some, may have been the springs sought by Ponce de Leon.

Largest incorporated places are Orange Park, Green Cove Springs, the county seat, and Keystone Heights.

COLLIER

Area: 2,119 square miles
Approx. elev: 4 ft.
Avg. temps: 68 Jan.
            82 Aug.
Avg. annual rain: 51.40 in.
1990 pop: 152,099
2000 pop: 251,377
2009 est. pop: 318,537

Collier is one of the state's fastest growing counties, its population increasing 65 percent in the past decade.

Known for its 10,000 islands, Collier County and its Everglades region offer one of the last large strands of cypress in the eastern U.S. The Everglades dominate much of Collier, and thus rampant development has been almost exclusively along the county's western boundary, on the Gulf of Mexico.

In the 1800s, Seminole Indians, in flight after losing battles with the U.S. Army, settled in the Everglades. Today many of the estimated 3,000 Seminoles in Florida live in Collier.

Major private employers are in health services and lodging. Major roads into the county are I-75 and U.S. 41. Nearest major air service is at Southwest Florida International Airport in Lee County to the north.

Largest incorporated places are Naples and Everglades City. County seat is in East Naples.

COLUMBIA

Area: 789 square miles
Approx. elev: 200 ft.
Avg. temps: 56 Jan.
81 Aug.
Avg. annual rain: 49.88 in.
1990 pop: 42,613
2000 pop: 56,513
2009 est. pop: 69,264

Among Columbia County's great natural resources are the Osceola National Forest and the bordering Suwannee River. The famous river enters Florida from the Okefenokee Swamp in Georgia near the Columbia County line, which borders the Peach State.

Largest private employers are in asphalt paving and mobile home manufacturing and sales.

Both I-10 and I-75 enter the county, but the nearest major airport, the Gainesville Regional Airport, is 42 miles to the south.

A popular visitor stop is the beautiful Ichetucknee River that provides swimming and canoeing. Its nearly three miles of slowly flowing spring water also make it one of the world's finest and most popular tubing sites.

Largest incorporated places are Lake City, the county seat, and Fort White.

DESOTO

Area: 721 square miles
Approx. elev: 56 ft.
Avg. temps: 63 Jan.
82 Aug.
Avg. annual rain: 50.66 in.
1990 pop: 23,865
2000 pop: 32,209
2009 est. pop: 35,297

A cattle and citrus region, DeSoto County is an inland county nearer the Gulf of Mexico than the Atlantic Ocean. It is primarily rural, sparsely populated, and proud of its annual All-Florida Rodeo held twice each year.

Flowing through DeSoto is one of Florida's two dozen major rivers, the Peace, noted for fishing and canoeing.

Private industry includes citrus, packing houses, and agriculture. I-75 is the primary driving route into the county, and for air service travelers favor the Sarasota/Bradenton International Airport 53 miles to the northeast.

Arcadia, the county seat, is the only notable populated city in DeSoto County.

DIXIE

Area: 709 square miles
Approx. elev: 42 ft.
Avg. temps: 55 Jan.
81 Aug.
Avg. annual rain: 58.20 in.
1990 pop: 10,585
2000 pop: 13,827
2009 est. pop: 14,824

One of the state's least densely populated counties with less than 20 persons per square mile, Dixie County fronts on the Gulf of Mexico but it does not have wide, attractive beaches. Instead, the region is more a favorite with deer, turkey, and wild pig hunters than with tourists.

Timber companies are Dixie's largest private employers. The major road into the county is U.S. 19, and air service is available 60 miles to the east at Gainesville Regional Airport.

The county's history includes

a battle at Old Town on U.S. 19, once a large Indian village where Chief Bowlegs encountered Andrew Jackson during Indian uprisings. Prior to the Civil War, Old Town was the site of a factory where Spanish moss was turned into clean, economical stuffing for mattresses and furniture.

Incorporated places are Cross City, the county seat, and Horseshoe Beach.

DUVAL

Area: 840 square miles
Approx. elev: 25 ft.
Avg. temps: 55 Jan.
    81 Aug.
Avg. annual rain: 58.20 in.
1990 pop: 672,971
2000 pop: 778,879
2009 est. pop: 857,040

Tucked into the northeast corner of Florida, Duval County has one of the nation's largest ports, used heavily by the U.S. Navy. During World War II, the port at Jacksonville was a busy military embarkation point. It still is a busy military site for the Air Force and Navy.

In 1967 the city of Jacksonville and Duval County consolidated into one large political entity, making Jacksonville the state's most populous city. Coursing through downtown Jacksonville is the north-flowing St. Johns River.

Largest private industries in Duval are retailing, banking, health care, insurance, communications, and shipping. The county is home to the University of North Florida. I-10 and I-95 enter the county, as do U.S. 1 and U.S. 90. Jacksonville International Airport provides air service.

Notable areas include the downtown urban core of Jacksonville, the government center, as well as Jacksonville Beach, Atlantic Beach, Neptune Beach, and Baldwin.

ESCAMBIA

Area: 762 square miles
Approx. elev: 20 ft.
Avg. temps: 53 Jan.
    81 Aug.
Avg. annual rain: 58.60 in.
1990 pop: 262,798
2000 pop: 294,410
2009 est. pop: 303,343

Spain, France, and England all owned portions of Escambia County at one time. It is the state's most western county. It is separated on the west from Alabama by the Perdido River; its southern boundaries front on the Gulf of Mexico.

Perdido Key and Santa Rosa Island stand between the Gulf and the county's major city, Pensacola. Also on the waterfront is the Pensacola Naval Air Station.

Pensacola is considered by many to be a military town because of its naval air station, numerous other, smaller, military installations in the county, and Eglin Air Force Base in adjoining Santa Rosa County.

Health care, chemicals, and paper products, along with tourism, are Escambia's other chief industries. The county hosts the University of West Florida. The major route into the county is I-10, with air service provided by Pensacola Regional Airport.

Largest incorporated places are Pensacola, the county seat, and Century.

FLAGLER

Area: 504 square miles
Approx. elev: 0-22 ft.
Avg. temps: 59 Jan.
        82 Aug.
Avg. annual rain: 50.74 in.
1990 pop: 28,701
2000 pop: 49,832
2009 est. pop: 91,622

Noted for its miles of pristine beaches, Flagler County is along the Atlantic Ocean on Florida's northeast coast.

Flagler, for the second consecutive decade, is Florida's fastest-growing county, its population jumping 74 percent over the past 10 years.

Yacht building, tourism, land development, and housing are the county's major industries. I-95 and U.S. 1 pass through the county. Air service is available 30 miles south at Daytona Beach Regional Airport.

Largest incorporated places are the new city of Palm Coast, already the second largest city in Northeast Florida; Flagler Beach; Bunnell, the county seat; and Beverly Beach.

FRANKLIN

Area: 565 square miles
Approx. elev: 0-24 ft.
Avg. temps: 54 Jan.
        82 Aug.
Avg. annual rain: 58.36 in.
1990 pop: 8,967
2000 pop: 11,057
2009 est. pop: 11,280

Sparsely populated Franklin County, in the Panhandle, is on Apalachicola Bay and buffered by the offshore St. George Island. Its interior is noted for the vast acreage of the Apalachicola National Forest and Tate's Hell Swamp.

Seafood is the county's primary industry. Passing near Franklin County is I-10. Its residents use air service at the Tallahassee Regional Airport 75 miles to the northeast.

Largest incorporated places are Apalachicola, the county seat, and Carrabelle.

GADSDEN

Area: 523 square miles
Approx. elev: 250-300 ft.
Avg. temps: 54 Jan.
        80 Aug.
Avg. annual rain: 56.02 in.
1990 pop: 41,105
2000 pop: 45,087
2009 est. pop: 47,474

Bordering the Georgia state line, Gadsden County was settled by wealthy slave owners, and the county is still famous for its large plantations and tobacco crop. The county harbors the huge Woodruff Dam, which now forms the headwaters of the Apalachicola River.

Gadsden is mostly rural, and its private employers include wholesale food distributors, mushroom growers, and makers of lumber, wire and nails, and furniture. Motoring routes into the county include I-10 and U.S. 90. Nearest air service is 20 miles away, at the Tallahassee Regional Airport.

Largest incorporated places are Quincy, the county seat, and Chattahoochee, Havana, Gretna, and Midway.

GILCHRIST

Area: 348 square miles
Approx. elev: 63 ft.
Avg. temps: 56 Jan.
          81 Aug.
Avg. annual rain: 54.76 in.
1990 pop: 9,667
2000 pop: 14,437
2009 est. pop: 17,116

A region of clear springs and rivers, Gilchrist County in north central Florida curves around both the Suwannee and Santa Fe rivers. It is a largely agricultural county, growing watermelons and dotted with dairies. It was the last of the state's counties to be formed.

Dairying and tourism are the county's primary industries. Because of its many crystal-clear springs, its rivers, and its uncrowded conditions, Gilchrist also is becoming a favorite homesite for retirees and for persons employed in nearby Gainesville. It is one of the few counties not traversed by a U.S. highway or Interstate. Nearest air service is 45 miles east at the Gainesville Regional Airport.

Largest incorporated places are Trenton, the county seat, Bell, and Fannin Springs.

GLADES

Area: 898 square miles
Approx. elev: 8-22 ft.
Avg. temps: 64 Jan.
          81.2 Aug.
Avg. annual rain: 49.95 in.
1990 pop: 7,591
2000 pop: 10,576
2009 est. pop: 10,950

One of five counties bordering Lake Okeechobee, Glades County also is the site of a large Seminole Indian reservation. Most of Glades' few residents live along the lakeshore. Its hinterland is occupied mostly by the Fisheating Creek Wildlife Refuge and Management Area. It is the least densely populated county on the peninsula with fewer than 12 persons per square mile.

Glades' largest product is sugarcane. U.S. 27, once the principal route through Florida, is the sole major highway through the county. Air service is either from Southwest Florida International far to the west, or Palm Beach International, far to the east.

Moore Haven, the only significant city in Glades County, is the county seat.

GULF

Area: 578 miles
Approx. elev: 15 ft.
Avg. temps: 54 Jan.
          82 Aug.
Avg. annual rain: 58.36 in.
1990 pop.: 11,504
2000 pop.: 13,332
2009 est. pop.: 15,755

Once an important cotton-shipping area, Gulf County also was the site of the state's first Constitutional Convention. It took place in 1838 in Port St. Joe, a city that was destroyed by a Yellow Fever epidemic and a tidal waves in 1841.

Gulf is a Panhandle county fronting on the Gulf of Mexico. But St. Joseph's Peninsula shelters much of its shoreline.

Paper is the county's biggest industry, followed by the transportation of crude oil, magnesium, and coal. The county's major motoring route is U.S. 98. Air service is available 40 miles to the west at the Northwest Florida Beaches

International Airport at Panama City.

Largest incorporated places rebuilt Port St. Joe, the county seat, and Wewahitchka.

HAMILTON

Area: 515 square miles
Approx. elev.: 152 ft.
Avg. temps: 54 Jan.
                81 Aug.
Avg. annual rain: 49.51 in.
1990 pop: 10,930
2000 pop: 13,327
2009 est. pop: 14,592

Site of the Stephen Foster Memorial and state park on the Suwannee River, Hamilton County shares its northern boundary with the state of Georgia. It is a small, lightly populated county, much of it covered in forests.

The primary private employer is the phosphate industry, although the county does have numerous vegetable-growing operations. The major thoroughfare through Hamilton is I-75 entering Florida through the county. The nearest large airport is Jacksonville International, some 90 miles to the east.

Canoeing the Suwannee River's whitewater shoals and the Withlacoochee River, the county's western boundary, are popular recreational activities.

Largest incorporated places are Jasper, the county seat, Jennings and White Springs.

HARDEE

Area: 630 square miles
Approx. elev.: 55 ft.
Avg. temps: 63 Jan.
                82 Aug.
Avg. annual rain: 58.07 in.
1990 pop.: 19,499
2000 pop.: 26,938
2009 est. pop.: 29, 415

Rural and locked into the south central section of the state, Hardee County is a citrus and cattle region. The county also calls itself the nation's cucumber capital.

Although agriculture in Florida is second in state income only to tourism, farm-rich Hardee's population decline in the 1980s but rebounded in the 1990s when it grew by 38 percent.

Largest industries are citrus growing and packing, and cattle ranching. The major highway through Hardee is U.S. 17, and the nearest air service is available either at Tampa International in adjoining Hillsborough County or at Sarasota/ Bradenton International in nearby Sarasota County.

Largest incorporated places are Wauchula, the county seat, Bowling Green and Zolfo Springs.

HENDRY

Area: 1,189 square miles
Approx. elev.: 12 ft.
Avg. temps: 64 Jan.
                81 Aug.
Avg. annual rain: 52.22 in.
1990 pop.: 25,773
2000 pop.: 36,210
2009 est. pop.: 39,594

Touching on Lake Okeechobee, Hendry County is best known for its rich mucklands and sugar

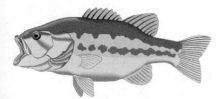

refineries. Big Cypress Seminole Indian reservation is in the county's southeast tip.

Sugar processing is by far the county's largest private industry, although employers also include truck cars and citrus growers.

It is the state's youngest county, with 30 percent of its population under the age of 15.

The county's only major highway is U.S. 27, which runs its northern boundary. Closest air service is 40 miles distant at the Southwest Regional Airport near Fort Myers.

Largest incorporated places are Clewiston and La Belle, the county seat.

HERNANDO

Area: 508 square miles
Approx. elev: 175 ft.
Avg. temps: 60 Jan.
　　　　81 Aug.
Avg. annual rain: 55.76 in.
1990 pop: 101,115
2000 pop: 130,802
2009 est. pop: 171,233

On the Gulf of Mexico and north of the Tampa Bay area, Hernando County's growth has been spurred by retirees and suburbanites. A considerable portion of the Withlacoochee State Forest is in the county, as is the famous Weekee Wachee Spring attraction.

Health care, electronics, mining and minerals, and tourism provide the county's economic base. I-75, U.S. 19, and the new Suncoast Parkway connect the county with the Tampa Bay metropolitan area to the south. Nearest major air service is at Tampa International, 45 miles distant.

Largest incorporated area is Brooksville, the county seat.

HIGHLANDS

Area: 1,119 square miles
Approx. elev: 150 ft.
Avg. temps: 63 Jan.
　　　　82 Aug.
Avg. annual rain: 52.22 in.
1990 pop: 68,432
2000 pop: 87,366
2009 est. pop: 98,704

Named for its rolling countryside, Highlands County in the south central area of Florida is the home of Sebring and that city's famous 24-hour auto endurance race. Near another of its cities, Avon Park, was a World War II air base that is now a tract for practice bombing.

The county is dotted with lakes, the largest being Lake Istokpoga near the city of Lake Placid. The county also is home to Highlands Hammock State Park, one of the nation's outstanding natural parks, with 3,800 acres of forests and plants.

Largest private employers are in health care, citrus, boat manufacturing, banking, and lawn supplies.

Major highways crossing the county are, from east to west, U.S. 98, and from north to south, U.S. 27. Air service is available at Orlando International, 80 miles to the north, and Sarasota/Bradenton International, 70 miles to the west.

Incorporated places include Sebring, the county seat, Avon Park and Lake Placid.

HILLSBOROUGH

Area: 1,062 square miles
Approx. elev: 15-121 ft.
Avg. temps: 60 Jan.
　　　　81.5 Aug.
Avg. annual rain: 48.48 in.
1990 pop: 834,054

2000 pop: 998,948
2009 est. pop: 1,195,317

Site of one of the state's most populous cities, Tampa, Hillsborough County on the state's west coast fronts on Tampa Bay, which funnels into the Gulf of Mexico. Tampa was once known as the Cigar City, and cigars still are hand-rolled there, but Tampa has become a primary service and financial center in the South.

Hillsborough also has a substantial international port in Tampa Bay and has what many travelers consider to be the nation's finest air terminal, Tampa International Airport.

Enthusiastic sports fans are entertained by professional sports and by being at the center of baseball's spring-training sites.

Private industry includes communications, air services, food processing, shipping, retail, banking, and tourism, with attractions such as Busch Gardens. Hillsborough also is home to the University of South Florida, second largest of the state's universities.

Major arteries into Hillsborough County include I-75 and I-4, U.S. 41 and 301, and the Suncoast Parkway.

Incorporated places in the county are Tampa, the county seat, Plant City, and Temple Terrace.

HOLMES

Area: 484 square miles
Approx. elev: 120 ft.
Avg. temps: 53 Jan.
            82 Aug.
Avg. annual rain: 57.40 in.
1990 pop: 15,778
2000 pop: 18,564
2009 est. pop: 19,099

Holmes County is in the Panhandle, bounded on the north by Alabama.

Rural and landlocked, Holmes depends on private employers in the clothing and health care fields for its economic base.

The major highway through Holmes is U.S. 90. Nearest air service is 45 miles away at Dothan, Alabama.

Largest incorporated places are Bonifay, the county seat, and Ponce de Leon, Esto, Westville, and Noma.

INDIAN RIVER

Area: 549 square miles
Approx. elev: 25 ft.
Avg. temps: 63 Jan.
            81 Aug.
Avg. annual rain: 52.84 in.
1990 pop: 90,208
2000 pop: 112,947
2009 est. pop: 135,167

Indian River County is halfway down the peninsula of Florida on the Atlantic Ocean and is most famous for its citrus products. Development has been along its eastern shore, with much of its increasing population settling across a causeway from the mainland to the ocean beachfront. The Indian River separates the mainland from the beach communities. Health care, airplane manufacturing, and citrus are the county's major industries.

Motoring routes into the county include I-95, U.S. 1, U.S. A1A, and Florida's Turnpike. Air service is available at the Vero Beach Municipal Airport and, 45 miles to the north, in adjacent Brevard County at Melbourne Regional Airport.

Largest incorporated places are Vero Beach, the county seat, and

Sebastian, Indian River Shores, Fellsmere, and Orchid.

JACKSON

Area: 938 square miles
Approx. elev: 120 ft.
Avg. temps: 53 Jan.
         81 Aug.
Avg. annual rain: 54.69 in.
1990 pop: 41,375
2000 pop: 46,755
2009 est. pop: 50,930

Jackson County is the only Florida county to border two states, Alabama and Georgia. It also is home to three scenic waterways—the Chattahoochee, the Flint, and the Apalachicola rivers.

The county also is known for Florida Caverns, a 1,217-acre state park. Indians used the caverns as refuge during skirmishes with U.S. Army troops, and those fleeing troops during the War Between the States also hid out in the underground chasms.

Major private industries in Jackson include the manufacturing of clothing, furniture, washing machines, and lumber. I-10 traverses the county, as does U.S. 90. The nearest airline service is 35 miles distant, at Dothan, Alabama.

Largest incorporated places are Marianna, the county seat, and Graceville, Sneads, Cottondale, and Malone.

JEFFERSON

Area: 609 square miles
Approx. elev: 202 ft.
Avg. temps: 53.5 Jan.
         80.5 Aug.
Avg. annual rain: 56.74 in.
1990 pop: 11,296
2000 pop: 12,902
2009 est. pop: 14,010

Jefferson County is the only county to extend from the Georgia state line to the Gulf of Mexico. Its largest city, and county seat, Monticello, is noted for its 19th-century architecture.

Like many north Florida counties, it is sparsely populated, mostly agricultural, and the rich solitude of its forests and streams remains largely undiscovered by tourists and retirees.

Major private employers are in clothing, nurseries, dairying, and food production. I-10 and U.S. 90 traverse the county. Nearest air service is 23 miles distant at the Tallahassee Regional Airport.

LAFAYETTE

Area: 554 square miles
Approx. elev: 69 ft.
Avg. temps: 55 Jan.
         81 Aug.
Avg. annual rain: 58.24 in.
1990 pop: 5,578
2000 pop: 7,022
2009 est. pop: 7,949

Considering Florida's tremendous growth since World War II, it is a near marvel that an area in the state more than 500 square miles in size has so few residents. Yet that is Lafayette County, in north central Florida.

One of the state's least densely populated counties, with only 13 people per square mile, Lafayette is known primarily for its hunting and fishing.

Flat and wooded, the county has many natural attractions, including numerous springs adjacent to the famous Suwannee River, which carves out Lafayette's eastern boundary. Employment, besides in agriculture (primarily dairying), centers on firms that build boats, pack seafood, and harvest timber.

The major artery into the county is U.S. 27. Air service is available at Gainesville Regional Airport about 65 miles to the east.

Mayo is the county's only incorporated city, and is the county seat.

LAKE

Area: 1,163 square miles
Approx. elev: 124 ft.
Avg. temps: 60 Jan.
82 Aug.
Avg. annual rain: 47.47 in.
1990 pop: 152,104
2000 pop: 210,528
2009 est. pop: 312,119

Centrally located in the state between the Gulf of Mexico and the Atlantic Ocean, Lake County is noted for its citrus groves and the estimated 1,440 lakes that dot its rolling landscape. Some residents swear that the county's relatively high altitude combined with its lakes produce warm winters and cool summers.

Major lakes such as Griffin, Yale, Eustis, Harris, Louisa, and Apopka make for excellent fishing in the county. Other recreational activity centers on the Ocala National Forest in Lake's northeast corner. Mount Dora is the state's antique capital.

Major private employment is in the citrus industry, but employers include those in metal fabrication, concrete, and mobile-home construction.

Florida's Turnpike and U.S. 27 are the county's major thoroughfares. Orlando International Airport, 45 miles distant, provides the nearest air service.

Largest incorporated places are Leesburg, Eustis, Mount Dora, Clermont, and Tavares, the county seat. Portions of the county are being drawn into the Orlando metropolitan area.

LEE

Area: 1,005 square miles
Approx. elev: 7 ft.
Avg. temps: 64 Jan.
81.5 Aug.
Avg. annual rain: 52.39 in.
1990 pop: 335,113
2000 pop: 440,888
2009 est. pop: 586,908

A well-known tourist center, Lee County is dominated by its major city, Fort Myers, famous as the winter home of inventor Thomas Edison. The southwest county fronting on the Gulf of Mexico also is known for its pair of enchanting offshore barrier islands, Sanibel and Captiva.

Lee's rapid growth, coupled with that of its neighboring counties, Charlotte and Collier, led to Lee being selected as the site of Florida Gulf Coast University.

The county's many bays and long coastline, along with the Caloo-sahatchee River (a waterway extending to the state's east coast), make Lee a paradise for water enthusiasts.

Major private employers are in health care, communications, foliage growing, and land developing.

Thoroughfares into the county include I-75 and U.S. 41. Residents are served by the area's Southwest Florida International Airport.

Largest incorporated places are Cape Coral, Sanibel, North Fort Myers and Fort Myers, the county seat.

LEON

Area: 696 square miles
Approx. elev: 192 ft.
Avg. temps: 52 Jan.
              81 Aug.
Avg. annual rain: 55.17 in.
1990 pop: 192,493
2000 pop: 239,452
2009 est. pop: 265,714

In what is known as the Big Bend area of the state and adjacent to the Georgia state line, Leon County is the site of the state's capital, Tallahassee. The site was so chosen because, at the time of achieving statehood in 1845, most Floridians lived in north Florida, and Tallahassee was midway between Pensacola and St. Augustine. It was the only state capital east of the Mississippi River not captured by Union forces during the War Between the States.

Leon is an old South county, with roads and farmland shaded by large oaks heavily draped in Spanish moss. Favorite fishing and boating spots are the Ochlockonee River, Lake Talquin, Lake Jackson, Lake Miccosukee, and the Apalachicola National Forest, which occupies roughly one-third of the county.

Largest employer is the state government and the two state universities in Tallahassee—Florida State and Florida A&M. Sizable private employers include those in health care, publishing, and printing.

Major roads into the county include I-10, U.S. 90, and U.S. 27. The county has its own airport, Tallahassee Regional.

Largest incorporated place is Tallahassee, both the county seat and the state capital.

LEVY

Area: 1,137 square miles
Approx. elev: 13-82 ft.
Avg. temps: 58 Jan.
              82 Aug.
Avg. annual rain: 45.30 in.
1990 pop: 25,923
2000 pop: 34,450
2009 est. pop: 39,147

A large, forested region, Levy County is a north central county on the Gulf of Mexico. Its famous offshore island, Cedar Key, used to be the southern terminus of the state's first railroad and now is a popular tourist retreat.

One of the state's most popular parks, Manatee Springs, is in Levy, along the Suwannee River that separates Levy from Dixie County.

Aside from agriculture and timber, private employers are few and mostly in services. The primary highway through Levy is U.S. 19, which runs southward from Tallahassee near the Georgia line to the Tampa Bay area. Air service is some 60 miles to the east, at Gainesville Regional Airport.

Largest incorporated places are Williston, Chiefland, Inglis, Cedar Key, and Bronson, the county seat.

LIBERTY

Area: 845 square miles
Approx. elev: 116 ft.
Avg. temps: 53 Jan.
              81.5 Aug.
Avg. annual rain: 58.94 in.
1990 pop: 5,569
2000 pop: 7,021
2009 est. pop: 7,983

Liberty County, in the Panhandle, is the state's least populated and least densely populated county with fewer than nine persons per square mile. Much of its area is devoted to forests and wildlife. Its quiet Southern charm makes it a paradise for woodlands lovers and botanists. The Apalachicola National Forest takes up more than half the county. Another large section is the Telogia Creek Wildlife Management Area. Torreya State Park also covers 1,063 acres of Liberty.

Adding to the county's undeveloped character is the Apalachicola River, Liberty's western boundary, and the Ochlockonee River, its eastern boundary. The Apalachicola River at one time was the main commercial water route through Florida from Georgia and Alabama to the Gulf of Mexico.

Largest employers are in health care and forestry. I-10 passes through Liberty County. The nearest air service is 45 miles distant, at the Tallahassee Regional Airport.

Bristol is the largest incorporated area and the county seat.

MADISON

Area: 708 square miles
Approx. elev: 133 ft.
Avg. temps: 55 Jan.
81 Aug.
Avg. annual rain: 52.50 in.
1990 pop: 16,569
2000 pop: 18,733
2009 est. pop: 18,901

Another largely agricultural Georgia border county, Madison County was on the route that Spanish explorer Hernando de Soto took northward into the U.S. hinterland. Near the county's main city, Madison, stood the Spanish mission of Santa Helena de Machaba. Madison County, like many north Florida counties, is geologically and socially more characteristic of the Deep South than of the Florida most tourists know.

Major private industries are in processed meats, poultry, and the manufacture of wheel covers, plywood, and furniture. I-10 and U.S. 90 are the county's primary highways and air service is available in the adjoining county at Tallahassee Regional Airport.

Incorporated places include Greenville, Lee, and Madison, the county seat.

MANATEE

Area: 772 square miles
Approx. elev: 9-17 ft.
Avg. temps: 61.5 Jan.
81 Aug.
Avg. annual rain: 54.60 in.
1990 pop: 211,707
2000 pop: 264,002
2009 est. pop: 318,361

Many believe Spanish explorer Hernando de Soto landed in Florida in Manatee County along the Manatee River near where it empties into the Gulf of Mexico.

The western and central regions of this coastal county, and Anna Maria Island are experiencing explosive growth while the county's eastern section remains agricultural.

The growth is fueled by the county's proximity to the adjacent Tampa Bay metropolitan area.

Major private employers produce citrus juice and boats, and provide health services. Thoroughfares through Manatee include I-75 and U.S. 41 and 301. Air service is provided by the Sarasota/ Bradenton International Airport.

Largest incorporated areas

are Bradenton, the county seat, Palmetto, Holmes Beach, Longboat Key, and Bradenton Beach.

MARION

Area: 1,652 square miles
Approx. elev: 100 ft.
Avg. temps: 59 Jan.
          81 Aug.
Avg. annual rain: 51.94 in.
1990 pop: 194,833
2000 pop: 258,916
2009 est. pop: 328,547

Marion County has become widely known as "Thoroughbred Country." Because of its peculiar limestone base soil, this central Florida county has proven an ideal place to breed and raise racehorses, several of them Kentucky Derby winners. It has more than 400 horse farms.

Marion, which grew by nearly a third in the 1990s, is the site of several nationally familiar attractions, including Silver Springs. Within its boundaries also is a large section of the Ocala National Forest.

Besides Thoroughbred breeders, private employers in Marion include those in lumber and wood, electronics, health care, fire and rescue equipment, van conversions, rubber hoses, and communication equipment.

Major thoroughfares are I-75, U.S. 441, 27 and 301. Metropolitan air service is available to the southeast at Orlando International Airport or to the north at Gainesville Regional Airport.

Incorporated areas include Ocala, the county seat, and Belleview, Dunnellon, Reddick, and McIntosh.

MARTIN

Area: 582 square miles
Approx. elev: 14 ft.
Avg. temps: 65 Jan.
          82 Aug.
Avg. annual rain: 49.79 in.
1990 pop: 100,900
2000 pop: 126,731
2009 est. pop: 139,794

On the lower east coast, Martin County is sandwiched by the Atlantic Ocean on the east and Lake Okeechobee on the west. Primary development of the county has occurred along the ocean coast. The population has nearly doubled in 20 years.

Residents take pride in the county's small but varied wildlife population, its high sand dunes along the shoreline, and its Hobe Sound National Wildlife Refuge.

Health care and aerospace, along with tourism, are the county's major private industries. Motor routes into Martin County include I-95, U.S. 1, and Florida's Turnpike. Air service is available 45 miles south at Palm Beach International Airport.

Incorporated areas include Stuart, the county seat, and Sewalls Point, Ocean Breeze Park, and Jupiter Island.

MIAMI-DADE

Area: 2,109 square miles
Approx. elev: 15 ft.
Avg. temps: 68 Jan.
          82 Aug.
Avg. annual rain: 57.77 in.
1990 pop: 1,937,094
2000 pop: 2,253,362
2009 est. pop: 2,500,625

Heart of the Gold Coast and most famous of Florida's regions is Miami-Dade County, its name recognizing its largest city and county seat. The area has become a truly cosmopolitan county, largely because of the influx of Cubans, West Indians, and Latin Americans. It is the state's largest county in population.

Professional sports fans enjoy local basketball, football, baseball, and hockey.

Like most east coast counties, Miami-Dade is heavily developed along its coast and sparsely populated in its western region because of massive wetlands.

Major private employers are centered on airlines, department stores, communications, banking, transportation, and food service. The county hosts Florida's largest private university, the University of Miami, as well as the state's Florida International University.

Highways into the county include I-95, U.S. 1, and Florida's Turnpike. Entering from the west is U.S. 41, the Tamiami Trail. The area is served by Miami International Airport.

Other incorporated places include Hialeah, Miami Beach, North Miami, and Coral Gables.

MONROE

Area: 1,418 square miles
Approx. elev: 10 ft.
Avg. temps: 70 Jan.
84 Aug.
Avg. annual rain: 38.03 in.
1990 pop: 78,024
2000 pop: 79,589
2009 est. pop: 73,165

The majority of Monroe County's land area is on the southwest tip of the Florida peninsula and separated from the county's Florida Keys, which comprise Monroe's main population centers.

The county portion on the

mainland is largely undeveloped and includes the Everglades National Park. The Florida Keys portion stretches some 100 miles into the Straits of Florida, which divide the Atlantic Ocean from the Gulf of Mexico.

Monroe enjoyed the slowest growth rate of any Florida county in the 1990s, its population increasing by only 2 percent. The population has fallen since the 2000 census.

Significant points of interest dot the Keys. They are the site of John Pennekamp Coral Reef State Park, featuring 100 square miles of living coral, and a half dozen wildlife refuges and other state parks. Dominating the county's seven Dry Tortugas Islands is the 19th-century Fort Jefferson, a massive coastal fort.

The Keys, particularly Key West, have blossomed from a sleepy, tropical paradise into a bustling spa where fishing, boating, and "good times" are primary pursuits.

Monroe is primarily a tourist area with few sizable employers or businesses. Access to the county is via U.S. 1, and air service is available at Key West International Airport or at Miami International to the north.

Incorporated areas include Key Colony Beach, Layton, and Key West, the county seat.

NASSAU

Area: 671 square miles
Approx. elev: 22 ft.
Avg. temps: 56 Jan.
81.5 Aug.
Avg. annual rain: 48.50 in.
1990 pop: 43,941
2000 pop: 57,663
2009 est. pop: 70,576

In the northeasternmost tip of the state, Nassau County is bordered on the east by the Atlantic Ocean, and on the north and west by the state of Georgia. The St. Mary's River forms the boundary between Georgia and Nassau County.

Nassau is steeped in history, and the area around one of its major attractions, Fort Clinch, has been under eight different flags.

Paper products and tourism are the area's primary economic ventures. Interstates 95 and 10, U.S. highways 1, 23, and 301, and State Highway A1A are the major thoroughfares into and through the county. The nearest airport, 25 miles to the south, is Jacksonville International.

Incorporated areas include Hilliard, Callahan, and Fernandina Beach, the county seat.

OKALOOSA

Area: 998 square miles
Approx. elev: 4-300 ft.
Avg. temps: 51 Jan.
            80 Aug.
Avg. annual rain: 63.70 in.
1990 pop: 143,776
2000 pop: 170,498
2009 est. pop: 178,473

Eglin Air Force Base embraces more than half of Okaloosa County, but the Panhandle county also is well known for its miles of beaches along the Gulf of Mexico and Choctawhatchee Bay. Its northern boundary is the state of Alabama. Development is restricted to the county's southeastern and central regions. Through the northern reaches flow the Yellow and Blackwater rivers, the latter coursing through the Blackwater River State Forest.

The beaches of Okaloosa are prized for their white quartz sand,

a much finer and whiter sand than that found on beaches in central and southern Florida.

Largest private employers are in electronics and health care. Major roads into the county are I-10, U.S. 98, and U.S. 90. Flights are available from the Okaloosa County Air Terminal.

Incorporated areas include Fort Walton Beach, Niceville, Valparaiso, Destin, and Crestview, the county seat.

OKEECHOBEE

Area: 780 square miles
Approx. elev: 27 ft.
Avg. temps: 63 Jan.
            81 Aug.
Avg. annual rain: 47.90 in.
1990 pop: 29,627
2000 pop: 35,910
2009 est. pop: 40,241

Named for the great lake that it borders, Okeechobee County in south central Florida is primarily agricultural. Its farms have rich organic soil and are noted for their winter vegetable crops.

Lake Okeechobee also provides commercial fishing. A shallow lake—its average depth measured at 14 feet—it is the largest U.S. lake without a natural outlet. The lake could be considered the county's sole tourist attraction since lake fishing is good the year around.

Okeechobee's economic base depends on agriculture and dairying, with the result that it has few sizable industries other than those associated with land use. Both Florida's Turnpike and U.S. 441 service motorists to the area. Air service is 56 miles distant at Palm Beach International Airport.

Largest incorporated area is Okeechobee, the county seat.

ORANGE

Area: 1,003 square miles
Approx. elev: 106 ft.
Avg. temps: 61 Jan.
        82 Aug.
Avg. annual rain: 52.35 in.
1990 pop: 677,491
2000 pop: 896,344
2009 est. pop: 1,086,480

Once noted almost entirely as a citrus center, Orange County, in central Florida, has been transformed into a highly urbanized area spurred by the many large tourist attractions that have located in its area, particularly Walt Disney World.

The millions of tourists flocking into Orange each year need not worry much about accommodations, because the county has more hotel rooms than New York City.

The county also boasts major private industries such as aerospace, communications, publishing, health care, and banking. It is the site of the University of Central Florida. Highways into the county include I-4, Florida's Turnpike, U.S. 17, and U.S. 441. The local airport is Orlando International Airport.

Largest incorporated areas are Winter Park, Ocoee, Apopka, Maitland, and Orlando, the county seat.

OSCEOLA

Area: 1,467 square miles
Approx. elev: 69 ft.
Avg. temps: 61 Jan.
        82 Aug.
Avg. annual rain: 50.06 in.
1990 pop: 107,728

2000 pop: 172,493
2009 est. pop: 270,618

Over the years Osceola County in central Florida has been devoted to cattle raising, but the county is rapidly being urbanized because of its proximity to Walt Disney World and other major attractions.

Cattle raising in past years covered two-thirds of Osceola, and the city of Kissimmee has been known as the "cow capital of Florida."

Western Osceola County is made up of Lake Kissimmee and the Kissimmee River, both important to the region's water resources.

Tourism, houseware products, electronics, molded injections, and food distribution, in addition to ranching, are the county's major industries.

I-4, Florida's Turnpike, and U.S. 192 are the county's primary roadways, with air service provided by nearby Orlando International Airport.

Incorporated areas include St. Cloud and Kissimmee, the county seat.

PALM BEACH

Area: 2,578 square miles
Approx. elev: 0-20 ft.
Avg. temps: 67 Jan.
        82 Aug.
Avg. annual rain: 59.44 in.
1990 pop: 863,518
2000 pop: 1,131,184
2009 est. pop: 1,279,950

Largest in size of all Florida counties, Palm Beach County runs to extremes—populous cities on the Atlantic coast and lush vegetable farms in its western region.

West Palm Beach on the inland waterway, and Palm Beach on the oceanfront, are well known to most tourists, but few visitors or residents venture into the county's vast hinterland that contains thousands of square miles of wetlands, wildlife refuges, and the Everglades.

Major private employers produce jet engines, computers, and sugar. Florida Atlantic University is located in Boca Raton. I-95, Florida's Turnpike, U.S. 1, and A1A are the county's major roads. Air service is available at Palm Beach International Airport.

Incorporated areas include Boca Raton, Boynton Beach, Delray Beach, Riviera Beach, and West Palm Beach, the county seat.

PASCO

Area: 772 square miles
Approx. elev: 0-100 ft.
Avg. temps: 60 Jan.
       81 Aug.
Avg. annual rain: 55 in.
1990 pop: 281,131
2000 pop: 344,765
2009 est. pop: 471,709

In the past 20 years large tracts that once were Pasco County farmland have been subdivided to provide homes for new residents in this fast-growing region in central Florida on the Gulf of Mexico.

Migration in past years has been mostly retirees, but more young families are moving in because the county's growth is fueling numerous service industries.

Melding into the metropolitan Tampa Bay area, Pasco also is home to thousands of workers who commute daily to St. Petersburg, Tampa and Lakeland.

Pasco is noted for the clarity and purity of its water. Major industries include citrus products, health care, and retailing. The southeast's largest Catholic university, St. Leo, is located here. Highways traversing Pasco are I-75, U.S. 19, 41 and 301, and the Suncoast Parkway. The nearest sizable airport is Tampa International, 35 miles to the south.

Incorporated areas include New Port Richey, Zephyrhills, Port Richey, St. Leo, San Antonio, and Dade City, the county seat.

PINELLAS

Area: 309 square miles
Approx. elev: 0-75 ft.
Avg. temps: 62 Jan.
       83 Aug.
Avg. annual rain: 54.53 in.
1990 pop: 851,659
2000 pop: 921,482
2009 est. pop: 909,013

A peninsula on the Florida peninsula, Pinellas County is nearly surrounded by water. To the east and south is Tampa Bay, to the west a string of barrier islands and the Gulf of Mexico. Pinellas has long been a favorite tourist and retirement center, but in the past decade has been luring the electronic and other clean industries for a more varied economic base.

Its major city, St. Petersburg, fronts on Tampa Bay and many rate the city's waterfront park facilities among the state's finest. A mile from the city's waterfront is the domed Tropicana Field, built at a cost of $138 million, home to the Tampa Bay Devil Rays major league baseball team.

Pinellas' vast waterfront, running south from Tarpon Springs past barrier islands and into Tampa Bay, has always been a major beacon for tourism. The unusual geography of the county also keeps attracting new residents, the result being that Pinellas is Florida's most densely populated county, with more than 3,000 people per square mile.

Largest private employers are in publishing, electronics, computers, and communications. Major highways into the county are I-275 and U.S. 19. St. Petersburg/Clearwater International Airport is mid-county; 15 miles to the east is Tampa International Airport.

Largest cities are St. Petersburg, Dunedin, Largo, Tarpon Springs, Pinellas Park, and Clearwater, the county seat.

POLK

Area: 2,048 square miles
Approx. elev: 115-215 ft.
Avg. temps: 61 Jan.
            82 Aug.
Avg. annual rain: 49.21 in.
1990 pop: 405,382
2000 pop: 483,924
2009 est. pop: 583,403

Midway between Tampa and Orlando, in central Florida, is Polk County, largest producer of citrus in the state.

A large county in size, Polk has varied assets for residents and tourists. Lakes proliferate in the region; the county is home to the Frank Lloyd Wright-designed Florida Southern College, and, together with Highlands County, it accommodates the military by providing it the Avon Park Bombing Range.

Polk's proximity to the Tampa Bay area and the Orlando area also has abetted the county's rapid development.

Besides citrus, major industries include phosphate mining, trucking, building supplies, and tourist attractions. I-4 and U.S. 27 are major routes through Polk County. Air service is available in the adjacent counties at Tampa International Airport and Orlando International Airport.

Incorporated areas include Lakeland, Winter Haven, Haines City, Lake Wales, and Bartow, the county seat.

PUTNAM

Area: 879 square miles
Approx. elev: 5 ft.
Avg. temps: 65 Jan.
            82 Aug.
Avg. annual rain: 49.79 in.
1990 pop: 65,070
2000 pop: 70,423
2009 est. pop: 72,893

Known for its bass fishing and azalea gardens, Putnam County in northeast Florida sidles along the St. Johns River. It is only 22 miles inland from the Atlantic Ocean, and 52 miles south of Jacksonville.

Part of the Ocala National Forest occupies Putnam, but the county is most sloganized as the "Bass Fishing Capital of the World." It is also famous for Ravine State Gardens, 182 acres of sub-tropical foliage highlighted by more than 100,000 azalea plants. Putnam is the center of the fern horticultural industry. Other major industries are pulp and paper making, and manufacturing of furniture, plywood, bags, boats, and concrete pipe.

The primary motoring route through Putnam is U.S. 17. Air service is available 70 miles to the north at Jacksonville International Airport.

Incorporated areas include Crescent City, Interlachen, Pomona Park, Welaka, and Palatka, the county seat.

ST. JOHNS

Area: 660 square miles
Approx. elev: 0-27 ft.
Avg. temps: 57 Jan.
             81 Aug.
Avg. annual rain: 48.25 in.
1990 pop: 83,829
2000 pop: 123,135
2009 est. pop.: 187,436

Steeped in exploration history, St. Johns County in northeast Florida on the Atlantic Ocean was fought for by the Spanish, the French, the English, and the Americans. The area around St. Augustine, the oldest city in the U.S., was first visited by Spanish explorer Ponce de Leon in 1513. The Castillo de San Marcos at St. Augustine is one of the best-preserved specimens of Middle Ages military architecture found in the New World.

Miles of unspoiled oceanfront beaches in St. Johns were "discovered" in the 1980s. The population grew 63 percent in that decade and again 47 percent in the last decade, setting off an almost continual battle between preservations and developers.

Tourism is a major industry, as are aeronautics, aluminum extrusion, auto parts manufacturing, and health food preparation. Major travel routes through the county are I-95, U.S. l, and A1A. Air service is 46 miles to the north at Jacksonville International Airport.

Incorporated places include Hastings, St. Augustine Beach, and St. Augustine, the county seat.

ST. LUCIE

Area: 626 square miles
Approx. elev: 5 ft.
Avg. temps: 65 Jan.
             82 Aug.
Avg. annual rain: 49.79 in.
1990 pop: 150,171
2000 pop: 192,695
2009 est. pop: 266,502

On the Atlantic Ocean, St. Lucie County has become a haven for tourists and new residents along its oceanfront, while its interior reaches remain used for citrus and truck crop production. St. Lucie's population growth rate has outpaced that of the state.

The Indian River separates the county's mainland from the main barrier island, Hutchinson.

Major private employers are in health care, communications, retailing, and citrus concentrate. Roadways traversing St. Lucie include I-95, Florida's Turnpike, and U.S. 1. Air service is available 60 miles to the south at Palm Beach International Airport.

Incorporated places include Port St. Lucie, St. Lucie Village, and Fort Pierce, the county seat.

SANTA ROSA

Area: 1,152 square miles
Approx. elev: 10 ft.
Avg. temps: 54 Jan.
             80.5 Aug.
Avg. annual rain: 58.85 in.
1990 pop: 81,608
2000 pop: 117,743
2005 est. pop: 151,759

Situated in the northwest Panhandle, Santa Rosa County is bounded on the north by Alabama and on the south by the Gulf of

Mexico. To its west is the busy Escambia River, and much of its eastern acreage is taken up by the Blackwater River State Forest.

Frontage on Santa Rosa Sound, part of the state's intracoastal waterway, is the county's main draw, although the county's economic base depends also on Eglin Air Force Base in the county's eastern region and Pensacola Naval Air Station in neighboring Escambia County. The Yellow and Blackwater rivers also course through the eastern area, emptying into East and Escambia bays.

Principal private industries include clothing, chemicals, medical services, oil and gas products, and agriculture. Motor routes into the county include I-10, U.S. 90, and U.S. 98, with air service provided by Pensacola Regional Airport 23 miles away.

Major incorporated areas are Jay, Gulf Breeze, and Milton, the county seat.

SARASOTA

Area: 563 square miles
Approx. elev: 18 ft.
Avg. temps: 61.5 Jan.
　　　　80 Aug.
Avg. annual rain: 57.11 in.
1990 pop: 277,776
2000 pop: 325,957
2009 est. pop: 369,765

Famous for its cultural activities and attractions such as the Ringling Museum of Art, Sarasota County on the central west coast of Florida also has some of the state's finest Gulf of Mexico beaches.

The county is known for its attractive barrier islands such as St. Armands Key, Longboat Key, Siesta Key, and Casey Key. All have been heavily developed the past 20 years. Population growth of the county also has spread eastward during the past decade into the county's woodlands, which feature the popular Myakka River State Park.

Tourism is a major industry, as are retailing, electronics, health care, banking, and real estate development. The state's New College is located in Sarasota. Major arteries into the county are I-75 and U.S. 41. Sarasota-Bradenton International provides air service.

Incorporated areas include North Port, its largest city; Venice; Longboat Key; and Sarasota, the county seat.

SEMINOLE

Area: 352 square miles
Approx. elev: 25 ft.
Avg. temps: 62 Jan.
　　　　82 Aug.
Avg. annual rain: 50.51 in.
1990 pop: 287,529
2000 pop: 365,196
2009 est. pop: 413,204

One of Florida's smaller counties, Seminole County is in the upper portion of central Florida near but not on the Atlantic Ocean. Its proximity to Orange County, with its Walt Disney World and other major attractions, and Brevard County with its space center, has changed Seminole County from an agricultural region to a cluster of urban centers, adding to metropolitan Orlando.

Industries include communications, food, electronics, housing, and telephone equipment. Motor routes through the county include I-4 and U.S. 17. Air service is available 15 miles away at Orlando International Airport. Its own Sanford-Orlando International Airport primarily serves as a gateway for foreign visitors.

Incorporated areas include Altamonte Springs, Winter Springs, Casselberry, Longwood, and Sanford, the county seat.

SUMTER

Area: 574 square miles
Approx. elev: 70 ft.
Avg. temps: 58 Jan.
          81 Aug.
Avg. annual rain: 51.44 in.
1990 pop: 31,577
2000 pop: 53,345
2009 est. pop: 77,681

Many Florida visitors have passed through Sumter County near the center of Florida's peninsula because it is the northern terminus of Florida's Turnpike. It has been known for decades for mining, principally limestone.

But in the past decade, visitors have stopped and stayed. The county's population grew another 20 percent since the last census as, primarily, retirees poured into its new, complete, communities.

The Dade Massacre occurred here in 1835, touching off the Second Seminole War in Florida. One of the state's four national military cemeteries, the Withlacoochee National Cemetery, is at Bushnell.

Home to the nation's largest federal prison complex and a major state prison, corrections is the county's biggest industry. Other industries include mining, rail transportation, trucking, meat products, pipe and tube manufacturing, and metal production. Both Florida's

Turnpike and I-75 traverse Sumter County, whose residents find the nearest air service 40 miles away at Orlando International Airport.

Incorporated areas include Wildwood, Coleman, Center Hill, Webster, and Bushnell, the county seat.

SUWANNEE

Area: 687 square miles
Approx. elev: 109 ft.
Avg. temps: 56 Jan.
          81 Aug.
Avg. annual rain: 49.60 in.
1990 pop: 26,780
2000 pop: 34,844
2009 est. pop: 40,149

Suwannee County is named after the famous river that forms the county's western boundary. Sparsely populated, the county is typical of many north Florida counties that have avoided over-population yet are rich in forests, rivers, lakes, and numerous clear springs.

Suwannee is best known among skin divers, fishermen, and hunters, but in recent years has attracted retirees from population centers such as Tampa, St. Petersburg, and Miami.

Major employers are in poultry, mining, boat manufacturing, and ornamental plants. I-10, I-75, and U.S. 90 are major roads through the county. Air service is available 60 miles away at Gainesville Regional Airport.

Incorporated places are Live Oak, the county seat, and Branford.

TAYLOR

Area: 1,052 square miles
Approx. elev: 47 ft.
Avg. temps: 56 Jan.
            81 Aug.
Avg. annual rain: 58.24 in.
1990 pop: 17,111
2000 pop: 19,256
2009 est. pop: 21,400

Calling itself the "Forest Capital of the World," Taylor County on the upper west coast of Florida has a vast Gulf of Mexico shoreline, but is known primarily as a county in which some 75 percent of its land area is in commercial forests.

Taylor also is popular among hunters, for much of the county is devoted to, besides forests, wildlife management refuges.

Industries include pulp and cellulose, construction, fencing and mulch, pyrotechnics, and lumber. The primary highway through the county is U.S. 19. Air facilities are available at Tallahassee Regional Airport 55 miles to the north.

Perry, the county seat, is the county's only sizable incorporated population center.

UNION

Area: 245 square miles
Approx. elev: 141 ft.
Avg. temps: 56 Jan.
            81 Aug.
Avg. annual rain: 49.40 in.
1990 pop: 10,252
2000 pop: 13,442
2009 est. pop: 14,584

Smallest of all Florida counties in area, Union County in north central Florida devotes most of its land to commercial forests. It also has several large state prison facilities, so that most of the county's labor force is employed by the state.

Industries center on lumber, clothing, trucking, and health care. No major highways traverse Union County, only state roads, and air service is 25 miles to the south at Gainesville Regional Airport.

Its incorporated places are Worthington Springs, Raiford, and Lake Butler, the county seat.

VOLUSIA

Area: 1,207 square miles
Approx. elev: 40 ft.
Avg. temps: 59 Jan.
            81.5 Aug.
Avg. annual rain: 53.36 in.
1990 pop: 370,712
2000 pop: 443,343
2009 est. pop: 496,890

Tourism is one of Volusia County's biggest assets, brought about primarily by the famous hard sand beaches at Daytona Beach. The county, on the northeast coast, has a vast Atlantic Ocean shoreline and is within a short distance of major attractions in Orange County and the space center in adjacent Brevard County.

Development has occurred on the county's east coast and in its western reaches, the central area dotted primarily by wetlands and wildlife refuges.

Primary industries are medical supplies, electronics, citrus juices, acoustics, plastics, and transportation. I-4 and I-95 pass through Volusia County, as do U.S. 1 and U.S. 92. The county has its own air services at Daytona Beach International Airport.

Incorporated areas include Daytona Beach, Port Orange,

Ormond Beach, New Smyrna Beach, and DeLand, the county seat.

WAKULLA

Area: 635 square miles
Approx. elev: 8 ft.
Avg. temps: 54 Jan.
          81 Aug.
Avg. annual rain: 54.03 in.
1990 pop: 14,202
2000 pop: 22,863
2009 est. pop: 32,815

A heavily wooded, still sparsely populated region, Wakulla County in the Panhandle saw its population grow 61 percent in the 1990s. It is famous for one of the world's largest spring basins, its low crime rate, its high graduation rate, and its relatively low cost of living. Much of the county is part of the Apalachicola National Forest, while its southern boundary on the Gulf of Mexico is noted for fishing and seafood.

New economy industry and suburban housing have joined commercial fishing in providing much of the area's revenue.

U.S. 90 runs across the county, which is served by air by the Tallahassee Regional Airport 25 miles to the north.

Incorporated places are Sopchoppy, St. Marks, and Crawfordsville, the county seat.

WALTON

Area: 1,135 square miles
Approx. elev: 266-345 ft.
Avg. temps: 53 Jan.
          81 Aug.
Avg. annual rain: 65.70 in.
1990 pop: 27,760
2000 pop: 40,601
2009 est. pop: 55,105

The highest elevation in Florida is in Walton County, at a site 345 feet above sea level. Much of the western portion of this Panhandle county is included in the sprawling Eglin Air Force Base.

Walton County is bordered on the north by Alabama, and on the south by the Gulf of Mexico. Its most famous attraction is Grayton Beach State Recreational Area, 356 acres of beach, sloping sand dunes, pine woodlands, and lakes.

Industries include poultry, clothing, orthopedic supplies, and health care. Major motoring routes through the county are I-10 and U.S. 90. Air service is available 35 miles away at Okaloosa County Air Terminal.

Incorporated places are Freeport, Paxton, and DeFuniak Springs, the county seat.

WASHINGTON

Area: 611 square miles
Approx. elev: 75 ft.
Avg. temps: 52.5 Jan.
          81 Aug.
Avg. annual rain: 60.20 in.
1990 pop: 16,919
2000 pop: 20,973
2009 est. pop: 23,916

Travelers through this modestly populated Panhandle county can become confused because the shape of Washington County is such that motorists leave Washington, enter Holmes County, then find themselves re-entering Washington County.

The county is populated by small towns, their surroundings devoted mostly to farms and rural pursuits. Its western boundary is the Choctawhatchee River.

Private employers include makers

of bed products, clothing, and turbine engines. I-10 and U.S. 90 cross the northern section of the county. Air travelers pick up flights 40 miles distant at the Northwest Florida Beaches International Airport.

Incorporated places are Vernon, Caryville, Wausau, Ebro, and Chipley, the county seat.

HURRICANE EVACUATION

Florida counties have hurricane evacuation plans established, but experts point out that such evacuations would likely take hours. In Key West, for instance, where only the Overseas Highway is available to motorists, officials estimate it would take more than 16 hours to remove a hurricane-threatened population. Panama City's limited access to the mainland would require more than 22 hours to completely evacuate, and it would take about 15 hours, estimate the experts, to move St. Petersburg/Clearwater residents safely inland.

PIEDMONT FLORIDA

Five Florida counties, Jackson, Gadsden, Leon, Jefferson, and Madison, all near the Georgia border, were dubbed "Piedmont Florida" by the 19th-century writer Sidney Lanier. This 150-mile stretch is one of the state's most beautiful regions, with rich red clay soils, numerous lakes, springs, and lush hills that display brilliant autumn colors.

DEADLY

Persons convicted of committing a capital crime in Florida are most likely to receive the death penalty in Pinellas County, according to a Columbia University Law School study.

OLDEST COUNTY

Collier County is the state's "oldest" with a median age of 53.9 years. Hendry County is the state's "youngest" with a median age of 29.57 years.

FORESTS

Florida's forests occupy 47 percent of the state's total land area. Over the past 50 years, however, Florida has experienced nearly a six-fold increase in population, particularly in the southeast. Land use changes associated with this population growth and urban buildup gradually have reduced the size of the state's forest resources.

With about 35 million acres of land, Florida has 14 of its 16 million forest acres classed as commercial. Most of this commercial timber acreage is held by thousands of private owners, 25 percent by governments. The most heavily forested area is the northwest section of the state, where commercial forests occupy 75 percent of the land area. Northeast Florida also is heavily forested, with 70 percent of its land occupied by commercial forests. Much timberland in this section of the state has been cleared for pasture. Reforesting involves planting 135 million trees per year and has kept forestland acreage stable since the 1980s.

Pulpwood remains Florida's leading forest product, accounting for 62 percent of each year's total timber output. More than 40,000 persons are directly employed by industries based on forest production in the state, including 99 sawmills and planning mills serving more than a thousand wood-product manufacturers. Forestry is a $6-billion annual industry in the state.

NATIONAL FORESTS

APALACHICOLA NATIONAL FOREST was established in 1936 and covers 564,000 acres in the northern section of the state. It is primarily a pine hardwood forest, and offers natural sinks, bottomland, and hardwood swamps along large rivers. The forest rivers and tributaries provide miles of fishing, mainly bass, bream, and perch. Other popular forest pursuits are hunting for quail, deer, and bear, as well as boating and swimming. Camping and picnic sites are numerous and hotels are not far away in the nearby towns of Apalachicola, Blountstown, Bristol, and Tallahassee.

CHOCTAWHATCHEE NATIONAL FOREST, in the Panhandle's Okaloosa and Walton counties, was deeded to the federal park system near the turn of the century, but in the 1940s much of its acreage was transferred to the War Department for use as Eglin Air Force Base. Only about 1,000 acres of the forest now remain outside the base. Rocky Bayou State Recreation Area, a state park, is in the forest so most of the forest's recreational activities are administered by the state park system.

OCALA NATIONAL FOREST, established in 1908, is a camper's paradise, mainly because of two famous springs, Juniper and Alexander. Other springs and large clear-flowing streams are scattered throughout the forest's 366,000 acres. A sub-tropical wilderness, the Ocala offers much botanical growth among its palms, hardwoods, and pines. Annual large game hunts are permitted in the forest by the wildlife management. Hunting camps, plus swimming and camping sites, are plentiful. The Paisley Woods Bicycle Trail offers a 22-mile run. Commercial accommodations are nearby just outside the forest.

OSCEOLA NATIONAL FOREST, near Jacksonville and Lake City, with 200,000 acres, is the smallest of the three major national forests. It is flat country, abundant with ponds, sinks, and cypress swamps, and a state breeding ground for game. Hunting of deer, quail, and dove is permitted but controlled. Best fishing is for bass, perch, and bream. Camping and picnicking sites are available.

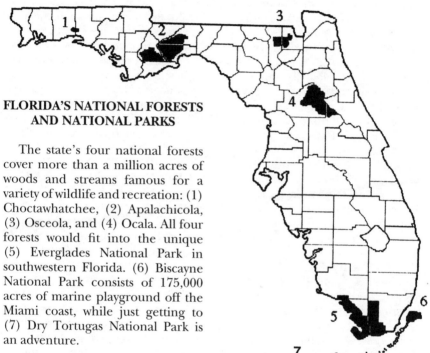

FLORIDA'S NATIONAL FORESTS AND NATIONAL PARKS

The state's four national forests cover more than a million acres of woods and streams famous for a variety of wildlife and recreation: (1) Choctawhatchee, (2) Apalachicola, (3) Osceola, and (4) Ocala. All four forests would fit into the unique (5) Everglades National Park in southwestern Florida. (6) Biscayne National Park consists of 175,000 acres of marine playground off the Miami coast, while just getting to (7) Dry Tortugas National Park is an adventure.

NATIONAL SEASHORES

CANAVERAL NATIONAL SEA-SHORE is a largely undeveloped wetland covering 57,000 acres in parts of two counties, Volusia and Brevard, next door to the Kennedy Space Center. Established by Congress in 1975, the preserve offers 26 miles of beaches along the Atlantic Ocean that include Playalinda, Apollo, and Klondike.

GULF ISLANDS NATIONAL SEASHORE, including Perdido Key, are offshore islands preserved by a 1971 congressional act setting aside these 139,776 acres along the northwest Florida Gulf coast, along with coastal acreage in Alabama and Mississippi. The Florida segment includes white-sand beaches and sea-oat-covered dunes along the shores of Escambia, Santa Rosa, and Okaloosa counties. Outstanding beaches include 14 miles of shoreline on Perdido Key, 17 miles of Gulf frontage at Fort Pickens, and 18 miles of beachfront on Santa Rosa Island. Eighty percent of the reserve is submerged.

NATIONAL PRESERVES

BIG CYPRESS NATIONAL PRE-SERVE was set aside by Congress in 1974 as a buffer zone to the northwest section of the adjacent Everglades National Park. Subtropical plant and animal life abounds in the preserve, the ancestral home of the Seminole and Miccosukee Indians.

TIMUCUAN NATIONAL PRE-SERVE is 46,000 acres at Jacksonville filled with historical sites including Kingsley Plantation, the last remaining plantation home in Florida, as well as its auxiliary buildings, including 23 remaining slave quarters. It also includes three significant and accessible natural areas, the Theodore Roosevelt Forest, Cedar Point and the Broward Islands, and the Thomas Creek historical Revolutionary War site. The Fort Caroline National Memorial is also in the Timucuan Preserve

NATIONAL PARKS

BISCAYNE NATIONAL PARK was set aside in 1968 as a national monument. Its 181,500 acres of water, reefs, and barrier islands were renamed a national park in 1980. Only 5 percent of the park consists of land, making it the largest marine park under the protection of the National Park Service. In the southern portion of Maimi-Dade County, Biscayne is best known for tropical fish, shipwrecks, living coral, and birds, and is a haven for scuba diving, fishing, and boating. Four presidents also have used the park as a vacation site.

EVERGLADES NATIONAL PARK, sprawling over more than 1.4 million acres, is the largest subtropical wilderness in the U.S. Concern for the Everglades led Congress in 1947 to declare the area in Florida's southern tip as a national park, the first park ever established for purely ecological reasons. Among the park's resources are more than 300 species of birds, 1,000 varieties of seed-bearing plants, 120 species of trees, 25 different types of orchids, 465,000 acres of sawgrass or freshwater marsh, and 230,000 acres of mangrove forest. All but 7 percent of the Everglades' million-plus acres are designated as wilderness. For park visitors, each season has its own advantage. The winter dry season is the best time to see abundant wildlife, while the summer's wet months provide calmer waters and better fishing.

FORT JEFFERSON AND DRY TORTUGAS NATIONAL PARK is one of the most unusual. The fort is the largest 19th-century coastal fort built in the U.S. It is 68 miles west of Key West at Tortugas Harbor on Garden Key. At one time, it was considered the "Key to the Gulf of Mexico."

The park's seven small islands are reachable only by commercial seaplane or ferry from Key West. Self-contained private boats may also visit, but only under stringent navigation and anchorage rules. Garden Key is open during daylight hours year round. The first tier of the fort may be toured, and it contains the park's visitors center, museum, and basic public facilities. A limited number of primitive campsites are sometimes available on Garden Key, and when camping is allowed, it is on a first-come first-served basis, with reservations strongly suggested. Loggerhead, East, and Middle keys are open during daylight hours year round, while Bush Key is closed to visitors from March through September to protect nesting birds.

Hospital and Long keys are closed at all times. There is no transportation provided to keys other than Garden. Because of its location, the park is vulnerable to winter and to tropical storms, leaving only April and May idyllic for visitors.

The six-sided brick fort, surrounded by a moat 70 feet wide and 30 feet deep, has a perimeter of one-half mile and covers most of the 16-acre key. From base to crown, its eight-foot-thick walls stand 50 feet high, its massive foundations resting on coral rock and sand 10 feet below sea level. It has three gun tiers designed for 450 cannons and was intended to garrison 1,500 men. Within the court are the foundations of the three-story officer and enlisted men's quarters, unfinished powder magazines, and two restored buildings.

Started by the U.S. in 1846, construction went on for nearly 30 years but was never completed. Obstacles were almost insurmountable—ships, money, and cargoes were lost in making the hazardous 1,500-mile voyage from eastern seaports. In addition, workmen found it difficult to withstand the subtropical heat, disease, and poor food. The site also was regularly swept by hurricanes.

The selection of Garden Key for the great fort was inevitable. Past this point sailed ships carrying the growing commerce of the Mississippi Valley and there were still keen memories of Gen. Andrew Jackson's fight with the British at New Orleans. Britain, too, in the mid-1800s was developing her West Indies possessions. And Texas, a new republic, seemed about to form an alliance with France or England and thus provide Europeans a foothold on the Gulf Coast.

Despite its strategic location, however, the fort never played a significant role in American history. The British ceased to be a threat in the northern Gulf region after their disastrous invasion attempt at New Orleans in 1815. Fort Jefferson was only half-completed when war broke out between the North and South, but to prevent its seizure by Florida secessionists, federal troops hurriedly occupied it. Following the war, little more was done to complete the fort. Engineers realized that the foundation was unstable as the huge structure settled and walls began to crack.

For almost 10 years after the war, the uncompleted Fort Jefferson was used as a prison. Among the prisoners sent there were four of the so-called "Lincoln Conspirators," those accused of plotting with John Wilkes Booth to kill the president and prominent members of his Cabinet.

Because of hurricane damage and persistent yellow fever outbreaks, Fort Jefferson finally was abandoned in 1874. It was reactivated briefly in 1898 as a naval base and was the departure point for the ill-fated battleship *Maine,* which blew up in Havana Harbor soon afterward. The mysterious explosion was blamed on Spain and precipitated the Spanish-American War. The fort has seen only sporadic and brief military use since World War I.

NATIONAL SANCTUARY

FLORIDA KEYS MARINE SANCTUARY was established by Congress in 1990 and is the nation's ninth and largest U.S. marine sanctuary, covering 2,800 nautical square miles. The designation calls Florida's coral reefs, mangrove islands, and seagrass beds "the marine equivalent of the tropical rain forests." Beginning at Biscayne National Park southeast of Miami, the sanctuary stretches along the Atlantic Ocean side of the Florida Keys all the way to Fort Jefferson National Monument some 70 miles west of Key West. On the Gulf of Mexico side, the sanctuary runs from Fort Jefferson to Everglades National Park on the tip of the Florida Peninsula. Boundaries of the sanctuary end where the water reaches a depth of 300 feet, which is about 10 miles out from shore on either side of the Keys.

STATE FORESTS

During the Great Depression, the federal government bought thousands of Florida acres for reclamation and resettlement projects. They became the nucleus of the state's forest system. Today, more than 837,000 Florida acres are set aside as state forests. In all, there are 34 such forests with more in development.

State Forest	Acreage	County
Blackwater River	189,594	Santa Rosa/Okaloosa
Withlacoochee	155,270	Citrus/Hernando/Pasco/Sumter
Tate's Hell	144,508	Franklin/Liberty
Picayune Strand	65,436	Collier
Goethe	50,177	Levy
John M. Bethea	37,736	Baker
Okaloacoochee Slough	32,039	Collier/Hendry
Tiger Bay	23,432	Volusia
Seminole	22,625	Lake
Jennings	20,623	Clay
Lake Wales Ridge	20,290	Polk
Lake George	19,610	Volusia
Lake Talquin	16,327	Gadsden/Leon
Point Washington	15,049	Walton
Twin Rivers	14,775	Hamilton/Madison/Suwanee
Four Creeks	13,147	Nassau
Belmore	8,736	Clay
Etoniah Creek	8,608	Putnam
Myakka	8,593	Charlotte/Sarasota
Pine Log	6,911	Bay/Washington
Ross Prairie	5,092	Marion

Little-Big Econ	5,045	Seminole
Matanzas	4,699	St. Johns
Ralph E. Simmons	3,638	Nassau
Cary	3,413	Nassau/Duval
Welaka	2,288	Putnam
Big Shoals	1,629	Hamilton
Wakulla	1,430	Wakulla
Deep Creek*	380	St. Johns
Carl Duval Moore	306	Putnam
Watson Island*	276	St. Johns
Woodville	73	Leon
Holopaw*	58	Osceola
Cottage Hill	31	Escambia
*Currently not accessible to public due to location		

SPECIES OF TREES

Florida is the most prolific tree flora state in the continental United States. There are about 314 species growing in this state, comprising almost half of all the varieties in North America north of Mexico.

The state's tree flora can be divided into four primary divisions: sweet gum, gum maple, tulip tree, and slash pine in the north; a southern division composed of longleaf pine, magnolia, and cypress; a Caribbean representation including royal palm, mahogany, and gumbo limbo; and an endemic representation such as Florida yew, dune holly, and Florida hickory.

Pine species generally are the most prolific, valuable, and versatile of all Florida tree species. Following are some of the most common trees found in the state.

AMERICAN BEECH occurs in alluvial soils in middle and western Florida. It is found scattered among other hardwood trees and sometimes makes small groups in pure stands. It drops its leaves in autumn but is one of the most beautiful of all trees, in summer or winter. The bark of this tree is perhaps its most distinctive characteristic, remaining an unbroken light gray throughout the tree's life. Wood of this tree is very hard and is of some value as lumber, although it will not stand up to weather or to being in soil.

ACACIA grows to only about 20 feet in height, but is a favorite in the southern regions in the state as a decorative tree. Its fernlike leaves and puffy, golden flowers make it pretty; its branches bear thorns. If kept trimmed, the acacia may also be used as a hedge.

AMERICAN ELM, sometimes called White Elm, is a famous shade tree that ranges from New England to the Rocky Mountains and southward to Texas. In low ground on river banks it is found in Florida to the Everglades. It reaches an average height of 60 to 70 feet and a diameter of four to five feet. The elm's wood is heavy, hard, strong, and difficult to split. It is used for wheel hubs, saddle trees, boats, barrel hoops, and as veneer for baskets and crates.

AMERICAN HOLLY is a Florida native evergreen that is becoming increasingly rare. It seldom reaches more than 30 feet tall, and has been considerably cut for Christmas decoration. Its leaves feature spiny points and in the fall it bears a red or yellow berry. Wood of the larger trees is favored for cabinetry.

AMERICAN SWEETGUM, or Red or Sweet Gum, is a large valuable forest tree. It occurs on hammocks, rich river bottoms, and in swamps, as well as on drier lands as far south as Cape Canaveral and Tampa Bay. It is usually abundant in second growth on old fields and in cutover woods. In the fall its coloring is brilliant, ranging from pale yellow through orange and red to a deep bronze. Wood of this tree is not durable, but is used for flooring, interior finish, and for pulp.

BALD CYPRESS is a swamp-dwelling tree found throughout the South. It can grow to 150 feet tall and is a member of the pine family. This tree's unusual feature is a "knee" that emerges from the water. These knees release oxygen and provide the mother tree with carbon dioxide. Bald cypress will grow on dry land, but do not have knees. These trees are virtually immune to serious pests and diseases. The wood is very durable and good for use in contact with soil and weathers very well for use in shingles or siding.

BIGLEAF MAGNOLIA is a magnolia with extraordinarily large leaves, 20 to 30 inches long with a 10-inch width. The tree is medium-sized, reaching a height of 30 to 40 feet, with a straight trunk up to 12 to 16 inches in diameter, ending in stout, noticeably wide-spreading branches. The tree is sparsely found over western and middle Florida in good soils with plenty of moisture. Flowers of this magnolia are white, nine to 12 inches across, with a pleasant fragrance.

BLACK WILLOW is common along streams throughout the northern part of the state. It grows to 65 feet in height and is usually found growing singly or in clumps along watercourses. The tree's bark is deeply divided into broad, flat ridges that separate into thick platelike scales. Older trees have a distinctly shaggy appearance. Its color varies from light brown tinged with orange to dark brown or nearly black. The wood is soft, light, and not strong. A high grade of charcoal, used in the manufacture of gunpowder, is obtained from willow wood, and it has been used in the manufacture of artificial limbs. The tree is especially valued for checking soil erosion along stream banks.

BLUEJACK OAK is a small, shrubby tree with a short, irregular, black trunk and an open crown. Spread by underground runners, it often forms thickets in well-drained sandy ridges and pineland flats in north-central Florida. Its most common use is for fuel.

BOXELDER is a fairly rapid-growing tree found sparsely in north Florida and in the upper part of the peninsula. It favors hammocks and river banks and is a true maple with the difference that it has a compound leaf. It is a tree of medium size, rarely reaching over 24 inches in diameter and 60 to 70 feet in height. It has been planted for shade because in good soil its growth is rapid. It is not long-lived or generally satisfactory for any purpose and reproduces quickly. It is often destroyed by grazing or cultivation.

BUCKWHEAT TREE, or Titi, a small tree, is common along Florida's swamps, ponds, and bays. In such areas it often forms dense thickets over the coastal region and somewhat inland over the pine barrens. Titi occasionally reach a height of 40 feet, but usually do not exceed 25 feet. The trunk is small, inclined, or crooked, and divides at a height of 10 to 15 feet into numerous branches.

CABBAGE PALMETTO is a member of the palm family. It is named from its large leaf-bud or "cabbage" at the top of the trunk, which can be cooked and eaten as a vegetable. The loss of the bud causes a branching, if not the tree's death. Like lilies, grasses, and corn, the palms grow outward from many bundles of tissues located centrally within the trunk. This is unlike the growth of pines, gums, oaks, and many other trees that yearly form a ring of wood. Cabbage Palmetto can grow 50 to 80 feet high with a straight, clear trunk up to two feet in diameter, covered with shallow ridges and fissures. It grows in sandy soil or hammocks over most of the coast, including the Keys north to the Apalachicola River.

CAROLINA LAURELCHERRY is a handsome tree with dark green leaves and much-planted for ornamental purposes. The laurel cherry, or mock orange, is native as far south as Biscayne Bay and the Kissimmee River. It prefers river banks and the borders of hammocks, and is abundant in the Orange County area. The trunk is straight or leaning, up to 40 feet in height. It is also some 10 inches in diameter, but the wood has no special uses.

CHICKASAW PLUM is found from central Florida north, usually in woodlands and hammocks. It is a spectacular spring flowering tree, with branches covered in small white blooms that precede the emergence of new leaves. In summer, a reddish-yellow berry becomes a favorite of birds. Although the fruit is acidic and sour, some persevering cooks create a tasty jam with it. These trees grow to about 25 feet tall.

CHINKAPIN is sometimes a shrub, but as a small tree, it grows up to 30 feet in height, with a trunk 18 inches in diameter. It forms dense thickets in sandy or rich soils at the edge of swamps or on hillsides in north and west Florida. Known for its durable wood, especially in contact with the ground, it's good for poles, posts, and crossties.

COMMON PERSIMMON, often called "simmon," is well known throughout the southern United States. It is usually medium sized, rarely exceeding 60 feet in height and 18 inches in diameter, and occurs throughout the state. It prefers open, sandy woods and is most abundant in old fields, though it may be found on hammocks and rich bottomlands. Timber from this tree is valued for making golf-stick heads.

COMMON SASSAFRAS is a small, aromatic tree, usually not over 40 feet in height or one foot in diameter. It is found throughout northern and central parts of the state in woods and fields and is one of the first broad-leaf trees to come up on abandoned fields, where the seeds are dropped by birds. It is closely related to red bay and the camphor tree of Japan. The root of this tree yields an aromatic oil used for flavoring.

FALSE MANGROVE, also called Buttonwood or White Mangrove, is a tree of the muddy tidal shores of bays and lagoons from Cape Canaveral on the east coast and Cedar Key on the west coast, south over the Keys, reaching greatest abundance and largest size in or near Monroe County. It attains heights up to 60 feet and diameters up to 20 inches, although generally smaller. Wood of this tree contains high amounts of tannin, used for tanning leather.

FLORIDA FISHFUDDLETREE, or Jamaica Dogwood, is one of the most abundant tropical trees and most valuable timber producers in subtropical Florida. It occurs on hammocks over the coastal shores and Keys from Bay Biscayne to Cape Sable. The tree grows rapidly and reaches heights up to 50 feet with trunks from two or three feet in diameter.

FLORIDA MAPLE, or Southern Sugar Maple, closely resembles the well-known northern sugar maple, and extends into the state from Georgia and Alabama. It is found on hammocks and good forest soil, reaching a height rarely over 50 feet, with a trunk up to two feet in diameter. Leaves turn yellow or scarlet during autumn.

FLORIDA POISONTREE, or Hog Gum, is a very common, medium-sized tree with poisonous properties. It is found on hammocks along the shores south from Bay Biscayne and over the Keys. It reaches heights of 30 to 40 feet with a short trunk up to two feet in diameter. The bark exudes a milky caustic or burning juice. It has emetic or purgative properties.

FLOWERING DOGWOOD, prevalent north of Orange County, is one of the state's most spectacular flowering trees. It is one of the most popular landscaping trees and its flowering habits tend to overwhelm the fact that its wood is valuable. This tree can be found on a wide variety of soils and will bloom heavily in gardens, street plantings, or in forests. In Florida west of the Ocklockonee River, an occasional fragrant specimen can be found; and a few rare trees bloom with pink or a light red color.

HAMMOCK HICKORY, or Florida Pignut, is a common hickory on the hammocks of Florida north of the Everglades. The tree usually reaches 40 to 80 feet, with a trunk of one to two feet in diameter. It is covered with medium gray, comparatively thin bark close and tight to the tree, and is broken into shallow furrows and small ridges. The branchlets are bright reddish-brown and smooth, which is one of the guides for identifying this tree.

HAWTHORN shows up with a number of species distributed throughout north and central portions of the state. About 50 species are known to occur in Florida on the poorest, richest, shallowest, and deepest soil regions, as well as on limestone hills or rich bottom and swamp land. Most forms have a common likeness, possessing thorns and bearing white blossoms and red or yellow fruit. Some species are planted as ornamentals, but otherwise the group is of little commercial value.

JUNGLEPLUM, Mastic or Wild

Olive, is a large, valuable timber tree growing along the state's coast from Brevard and Lee counties south into the Keys. It grows to 70 feet high with a large, straight trunk from three to four feet in diameter. Fruit of this tree is enjoyed by some people and its wood is used for boat building.

LAUREL OAK, a common but beautiful oak, is generally distributed and found on stream banks except in the extreme southern regions of the state. Laurel Oaks can reach 100 feet with a three- to four-foot diameter. It is especially valued as a shade tree.

LINDEN, also called Basswood or Wahoo, is a distinctive forest tree that appears in at least four species over northern or central Florida and into the Panhandle. They are common and valuable timber trees that attain heights of 70 feet and diameters of two feet. Outer bark from this tree is used for making rough camp buildings.

LIVE OAK can be found throughout Florida except for some of the Keys. Its habit of spreading, sometimes to 100 feet, makes it a striking shade tree. Live oak trunks may be three to four feet in diameter and divide into many limbs. This tree is slow growing but highly desirable.

LOBLOLLY PINE is also called Oldfield Pine and is an important tree throughout most of the South. Loblolly is most common in north Florida, often along streams and rivers, but can be found from central Florida northward. Loblolly has much shorter needles than slash pine and the needles grow three in a sheath. The loblolly cone is very prickly and elongated.

LONGLEAF PINE is a striking tree found throughout the state. As its name suggests, the needles of this tree are from 10 to 15 inches long. Wood of this pine is a favorite because it is strong and durable. The tree's gum is used to produce rosin, tar, and turpentine. It is also called the pitch pine, the yellow pine, and the southern pine.

PIGEON SEAGRAPE, or Pigeon Plum, is the only tree member of the buckwheat family of plants. It is a large tree, up to 70 feet in height with a tall, straight trunk up to two feet in diameter. It is found most often on hammocks of the Keys, but its range is from Cape Canaveral around to Cape Sable.

POND APPLE is abundant near waterways and along the borders of Lake Okeechobee. Also called the Alligator Apple, it is related to the paw paw, and grows to a height of 50 or 60 feet. It has a sturdy, often buttressed base, and a short, clear trunk that is often irregularly shaped. This tree's fruit is yellow when ripe and is aromatic, but does not taste good and is not recommended for eating.

PUMPKIN ASH grows in deep-river swamps of central and western Florida. It reaches heights of nearly 100 feet with a somewhat slender trunk of up to three feet in diameter. It resembles tupelo or cypress in that its trunk has an enlarged base.

RED MULBERRY trees occur nearly throughout the state and are the state's only native mulberry. White and black mulberry species are also found in the state but they were imported from elsewhere. This tree rarely grows higher than 50 feet with a trunk that is two feet in diameter. Fruit is a dark red, almost black color, and is sweet and edible. The tree is a particular favorite of birds.

REDBUD is an exotic-looking tree, especially in spring when its branches are covered in tiny pinkish-red blooms. It prefers the northern regions of the state, but a few individuals can be found as far south as Tampa. It is an ideal candidate for beautification projects along streets or highways as it requires very little maintenance.

RIVER RED GUM is one of several Eucalyptus introduced from Australia. It is tall—110 feet—with a shapely form. This tree has been used for reforestation because it grows so rapidly, about 10-15 feet per year. It is tolerant of poor soil and makes a good shade tree in the warmer regions of the state, south of a line from Tampa to Vero Beach.

ROYAL PALMS Both the Cuban Royal Palm and the Florida Royal Palm are considered native to Florida and both thrive in the moist heat of the Everglades and point south. Neither is cold tolerant, becoming vulnerable at 35 degrees. The Royals are noted for their slightly bulbous bases and their great height. The Cuban at maturity is routinely 50 feet straight, and true, tall and hardy specimens can grow to 75 feet. The Florida routinely grows to 75 feet and can top out at more than 80 feet. They are sometimes called Boulevard Palms for their use as impressive roadside landscapes.

SAND PINE flourishes in very sandy soils throughout Florida, except in the hottest areas. It is most abundant in the eastern and central portions of the peninsula. Two varieties of this pine are found in Florida: the Choctawhatchee and the central or Ocala type, which is found in the Ocala National forest.

SHORTLEAF PINE is also called the yellow or rosemary pine. It is widely distributed throughout the South and is found most often in north Florida. Once mature, this tree has a tall, straight trunk and an oval crown and may reach heights of 60 feet and a diameter of about two and one-half feet.

SLASH PINE is a fast-growing tree common to all of Florida. Second growth stands of slash pine form a large part of the state's pine forests. This pine is an excellent timber tree and its gum is used to produce turpentine and other products.

SOUTHERN MAGNOLIA is a beautiful forest tree that occurs naturally in the hammocks and swamps of Florida. It attains heights generally of 60 to 80 feet and has a trunk diameter of about four feet. It is also called the Evergreen Magnolia and bears beautiful flowers that are white with a lavender center and a pleasing aroma.

SOUTHERN RED CEDAR occupies the same range and is often confused with West Indies Juniper. This tree is evergreen, fragrant, and occurs through most of the state south to Sarasota County. It tolerates a wide range of soils and reaches heights of up to 50 feet. Its aromatic woods are used to line closets and chests.

SOUTHERN WAXMYRTLE attains a height of about 40 feet and is found over most of the state. It is a small tree with a slender upright trunk and its spreading branches form a round-shaped head. It is found largely in swampy areas.

TURKEY OAK is found abundantly throughout the scrub woodlands of Florida. It is usually no taller than 20 or 30 feet, although a few individuals reach 60 feet in height. Its leaves are deeply divided into three or five lobes and are quite characteristic of only this tree. Its wood is used primarily for fuel. Another name for this oak is Blackjack. Usually growing with this oak is another oak that is dubbed a "turkey" oak, but which has oblong leaves and is more properly termed "bluejack" or Upland Willow Oak.

WATER OAK inhabits in north and into central Florida. It is a tall, slender tree growing from 50 to 80 feet in height, with ascending branches that form a round-topped, symmetrical crown. It is a bottomland species, although it may occur in permanent swamps. Where it appears, it tends to dominate hardwood stands. Although not a particularly sturdy or long-lived tree, transplanted or cultivated, it is a favored landscape tree.

WEST INDIAN MAHOGANY can attain a height of 50 feet. It is deciduous and found only in south Florida. It is fast growing and provides ample shade with spreading, densely foliaged branches. Wood of this tree tends to be brittle and may be damaged during hurricanes.

WEST INDIES JUNIPER is common in the state except in the southern areas. It also is called Red Cedar and its aromatic heartwood is used to make closet linings and cedar chests. Durable, especially in contact with the soil, this tree provides long-lasting fence posts or poles.

WHITE OAK is a shapely oak that can reach 100 feet tall. It is an important timber tree with a trunk diameter of two or three feet. It is found in the middle and western parts of Florida. In open fields, this tree develops a broad crown and reaching limbs and can be a most attractive shade tree.

RARE TREES

FLORIDA TORREYA is a relatively small tree but can grow to 40 feet tall and up to two feet in trunk diameter. A short bole and an open, pyramidal crown with whorls and spread branches characterize it. The bark is irregularly fissured and scaly, dark brown, and often tinged with orange. It is a rare tree, with its native habitat being along the banks of the Apalachicola River and Panhandle tributaries. Cultivated, it is a favorite ornamental in and around Tallahassee and is noted for its odor, that of crushed tomato leaves.

FLORIDA YEW is one of the world's rarest trees. It occurs naturally only in an area of bluffs and ravines east of the Apalachicola River. Pessimists believe its entire population numbers in the dozens, while optimists estimate the number to be in the hundreds. Closely related to and resembling the Florida torreya, it shares much the same range, and like the torreya, it is listed as endangered. The yew is a small tree, rarely taller than 25 feet, growing most commonly to 15 feet. The trunk is short and slender, with numerous spreading branches, giving the tree a shabby look. Both the Florida torreya and the Florida yew benefit by having most of their growth within the confines of Torreya State Park.

A POTPOURRI OF PALMS

The world boasts some 4,000 species of palms and while Florida has only a small percentage of that number, perhaps several hundred, it does have more than any other state. In fact, most of the palms native to the U.S. are found in Florida. They range from dwarf shrubby types to magnificent trees reaching 100 feet tall. Some species are erect in habit of growth, others are leaning; some have but a single trunk, others have numerous stems forming clumps of different sizes.

All palms can be divided according to leaf type into two main classes: pinnate or feather leaved, and palmate or fan leaved. By far the larger number of species belong to the pinnate class. The greatest threat to Florida's palm trees is a disease called lethal yellowing that has struck hard at coconut palms and numerous other species, including the Christmas palm and the date palm. The disease hit Florida in 1955, spreading from Key West to the mainland. In the 1970s it had killed an estimated 5 million palms in the Miami area, including 90 percent of the city's coconut palms. By 2007, the disease had reached as far north as Manatee County.

The disease is caused by microorganisms carried from tree to tree by insects called planthoppers. Plant pathologists have discovered planthoppers are not cold tolerant and recent harsh winters are expected to roll back the disease. If trees sicken and die, tree experts are urging residents to replant with Malayan Dwarf and the hybrid Maypan palms, both proven resistant to lethal yellowing and producing coconuts. Royal palm and cabbage palmetto, native to Florida, also appear immune.

The latest palm plague doesn't affect palms in the least. But a tiny insect is eating its way through the state's sago palm, which is not a palm at all but looks like one. The sago, a cycad, is a highly popular landscape plant.

The enemy is Asian Cycad Scale, and it is now busy destroying sago palms throughout central Florida. Believed to have been introduced unknowingly by a botanical expedition returning to Miami from China in the early 1990s, the scale has destroyed 60 percent of the sago palms in South Florida.

Asian Scale is a very small but armored white insect that can cover a sago at the rate of 3,000 per square inch. A besieged plant can appear laden with snow. The scale also imbeds itself in the plant's roots. It inserts its strawlike mouth into the plant and feeds until the insect dies. Infestation can destroy the plant.

Ordinary garden insecticides have little effect on the scale. Special mixtures of horticultural oil and the deadliest insect killers available can be effective. But the process involves drenching the plant and its roots repeatedly and vigilantly over a long period of time. Severe pruning, with burning, double-bagging, or burying of the debris, also has some benefit. The scale is spread by the wind and can travel a half-mile a day.

State scientists have been working on the problem in central Florida since spring 2002, and the Florida Division of Plant Industry has released imported tiny parasitic wasps that feed on the scale, but it will take years for the wasp population to grow to sufficient numbers to check the insects.

Sale of the sago has not been banned, but many nurseries and landscape architects have stopped promoting or using the plant until a time when the scale invasion comes under control.

CHAMPION TREES

Hundreds of tree species thrive in Florida because of the diversity of its climate. The American Forestry Association, along with the Florida Department of Agriculture and Consumer Services, seeks to locate and record the largest specimens of each species.

Some species known to grow

in the state have never been nominated and thus may not appear on this list of national champion trees in Florida. Anyone wishing to nominate a tree should contact the local county forester.

The champion tree list that follows is compiled by the American Forestry Association in cooperation with Florida officials. It lists those trees in Florida that are known to be of record size nationally.

Measurements are given in inches for circumference, in feet for height, and in feet for average crown spread. To determine the largest tree, one point is allowed for each inch of circumference, each foot of height, and each four feet of average crown spread.

Species	Circ. (in.)	Height (ft.)	Spread (ft.)	County
Alvaradoa, Mexican*	53	35	30	Miami-Dade
Ash Magnolia	25	34	32	Wakulla
Balsom Apple*	31	32	26	Broward
Balsom Torchwood*	21	25	71	Monroe
Beech	130	130	78	Wakulla
Bitterbush	13	15	22	Miami-Dade
Blackbeard, catclaw*	175	78	93	Manatee
Black Gum	76	89	40	Wakulla
Black mangrove*	85	58	44	Monroe
Black Walnut	120	67	70	Putnam
Blue Beech	40	37	36	Union
Box Elder	80	64	53	Alachua
Brittle Thatch Palm*	20	20	7	Miami-Dade
Buckhorn	14	27	14	Alachua
Buckhorn, tropical	35	22	28	Monroe
Buckthorne, smooth	30	37	20	Nassau
Buckthorne, tough*	41	38	38	Duval
Buckwheat tree*	59	41	34	Wakulla
Bustic, willow	54	57	18	Miami-Dade
Butterbough*	47	47	28	Monroe
Buttonbush	53	24	25	Alachua
Buttonwood, Green	207	25	70	Monroe
Buttonwood, Silver	159	45	62	Monroe
Byrsonima*	35	20	20	Monroe
Cabbage Palm*	69	60	14	Lafayette

Carolina Basswood*	118	111	70	Wakulla
Carolina Willow	62	24	44	Alachua
Catalpa	173	68	82	Hamilton
Cedar, Atlantic white	45	52	26	Okalooosa
Cedar, bay*	8	14	16	Monroe
Cedar, Southern red*	212	77	55	Alachua
Cherry, Alabama	41	26	25	Liberty
Cherry, Black	134	99	69	Hamilton
Cherry, West Indies*	73	41	23	Miami-Dade
Chinquapin, ashe*	76	42	47	Columbia
Coral bean	36	26	26	Brevard
Corkwood*	8	16	7	Levy
Cottonwood, Western	127	84	90	Levy
Cypress, bald	424	107	60	Seminole
Cypress, pond	39	19	22	Lafayette
Cyrilla, swamp*	60	50	12	Washington
Darling plum*	23	119	16	Monroe
Devils Walking Stick	12	23	5	Alachua
Devilwood*	88	39	42	Clay
Dogwood, flowering	71	54	31	Leon
Dogwood, Jamaica*	123	50	62	Monroe
Downy Serviceberry	24	43	22	Leon
Eastern Redbud	29	78	24	Wakulla
Elderberry	17	15	6	Lake
Elm, cedar*	118	92	60	Marion
Elm, Florida*	169	79	64	Duval
Elm, slippery	39	70	31	Gadsden
Elm, water*	207	66	61	Gilchrist
Elm, winged	120	83	89	Alachua
False boxwood	10	19	13	Monroe
Falsemastic*	112	75	94	Monroe
Farkieberry	48	27	39	Walton
Fiddlewood*	39	25	24	Miami-Dade
Fig, Fla. Strangler*	399	67	77	Miami-Dade
Fig, shortleafed*	444	48	76	Monroe

Fire-bush*	18	14	16	Brevard
Florida Banana Shrub*	8	18	9	Marion
Florida Maple	68	95	38	Gadsden
Florida Royal Palm*	55	93	14	Collier
Florida Torreya	64	44	40	Madison
Florida Tetrazygia*	24	22	15	Miami-Dade
Florida Trema	17	18	16	Collier
Fringetree	41	36	39	Suwannee
Geiger tree* (tie)	37	24	17	Lee
Geiger tree* (tie)	39	19	22	Palm Beach
Gumbo limbo*	173	43	63	Manatee
Hackberry, spiny	12	22	22	Lee
Haw, green	48	53	55	Gilchrist
Haw, summer* (tie)	43	27`	45	Alachua
Haw, summer* (tie)	30	45	32	Nassau
Hercules-club	52	62	36	Wakulla
Hickory, butternut	111	103	70	Wakulla
Hickory. Mockernut	179	102	112	Hamilton
Hickory, pignut	122	119	48	Alachua
Hickory, water	234	85	86	Volusia
Holly, American	101	72	51	Putnam
Holly, dahoon*	79	46	36	Palm Beach
Holly, myrtle*	77	60	39	Wakulla
Ironwood, black*	73	28	30	Monroe
Ironwood, hop (tie)	62	40	28	Taylor
Ironwood, hop (tie)	45	58	23	Washington
Ironwood, white*	79	45	38	Monroe
Jamaica Caper*	23	33	23	Monroe
Joe-wood	60	13	13	Lee
Lidflower, pale	18	33	18.5	Monroe
Lignum vitae, rough*	97	36	35	Monroe
Loblolly bay* (tie)	132	89	49	Duval
Loblolly bay* (tie)	143	80	48	Duval
Locust, honey	63	66	38	Lafayette
Locust, water	106	86	51	Gilchrist

Mahogany, W. Indies*	164	70	92	Monroe
Manchineel*	57	25	14	Monroe
Mango	151	39	46	Miami-Dade
Marlberry	23	28	12	Miami-Dade
Mayhaw	27	31	29	Gadsden
Milkbark	41	37	15	Monroe
Myrtle-of-the-river*	10	28	7	Monroe
Oak, black	89	105	32	Lafayette
Oak, blackjack	62	60	40	Jackson
Oak, bludjack	72	55	43	Dixie
Oak, bluff	127	129	64	Wakulla
Oak, Chapman	85	45	46	Alachua
Oak, cherrybark	159	99	90	Jackson
Oak, chinquapin	124	116	68	Jackson
Oak, laurel	231	38	108	Okaloosa
Oak, live	368	85	155	Alachua
Oak, overcup	180	105	101	Gilchrist
Oak, post	200	95	85	Jackson
Oak, sand live*	193	64	104	Alachua
Oak, sand post*	162	86	97	Jackson
Oak, shumard (tie)	160	117	68	Marion
Oak, shumard (tie)	164	110	80	Wakulla
Oak, southern red	225	111	98	Marion
Oak, swamp chestnut	155	135	73	Wakulla
Oak, swamp laurel	200	100	80	Alachua
Oak, turkey	134	64	65	Pasco
Oak, water	205	89	108	Washington
Oak, white	139	146	84	Wakulla
Ogeechee	167	91	42	Wakulla
Olive, black	57	31	40	Broward
Olive, scrub wild	19	30	13	Monroe
Osage Orange	110	68	60	Gadsden
Oysterwood*	17	33	8	Monroe
Papaya	36	40	10	Sarasota
Paradise tree	67	55	44	Miami-Dade

Paurotis palm*	10	35	5	Miami-Dade
Pecan	250	108	125	Alachua
Persimmon	68	105	52	Columbia
Pigeon Plum*	66	42	40	Monroe
Pine, loblolly	173	102	158	Nassau
Pine, longleaf	105	105	50	Marion
Pine, pond*	188	120	65	Putnam
Pine, sand	91	94	39	Pasco
Pine, shortleaf	111	96	49	Leon
Pine, slash*	144	138	55	Duval
Pine, So. Fla. Slash*	149	69	60	Lee
Pine, spruce	130	120	70	Wakulla
Pisonia	40	27	12	Monroe
Poisontree, Florida*	76	47	24	Monroe
Pond Apple	130	42	38	Palm Beach
Potato tree	62	22	17	Lake
Prickly ash, lime*	65	16	33	Lee
Princewood*	26	36	10	Monroe
Pyramid Magnolia	59	87	36	Gadsden
Red Bay*	146	94	45	Hamilton
Redberry, Eugenia*	61	41	20	Miami-Dade
Red Buckeye	30	20	25	Putnam
Red Maple	145	102	57.5	Citrus
Red Mulberry	60	58	38	Manatee
River Birch	94	82	39	Gadsden
Royal Poinciana	182	62	61	Hendry
Rusty Blackhaw	11	15	1`4	Alachua
Rusty Lyonia	27	35	34	Wakulla
Sassafras	89	113	34	Wakulla
Satinleaf*	72	45	45	Miami-Dade
Satinwood*	95	30	36	Monroe
Saw palmetto* (tie)	21	23	8	St. Lucie
Saw Palmetto* (tie)	22	20	13	Sumter
Sea Grape*	288	80	80	Miami-Dade
Silk Bay*	66	41	39	Marion

Silver Maple	56	102	28	Gadsden
Silverpalm, Florida*	19	33	4	Monroe
Soldier wood*	86	28	24	Monroe
Southern Magnolia* (tie)	220	80	92	Clay
Southern Magnolia* (tie)	214	88	65	St. Johns
Stopper, Simpson's*	34	38	23	Okeechobee
Stopper, Spanish*	12	25	10	Monroe
Stopper, red	28	11	50	Monroe
Stopper, white*	17	25	7	Lee
Strongback, Bahama*	37	33	18	Monroe
Sugerberry	243	74	93	Hamilton
Sweetbay	129	96	54	Wakulla
Sweet Gum	163	133	87	Liberty
Sycamore	192	83	54	Orange
Tallow-wood*	31	23	10	Monroe
Tamarind*	85	38	44	Monroe
Thatchpalm, Florida*	17	34	10	Broward
Torchwood*	0	30	14	Monroe
Tropical Almond	135	61	71	Monroe
Tupelo, swamp	197	91	58	Alachua
Tupelo, water* (tie)	158	105	54	Liberty
Tupelo, water* (tie)	158	105	54	Jackson
Velvet-seed*	38	34	20	Monroe
Velvet-seed, rough*	13	30	12	Monroe
White Ash	126	115	72	Jackson
White mangrove	80	38	44	Monroe
Whitewood*	7	14	7	Monroe
Wild Cinnamon*	26	38	21	Monroe
Wild Crab Apple	17	40	20	Jackson
Wild Dilly	22	21	32	Monroe
Wild plum	40	30	11	Gadsden
Yau Pon*	65	45	26	Putnam
Yellow Poplar	222	112	67	Putnam
Yew, Florida*	27	22	15	Liberty
indicates National Champion				

FLORIDA NATIONAL SCENIC TRAIL MAP

FLORIDA TRAIL

A 1,300-mile wilderness trail through Florida, from the Everglades to the far reaches of the Panhandle, has been carved out by and for ardent outdoors people. The Florida Trail is designated as a national scenic trail.

The blazed way is a two-and-one-half-foot-wide footpath across public land for the most part and ties into numerous state and federal paths. Portions of the trail cross private land, some requiring advance notice, while others follow roadways for relatively short distances.

A full-system hike takes a walker through the state's varied topography from the Big Cypress Swamp in southwest Florida, up the spine of the peninsula, and through the hardwood stands of north Florida to the sands of the Gulf Islands National Seashore, south of Pensacola.

Because portions of the trail cross prime hunting grounds, hikers are encouraged to be aware of activities along their way.

Hiking season in Florida is November through April, although access to the Florida Trail and other pathways is year round.

The Florida National Scenic Trail was developed and is maintained by the Florida Trail Association and other volunteer organizations.

SPANISH MOSS

Spanish moss is not a moss but a member of the bromeliaceae family of plants, best known of which is the pineapple. An air plant, growing throughout Florida and a hallmark of much of the South, it needs no roots, but traps and absorbs water through its leaves. For food, the moss combines water with carbon dioxide from the air and manufactures its own food by photosynthesis. Spanish moss is not a parasite on trees, but uses trees only for mechanical support.

In the summer, the long strands of moss produce tiny yellow-green flowers. When ripe seeds are cast off they are spread by the wind to other trees nearby. In high winds, thousands of pieces of the plant will be snapped off and carried great distances. Some will be forcefully driven into cracks in trees and telephone poles; others will be stopped by buildings, rooftops, and other structures, where they grow into mature, healthy plants. Scientists believe hurricanes, with their tremendous winds, are a major means of spreading Spanish moss, which has the widest range of any bromeliad.

Hardwoods, especially live oaks, are most likely to harbor the moss though no tree is immune to it. In north Florida, for example, pecan groves must be de-mossed regularly if they are to produce their best nut crops. Pecan trees, like live oaks, offer excellent growing conditions for the moss because they provide open crowns and horizontal branches.

Of course, too much moss in any tree is not good. Because it can absorb several times its own weight in water when it rains, moss tends to make branches sag, split, and break off under its great weight. At the same time, its rain-holding characteristic can be an asset to the tree. Moss reduces rain runoff and holds water in reserve so that when a dry season hits, the trapped water slowly evaporates, creating an air of humidity around the tree.

It has other benefits. Spanish moss can block out much sunlight and thereby influences the type of ground plants that grow under trees. Several tree-living species use the moss for roosting and rearing of their young; others, like the warblers, carry away the plant for nesting material. Raccoons and squirrels make use of the moss for nest building or protective cover. It

also is a haven for bugs, spiders, and even bats.

Harvesting moss was a big industry in Florida at one time. At the industry's peak in 1936, dozens of gins dried, combed, and sold the plant. Collected by hand, usually with the aid of a hook or blades, the moss was piled in large heaps or buried in long, shallow pits. This allowed the gray outer portions of the strands to rot away, and what remained was a central black fiber, tough and resilient. It was used to fill cushions of automobiles and railway coach seats, mattresses, chairs, couches, even horse collars. The industry thrived until the late 1950s when less-expensive foam upholstering materials were invented.

Today, the gins are gone, and for a while, there was fear that Spanish moss might eventually follow. A die-off of the plant in 1968 in Florida was blamed on air pollution, to which it is susceptible. But time and further research point to a virus, which the hardy plant appears to have overcome.

Long used in folk medicine, Spanish moss is the subject of much new medical research.

POISONOUS PLANTS

Florida's wide variety of flora harbors numerous poisonous plants. Following is a list and description of such plants most frequently encountered. Fortunately, most have such an unpleasant taste or consistency that it is not likely anyone would chew them for long or swallow any part of them. Should a person do so, however, and begin suffering effects, a call or trip to the nearest poison control center would be wise.

ANGEL'S TRUMPET is a beautiful

flowering plant with a long history in folklore as having hallucinogenic properties. In fact, the flower and seeds deliver a deadly poison that has sickened or killed numerous Florida teenagers in the past decade.

AZALEA is a popular landscaping plant, but all of the plant is poisonous if eaten.

BARBADOS NUT, also called French Purge Nut or Curcas Bean, is a coarse annual plant or small tree up to 15 feet tall. The leaves are thick, six inches or more wide, heart-shaped or coarsely three to five-lobed. The seeds are a purgative and toxic.

BITTERWEED is a flowering plant that ranges in height from six inches to three feet. Leaves are about an inch long, very narrow, and found on multiple stems and branches. Flowers look like black-eyed susans, with yellow petals, but the centers are also yellow. It is found primarily in north and central Florida along roadsides and in fields. As its name suggests, it tastes bitter, but all parts of the plant are poisonous.

BOXWOOD is an ornamental shrub rarely over five feet tall with bright green, shiny leaves. Both the bark and leaves of this shrub contain an alkaloid substance that causes severe abdominal pain, and in some instances, convulsions.

BRACKEN FERN is a long-stemmed, coarse fern found most often in open woods or in fields from Lake Okeechobee north. Its leaves are lacy and form a clearly triangular shape. Livestock may be poisoned by this plant if it is accidentally baled with hay.

BRAZILIAN PEPPER is a major invasive exotic tree that can spread bushlike to an area 40 by 40 feet. On Florida's prohibited plant list, it is illegal to cultivate, sell, or transport. But still it thrives. In addition to its other bad qualities, the entire tree is dangerous to humans. Related to poison ivy, poison oak, and poison sumac, its toxins cause skin itching and inflammation by contact. Its pollen causes respiratory irritation, as does smoke from burning it. Clothes in contact with the tree will remain toxic until washed.

CAROLINA JESSAMINE is a showy vine featuring dark, oval leaves that are one-half to two and one-half inches long. This plant often is used in landscaping as it is an evergreen and bears clusters of fragrant yellow trumpet-like flowers all summer. The flowers, leaves, and roots contain a poison that can affect nerve endings of the body. Also called the Evening Trumpet Flower.

CASTOR BEAN, also called Palma Crista or Castor Oil Plant, is a robust annual herb growing to the size of a small tree. The strong stems are green or red to purple. Leaves are star-shaped with five to nine or more lobes, thin and finely toothed along the margin. Castor bean contains a poisonous principle, ricin, which is a true protein, plus ricinoleic acid and oliec acid. This plant also is used as an ornamental and is abundant as a wild plant in the Lake Okeechobee area.

CRAPE JASMINE is a rather succulent shrub, three to eight feet tall. The flowers, one to two inches across, are produced in small clusters. They are pure white with a yellowish tubular base. The roots, bark, and flower may be harmful if eaten.

CROATALARIA ranges from three to six feet tall and is found all over the state. It has large, waxy leaves four to seven inches long that may have a bristle at the tip. A spike of yellow flowers grows snapdragon-like on a stalk within the plant. Livestock may be poisoned by this plant, which is often found in abandoned or neglected fields.

CROWN OF THORNS is a low-growing shrub with thorny stems and branches. They are purplish in color and armed with numerous stiff, sharp-pointed spines. The milky sap or latex is quite irritating to the skin of some people. The root contains an unclassified toxic substance.

DEADLY NIGHTSHADE is a two-foot-tall plant with black berries and white flowers. All parts are poisonous if eaten.

DIEFFENBACHIA, or Dumb Cane, is a tender house plant. The green stems, three to six feet tall, are fleshy and the green leaves, usually a foot long, may be spotted. Chewing or swallowing any of these parts, which contain calcium oxalate, is quite harmful and can cause severe swelling of the throat or tongue.

ELDERBERRY is a widespread plant featuring small white flowers and purple berries, but its roots, bark, stem, and leaves are poisonous if eaten.

ELEPHANT EAR is a large-leaved plant that can reach enormous proportions. It is a favorite for Florida landscapes and is often seen in the wild. Ironically, it is a food source in some parts of the tropical world. But its roots and rhizomes require very careful and knowledgeable preparation. Raw, all parts of this plant deliver a stinging toxin. It is one of the most frequently reported causes of plant poisoning in Florida.

ERYTHRINA leaves and flowers, when cooked, are edible, but its raw seeds are highly poisonous.

GLORIOSA, or Climbing Lily, is a tender, herbaceous plant. The weak stems, upright at first, attain a height of five to seven feet. The numerous narrow leaves grow in pairs all along the stem. These leaf ends act as tendrils, twining around any suitable support. Each flower is crinkled along the edges, is yellow or yellow and red in color, or becomes red all over as the flower fades. All parts of this plant are poisonous, with the highest concentration of toxic materials in the tubers. Death has been reported to have occurred within four hours after tubers were eaten.

HYDRANGEA is a stiff, stout shrub three to 12 feet tall. The flowers are borne at the end of the stems in dense, rounded clusters sometimes a foot in diameter. The individual flowers are pink, blue, or almost white. All parts of the plant are poisonous.

JIMSON WEED, also called Jamestown Weed or Thorn Apple, is a large annual weed, three to five feet tall, with several widespreading branches near the top of the stem. The erect flowers are short-stalked, funnel-shaped, and white or pale bluish-purple in color. All parts of the plant, particularly the seeds, are poisonous. Children have been poisoned by eating the fruit or sucking the flowers.

LANTANA is a native Florida shrub that is increasingly used as an ornamental. It reaches three to five feet in height. Oval leaves, pointed at one end, are scalloped along the edges and toxic. Children may be attracted by the dainty flowers of white, yellow, pink, orange, or scarlet that are clustered into tiny "bouquets." Immature berries are deadly.

LARKSPUR (ANNUAL OR ROCKET)

is an upright annual garden plant grown for its flowers. Young plants form dense rosettes five to 10 inches across. Flowers vary in color from white to pink, rose, blue, or purple, or may be striped. The fruits are urn-shaped capsules. All plant parts are poisonous.

LARKSPUR (HARDY) is a perennial plant often used in flower gardens. The pale blue flowers scattered along the flowering stems are slender-stalked. If eaten in large quantities it could be hazardous.

MANGO is a large, tropical fruit tree that grows up to 60 feet in height. Because mango is related botanically to poison ivy, susceptible individuals who come in contact with the plant can develop a dermatitis similar to ivy poisoning. Handling any part of the plant may result in the poisoning. Many people are not affected by mangoes; in fact, it is an unusually delicious fruit that can be purchased at supermarkets. But those persons suffering a reaction to mangoes may lessen the poisoning effect by cooking the fruit, which destroys its inflammatory contents.

MILK BUSH, also called Pencil Cactus or Malabartree, is a shrub or small, multi-branched tree up to 15 feet tall. On old plants the trunk, three inches or more in diameter, is grayish but all of the rest of the plant is green. The twigs are produced in whorl-like clusters at the ends of each flush of growth. If eaten, the plant parts are reputed to be dangerously toxic.

MISTLETOE has white berries that, if eaten, can cause acute stomach pains, cramps, vomiting, and heart failure.

OLEANDER (COMMON) is a woody shrub or small tree from five to 25 feet in height. The flowers vary in color from white through pink, creamy yellow, rose, and deep red. All plant parts are poisonous if eaten. One leaf is reported to be sufficient to kill an adult. Children may be poisoned by carrying flowers around in their mouths in play. Some people have suffered poisoning after eating frankfurters roasted on oleander stems. Inhaling smoke from burning oleander stems and leaves has caused symptoms of poisoning.

POINSETTIA, a favorite holiday plant, has leaves and seeds that can cause burning, inflammation, and blistering if eaten.

POKEWEED, also called Poke or Pokeberry, is a robust herbaceous plant growing six feet tall. The lower leaves are a foot or more long, gradually diminishing until the upper leaves are about three inches in length. All are spear-shaped. The flowers, produced all summer, are white. The flattened, purple-black, juicy berries contain several seeds. All plant parts, particularly the berries and roots, are considered toxic. Symptoms occur about two hours after the plant has been consumed. The young sprouts of this plant, called Poke (or Polk) Salad, are edible as greens, but harvesting and cooking them is best left to the experts.

PRIMROSE (TOP) is a winter-flowering greenhouse ornamental plant with leaves growing in a dense rosette. Individual leaves are nearly round, two to four inches long, and heart-shaped at the base. The pale pink to rose-colored flowers are produced at the top of the flower stalk. Handling primrose plants results in an itching dermatitis in some individuals. The irritation resembles ivy-poisoning but is usually less severe.

PRIVET (LIGUSTRUM) is a glossy

shrub or small tree, five to 25 feet tall, and commonly used as a hedge plant. Records of poisonings by privet seem to be rare in the U.S., but in Europe children have died from eating the plant's fruits.

RHUBARB is a popular garden plant. Its stalk is edible, but leaf blades are toxic if eaten.

ROSARY PEA, also called Crabeye or Jequirity Pea, is a woody vine climbing to a height of 10 to 20 feet on other plants, arbors, or other support. The pods split along one side and show the two rows of bright red seeds that are black on one end. One seed thoroughly chewed and swallowed is sufficient to cause fatal poisoning of an adult.

RUBBER PLANT, used for interior decoration, contains latex in its stems and leaves that can cause burning, itching and blistering.

STINGING NETTLE is found in sandy areas, and its stiff hairs inject an irritant causing redness, intense itching, and swelling.

TREE TOBACCO is a shrub or small tree 10 to 15 feet tall with tubular flowers that either are erect or drooping, and borne in open clusters or panicles. The individual flowers, one to two inches long, are yellow or greenish yellow, and only slightly flared open at the ends. Cattle are reported to have been poisoned by this plant.

TRUMPET VINE has leaves and flowers that are poisonous if touched, resulting in skin inflammation and burning.

TUNG-OIL TREE, also called Tung Tree or Tung Nut, is a small, deciduous tree with smooth bark. The leaf-stalk bears two reddish or brownish glands or small knobs close to the leaf blades. The flowers are produced in large clusters before the leaves appear. They are pale pink or white and have reddish-brown bases. The fruits are nearly global and dark green, later turning brown. Each fruit contains three to seven large, hard, rough-coated seeds with white flesh. Cases of tung poisoning have occurred from eating the nuts.

WATER HEMLOCK grows in water and, if eaten, all parts of the plant can cause nausea, delirium, convulsions, and even death.

WILD CHERRY leaves contain cyanide poisoning that can cause convulsions and coma.

YELLOW ALLAMANDA is a vigorous vine or weak-stemmed shrub with leafy stems growing as much as 15 feet in a season. The large yellow flowers are produced in clusters near the ends of the branches. All parts of the plant cause vomiting if ingested.

YELLOW OLEANDER is a shrub with a dense crown. Its dark leaves are three to six inches long, about a quarter-inch wide, glossy above, and paler beneath. The yellow to dull orange flowers are produced in small clusters near the tips of the twigs. The fruits are somewhat triangular. All plant parts are poisonous if eaten.

PLANT SAVERS

Joining 18 other major gardens in the U.S. in preserving nearly 3,000 species of plants near extinction are two Florida gardens, Bok Tower Gardens at Lake Wales and Fairchild Tropical Gardens at Miami. Fewer than 20 percent of these plants now receive any kind of protection, and fewer than 10 percent have been cultivated.

FLOWERS

They don't call Florida "Florida" for nothing. Discoverer Ponce de Leon was so overwhelmed by the extent and variety of the flora he encountered that he named the area, and subsequently the state, "Florida"—the land of flowers.

Today, botanists have identified more than 3,500 species of plant life in the state, providing an explosion of color throughout the year. Whether native, imported or escaped, or representing the southern reaches of northern temperate zone flowering plants or the northernmost outpost of the flowers of the tropics, most of the world's flowering plants thrive in some part of the state.

Gardening is a major activity of Floridians, especially new Floridians, although they may have to change the timing, care, and feeding of their favorite flowers from "back home." Flower shows are regularly held throughout the state and are heavily attended. The annual explosion of simple phlox along roadsides and in open fields is a tourist attraction similar to the turning of the leaves in northern climes.

The flowers of Florida can be divided into native plants and imported plants. The native plants include those endemic to Florida, temperate plants for which Florida is the southernmost range, and tropical plants for which Florida is the northernmost range. Many plants imported for landscaping have escaped into the wild. Some fare poorly, others have taken on a new and evolving life. Others still have become nuisance plants.

NATIVE FLOWERS

Duck Potato	Catbrier	Sweet Shrub
Arrowhead	Purple Flat Iris	Spice Bush
Colic Root	Southern Blue Flag	Carolina Bay
Yellow Colic Root	Blue-eyed Grass	Peperomia
Wild Onion	Golden Club	Lizard's Tail
Devil's Bit	Cattail	Columbine
String Lily	Yellow-eyed Grass	Leather Flower
Dogtooth Violet	Pickerel Weed	Rue Anemone
Spider Lily	Sedge	Prickly Poppy
Alligator Lily	White Bracted Sedge	Watershield
Pine Lily	Day Flower	Lotus
False Garlic	Pink Spiderwort	Water Lily
Wake Robin	Spiderwort	Loblolly Bay
Bellwort	Hat Pins	Possum Haw
Atamasco Lily	Bog Buttons	Yaupon
Crow Poison	Wild Rice	Sweet Pepperbush
Snakeroot	Canna	Black Ti-ti
Manfreda	Arrowroot	Ti-ti
Yucca	Star Anise	St. John's Wort
Redroot	Pawpaw	Hypericum
Goldcrest	Flag Pawpaw	Tartflower

Dwarf Huckleberry
Hairy Laurel
Fetterbush
Indian Pipes
Wild Azalea
Shiny Blueberry
Low Bush Blueberry
Rosemary
Snowbell
Marlberry
Florida Violet
Long-leaf Violet
Field Pansy
Sea Rocket
Waltheria
Poppy Mallow
Swamp Mallow
Salt March Mallow
Turk's-cap
New Jersey Tea
Spurge
Tread Softly
Pineland Croton
Painted Leaf
Jimson Weed
Narrow Leaf Ground
    Cherry
Seaside Ground Cherry
Common Nightshade
Horse Nettle
Blodgett's Nightshade
Creeping Morning
    Glory
Annual Phlox
Cardinal Flower
Glades Lobelia
Venus' Looking-glass
Oxalis
Crane's Bill
Locust Berry
White Bachelor-button
Tall Milkwort
Large-Flower Polygala
Candyweed
Polygala
Winged Sumac
Red Buckeye
Prickly Pear

Pink Purslane
Bloodleaf
Chickweed
Wild Buckwheat
Red Chokeberry
Gopher Apple
Hog Plum
Swamp Rose
Sand Blackberry
White Indigo
Pineland Baptisia
Cassia
Rabbit Bells
Dalea
Summer Farewell
Beggar's Lice
Lupine
Dollar-weed
Pencil Flower
Tephrosia
Oak-leaf Hydrangea
Virginia Willow
Sundew
Dew Threads
Tall Meadow Beauty
Ludwigia
Primrose Willow
Evening Primrose
Button Bush
Diodia
Beach Creeper
Firebush
Partridge Berry
Richardia
Pineland Allamanda
Blue Star
Wild Allamanda
Seaside Gentian
Gatesby Gentian
Sabatia
Agalinis
False Foxglove
Water Hyssop
Buchnera
Indian Paint Brush
Lousewort
Seymeria
Beech Drops

Orobanche
Meadow Parsnip
Florida Elder
Possom Haw
Black Haw
Sky-flower
Scorpion-tail
Puccoon
Beauty Berry
Lantana
Blue Porterweed
Conradina
Lion's Ear
Blue Sage
Tropical Sage
Lyre-leaf Sage
Skullcap
Hedge-nettle
Frost Aster
White-top Aster
Sea Myrtle
Honeycomb Head
Greeneyes
Spanish Nettles
Bigelowia
Sea Daisy
Deer Tongue
Thistle
Tickseed
Swamp Coreopsis
Ageratum
Flat-topped Goldenrod
Gaillardia
Garberia
Rabbit Tobacco
Bitterweed
Beach Sunflower
Rayless Sunflower
Blazing Star
Roserush
Barbara's Buttons
Palafoxia
Golden Aster
Camphor Weed
Blackroot
Sow Thistle
Stokesia
Ironweed

IMPORTED FLOWERS

Brazilian Elodia
Spanish Bayonet
Water Hyacinth
Mexican Poppy
Banana Water Lily
Pimpernel
Annatto
Begonia
Watercress
Wild Radish
Poinsettia
Angel Trumpet

Nightshade
Wahlenbergia
Puncture Weed
Alligator Weed
Mock Strawberry
Crimson Clover
Lavender Scallops
Life Plant
Primrose
Butterfly Bush
Madagascar Periwinkle
Oleander

Mullen
English Plantain
Bush Dogwood
Angelica
Japanese Honeysuckle
Glorybower
Verbena
Chamomile
Tasselflower
Cat's Ear
Wild Marigold

Florida is also home to many endangered flowers protected by either federal or state law. While many have become very rare, other protected flowers, rare elsewhere, are known to grow in abundance in Florida. Either way, protected flowers may not be disturbed.

ENDANGERED FLOWERS

Celestial Lily
Delicate Ionopsis
Pale Grass Pink
Grass Pink
Thickroot Orchid
Rosebud Orchid
Spider Orchid
White Fringed Orchid
Crested Fringed
   Orchid
Snowy Orchid
Spring Coral Root
Shell Orchid
Green-fly Orchid
Long-horned Orchid
Vanilla Orchid
Water-spider Orchid

Dingy Epidendrum
Rigid Epidendrum
Rose Pogonia
Scarlet Ladies Tresses
Fragrant Ladies'
   Tresses
Lesser Ladies' Tresses
Grass-leaf Ladies'
   Tresses
Quail-Leaf
Texas Anemone
Trumpets
White Top Pitcher
   Plant
Hooded Pitcher Plant
Sweet Pitcher Plant
Pine-sap

Chapman's
   Rhododendron
Halberd Leaf Violet
Yellow Rhexia
Tetrazygia
Black Mangrove
Red Mangrove
Sea Lavender
Four-petal Paw-paw
Purple Flower Pink
   Root
Britton's Bear-grass
Stawberry Spiderhead
Needle-leaf
   Spiderhead
Graceful Spiderhead
Trident Spiderhead

GARDENING

Florida is also home to numerous flowering trees; brilliantly flowering vines, ferns, and bromeliads; plants which fruit rather than flower; and a wide variety of natural grasses and herbs.

The state's perennial plants are likely to show up almost any time, almost anywhere. But for gardeners who prefer order in their lives and in their gardens, it takes long experience or reeducation to make a garden grow in the way the gardener expects and desires. What worked back home is unlikely to work in Florida.

The first observation a gardener will make is that Florida's soil is basically sand, requiring careful preparation for success. The gardener must also be aware of where in Florida the garden is located. Much of what thrives in the Everglades will not survive in the Panhandle and vice versa. Central Florida treads the thin line between the two extremes, enjoying both the benefits and the dangers of being caught in the middle. Florida also has some interesting pests that also vary from one region to another. Still, most Florida gardeners will find themselves and their plots overrun with color.

Again depending on location, many flowering favorites can be planted almost any time. This monthly schedule, starting at the beginning of the year, indicates Florida's earliest prudent planting dates. The further north one plants, the later seeds, bulbs, cuttings, and plants should go into the ground. Gardeners should also be aware of a plant's salt tolerance. Nowhere in Florida is very far from the coast.

MONTHLY PLANTING SCHEDULE

January-February

Flowers
Aster
Baby's Breath
Bachelor Button
Balsam
Calendula
Candyturf
Carnation
Cosmos
Cockscomb
Daisy
Forget-Me-Not
Gaillardia
Globe
   Amaranth
Hollyhock
Lace Flower
Larkspur
Lobelias
Lupins
Marigolds
Morning Glory
Nasturtium
Pansy
Periwinkle
Petunia

Phlox
Pinks
Poppies
Portulacas
Salvia
Scabiosa
Snapdraggon
Statice
Stock
Strawflower
Sweet Pea
Sweet William
Verbenas

Bulbs
Amaryllis
Caladium
Callas
Cannas
Dahlias
Gladiolus
Iris
Lillies
Narcissus
Tuberose
Zephyranthes

March-April

Flowers
Zinnias

Bulbs
Archimines
Begonias
Caladiums
Gloxinias

May

Flowers
Four-o'clock

June

Flowers
Dianthus

July

Your "spring" planting is now complete, but it's still not too late to plant Cosmos, Cockscomb, Gailladias, Salvia, Strawflowers, Verbenas, and Zinnias.

August

Flowers
Tithonias

September-October

Flowers and Bulbs
Much of what was planted in

January-February can be planted again, with the exception of Larkspur and Morning Glory. Plant Pansy, Periwinkle, Petunia, Phlox, Poppies, and Portulacas late in this period rather than early. Bulbs that can again go back into the ground in October include Amaryllis, Callas, Gladiolus, Lillies, Narcissus, and Zephyranthes. October is also the time to put Eucharis and Gloriosas into the ground.

November-December Flowers and Bulbs

Keep on planting. Again, what was good for January and February is good for November-December, with the exceptions of Larkspur, Morning Glory, and Pinks. You can continue to plant Dianthus but not Zinnias. You may continue your bulb planting with Amaryllis, Callas, Gladiolus, Lilies, and Zephyranthes. This also is the time to add Dahlia Tubers and Easter Lilies.

The hurricane season continues through November, but real summer is pretty much over. Near the end of the year, earlier is better than later in much of Florida.

Many casual gardeners prefer to plant by cuttings using the old standbys: Hibiscus, Azalea, Crepe Jasmin, and Poinsettias. In much of Florida it really is just a matter of snipping off the end of an existing plant, sticking it in the ground, going away, and coming back to find a magnificently flowering plant.

FREEZE AND FROST

Frost and hard freeze (28 degrees for more than four hours) is a regular occurrence in north Florida, which has a winter. Both are rare in south Florida and unheard of in extreme south Florida. But they are likely occurrences at various points of winter in central Florida. Frost and even a light freeze can be handled often by simply covering plants. But a hard freeze leaves devastation, or apparent devastation. The first instinct of gardeners, especially those new to Florida, is to cut back and even uproot the damage. Don't. The first order of business is to pick up only loose debris and then live with an unsightly garden, because much of what appears dead is not. Many plants will come back either from apparently dead stalks or from the roots, but not if they are cut back and subjected to another freeze. March 1, when the danger of freeze and frost is most likely over, has become the unofficial "cut back" day in much of Florida.

WATER

Many areas of Florida are under water restriction of one type or another. Violations carry penalties, usually fines. Because of the summer heat and the inherent tendency of many plants to wither in that heat and under the direct rays of the sun, many gardeners, especially those new to Florida, tend to overwater. Those same plants, however, come back almost daily when the heat is broken and the sun is blocked, most often by regular, even daily, rain. Overwatering in Florida not only tempts the law, but it can kill the garden.

STATE PARKS

Florida's state park system, consisting of more than 150 recreational areas comprising 724,600 acres and 100 miles of beaches, is among the nation's finest. It won the 2005 Gold Medal from the National Recreation and Parks Association as the nation's best state park service. The parks offer fishing, boating, camping, backpacking, swimming, scuba diving, snorkeling, horseback riding, cycling, nature and canoe trails, and scores of historic sites. They draw more than 21 million visitors a year.

Many of the parks front on the Atlantic Ocean or the Gulf of Mexico, providing a variety of landscapes. In the Panhandle are mounds of white sand dunes, while the state's subtropical southern tip is famous for its coral reefs and mangroves.

Coursing through the parks are more than two dozen rivers, explorable by boat, canoe, kayak, or tubing. Along the shore grow record-sized trees and rare plants, some lining ravines and sinkholes. More than 300 springs, many of them acquired by the state for public use and preservation, are found at park sites in north and north central Florida.

Most state parks open at 8 a.m. and close at sunset year round; museum hours vary.

Freshwater and saltwater fishing licenses are required, and can be purchased at a county tax collector's office or from a local bait and tackle shop. Park visitors bringing their own horses into a park that offers riding trails must bring proof of their horse's negative Coggins test. In parks that are preserves, no flora, fauna, or fossils may be removed.

Many parks offer accommodations, including campsites. Reservations are available only through ReserveAmerica.

Parks in areas traditionally hit by wildfires in spring abide by local fire regulations, usually banning open burning.

Following is a brief profile of each park. The accompanying map and code are included for quick reference to parks in different regions of the state.

A—NORTHWEST

BIG LAGOON STATE PARK, in Escambia County, is noted for its sandy beaches and salt marshes, important habitats for numerous birds and animals. An observation tower at the east beach offers a panoramic view of Big Lagoon and Gulf Islands National Seashore across the intracoastal waterway. Available are swimming, fishing, boating, camping, and picnicking. The 712-acre park is on Gulf Beach Highway, about 10 miles southwest of Pensacola.

BLACKWATER RIVER STATE PARK, in Santa Rosa County, features one of the world's purest sandbottom rivers. The park's pristine conditions are especially attractive to nature lovers. The river and its banks offer camping, picnicking, fishing, boating, and canoeing. From the town of Harold, the 590-acre park is three miles down Deaton Bridge Road.

CAMP HELEN STATE PARK is a small park, 180 acres, consisting of undisturbed dunes on Santa Rosa Island. Major activities are swimming,

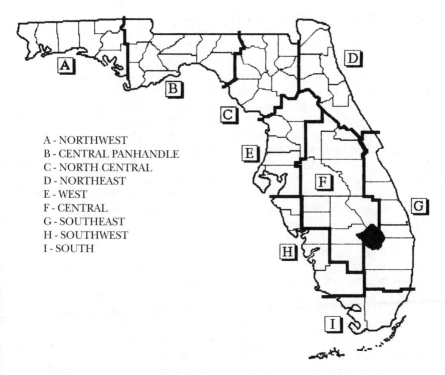

A - NORTHWEST
B - CENTRAL PANHANDLE
C - NORTH CENTRAL
D - NORTHEAST
E - WEST
F - CENTRAL
G - SOUTHEAST
H - SOUTHWEST
I - SOUTH

boating, fishing, nature trails, and picnicking. It is located on U.S. 98 west, about 100 yards past the inlet/ lake bridge. Fifteen cabins are available for overnight stays.

CONSTITUTION CONVENTION MUSEUM STATE PARK, in Gulf County, commemorates the work of 86 territorial delegates who drafted Florida's first constitution. The site, St. Joe, was a boom town created in 1835 to compete as a trading port with the town of Apalachicola. It vanished, however, in the mid-1800s when besieged by yellow fever and storms. The museum is at 200 Allen Memorial Way, Port St. Joe.

DEER LAKE STATE PARK is a 1,920-acre facility on Santa Rosa Beach and is named after a freshwater coastal dune lake within its boundaries. Trail access to the Gulf of Mexico opens to a magnificent dune field and to a pristine section of beach. A new boardwalk spans the dunes. One of the state's least-known parks, it offers lake and river swimming, fishing, and hiking opportunities. Entrance is on CR 30A.

EDEN GARDENS STATE PARK in Walton County was the property of an early Florida lumbering family. Visitors may tour both the Southern mansion and surrounding grounds. A picnic area is provided. The gardens are in Point Washington off U.S. 98 on County Road 395.

FALLING WATERS STATE PARK in Washington County gets its name from its most dramatic feature, a 67-foot waterfall. On the site is a 100-foot-deep sink into which flows a small stream. The area covers 171 acres and offers camping, picnicking, and nature trails. The park is three miles south of Chipley off State Road 77A.

FRED GANNON ROCKY BAYOU STATE RECREATION AREA in Okaloosa County is known as a peaceful camping, hiking, and fishing area, its 357 acres noted for extensive sand pine forests and plant and animal life. Canoeing along the park's aquatic preserve is available. The park is five miles east of Niceville on State Road 20.

GRAYTON BEACH STATE PARK in Walton County is one of northwest Florida's most popular parks because its 336 acres offers all types of recreational activity, including surf fishing. The park is near Grayton Beach on State Road 30A south of U.S. 98.

HENDERSON BEACH STATE PARK in Okaloosa County features 1.3 miles of white-sand beach along the Gulf of Mexico. Available are camping, RV, and picnic facilities, a pavilion, and a boardwalk. The park is just east of downtown Destin on U.S. 98.

PERDIDO KEY STATE PARK in Escambia County is a 247-acre barrier island near Pensacola on the Gulf of Mexico. It not only protects the mainland from storms, but provides a habitat for shorebirds and other coastal animals. Popular are its wide, white sand beaches and rolling sea-oat-covered dunes. The park is 15 miles southwest of Pensacola off State Road 292.

PONCE DE LEON SPRINGS STATE PARK in Holmes County is the site of several natural springs. The sources of the main spring are two flows from a limestone cavity. The two flows produce 14 million gallons of crystal-clear water daily, all of which empties into the Choctawhatchee River and from there into the nearby Gulf of Mexico. The park is a half-mile south of U.S. 90 on County Road 181A.

ST. ANDREWS STATE PARK in Bay County consists of 1,260 acres and offers waterfront camping. Fishing is popular off two piers, jetties, and offshore. Picnic sites are provided on the Gulf beach and on Grand Lagoon. An Environmental Interpretation Center is featured. The park is three miles east of Panama City off State Road 392.

TARKIN BAYOU PRESERVE STATE PARK in Escambia County is home to four species of endangered pitcher plants along with other rare and endangered plant species. A boardwalk takes visitors to the wild bayou. Picnicking and nature trail hiking also are available. The park is located south of the intersection of U.S. 98 and SR 293

TOPSAIL HILL PRESERVE STATE PARK is east of Destin in Okaloosa County on Santa Rosa Beach, off Scenic Highway 30A. The park is named for Topsail Hill, a high, picturesque dune standing 25 feet above sea level. The preserve has 14 natural wild-plant communities from beach dunes to pine flatwoods and holds such rare communities as coastal dune lakes, wet prairies, and maritime hammocks. The Beach Dune community provides habitat for the endangered Choctawhatchee beach mouse. Sea turtles come ashore late spring and summer to nest at the park, while rookeries of herons and egrets are found within the cypress swamps. White-tailed deer, fox, coyote, raccoon, and gopher tortoises are common. The 1,637-acre park is very popular with RVers and contains 156 full-hookup, big-rig sites on paved roads. Furnished bungalows are also available. A tram takes swimmers through the forest to the beach, while fishing is available in six freshwater lakes.

YELLOW RIVER MARSH PRESERVE STATE PARK, in Santa Rosa County on Garcon Point separating Escambia Bay from Blackwater Bay, protects one of the state's last remaining tracts of wet prairie including the largest community of carnivorous pitcher plants in Florida. There are no recreational facilities, but the park offers rare photography opportunities. The park's public access point is on Dickerson City Rd. one mile north of CR 281.

B—CENTRAL PANHANDLE

ALFRED B. MACLAY GARDENS STATE PARK features beautiful ornamental gardens, considered a masterpiece of floral architecture on the portion of the park's 1,076 upland acres at Tallahassee. The gardens, first planted by the Maclays in 1923, features a brick walkway, a secret garden, a reflection pool, a walled garden, and hundreds of azaleas and camellia plants. Park activities include swimming, fishing, canoeing and kayaking, picnicking facilities, and nature trails on Lake Hall, and five miles of multi-use trails for hikers, cyclists, and equestrians surround Lake Overstreet adjacent to the gardens. While the park and gardens are open everyday during daylight, an additional admission to the gardens is required during the blooming season, January through April. The park, which also features facilities for meetings and weddings, is located five miles from downtown at 3540 Thomasville Road.

BALD POINT STATE PARK is located on the eastern tip of the St. James Peninsula in Franklin County, where the Ochlockonee River meets Apalachee Bay. The entrance is on Bald Point Road, off SR 370. The coastal park has more than 3,600 varied acres, including timber flats and upland marshes. Wildlife in the park ranges from the Florida black bear to rare sea turtles. Monarch butterflies rest at the park each autumn before undertaking their annual trek across the Gulf to Mexico. Birding and hiking are major activities for those drawn off the park's white-sand beaches. Canoeing, kayaking, windsurfing, and fishing from the park dock also are popular activities. An observation boardwalk overlooks the park's pristine marshes.

DR. JULIAN G. BRUCE ST. GEORGE ISLAND STATE PARK in Franklin County is a coastal barrier island adjacent to the Gulf of Mexico and Apalachicola Bay. Nine miles of beaches make up the park, which is noted for bird watching, swimming, camping, picnicking, hiking, and shelling. Boardwalks and observation platforms aid visitors in enjoying the area. The park is on St. George Island 10 miles southeast of Eastpoint off U.S. 98.

ECONFINA RIVER STATE PARK is located on the Gulf of Mexico and consists of 3,377 acres of greatly varied landscapes, from pine flatlands, to oak/palm forests, to broad expanses of salt marsh dotted with pine islands, the park offers spectacular vistas and scenic beauty. Primary recreational activities include picnicking, canoeing, boating, and fishing. Unimproved hiking and equestrian trails are also available. It is located in Taylor County at the end of SR 14, south of U.S. 98.

ED BALL WAKULLA SPRINGS

STATE PARK in Wakulla County is the site of one of the world's largest and deepest springs. The Wakulla Springs Lodge and Conference Center offers excellent, comfortable accommodations overlooking the spring, and glass-bottom boats that cruise the park. Picnicking, swimming, scuba diving, and snorkeling are favorite visitor activities. The very popular Wakulla Wildlife Festival is held in the park each April. The park is 14 miles south of Tallahassee on State Road 267.

FLORIDA CAVERNS STATE PARK in Jackson County is 1,280 acres of hammock, floodplain, and limestone outcroppings that feature a series of connecting caves. Guided tours of the caves are given daily. Other activities include picnicking, camping, swimming, fishing, boating, and horse trails. The park is three miles north of Marianna on State Road 166.

FOREST CAPITAL MUSEUM STATE PARK in Taylor County celebrates the importance of forestry to the region. The museum is filled with exhibits of different kinds of woods, and depicts the techniques used to harvest forests. The museum is south of Perry on U.S. 19.

JOHN GORRIE MUSEUM STATE PARK in Franklin County cites the work of John Gorrie, a leading Apalachicola citizen in the early 1800s who invented an ice machine to cool rooms. Some credit him with discovering air conditioning. A replica of his machine is in the museum. The park is on Sixth Street in Apalachicola one block off U.S. 98.

LAKE JACKSON MOUNDS ARCHAEOLOGICAL STATE PARK in Leon County is a complex of six Indian earth temple mounds. Guided tours and interpretive programs are available. The park is off U.S. 27 two miles north of I-10 in Tallahassee.

LAKE TALQUIN STATE PARK holds 30,000 acres ten miles west of Tallahassee, off SR 20 on Jack Vause Road. The lake was created in 1927 by the Jackson Bluff Dam to produce hydroelectric power. The lake—stocked with largemouth bass, shellcracker, and speckled perch—is known for its outstanding fishing. Because the lake is filled with logs and stumps, no swimming is permitted. Boating, hiking, and picnicking are favorite activities. The park is very popular as a site for large gatherings such as family reunions and is open after hours for such events. Very large meets can close the park to the public.

LETCHWORTH/LOVE MOUNDS STATE PARK in Jefferson and Leon Counties features Florida's tallest Native American ceremonial mound, believed built between 200 and 800 AD. The park offers picnicking, birding, and hiking. Located 15 miles east of Tallahassee, off U.S 90 at 4500 Sunray Rd. S.

MADISON BLUE SPRING STATE PARK is in Madison County and centers on its first magnitude spring. Hardwoods and pines are the setting for picnicking. Swimming and snorkeling the springs, river fishing, and paddling the Withlacoochee River are popular activities. Walk-in camping is also available. The park is located east of Madison on SR 6 and the river.

NATURAL BRIDGE BATTLE-FIELD HISTORIC STATE PARK in Wakulla County is the site of a confrontation between Union and Confederate forces during the War

Between the States. Union forces arriving in Apalachee Bay planned to move north and take Tallahassee. The two sides fought at the natural bridge spanning the St. Marks River. After several hours fighting, Union forces retreated. The park is six miles east of Woodville off State Road 363.

OCHLOCKONEE RIVER STATE PARK in Wakulla County is a 392-acre setting of grassy ponds and oak thickets, ideal for wildlife. Picnicking, boating, and fishing are available along the river's banks. The park is four miles south of Sopchoppy on U.S. 319.

ORMAN HOUSE HISTORIC STATE PARK, off U.S. 98 in Apalachicola, was premanufactured in New York and then assembled on the bluff overlooking the estuary and bay of the Apalachicola River in 1838. The two-story home is one of the oldest and most history-filled in Florida. With its grounds officially a state park, the house is open from 9 a.m. to 5 p.m. Thursday through Monday.

SAN MARCOS DE APALACHE HISTORIC STATE PARK in Wakulla County is the site of the first fort built at the junction of the Wakulla and St. Marks rivers. On the site is a museum featuring exhibits and history of the original fort. The park is in St. Marks off State Road 363 on Old Fort Rd.

THREE RIVERS STATE PARK in Jackson County is at the meeting of the Apalachicola, Flint, and Chattahoochee rivers. In its midst is Lake Seminole, a reservoir noted for bass, panfish, and catfish angling. The area also is a favorite for picnicking, camping, hiking, and boating. The park is two miles north of Sneads on State Road 271.

T.H. STONE MEMORIAL ST. JOSEPH PENINSULA STATE PARK in Gulf County offers miles of natural beach in the 2,516-acre park bordered by St. Joseph Bay and the Gulf of Mexico. It is an "index beach" for nesting sea turtles. The park provides excellent bird watching, camping, fishing, hiking, boating, and swimming. The park is near Port St. Joe off County Road 30-E near U.S. 98.

TORREYA STATE PARK in Liberty County is named for a rare species of tree that grows only along and near the Apalachicola River. Special about the park is its steep, 150-foot bluffs along the river. Available are amenities for camping, hiking, and picnicking. The park is 13 miles north of Bristol off State Road 12 on CR 1641.

C—NORTH CENTRAL

BIG SHOALS STATE PARK is a 3,782-acre preserve near White Springs featuring the largest whitewater rapids in Florida. It has 33 miles of trails, with activities including hiking, bird watching, picnicking, bicycling, and horseback riding, plus canoeing, kayaking, and fishing on the Suwannee River. Limited hunting is also available. Big Shoals rapids earns a Class III whitewater classification for kayaking. The downstream Little Shoals are navigable only at high water. Both Little Shoals and Big Shoals have their own entrances off Highway 135.

CEDAR KEY MUSEUM STATE PARK in Levy County celebrates the days Cedar Key thrived as the terminus of the state's first cross-state railroad. The track was used to ship cotton, lumber, and turpentine to Fernandina on the east coast.

These days Cedar Key is attractive to tourists as a rustic island best known for fishing. The museum is in Cedar Key at 12231 SW 168th Ct. off State Road 24.

CEDAR KEY SCRUB STATE RESERVE is located on the western edge of Levy County, six miles northeast of Cedar Key, on SR 24. Oaks, along with saw palmetto, dominate the scrub. It sustains numerous wild flowers native to the area, which also supports the Florida scrub jay, the bald eagle, and the osprey. The 5,028-acre park contains more than 12 miles of trails. Its shallows and numerous creeks are fine for canoeing and kayaking, and saltwater fishing is popular in the adjacent waters. The park has a small picnic area but no campsites.

DEVIL'S MILLHOPPER GEO-LOGICAL STATE PARK in Alachua County features a giant sinkhole, into which visitors may descend via a wooden staircase. The park is located on Millhopper Rd. off 43rd St. in Gainesville.

DUDLEY FARM HISTORIC STATE PARK is located four miles east of Newberry on SR 26 and is open Wednesday through Sunday from 9 a.m. to 5 p.m. It is a living history exhibit of an Old Florida homestead, including original crops, now-antique plants and cracker cows on its 325 acres.

FANNING SPRINGS STATE PARK is on U.S. 1⅜, where it meets the Suwannee River in the town of Fanning Springs in Levy County. The park surrounds one of Florida's first magnitude springs. On the bank of the Suwannee River, the springs release 50 million gallons of water a day at a constant 72 degrees, the average yearly air temperature in the park. The park is a launch site

for river activities, including boating, canoeing, swimming, fishing, scuba diving, and picnicking. There are no campsites in the park.

GAINESVILLE-HAWTHORNE STATE TRAIL runs 16 miles from Boulware Springs Park in Gainesville through Paynes Prairie Preserve State Park and the Lochloosa Wildlife Management Area to Hawthorne. The trail is designed for walking, cycling, and horseback riding. Parking is at the three trailheads at 3300 SE 15th Street in Gainesville, CR 2082 west of Hawthorne, and 2182 SE 71st Avenue in Hawthorne.

ICHETUCKNEE SPRINGS STATE PARK, in Columbia County, is rated by some as the world's finest site for tubing. Springs discharge 233 million gallons of water to make the Ichetucknee, which flows into the Santa Fe River. The Ichetucknee is an outstanding riverfront park that offers canoeing, swimming, scuba diving, hiking, picnicking, nature study, and, especially, tubing. The 2,241-acre park is four miles northwest of Fort White, off state roads 47 and 238. The south entrance is east of Fort White off U.S. 27.

LAFAYETTE BLUE SPRING STATE PARK features a first magnitude spring and a natural limestone bridge that crosses the spring run flowing into the Suwannee River. Fishing, canoeing on the river, swimming, cycling, hiking, and wildlife viewing are among the activities available as is picnicking. Two pavilions are popular for family reunions and parties. The park has a boat ramp. Cabins on stilts above the spring are available as is walk-in tent camping in the park's full-service campground, which also serves as a river camp for travelers along the Suwannee River Wilderness Trail. The park is located at 799 N.W. Blue Spring Road in Mayo.

MANATEE SPRINGS STATE PARK in Levy County is the site of a first magnitude spring that flows into the nearby Suwannee River. More than 2,000 park acres provide hiking, camping, swimming, canoeing, fishing, and scuba diving. The park is six miles west of Chiefland at the end of State Road 320 off U.S. 98.

MARJORIE KINNAN RAWLINGS HISTORIC STATE PARK in Alachua County is in the famous community of Cross Creek, the home of novelist Marjorie Kinnan Rawlings. Her home and its grounds are preserved as a historic site. There are guided tours Thursday through Sunday from October through July. The park is in Cross Creek off State Road 325.

O'LENO STATE PARK in Alachua County is bisected by the Santa Fe River, which disappears underground in the park only to resurface miles to the south where it flows into the Suwannee River. In Depression days, the Civilian Conservation Corps built the park, including its pavilions and still-in-use suspension bridge. It is a unique spot for swimming, canoeing, fishing, hiking, and horseback riding. Numerous cabins, plus a dining hall and kitchen, are available to groups. Primitive and full-facility campsites are also available. The park is six miles north of High Springs on U.S. 441.

OLUSTEE BATTLEFIELD HISTORIC STATE PARK in Baker County is the site of a Civil War battle between Union and Confederate troops. The site is marked by a trail and signs. Every February the battle, which claimed nearly 3,000 casualties, is reenacted on the grounds. The park is two miles east of Olustee on U.S. 90.

PAYNES PRAIRIE PRESERVE STATE PARK in Alachua County is 18,000 acres of prairie, marsh pine flatwoods, hammocks, swamps, and ponds, all teeming with wildlife. Activities for visitors include camping, fishing, swimming, picnicking, hiking, and bridle trails. The park is south of Gainesville on U.S. 441.

PEACOCK SPRINGS STATE PARK in Columbia County includes two major springs and numerous sinks and depressions. It has one of the continent's longest underwater cave systems. Swimming, picnicking, and certified diving are popular. The park is 16 miles southwest of Live Oak off State Road 51.

RIVER RISE PRESERVE STATE PARK is within O'Leno State Park, on U.S. 441, six miles north of High Springs. The Santa Fe River disappears in the O'Leno and reappears again at River Rise. Together, the parks encompass more than 6,000 acres in Alachua and Columbia counties. Activities at River Rise include primitive camping, horse trails, and picnicking. The park's own entrance is on U.S. 27, two miles west of High Springs.

SAN FELASCO HAMMOCK PRESERVE STATE PARK in Alachua County is 6,000 acres of hammock, limestone outcrops, sinkholes, and springs. It shelters one of the few remaining mature forests in the state. Park rangers offer group hikes. Riders may take horses in the park upon request. The southern two-thirds of the park is reserved for hikers. The park is four miles northwest of Gainesville on State Road 232.

STEPHEN FOSTER FOLK CULTURE CENTER STATE PARK in Hamilton County pays homage to composer Stephen Foster, who penned the official state song. It is bordered by the Suwannee River, and is the site each year of folk festivals and programs. The park is in White Springs off U.S. 41 N.

SUWANNEE RIVER STATE PARK in Suwannee County consists of 1,800 acres at the junction of the Withlacoochee and Suwannee rivers. Wildlife is abundant, and visitors can enjoy camping, fishing, canoeing, hiking, and swimming. The park is 13 miles west of Live Oak off U.S. 90.

TROY SPRING STATE PARK, six miles northwest of Branford and 13 miles southeast of Mayo, off U.S. 27 and CR 425 in Lafayette County, surrounds the first magnitude spring, which is about 70-feet deep, with a 900-foot run bordering the Suwannee River. The park includes a half-mile of Suwannee shoreline. The Civil War scuttled steamship Madison can be seen beneath the waters of the run. Swimming, snorkeling, scuba diving, and picnicking are activities in the park, which also can be reached by boat on the Suwannee. Fishing is also available on the river. As in other parks where scuba is permitted, all such divers must be certified, but at Troy Spring, no solo diving or cave exploring is allowed.

WACCASASSA BAY PRESERVE STATE PARK, on the Gulf of Mexico in Levy County, is 32,128 acres of salt marsh, wooded islands, and tidal creeks extending from Cedar Key to Yankeetown and is accessible only by boat. Many endangered species live in the preserve, making the area of special interest to environmentalists.

D—NORTHEAST

AMELIA ISLAND STATE PARK in Nassau County is 200 acres of unspoiled beach along the Atlantic Ocean. It is an ideal area for beach horseback riding, picnicking, hiking, and coastal fishing. The park is eight miles south of Fernandina Beach on A1A.

ANASTASIA STATE PARK in St. Johns County is an excellent bird watching park, with numerous salt and freshwater species along the beaches, lagoons and tidal marshes. Ocean swimming and surfing are popular sports. The park, with a full-facility campground, is at St. Augustine Beach off A1A at State Road 3.

BIG TALBOT ISLAND STATE PARK in Duval County is a barrier island suited to a variety of recreation, including swimming, picnicking, surfing, hiking, fishing, and photography with "the Bluffs" being a top-rated vantage point, The park is 20 miles east of downtown Jacksonville on A1A.

BLUE SPRING STATE PARK in Volusia County is adjacent to the St. Johns River and to Blue Spring Run, both offering boating and fishing. The park also is a winter home for the endangered manatee, which can be seen from an observation platform. Swimming and scuba are not permitted in a manatee area. The park offers cabins and full-facility camping, but primitive camping requires a four-mile hike to the site. The park entrance is two miles west of 17-92, on French Avenue in Orange City.

BULOW CREEK STATE PARK in Flagler County was once the site of two plantations. Today it is a pleasant oasis with a nature trail showing off a variety of plant and animal life. The park harbors one of the largest remaining stands of Southeast Live Oak forest on the state's east coast. It is off old Dixie Highway near the Volusia/Flagler County line.

BULOW PLANTATION RUINS HISTORIC STATE PARK in Flagler County once was the site of a plantation growing sugarcane and cotton. It was destroyed in the Second Seminole War. Picnicking, fishing, and canoeing are available near the ruins. The park is three miles west of Flagler Beach on CR2001.

DE LEON SPRINGS STATE PARK in Volusia County is named for the park's second magnitude springs, around which visitors may swim, picnic, and canoe. The park is in De Leon at the junction of Ponce de Leon and Burt Parks roads.

Eight in One

Eight parks collectively comprise Talbot Islands State Parks: Pumpkin Hill Creek Preserve State Park, Amelia Island State Park, George Crady Bridge Fishing Pier, Little Talbot Island State Park, Fort George Island Cultural State Park, Yellow Bluff Fort Historic State Park, and Big Talbot Island State Park.

DUNNS CREEK STATE PARK is 15 miles south of Palatka between Pomona Park and Satsuma. Situated south of a sharp bend in the St. Johns River, its sand hills are covered by longleaf pines and wiregrass along with sand pine scrub. A 1.5-mile trail takes hikers and bicyclists to Blue Pond.

FAVER-DYKES STATE PARK in St. Johns County is a tranquil, 752-acre park that runs along an aquatic preserve, Pellicer Creek. The creek area teems with wildlife. Fishing, picnicking, and hiking are favorite activities. The park is 15 miles south of St. Augustine near the junction of I-95 and U.S. 1.

FORT CLINCH STATE PARK in Nassau County was the site of a fort built nearly two centuries ago to protect shipping in the adjacent St. Mary's River. The fort was occupied by both Union and Confederate forces during the War Between the States. It is one of the state's oldest parks, its structures built by the Civilian Conservation Corps in the 1930s. The site's 1,100 acres offer camping, swimming, surf and pier fishing, and hiking. The park is north of Fernandina Beach off A1A.

FORT GEORGE ISLAND CULTURAL STATE PARK on Fort George Island, home to another of the units in the Talbot Islands GEOpark complex, has been occupied continuously by man for over 5,000 years, and traces remain of each occupation period. Several plant species occur here far beyond their normal range and Mount Cornelia, at 65 feet, is the highest point along the Atlantic coast south of Sandy Hook, New Jersey. Bicycling or hiking are activities along the island's tree-lined and canopied roads and trails. The site lies approximately 16 miles east of downtown Jacksonville on State Road A1A, or three miles south of Little Talbot Island State Park.

FORT MOSE HISTORIC STATE PARK is on the site of the African community and fortress chartered by the Spanish in 1738 to help guard the approaches to St. Augustine. The community migrated to Cuba when the British took over in 1763. Although nothing remains of the fort, a new visitor's center and the park commemorates the settlement. It is located two miles north of St. Augustine's city gates off U.S. 1.

GAMBLE ROGERS MEMORIAL STATE AREA at Flagler Beach is bordered by the Atlantic Ocean to the east and the Intracoastal waterway on the west. This 145-acre shadeless park offers coastal camping, picnicking, boating, fishing, nature trailing and scenic relaxation. Its 34 modern campsites are on the Atlantic and are among the most popular in the state. Reservations may and should be made 11 months in advance. The beach is nesting home to several species of endangered turtles. Boating facilities are on the Intracoastal. The park is located three miles south of Flagler Beach and 18 miles north of Daytona Beach on Hwy. A1A which divides the park.

GEORGE CRADY BRIDGE FISHING PIER is a one-mile long, pedestrian-only span across Nassau Sound in Jacksonville. It also spans one of the best fishing areas in Northeast Florida, especially good for whiting, jacks, drum, and tarpon. It is open 24 hours a day, every day. Access to the bridge is through Amelia Island State Park.

HONTOON ISLAND STATE PARK in Volusia County, once was home to the Timucuan Indians, a boatyard, a cattle ranch, and a pioneer family. Remote and rustic, its 1,650 acres are accessible only by private boat or by ferry. Camping, nature study, boating, canoeing, picnicking, cabin rental, tent camping, and fishing are available. The park is six miles west of DeLand, off SR 44.

LITTLE TALBOT ISLAND STATE PARK in Duval County is a barrier island on the Atlantic coast that offers five miles of wide beaches, sand dunes, and salt marshes. The site is busy with wild animals, particularly along the adjacent Fort George River. Recreation includes fishing, camping, hiking, picnicking, surfing, and swimming. The park is 17 miles northeast of Jacksonville off A1A.

MIKE ROESS GOLD HEAD BRANCH STATE PARK in Clay County is a 1,562-acre site built on sand hills. Ravines cut through the rolling hills and are cooled by a spring-fed stream that flows into Lake Johnson. Four trails course through the park, whose buildings were erected by the Civilian Conservation Corps. Available is swimming, boating, fishing, camping, and hiking. The park is six miles northeast of Keystone Heights on State Road 21.

NORTH PENINSULA STATE PARK in Volusia County offers two miles of unspoiled Atlantic beach for swimming, sunning, and surf fishing, while "across the road" it shelters numerous rare animal species. Watching for both native and migratory birds is a prized activity. A county park is adjacent. The park is located on A1A four miles south of Flagler Beach.

PUMPKIN HILL CREEK PRESERVE STATE PARK in Duval County protects a 5,000-acre swath of contiguous coastal uplands. Equestrians, hikers, and off-road bicyclists can explore five miles of multi-use trails. The park has a canoe/kayak launch to marshes. The park is east of Jacksonville on Pumpkin Hill Rd.

RAVINE GARDENS STATE PARK in Putnam County was created in 1933 by a federal works project at the site of a steep ravine. The ravine occurred from water flowing under sandy ridges along the west bank of the St. Johns River. Peak flowering season is spring. The park is off Twigg Street in Palatka.

TOMOKA STATE PARK in Volusia County is graced with huge oaks where the Tooka and Halifax rivers merge. Park activities include camping, hiking, fishing, boating, and picnicking. The park is three miles north of Ormond Beach on North Beach Street.

WASHINGTON OAKS GARDENS STATE PARK in Flagler County is a 389-acre park bounded by the Matanzas River and the Atlantic Ocean. Formal gardens are the park's centerpiece, but it is also known for its unique coquina rock Atlantic shoreline. Visitors also can enjoy fishing and picnicking. The park is three miles south of Marineland off A1A.

YELLOW BLUFF FORT HISTORIC STATE PARK is in north Jacksonville off New Berlin Road. It is open 24 hours and free to the public. Its earthworks, commanding the St. Johns River and used by both sides in the War Between the States, draw history buffs. It has a small picnic area.

E—WEST

ALAFIA RIVER STATE PARK is at Picnic in southern Hillsborough County. The park is on more than 6,000 acres of reclaimed phosphate land on the river's south prong. It offers 32 miles of trails, including 18 miles for horses. There's RV, tent, and horse camping as well. Entrance is on SR 39, south of Lithia.

ANCLOTE KEY PRESERVE STATE PARK in Pinellas County features four miles of beach, an 1887 lighthouse, and active wildlife habitats. This pristine preserve provides swimming, nature study, and primitive camping. This park is three miles off Tarpon Springs and is accessible only by private boat. Visitors must bring their own water and supplies.

CALADESI ISLAND STATE PARK in Pinellas County is one of the Gulf coast's few undeveloped barrier islands. Arrivals are by private boat or a ferry that operates from nearby Honeymoon Island off Dunedin. Because the pass between them has filled, it is possible to walk to the park from the north end of Clearwater Beach. Swimming and shelling on one of the proclaimed "nation's best beaches" and strolling the nature trails are favorite activities. Boaters must register before sundown to stay anchored overnight.

CRYSTAL RIVER ARCHAEOLOGICAL STATE PARK in Citrus County features a pre-Columbian Indian mound complex dating back to 200 B.C. The 61-acre site is heavily wooded. Methods used to excavate the mounds, as well as artifacts from the site, are on display. The park is at 3400 N. Museum Point in Crystal River.

CRYSTAL RIVER PRESERVE STATE PARK in Citrus County borders 20 miles of the Gulf coast between Yankeetown and Homosassa. Hiking and biking over nine miles of trails, canoeing and kayaking on the Crystal River, and fishing at the Mullet Hole are popular activities. The park is located west of U.S. 19 in Crystal River.

DADE BATTLEFIELD HISTORIC STATE PARK in Sumter County provides a history lesson to visitors who learn how more than 100 soldiers were killed in a battle that launched Florida's Second Seminole War. An interpretive trail and visitor's center are set among pine flatwoods. Picnickers are welcome. The park is off State Road 476 west of Highway 301.

EGMONT KEY STATE PARK guards the mouth of Tampa Bay. Its past is mainly military and strategic. Visitors can swim from its beaches or walk its historic sites. The island is a haven for the gopher tortoise and other species. Although nowhere near it, the key is in Hillsborough County and located out in the Gulf directly west before the bay. It is accessible only by private boat and activities are heavily monitored.

ELLIE SCHILLER HOMOSASSA SPRINGS WILDLIFE STATE PARK in Citrus County accents Florida's unique wildlife. A display exhibits black bears, alligators, wild birds, and small mammals. In an underwater viewing station, visitors can watch endangered manatees that live at the spring. Pets and smoking are banned in the park. It is at Homosassa Springs off U.S. 19 about five miles south of Crystal River.

FORT COOPER STATE PARK in Citrus County was a refuge during the Second Seminole War and is situated in a hardwood forest dotted with swamp and marsh. Ten miles of trails delight nature lovers and equestrians. Fishing, picnicking, swimming, and canoeing also

are available. During April, a Seminole Indian War reenactment is portrayed by park personnel. The park is on State Road 39 two miles southeast of Inverness.

FORT FOSTER STATE HISTORIC SITE is contained within Hillsborough River State Park. The Second Seminole War fort reconstruction is open only for reserved guided tours and special events.

HILLSBOROUGH RIVER STATE PARK in Hillsborough County has more than 3,300 acres, affording a range of natural beauty. Five trails, including one exclusively for cyclists, wander through it. Swimming, canoeing, and fishing are popular activities. Full-facility RV and tent camping are available, as is, unusually, a man-made swimming pool. The park is 12 miles north of Tampa and six miles south of Zephyrhills on U.S. 301.

HONEYMOON ISLAND STATE PARK in Pinellas County is Florida's most popular state park, drawing more than a million visitors a year. Its main attraction is its Gulf beach. The park also provides diverse ecosystems, from tidal marsh to pinelands. It offers fishing, swimming, picnicking, and boating. The site has been a favorite leisure spot since 1939 when the island, originally called Hog Island, was developed. The park is at the west end of State Road 586 causeway north of Dunedin.

LITTLE MANATEE RIVER STATE PARK in Hillsborough County highlights a river that takes canoers more than four miles through this park. Horseback-riding enthusiasts can enjoy 12 miles of trails in this 1,638-acre facility. A six-mile wilderness trail is available to hikers.

The park is four miles south of Sun City Center off U.S. 301 on Lightfoot Road.

RAINBOW SPRINGS STATE PARK, once the site of an old tourist attraction, is Florida's fourth largest spring. The springs start the Rainbow River. The park's azalea gardens, the river wetlands, and sandhill pine forest are home to many species of plants and animals. Man has been at the springs for 10,000 years. Activities include camping, swimming, picnicking, canoeing and tubing. The azalea gardens bloom in February and March. The park is located three miles north of Dunnellon in Marion County, off U.S. Highway 41. The camping entrance is located 2½ miles north on CR 484 off Dunnellon's S.W. 180th Avenue.

SILVER RIVER STATE PARK in Marion County is 2,300 acres featuring 14 different plant communities, plus riverbeds and springs. Silver Springs is at the headwater of the Silver River, which flows into the Oklawaha River. Canoeing, hiking, and biking are among the park's activities. It also features a cracker village, a museum, and an environmental education center. A full-facility campground and luxury cabins are on the grounds. The park is a mile south of Silver Springs on County Road 35.

SKYWAY FISHING PIER STATE PARK in Pinellas and Manatee Counties is the world's longest fishing pier, the north and south remnants of the old Sunshine Skyway Bridge. With handy parking and lights at night, it's open 24 hours a day every day.

WEEKI WACHEE SPRINGS STATE PARK is the famous "home of live mermaids" that has delighted visitors since 1947. The 538-acre park includes the first-magnitude spring with its 400-seat underwater theater where the mermaids still perform. Visitors may enjoy the white sand beach, the educational shows, take a riverboat cruise, or canoe and kayak on the Weeki Wachee River. Or they can enjoy the Buccaneer Bay water park with its famed flume ride. The park is located at the intersection of U.S. 19 and SR 50, west of Brooksville, north of Spring Hill and South of Homosassa Springs. The park is open Thursday through Sunday, January and February; open daily March through September; and Thursday through Sunday, October through December. The park is closed on Thanksgiving and Christmas Day but open daily Dec. 26-Jan. 2. Buccaneer Bay is closed from October to March, open on Saturday and Sunday and daily for spring break and high summer. Costs to enter the state park and its water park are considerably higher than at other parks

WERNER-BOYCE SALT SPRINGS STATE PARK is on western Pasco County's Gulf Shore near New Port Richey, off U.S. 19. Most of its 3,400 acres are wetlands or are submerged, but it does have four miles of pristine coastline as well as a picnic area and a short hiking trail. Despite its location on the edge of a large metropolitan area, the park is already noted for its large number of wildlife of all kinds. The salt spring for which it is named is not visually impressive, but it does have a documented depth of 320 feet.

YBOR CITY MUSEUM STATE PARK in Hillsborough County focuses on Tampa's rich Latin history in a building that once housed a bakery. A unique and colorful culture, as well as world-renowned cigars, are entertainingly featured. The museum is at the corner of 9th Avenue and 19th Street in Tampa.

YULEE SUGAR MILL RUINS HISTORIC STATE PARK in Citrus County offers a glimpse of plantation Florida when slaves worked David Yulee's 5,100 acres to produce sugar. Yulee served in the U.S. Congress before the War Between the States. The park, open free to the public, is on State Road 490 west of U.S. 1 in Homosassa.

F—CENTRAL

ALLEN DAVID BROUSSARD CATFISH CREEK PRESERVE STATE PARK in Polk County is home to numerous rare plants and protected animal species. Horseback riding, hiking, and wildlife viewing are activities along the preserves' challenging rugged trails. Visitors are advised to bring plenty of their own water. The park entrance is at 3950 Firetower Rd., Haines City.

COLT CREEK STATE PARK is a new 5,067-acre site within the Green Swamp Wilderness Area. The acreage was operated as a cattle ranch with auxiliary operations including lime rock mining, timber, and citrus. The park consists of pine flatwoods, cypress domes, and open pasture land and is home to numerous animal species. Activities include picnicking, fishing, nature study, and hiking or horseback riding over 12 miles of trails. Cycling is limited to service roads. Three primitive campsites are available to organized youth groups. The park, open every day during daylight, is located on a lime rocking mining road off State Road 471, Lakeland.

HIGHLANDS HAMMOCK STATE PARK in Highlands County is a 9,000-acre site that was acquired privately for the public in the 1930s. The Civilian Conservation Corps built a botanical garden next door, and the two sites merged in 1941. Walking the boardwalks through the park exposes visitors to wildlife and various plant communities. The available recreation is hiking and horse trails. The park is four miles west of Sebring on State Road 634.

KISSIMMEE PRAIRIE PRESERVE STATE PARK is 25 miles north of the city of Okeechobee and five miles north of the western end of Okeechobee CR 724. The road that reaches the park is shell, not paved. Five more miles from the entrance of the 84-square-mile park is its Hammock campgrounds, including primitive camps, family camps with electricity and facilities, and a camp for horseback riders. Horseback is one of the best ways to see the park, with over 110 miles of two-trail road. No vehicle traffic is allowed beyond the horseback camp. Hikers and bicycle riders are also welcome on the trails that wander through dry prairie, wetlands, and hammocks. One unusual activity at the park is stargazing. Few locations in Florida are further removed from urban and suburban light pollution.

LAKE GRIFFIN STATE PARK in Lake County is best noted for its bass fishing. Full-facility camping, canoeing, and nature study also attract visitors. The park is on U.S. 441 in Fruitland Park, three miles north of Leesburg.

LAKE KISSIMMEE STATE PARK in Polk County is on the shores of Lakes Kissimmee, Rosalie, and Tiger, all of which offer outstanding fishing, boating, and camping. Hiking along

13 miles of trails brings visitors in contact with deer, eagles, cranes, and turkeys. An 1876 "cow camp" is re-created on the grounds. The park is 15 miles east of Lake Wales off State Road 60.

LAKE LOUISA STATE PARK in Lake County is 4,372 acres on the shores of Lake Louisa. The lake, on the rim of the Green Swamp, is part of a chain of lakes that connect with the Palatlakaha River. The park is noted for its hardwood forests, marshes, swamps, streams, and hammocks. Summer swimming and year-round picnicking, fishing, canoeing, kayaking, and horseback riding are popular. Full-facility and primitive camping along with cabins are available. The park is on U.S. 27, seven miles south of SR 50.

LOWER WEKIVA RIVER PRESERVE STATE PARK in Seminole County is noted for its blackwater streams and wetlands, which provide habitat for bear, otter, wood stork, cranes, and alligators. It is a 4,636-acre park bordering two miles of St. Johns Creek and four miles of the Wekiva River and Blackwater Creek. It is rich in plant life. Available are canoeing, camping, hiking, and horse trails. Equestrian camping is popular. The park is nine miles west of Sanford on State Road 46.

PAYNES CREEK HISTORIC STATE PARK in Hardee County commemorates a fort and trading post established here to protect early white settlers from Seminole Indian attacks. The structures were abandoned after a malaria outbreak. Exhibits about the Seminoles and the fort and trading post are on the grounds. Picnicking and fishing are available. The park is a half-mile southeast of Bowling Green on Lake Branch Rd.

ROCK SPRINGS RUN STATE PRESERVE in Lake County features 12 miles of unspoiled frontage on the Wekiva River and Rock Springs Run. Hiking, primitive backpacking, camping, nature study, canoeing, and horseback riding are permitted, but no swimming is allowed. The park is in Sorrento on State Road 46 via State Road 433.

WEKIWA SPRINGS STATE PARK, in Orange County is 6,397 acres, holding 13 miles of hiking trails. The park's springs are the headwaters for the Wekiwa River, which flows 15 miles into the St. Johns River. Other activities include swimming, canoeing, picnicking, and camping. Horse trails also are available. The park is very popular and sometimes closes on weekends to prevent overcrowding. It is near Apopka on Wekiwa Springs Road off State Roads 434 or 436.

G—SOUTHEAST

AVALON STATE PARK in St. Lucie County is a seaside park and offers more than a mile of undeveloped beachfront. Boardwalks take swimmers, snorkelers, sunbathers, and picnickers over the park's fragile dunes. Swimming and snorkeling do require extra care for offshore there are the underwater obstacles left over from World War II amphibious warfare exercises. The park is located along Highway AIA on North Hutchinson Island.

FORT PIERCE INLET STATE PARK in St. Lucie County is a 340-acre spa along the Atlantic Ocean and intracoastal waterway that is excellent for swimming, picnicking, hiking, and surfing. Bird watchers are entertained by numerous species on adjacent Jack Island. The park is four miles east of Fort Pierce via the North Causeway to Atlantic Beach Boulevard.

HUGH TAYLOR BIRCH STATE PARK in Broward County is a 180-acre oasis in the Fort Lauderdale metropolitan area. It is nestled between the Atlantic Ocean and the intracoastal waterway. Swimming, picnicking, fishing, canoeing, and hiking are available. For joggers the park provides a two-mile run. Facilities include cabins, meeting and dining rooms, and a kitchen. The park is on East Sunrise Boulevard off A1A in Fort Lauderdale.

JOHN D. MACARTHUR BEACH STATE PARK in Palm Beach County is a barrier island fronting on the Atlantic Ocean. Its mixture of hammock, mangroves, and rare plant species beckons visitors, as do its excellent swimming, fishing, snorkeling, and shell collecting. The park is three miles south of the intersection of U.S.1 and PGA Boulevard on A1A.

JOHN U. LLOYD BEACH STATE PARK in Broward County is a 244-acre site dotted by sand dunes, coastal hammocks, and mangroves. Recreation is abundant, including ocean swimming, fishing from jetties, hiking, boating, and picnicking. The park is in Dania off A1A.

JONATHAN DICKINSON STATE PARK in Martin County is a mammoth site of woods, mangroves, swamps, plants, and wildlife. At 11,500 acres, it is one of the state's largest parks. It is home to the Loxahatchee River, designated a national wild and scenic river, on which tours are given aboard a 30-passenger boat. Recreation includes fishing, boating, hiking, cycling, and canoeing. Horse trails

wind through the grounds. Cabins and full-facility and primitive camping are available. The park is 12 miles south of Stuart on U.S. 1.

ST. LUCIE INLET PRESERVE STATE PARK in Martin County is a barrier island accessible only by private boat. Visitors may stroll along a 3,300-foot boardwalk through coastal hammocks lush with palms, ferns, and wild fruit. Miles of Atlantic Ocean beachfront are perfect for swimming, fishing, and picnicking. The park is in Port Salerno and is reached by boat across the intracoastal waterway.

ST. SEBASTIAN RIVER PRESERVE STATE PARK in Brevard and Indian River Counties reserves open forests of longleaf pine once common in Florida. The flatwoods harbor other topographies including a strand swamp. The park is home to more than 50 protected species. Photographers, bird-watchers, and nature enthusiasts can explore along miles of trails on foot, horseback, or bicycle. Canoeing, boating, and fishing are available along the river from launching sites outside the park. The park has two entrances, on CR 507 just north of the C-54 Canal, and off CR 512, nearly two miles east of I-95.

SAVANNAS PRESERVE STATE PARK holds more than 5,000 acres and stretches more than 10 miles from Ft. Pierce to Jensen Beach. Its Environmental Education Center is located on Walton Road in Port St. Lucie. The preserve is the largest freshwater marsh system along the southeast coast of Florida. With more than eight miles of multiuse trails, activities include bicycling, hiking, horseback riding, canoeing, and fishing.

SEABRANCH PRESERVE STATE

PARK in Martin County offers several different natural communities in close proximity. Open but still under development, its main attraction is hiking. The park is located near Hobe Sound on SR A1A about ten miles south of Stuart.

SEBASTIAN INLET STATE PARK in Brevard County offers jetties into the Atlantic Ocean, a beach area, and the Indian River, all famous for fishing for snook, bluefish, redfish, and Spanish mackerel. Campsites along the inlet provide water and electricity. Swimming, surfing, boating, and scuba diving are popular sports. For the less active, a visitor's center features information about a nearby wrecked Spanish treasure fleet. Bird watchers also are treated to countless shore and wading birds. The park is in Melbourne Beach on A1A.

THE BARNACLE HISTORIC STATE PARK in Broward County is named after a home on the grounds called The Barnacle. Visitors may tour the home and picnic on the grounds. A footpath leads visitors to the early Coconut Grove of the 1880s, before Miami was developed. The park is at 3485 Main Highway in present-day Coconut Grove.

H—SOUTHWEST

CAYO COSTA STATE PARK in Lee County is called by some the state's most beautiful subtropical beach park. Cayo Costa is an island, accessible only by private boat or ferry, that is one island in a barrier chain that protects the Florida mainland from storms blowing in from the Gulf of Mexico. The island shelters Pine Island South and Charlotte Harbor with miles of beaches, pine forests, hammocks, and mangrove swamps. Birds proliferate, and shell collecting is ideal during the winter months. Other recreation includes swimming, fishing, boating, picnicking, and primitive, cabin, and tent camping. The park is on Cayo Costa Island, directly south of Boca Grande.

CHARLOTTE HARBOR PRESERVE STATE PARK in Charlotte County rings Charlotte Harbor with a necklace of mangroves. The mangrove forest and salt marshes make up most of the park area, but there are six miles of trails. Visitors may go anywhere in the park except posted areas. Many areas of the park are remote and primitive wilderness, and visitors should take a compass and drinking water with them and be prepared for heat, mud, and mosquitoes. The park has numerous access points. The Old Datsun Trail is at 12301 Burnt Store Rd. in Punta Gorda; additional access is available in Cape Coral, Cape Haze, El Jobean, Little Pine Island, and Rotonda.

COLLIER-SEMINOLE STATE PARK in Collier County is best known for the many threatened and endangered species that populate this park in the Everglades region. Vegetation is characteristic of the coastal forests of the Yucatan and the West Indies. The otherwise rare Florida Royal Palm is common in the park. It is also home to the Bay City Walking Dredge, which built the Tamiami Trail through the Everglades. A six-mile nature trail takes visitors into the park's hinterland, which is popular with primitive campers. Fishing and boating are available. The 4,760-acre park is 17 miles south of Naples on U.S. 41, the Tamiami Trail.

DELNOR-WIGGINS PASS STATE PARK in Collier County is a tropical setting on the Gulf of Mexico. It is a narrow barrier island offering swimming, fishing, boating, picnicking, and cycling. Separating the park from the mainland are mangrove swamps and tidal creeks. The park is in North Naples on CR 901 off U.S. 41.

DON PEDRO ISLAND STATE PARK in Charlotte County is a barrier island park between Little Gasparilla Island and Knight Island. It is reached only by private boat. Recreation includes picnicking, shelling, swimming, fishing, and nature study. Park docks are provided on the bay side via a channel south of the Cape Haze powerline crossing.

ESTERO BAY PRESERVE STATE PARK in Collier County was the first aquatic preserve established by the state. It protects the water, inlets, and islands along 10 miles of Estero Bay. There are miles of trails for visitors to hike or ride. Camping available at nearby Koreshean Historic Site State Park. Estero Bay is located near Estero between Fort Myers and Naples, off U.S. 41 on Broadway West.

FAKAHATCHEE STRAND PRESERVE STATE PARK in Collier County is a major drainage slough of the Big Cypress Swamp. The Strand, a linear swamp forest of cypress, royal palms, and epiphytic plants, may be greater than in any other region of Florida. Besides extremely rare plants, the park is home to abundant wildlife including rarely seen Florida black bears, Florida panthers, and wood storks. Facilities are minimal, with only a boardwalk and hiking trails providing access into the interior. The park is west of Copeland on Janes Memorial Scenic Drive, SR 29.

GAMBLE PLANTATION HISTORIC STATE PARK in Manatee County features the only plantation home in south Florida. It once was headquarters for an extensive sugar plantation. After the Civil War, the Confederate secretary of state took refuge here before fleeing to England. Today, the mansion and its 16 acres are kept in the style of a 19th-century plantation with guided tours Thursday through Monday. Picnicking on the grounds is permitted. The park is in Ellenton on U.S. 301.

GASPARILLA ISLAND STATE PARK in Lee/Charlotte counties is a barrier island on the Gulf of Mexico that, legend has it, was a base for the legendary pirate Jose Gaspar. Picnicking, swimming, fishing, and shelling during winter months are popular activities. A museum, chapel, and the restored 1890 Boca Grande lighthouse are features. The park can be reached via the toll Boca Grande Causeway at Placida and County Road 775.

KORESHAN STATE HISTORIC SITE in Lee County once was the "New Jerusalem" of the followers of Koreshanity, a religion based on celibacy, separation of sexes, and communal ownership of all property. The community took shape in 1894, but by 1961 was down to four members, who deeded the site to the state. Guided walks and campfire programs are scheduled, and full-facility camping, fishing, and boating are available. The park is at Estero on U.S. 41 at Corkscrew Rd.

LAKE JUNE-IN-WINTER SCRUB STATE PARK in Highlands County is an 845-acre area of sand scrub—Florida's Desert—which contains the highest concentration of rare plants and animals in North America. The eco-system is so rare that visitors are urged to stick to the half-mile nature trail and fire lanes. They are also urged to bring drinking water, a compass, a hat, very sturdy shoes, and a companion or a cell phone. Canoeing, kayaking, and fishing are available at the lake. The park is in Lake Placid on Daffodil Rd.

LAKE MANATEE STATE PARK in Manatee County is a 556-acre park on three miles of Lake Manatee's south shore. Mostly woods and marshes, the acreage does offer swimming, camping, fishing, boating, and picnicking. The park is 15 miles east of Bradenton on State Road 64.

LOVERS KEY STATE PARK in Lee County consists of four islands and 1,616 acres. It has two miles of beachfront and is famous, too, for birding. The park is entered on Fort Myers Beach via Estero Blvd.

MADIRA BICKEL MOUND ARCHAEOLOGICAL STATE PARK in Manatee County features a flat-topped ceremonial mound measuring 100 by 170 feet containing at least three periods of Native American culture, the earliest estimated to go back 2,000 years. Although the state has owned the site since 1948, it is just now being developed into a park, and picnicking is its only practical activity. It is located in Palmetto on Bayshore Drive.

MOUND KEY ARCHAEOLOGICAL STATE PARK in Lee County is on Terra Ceia Island, within Koreshan State Historic Site, at Estero, off U.S. 41. It is reachable only by boat, either from the Site's boat ramp on the Estero River or from the Lovers Key State Park boat ramp on Estero Island. Boat and guided tours are provided by the Koreshan staff. A primary feature of the park is a 20-foot-tall, flat-topped temple or ceremonial mound. Activities are those of the Site, and fishing is popular in local waters. There are no facilities at the Mound park.

MYAKKA RIVER STATE PARK in Sarasota County covers 28,875 acres and is one of the state's largest park. It is named for the Myakka River, which flows for 12 miles through its grounds. It has a large wildlife population. The natural landscape includes hammocks, marshes, sloughs, abundant plants, and the Upper Myakka Lake. Available are camping, backpacking, fishing, horse trails, and canoeing. The park is nine miles east of Sarasota on State Road 72.

OSCAR SCHERER STATE PARK in Sarasota County is home to several declining species such as the scrub jay, indigo snake, and gopher tortoise. Swimming is popular in a freshwater lake, and fishing and canoeing are available in the park's tidal creek. Full-facility camping is available on the park's nearly 1,400 acres in a rapidly developing area. The park is two miles south of Osprey on U.S. 41.

STUMP PASS BEACH STATE PARK is at the south end of Manasota Key in the town of Englewood. The 245-acre park consists of three islands—the southernmost mile of Manasota Key, Peterson Island, and Whidden Island—and the protected channels between them. The islands provide a unique area for fishing, picnicking, shelling, and year-round swimming on a mile-long beach along the Gulf of Mexico. Only the portions of shoreline along Manasota Key are accessible by vehicle. The protected waters of the bay are ideal for small-boat cruising, sailing, and water-skiing. Boat-launching sites are located within one mile of Stump Pass and the nearby islands. The southern tip of Manasota Key, abutting Stump Pass, is also a popular anchor. Fishing is good around Stump Pass and on nearby grass flats. The park offers many recreational opportunities to visitors with disabilities.

I—SOUTH

BAHIA HONDA STATE PARK in Monroe County boasts plants and animal species closely aligned with the Caribbean. It has excellent swimming on both its shores—the Atlantic Ocean and Florida Straits. Also offered are camping, boating, and fishing. The park is 12 miles south of Marathon.

BILL BAGGS CAPE FLORIDA STATE PARK in Miami-Dade County is a 406-acre park that fills to capacity early each day. It is on the southern tip of a barrier island, Key Biscayne. Picnicking and hiking are favorite activities. Its historic lighthouse is the oldest standing structure in the county. The park is south of downtown Miami on Key Biscayne off the Rickenbacker Causeway.

CURRY HAMMOCK STATE PARK in Monroe County is made up of a group of islands in the middle keys. With facilities for swimming and picnicking on Little Crawl Key, its hardwood hammocks, mangrove swamps, seagrass beds, and wetlands are of interest to naturalists. Located along both sides of U.S. 1 starting at Little Crawl Key, Mile Marker 56.2, 11 miles west of Long Key. The facilities entrance is on the ocean side of U.S. 1.

DAGNY JOHNSON KEY LARGO HAMMOCK BOTANTCAL STATE PARK in Monroe County was rescued from condominium development and contains one of the largest tracts of West Indian tropical hardwood hammock in the United States. It's home to 84 protected species. Most of the park's six miles of trails are paved and lure birdwatchers, photographers, and bicyclists. The park is located on CR 905, a quarter-mile north of its intersection with the Overseas Highway, U.S. 1.

FORT ZACHARY TAYLOR HISTORIC STATE PARK in Monroe County is named for the president in office when this fort was being built. It took 21 years to complete the three-story fortification, which during the Civil War remained in Union hands. Swimming and fishing are available around the national landmark. The park is in Key West at the end of Southard Street on Truman Annex.

INDIAN KEY HISTORIC STATE PARK in Monroe County is an island reached only by private boat. It was inhabited by Indians for centuries, but became the site of a ship salvaging business in the early 1800s. A prosperous island, its development was halted in 1840 when the settlement was burned by Indians during the Second Seminole War. Remains of the key's early history still can be seen. The park is on the ocean side of U.S. 1 at Mile Marker 78.5.

JOHN PENNEKAMP CORAL REEF STATE PARK in Monroe County covers 70 nautical square miles of coral reefs, seagrass beds, and mangroves. It was established to preserve the only living coral reef in the U.S. Park submerged land covers 53,661 acres, and offers snorkeling, swimming, fishing, boating, and full-facility camping. Uplands of 2,350 acres are home to rare plants. The park is north of Key Largo at Mile Marker 102.5.

LIGNUMVITAE KEY BOTANICAL STATE PARK in Monroe County is an example of life decades ago in the Florida Keys. The park is a 280-acre island featuring trees native to tropical forests. On the grounds and open to the public is the Matheson House, whose owner bought and developed the island in 1919. Access is by private or charter boat. The park is one mile west of U.S. 1 at Mile Marker 78.5.

LONG KEY STATE PARK in Monroe County is halfway down the chain of Florida Keys, and is billed as a sun-drenched tropical paradise. Tropical trees and marine and birdlife are abundant and observable along two nature trails. Fishing, camping, swimming, picnicking, canoeing, and hiking are offered. A family campground allows pets. The park is at Mile Marker 67.5 on the Overseas Highway.

OLETA RIVER STATE PARK in Miami-Dade County is an oasis in heavily urbanized North Miami. Mangrove forests and aquatic areas offer biking, picnicking, fresh and saltwater fishing, canoeing, and swimming along a 1,200-foot beach on the Oleta River and intracoastal waterway. The park, the state's largest in an urban area, is at 3400 NE 163rd Street.

SAN PEDRO UNDERWATER ARCHAEOLOGICAL PRESERVE STATE PARK is under 18 feet of water. The *San Pedro*, a 287-ton, Dutch-built ship that sailed and sank as part of the New Spain fleet in 1733, was rediscovered in the 1960s in Hawk Channel. It is among the most picturesque of the 1733 wreck sites, due to her location in a white sand pocket surrounded by turtle grass. A large pile of ballast stones, 90-feet long and 30-feet wide, marks her final resting place. The site has been enhanced with seven replica cannons, an anchor and an information plaque. It is located approximately 1.25 nautical miles south from Indian Key at GPS coordinates 24 degrees 51.802'N and 80 degrees 40.795'W. Anchoring is at mooring buoys to prevent anchor damage to the site.

WINDLEY KEY FOSSIL REEF GEOLOGICAL STATE PARK is on the bay side of the Florida Keys at Mile Mark 85.5, near Islamorada. It was used as a quarry by Henry Flagler in building the overseas railroad, and its precisely cut stone allows for a close look at the ancient coral reef formation that made the Keys. The 32-acre site has three quarries and 1.5 miles of trail. Picnic tables, but not much shade, are available. Despite its location, there is no access to the shore.

FEES AND REGULATIONS

Entrance Fees	Charge
Admission range	$0.00-$10.00
Vehicle and driver (up to 8 people)	$5.00-$10.00
Selected parks	$13.00

Each additional passenger	$1.00
Selected parks, single occupant vehicle	$3.00
Pedestrian, bicyclist	$2.00-$5.00
Honor parks, per vehicle	$2.00-$10.00
Economically disadvantaged	Half-price
Bus tours	The lesser of $60.00 of $2.00 per person
Annual individual and family passes	$60, $100
Sunset admission	$4.00-$6.00
Children under 6	Free
Children of Military	Free
Picnic Pavilions	Group rental is available, with fees ranging from $10 to $2,500 depending on park and size of pavilion.
Miscellaneous	**Charge**
Museum fee (selected parks)—per person	$2.00-$10.00
Boat launching—per boat (selected parks)	$4.00-$15.00
RV overnight parking	$10.00-$20.00

Cabins

Sixteen Florida state parks offer vacation cabins. The cabins are situated in pristine settings and are convenient to other park facilities and use areas. Parks offering cabins are Gold Head Branch, Jonathan Dickinson, Oleta River, Myakka River, Bahia Honda, Hontoon Island, Cayo Costa, Grayton Beach, Silver River, Fanning Springs, Lafayette Blue Spring, Lake Louisa, Stephen Foster, Suwanee River, Three Rivers, Topsail Hill and St. Joseph Peninsula. Charges range from $30 per day to $180 per day. Wakulla Springs operates a lodge and conference center. Rates range from $95 to $150.

Camping

Full-facility camping fees vary according to season, length of stay, site location, extra vehicles, electricity use, and extra persons. Reservations may be made 11 months in advance. Camping fees range from $1 to $60. Discounts are available. No reservations are required for primitive campground sites.

Reservations

Reservations for full-facility camp-sites, including RV sites, and for cabins must be made through the ReserveAmerica system.

Pets in the Parks

Pets in Florida's state parks are restricted from certain park areas for sanitary reasons and to ensure a more relaxing retreat for visitors. Pets are not allowed in the camping areas, on beaches, in concession facilities, and may be restricted in other designated park areas such as wildlife sanctuaries. Where pets are allowed they must be kept on a six-foot, hand-held leash. Service dogs are welcome in all areas of the parks. Pets must be vaccinated against rabies, and proof must be provided. .

Management and Protection

Florida State Parks are managed as natural systems. All plant and animal life is protected in state parks. Hunting, livestock grazing and timber removal are not permitted. Natural resources, including fossils and artifacts, may not be removed, defaced, mutilated, or molested. For safety, animals are not to be fed. Intoxicants and firearms are prohibited from state parks.

FLORIDA'S MOST POPULAR STATE PARKS
BASED ON ANNUAL ATTENDANCE

Park	Number in Attendance
Honeymoon Island State Park, Dunedin	1,200,000
St. Andrews State Park, Panama City Beach	910,000
Bill Baggs Cape Florida State Park, Key Biscayne	909,000
Gasparilla Island State Park, Boca Grande	846,000
Sebastian Inlet State Park, Melbourne Beach	796,000

BIG PINE FOREST
Blackwater River State Forest, along with Alabama's adjacent Conecuh National Forest and Eglin Air Force Base, makes for the largest forest of longleaf pine trees in the world.

WILDLIFE

No state offers a variety of wildlife as diverse as Florida. Its subtropical climate is suited to creatures found nowhere else in the contiguous U.S., from the placid and endearing manatees to the aggressive and feared alligators and crocodiles. Even the state's birds are enticingly different from winged creatures found elsewhere. Below are details on some of the more famous, and notorious, residents of the state's woods, rivers, lakes, and shores.

MAJOR SPECIES OF MAMMALS

ARMADILLOS are a good example of an exotic species run amok in Florida. The large armadillo population resulted from animals migrating from Texas and being intentionally released. The nine-banded armadillo now lives everywhere in Florida except the Everglades and coastal islands. About house cat-sized, armadillos are uniquely hard-shelled. They grow to nearly three feet long and can weigh 14 pounds. They burrow and their tunnels can also house rats, opossums, snakes, and spiders. Mostly nocturnal, armadillos forage all night for insects and grubs. They always bear four young of the same sex that are born in March and April. Although their sharp-toed front feet cause extensive lawn damage, they help the state by their greedy consumption of many grubs and insects. Some people eat armadillos and report the taste to be like pork. However, armadillos are the only mammals besides humans that are vulnerable to leprosy, and are now used in leprosy vaccine research. For this reason, it is recommended that contact with them be avoided.

BAT species in Florida include the gray myotis, keen myotis, mastiff, big brown, eastern pipistrel, red, hoary, Seminole, eastern yellow, evening, eastern big-eared, and Mexican freetailed. Some species such as the evening and yellow bats may live alone or in small groups in trees without attracting much attention. Colonial bats such as the Mexican freetailed will gather by the thousands in caves or other hollow outcroppings. Caves serve as maternity wards for such species as the gray myotis, which bears one to three young, usually from May to July. Bats eat insects by the thousands during each evening's outing. Moths, mosquitoes, and other insects are the bats' diet staple. Like any mammal, bats can carry rabies, although their secretive habits make them less likely than dogs to spread the disease to humans. It is illegal to kill a bat in Florida, even a rabid one. Florida has no indigenous vampire bats.

BLACK BEARS are limited mostly to unpopulated wilderness areas of the state, primarily in the Osceola National Forest, the Apalachicola National Forest, on the Georgia border in the Okefenokee Swamp, and increasingly are found in the southern parts of the state including the Everglades. Bears make dens beneath trees, in hollow logs, or in caves or rock outcroppings. Females generally bear one to three cubs every other year and the young remain with their mother for about 12 months. The bears' diet ranges from berries and plants to insects and small mammals. They will invade camping areas and garbage sites in search of food. An adult male black bear may roam a territory of 15 miles. Bears have moderately good hearing and an excellent sense of smell. The Florida black bear is a subspecies of other black bear species.

BOBCATS are found nearly everywhere in the unpopulated regions of Florida. Scrappy hunters with razor-sharp claws and needle-like teeth, bobcats prefer a diet of birds and small mammals, although occasionally opportunistic individuals may raid chicken coops. A litter of two to four kittens are usually born in spring and leave their mother within a year. This cat's fur is varying shades of brown and its distinctive bobtail makes it easy to identify. Most bobcats weigh between 15 and 35 pounds and travel alone, unless with kittens, on a range of 25 to 50 miles. Stealth and keen eyesight are the major aids to this primarily nocturnal animal.

COYOTE populations are growing in Florida, with every county providing habitat to these wild canines. Coyotes are durable newcomers. Males weigh about 30 pounds and females weigh 20 to 25. After mating in January and February, female coyotes bear 5 to 10 pups, and occasionally mate with domestic dogs to produce what are called "coy dogs." Food is rarely a problem for coyotes because they eat virtually anything and have a particular liking for watermelon. Florida farmers are concerned about losing livestock to coyotes and blame the wild canines for losses of chickens, goats, pigs, sheep, and calves. But Smithsonian Institution studies reported the coyote's diet is similar to that of foxes, with prey primarily being small rodents such as rabbits. It is legal in Florida to hunt coyotes and they may be trapped with steel leg-hold traps if a proper permit has been obtained from the Fish and Wildlife Conservation Commission. Coyote pens afford a legal new sporting use of captive coyotes, which are chased by dogs until they are killed or escape.

FLORIDA PANTHERS, official symbols of the state, are Florida's most highly endangered species, with a population officially estimated to be approximately 100. Florida's panther is a unique relative of the mountain lion or puma found in other states. The state's largest wild cat, it is identified by a kinked tail, some white spotting, and a peculiar swirl of fur in the middle of its back.

The panther is a good-sized cat, about six feet long, standing 24 to 28 inches tall at the shoulder, and weighing 60 to 80 pounds (females) or 100 to 130 pounds (males). Its range is from 50 to 100 miles, and some panthers are known to have traveled 20 miles in a 24-hour period.

Habitat destruction is the prime reason for the panther's decline. It once ranged throughout the state, but now lives almost entirely in either the Big Cypress Swamp or the Everglades regions of south Florida. Human encroachment has decreased availability of food such as white-tailed deer, and many of the big cats are killed trying to cross highways.

Another snag in panther survival is the animal's low birth rate—two to four kittens every other year. Scientists recently learned that the gene pool of some panther groups is growing severely limited as the small number of animals inbreed. Long-term effects of this are not precisely known, but researchers say male panthers are revealing a high incidence of reproductive abnormality, which could affect birth rates.

In addition, a 1990 U.S. Fish and Wildlife Service study reported high levels of mercury in panthers that live in the Fakahatchee Strand and East Everglades. Scientists believe the mercury is coming from contaminated small prey, such as raccoons, which the panthers eat. Mercury also reduces fertility.

During 1988 and 1989, scientists released a half-dozen sterilized Texas cougars in north Florida to study how well these cousins of the Florida panthers would survive. The cougars adapted well, but by spring 1989 most had been killed by hunters. The remaining cougars were recaptured and the study was aborted.

But the introduction of eight female panthers from Texas in this century is credited with a 20 percent increase in the population. Young panthers also appear hardier.

Panther crossing sign

The U.S. Wildlife Service and the state's Fish and Wildlife Conservation Commission are now studying a new plan to breed captive Florida panthers in an effort to expand the gene pool.

The Florida panther was federally listed as endangered in 1973, and in 1976 the U.S. Fish and Wildlife Service appointed a Recovery Team to draw up a panther recovery program. The legislature named the panther to be the state animal in 1978. It is a felony to kill one in the wild, punishable by a heavy fine, lengthy imprisonment, or both. Persons are asked to report the deaths of Florida panthers by calling 1-800-342-8105.

FLYING SQUIRRELS are tennis ball-sized cousins of the common gray squirrel and are found from north Florida south to the Lake Okeechobee area. These tiny rodents are exceedingly shy and nocturnal. They do not fly like birds, but rather glide from a high branch to a lower limb through use of a skin flap that balloons out from the body. A glide of about 80 feet is optimum. They nest in tree cavities, and mate in February, March, June, and July, with two to six young born slightly more than a month after mating. They eat insects, bird eggs, seeds, and nuts. Their primary predators are owls.

FOX in Florida are either of the gray or red variety. The gray fox is found throughout the state. Only 15 inches tall, it has a silvery gray coat highlighted with reddish brown on its underbelly, legs, under its bushy tail, and around its white face. A hallmark is the black stripe atop the length of its tail. The gray fox is a good climber and will scramble up a tree to be rid of pursuers.

The red fox is found in north Florida down to Polk County. It is vividly orangish red with a white underbelly, black feet, and a white tail tip.

These small members of the dog family are mostly nocturnal. After mating in February or March, they bear litters of three to seven pups. Foxes eat almost anything, including acorns, birds, eggs, small mammals, and insects. They den in hollow logs or in ground burrows.

KEY DEER are confined to Florida's Keys, with most of the population on Big Pine and No Name keys. These "toy" members of the white tail deer family weigh 50-80 pounds and are only two feet tall. They are thought to have miniaturized as a result of adapting to their reduced range, where smaller rather than larger deer survived to breed. Key deer numbered just 25 animals in 1955, but protection has increased their numbers to between 250 and 300 today. Development, highway traffic and dogs continue to threaten their future. They eat grasses, shrubs, and twigs in the wild, but humans often feed the endearing creatures unusual foods but to do so is a violation of state and federal law. Key deer bear one to two young once a year.

MINK, a valuable fur-bearing animal, exists in Florida in two subspecies—the Florida mink in northern areas, and the Everglades mink in the southern region. Minks inhabit the state's freshwater marshes where such food as fish, frogs, turtles, snakes, birds, insects, and mice are available. Female minks bear a single litter of three to four young, usually in May. The Everglades mink is protected from human hunters but not from such natural predators as bobcats, owls, hawks, and foxes.

OPOSSUMS, the state's only marsupial, can be found throughout the state's woodlands. They seek shelter in old logs or brushpiles and are nocturnal hunters of berries, eggs, insects, and carrion. Opossum are prolific and may bear up to 14 young once or twice a year, which are carried in a stomach pouch for the first two months of their lives. Young 'possums later travel on their mother's back. Adult opossums are often hunted for their meat, which has a high nutritional value.

POCKET GOPHERS are often called salamanders by Florida natives. True salamanders are amphibians, while pocket gophers are small mammals about half the size of a rat. It is easy to see the gopher's work—mounds of piled sand. Seeing the worker is more difficult because gophers are solitary and nocturnal. Male gophers dig yards-long tunnels that intersect with females' tunnels. In spring, litters of three to seven babies are born. Gophers feed on roots and other vegetation, and are rated beneficial by most researchers. Gopher tunneling aerates and turns soil over.

WEST INDIAN MANATEES are alive and well and thriving in Florida. For manatees, the 2010 prolonged January cold snap brought news that was both incredibly good and incredibly bad. During and immediately after the cold wave, 431 manatees died, a number in the year's first quarter greater than the record number of manatee deaths from all causes the entire year before, 429. Scientist attributed the deaths to just one cause: cold stress. By contrast, only 42 manatees died of cold stress the year before.

The good news was that the cold forced manatees side by side into the state's springs, rivers, estuaries, and power plant outflows in an attempt to stay warm. By happenstance, the annual one-day manatee census came at the height of the cold and it revealed an astounding 5,067 manatees gathered in the state. The number eclipsed the prior year's count, 3,087. The 2010 record represents a manatee population greater than scientists have long held the state could support. Manatees remain on both the federal and the state's lists of endangered mammals. A federal proposal to designate the manatee as "threatened" rather than "endangered" remains in the process of waiting for a decision. When Florida's Fish and Wildlife Conservation Commission moved forward separately with a similar decision, arrived at before the record-setting census count, it aroused such political controversy that the governor asked the agency to delay its decision indefinitely.

Manatees, another official symbol of Florida, grow to be between 10 and 13 feet long and between 1,200 and 3,500 pounds. They reproduce very slowly, with females bearing one calf every three to five years.

Manatees are slow-moving creatures who enjoy the warmth of Florida's waters in winter. The animals have no fear of man and spend their days placidly grazing the water surface, ingesting about 100 pounds of vegetation daily. This dietary habit exposes the manatee to the propeller blades of boats.

Besides boaters, increasing numbers of divers present a harassment to the giant sea cow.

Discarded fishing lines subject the manatees to entanglement. And fishhooks have been found in the lips of manatees.

Various sovereigns have banned the killing of manatees since the 1700s. Florida again banned the killing of manatees in 1893. The modern Manatee Sanctuary Act proclaims the entire state of Florida as a refuge and sanctuary for manatees and extends the ban to molesting or knowingly causing physical harm to a manatee. Violations are a first-degree misdemeanor and punishment can include prison and fines.

Manatee-saving actions, besides slow boat speed, urged by the Florida Fish and Wildlife Conservation Commission, include:

—Wearing polarized glasses while operating a boat to make it easier to see a manatee swimming under water

—Staying in marked boating channels, the depth of which helps protect manatees

—Keeping boats out of seagrasses where manatees graze

—No discarding fishing gear in the water

—No approaching or touching of manatees by divers

To report injured, killed, or cold-affected manatees, persons are asked to call 1-800-DIAL-FMP (1-800-342-5367).

WHITETAIL DEER are a normally shy and retiring species that has adapted to the state's increasing human population. They live throughout the state, except in the most urbanized areas. Deer are browsers and eat twigs, acorns, shrubs, fungi, and grass. They generally bear two fawns once or twice a year. Because they enjoy leafy plants, deer can cause considerable damage to crops if their numbers grow too large. This often occurs because such natural predators as wolves and panthers are no longer available to balance the population. In-season hunting is a partial control over deer populations in specified areas of the state.

MAJOR SPECIES OF REPTILES AND SNAKES

ALLIGATORS were once relentlessly hunted for their hides, and had become nearly extinct in Florida by the 1960s. In 1967, the federal government declared alligators to be an Endangered Species and prohibited gator hunting and the sale of hides. The alligator responded and by the mid-1970s, the reptile numbers soared to an estimated half-million. In 1977, the alligator's status was upgraded from "endangered" to "threatened," which legalized the killing of the creatures if they were deemed dangerous. Today, the alligator is a Species of Special Concern and the state sanctions tightly regulated hunts to keep a check on alligator numbers, now estimated to more than a million.

Scientists estimate the alligator has undergone few physical changes in the past 200 million years. It is highly adapted to watery habitats of the southeastern U.S. In size, the alligator can grow up to 16 feet, although a 19-foot record length is listed in some references. Well-formed jaws provide ample crushing power for the alligator to eat about anything it wants at a rate of 150 to 200 pounds a day, except during the winter months' dormancy period. Usual diet includes fish, frogs, birds, and snakes, although larger alligators will take raccoons, muskrats, large wading birds, and an occasional wild hog.

With its thick, rudder-like tail and eyes that are protected by a clear lid, the alligator is adept in or under water and can remain submerged for up to a half hour. On land, the alligator is most commonly seen basking in the sun. An aroused alligator, however, can move with amazing speed to seize prey or to protect its nest.

Egg-laying reptiles, alligators generally nest in piles of plant debris mounded up along the bank of a waterway. Nests can measure four to seven feet in diameter and contain a dozen or more eggs. Only an estimated 20 percent of the eggs survive to hatch and predators such as birds, bass, and other alligators take a heavy toll on hatchlings.

Although alligators can be dangerous, they provide a great benefit to creatures with whom they share the wilds. Holes dug by alligators soon become water sources for all animals during droughts. And birds nesting near an alligator nest reap the benefit of a watchful mother alligator that keeps raccoons and other predators from the vicinity. Alligators also feed on the poisonous cottonmouth water moccasins and help control the snake's population.

As Florida's population grows, the alligator's habitat shrinks. The result is that thousands of "nuisance" alligator calls are made to state game officials when wandering alligators are found in carports, swimming pools, storm drains, or on lawns. Wildlife officers relocate creatures less than four feet in length to the more remote swamplands.

Alligators will seek food wherever they find it, so ducks, pets, and even small children may be attacked. Game officials report that since 1948 nearly 250 unprovoked alligator attacks on humans have occurred. Twelve deaths have been linked to alligators in the past decade. Parents and homeowners living near natural alligator habitats are warned to keep children and pets under a watchful eye and to report immediately any alligator sightings that could result in life-threatening situations.

The largest alligator documented by Florida game officials was a 1,043-pounder removed in 1989 from Orange Lake in Alachua County. It measured 13 feet, 10 ½ inches long, and produced 294 pounds of meat and 15 feet of hide for a total of $2,500 in wholesale value. The longest alligator, taken in 1997 from Lake Monroe near Sanford, measured a fraction over 14 feet. A state-operated annual alligator harvest is held each fall, with about 200 participants issued permits. In recent years, alligator hides have sold for about $5 per foot, with meat selling for roughly $5 per pound.

Record Gator

The longest alligator ever captured in Florida was taken in November 2010, by Orlando hobby trapper Tres Ammerman in Lake Washington in Brevard County. It measured 14 feet, 3.5 inches. The previous record was a 14-foot, ⅝-inch alligator taken from Lake Monroe in Seminole County. Alligators at or near the 14-foot mark are extremely rare in Florida. The Florida Fish and Wildlife Commission confirmed the record.

CROCODILES often are confused with alligators, but can be distinguished by their pointier snout and two large teeth protruding from both sides of the snout. Crocodiles are listed by both the state and federal governments as an Endangered Species, and the only place in the United States where they are found is in south Florida. Originally in the Keys, crocodiles spread into Dade County, then across the Everglades as far west as Collier County. They have been found most recently as far north as Manatee County on the Gulf Coast.

Crocodiles bury their eggs in sand mounds and the females usually return to the nests at night. The number of eggs range between 21 and 56, and they hatch in about three months. These reptiles are slightly smaller than alligators, attaining an average length of 10 feet (a record length is 15 feet). They are ferocious fighters, however, and people should avoid approaching them. Their diet is basically the same as alligators: any living creature within reach of its powerful jaws is fair game. However, there have been no crocodile attacks on humans reported in Florida.

GOPHER TORTOISES, large land turtles, have been plodding, natural inhabitants of Florida for centuries. Just 30 years ago, more tortoises than people lived in the state. Today, it is estimated Florida is home to about 1 million tortoises, but their numbers are dwindling as habitats are being gobbled up by developers. The creatures have been listed by the state as a Species of Special Concern since 1978.

Gopher tortoises (called gophers by native Floridians) live in deep burrows in open fields or woodlands. The holes also provide housing for burrowing owls, opossums, toads, indigo snakes, pine snakes, frogs, and mice—some of which are only found in tortoise burrows.

Gopher breeding begins when they are 10 to 15 years old. Females lay 5 to 10 hardshelled eggs in a sand mound near the burrow between February and September. Eggs hatch after about three months, but the hatchlings are preyed upon by many animals, including fire ants, raccoons, and armadillos. Gopher tortoises can live up to 60 years.

Few tortoises live that long. Many are killed when their burrows are excavated to find rattlesnakes during scheduled hunts known as "round-ups," although researchers claim few rattlesnakes live in gopher holes. Hunting gophers, however, is prohibited.

SEA TURTLES of five species are to be found in Florida's coastal water. They are

• **Leatherback Turtle**—the largest of sea turtles. It can mature at six feet in length and weigh up to 1,300 pounds. It is easily identified by its top shell, which is divided longitudinally into six sections by prominent ridges called keels. Coloring is predominately black with white spots.

Leatherbacks have strong front flippers that aid it as a long-distance swimmer in the open sea. These turtles are known to travel more than 3,000 miles to nesting sites. Jellyfish is a staple of leatherbacks and the discovery of deep-water jellyfish in turtle stomachs has led to the belief that these turtles dive to great depths. Leatherbacks range throughout the Atlantic, Pacific, and Indian oceans and some nest in Florida each year.

This turtle's flesh is not particularly tasty. Although some slaughter for meat occurs, the biggest threat to its survival is the taking of eggs for food. They do not thrive in captivity.

• **Green Turtle**—likely the most economically important sea turtle. It is typically about 39 inches long and weighs about 300 pounds. It gets its name from its green coloring, although some locals generically refer to it as the black turtle. Green turtles are found in the Atlantic, Pacific, and Indian oceans, but usually in warm climates. They are known to migrate 1,400 miles in open ocean to reach nesting sites, some of which are along Florida's Atlantic coast. They are plant feeders, grazing on seagrass and sometimes on algae. Green turtles are in danger from human consumption of turtle meat and eggs, and use of turtle leather and shell. Many of these turtles drown in shrimp trawls.

• **Loggerhead Turtle**—a reddish-brown turtle that grows to a length of about 38 inches and a weight of from 200 to 350 pounds. The turtle is named for its large-sized head. Loggerheads are slow swimmers who range about 500 miles out to sea. Florida's nesting population is sizable, with most placing their eggs along the Atlantic coast from Volusia County south to Broward County, and on the west coast in the Cape Sable area. The loggerhead diet is varied and includes crabs, shrimp, jellyfish, and plant matter. Humans have long enjoyed these turtles for food; raccoons enjoy the turtle eggs. Shrimp trawlers and destruction of habitat are other key threats to loggerheads.

• **Kemp's Ridley**—the most endangered of sea turtles. It is a cream and black creature, small in comparison to other sea turtles, measuring about 30 inches long and weighing 85 to 100 pounds. For decades, Kemp's Ridleys were often seen in southeastern waters but the whereabouts of their nesting sites were a mystery. In 1947, a Mexican engineer's film revealed ridleys nested on a remote sand bar beach off the Mexican coast. Numbers so declined, however, that the 1947 population estimate of 40,000 turtles had been reduced to between 400 and 600 females.

Conservation efforts since 1978 on the part of Mexico and the U.S. include beach patrols and tagging. The most recent count on Mexico's now protected beach havens charted 6,000 nests. The ridley's diet includes fish, jellyfish, crustaceans, swimming crabs, and mollusks.

• **Hawksbill Turtle**—readily identified by its birdlike beak. The hawksbill grows to a length of three feet and weighs about 100 pounds when mature. It is found throughout the world in shallow waters where it dines on vegetation and may consume sponges.

Only a few Florida nesting sites have been documented, most of them on offshore reefs and in the Keys. These turtles historically have been prized for their attractively marked shells used for ornaments or jewelry, especially in Japan, to which an estimated 40 percent of the Caribbean based hawksbill turtle shell is shipped. Most serious depletion of hawksbill population occurs in southeast Asia, where

some 65,000 turtles are killed each year for their shells.

Declining sea turtle numbers prompted the federal government in 1988 to enact a law requiring use of Turtle Excluder Devices (TEDS) in Florida waters from May 1 through August 31. These devices allow sea turtles to escape from shrimp trawling nets and are required on all domestic trawlers over a certain length plying U.S. coastal waters. Stiff penalties await those who do not conform to the regulations.

Currently, the leatherback, Kemp's Ridley, and hawksbill turtles are included on federal Endangered Species lists, and the green turtle is Endangered on the state's list. They are protected by federal and state laws, so it is illegal to import, sell, or transport these turtles or their products in interstate or foreign commerce without special permits. It is also unlawful to tamper with nesting turtles or eggs.

SNAKES are plentiful in Florida. The state has more snake species than any other. By far, most varieties are harmless consumers of worms, lizards, and frogs. Only six species in Florida are poisonous, three of them members of the rattlesnake family. All six are capable of causing painful bites that are seldom fatal. Nationally, for example, of the approximate 6,000 persons bitten by poisonous snakes each year, fewer than a dozen die. Most bites occur during the warm spring and summer months when the snakes are most active.

The best precaution that can be taken against being bitten by poisonous snakes is to familiarize yourself with these species and give them a wide berth when you see them. Memorize what they look like, where their habitats are most likely to be found, and always look down toward the ground when treading in the woods and swamplands they habitate. Whenever possible, step over rather than on hollow logs, debris piles, and other likely snake nesting sites. As a rule, snakes are more afraid of us than we are of them and will normally run from us, but don't count on it in all cases. They will bite if stepped on, molested, cornered, or if they are defending a nest. When hiking in the woods or swamps, thick high boots are recommended. When cleaning up long-standing piles of wood, boards, leaves, trash, or other debris around the house or farm, turning them with a long-handled rake at first is safer than reaching in with your bare hands.

If a snakebite does occur, there are recommended immediate procedures that can and should be taken prior to admission to the hospital. These emergency procedures are often published in brochures given out free by pharmacies, hospitals, state agencies, or other public service organizations. These brochures should be kept in a convenient location in the house and carried on all outings into snake habitats.

Florida's poisonous snakes are
• **Diamondback Rattlesnake**— the largest, most dangerous snake native to Florida. Its large body size, quantity of venom, aggressive defensive tactics, and blazingly accurate striking speed make it a snake to be treated with utmost respect.

The diamondback is recognized by a distinctive pattern of yellow-bordered, diamond-shaped body markings. Brittle, button-shaped segments form a rattle at the end of the tail. The arrow-shaped head is much wider than the neck.

Found in every county in Florida, the diamondback also inhabits many of the coastal islands. It may be encountered in almost any habitat, but most commonly frequents palmetto flatlands, pinewoods, abandoned fields, and brushy, grassy areas. In most situations the snake is difficult to spot because its color pattern blends into the background.

When disturbed the rattler assumes a defensive posture with body coiled, head and neck raised, rattle free and elevated to sound a warning. From this stance, if the target is close, the rattler can repeatedly deliver a stabbing strike. Its optimum striking distance is from one-third to more than one-half its body length.

Recurving fangs lying folded inside the roof of the rattler's mouth become erect when the mouth is opened wide during a strike. As the fangs pierce a victim, pressure is exerted on poison sacs and the venom is pumped into the wound. The rattler does not have to be coiled to strike; it can strike from any position, in any direction. When disturbed or when protecting a nest, it may sound a warning rattle, but not always.

Diamondback rattlers shed skin three to five times a year, depending on the amount of food it takes in, which governs its growth. A new segment is added to the rattle at each shedding, a phenomenon that allows herpitologists to estimate a rattler's age. Although it may attain a length of more than eight feet, it is rare to find a rattler longer than seven feet. Rattlesnakes feed mainly on small mammals such as rabbits, squirrels, rats, mice, shrews, and sometimes birds.

Rattlers bear 9 to 15 young at a time. Newborn rattlers are equipped with venom and the fangs to inject it.

This species is commercially valued for its hide, meat, and venom, and for exhibition purposes. It renders valuable service to farmers by preying on crop-destroying rodents. Besides large birds, the rattler's natural predators include the indigo snake and the scarlet king snake.

• **Canebrake Rattlesnake**—found mainly in north Florida, but reported as far south as Alachua County. This snake is the southern counterpart of the timber rattler found in other parts of the U.S.

The canebrake is recognized by a grayish-brown or pinkish-buff color, with dark bands across its body, an orange or rusty-red stripe down the middle of its back, and a brown or black tail that bears a rattle. As with other rattlers, the canebrake's head is much wider than its neck, but it is more slender than the average diamondback. Florida specimens rarely measure more than five feet long.

This snake is commonly found in flatwoods, river bottoms and hammocks, and may be found in abandoned fields and around farms. During hot weather, it may seek low, swampy ground.

• **Pygmy Rattlesnake**—also called the ground rattler. It is commonly found in all of Florida's counties and on some offshore islands. Its rattle is small and slender and produces a buzzing sound like an insect. This signal can be heard from no more than a few feet away.

Stout-bodied for its diminutive size of less than 18 inches, the pygmy is gray and prominently marked with roundish dusky-colored spots. At the base of its head, red spots alternate with black along the midline on the back.

Pygmy rattlers feed on small frogs, lizards, mice, and other snakes. Like other members of the pit viper family, it does not lay eggs, but gives birth to live young.

These snakes are encountered primarily in wetlands, in palmetto flatwoods, or in areas of slash pine and wire grass. For its size, the pygmy rattler has a feisty disposition and is quick to strike. Its bite produces pain and swelling that normally subsides in a few days. It can be fatal to humans under some circumstances, but no deaths from a pygmy rattler bite have been recorded.

• **Cottonmouth (Water Moccasin)**— the only poisonous water-dwelling snake in North America. The cottonmouth is a pit viper that has no rattles and grows to a large size, usually more than five feet. Most Florida specimens average about three feet and are found in every county and on many coastal islands.

Coloring of the cottonmouth varies from olive-brown to black, with or without dark crossbands on the body. It is stoutly shaped, with an abruptly tapering tail and a broad head much wider than its neck. A distinctive mark is a dark band extending from the eye to the rear of the jaw. A drooping mouthline and protective shields over its eyes give it a sullen expression.

A disturbed cottonmouth often draws into a loose coil, cocks its head up, and opens its mouth wide to reveal a white interior, hence the name cottonmouth. From this pose it lunges out in a fast strike to imbed its poisonous fangs. It usually keeps a hold on prey, chewing in order to drive its fangs deeper. It does not have to be coiled to strike, but can deliver a bite from almost any position, in or out of water. It is unpredictable and may behave calm and sluggish, or aggressive.

As a water snake, the cottonmouth is usually found along the edges of lakes, swamps, and marshes, where it hides in brushy areas or in low trees overhanging the water. It forages at night for fish, frogs, other snakes, lizards, and small mammals.

Cottonmouth young, 6 to 12 of them in the average litter, are born with poison sacs loaded and ready. The little snakes are boldly marked with red-brown crossbands and bright yellow tails. At this stage they can be mistaken for another poisonous species, the copperhead.

Poison of the cottonmouth causes much pain and swelling. But with immediate medical treatment, the bite is only occasionally fatal to humans.

• **Copperhead**—found only rarely in Florida in a few northwestern Panhandle counties. This is a primarily northern mountain and wilderness snake that hibernates in the winter. Reports of bites from this snake are rare in Florida, and no deaths have ever been attributed to the copperhead by state health agencies.

The copperhead is a handsome snake, with pinkish-tan body color and reddish-brown crossbands. The bands are wide along the sides and narrow along the back, forming something of an hourglass shape. The copper-colored head from which it receives its name is wider than the neck. Its average length is less than three feet. The copperhead's coloration is so similar to that of young cottonmouths that the two are often confused with one another.

• **Coral Snake**—brightly colored and the most deadly venomous snake in North America. Corals are related to the cobras, kraits, and mambas found in tropical countries. Fortunately, most coral snakes are shy and secretive and will not bite unless startled, tormented, or hurt. It has short fangs and a small mouth and does not strike like the pit vipers, but bites and chews to inject its poison.

Most bites from coral snakes occur when people pick up or attempt to touch one. As a result, fingers are the most frequent target for the coral's venom, although toes and other parts of the feet may be attacked if a person steps on or near the snake.

Coral snakes often are confused with the harmless scarlet king snake. Both snakes have brightly colored bands of red, black, and yellow. However, the red rings of the coral snake border the yellow, whereas the red rings of the non-poisonous king snake border black. A helpful rhyme goes: "Red touch yellow, kill a fellow; red touch black, good for Jack." The coral snake also has a black nose; the king snake has a red nose.

The largest coral snake recorded was 47 inches long, but most specimens are less than two feet. The coral's body is small and slender, and it has a narrow head more commonly found on non-poisonous species of snakes.

Pine woods, under rotting logs or brush piles, along pond or lake borders, or dense hammock areas

are the most common sites of coral snake nests. It eats frogs, lizards, and other snakes, and lays up to half a dozen eggs that hatch in two to three months.
CONSTRICTORS Burmese Pythons, escaped or abandoned legal pets, and their offspring are thriving in the Everglades and causing a serious danger to the bioenvironment and perhaps people. Wildlife officials have already witnessed epic battles between pythons and alligators and while the protected state symbol usually wins, experts fear it may someday be outnumbered. Pythons can routinely grow from 15 feet to 20 feet in length and weigh more than 200 pounds. Everglades National Park officials removed 52 pythons from the park prior to 2003. But in 2004 alone, they removed 61, and in 2005, the constrictor was being dispatched at a rate of 15 a month. Anything that moves is prey to the python including all Everglades wildlife. There are serious concerns about human safety as well. Large African Monitor lizards are also making their way into the Everglades and breeding. Although the 2010 cold snap killed nine of every ten pythons banded by the state for tracking, estimates are that it killed only half the deadly population and a quick rebound is expected. And the Burmese python is not alone. Also surviving and making their way through the Everglades are other, more aggressive constrictors including the Indian python, the reticulated python, and the northern and the southern African rock pythons, the Amethystine or scrub python, and the green anaconda.

MAJOR SPECIES OF BIRDS

BROWN PELICANS are commonly seen along Florida's coast, and this expert diver is easily recognized by the large pouch underneath its long bill. Its pouch is not used to carry or store fish, but rather acts as a scooping strainer as the pelican gathers the fish.

A stocky bird, the brown pelican's wingspan can reach 90 inches. They are aggressive and noisy companions at nearly every fishing dock, where they await castoff bait or scraps of fish.

In Florida, the brown pelican is a Species of Special Concern because its numbers have declined in past decades. Studies have attributed this to the use of insecticides that, when ingested, weaken egg walls causing them to break before hatching. Brown pelicans lay two or three white eggs in a nest of sticks or grass in trees or low bushes. Some individuals may lay eggs on the ground. Loss of habitat and harassment has added to the decline of this bird's numbers. As Florida's human population has grown, and more and more coastal islands have been developed, greater numbers of Floridians are boating and fishing. These encroachments have been detrimental to the brown pelican population, currently estimated in Florida to be around 6,000 nesting pairs.
CRANES, specifically the sandhill specimen, are a most spectacular Florida resident. They once were plentiful all over the United States, but today can be found only in isolated areas. These cranes stand up to four feet tall and have a wingspan of about 80 inches. After an elaborate mating ritual, the female lays two buff-colored eggs in a grassy nest in marshlands. It is a Threatened Species and experts fear it will eventually decline, as did the whooping crane.

CRESTED CARACARA is rapidly declining in its habitat north and west of Lake Okeechobee. This long-legged raptor stands 20 to 25 inches from head to tail and has a 4-foot wingspan. It is boldly patterned with vulture-like red skin on its face and a distinguishing crest of dark brown. Primary prey includes reptiles, other birds, mammals, and carrion. Nests are built of twigs and limbs in cabbage palms, but only 250 nesting pairs of the crested caracara, also called the Mexican eagle, are believed to exist in Florida. It is on both the state and federal threatened species lists.

EAGLES, the national bird, are enjoying a resurgence in Florida. With more than 1,100 nesting pairs, the state is the largest eagle breeding ground in the country outside Alaska.

Florida classifies the southern bald eagle as a Threatened Species, although the federal government has removed eagles from the Endangered list. Consequently, land development in Florida is restricted within a mile of an eagle's nest. In Florida, where wildlife officials estimate 75 percent of the eagle population lives on privately owned land, this has created land-use problems.

The state's eagle population generally mates in the fall, with about two eggs appearing in nests between October and February. The eggs require about a month to hatch and young spend nearly four months maturing. An average of one eaglet survives in most nests.

A most regal bird, the southern bald eagle boasts a wingspan of up to 90 inches. Eagles are meat eaters and they prefer fresh-killed prey such as rodents, squirrels, land reptiles, and other birds.

Human-eye view of some of Florida's most graceful large birds as they soar overhead. Top to bottom: bald eagle, turkey vulture, osprey, and red-tailed hawk.

EGRETS of several varieties live in Florida all or most of the year. The great egret, the snowy egret, the reddish egret, and the smaller cattle egret all breed in the state.

HERONS such as the great blue, the great white, the tri-colored, the little blue, and the green-backed live in Florida year-round. Their plumage and grace makes them great favorites of bird lovers. Several are Species of Special Concern.

One of Florida's most famous and beautiful birds, the pink flamingo, is a member of the heron family. Once highly sought after by plume hunters, they are found in especially large numbers in the Everglades, where they are protected.

KITES in Florida are primarily the Everglades species. This species is a sleek gray (male) or brown (female) bird that feeds exclusively on snails and is often listed as the snail kite. It is a shy bird, seldom seen or heard, and is highly endangered because of the invasion of Florida's waterways by water hyacinths, which effectively hide snails from the kite. Recent surveys report the kite population to be stable.

OSPREYS, hawklike brown birds, are another of Florida's Species of Special Concern. Ospreys are adept at fishing with their feet, which are equipped with sharp spikes that aid in carrying a fish back to the nest.

Wherever there is water there is likely an osprey. Nests are easily spotted masses of twigs and sticks often in trees, but just as often stuck on a light pole, a channel marker, or a telephone pole. As with other fish-eating birds, the osprey's numbers declined because of pesticide use.

OWLS are predominantly nocturnal and are sure to delight any camper or bird watcher. The state is home to several species, including the great horned owl, barred owls, barn owls, and burrowing owls.

Environmentally important, owls eat snakes, roaches, grasshoppers, and small rodents. Many species live in dead trees or, if possible, in vacant outbuildings. The burrowing owl, which makes its home in ground holes, is a Species of Special Concern.

SCRUB JAYS are a crestless and more brilliant type of jay than the common blue. The scrub jay is classified as a Threatened Species. It is to be found only in the state's more isolated areas where it feeds on insects, acorns, and berries. Scrub jays mate for life.

SONGBIRDS by the thousands either live in Florida or visit during winter. Major species include larks, jays, titmice, wrens, warblers, thrushes, vireos, cardinals, sparrows, orioles, mockingbirds, and finches.

VULTURES, winged scavengers, are often looked upon with disdain because they feed on carrion. This is a vital natural function, however, which keeps the environment healthy. Often called "nature's cleanup crew," vultures can be seen circling slowly, searching for food while riding the thermal air currents.

The turkey vulture is nearly the size of an eagle and frequents forests and farmlands. Vultures nest in fallen logs or in hollow trees, laying a couple of brown and white eggs inside the crevice with no nesting material.

Black vultures are slightly less common and are smaller than the turkey vulture but their nesting habits are similar. The species recently has come under state protection.

WILD TURKEYS are popular hunting fare in Florida. They are similar to domestic turkeys, but are much more wary and are of a sleeker build. They are found throughout the state, but are scarce in the Everglades. Mating activity begins in March and an average nest contains 8 to 11 eggs. Although Florida is ranked as a leading turkey hunting state, destruction of habitat is expected to affect their numbers in the wild.

WOOD STORKS, gracefully large wading birds, boast a wingspan of over five feet. Wings have conspicuous black marks, as does the tail. Colonies of thousands of wood storks once roosted in the cypress and mangrove swamps of Florida. This bird is listed as endangered because its population declined rapidly from more than 70,000 in the 1930s to about 16,000 today. The primary reason for the population decrease is the draining of wetlands and logging activities, as well as the destruction of mangroves. It is North America's only true stork.

WOODPECKERS abound in Florida, ranging from the rather small, colorful redheaded woodpecker to the pileated woodpecker whose body is 17 inches long. The ivory-billed woodpecker is endangered and may be extinct. No reliable sightings of this magnificent bird have been reported in more than 10 years. Numbers of the red-cockaded woodpecker are also dwindling as stands of old-growth pine are timbered. This 8-inch bird lives only in live pine trees, where resin drips protect the nest from predators such as the pine snake. But it can take years for red-cockaded woodpeckers to peck out a nesting cavity, so humans are helping by installing pre-constructed nesting boxes in pine trees.

Hooked or Tangled Sea Birds

Seabirds tangled in discarded fishing lines are not an uncommon sight along the shore of Florida. In most cases, the bird, often a pelican, has been unknowingly snared by a careless fisherman's discards. Unless attended to, the bird probably will suffer a slow, torturous death. Under no conditions should a line, nor a multiple hook, be left in a bird. Wildlife officers have some suggestions for helping a hooked bird.

They urge that the bird be captured. If the victim is in the water, a large hoop net is recommended. If on land, the victim should be gathered in a towel, shirt, blanket, or other cloth. Removing a hook is not difficult. In the case of a pelican that is hooked in the pouch below the bill, for example, hold the bill and cut off the hook barb; then back the hook out. Never cut the line and expect the bird to free itself. Leaving a trailing monofilament line on a bird can be disastrous. The bird very likely will accidentally hang itself from the line at its nightly roost.

Once the hook and line have been removed, ideally the bird should be brought to a bird sanctuary for further treatment and extended care.

To prevent hook and line injuries, several precautions should be taken. Among them: Be aware of pelicans and seabirds when fishing, and always avoid casting while birds are in the vicinity. Do not leave fishing lines unattended, especially when they are baited. Do not throw waste line overboard. And do not leave a rod with the line reeled up and hook dangling—birds can fly into dangling hooks or lines and become tangled.

Another danger to seabirds is six-pack plastic rings. Water birds and ducks have been known to stick their heads into one of the rings and not be able to shake it loose. Slow starvation often results if the plastic ring restricts feeding and flying. To discard six-pack plastic rings, cut all connections of plastic to "open" the rings and dispose of the remains in proper trash receptacles.

VENOMOUS SPIDERS

There are few poisonous spiders in Florida. Only two species, in fact, can cause serious injury or death, but their bites are nonetheless painful and immediate hospital treatment is recommended for victims. As is the case with poisonous snakes, the best assurance against being bitten is visual recognition of the harmful species and avoiding them on sight. Observing caution around their most likely habitats is also recommended, including checking under toilet seats in unfamiliar places before sitting down.

The venomous spiders found in Florida are

• **Brown Recluse**—most commonly found in the yard or house. Indoors, this spider prefers to hide behind books, furniture, in shoes, clothing, in folded towels, and under items left lying on the floor. Outdoors, the brown recluse, as its name implies, hides under rocks, loose bark, and any other secretive areas.

This rusty-brown spider also is called the violin spider because it has such a shape outlined in darker brown shades on its back. Including legs, the brown recluse is about the size of a half-dollar.

The source of its painful bite is a nerve poison that kills cells as it spreads through tissue. The longer the poison remains in the victim's system, the greater the tissue damage, and some severe bites may take months to heal. Instances of red blood cell destruction have been reported which resulted in kidney or liver problems in victims, particularly in children and in elderly persons. A telltale symptom of the brown recluse bite is a crusty wound that forms a reddish-purple

zone on the flesh surrounding the site. Bite victims should try to remain calm, since panic results in a more rapid flow of blood and the poison carried in it through the body. Emergency hospital treatment should be sought immediately.

• **Widows**—native to Florida in four species. All are potently poisonous, but reports of serious encounters have involved only the southern black widow. The bite of these spiders is a needle-like pang that is followed in about 15 minutes by muscle cramps, usually in the shoulder, thighs, and back. Severe pain later spreads to the abdomen, and weakness and tremors follow. Breathing may grow difficult, and the skin becomes cold and clammy. In severe instances, shock and vomiting may occur. Medical treatment should be sought immediately. Treatment with antivenin is effective. Reported deaths occurred because the victim suffered from an additional health problem such as heart disease. In one case, the victim was bitten at the base of the skull and the spider's venom traveled rapidly to the brain.

Florida's widows species are:

—**Southern black widows,** a glossy black or dark reddish-brown-colored spider with a distinctively bright orange hourglass marking on the frontal abdomen. The southern black widow is the most widespread of Florida's widow spiders and can be found in stumps, pipes, building materials, under stones, in storm sewers, in water meter boxes, and under the ledges of seawalls throughout the state.

—**Northern black widows,** which behave and appear nearly the same as the southern version, except that they have two red-orange barlike designs on the frontal abdomen instead of the more obvious hourglass. The northern widow has been found only in the state's Panhandle, usually west of Tallahassee.

—**Red widows,** which prefer the palmettos of pine scrublands in central and southeastern Florida. This is an exotic-looking spider, red everywhere except on the abdomen, which is dark brown and often has several yellow or orange spots.

—**Brown widows,** varying in color from light gray or brown to almost black. The abdomen is usually highly marked with spots or lines of white, red, and yellow. The frontal abdomen includes the classic red-orange hourglass. This spider lives in the state's southeastern coastal regions, rarely north of Daytona Beach, and prefers well-lighted haunts such as automobile service stations.

MAJOR INSECT PESTS

AFRICANIZED BEES have permeated Florida since arriving in 2002. The newcomers are mingling with the state's European honeybees. They appear to be dominating hives in the wild but being dominated in the managed hives that are the basis of the multi-million dollar honey and pollination industry. Africanized bees produce less honey than European honeybees and are less easily managed by beekeepers, factors that could cause costs to rise. The state's plan to minimize the impact of Africanized bees focuses on diluting the African strain by crossbreeding. Africanized bees have been dubbed "killers" because they have caused some 350 deaths in Latin America. Africanized bee venom is no more potent than that of other bees, but this species swarms angrily and will pursue those disturbing their nests for greater distances than their more docile European cousins. Most reported deaths have occurred because of massive numbers of stings. Africanized bees are slightly smaller and darker colored than other varieties.

CHIGGERS are minor Florida pests found in underbrush. They burrow under skin and can cause severe itching and possible secondary infections. Tree bark, moss, even wooden picnic benches can harbor chiggers. Preventative insect repellents help, and an after-hiking bath is recommended. Clear nail polish dabbed on chigger bites is reputed to smother the insects.

FIRE ANTS are to be found throughout Florida. Contrary to many notions, fire ants are not unusually large. They measure from one-sixteenth to one-fourth of an inch long. Such small sizes belie the ferocity of this ant's sting and at least one infant death has been reported due to massive numbers of ant bites. Fire ants are reddish-black and have proportionately large heads. Their mounds or nests are excavations usually found in woods or fields and often are placed near protective shrubs, but they are a problem for homeowners' lawns as well. Some nests may contain up to a half-million ants and, when their nests are stepped on, they may swarm up the person's leg and attack in force.

These ants can cause severe problems among farmers because newly born calves, lambs, or foals may become targets of the insects, which are attracted to the mucous membranes of the young animals.

Pet owners should protect newborn puppies or kittens from fire ants.

Medical problems from fire ant bites can be severe. After the initial, painful bite, secondary infection or allergic reactions may occur.

Scientists are investigating several natural fire ant eradication methods. Boiling water, while initially killing some ants, will usually just prompt surviving ants to move the nest to another location. Commercial baits work well when worker ants carry the bait into the nest to the queen.

FLEAS affect Florida pets and their owners, especially in warm months. Dogs need frequent bathing and insecticidal sprays or dips may be necessary. Frequent vacuum cleaning as well as household flea sprays and applications of boric acid may be necessary to prevent infestations of dwellings.

FRUIT FLIES, particularly the Mediterranean, are the bane of Florida's citrus industry. Fruit fly (also called Medfly) infestations have damaged Florida citrus crops in the 1920s, the 1950s, the 1960s, the 1980s, the 1990s, and most recently in 2010. The fly's damage is done when larvae feed on the ripening fruit and it falls to the ground. Not only citrus is vulnerable to Medfly damage. Watermelon, papaya, Surinam cherry, and mango can be affected. There are more than 100 known species of fruit plants that Medflies infest.

In the past, the most effective means of eradicating Medflies was aerial spraying of the chemical malathion. Concern about the pesticide's effect on humans, however, has prompted further investigation into producing safer sprays and finding methods of early detection of the flies.

LOVE BUGS are the sticky little pests that cover Florida cars for about four weeks every May and September. They develop in moist hammocks or wooded areas where larvae or young feed on decaying vegetation. Their name derives from their flight, which occurs in mating tandem. After a couple of days, the male dies and is shaken loose by the female, who seeks out a new mate. After about three matings, the female dies. Fortunately, love bugs do not bite, sting, or feed on plants. They are simply annoying. To minimize damage to automobile paint, crushed bugs should be washed off as quickly as possible.

MOSQUITOES have been slapped at by Floridians since the state was discovered. It is the female mosquito that bites, for she must have a blood meal before she can produce eggs. Florida has several types of mosquitoes, all of which lay eggs in stagnant water. For that reason, old tires, tubs, or other containers should be kept drained. Diseases that can be spread by mosquitoes include malaria, yellow fever, encephalitis, and West Nile virus. Any of Florida's woodlands and marshes harbor mosquitoes, especially in summer. A good insect repellent containing Deet is advised before venturing outside.

ROACHES have been around for an estimated 350 million years, and Florida is home to 56 of the known 3,500 species. A most noticeable Florida roach is the American Cockroach, called "Palmetto Bug" by polite folks. These large (up to two inches long) and speedy bugs fly well, live in palm and oak trees, and enjoy the indoors, especially kitchens. A smaller but even more common roach is the German, which is lighter colored than the American version. A third common roach is the Oriental model, which is nearly black and is about one and one-half inches long. All of these varieties shun light.

These repugnant regulars have been joined by a new roach variety, the Asian, which flies and is more silvery-colored. This new roach is attracted to light and, should it thrive, promises to put a damper on outdoor barbecues. All roaches thrive in garbage and pet food, and will eat virtually anything. Researchers report some species of roaches can live on little more than dust; others resort to cannibalism if left with nothing else to eat. Many are virtually immune to insecticides. Known natural predators of roaches include some spiders, lizards, and snakes.

TERMITES cause millions of dollars of damage to Florida homes each year, and with the introduction of a fourth major species, it is likely to get worse. Florida is plagued by its native variety, three subspecies of the Eastern subterranean termite, or "dampwood termite," that travel through the ground to get to and eat deeply into wood. Swarming in daylight, and thriving on moisture and humidity, they eat homes from the ground up. They nest in both decayed and living wood. The drywood termite lives in the wood it eats and doesn't require contact with the ground. It can arrive through the air and needs far less moisture than the dampwood species. The recently introduced but thriving-throughout-the-state Formosan termite is known, with regret, for its voracious appetite and the size of its colonies—up to 10 million insects—more than twice the size

of the largest Eastern subterranean colony. It swarms at night and can eat a home from the top down. It is believed, and is proving, to be 10 times more aggressive and destructive than the native variety. It also enjoys citrus and mango trees and sugarcane. The new plague, discovered in 2001 near Dania Beach on the lower east coast, is the tree termite, dubbed for its nesting at the base of trees, often in nests as large as three feet in diameter. Unlike others, the tree termite builds clearly visible tubes toward and on wood. They eat anything, large or small, made of wood. In 2003, the infestation was still contained in a 50-acre plot containing 20 homes and businesses. It also contained 63 identified nests, the most concentrated termite infestation ever discovered in Florida. Should the tree termite, native to the Caribbean, escape from the cordon, officials believe it will spread throughout the state. Traditional chemical controls are being used against the variety of termites, with new ones being developed to deal with the specific threats. Thus far, chemical approaches to combating tree termites have been ineffective. Although termites are a major and costly threat throughout the state, south and central Florida are considered particularly vulnerable.

TICKS have long pestered Florida dogs and cats. A few species, such as the soft mammal tick or the Eastern wood tick, are known to spread disease. More recently, the black-legged tick, a mite-sized, hard-bodied insect, has been linked to Lyme Disease, which is thought to prompt arthritis in some affected people. Florida's warm weather provides a near year-round tick season. Insect repellent should be used and all clothing should be washed immediately after visiting the state's woodlands.

YELLOW JACKETS have killed several Floridians in recent years, and the discovery of a nest has risen to the level of a public-safety emergency. Built on and under ground, a nest can contain tens of thousands of the stinging wasps and reach immense size. A nest discovered near a playground at Clermont measured a visible 8 x 6 feet. When the nest is disturbed, yellow jackets, capable of stinging again and again, swarm and attack to protect the nest. Wasp venom is toxic, and while one sting can kill a person with a severe allergic reaction, experts believe it takes approximately 1,500 nearly simultaneous stings to kill the average adult male. Private citizens are advised not to attempt dealing with a nest on their own. The reason yellow-jacket colonies and their nests achieve such immense size in Florida is because few colonies experience the near-complete winter die-off common elsewhere.

FRESHWATER FISH

An estimated 675 strictly freshwater fish species inhabit lakes and rivers in North America, and another 100 regularly enter fresh waters in the U.S. and Canada from the sea. Floridians are told they have 115 native freshwater fish species in the state's lakes and streams, plus another 175 marine, migratory, and exotic species that invade the state's streams.

The Panhandle rivers and streams, because that area was never completely flooded thousands of years ago, retain more species of mainland fishes than the peninsula. In fact, about one-half of the native freshwater fish species of Florida occur only in, or west of, the Suwannee River system.

Containing the largest variety of freshwater species are the Apalachicola and Escambia rivers, both in the Panhandle. Wildlife officials have recorded 83 different kinds of fish in the Apalachicola and 81 in the Escambia.

Following are descriptions of some of the state's best-known species:

BLACK BASS in Florida are the largest in the world. Four varieties are recognized:

• **Largemouth bass** average four pounds, although 12 to 14-pound catches are not rare. Color varies according to water color, but these bass always have a dark side stripe from tail to gill. They will strike almost any artificial lure and are considered fighters.

• **Smallmouth bass** are present but have never thrived in Florida. Coloring is similar to the largemouth bass, but the smallmouth has more rows of scales and, as the name implies, a smaller mouth.

• **Spotted bass** are easily confused with largemouth, but have regular rows of black spots instead of irregular blotches below the lateral line. They are found in cool, clear streams with gravel and sand bottoms. Averages 10 inches in length.

• **Suwannee bass** are found in its namesake river and tributaries.

BLACK CRAPPIE is also known as Speckled Perch and is not a hot-weather fish, but does offer much sport to cane pole fishermen. A member of the sunfish family, the crappie is flat with an irregular pattern of black dots on a silver background. The average weight is 12 ounces for landed fish, but an adult specimen may reach three pounds.

BREAM is also called Bluegill, and like the bass, the color of this fish varies with water conditions. It is sunfish shaped and usually olive-green on the back with a purplish, chain mail effect. Best bream fishing is spring and early summer, but this fish is caught statewide year round. Both bluegill and the shellcracker bream may weigh in at three pounds. Both are popular panfish.

CATFISH come in three popular varieties in Florida. They are:

• **Channel cat,** slate gray to blue with a forked tail and averaging about four pounds. It is found in rivers, lakes, and waterways and is considered one of the state's best-tasting freshwater fish.

• **Bullheads,** usually weighing in at about one pound. This catfish is dark yellow or brownish and is found throughout the state. A variation of the species has a mottled gray-black coloring and reaches four pounds. Both have square-shaped tails and are edible.

• **White cat,** gray-blue with a white belly, but with no deeply-forked tail. It is found throughout the state and weighs about one pound. Known specimens have reached nine pounds, but this size is rare. It has good food value.

GARFISH is one of the least popular Florida fish. It is ugly and seldom eaten. When hooked, they are fighters and are just not worth the effort it takes to land them. The alligator gar is the largest and can reach 100 pounds, but averages about 18 pounds. It is found in sloughs and streams in western Florida. The long-nose gar may reach 50 pounds and its average length is two feet. It is most common in central Florida, but is found in all but the southernmost regions. A third variety, spotted gars, seldom exceed five pounds and are found statewide.

MUDFISH is also known as Bowfin or Dogfish, and has little sport or commercial value. Its color is mottled olive and its average weight is one pound. It is found in lakes, rivers, and ponds throughout the state.

PICKEREL, also called Pike, comes in two types in Florida, the chain pickerel (jackfish) and the small redfin. Some outdoor writers refer to the jackfish as an eastern pickerel and say the term "chain pickerel" is a misnomer, preferring the term pike or redfin pike. The fish is a brownish-green on its back, fading to greenish-yellow on the sides and belly, with chain-like olive blotches. Average weight is eight pounds and it is found throughout the state.

SHAD, also called Herring, is a popular freshwater fish that makes good eating. Some shad varieties are considered gamefish and some are worthless. One of the most numerous varieties in Florida is the gizzard shad with an average size of nine inches and a three to four-pound average weight. It is inedible and used for bait. Two other members of the shad family are fairly common in Florida streams—the American (white) shad, which is bluish above with silver sides and reaches a weight of about five pounds, and the Alabama shad, which seldom exceeds one pound.

Both are valued for their flesh and roe.

STURGEON, endangered but with a prehistoric lineage, spawn in rivers and streams entering the Gulf. Average size is three feet, although it reaches weights of several hundred pounds and "leaping" sturgeon have injured numerous boaters. It is easily recognized by bony plates that cover it. Its food value is only fair, but the sturgeon is prized for its roe, which is processed for caviar.

SALTWATER FISH

BARRACUDA is a formidable fish with sharp, double-edged teeth. It is rarely dangerous unless bothered. An average barracuda in south Florida waters will weigh up to 10 pounds with 15 and 20 pounds fairly common offshore. The fish is smoky to dark gray on back and shaped like a torpedo. It is not considered edible because it occasionally dines on smaller reef fish whose organs are toxic.

BONEFISH is a small, inedible, powerful fish that is highly regarded by fishermen. It is the fastest of shallow water game fish and is seldom caught until it moves onto the flats for dinner. Bonefish prefer the warmer waters of southern Florida, where they grow to an average weight of about five pounds, with eight- or nine-pound fish not uncommon.

BONITA is a small cousin of the blue fin tuna sometimes called "little tunny." This superb game fish has been known to reach 20 pounds, but three to five pounds is average. They are caught year round in Florida. Food value is low, but the sporting fish strike and fight hard.

It makes good bait for sharks and other large game fish. Gill plates of the bonita are extra sensitive and care should be used when releasing this fish.

DOLPHIN, not to be confused with the porpoise, is a hard striking animal usually weighing about five pounds, although 30- or 40-pounders are not rare. A surface-feeding fish, the dolphin likes warm water and its iridescent coloring seems to change when it is excited.

JACKS are considered by many the gamest of all reef fish, even though most Jack family fish are poor to fair in food value. They are most tasty when served smoked. The amberjack is streamlined and a powerful underwater fighter. Its average weight is 20 to 30 pounds, but catches twice that size are fairly common. The yellow or bar jack is a small cousin of the amberjack that averages between three and eight pounds.

Another variety, Jack crevelles, has been dubbed the bulldogs of the sea for the fight they wage when hooked. Their average size is just five pounds, but they seem much bigger while being hooked.

Of all the Jacks, however, the African pompano is the most prized. It is prevalent in Cuban water, averages 12 pounds, and makes an excellent trophy fish.

Other members of the Jack family are the blue runner, an avid fighter, and the permits. Permits are elusive and require patience. Their speed and agility are similar to the bonefish. Florida permit average 11 pounds, with 20 to 30 pounds considered a good day's work.

LADYFISH rarely exceed five pounds, but this fish is a surprisingly powerful member of the tarpon and bonefish family. It can be found in all Florida water, including brackish, and prefers the bays and channels near grass feeding beds.

MARLIN come in two types, the blue and the white, and both can be caught off Florida coasts. The blue averages between 150 and 200 pounds and requires an experienced angler equipped with heavy gear. This fish's spearing nose and lashing tail can be dangerous if encountered. The white marlin is smaller and not as common in Florida waters and is occasionally hooked while trolling for sailfish. Most white marlin catches are made from March to May, whereas blue marlin fishing peaks between May and July.

REDFISH are known by several names, such as red, bull red, puppy drum, and channel bass. It is a sporting fish and, at 10 pounds or less, is excellent table fare. The average Florida red is smaller than its northern cousins and weighs between three and eight pounds. The adult fish is solid red with a large black spot at the base of its tail, and is generally caught in shallow waters.

SAILFISH is a most enticing and sought-after game fish that can average over seven feet in length. It was rarely caught until discovery of the drop-back technique in which the angler lets his bait drop toward the bottom for about 10 seconds. The fish supposedly thinks it has stunned or killed the bait. This delayed procedure allows the fish to inhale the live bait and the hook. Sails can be easily released by snipping the leader wire near the mouth. The hook dissolves. Badly injured fish may be served smoked.

SHARKS come in about 350 varieties, worldwide, but only about 24 are considered dangerous to man. Of that two dozen, only seven "man-eating" varieties are known to venture into Florida waters.

Sharks are unpredictable scavengers who track their targets to within visual range and begin circling. A circling shark sometimes will spiral in and bump its nose against its prey. If the quarry does not strike back, the shark may attack. Once blood flows, more sharks will usually arrive to share the kill in a feeding frenzy.

The shark is among the most efficient killers found in nature. Rows of teeth, as many as 19, can tear prey apart. In some species, such as the great white, the upper jaw moves forward and upward to better seize, shake, and hold the victim while it prepares to eat. Sharks' skin is also dangerously abrasive and even a brush by a small shark can remove human skin and sometimes the muscle layer beneath.

The following shark varieties found in Florida are listed here in order of reported incidents of attacks:

• **Sand,** common in shallow waters, eats mostly small fish, but may bite if stepped on. Reaches a length of 8 to 10 feet.

• **Bull,** averages nine feet, weighs about 500 pounds, and can be dangerous.

• **Mako,** considered a man-eater with an average 12-foot length. It is fast swimming and has reportedly attacked boats. Weighs approximately 1,000 pounds.

• **Hammerhead,** easily identified by its unusual head shape. It averages nine feet.

• **Tiger,** also a man-eating shark, will attain a length of more than 15 feet and weighs about 1,800 pounds. Has been known to attack boats.

• **Lemon,** averages nine feet long, 800 pounds weight, and considered dangerous.

• **White,** dangerous to the point of being legendary. Averages 18 feet in length, but seen only occasionally in Florida waters. It is highly aggressive, will attack boats, and is capable of eating humans. Usual weight is about 1,700 pounds. Females generally outweigh males.

• **Black-tipped,** also called the spinner shark. It often travels in schools and leaps from the water. Common in Florida waters and may exceed eight feet in length, but is seldom more than 150 pounds.

• **Nurse,** found in shallow waters near mangroves in Florida. Very sluggish, this shark is dangerous only when stepped on. Weighs 200-400 pounds and averages about 10 feet long.

• **Porbeagle,** prefers colder waters, averages eight feet in length, and weighs about 400 pounds.

• **Thresher,** can exceed 15 feet in length with a weight of about 900 pounds. Usually attacks only when provoked.

• **Dogfish,** common to Florida waters and only about four feet long. It will bite if tormented and its sandpapery hide can scrape off human skin if it brushes past and makes contact.

The International Game Fish Association recognizes six shark species as gamefish: blue, mako, porbeagle, thresher, tiger, and white, with the mako the most popular. It gives anglers a battle with long runs and spectacular leaps.

Food value of sharks is debatable, although consumers may unknowingly purchase shark labeled as "steak-fish." The shark's liver is a source of high vitamin A content and sharkskin is used for luggage, wallets, and handbags.

SHEEPSHEAD is a lightly-nibbling common fish along Florida's West Coast. It tends to inhale bait and must be given time to nibble its way to the hook. It is good eating and weighs one or two pounds.

TARPON are a most popular and exciting fish to catch. Tarpon are acrobats and have an uncanny knack for shaking free of hooks. They are widespread along the Gulf Coast and in the Keys. The average tarpon weighs 68 pounds and the species is not considered edible. They are valued more for the sport than the palate, and tarpon "round-ups" (or "rodeos") are held in Florida and in other Gulf states.

WAHOO is a spunky fish rarely hooked in Florida waters. Its average weight is 15 to 20 pounds, and like its smaller cousin, the king mackerel, the wahoo's food value is good. It is a popular trophy fish.

SALTWATER FOOD FISH

BLUEFISH are strong, swift fish that migrate along the Atlantic coast. Excellent eating, bluefish are most commonly caught from mid-December to May. The species is voracious while schooling and will bite anything.

CREVELLE is a close relative to the blue runner and pompano. It is good eating, and is most common during winter months. The fish is most abundant on Florida's west coast. Anglers catch this fish by trolling. Average weight is about a pound.

GROUPER is one of the largest,

most widely distributed fish families in the world. Largest member of the family, the Goliath, can weigh up to 600 pounds.

There are a number of grouper species including the Black, Yellow, Nassau, Rockhind, Gag, Rock, and Red. All are fine food, but the red is the most abundant and the most commercially important. All are found on the Gulf Coast but can be caught along the state's entire coastline. They are found mostly on offshore banks and reefs, usually near a rock bottom.

Red groupers are solitary fish and seldom school. They are caught throughout the year and, when fully grown, will weigh as much as 50 pounds.

Because of overfishing, periodic restrictions are imposed on grouper fishing. The taking of Goliath and Nassau is prohibited.

KINGFISH (KING MACKEREL) is a large relative of the Spanish Mackerel and ranks as a top game fish. It is slightly less desirable than its smaller cousin for eating. Kings are most common in February and March where they are caught along both Florida coasts. The fish is a fighter and may leap 10 or more feet out of the water when hooked. Drifting over a reef using live shrimp bait is a successful way to catch king.

LISA, more commonly called mullet, is one of the important food fish of the South. Only menhaden and shrimp exceed catch of mullet. It has firm, tender flesh with a mild flavor. Its roe is also eaten.

Lisa (a name coined by marketers) frequent coastal waters near brackish river mouths and may be found in freshwater. There are about 100 species of Lisa, but the striped or jumping is the most abundant. White Lisa is taken in just a few locales such as the Keys.

Most often netted, Lisa or mullet are easily spotted because they jump. Best catches are from April through November with heaviest runs in September.

POMPANO is a choice food fish. Height of the season is summer through fall. Pompano is a thin fish with a forked tail and is dark blue at the top, shading to bright silver on the sides. The average market size is about 24 ounces. They are found in all Florida coastal waters in areas with sandy bottoms near the shore, or in channels near flats. Anglers report success with yellow feather jigs that are bumped rapidly on the bottom or under bridges or docks. Light tackle can be used, but be ready for a fight.

SNAPPER include several species, all available in Gulf waters but rarely found on the Atlantic coast. Red, Yellowtail, Gray, Cubera, Dog, Schoolmaster, Mangrove, Mutton, and Vermillion are a few. Snapper is one of the most widely known of all fishes and lives offshore in rock gullies. Small specimens come close to shore. They are excellent food fish and average 5 to 10 pounds. Red snapper usually are caught in deep water with heavy rods or handlines, using cut mullet or small fish for bait.

SNOOK, also called the robalo or sergeant fish, is common along the southwest Florida coast. It is a good food fish. Average size is 3 to 5 pounds. Snook are found in a variety of waters and can be caught from bridges, from a boat in an inlet, or close to shore. They can be found in brackish and fresh waters. Shrimp, dead or alive, and strip-cut mullet make good bait.

SPANISH MACKEREL is a schooling, migrating fish found along the entire coast of Florida where it feeds on smaller fish and squid. It is a good, sporty food fish most often caught between October and March.

TROUT, or sea trout, belong to the croaker family and are related to the spots and drums. The Spotted sea trout, the most important of the group, is an excellent game and food fish. This fish remains in shallow waters throughout the year. Larger trout travel in large schools and swim low in the water. When close to shore, they usually come in with the tide. Trout like grass beds, sand patches, and mud flats, and are found around bays and inland waters, sometimes in the ocean.

Fishermen usually anchor, but drifting often gets results. Bait may be live shrimp, spoons, or jigs. The Gray sea trout is relatively scarce in Florida waters, occurring occasionally in the Gulf. The White or Sand trout is found only in the Gulf and is a good pan fish, about 11 to 15 inches.

OTHER MAJOR MARINE SPECIES

Poisonous Species

JELLYFISH are blobby floating creatures that periodically invade Florida's waters. Two common jellyfish varieties are the Moon Jelly and the Lion's Mane. A third, potentially dangerous type is the Portuguese man-of-war, found most often on the Atlantic coast. It floats along, its presence revealed only by a bluish air bladder that acts as a sail. Under-water, the man-of-war trails tentacle-like streamers that may be 40 feet long. These tentacles contain sensors that signal if a fish (or human) is nearby, and the tentacles literally shoot a microscopic thread that contains nerve poison.

The poison paralyzes the man-of-war's fish dinner, but usually does no more to humans than zap them with a hefty sting. Of course, some people are allergic to the toxin and, as with a bee sting, can develop complications. A chief predator of the man-of-war is the loggerhead turtle, whose tough skin and beak protect it from man-of-war toxin.

The Moon Jellyfish is whitish-clear and can inflict a tingling sting if encountered, while the pinkish-colored Lion's Mane is rarely potent enough to be of concern.

Jellyfish venom, say scientists, is protein-based and stings can quickly be relieved by use of chemicals such as ammonia or meat tenderizing powder that break down proteins. Beachwalkers should beware of stepping on them, however, since the venom remains in the tentacles even after the jellyfish are dead.

STINGRAYS are dangerous residents of Florida's coastal waters. Marine biologists estimate that some 1,500 people are injured by stingrays each year in the U.S., most occurring in summer when rays invade shallow waters for breeding. It usually burrows in sand or mud with only its eyes and tail exposed and is difficult to see. A serrated barb on the ray's tail contains a poison that produces a painful sting if a bather steps on it.

Stingrays are actually docile and their inflicted injuries on people are usually accidental. However, the stings can produce symptoms such as low blood pressure, rapid heartbeat, vomiting, diarrhea, and sweating. Fatalities are rare, but medical treatment should be sought immediately.

Emergency treatment should include washing the wound site with saltwater and removing the barb if it remains in the skin. Hot water for 30 to 90 minutes also reduces the pain. Swimmers and beachwalkers can lessen the risk of stepping on a stingray if they shuffle their feet as they wade. This will dislodge the ray. Fishermen catching stingrays on their lines are advised to cut the lines immediately, keeping a safe distance from the ray's whipping tail. Never attempt to bring one into a boat, live or dead.

The most common ray in Florida waters is the Southern stingray, which reaches a width of five feet and a length of about seven feet.

Shellfish

Shellfish found in Florida waters consist of several varieties of crustaceans and mollusks. Pollution has blighted some of the ocean beds where these creatures live. Among the varieties inhabiting Florida waters are:

BLUE CRAB, a blue-colored crustacean found all along the Gulf Coast and the South Atlantic. It prefers brackish waters. One time-tested method for snaring these crabs is to lower a string to which a bread ball or a chunk of chicken has been attached. In shallow water, a crab will likely give the string a tug. Pull the string (and crab) up evenly and gently so the crab doesn't let go. Dump the catch in a bucket of salty water. Eat by boiling as soon as possible.

SOFT-SHELLED CRAB is actually a blue crab that is growing a new shell. The popular King and Dungeness crabs are not found in Florida's warm waters.

CLAMS in Florida are edible. Quahogs can be found buried in coastal mud or sand. When hunting the clam, look for them in shallow water and at low tide along sandbars. Discard any clam that does not close when picked up. One that does not open after being steamed also should be discarded. When opening a clam, use a thin, sharp knife and place it between the shell half, cutting around the clam and twisting to pry open the shell. Then cut muscles from the two shell halves. Boiling in water about 10 minutes usually will open shells.

CONCHS, pronounced "konks," are found in the Keys and are among the largest in North America. The animal inside the conch shell retreats inside when approached. It can be removed by cutting the pointed end of the shell and inserting a knife. After removing, the conch must be skinned before cooking.

COQUINA are pretty, tiny shells found along Florida beaches and are related to oysters and clams. There is a tiny animal inside the kernel-sized shells which, if boiled in enough quantity, produces a tasty chowder broth. It is nearly impossible to rinse all the sand from coquina shells, and many people dislike coquina chowder's grit.

LOBSTER, Florida-style, is a cousin of the more famous Maine lobster, and is smaller, usually one to two pounds. It also lacks meat in the claw. Popularity of this tasty crawfish has led to lobster season changes, so local game and fish officials should be contacted to make sure lobster beds are open.

OYSTER beds once surrounded Florida on a vast scale, but habitat destruction and pollution have narrowed the commercial harvest to the Apalachicola region of the Gulf Coast. Some oyster lovers contend that summer oysters are less tasty than those harvested in cooler months, and any oysters that are open when gathered should be discarded.

SCALLOPS are found in shallow bays and inland waters, especially in July and August. They are feisty little mollusks and will swim away from pursuers by opening and closing their shells. The muscle is the desired edible bit of the scallop. Bay scallops are smaller than Deep Sea scallops, which are found in deeper, colder waters. It is easy to shuck a scallop by prying the shell open with a knife, cutting the pinkish muscle out, and storing it in a tub of salt water.

SHRIMP are probably the most popular shellfish and among the easiest to catch. Armed with a net and a light (shrimp are nocturnal), wade out to waters where shrimp school and scoop them up. They are constantly moving. Florida's shrimp are either pink or white. If overcooked, shrimp will be either rubbery or will have a mealy texture. The best steaming time is about five minutes in either beer or herbal-seasoned water.

STONE CRABS are rock-hard and have one large and one small claw. They can be found along rocks near beaches and inland waters. The usual method of taking stone crabs is a long-handled pole that has a wire hook on the end. Stone crab catches are restricted and no females may be taken. Some enthusiasts keep the meaty large claw and return the crab to the water to grow a new claw.

Whales Along the Coasts

Anyone venturing into the deep waters some 125 miles off the Florida coasts has the chance of seeing any of a dozen whale species known to travel past the state. Unfortunately, most of these creatures go unseen unless they have stranded themselves on coastal or island beaches. Because studying whales is a difficult and often expensive scientific undertaking, not much is known about the habits of some species. But all whales, being warm-blooded mammals, give live birth, usually not more than every two years, to single young called calves.

The following whale species seen off Florida's coasts are listed as endangered by Florida's Fish and Wildlife Conservation Commission and the federal government:

• **The great sperm whale** is a giant. Males can grow to 62 feet long and weigh 35 to 51 tons. Females are usually 38 feet long and 38 tons in weight. Females give birth to one 11-to-14-foot calf after 16 months of gestation. The species eats primarily squid, shark, octopus, and seals.

• **The right whale** lacks a dorsal fin. It is a baleen whale, that is, the whale's mouth contains not teeth but horn-like material that filters tiny plankton from seawater. Up to 50 feet long and 50 feet in circumference, this species has been heavily hunted. A single calf is born after a year's gestation.

• **Humpbacked whales** average about 40 feet long with 30 tons of heft. This baleen whale is named for a triangular, fin-like bump on its back. Single calves are born after 11 months of gestation. One of the most studied whales, it is admired for its playfulness, rowdy mating games, and singing.

• **The fin whale** is an aerodynamic baleen whale that swims about 25 miles per hour. Usually 65 to 80 feet long, the species can weigh 80 tons. Calves, up to 21 feet long, are born after the whales have come south to winter. It is also called the finbacked whale.

• **The sei whale,** sometimes called the sardine whale, resembles the fin whale but is smaller. The species skims the water's surface for tiny sea creatures to eat and tends to prefer temperate climes. Its name is properly pronounced "say" whale.

Other whale and dolphin species have been found beached along Florida's coastline, including rarely seen pygmy sperm and dwarf sperm whales.

The spectacular killer whales, now popular performance animals, are actually large dolphins. Their name is deserved, as they are adept hunters of seal, tuna, penguin, sea otter, walrus, and an occasional great white shark.

Pilot whales, another member of the dolphin family, are among the most numerous of the reported strandings. An encounter with killer whales can panic a herd of pilot whales into beaching themselves, but scientists believe most beachings are due to parasite infestations.

Comparative sizes of aquatic mammals found around Florida range from (top to bottom) the 80-foot-long fin whale to the humpback whale, the killer whale, the pilot whale, and the 12-foot-long bottlenose dolphin.

CORAL REEFS

Florida's spectacular living coral reefs stretch south from Miami to the Dry Tortugas, 65 miles west of Key West. Visitors may see coral reefs firsthand by visiting Biscayne National Park, John Pennekamp Coral Reef State Park, or the Looe Key and Key Largo Marine Sanctuaries. Though reefs appear to be nothing more than rocky fish refuges, they are living creatures that support an amazing array of sea life. Florida's coral reefs are the only true coral reefs in U.S. continental waters.

Stony corals are hard-plated layers of calcium carbonate that is secreted by the coral polyp, a living animal that is a member of the jellyfish and sea anemone family. A reef is formed as the coral forms large colonies welded together by chemicals and sea algae. Coral colors range from whitish cream to green and brown.

Coral reefs support a wide assortment of other sea creatures. Spotted, striped, and peacock-hued fish varieties include the Blue Tang, Parrotfish, French Angels, Triggerfish, and Damselfishes, in all, more than 150 species of tropical fish.

Other, less recognizable species found in and around the coral reefs are sea anemones, colorful marine worms and mollusks, starfish, sponges, fans, and sea plumes. Turtles, shrimp, conchs, and octopus also frequent the reefs.

Scientists are growing increasingly concerned that the state's coral reefs are rapidly declining. Many species are displaying tumors, black band disease, and bleached patches where the coral polyps have died. A virus has begun to attack the reefs and no way has been determined to stop it. The reefs have declined at a rate of 10 percent a year for the past three years.

The coral has a few natural enemies, such as fish or worms that nibble away at the polyps. Also responsible for reef destruction are recreational scuba divers. More than a half million swimmers, snorkelers, and scuba enthusiasts visit Florida's state reefs each year. With them come boat propellers, anchors, fishing, and diving gear. The sheer numbers of people who prop to rest or to take photographs on the coral kill the delicate creatures. Pollution from the burgeoning Keys with their gallons of poorly treated sewage, tons of garbage, and the petroleum contamination from the area's hundreds of boats continue to threaten the reef environment. Coral preservation was a major consideration in Florida's declaring a moratorium on offshore oil drilling. However, the 20-year-old ban was successfully challenged in court in 1996 and the state lifted it. But no drilling has taken place and the state has taken other legal and political means to prevent it.

Should the coral reefs die, it would spell the end of an entire Florida ecosystem.

ENDANGERED SPECIES

The Florida animals in this list are either Endangered (E), Threatened (T), or are a Species of Special Concern (SSC) because of declining numbers, as determined by the Florida Fish and Wildlife Conservation Commission. Species that are listed on both the commission's list and the list of the U.S. Fish and Wildlife Service are indicated with an asterisk.

MAMMALS	
Right whale	E*
Finback whale	E*
Florida mastiff bat	E
Florida panther	E*
Humpback whale	E*
Gray bat	E*
Key deer; toy deer	E*
Key Largo cotton mouse	E*
Anastasia Island beach mouse	E*
Choctawhatchee beach mouse	E*
Perdido Key beach mouse	E*
Lower Keys marsh rabbit	E*
Silver rice rat	E*
St. Andrews beach mouse	E*
Key Largo woodrat	E*
Florida saltmarsh vole	E*
West Indian manatee	E*
Sei whale	E
Sperm whale	E
Indiana bat	E
Big Cypress fox squirrel	T
Everglades mink	T
Florida black bear	T
Southeastern beach mouse	T
Sherman's Short-tailed shrew	SSC
Sanibel Island rice rat	SSC
Florida mouse	SSC
Sherman's fox squirrel	SSC
Homosassa shrew	SSC
Eastern chipmunk	SSC

BIRDS	
Cape Sable seaside sparrow	E*
Florida grasshopper sparrow	E*
Kirtland's warbler	E*
Wood stork	E*
Ivory-billed woodpecker	E
Snail kite	E
Bachman's warbler	E
Arctic peregrine falcon	E
Piping plover	T*
Florida scrub jay	T*
Crested caracara	T*
Roseate tern	T*
Bald eagle	T
Red-cockaded woodpecker	T
Southeastern snowy plover	T
White-crowned pigeon	T
Southeastern American kestrel	T
Florida sandhill crane	T
Least tern	T
Whooping Crane	T
Black skimmer	SSC
Roseate spoonbill	SSC
Wakulla seaside sparrow	SSC
Scott's seaside sparrow	SSC
Limpkin	SSC
Burrowing owl	SSC
Worthington's marsh wren	SSC
Marian's marsh wren	SSC
Little blue heron	SSC
Reddish egret	SSC
Snowy egret	SSC
Tricolored heron	SSC
American oystercatcher	SSC
Brown pelican	SSC

Osprey	SSC
White ibis	SSC

FISH	
Shortnose sturgeon	E*
Okaloosa darter	E*
Blackmouth shiner	E
Crystal darter	T
Key silverside	T
Atlantic sturgeon	SSC*
Lake Eustis pupfish	SSC
Harlequin darter	SSC
Southern tessellated darter	SSC
Saltmarsh topminnow	SSC
Suwannee bass	SSC
Shoal bass; Chipola bass	SSC
Bluenose shiner	SSC
Mangrove rivulus	SSC
Key blenny	SSC
Johnny darter	SSC

AMPHIBIANS AND REPTILES	
Atlantic green turtle	E*
American crocodile	E*
Leatherback turtle	E*
Atlantic hawksbill turtle	E*
Kemp's ridley turtle	E*
Striped mud turtle	E
Atlantic loggerhead turtle	T*
Eastern indigo snake	T*
Atlantic salt marsh snake	T*

Sand skink	T*
Key ringneck snake	T
Short-tailed snake	T
Miami rock crown snake	T
Florida brown snake	T
Florida ribbon snake	T
Gopher tortoise	T
Blue-tailed mole skink	SSC
American alligator	SSC
Alligator snapping turtle	SSC
Suwannee cooter	SSC
Red rat snake; corn snake	SSC
Florida Keys mole skink	SSC
Barbour's map turtle	SSC
Flatwoods Salamander	SSC
Georgia blind salamander	SSC
Pine Barrens treefrog	SSC
Florida pine snake	SSC
Dusky gopher frog	SSC
Florida gopher frog	SSC
Bog frog	SSC

INVERTEBRATES	
Schaus' swallowtail butterfly	E*
Pillar coral	E
Stock Island tree snail	E
Miami blue butterfly	T
Florida tree snail	SSC
Sims Sink crayfish	SSC
Black Creek crayfish	SSC
Panama City crayfish	SSC

DEAD BIRDS

Birds are occasionally killed when they encounter toxic pesticides. If you find a number of dead birds in a single locale, report it to the local Florida Fish and Wildlife Conservation Commission office. Individual dead birds should be reported to the local county health department monitoring West Nile and Bird Flu viruses.

WILDLIFE ALERT

Citizens witnessing violations of Florida's wildlife or marine laws are urged to call "Wildlife Alert," a toll-free number to the Florida Fish and Wildlife Conservation Commission. Investigators are sent to the scene, and if an arrest is made, the caller is eligible for a cash reward ranging from $25 to $1,000.

The reward program was established in 1980 as the commission's way for private citizens to assist state wildlife and marine officers in law enforcement. Reward money comes not from tax funds but from donations by conservation-minded organizations and individuals. In addition, convicted violators often are ordered by judges to contribute to the "Wildlife Alert" fund as part of their punishment.

Most rewards are given in connection with fishing, hunting, and marine regulations, with the largest money awarded those callers who give information leading to arrests of persons killing or harming the state's endangered species.

Citizens witnessing violations are asked to obtain, if possible, names, addresses, descriptions of persons and vehicles involved, and location.

Toll-free numbers to call are (888) 404-3922. Cellular users dial *FMP.

EXOTIC WILDLIFE

Florida's wildlife systems constantly change. Just as some species dwindle, others appear—either by migrating or through accidental or deliberate introduction. Climate, particularly in south Florida, provides for bountiful breeding of the exotics.

Scientists are growing concerned that exotic species will replace Florida's native species by out-breeding and out-competing native species for the available habitat and food. In addition, predators that control native species often dislike the exotics, so the new arrivals thrive while the predators go hungry.

Laws attempt to control importation and selling of exotic species in Florida, but no agency has the sole responsibility of monitoring the state's wild exotic populations. Moreover, say some biologists, such monitoring would be difficult because deciding precisely which species are native or exotic has just begun.

Scientists do know, however, that some animals imported to Florida from foreign countries are affecting the state's traditional species and crops.

The ten-pound Burmese rat, confined thus far to two small keys in Monroe County, is aggressively being hunted down and eradicated. Should these rodents make it to the mainland, they are projected to devastate the state's winter vegetable crop, which supplies half the nation's supply.

Some 23 non-native bird species thrive mostly in south Florida. Colorful and attractive, the birds delight watchers, but biologists consider the newcomers as biological pollution. So far, not much data has recorded damage caused by exotic birds such as the Spot-breasted Oriole and the Blue-gray Tanager, but some, such as the Monk Parakeet, are known fruit crop destroyers in their homelands.

The ecological or financial impact of some other imports

are not yet known, but they are decidedly unwanted. The giant "Bufo" toad, popular in the pet trade, is but one of 25 species of frogs, lizards, and snakes estimated to now inhabit Florida. These large toads can poison domestic dogs.

During the 1970s, wildlife officers near Miami captured individual specimens of Siamese, Egyptian, and Ceylonese cobras thought to have been purposely released by a religious sect.

Undesirable fish species also have easily found their way into Florida waters. They range from unwanted aquarium fish that are released by homeowners, to fish farm escapees, to species that were released to control some other unwanted biological pest.

The walking catfish strolled away from a Broward County fish farm in the 1960s and now inhabits most of south Florida's freshwater bodies. Fish farmers erect fences to prevent these catfish from preying on aquarium species.

The Spotted Tilapia, a West African fish, is presumed to have escaped from a Miami-Dade County fish farm in the 1970s. Since then, it has aggressively overtaken native fish and some studies have found some canals contain few fish species other than Spotted Tilapia.

Another invader is the Indo-Pacific green mussel, discovered in Tampa Bay in 1999. It has already spread down the Gulf Coast and is expected to thrive in the subtropical Gulf and Atlantic Ocean as well as the Caribbean.

Exotic mammals have not presented as great a problem and their presence appears to be benignly tolerated. Two colonies of Rhesus monkeys at Ocala's Silver Springs are popular residents whose threatened removal prompted a citizen protest. Jaguarundi and ocelots are so shy as to be seldom noticed. Armadillos are firmly entrenched with virtually no predators.

But exotics cost money to control. The Giant African Snail, released by a North Miami resident in 1966, reproduced rapidly and soon began consuming shrubs and trees. The snails soon demanded attention when they began eating paint off stucco buildings, probably in a search for needed calcium. After two eradication programs finally seemed to work, the bill tallied nearly $650,000.

Wildlife officials see no end to the constant battle of incoming exotic species. Current quarantine procedures catch only an estimated 10 percent of the unwanted creatures.

HUNTING FEES AND REGULATIONS

For the purpose of hunting in Florida, a resident is a person who has lived continuously in Florida for six months. Active military personnel stationed in Florida and full-time students in a Florida school are considered residents when purchasing a Hunting License Stamp or permit stamps.

To increase hunting safety in Florida, the state requires that any hunters born on or after June 1, 1975, complete a hunter safety course before they may hunt with a firearm, bow or crossbow. Exempt from this law are persons hunting in their county of residence, on their homestead or the homestead of their spouse or minor child, or any minor child hunting on the homestead of his or her parent.

Firearm-related hunting accidents in Florida in 2008 accounted for two fatalities.

Licensing/Stamps

A Hunting License Stamp or a Gold Sportsman's or Sportsman's License Stamp is required of anyone hunting furbearing animals.

To trap furbearing animals a person must have a Trapping License Stamp.

An Archery Stamp is required in addition to a Hunting License Stamp if one wishes to participate in archery season, although such a stamp is not required for Gold Sportsman's or Sportsman's License holders.

For a person participating in a muzzleloading gun season, a Muzzleloading Gun Stamp is required unless that person already holds one of the sportsman's licenses.

To hunt waterfowl, hunters must purchase a federal Migratory Bird Hunting and Conservation Stamp and a Florida Waterfowl Stamp, in addition to a Hunting License Stamp. The Florida Waterfowl Stamp is not required for either sportsman's license holders, but the federal stamp is.

For turkey hunters, a Florida Turkey Stamp must be purchased, in addition to a Hunting License Stamp, unless the hunter already has purchased one of the sportsman's licenses.

All the above stamps, except federal waterfowl stamps, may be purchased from a county tax collector or their subagents. Subagents may charge an addition 50 cent fee. Subagents are primarily

hunting and fishing equipment retailers. The federal stamps are available at U.S. post offices.

Persons hunting in their county of residence, on their homestead, are not required to have a Hunting License Stamp, Turkey Stamp, Archery Stamp, Muzzleloading Stamp, or Florida Waterfowl Stamp. Nor are residents 65 years of age or more who possess a Resident Senior Citizen Hunting and Fishing Certificate. The stamps also are not required of totally and permanently disabled persons who have bought a Florida Resident Disabled Person Hunting and Fishing License, nor do children under age 16 need to purchase the stamps.

License Costs, annual

Gold Sportsman's License (includes hunting, saltwater fishing, and freshwater fishing licenses; Type I Wildlife Management area permit; archery, muzzleloading, turkey, Florida waterfowl, snook, and crawfish permits; does not include federal permits)	$100.00
Military Gold Sportsman	$20.00
Sportsman's License (includes all of the above except saltwater license; snook and crawfish permits)	$80.50
Resident 64+ Sportsman	$13.50
Statewide Hunting	$17.00
Statewide Hunting/Fishing	$32.50
Five-year Hunting	$79.00
Hunting and Freshwater Fishing	$32.50
Hunting, Fresh and Saltwater Fishing	$48.00
Resident and Nonresident Trapping	$46.50
Nonresident State Hunting	$151.50
Nonresident 10-Day	$46.50
Wildlife Management Area Stamp	$26.50
Management area five-year, resident	$126.50
Archery Stamp	$5.00
Archery five-year, resident	$25.00
Muzzleloading Gun Stamp	$5.00
Muzzleloading, five-year, resident	$25.00
Florida Waterfowl Permit	$3.00
Fla. Waterfowl five-year, resident	$25.00

Florida Turkey Permit	$10.00
Florida Turkey five-year, resident	$50.00
Turkey non-resident	$125.00
Resident Senior Citizen Certificate	Free
Resident Disabled Person Certificate	Free
Migratory Bird Permit	Free
Fur-bearer Trapping	$26.50

Lifetime Sportsman's License

The state now issues an all-inclusive Sportsman License, as well as a lifetime license and a five-year license to Floridians for hunting and fishing, both saltwater and freshwater.

This license is good for a sportsman's lifetime and includes hunting, fresh- and saltwater fishing, Wildlife Management Area, archery, muzzleloading gun, turkey, Florida waterfowl, snook, and crawfish. Costs are

Age	Fee
4 years or younger	$401.50
5 to 12 years old	$701.50
13 to 63 years old	$1,001.50

Lifetime License

A lifetime license for hunting includes stamps for Wildlife Management Area, archery, muzzleloading gun, turkey, and Florida waterfowl.

Age	Fee
4 years or younger	$201.50
5 to 12 years	$351.50
13 years or older	$501.50

TRESPASS

A Florida hunting license does not authorize trespass. Landowner permission must be obtained before entering private land. Trespass while in possession of a firearm is punishable by imprisonment for up to five years and/or a fine up to $5,000.

Hunter Orange

Any person hunting deer with a firearm, or accompanying another person hunting deer with a firearm, on public lands must wear not less than 500 square inches of daylight fluorescent-orange material as an outer garment above the waist—that may include a head covering.

LEGAL METHODS OF TAKING GAMES

For taking resident game birds and mammals: Rifles, shotguns, pistols and birds of prey (falcons, owls, and hawks), may be used. Longbows, compound bows, recurved bows, and crossbows must have a minimum draw weight of 35 pounds. Hand-held releases may be used. Broadheads must have two sharpened edges with a minimum width of 7/8 inch.

For hunting deer: Muzzleloading guns firing a single bullet must be at least .40-caliber. Those firing two or more balls must be 20-gauge or larger. For taking migratory game birds: Shotguns (not larger than 10-gauge and plugged to a three-shell capacity with a filler, which cannot be removed without disassembling the gun), birds of prey and bows may be used.

All other methods and equipment are prohibited.

Children and Guns

A minor under 18 years of age may not possess a firearm other than an unloaded firearm at his or her home, unless

• the minor is engaged in a lawful hunting activity and is at least 16 years of age or is under 16 and supervised by an adult
• the minor is engaged in a lawful marksmanship competition or practice or other lawful recreational shooting activity and is at least 16 years of age or under 16 years old and under the supervision of an adult acting with the consent of a parent or guardian. The minor may transport an unloaded firearm to such an event

In other circumstances, allowing a minor to possess a loaded firearm, or to knowingly or unknowingly allow a minor access to a loaded firearm, is a third-degree felony.

Florida Wildlife Harvest Data State Management Areas (2009-2010 Hunting Season)

Deer	3,443
Hog	3,258
Duck	32,538
Dove	5,598
Snipe	3,237
Quail	2,147
Rabbit	197
Squirrel	7,471
Bobcat	5
Raccoon	123
Turkey	785
Woodcock	4
Otter	4

Bag Limits

	Daily	Season limit	Possession
Deer (antlered)	2	None	4
Deer (antlerless)	2	Permit	4
Deer (antlered-archery season)	2	None	4
Deer (antlerless-archery season)	1	None	2
Wild Hog	None	None	No limit
Turkey (fall season)	1	2	2
Turkey (spring season)	1	2	2
Quail	12	None	24
Gray Squirrel	12	None	24
Rabbit	12	None	24
Raccoon, Opossum, Bobcat, Otter, Coyote, Nutria, Skunk, Beaver: No bag or possession limit			

Prohibited

Florida law prohibits hunters from shooting wildlife from rights of way along paved or graded roads. Penalty for violation is a $500 fine and/or 60 days in jail. It is also illegal to release dogs on road rights of way so that they may chase game across private property.

Licenses via Phone

Florida hunting and fishing licenses may be obtained from anywhere in the U.S. and Canada by telephone with a credit card. A valid temporary license number is issued immediately over the phone and a hard copy will follow. There is an addition $3.95 "convenience" charge for the service which is available toll-free at 1-888-486-8356 (hunting) or at 1-888-347-4356 (fishing).

FRESHWATER FISHING FEES AND REGULATIONS

A freshwater fishing license stamp is required for all residents between 16 and 65 years of age, and all nonresidents of 16 or more years of age, to fish by any method, including cane poles.

Defined as a resident is a person who has lived in Florida for six continuous months.

Military personnel who are home on leave in Florida for 30 days or less may sport fish without a fishing license.

The state's "cane pole law" permits a resident to fish in the county of residence without a license, but he must buy a license if cane pole fishing in a Fish Management Area.

Game fish as defined by the state include but are not limited to black bass, black crappie, bluegill, redear sunfish, warmouth, redbreast sunfish, spotted sunfish, chain pickerel, redfin pickerel, peacock bass, white bass, striped bass, and sunshine bass. Non-game fish include bowfin, common carp, catfish, eels, gar, shad, shiners, tilapia, killifish, suckers, top-minnows, and fish not listed as freshwater game fish and not taken for sport.

Freshwater fishing reciprocity between Florida and Georgia for seniors has ended. Both states now require a non-resident license. Residents of Georgia fishing in the St. Mary's River or Lake Seminole must have a Georgia license.

License Costs

Gold Sportsman's License (includes hunting, saltwater fishing, and freshwater fishing licenses; Type I Wildlife Management area permit; archery, muzzleloading, turkey, Florida waterfowl, snook, and crawfish permits; does not include Federal permits)	$100.00
Military Gold Sportsman's License	$20.00
Sportsman's License (includes all of the above except saltwater license; snook and crawfish permits)	$80.00
Resident 64+ Sportsman's	$13.50
Resident Fishing/Hunting	$32.50
Resident 12-Month Fishing	$3.50
Resident 5-year fishing	$47.00
Resident freshwater/saltwater fishing/hunting combo	$48.00

Nonresident 12-Month Fishing	$47.00
Nonresident 7-Day Fishing	$30.00
Nonresident 3-day fishing	$17.00
Resident Senior Citizen Certificate	Free
Resident Disabled Person Certificate	Free

Sportsman's License includes all resident hunting and fishing licenses and stamps except a few special stamps. In addition to fees above, tax collectors and authorized agents selling licenses are entitled to a $.50 to $1 surcharge.

The state now issues an all-inclusive Sportsman License, as well as lifetime and five-year licenses to Florida residents for hunting and fishing, both saltwater and freshwater.

Lifetime Sportsman's License

This license is good for a sportsman's lifetime and includes hunting, fresh- and saltwater fishing, Wildlife Management Areas, archery, muzzleloading gun, turkey, Florida waterfowl, snook, and crawfish. Costs are:

Age	Fee
4 years or younger	$401.50
5 to 12 years	$701.50
13 to 63 years	$1,001.50

Lifetime Freshwater or Saltwater Fishing License

Age	Fee
4 years or younger	$126.50
5 to 12 years	$226.50
13 years or older	$301.50

A five-year freshwater or saltwater fishing license costs $61.50. The five-year saltwater license does not include snook, crawfish, or tarpon.

Bag Limits

• 5 Black Bass (largemouth, Suwannee, redeye, spotted, and shoal basses individually or total), of which only one may be 22 inches or longer in total length
• 20 striped bass, white bass, and sunshine bass (individually or in total), of which no more than six may exceed 24 inches in total length
• 15 Chain pickerel
• 50 panfish (for example: blue-gill, shellcracker, spotted sunfish, warmouth and redfin pickerel individually or in total)
• 25 black crappie (speckled perch and/or white crappie)
• 2 butterfly peacock bass, only one of which may be longer than 17 inches in total length
• 0 Speckled peacock bass. Immediately release unharmed all speckled peacock bass
Total possession limit for the above fish is two days' bag limit.
Special bag and length limits apply in some areas.

Commercial Licenses
(excluding issuing fees)

Resident Commercial	$50.00
Resident Freshwater Fish Dealer	$70.00
Nonresident Commercial Fishing	$200.00
Nonresident Retail Fish Dealer	$250.00
Nonresident Wholesale Fish Dealer	$1,100.00

Resident Commercial fishing license stamps are issued by the county tax collector; all other commercial fishing licenses are issued only by the Florida Fish and Wildlife Conservation Commission. Additional fees, beyond issuing, for licenses, permits and certificates may apply.

FLORIDA RECORD FRESHWATER FISH CATCHES
(As of 2010)

Species	Weight	Place	Year
Bass, largemouth	17 lb. 4½ oz.	Polk County	1986
Bass, largemouth	20 lb. 2 oz.	Pasco County	1923*
Bass, redeye	7 lb. 13¼ oz.	Apalachicola River	1989
Bass, spotted	3 lb. 12 oz.	Apalachicola River	1985
Bass, striped	42 lb. 4 oz.	Apalachicola River	1993
Bass, sunshine	16 lb. 5 oz.	Lake Seminole	1985
Bass, Suwannee	3 lb. 14¼ oz.	Suwannee River	1985
Bass, white	4 lb. 11 oz.	Apalachicola River	1982
Bass, butterfly peacock	9 lb. ¼ oz.	Miami-Dade County	1993
Black crappie	3 lb. 8 oz.	Lake Talquin	1992
Bluegill	2 lb. 15¼ oz.	Washington County	1989
Bowfin	19 lb.	Lake Kissimmee	1984
Bullhead, brown	5 lb. 11 oz.	Duval County	1995
Bullhead, yellow	2.91 lb.	Withlacochee River	2007
Catfish, blue	64 lb. 8 oz.	Choctawatchee River	2008
Catfish, channel	44 lb. 8 oz.	Lake County	1985
Catfish, flathead	49.39 lb.	Apalachicola River	2004
Catfish, flathead	57 lb., 8 oz.	Hillsborough River	1975*
Catfish, white	18 lb. 13 oz.	Withlacoochee River	1991
Common carp	40 lb. 8½ oz.	Gadsden County	1981
Flier	1 lb. 4 oz.	Lake Iamonia	1992
Gar, alligator	123 lb.	Choctawhatchee River	1995
Gar, Florida	9.44 lb.	Orange County	2001
Gar, longnose	41 lb.	Lake Panasoffkee	1985
Oscar	2 lb. 5¼ oz.	Lake Okeechobee	1994
Pickerel, chain	6.96 lb.	Gadsden County	2004
Pickerel, chain	8 lb.	Gadsden County	1971*
Pickerel, redfin	1 lb. 1 oz.	Bradford County	1993
Shad, American (tie)	5 lb. 3 oz.	St. Johns River	1992
Shad, American (tie)	5 lb. 3 oz.	St. Johns River	1990

Sunfish, redbreast	2 lb. 1¼ oz.	Suwannee River	1988
Sunfish, redear	4 lb. 13¾ oz.	Jackson County	1986
Sunfish, spotted	0 lb. 13¼ oz.	Suwannee River	1984
Warmouth	2 lb. 7 oz.	Okaloosa County	1985
*Witnessed but not certified			

SALTWATER FISHING FEES AND REGULATIONS

Florida residents, nonresidents, and recreational divers must have a saltwater fishing license to take fish in saltwater unless covered by one of the following exemptions:

—Any individual under 16 years of age;

—Any Florida resident fishing in saltwater from land or from a structure fixed to the land;

—Any individual fishing from a vessel issued a Vessel Saltwater Fishing License;

—Fishing aboard a vessel that has a valid saltwater products license;

—Any person 65 years of age or older who holds a valid Florida driver's license or Florida voter registration card;

—Any Florida resident who is a member of the Armed Forces while home on leave for 30 days or less, with valid orders in his or her possession;

—Any individual who has been accepted by the Florida Department of Children and Families for developmental services;

—Any individual fishing from a licensed fishing pier;

—A Florida resident who is certified as totally and permanently disabled is entitled, without charge, to a permanent saltwater fishing license.

License Costs, annual (excluding issuing fee)

Shoreline (permit required)	Free
Lifetime saltwater fishing license (including snook and lobster permits):	
4 years or younger	$126.50
5-12 years	$226.50
13 years or older	$301.50
Resident annual license	$13.50
Resident, five year	$61.50
Nonresident annual license	$31.50
Nonresident 7-Day	$16.50
Nonresident 3-Day	$6.50

The state now issues lifetime and five-year saltwater fishing licenses. For details, see freshwater license fees above.

In addition to the saltwater fishing license, any person required to have the license who takes or possesses snook or crawfish must have a snook or crawfish stamp affixed to the license. Each stamp costs $2.

Taking tarpon requires a $50.00 tag. There are no exceptions.

A line of demarcation between salt and fresh water has been established in the rivers, streams, and bayous of the coastal regions. If planning to fish in these areas, inquire locally for the point beyond which a freshwater fishing license is required.

Florida's state waters consist of all waters within nine nautical miles of the shoreline in the Gulf of

Mexico and three nautical miles of the shoreline in the Atlantic Ocean. For fisheries purposes, the federal waters are the waters 200 miles seaward of state waters.

Saltwater food fish not used must be returned to the water alive. No size limits on saltwater fish are stated with the exceptions of those listed below. Not permitted to be taken, injured, or killed are marine turtles, porpoise, rays, manatees, or coral. In addition, it is illegal to spearfish in Pennekamp Coral Reef State Park, Collier County, that part of Monroe County from Long Key north to the Miami-Dade County line, and in the immediate area of all public bathing beaches, commercial or public fishing piers, bridge catwalks, and jetties. It also is illegal to spearfish in fresh water or for freshwater fish in brackish water.

Minimum Legal Lengths, Bag Limits

(Note—All fish measured from tip of nose to rear center of tail. Sizes and bag limits subject to change; check most current regulations. The following also apply only to coastal waters within three nautical miles of the east coast, and nine nautical miles of the west coast.)

Species	Size Limit	Bag Limit Per Day
Amberjack, greater	30"	One
Amberjack, lesser	14-22"	Five
Black drum	14-24"	Five
Red drum	18-27"	One
Sea bass	10"	Twenty
Bluefish	12"	Ten
Bonefish	18"	One
Cobia	33"	One
Dolphin	20"	Ten

Flounder	12"	Ten
Hogfish	12"	Five
Grouper	22-24"	Two
Grouper, yellow	20"	Five
King mackerel	24"	Two
Spanish mackerel	12"	Fifteen
Marlin, blue	99"	One
Marlin, white	66"	One
Black mullet	None	Fifty
Pompano	11-20"	Six
Redfish	18-27"	One
Sailfish	63"	One
Shad	None	Ten
Shark	54"	One
Snapper	16"	Two
Snook	28-32"	One*
Sea trout	15-20"	Five
Swordfish	47"**	One
Tarpon	None	Two***
Triggerfish	14"	Two
Wahoo	None	Two
Weakfish	12"	Four
*permit required		
** lower jaw length		
*** $50 tag required to harvest or possess		

It is unlawful to harvest, possess, land, purchase, sell, or exchange Nassau or Goliath grouper, sawfish, manta, or spotted eagle rays or sturgeon (also basking, whale, white, sand tiger, or big eye sand tiger sharks).

Although most of Florida's saltwater fish occur throughout the state's long coastline, fishing for any particular species may be better in one area than in another. Following is a brief listing of species often encountered in each area:

Northeast Atlantic Coast—Surf casting for redfish, blues, drum. Inside bays and inlets for trout, redfish, drum, bluefish, and tarpon.

Central East Coast—Trout; redfish in the surf and inshore;

drum, tripletail, jack crevalle. Lower areas for sailfish and snook.

Lower East Coast—Sailfishing entire area but particularly off Stuart and Palm Beach. In Gulf Stream, sailfish, marlin, tuna, mako shark, dolphin. Along shoreline, snook, tarpon, blues, trout, and mackerel during runs.

The Keys—Upper Keys produce trout, redfish, snapper, and noted for bonefish. Area also good for permit, tarpon, grouper, amberjack, barracuda, and wahoo.

Northwest Gulf Coast—Red snapper, flounder, cobia, trout, blue runner, and grouper.

Upper Gulf Coast—Trout, redfish, flounder, grouper, tarpon in summer; mangrove snapper in fall; offshore runs of cobia, kingfish, and mackerel in spring.

Middle Gulf Coast—Tarpon from the Homosassa River to Boca Grande, grouper and jack offshore, and snook, cobia, trout, kingfish, mackerel.

Lower Gulf Coast—Tarpon, snook, redfish, and pompano; mackerel during runs.

FLORIDA RECORD SALTWATER FISH CATCHES
(All tackle—as of 2010)

Species	Weight	Place	Year
Amberjack	142 lb.	Islamorada	1979
Barjack	7 lb. 12 oz.	Miami	1999
Barracuda	67 lb.	Islamorada	1949
Bass, black sea	5 lb. 1 oz.	Panama City	1956
Bass, striped	43 lb. 9 oz.	Indian River	2004
Bluefish	22 lb. 2 oz.	Jensen Beach	1973
Blue runner	8 lb. 5 oz.	Pensacola	1995
Bonefish	16 lb. 3 oz.	Islamorada	2007
Catfish, gafftopsail	8 lb. 14 oz.	Titusville	1996
Catfish, hardhead	3 lb. 5 oz.	Sebastian	1993
Cobia	130 lb. 1 oz.	Destin	1997
Croaker	4 lb. 15 oz.	St. Lucie	2002
Dolphin	81 lb. 1 oz.	Lantana	2007
Drum, black	96 lb.	Fernandina Beach	2001
Drum, red	52 lb. 5 oz.	Cocoa	1996
Flounder	20 lb. 9 oz.	Nassau County	1983
Grouper, black	113 lb. 6 oz.	Dry Tortugas	1990
Grouper, gag	80 lb. 6 oz.	Destin	1993
Grouper, Goliath	680 lb.	Fernandina Beach	1961
Grouper, Nassau	9 lb.	Marathon	2007

Grouper, red	42 lb. 4 oz.	St. Augustine	1997
Grouper, Warsaw	436 lb. 12 oz.	Destin	1985
Grouper, yellowfin	34 lb. 6 oz.	Key Largo	1988
Grunts, margates	15 lb. 8 oz.	Key West	2001
Hind, speckled	52 lb. 8 oz.	Destin	1994
Hogfish	19 lb. 8 oz.	Daytona Beach	1962
Jack, bar	7 lb. 12 oz.	Miami	1996
Jack, Crevalle	57 lb.	Jupiter	1993
Jack, horse-eye	25 lb. 12 oz.	Palm Beach	1997
Ladyfish	6 lb. 4 oz.	Cocoa Beach	2005
Mackerel, cero	17 lb. 2 oz.	Islamorada	1986
Mackerel, king	90 lb.	Key West	1976
Mackerel, Spanish	12 lb.	Fort Pierce	1984
Marlin, blue	1,046 lb.	Panama City	2001
Marlin, white	161 lb.	Miami Beach	1938
Permit	56 lb. 2 oz.	Fort Lauderdale	1997
Pompano, African	50 lb. 8 oz.	Daytona Beach	1990
Pompano, Florida	8 lb. 4 oz.	Port St. Joe	1999
Runner, blue	8 lb. 5 oz.	Pensacola	1995
Runner, rainbow	23 lb.	Boynton Beach	2003
Sailfish, Atlantic	126 lb.	Big Pine Key	2009
Scamp	28 lb. 6 oz.	Mayport	2002
Seatrout, spotted	17 lb. 7 oz.	Ft. Pierce	1995
Shark, blacktip	152 lb.	Sebastian	1987
Shark, bull	517 lb.	Panama City Beach	1981
Shark, dusky	764 lb.	Longboat Key	1982
Shark, hammerhead	1,060 lb.	Boca Grande	2009
Shark, lemon	397 lb.	Dunedin	1977
Shark, mako	911 lb. 12 oz.	Palm Beach	1962
Shark, spinner	190 lb.	Flagler Beach	1986
Shark, thresher	544 lb. 8 oz.	Destin	1984
Shark, tiger	1,065 lb.	Pensacola	1981
Shark, white	686 lb.	Key West	1988

Sheepshead	15 lb. 2 oz.	Homosassa	1981
Snapper, cubera	116 lb.	Clearwater	1979
Snapper, gray	17 lb.	Port Canaveral	1992
Snapper, lane	6 lb. 6 oz.	Pensacola	1991
Snapper, mutton	30 lb. 4 oz.	Dry Tortugas	1998
Snapper, red	46 lb. 8 oz.	Destin	1985
Snapper, yellowtail	8 lb. 9 oz.	Fort Myers	1996
Snook	44 lb. 3 oz.	Fort Myers	1984
Spearfish, longnose	61 lb. 8 oz.	Islamorada	1981
Swordfish	612 lb. 12 oz.	Key Largo	1978
Tarpon	243 lb.	Key West	1975
Triggerfish, gray	12 lb. 7 oz.	Pensacola	2001
Tripletail	40 lb. 13 oz.	Fort Pierce	1998
Tuna, bigeye	167 lb.	Miami Beach	1957
Tuna, blackfin	45 lb. 8 oz.	Key West	1996
Tuna, skipjack	33 lb. 8 oz.	Islamorada	1998
Tuna, yellowfin	240 lb.	Key West	2002
Tunny, little	27 lb.	Key Largo	1976
Wahoo	139 lb.	Marathon	1960
Weakfish	10 lb.	Port Canaveral	1987

INJURED WILDLIFE

Any encountered injured wildlife, especially large species such as manatees, should be reported to the Florida Fish and Wildlife Conservation Commission. In some instances, for seabirds, raptors (hawks, owls, eagles), or small mammals, the local Animal Control office or Humane Society can direct you to an animal rehabilitation site. It is not advisable to attempt home nursing for two reasons: the success rate is about nil and state law prohibits possessing wildlife.

FLORIDA SHARK ATTACKS

Most shark attacks in the United States occur in Florida, and most in Florida occur off Volusia County.

Year	Fatal	Non-fatal
1990	0	9
1991	0	12
1992	0	12
1993	0	8
1994	0	23
1995	0	31
1996	0	13
1997	0	25
1998	1	18
1999	0	25
2000	1	37
2001	0	37
2002	0	29
2003	0	31
2004	0	12
2005	1	17
2006	0	23
2007	0	32
2008	0	32
2009	0	19

WATERWAYS AND BOATING

INTRACOASTAL WATERWAY

Florida, with more coastline than any state except Alaska, and with hundreds of navigable rivers and lakes, offers unlimited opportunities for sailing, pleasure cruising, canoeing, kayaking, and exploring. Among the most widely traveled and enjoyable water highways is the state's intracoastal waterway. It is in three parcels—the Atlantic section, the Okeechobee section, and the west coast section. The trio makes up the Intracoastal Waterway of Florida, which extends from Jacksonville in northeast Florida, down the east coast, across the southern peninsula to the west coast, and northward to Tarpon Springs.

Atlantic Intracoastal Waterway

Construction of the Intracoastal Waterway of Florida was the outgrowth of a desire to connect the chain of rivers, lakes, and lagoons along Florida's east coast into a continuous waterway. The original construction was done by the Florida East Coast Canal Company under a state statute that provided for grants of land to railroad and canal companies.

Actual construction began in 1881 on a channel that was to be five feet deep and 50 feet wide, extending from Jacksonville to Miami. The work was completed in 1912, but the channel dimensions were never attained in full, and it was seldom maintained. Tolls were charged, but operation was not profitable, and in 1923 the canal went into receivership.

Prodding from the chambers of commerce along the east coast prompted the Legislature in 1927 to create the Florida Inland Navigation District, a special taxing district consisting of 11 east coast counties from Duval to Miami-Dade. It soon became part of a more widely proposed federal project by the Corps of Engineers so that the Florida section actually was constructed and is maintained by the U.S. Army Corps of Engineers District in Jacksonville, in cooperation with the Florida Inland Navigation District.

The original Florida east coast waterway today is part of the Atlantic Intracoastal Waterway, a continuous and connected system of sheltered inland channels for commercial barges and pleasure boats that actually extends 1,391 miles between Trenton, N.J., on the Delaware River, to Miami. The channels are between 10 and 12 feet deep, and have a bottom width of 90 feet or more.

Florida's Atlantic Intracoastal Waterway starts at Fernandina Beach and follows coastal rivers and lagoons through the resorts of Jacksonville Beach, St. Augustine, Daytona Beach, and close to the Kennedy Space Center at Cape Canaveral. It then continues through the resort cities of Cocoa, Melbourne, Vero Beach, Fort Pierce, Jensen Beach, West Palm Beach, Fort Lauderdale, and many other Gold Coast cities, ending at Biscayne Bay between Miami Beach and Miami.

The Atlantic waterway has a channel of 12-foot depth at low water south to Fort Pierce, and thence a 10-foot depth south to Miami.

From Fernandina Beach to

Miami the waterway is generally protected from strong winds and rough water, with the exceptions of Mosquito Lagoon, Indian River, and Lake Worth, where conditions can become quite choppy. Fixed bridges over the entire Intracoastal Waterway in Florida generally provide a minimum vertical clearance of 65 feet at mean high water, and horizontal clearance of 90 feet between fenders. Several exceptions exist in the Miami area, and boaters are urged to obtain a summary of bridge clearance data from the Florida Inland Navigation District. In addition, there are many lift-type bridges all along the ICW that have to be opened for captains of larger boats to clear. It is recommended that boaters use a reliable cruising guide to find out what times these spans are opened.

Okeechobee Intracoastal Waterway

The Okeechobee section extends from Stuart on the east coast to Fort Myers on the west coast, and was opened in 1937. It covers more than 150 miles and is the state's only cross state waterway connecting the Atlantic Ocean with the Gulf of Mexico.

The Okeechobee waterway is made up of three areas, each different—the first 38 miles from the east are in the St. Lucie Canal, the center area is actually Lake Okeechobee, and the third area is made up of the Caloosahatchee Canal and River that leads into the Gulf.

The route from Stuart is well protected and feeds into Lake Okeechobee through a system of locks. On entering the lake, boaters have two routes to choose from. They have the direct route

option of crossing unprotected Lake Okeechobee, the second largest body of freshwater in the U.S., or the partially protected "Rim Route" that hugs the huge lake's southern shore. The direct route is 22 nautical miles (approximately 40 statute miles) and the Rim Route about eight or nine nautical miles longer. Both arrive at Moore Haven, a city on the lake's western edge.

Depths on Lake Okeechobee and its connecting canals can vary substantially from those shown on charts, depending on rainfall. Charted depths are based on a "normal" low water level of 12.5 feet above sea level. In a wet year the lake may be three or four feet deeper than the chart shows, and in dry spells it can be as much as two feet shallower than the chart figure. Current available depths are posted at every lock.

For the neophyte boater, the Okeechobee Intracoastal Waterway is an ideal cruise, presenting no navigation problems. The entire distance of 150 miles consists simply of hopping through canals and rivers. And there is little chance of getting into trouble because a boater is never more than a short distance from a highway or village. On-shore services and accommodations are everywhere, including motels, restaurants, marinas, and camps. Those choosing to "anchor off" have a good many sheltered coves and anchorages in which to drop the hook.

The waterway has five locks and more than 20 bridges. Passing through the locks is quite simple. Each lock can be reached by telephone, if a boater wishes information about the route, depths, clearances, and general conditions.

No currents must be contended with along the Okeechobee Intracoastal Waterway. Tides at both Stuart and Fort Myers are only one foot and therefore create no problem.

West Coast Intracoastal Waterway

Marine interests along the west coast petitioned Congress in 1934 for an inland waterway adjacent to the Gulf of Mexico. In 1939, after a study, the Corps of Engineers recommended such a waterway from the Caloosahatchee River in Lee County to the Anclote River in Pinellas County. The project was put on hold during World War II, but in 1945 Congress enacted legislation calling for a nine-foot channel, 100 feet wide, and approximately 100 miles long.

The channel was to run through six counties, thereby necessitating formation of the West Coast Inland Navigation District in 1947. Represented were the counties of Lee, Charlotte, Sarasota, Manatee, Hillsborough, and Pinellas.

In the mid-1950s, the district began acquiring thousands of acres of right-of-way and spoil areas necessary for the project. The first dredging began in 1960, from the Caloosahatchee River northward toward Boca Grande. In 1961 another dredge worked south from the Anclote River toward Tampa Bay. Another dredge in 1962 dug south from Tampa Bay toward Venice, and two years later dredging started from Boca Grande toward Venice. The complex Venice overland cut was commenced in 1965 and finished three years later, linking the previously dug sections of channel and in effect completing the 150-mile waterway.

Since the project was authorized, additional channels have been incorporated, including the Venice Inlet, Cats Point Channel connecting Gulfport to the waterway, and the Sunshine Skyway Channel connecting lower Tampa Bay with Boca Ciega Bay. Total cost of the West Coast Intracoastal Waterway was more than $10 million.

From the Caloosahatchee River the waterway winds northward to the Anclote River west of Tarpon Springs in a bending course, utilizing dug channels, natural bays and passes, harbors and sounds—frequently challenging the navigational skills of a boater. The waterway is nine feet deep and 100 feet wide, except in the Cats Point Channel that links Gulfport with the waterway; there the depth is six feet and the width 80 feet.

The west coast waterway is generally protected from high winds and rough water, with the exceptions of open waters of San Carlos Bay, Sarasota Bay, Tampa Bay, Clearwater Harbor, and St. Joseph Sound. Passes should be entered on a rising tide and the best time is during mid-day, when the sun is high and the bright light shows up shoal areas and shallow waters.

Some of the most beautiful and unspoiled coastlands in Florida are found along the west coast waterway. It is an ecological wonderland. Side trip possibilities are endless, including trips to Sanibel and Captiva islands for shell hunting. Boats also can cruise up the numerous wide rivers in the region, such as the Peace, the Manatee, the Hillsborough, and the Myakka.

The Missing Link

No inland route along the coast has been dredged for the Intracoastal Waterway from the Anclote River at Tarpon Springs to the Panhandle region. The section often is referred to as "the missing link" in the waterway. Construction of this section has been authorized by Congress but has not yet begun. Boats traveling this route have the option of hugging the unpopulated shoreline northward or taking a more direct route by angling across the open Gulf of Mexico. The waterway resumes on the northern Gulf shore between St. Mark's Light and Carrabelle. The distance from Tarpon Springs to St. Mark's Light is 145 miles and is not recommended for novice boaters or captains of smaller craft.

MAJOR CANALS

Miami Canal	85 miles long
Caloosahatchee River (Lake Okeechobee to Gulf of Mexico)	65 miles long
North New River Canal	58 miles long
Hillsboro Canal	52 miles long
West Palm Beach Canal	42 miles long
St. Lucie (Lake Okeechobee to Atlantic Ocean)	40 miles long

LIGHTHOUSES

Thirty-three operating lighthouses rim the Florida coastline. Keeping them functioning is the responsibility of the U.S. Coast Guard. Lighthouses in the Panhandle are maintained by the Coast Guard station in New Orleans; those on the peninsula and the Keys by the Miami station. Nearly half of Florida's lighthouses are in the Keys. The traditional lighthouse, with its keeper living on the site and regularly polishing the lamps, disappeared in the 1960s. Today, lighthouses are turned on and off by photocells and electric timers.

Name	General Location	Height (feet) above Water
Alligator Reef	Florida Keys	136
Amelia Island	Fernandina Beach	107
American Shoal	Lower Florida Keys	109
Anclote Key	Tarpon Springs	101
Boca Grande Rear	Gasparilla Island	105
Cape Canaveral	Cape Canaveral	137
Cape Florida	Key Biscayne	95
Cape San Blas	Port St. Joe	101
Cape St. George	Off Apalachicola	72
Carysfort Reef	Upper Florida Keys	100
Cosgrove Shoal	Florida Keys	49
Crooked River	Carrabelle	115

Dry Tortugas	Florida Keys	151
Egmont Key	Off Tampa Bay	85
Fowey Rocks	Upper Florida Keys	110
Hillsboro Inlet	Deerfield Beach	136
Jupiter Inlet	Jupiter	146
Key West	Lower Florida Keys	91
Molasses Reef	Florida Keys	45
Pacific Reef	Florida Keys	44
Pensacola	Pensacola	191
Ponce de Leon Inlet	New Smyrna Beach	159
Port Boca Grande	Gasparilla Island	41
Pulaski Shoal	Florida Keys	49
Rebecca Shoal	Florida Keys	66
Sand Key	Lower Florida Keys	109
Sanibel Island	Off Fort Myers	98
Smith Shoal	Florida Keys	47
Sombrero Key	Upper Florida Keys	142
St. Augustine	St. Augustine	161
St. Johns	Jacksonville	83
St. Marks	St. Marks	82
Tennessee Reef	Florida Keys	49

BOAT FEES AND REGULATIONS

All vessels operated on Florida waters must be registered and/or numbered in Florida except:

—vessels used exclusively on private lakes or ponds

—vessels owned by the federal government

—vessels used exclusively as life boats

—non-motor-powered vessels

—vessels with a current number from another state or from another country temporarily using Florida waters (less than 90 consecutive days).

—vessels newly purchased in Florida (less than 30 days)

In addition, all vessels except those documented vessels and non-motor-powered boats less than 16 feet in length must be titled in Florida.

Boat titles and registrations are made at county tax collector offices. Applicants must provide proof of ownership. Registration must be renewed each year in the birth month of the owner.

Annual registration fees are:	
Class A-1 (less than 12 feet)	$7.25
Class A-2 (12 feet to less than 16 feet)	$14.25
Class 1(16 feet to less than 26 feet)	$22.25
Class 2 (26 feet to less than 40 feet)	$54.25
Class 3 (40 feet to less than 65 feet)	$86.25
Class 4 (65 feet to less than 110 feet)	$102.25
Class 5 (110 feet and over)	$126.25
Some counties impose an additional fee.	

Upon receipt and approval of registration, the owner is issued a certificate of number and a validation decal. The certificate must be on board whenever the boat is used and the decal must be properly displayed on the bow.

Fee for titling a vessel is $5.25. There is an additional $1 fee to record each existing lien and an additional $4 fee for titling a vessel previously registered out of state. The owner must show proof of payment of sales tax for the vessel, motor, and trailer.

Transferring a title from one owner to another carries a fee of $6.50.

Documented Boats

Florida law requires titling of undocumented vessels, but owners of larger boats can document their vessels with the U.S. Coast Guard. A marine document is proof of ownership and is recognized internationally. A person owning a documented boat for use in Florida still must register it in Florida. Documented vessels must display the validation decal on the windshield or port side window.

Hull ID Number

All boats built since 1972 must have a hull identification number permanently attached to the transom on the starboard side above the waterline. A later regulation, in 1984, requires the number also be permanently attached in a second, unexposed location. Owners of homemade boats should contact the Florida Fish and Wildlife Conservation Commission for a hull number. The number is similar to the VIN number on a car.

Law Enforcement

Florida ranked second among the states in the number of boating accidents involving fatalities. In 2009, with more than 982,000 boats registered, 65 people were killed in just 51 accidents. Surprisingly, most fatal accidents involved older, experienced boaters.

The state closely monitors the use of alcohol by boaters.

By operating on Florida waterways, a person is deemed to have given consent to be tested for alcohol if arrested for operating under the influence. Penalties for operating a vessel under the influence of alcohol or drugs include fines of up to $2,500, imprisonment of up to one year, nonpaid public service work, and mandatory substance abuse counseling.

Sentencing is mandatory; the "suspended sentence" is a thing of the past for impaired boat operators. If a drunken operator kills another person, the penalty jumps to 15 years in prison and a fine of up to $10,000.

Florida has a chemical test law for boat operators. Refusal to submit to a breath or urine test can incur a fine of $500. If an operator causes death or serious injury to someone, police may use reasonable force to require the operator to submit to a blood test.

Any sworn law-enforcement officer may enforce boating laws and regulations. Most violations are misdemeanors.

ADDITIONAL BOATING REGULATIONS

Florida maintains boating regulations that are in addition to federal rules and requirements. Among them

Age Restrictions

—Persons less than 14 years of age shall not operate a Personal Watercraft. No one under the age of 18 may rent a Personal Watercraft in Florida.

—No person born after January 1, 1988, may operate a vessel powered by a motor of 10 horsepower or greater unless he or she has in their possession a photographic identification and a boater safety identification card issued for successful completion of an approved boating safety course.

Personal Flotation Devices

Every child under 6 years of age must wear a USCG approved Personal Flotation Device on a vessel less than 26' while the vessel is underway. Personal Watercraft operators and passengers must wear an approved Type I, II, III, or V PFD. Required PFDs must be readily accessible. Inflatable PFDs are prohibited.

Speed Limits and Reckless Operation

No vessel can be operated within Florida in a reckless or negligent manner, including excessive speed in regulated or congested areas, operating in a manner that may cause an accident, operating in a swimming area with bathers present, towing water skiers where obstructions exist or a fall might cause them to be injured, bow riding or riding on the gunwale or transom where no seating is provided, endangering life or property. Reckless operation is a first-degree misdemeanor. Boats may not tow water skiers, aquaplanes or similar devices without a wide-angle rear view mirror or an observer on board and may not tow in darkness. Boaters must be aware of and obey manatee protection restrictions.

Accident Reporting

Any accident involving death, disappearance or personal injury, or damage greater than $500 must be reported. A "boating accident" includes, but is not limited to, capsizing, collision, foundering, flooding, fire, explosion and the disappearance of a vessel other than by theft. Accidents must be reported immediately to the nearest office of the Florida Fish and Wildlife Conservation Commission office or the Florida Marine Patrol.

RED TIDE

Few natural phenomena are so disastrous to Florida's waters, coasts, fishing, and tourist industry, and so unpleasant to its residents, as what is known as Red Tide. It has been around for hundreds, perhaps thousands, of years, all over the world. A 1996 outbreak was the worst ever recorded in Florida waters.

Red Tide is the popular name given a peculiar discoloration of sea water caused by microscopic organisms. Usually these discolorations are observed along coasts where they are frequently accompanied by the widespread death of fish and other marine animals.

Scientists find that the color and slimy consistency of the water during Red Tide is partly due to the presence of a microscopic form of life. It is one-thousandth of an inch across and travels about the water by means of two whiplike threads, one trailing behind it and one running around its middle.

A single-celled creature with both animal and plant characteristics, it is present in sea water off the west coast of Florida in quantities of less than 1,000 to the quart. In this concentration it appears to be harmless. During periods of Red Tide, however, it has increased its numbers to 60 million and higher to the quart. In this concentration it is violently poisonous to fish and marine mammals.

Odorless, colorless gases irritating a person's eyes, nose, and throat often occur in conjunction with outbreaks of Red Tide. These irritant gases are given off when samples of Red Tide water are heated or violently shaken.

Because the organism behaves somewhat like a plant, it appears to require fertilizer for growth. Normally the most important of these in the ocean are phosphates. With a normal phosphate level, the one-cell creature remains in a normal balance in the ocean. It is when some additional nutrients appear in the water that the creature seems to multiply. What these nutrients are remains open to study. More than a dozen theories regarding the cause of Red Tide outbreaks have been offered by scientists. To date, all are just theories.

CROSS-FLORIDA BARGE CANAL

The saga of the Cross-Florida Barge Canal began early in the 19th century when in 1818 Secretary of War John Calhoun "directed some partial examination near the headwaters of the St. Mary's River and the Suwannee River with the view to inland communication between the Atlantic and Gulf."

Between 1825 and 1923 the subject became an almost annual debate in Congress. Pro arguments dwelled on protecting wartime commerce and avoiding attacks by pirates. In 1825 the annual losses due to wrecks in the Florida Keys and shoals was about $500,000, a sum considered "almost sufficient" to build a canal across the peninsula. At that time, however, the recommended route united "the waters of the St. Johns River with those of the river Suwannee requiring a canal of not more than 20 miles in length."

In 1829, Congress decided to ascertain "the most eligible route for a canal." Use of the Oklawaha River north of Ocala was prominently mentioned. But surveyors recommended dismissal of the idea because of impractability.

Surveys and debate did not cease, however, and finally in the 1930s, construction was started as Depression-work. A Florida water conservation committee promptly filed a brief against the proposed canal and in 1936 work was halted. Some 4,000 acres of land had been cleared, 12 million cubic yards of dirt moved, and $5.4 million expended.

Then, in 1942, Congress authorized a lock-type, high-level canal across north-central Florida. It was assigned to the Corps of Engineers, but no money was appropriated. When World War II ended, the corps did design a ship canal but no work was done.

Presidential candidate John Kennedy in 1960 saw the canal as a popular issue in Florida and endorsed the idea. A study by the Corps of Engineers stated that the canal would show a profit of 17 cents on each dollar it cost. Congress was impressed and in 1963 voted a million-dollar construction appropriation. Work began in 1964 with President Lyndon Johnson detonating an explosive charge near Palatka.

For five years the protests of conservationists were isolated and ineffective. Then, aroused by what had been termed the "rape of the Oklawaha," organized groups of university professors and ecologists began to make themselves heard. The canal became a major issue in the 1970 election campaigns.

To appease the conservationists, President Richard Nixon stopped work on the canal. Some 300 acres of wildlife habitat already had been written off by conservationists as the result of earlier work, but they urged authorities to draw down the 13,000-acre Rodman Reservoir to save an estimated 700 acres of trees inundated when the basin was flooded in 1969.

The federal government and a federal judge supported the drawdown but a Jacksonville judge issued an injunction preventing it. More years of legal maneuvering followed. In 1974 Federal Judge Harvey Johnsen ruled that President Nixon had no authority to stop canal work and that only Congress had the power.

But in 1976 the state cabinet voted 6-1 to ask Congress to abandon the project. It further asked Congress to restore the Oklawaha River and to use the already completed portion of the canal for public recreation. (The 110-mile-long canal, between Jacksonville and Yankeetown, was to be 12 feet deep and 150 feet wide. Completed were three of five navigational locks, three dams, and four of 11 planned bridges.)

In 1986, Congress de-authorized the canal, and cut off any more construction funds. It also agreed to buy, for $32 million, the canal right-of-way lands through Duval, Marion, Putnam, Citrus, Clay, and

Levy counties that the state had purchased.

Florida balked at the suggested reimbursement, however, contending the land now was worth closer to $100 million. State officials also worried that signing over the right of way to the federal government risked the project being revived some day. Instead, Florida political leaders and conservationists asked to keep title to the vast right-of-way and use it for parks and nature trails. They also beseeched the Corps of Engineers to tear down the locks and dams and return the Oklawaha River to its original state.

Finally, in November 1990, nearly 20 years after President Nixon halted canal construction, President George Bush signed legislation that officially killed the project and turned the route over to the state. It gave Florida control of the 110-mile-long waterway under the condition that it be preserved as a "greenway" for conservation and recreation.

Two months later, in January 1991, Florida Governor Lawton Chiles and the Cabinet approved a resolution signaling the demise of the canal and the beginning of plans to convert 77,000 acres of canal land into a huge state park.

When deauthorized in 1986, the project had used up $70 million, destroyed 4,000 acres of hardwood forests, and done irreparable damage to the Oklawaha River.

MAJOR BRIDGES

Bridge	Spans	Length (Feet)	Vertical Clearance (Feet)	Date
Seven-Mile	Money Key Channel	35,716	28	1938
Sunshine Skyway	Tampa Bay	21,640	175	1987
Buckman	St. Johns River	16,300	65	1969
Howard Frankland	Tampa Bay (old span)	15,893	43	1958
	(new span)	15,893	49	1989
Pensacola Bay	Pensacola Bay	15,640	50	1960
Gandy	Tampa Bay (old span)	14,784	43	1975
	(new span)	13,886	43	1997
Escambia	Escambia Bay	13,577	50	1970
Napoleon Broward	St. Johns River	10,646	175	1989
John Mathews	St. Johns River	7,375	149	1953
New Shands	St. Johns River	6,662	45	1961
Fuller Warren	St. Johns River	7,500	75	2002
Bahia Honda	Bahia Honda Channel	5,356	55	1938
Caloosahatchee	Caloosahatchee River	4,966	55	1962
Arthur Sollee	Intracoastal Canal	4,594	65	1988
Acosta	St. Johns River	3,740	57	1922
Fuller Warren	St. Johns River	3,667	37	1954
Hathaway	West Bay	3,358	50	1960

Courtney Campbell	Tampa Bay	3,274	45	1974
Ringing	Sarasota Bay	3,097	65	2003
Blackwater Bay	Blackwater Bay	2,931	45	1968
Dunn's Creek	U.S. 1	2,699	—	1987
St. Johns	St. Johns River	2,655	45	1961
Navarre	Santa Rosa Sound	2,640	50	1960
Memorial	Clearwater Bay	2,340	74	2005
Isaiah Hart	St. Johns River	2,504	30	1968
Manatee	Manatee River	2,225	40	1957
East MacArthur	Biscayne Bay	2,155	35	1958
Julia Tuttle Causeway	Biscayne Bay	2,150	64	1959
West MacArthur	Intracoastal Canal	2,114	35	1961
Main Street	St. Johns River	1,900	38	1941
Trout River (I-95)	Trout River	1,835	30	1959
Apalachicola River	Apalachicola River	1,636	35	1959
Trout River (U.S. 17)	Trout River	1,458	30	1958
36th Street	Biscayne Bay	1,138	41	1959
Trout River	I-295	1,105	8	1976
East Las Olas	Intracoastal Canal	1,095	33	1958

The Sunshine Skyway

One of Florida's most spectacular bridges, the Sunshine Skyway, opened in May 1987 across the mouth of Tampa Bay, connecting Pinellas County with the northern end of Manatee County. The center of the span is in Hillsborough County.

It took five years to build and cost $244 million. The new bridge replaced the original Skyway, a twin- span structure, half of which was built in 1954 and the other span in 1971. One of those spans collapsed in May 1980 when struck by a freighter. The tragedy caused 35 deaths when a Greyhound bus and several passenger cars dropped 150 feet into Tampa Bay.

The new bridge has a main span of 1,200 feet, compared with 864 feet for the old Skyway. Total length of the new bridge is 4.1 miles. The twin cable towers are 432 feet tall and the roadway is 192 feet above the water at its peak. Designed by engineer Jean Muller, the new Sunshine Skyway is a superstructure of hollow concrete segments strung together with steel cables attached to two tall pylons. It will survive winds of 135 mph, although wind tunnel tests have shown it could withstand winds as high as 236 mph.

Muller's Skyway won a 1988 Presidential Award for Design Excellence and was declared by the award jurors "a work of art."

CANOE TRAILS

The Florida Canoe Trail system was established by the state to offer the public a way to discover and explore the state's unique environment. The system currently consists of 39 canoe trails, totaling 2,600 miles of scenic waterways.

With the exception of saltwater courses, a canoe trail is a publicly owned stream, often flowing through private property. In most cases the river banks are privately owned and not open to public use so canoeists are required not to trespass, abuse, or litter the banks and shorelines of a canoe trail. Being public waters, the canoe trails are open to many kinds of users, including motorboaters.

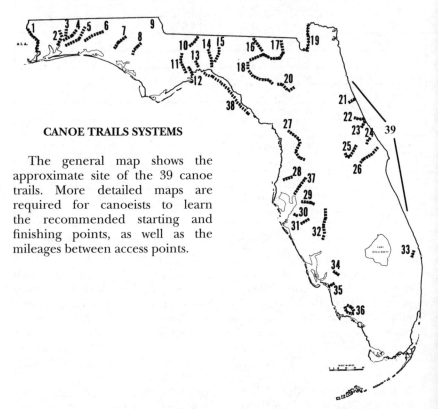

CANOE TRAILS SYSTEMS

The general map shows the approximate site of the 39 canoe trails. More detailed maps are required for canoeists to learn the recommended starting and finishing points, as well as the mileages between access points.

1. PERDIDO RIVER. Forming the border between Florida and Alabama, the Perdido River gently curves past woodlands of pine, cypress, and juniper. Several small ponds or sloughs, hidden along the banks, provide additional canoeing opportunities.

2. COLDWATER CREEK. This Panhandle river features crystal clear water and white sand bottoms along its 20-mile course. Dotted along the banks are sandbars perfect for camping or picnicking.

Like other west Florida streams, the current of this creek can be faster than many peninsular Florida rivers.

3. SWEETWATER/JUNIPER CREEKS. Sweetwater Creek is narrow and swift with winding curves, but after it joins Juniper Creek the curves become gentler and the creek widens. Spring runs trickle into this clear stream. The water level fluctuates rapidly after heavy rains.

4. BLACKWATER RIVER. The dark, tannin-stained waters of the

Blackwater contrast with the pure white sandbars found along its bends. Flowing 31 miles through the western highlands, this beautiful trail is lined with cedar, maple, and cypress.

5. YELLOW RIVER. The upper portion of the Yellow River is a fast flowing stream draining the western highlands and Florida's highest elevation. Hardwood forests and high sandy banks frame the river. Downstream the river deepens and slows as it passes through cypress and gum swamps. Part of the trail borders Eglin Air Force Base.

6. SHOAL RIVER. A nature lover's dream, the Shoal River threads its way through northwest Florida wilderness. This 27-mile, narrow, shallow course passes by sandbanks and broad sand bars. The surrounding forest is a mixture of maple, oak, gum, and cypress.

7. HOLMES CREEK. In contrast with other streams of west Florida, Holmes Creek slowly winds its way past high sandy banks and through lush swamplands. Many low-hanging branches and sharp twisting bends add a bit of challenge to canoeists.

8. ECONFINA CREEK. Experienced canoeists will find this virtually unspoiled and ever-changing stream a technical paddling challenge. It flows through scenic river swamps, hammocks, and pine flatwoods. The springs that feed this swift-flowing stream have cut deep canyons in the limestone.

9. CHIPOLA RIVER. Beginning in Marianna, this trail passes through 51 miles of river swamps and hardwood forests. Limestone bluffs and caves are visible from the river. Some rapids, including "Look and Tremble Falls," challenge even experienced canoeists.

10. OCHLOCKONEE RIVER (UPPER). Beginning near the Georgia line, the narrow portion of the Ochlockonee twists around cypress knees and blowdowns toward Lake Talquin. Low water requires some portaging.

11. OCHLOCKONEE RIVER (LOWER). More than 50 miles of this trail wind through the Apalachicola National Forest, past high pine bluffs and dense hardwoods. Near the Ochlockonee River State Park, the end of the trail, the river widens and motor boats are common. Releases from Jackson Bluff Dam vary the river level.

12. SOPCHOPPY RIVER. This dark-colored river twists and bends its way around cypress knees as it swiftly courses through the Apalachicola National Forest. At low water levels, the trip requires many pullovers and some wading.

13. WAKULLA RIVER. This beautiful spring-fed, cypress-lined river makes for an unhurried half-day trip over four- and six-mile courses below Wakulla Springs State Park. The slow current makes a round-trip easy. Wildlife, including manatees, is abundant along the river.

14. WACISSA RIVER. The sparkling waters of the narrow, swift Wacissa twist and turn through the Aucilla Wildlife Management Area. The entrance to the lower section of the trail is obscured by aquatic plants and over-hanging willow trees.

15. AUCILLA RIVER. This dark but clear river is recommended for experienced canoeists. Whitewater along the 25-mile navigable trail starting near Lamont can be a challenge, and they become more numerous and hazardous during low water.

16. WITHLACOOCHEE RIVER (NORTH). Flowing through Twin Rivers State Forest and past sandy beaches and limestone outcrops, the trail contains several shoal areas. The trail ends at Suwannee River State Park. Primitive camping on forest land is allowed without a permit.

17. SUWANNEE RIVER (UPPER). The Suwannee River flows through areas of pristine river swamp and along wide sandy banks. There are numerous access points offering a choice of one-day excursions. Even experienced canoeists are recommended to portage "Big Shoals" rapids, the only Class III rapids in Florida. The Stephen Foster State Folk Culture Center is accessible from the trail, and the Suwannee River State Park marks the trail's end.

18. SUWANNEE RIVER (LOWER). Continuing from Suwannee River State Park, the lower section of the Suwannee River also contains numerous shoals during low water. Portage may be necessary. Abundant wildlife and beautiful scenery make this a popular trail.

19. ST. MARY'S RIVER. The many snow-white sandbars along this river make camping easy and enjoyable. Forming the state border, the St. Mary's gently curves through the wilderness of north Florida and south Georgia. There are several access points along the 60-mile course.

20. SANTA FE RIVER. This trail begins just below River Rise State Preserve where the Santa Fe returns to the surface after a three-mile-long underground journey. The lazy current and gentle curves over 30 miles makes the Santa Fe a good beginner's canoe trail. There are some small shoals during low water, but they are almost always passable.

21. PELLICER CREEK. This four-mile trail makes an easy half-day canoe trip.

22. BULOW CREEK. The 13-mile Bulow Creek trail loops upstream from Bulow Plantation Ruins State Historic Site, then returns to the trailhead before continuing on to the Intracoastal Waterway where it ends. The creek flows through grassy coastal marshes characteristic of the Atlantic Coast. Weather is often a factor on the course.

23. TOMOKA RIVER. This 130-mile trail loops upstream from the trailhead where the narrow river threads its way among cypress trees. Moving downstream, the river widens as it flows through open coastal marsh and then into Tomoka State Park.

24. SPRUCE CREEK. This east-central Florida trail passes through several habitats including dense hardwood forests and coastal saltwater marsh. Two loops, a five-mile round trip upstream and a nine-mile round trip downstream, make up this trail. Both loops begin and end at Moody Bridge.

25. WEKIVA RIVER/ROCK SPRINGS RUNS. Rock Springs Run forms the border between Wekiva Springs State Park and Rocks Springs Run State Preserve. The run meets the Wekiva River at the park. The tannin-stained waters of the Wekiva River twist through pine and hardwood uplands and dense swamplands, and pass through the Lower Wekiva River State Preserve before flowing into the St. Johns River. The course offers both swift and placid waters, making for frequent changes of pace.

26. ECONLOCKHATCHEE RIVER. Generally untouched by development, the "Econ" winds past white sandy beaches and through oak-palm hammocks. The beginning is narrow, shallow, and cypress-lined. Downstream, the river broadens and deepens, and the curves become gentler.

27. WITHLACOOCHEE RIVER (SOUTH). Flowing out of the Green Swamp in west-central Florida, the Withlachoochee River trail twists and winds northward through lush cypress swamps, hardwood and pine forests, and scattered residential areas. Birds and other wildlife abound along the 83-mile trail with numerous access points. Paddlers may need to maneuver or portage around log or hyacinth jams in dry periods.

28. PITHLACHASCOTEE RIVER. This short trail is recommended for canoeists with some experience. The Pithlachascotee has tight curves in the narrow upper segment that demand technical paddling skills. It widens to long straight stretches on the lower section.

29. ALAFIA RIVER. Meanders under a spreading canopy of pine, cypress, and cedar trees. The river flows swiftly over a limestone bed that exposes shoals in low water.

30. LITTLE MANATEE RIVER. The seven-mile trail on this pristine river winds through a variety of habitats including sand pine scrub, willow marsh, and hardwood forests on its way to the take-out at Little Manatee State Recreation Area. It makes a good half-day trip.

31. UPPER MANATEE RIVER. Subtropical vegetation lines the banks of this gently winding trail. It is an easy half-day trip. Water levels and flow vary with releases from Lake Manatee Dam.

32. PEACE RIVER. As the name implies, this ideal canoe trail offers a peaceful meandering trip away from civilization. The river originates in the Green Swamp and is alternately bordered by sand bluffs, grassy areas, and dense forests. The opportunities for nature observation, especially birding, are abundant. The 67-mile trail runs from Ft. Meade to Arcadia.

33. LOXAHATCHEE RIVER. This beautiful nine-mile trail winds through a cypress swamp lush with ferns and orchids. Within Jonathan Dickinson State Park, the river twists through mangrove swamps. A variety of wildlife species make their homes along the banks. The Loxahatchree is Florida's first Natural Wild and Scenic River.

34. HICKEY CREEK. An easy half-day trip, Hickey Creek trail flows through subtropical hammocks. The trail ends at the locks on the Caloosahatchee River.

35. ESTERO RIVER. This trail offers an easy, one-day adventure from Koreshan State Historic Site among mangrove islands and coves. When the trail opens into Estero Bay, canoeists can select a variety of routes to explore the mangrove islands before returning upstream.

36. BLACKWATER RIVER/ ROYAL PALM HAMMOCK. This 13-mile loop trail through Collier-Seminole State Park is a good trail for beginning canoeists. The tidal creeks and mangrove wilderness areas are quiet and pristine.

37. HILLSBOROUGH RIVER. This 32-mile tannin-laden course starts in the wilderness and ends in the city. It's upper stage, from Crystal Springs to the Hillsborough River State Park with rapids, portage and numerous blind branches, is not for the inexperienced. But the remainder is an easy, scenic meander through transitioning landscape.

38. HISTORIC BIG BEND PADDLING TRAIL. Florida's first "outside" course, runs in the Gulf of Mexico from the St. Marks River lighthouse to the Suwannee River along the largely undeveloped Big Bend coast. Although navigable by canoe, modern sea kayaks as well as NOAA and Coast Guard charts are recommended.

39. FLORIDA CIRCUMNAVI-GATIONAL SALTWATER PAD-DLING TRAIL. This new trail is a 1,500-mile trek around the state. Beginning at Big Lagoon State Park near Pensacola on the Gulf of Mexico, it runs along the shore all the way to Fort Clinch State Park north of Amelia Island on the Atlantic Ocean. Sea Kayaks are recommended as is pre-planning since

segment skills range from beginner to experienced.

WATER MANAGEMENT DISTRICTS

Five water management districts covering the entire state are at the forefront of agencies assigned to preserve the state's natural resources.

Created in 1972, their mission is to preserve, conserve, and provide for public use of the state's waterways. They pursue that mission by regulation of waterways, by land acquisitions, by promoting public awareness of waterways, by assuring that the public's need for water is met, by setting standards to reduce flood damage, by regulating location and construction of wells and septic tanks, and by controlling

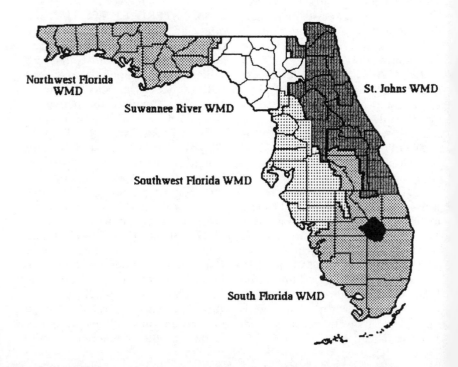

Northwest Florida WMD

Suwannee River WMD

St. Johns WMD

Southwest Florida WMD

South Florida WMD

withdrawal or diversion of water from rivers.

The districts obtain most of their revenue from property taxes and a percentage of the state's documentary stamp tax. Much of the money goes for purchase of frontage along the state's rivers. The frontage assures continued quality of the waterways, and provides scores of recreational parks for the public. For example, the Suwannee River Water Management District has purchased thousands of acres along the Suwannee so that today the public is the largest landowner along the famous river.

The map shows the counties served by each of the five water-management districts.

MOTORING

DRIVER'S LICENSING

A person is required to obtain a Florida driver's license if that person has children enrolled in the state's public schools, or is registered to vote, or has filed for homestead exemption, or accepts employment in the state, or has lived in Florida more than six consecutive months. Anyone moving to Florida with a valid driver's license from another state must get a Florida license within 30 days of becoming a Florida resident.

The following persons may drive in Florida without having a Florida license if they have a valid license from another state or country:

—Any nonresident who is at least 16 years old

—Persons employed by the U.S. government driving a government vehicle on official business

—A nonresident working for a firm on contract with the U.S. government

—A nonresident attending college in Florida

—Persons who drive only vehicles such as farm tractors or road machines

—A licensed driver who lives in another state and travels regularly into Florida

—Nonresident migrant farm workers, even if they have children in Florida public schools or are employed, providing they have a valid driver's license from their home state

—Members of armed forces stationed in Florida who are otherwise nonresidents.

Identification Requirements

Stringent new requirements have been instituted to obtain a Florida driver license. In addition to the traditional road, vision, and written tests when required, an applicant must provide extraordinary proof of identity and residence.

To obtain an original Florida driver license or to renew a Florida driver license, requiring physical presence, or to obtain an official Florida identification card, the following identification documents are required.

U.S. citizens must provide as their primary document an original or certified U.S. birth certificate or a valid U.S. Passport or Passport Card or a Consular Report of Birth Abroad or a Certificate of Naturalization of a Certificate of Citizenship.

When necessary, a marriage certificate, court orders, or divorce decrees must be provided to correct the name of the applicant on the primary identification to the name the applicant would like on the driver license or identification card.

Also required: Proof of a Social Security number as displayed on a Social Security card, W-2 form, paycheck, or 1099 form. Applicants without a Social Security number must provide a letter from the Social Security Administration attesting that the applicant was never issued one.

In addition, an applicant must provide at least one other form of identification, which may include an on-record Florida license or identification card; a driver license or identification card issued by other U.S. states, territories, or the District of Columbia; a U.S. Military or Military Dependent identification card; a valid Military Record; a draft card; a Florida Vehicle Registration certificate or registration from another state; a transcript of the applicant's birth record filed with appropriate authorities; a registrar-signed school record stating date of birth; a baptismal certificate showing date of birth and place of baptism; a family Bible record or birth announcement in a "baby book"; an insurance policy on the applicant's life that displays date of birth and which has been in force for at least two years; a receipt copy of the applicant's last driver license issuance; an Immigration form I-571; a marriage certificate; a court order including legal name; a government-issued out-of-country passport, driver license, or identification card; and, for minors, a signed parental consent form.

However, an applicant is not through yet.

Also required are an additional two proofs of residence that may include a deed mortgage, monthly mortgage statements, payment booklet, or residential rental or lease agreement; a Florida Voter Registration card; a Florida vehicle registration or title; utility bills no more than two months old; a utility hook-up or work order dated within 60 days of application; mail from a financial institution or from a government agency at any level not more than two months old; an automobile payment booklet; a draft card; a medical or health card with address listed; a current homeowners or auto insurance policy; an educational institution transcript for the current school year; a current professional license issued by a government agency in the United States; a W-2 or 1099 form; a certificate of eligibility of an exchange visitor J-1 status; a letter from a homeless shelter, transitional service provider, or half-way house verifying an applicant's address; or a transients Sexual Offender/Predator/Career Offender FDLE registration form completed by the local sheriff's department.

An applicant living on a boat or houseboat may provide a Florida boat registration or title as one proof of residency. An applicant who is a minor requires a statement from a parent, step-parent, or legal guardian living at the same address as one proof of residency. Internet printouts or faxes of proof of residency are acceptable.

Immigrants applying for a Florida driver license must provide proof of a Social Security number and the similar two proofs of residency required of citizens.

In addition, an immigrant applicant must provide one original or certified copy of either a Green Card; an I-551 stamp in passport; an I-94; an immigration judge's order with the applicants A- number granting asylum; an I-797 with the applicant's A- number stating the applicant has been granted asylum; or another form from the Bureau of Customs and Immigration Services with the applicants A- number stating the applicant's application for refugee status has been approved.

Non-immigrants must provide proof of a Social Security number and two proofs of residency similar to those required of citizens and immigrants.

A non-immigrant also must provide one original or certified copy of any employment authorization card issued by the U.S. Department of Homeland Security or proof of non-immigrant classification provided by Homeland Security, i.e., a valid form I-94 with required supporting attachment or attachments. If as an applicant a person is in doubt as to required documents, they should bring them all. An I-94 must be accompanied by a passport. Certain classifications of non-immigrants require additional documentation. Those classified F-1 or M-1 must also provide an I-20 form. Those designated J-1 or J-2 must provide a DS2019. Those with refugee, asylee, or parolee classifications must provide additional documentation, which may include an I-571 travel document/refugee travel permit, an I-512 parolee letter accepted, or a IJO, asylum or cancellation of removal, an immigration judge's order granting asylum or cancellation of removal.

These documents will only be accepted with a supporting document including but not limited to a passport, a Florida driver license or identification card, a driver license from another state, an employment authorization card, an employer's identification, identification from the applicant's home country, identification from a school or college, or a Social Security card. All required and supporting documents must be original or certified and must be valid for more than 30 days from the date of issuances

Non-U.S. citizens applying for an original driver license will be issued a 30-day, no photo, paper temporary permit and a receipt. ID card applicants receive only a receipt.

All submitted records are transmitted to Tallahassee, where the information will be examined and run against Florida Department of Law Enforcement, FBI ,and Federal Bureau of Customs and Immigration Service's databases. Upon verification, a driver license or identification card will be issued within 30 days from Tallahassee and mailed to the address on record. They will be issued for the period of time specified by the BCIS record up to a maximum of one year. If there is a problem, a denial of issuance letter will be mailed to the applicant.

Canadian citizens applying for a Florida driver license or State of Florida ID card must provide proof of a Social Security number and two proofs of residency the same as all others. Canadian applicants also must provide one original or certified copy of either a valid Canadian passport, original or certified birth certificate, a Canadian Naturalization Certificate, or a Canadian Certificate of Citizenship.

Restricted Driver's License

A person learning to drive must obtain a restricted operator's license, or learner's license, even when learning in the company of an adult licensed driver. Applicants for a restricted license must be at least 15 years old; must pass a vision, road signs, and road rules test; must have the signature of one parent on a consent form if under age 18; must show proof of a traffic law and substance abuse education course or a license from another jurisdiction; and must produce two official forms of identification. Names on documents must match exactly.

A restricted license permits driving only during daytime hours for three months following issue dates at which time driving hours are expanded, 6 a.m. to 10 p.m. Accompanying a restricted license driver must be a licensed driver at least 21 years of age, seated in the passenger side of the front seat. A driver with a learner's license is ineligible for a motorcycle endorsement.

Sixteen-year-olds may have a full license but may not drive between 11 p.m. and 6 a.m. without a licensed 21-year-old driver accompanying or unless driving to or from work. Seventeen-year-old drivers are similarly restricted from 1 a.m. to 5 a.m.

In addition, teenagers applying for the license must have held a learner's license for 12 months, not incurred any traffic convictions, and logged at least 50 hours of driving including at least 10 hours at night.

Under 18-year-olds can lose their driving privileges for fewer violation points than adult drivers and for a growing list of school-related infractions including unexcused absences.

All drivers under the age of 21 can have licenses suspended immediately for six months for any infraction involving alcohol at a .02 level.

The license does not permit the learner to operate a motorcycle with more than 150 cubic centimeter displacement until the sixteenth birthday. .

Restrictions Entered on Licenses

Various restrictions may be printed on a person's driver's license. They include:

—Motorcycle only, meaning the person has passed the tests only for motorcycle licensing

—Corrective lenses, meaning the person cannot pass the vision test without glasses or contact lenses

—Outside mirror (left side), when a person cannot hear an ordinary horn or is blind in one eye

—Steering wheel knob or power steering, when a person does not have full use of both hands or has only one hand

—Mechanical turn indicator, when a person has lost the use of either arm

—Daylight only, when a person has difficulty seeing at night and an eye doctor recommends no night driving

—Automatic transmission, when a person, because of physical condition, requires an automatic transmission to pass the driving test

—Business purposes, when the person is licensed to drive only to and from work, to a job, or for educational, church, or medical purposes

—Employment purposes, when a person is licensed to drive only to and from work or for job training

Test Requirements and Fees

Applicants for an original Florida license must take a test that covers vision, road signs, and road rules. The applicant must provide the vehicle, which will be inspected to make sure it is safe and in good working order.

New residents holding a valid license from other states, U.S. possessions, Canada, and France are required to pass the vision test only for a Florida license. Persons holding a license from Germany or Taiwan must take the vision, hearing, and written exams.

Following the test the driver examiner may or may not approve the application. If the applicant is not approved, the test may be taken again at another time.

Appointments for taking the driver's test are urged, but not required, at all 157 driver's license offices. Days and hours of each office vary.

Fees

Initial License Fee for first Florida license	$20.00
Learner's License	$20.00
License Renewal	$15.00
Commercial License	$50.00
Duplicate License (if original lost or stolen)	$10.00
Commercial Endorsements	$5.00
Motorcycle Endorsement	$5.00
License address change	$10.00
Replacement License (stolen, with police report)	free
Replacement License (must turn in incorrect license)	$10.00
Delinquent Fee (for renewals if license expired less than 12 months before renewal application)	$1.00
Re-test, written	$5.00
Re-test, skills	$10.00
Identification Card*	$3.00
Identification card renewal	$10.00
Identification card duplicate	$10.00
Identification card address change	$10.00
Duplicate ID Card (if original lost or stolen)	$10.00
Motorcycle Endorsement (for licenses that required applicant pass written cycle test and on-cycle test)	$5.00
Administrative Fee, Alcohol and Drug-Related Offenses	$115.00
Service Fee after license has been revoked	$60.00
Service Fee after license has been suspended	$35.00
Service Fee after license has been disqualified	$60.00
Service Fee after financial responsibility suspension	$15.00-$500.00

Some driver's license services delivered at tax collector offices carry an additional $5.25 fee.

A person who does not have a driver's license but needs an identification card may obtain one at a driver's license office. Requirements are the applicant is 12 years of age or older, present a Social Security number, and have two items of identification. The card includes a color photo, name, sex, race, address, date of birth, and physical description. It is valid for four years.

License Renewal

A driver's license is valid for four or six years. Applicants who have a conviction-free record for the previous three years can obtain a six-year license, and must pass a required examination. A four-year renewal is available by mail.

A notice warning that a license will soon expire is mailed to each driver 30 days before the birthday expiration date. Licenses must be renewed on or before a person's birthday.

Persons Ineligible for Licenses

A Florida license is not issued to a person whose license is under suspension or revocation in any state, who is addicted to drugs or alcohol, who cannot drive because of mental or physical problems, or who is under the legal age for licensing.

A license can be suspended in Florida if the driver:

—Makes a fraudulent driver license application

—Is unable to drive safely

—Allows license to be used for illegal purposes

—Has license ordered suspended by court

—Refuses to take an alcohol or drug test if ordered to

—Misuses a restricted license

—Earns a certain number of traffic offenses points

—Fails to pay fine after breaking traffic law

A license can be revoked for up to six months if a driver is found guilty or motor vehicle records show:

—Driving under influence of alcohol or drugs

—A felony in which a motor vehicle is used

—Not stopping to help when the vehicle is in an accident and causes injury

—Lying about ownership or operation of vehicle

—Three cases of reckless driving in one year

—An immoral act in which a motor vehicle is used

—Three major offenses or 15 point-receiving offenses within five years

—A felony for drug possession

—Vision worse than standard minimum

A driver's license will be revoked for a minimum three years when the motorist, because of reckless driving, kills someone, or when the motorist kills someone because of driving under the influence of alcohol or drugs or other controlled substances. And a lifetime revocation can occur if a motorist is convicted in a manslaughter case involving a vehicle and also accumulates four convictions of driving under the influence.

A person found guilty of driving after a license has been suspended or revoked can be jailed.

Point System

The state assesses points against drivers for various violations. Points can lead to suspension of a license.

Violation	Points
Leaving scene of accident	6
Unlawful speed resulting in an accident	6
Reckless driving	4
Moving violation resulting in an accident	4
Passing a stopped school bus	4
Unlawful speed, 16 mph or more over posted limit	4
Unlawful speed, 15 mph or less over posted limit	3
Ignoring traffic control signals	4
Minor driving during restricted hours	3
Curfew violations	3
Open container	3
All other moving violations	3
Littering	3
Violation of child-restraint laws	3

A license will be suspended 30 days if the driver accumulates 12 points in a 12-month period. Accumulating 18 points within 18 months draws a three-month suspension. A total of 24 points within 36 months is punished by a one-year suspension.

Driving Under the Influence

The unlawful blood alcohol content level in Florida is .08 or higher. Penalties include:

•**First conviction**—a minimum 180 days license revocation, minimum $250 fine, possible imprisonment up to six months plus a year's probation and 50 hours of community service, and attendance in substance abuse course. If offense results in serious injury, a three-year suspension.

• **Second conviction**—a minimum five years license revocation (if offense within five years of first conviction), minimum $500 fine, minimum 10 days in jail (if offense within three years of first conviction).

• **Third conviction**—a minimum 10 years license revocation (if offense within 10 years of first conviction), minimum $1,000 fine, minimum 30 days in jail (if offense within five years of first conviction).

• **Fourth Conviction**—results in permanent revocation of license with no provision for hardship appeal.

• A single conviction for DUI manslaughter results in permanent revocation of license; with a prior DUI conviction, no provision for hardship appeal.

It is illegal for motorists to drink alcoholic beverages while they drive, and possession of an open alcohol container in a moving vehicle is punishable by a fine and points.

Fines and imprisonment are higher if blood alcohol level is .20 or higher or if a minor is in the vehicle.

Implied Consent Law

By driving in Florida, a motorist stopped for possible driving under the influence has agreed to take, if asked, a blood test, urine test, or breath test. To refuse means to risk a driver's license being suspended for one year.

In driving under the influence cases involving death or injury, a driver can be required to take a blood test. If a driver is unconscious or in no condition to refuse the blood test, samples of the motorist's blood may be withdrawn.

VEHICLE INSURANCE

Florida's Financial Responsibility law requires owners and operators of motor vehicles to be financially responsible for damages or injuries they may cause to others in an accident. Coverage required is

$10,000 Bodily Injury Liability, $20,000 Bodily Injury Liability to two or more persons, and $10,000 Property Damage Liability. To have an accident without this coverage can result in suspension of driver's license and tags for up to three years.

VEHICLE INSPECTIONS

Florida does not require vehicle inspections.

SEAT BELTS

Driver and front seat passengers are required by Florida law to wear seat belts. Violation is punishable by a $30 fine. Children, including teenagers, riding in the back seat are required to have the appropriate restraints, seat belts or child restraint seat. An unrestrained child violation is $60. The driver is responsible. The requirements are actively enforced.

LITTERING

People who throw trash from their vehicles onto public streets or highways are subject to a fine up to $500 or a jail term up to 60 days. Because of the number of wildfires caused by tossed cigarette butts during Florida's prolonged drought, the littering law is strictly enforced.

BICYCLES, MOPEDS, SCOOTERS

Bicycle riders have rights and responsibilities as motor vehicle operators and do receive tickets for traffic violations. Children's safety helmets are required. Moped riders must hold a valid driver's license but no motorcycle endorsement is required. Mopeds must be registered at the county tax collector's office annually. Depending on the model, a scooter may be a moped or a motorcycle. If a motorcycle, a license endorsement is required.

NO HEADPHONES

Florida law bans the wearing of earphones including ear buds while operating a vehicle including bicycles.

LICENSE TAG RATES

Classification	Pounds	Rates
Automobile or lightweight truck, private use	under 2,500	$46.15
Automobile or lightweight truck, private use	2,500-3,499	$57.15
Automobile or lightweight truck, private use	3,500 up	$70.65
Transferring tag		$4.60
New metal tag		$10.00
Utility trailer	under 500	$16.75
Fifth wheel travel trailer		$21.60
Travel trailers over 35 feet		$36.60
Camp trailer (folding walls)		$38.65

Chassis Mount camper	through 4,499	$52.15
Chassis Mount camper	4,500 up	$72.40
Motor home or motor coach, self-propelled	through 4,499	$52.15
Motor home, or motor coach, self-propelled	4,500 up	$72.40
Motorcycles		$41.50
Moped		$34.40
Antiques (passenger cars or trucks)		$36.90
Disabled access vehicles		$41.15
Classification	**Pounds**	**Rates**
Mobile homes	up to 35 ft	$30.35
Mobile homes	36 to 40 ft	$35.35
Mobile homes	41 to 45 ft	$40.35
Mobile homes	46 to 50 ft	$45.35
Mobile homes	51 to 55 ft	$50.35
Mobile homes	56 to 60 ft	$55.35
Mobile homes	61 to 65 ft	$60.35
Mobile homes	over 65 ft	$90.35

Additional fees totaling more than $30 are added to the rates.

Florida charges a $225 fee for "new wheels," vehicles that do not replace a previously registered vehicle. The charge also applies to out-of-state vehicles being registered in the state for the first time. The state also charges $28 for a metal plate.

A mobile home on property of the owner and affixed to the land does not require a license tag. It is, however, subject to ad valorum property tax.

Specialty Tags

In 1987, the state began selling a special license tag that honored the crew of the ill-fated *Challenger* spacecraft. Motorists wishing to buy the tag in lieu of a regular vehicle tag were asked to pay an additional fee, which was used to build a memorial for the astronauts killed in the tragedy.

Sales were so successful that every year thereafter the state has offered more specialty license tags, so that by 1994 there were approximately 55 available. In 2009, there were 114 such tags authorized.

Not all were issued after 1987; some, such as those for veterans and horseless carriages, have been available for decades. Most of these older specialty tags carry no added fee. But with the *Challenger/Columbia* tag and the numerous other recent specialty tags, revenue from the added fee is passed on to the group or institution honored on the tag.

Below is a list of major specialty tags now being offered. Figures are as of 2009. The fee listed is, of course, in addition to the cost of a regular tag, per year for five years. University tags also carry a $2.00 processing fee.

Type	Special Fee	Issued 2009
Univ. of Florida	$25	120,858
Sea Turtles	$17.50	76,804
Florida State Univ.	$25	76,216
Dolphins	$20	75,912
Panther	$25	73,060
Manatee	$20	63,263
Marine Corps	$15	45,253
Protect Reefs	$25	42,047
Choose Life	$20	39,518
Support Education	$15	32,890
Save Our Seas	$25	33,665
Challenger/Columbia	$25	31,401
Golf	$25	29,295
Univ. of Miami	$25	28,990
Florida Arts	$20	26,852
Salute Firefighters	$20	26,103
U.S. Army	$15	25,655
Wildlife	$15	25,570
Florida Salutes Veterans	$15	24,367
Breast Cancer	$25	24,150
Fish Florida	$22	24,001
Florida A&M Univ.	$25	21,594
U.S. Air Force	$15	21,093
Indian River Lagoon	$15	20,948
Animal Friend	$25	20,281
U.S. Navy	$15	20,250
Protect Florida Whales	$25	19,255
Motorcycle (specialty)	$20	18,530
Invest in Children	$20	18,184
Wildflower	$15	17,952
Agriculture	$20	17,932
Police Athletic League	$20	17,599
Aquaculture	$25	17,027

Univ. of South Florida	$25	16,636
Discover Florida Oceans	$25	16,183
United We Stand	$25	15,811
Univ. of Central Florida	$25	15,545
Police Benevolent Association	$20	15,508
Large Mouth Bass	$25	15,437
Hospice	$25	14,631
Everglades	$20	14,011
Imagine	$25	13,660
Sportsman Land Trust	$25	12,930
Share the Road (Bicycling)	$15	12,460
Heart Disease	$25	11,839
Tampa Bay Estuary	$15	9,529
Stop Child Abuse	$25	9,248
U.S. Coast Guard	$15	8,337
U.S. Olympics	$15	8,251
Drug Free Kids	$25	8,183
Family First	$25	8,126
Live the Dream	$25	7,044
Bethune-Cookman	$25	6,672
Support Soccer	$25	6,131
Sheriffs Youth Ranches	$20	6,045
U.S. Paratroopers	$20	5,935
In God We Trust	$25	5,270
U.S. Special Olympics	$15	5,058
NASCAR	$25	3,526
Boy Scouts	$20	3,434
Support Home Ownership	$25	3,108
Protect Florida Springs	$25	3,107
Florida International Univ.	$25	3,001
Trees Are Cool	$25	2,688
Family Values	$25	2,671
Florida Atlantic Univ.	$25	2,643
Nova Southeastern University	$25	2,578
Support Our Troops	$25	2,443
Parents Make a Difference	$25	2,327

A State of Vision	$25	2,100
Donate Organs	$25	2,053
Kids Deserve Justice	$25	1,927
Univ. of North Florida	$25	1,858
Embry-Riddle Aero University	$25	1,840
Play Tennis	$25	1,797
Rollins College	$25	1,775
Visit Our Lights	$25	1,738
Stetson University	$25	1,703
Flagler College	$25	1,652
Florida Gulf Coast Univ.	$25	1,645
Florida Institute of Technology	$25	1,600
University of Tampa	$25	1,564
Agriculture Education	$25	1,436
Horse Country	$25	1,381
Univ. of West Florida	$25	1,379
Barry University	$25	1,327
Jacksonville University	$25	1,281
Florida Memorial College	$25	1,271
American Red Cross	$25	1,181
Edward Waters College	$25	1,066
St. Leo University	$25	804
New College	$25	800
Florida Southern College	$25	714
Ringling School of Art	$25	535
Eckerd College	$25	514
Florida College	$25	372
Corrections Foundation	$25	342
Palm Beach Atlantic University	$25	321
St. Thomas University	$25	281
Lynn College	$25	264
Southeastern University	$25	206
Support Autism Programs	$25	177
Warner Southern	$25	176
Florida Hospital College	$25	166
Clearwater Christian College	$25	75

Florida also issues specialty tags for fans of the state's professional sports teams with revenues going not to the teams but to the state's Professional Sports Development Trust and to the Florida Sports Foundation.

Type	Special Fee	Issued 2009
Tampa Bay Buccaneers	$25	35,463
Miami Dolphins	$25	21,929
Miami Heat	$25	20,874
Jacksonville Jaguars	$25	11,352
Tampa Bay Lightning	$25	4,869
Orlando Magic	$25	4,032
Tampa Bay Rays	$25	3,155
Florida Marlins	$25	2,891
Florida Panthers	$25	2,710

Florida also issues specialty tags for vehicles or drivers meeting specific criteria. Special vehicle tags include those for Horseless Carriages and other antique cars. Eligible drivers may purchase tags identifying them as Congressional Medal of Honor recipients, National Guardsmen, members of U.S. Reserve armed forces, ex-prisoners of war, paralyzed veterans, disabled veterans, disabled wheelchair veterans, the wheelchair-bound, Seminole or Miccosukee Indians, amateur radio operators, Purple Heart recipients and their widows, or Pearl Harbor survivors. These tags involve only a nominal fee. More than 80,000 Florida vehicles carry such specialty tags.

Additional fees are collected annually. Florida license plates, including specialty tags, have a five-year lifetime and are updated by decals. The state gives a specialty tag five years to attract 10,000 vehicles. If it does not, it is dropped from the list. An exception is made for colleges and universities.

TRAFFIC STATISTICS

Year	Licensed Drivers	Registered Vehicles	Mileage (Millions)	Death Accidents	Death (Thousands)	Mileage Death Rate*
1960	2,710,665	2,717,121	21,171	124,630	1,245	5.9
1965	3,358,747	3,460,096	27,737	169,408	1,665	6
1970	4,143,442	4,730,034	39,992	238,740	2,170	5.4
1975	6,320,822	6,995,683	61,715	283,086	2,040	3.3
1980	7,809,423	7,797,375	75,281	201,385	2,879	3.8
1985	9,630,975	10,827,693	87,000	216,596	2,870	3.3

1990	11,612,402	12,465,790	109,997	216,245	2,951	2.7
1991	12,170,821	11,184,146**	113,484	195,312	2,523	2.2
1992	11,440,126**	11,205,320	NA	169,233	2,271	NA
1993	11,767,409	11,159,938	119,768	199,039	2,719	2.3
1994	11,992,578	11,393,982	120,929	206,183	2,722	2.3
1995	12,019,156	12,062,731	127,800	228,589	2,847	2.2
1996	12,343,598	12,003,929	129,637	241,377	2,847	2.2
1997	12,691,835	12,170,375	133,276	240,639	2,811	2.1
1998	13,012,132	11,277,808	136,680	245,440	2,889	2.1
1999	13,398,895	11,611,993	139,329	243,409	2,920	2.1
2000	14,041,846	11,948,485	149,857	246,541	2,316	2
2001	14,346,373	13,448,202	171,029	256,169	3,013	1.76
2002	14,604,720	12,989,278	178,680	250,470	3,143	1.76
2003	14,847,416	14,080,866	185,642	243,294	3,179	1.71
2004	15,007,005	14,512,264	196,722	252,902	3,257	1.66
2005	15,272,680	15,062,993	200,974	268,605	3,535	1.76
2006	15,491,878	15,612,161	203,783	256,206	3,365	1.65
2007	15,579,603	14,858,332	205,421	256,206	3,221	1.57
2008	15,556,658	15,966,287	196,494	243,342	2,983	1.5
2009	15,533,387	14,983,437	196,402	235,778	2,563	1.3

*Per million miles
**Decrease represents change in accounting procedures
NA: Not available

AMTRAK STATIONS

Passenger train service is available in Florida through the following Amtrak stations:

Chipley
Crestview
Deerfield Beach
DeLand
Delray Beach
Fort Lauderdale
Hollywood
Jacksonville

Kissimmee
Lake City
Lakeland
Madison
Miami
Okeechobee
Orlando
Palatka

Pensacola
Sanford
Sebring
Tallahassee
Tampa
West Palm Beach
Winter Haven
Winter Park

INTERSTATE HIGHWAY SYSTEM

Four main interstate routes traverse Florida. The longest is Interstate 75, extending from the Georgia line south through Lake City and Ocala, into the Tampa Bay area, and southward adjacent to Bradenton, Sarasota, Venice, Fort Myers, and Naples. From Naples, an eastward route, designated I-75 but known as Alligator Alley, crosses the lower peninsula to connect with the east coast in Broward County. Various spurs such as I-275 lead off I-75, acting as a beltway into the nearby cities of Tampa and St. Petersburg and across the Sunshine Skyway to Bradenton and Sarasota.

Interstate 10 is a 362-mile highway between Jacksonville on the east coast and the Alabama state line near Pensacola. The route is a nearly straight line across northern Florida.

Running the depth of the state along the east coast is Interstate 95, a heavily traveled corridor taking the traveler from Jacksonville all the way to Miami, a drive of 347 miles. Numerous spurs exit traffic to the dozens of metropolitan areas fronting on the Atlantic Ocean.

The state's fourth major artery is Interstate 4, a 132-mile segment cutting across the mid-peninsula and connecting the Tampa Bay area with the east coast area of Daytona Beach, after passing through Orlando.

FLORIDA TURNPIKE

Started in 1953, the Florida Turnpike, officially the Ronald Reagan Parkway, is a 309.58-mile trip from its entrance off I-75 north of Wildwood, and south of Ocala, to Miami and on through its 47-mile extention to Homestead, south of Miami.

The turnpike handles the bulk of traffic leading from the Central Florida area of Ocala to the Gold Coast farther south.

The turnpike consists of 65 interchanges with toll booths collecting fares, charged according to the number of axles on a vehicle.

Class 2 tolls indicating two axles, refers to passenger cars and light trucks. Vehicles with more axles, such as heavy trucks, pay higher fares.

Among Florida's other toll roads are Alligator Alley, the I-75 corridor between Naples and Fort Lauderdale, the Sawgrass Expressway in Broward County, the Seminole Expressway in Seminole County, the Veterans and Crosstown Expressways in Hillsborough County, the Suncoast Parkway on the West Coast, the Beach Line Expressway, the Western Beltway and the Osceola Parkway in the Orlando area, the Polk Parkway around Lakeland in Polk County, the Bayway in Pinellas County, and the Sunshine Skyway Bridge across the mouth of Tampa Bay.

Emergency Call Boxes

Motorists traveling Florida's interstates have available to them emergency call boxes placed every mile along the roadways. They communicate with the nearest Florida Highway Patrol station.

A motorist needing help can stop at a box, open the door, and press one of the three buttons inside. One signals the need for a tow truck, a second for police, and a third for medical help. The signal is transmitted by microwave to the patrol station. Help then is dispatched to the numbered box.

The boxes are installed along Interstates 4, 10, and 75, on remote stretches of the Bee Line Expressway in east-central Florida, and along Florida's Turnpike.

In many areas, well posted, the highway patrol can also be contacted in an emergency via cellular phone by dialing *FHP.

Road Rangers

"Road Rangers" is a free Department of Transportation program that comes to the aid of stranded motorists along the state's busiest urban highways. The clearly marked roving vehicles carry necessary equipment to get a stalled motorist moving again or to insure that help is on the way. In 2009, the program assisted more than 296,000 drivers.

In addition to roving, Road Rangers are dispatched by the Florida Highway Patrol (call *FHP). The State Farm Safety Patrol performs the same duties along the Florida Turnpike and the Sawgrass Expressway.

Electronic Collection

Modern electronic collection systems are in the process of being installed on Florida Toll Roads.

AIRPORTS

Commercial Airports
2009

Enplanements	
Orlando International	16,658,718
Miami International	16,371,016
Fort Lauderdale/Hollywood International	10,234,872
Tampa International	8,263,294
Southwest Florida International (Ft. Myers)	3,668,279
Palm Beach International	3,004,076
Jacksonville International	2,777,041
Orlando/Sanford International	815,137
Pensacola Regional	694,786
Sarasota/Bradenton International	675,969
St. Petersburg/Clearwater International	381,029
Okaloosa Regional	374,220
Tallahassee Regional	360,441
Key West International	234,322
Daytona Beach International	200,417
Panama City-Bay County International	150,401*
Gainesville Regional	130,166
Melbourne International	110,510
Charlotte County	52,638
Total	65,157,332

The Panama City-Bay County International Airport closed in 2010. In its place stands the Florida Northwestern Beaches International Airport, the first major airport to be built in the U.S. in a decade.

OTHER PUBLIC AIRPORTS

Airport	Associated City	Distance and Direction from City
Airglades	Clewiston	6 W
Albert Whitted Municipal	St. Petersburg	1 E
Ames Field	Trenton	3 W

Apalachicola Municipal	Apalachicola	2 W
Arcadia Municipal	Arcadia	2 SE
Arthur Dunn Airport	Titusville	2 NW
Avon Park Municipal	Avon Park	1 SW
Bartow Municipal	Bartow	4 NE
Belle Glade	Belle Glade	1 NE
Bob Lee Airport	DeLand	5 N
Bob Sikes Airport	Crestview	3 NE
Bob White Airport	Zellwood	1 W
Boca Raton	Boca Raton	2 NW
Buchan Airport	Englewood	2 N
Calhoun County	Blountstown	2 E
Carrabelle-Thompson	Carrabelle	2 W
Cecil Field	Jacksonville	16 SW
Chalet Suzanne	Lake Wales	5 NW
Charlotte County	Punta Gorda	3 SE
Clearwater Airpark	Clearwater	2 NE
Coastal Airport	Pensacola	12 NW
Costin Airport	Port St. Joe	2 S
Craig Field	Jacksonville	9 E
Cross City	Cross City	1 E
Crystal River	Crystal River	3 SE
DeFuniak Springs Municipal	DeFuniak Springs	2 W
DeLand Municipal	DeLand	3 NE
Destin-Fort Walton Beach	Destin	1 E
Downtown Fort Lauderdale Heliport	Fort Lauderdale	0
Dunnellon-Marion County	Dunnellon	5 E
Everglades	Everglades	1 SW
Ferguson Airport	Pensacola	8 SW
Fernandina Beach Municipal	Fernandina Beach	4 S
Flagler County	Bunnel	3 E
Florida Keys Marathon Airport	Marathon	E

Flying Ten Airport	Gainesville	10 W
Fort Lauderdale Executive	Fort Lauderdale	6 N
Fort Walton Beach Airport	Fort Walton Beach/Navarre	2 E
Gainesville Regional	Gainesville	4 NE
George T. Lewis	Cedar Key	1 W
Herlong Municipal	Jacksonville	9 SW
Hernando County Airpark	Brooksville	7 SW
Hilliard Airpark	Hilliard	1 E
Homestead General Aviation	Homestead	5 NW
Homestead Regional	Homestead	1E
Immokalee Regional	Immokalee	1 NE
Indiantown	Indiantown	3 NE
Inverness	Inverness	2 SE
Jack Brown's SPB*	Winter Haven	3 NW
Kay Larkin Airport	Palatka	3 W
Kendell-Tamiami	Miami	15 SW
Keystone Airpark	Keystone Heights	5 N
Kissimmee Municipal	Kissimmee	2 W
La Belle Municipal	La Belle	1 S
Lake City Municipal	Lake City	3 E
Lakeland-Linder Regional	Lakeland	5 SW
Lake Wales Municipal	Lake Wales	2 W
Leesburg Regional	Leesburg	4 E
Marco Island Executive	Marco Island	10 NE
Marianna Municipal	Marianna	5 NE
Massey Ranch Airpark	New Smyrna Beach	3 S
Melbourne International	Melbourne	2 NW
Merritt Island	Cocoa	25 E
Miami Heliport	Miami	0
Mid-Florida	Eustis	3 E
New Hibiscus Airpark	Vero Beach	9 W

New Smyrna Beach Municipal	New Smyrna Beach	3 NW
North Palm Beach	Palm Beach Gardens	1 NW
North Perry	Hollywood	6 W
Ocala International	Ocala	2 W
Okeechobee County	Okeechobee	3 NW
Opa-Locka Airport	Miami	1 N
Opa-Locka West	Miami	14 NW
Orlando Country Airport	Plymouth-Apopka	4 NE
Orlando Executive Airport	Orlando	3 E
Ormond Beach Municipal	Ormond Beach	3 NW
Page Field	Fort Myers	4 S
Palm Beach County Glades	Pahokee	3 W
Palm Beach County Park	West Palm Beach	5 SW
Panama City-Bay County	Panama City	4 NW
Perry-Foley	Perry	3 S
Peter O. Knight	Tampa	2 S
Peter Prince Field	Milton	3 E
Pierson Municipal	Pierson	1 N
Pilot Country Airport	Brooksville	15 S
Plant City Airport	Plant City	5 W
Pompano Beach Airpark	Pompano Beach	1 NE
Quincy Municipal	Quincy	2 NE
River Ranch	Lake Wales	22 E
Rudy's Airport	High Springs	8 SW
St. Augustine Airport	St. Augustine	5 N
St. George Island	Apalachicola	8 SE
St. Lucie County International	Fort Pierce	3 NW
Sebastian Municipal	Sebastian	1 W
Sebring Regional	Sebring	7 SE
Shell Creek Airpark	Punta Gorda	8 NE
South Lakeland Airport	Mulberry	4 W

Southwest Florida Regional	Fort Myers	8 SE
Space Coast Regional	Titusville	6 S
Suwannee County	Live Oak	2 W
Tallahassee Commercial	Tallahassee	7 NW
Tampa North Aeropark	Lutz	21 N
Tri-County	Bonifay	7 NE
Umatilla Municipal	Umatilla	1 E
Valkaria Field	Valkaria	1 W
Vandenberg	Tampa	7 E
Venice Municipal	Venice	1 N
Vero Beach Municipal	Vero Beach	1 NW
Wakulla County	Panacea	3 S
Watson Island Heliport and SPB* **	Miami	1 E
Wauchula Municipal	Wauchula	5 SW
Williston Municipal	Williston	2 SW
Winter Haven Municipal	Winter Haven	3 NW
Witham Field	Stuart	1 SE
Zephyrhills Municipal	Zephyrhills	1 SE

*SPB—sea plane base
**also dirigible landing base

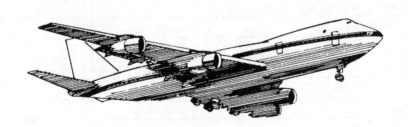

ORGAN DONATIONS

Florida allows motorists to indicate on their driver's licenses or identification cards that they wish to donate organs or tissues after their death.

TOURISM

Despite a poor economy and the perceptions spawned by the Gulf Oil Spill disaster, which did dampen enthusiasm for Florida's renowned beaches, the state's all important tourist industry stayed steady, drawing more than 80 million visitors annually every year since 2005.

Tourism generates more than $65 billion a year and directly accounts for more than a million jobs. It also provides more than $3.5 billion directly to the state's coffers via the state sales tax.

The economy was seen as the main cause for the decrease in domestic travel to Florida in 2008, but it was more than made up for by foreign tourists, not affected by the U.S. slowdown. More than 5 million tourists arrived from outside the U.S., the most in a single year since 2001.

"Snowbird" tourism, the annual migration of Canadians to what is often called that nation's southernmost province, increased by 14 percent. Nearly 3 million Canadians came to Florida in 2008, an all-time high.

The number of both Canadian and foreign tourists each jumped by more than another 10 percent in both 2009 and 2010. The number of tourists from Brazil jumped 29 percent in 2009, making Brazilians third among international visitors with more than a quarter million visiting just in early 2010. Only Canadian and British tourists outnumbered them.

The 2010 season was up from the year before as the industry adjusted to economic realities and made visiting the state more affordable. A majority of visitors to the state, 51 percent, arrived by air.

TOP TEN PLACES OF ORIGIN (DOMESTIC) 2009	TOP TEN PLACES OF ORIGIN (INTERNATIONAL) 2009
1. Georgia	1. Canada
2. New York	2. United Kingdom
3. New Jersey	3. Brazil
4. North Carolina	4. South America*
5. Texas	5. Germany
6. Ohio	6. Australia
7. Illinois	7. Japan
8. Alabama	8. France
9. California	9. Spain
10. Tennessee	10. Italy

Primarily Argentina, Colombia, and Venezuela

January through March and April through June were the most popular periods to visit the state in 2008. The first quarter drew 29 percent of the year's visitors while the second quarter drew 26 percent. The high summer period of July through September drew 24 percent with 21 percent arriving in the last quarter of the year.

The state once counted tourists as they entered the state through the air, on the highway, and by rail. The volume of visitors has made that impractical, and much tourism information is gleaned from surveys.

In 2008, surveys indicated the primary reason domestic visitors came to the state was leisure. The major type of lodging for more than 46 percent was hotels or similar accommodations. They stayed on average just more than five nights with air travelers staying about a half-day longer than those who drove. They listed their favorite activities as going to the beach, shopping, and visiting theme parks.

Nearly 80 percent of Canadian visitors also came for a vacation, and 29 percent of them stayed in hotels. The average stay for Canadian visitors was just over 17 nights, but the median length of stay was nine nights.

Seventy-two percent of overseas visitors stayed in hotels, but their main reason for coming, too, was vacation. They stayed on average more than 11 nights, and their median stay was nine nights.

Orlando, with its concentration of family-friendly attractions, continued to be the state's top destination, followed, in keeping with the recent surpassing popularity of the beach, by the state's vast array of shorelines.

AU NATURAL

Land O'Lakes in Pasco County is the U.S. capital of nudist resorts. Five *au natural* resorts draw more than 100,000 visitors annually. The area has proved so popular that developers are building communities for enthusiasts in and around the resorts.

MAJOR ATTRACTIONS

Most major attractions are members of the Florida Attractions Association, an organization committed to providing fair admission, courtesy, cleanliness, ethical operation, and quality exhibits and entertainment. They are:

Adventure Island is Tampa Bay's only recreational water park and is home to a championship volleyball complex, adjacent to Busch Gardens in Tampa.

Ah-Tha-Thi-Ki Museums at Hollywood and at Clewiston feature the history and culture of Florida's Seminole Indians.

Babcock Wilderness Adventures at Punta Gorda offers swamp-buggy rides through Florida's hinterlands.

Billie Swamp Safari offers swamp-buggy eco-tours deep in the Everglades, midway between Ft. Lauderdale and Naples off I-75.

Brevard Zoo at Melbourne is a small community zoo that has built a major reputation through its environmental program and unique presentations and activities.

Broadway Palm Dinner Theater offers professional plays and musicals in Fort Myers.

Busch Gardens at Tampa is a 300-acre period Africa theme park with the world's largest inverted roller-coaster.

Butterfly World at Coconut Creek is a tropical rain forest with botanical gardens and thousands of exotic butterflies.

Canoe Outpost-Peace River at Arcadia is a paradise for paddlers through this stretch of Old Florida.

Captain Doug's Florida Airboat Tours at Everglades City conducts escorted and narrated scenic tours of the Everglades

Central Florida Zoo and Botanical Gardens at Sanford is a child-friendly park devoted to exotic animals and native Florida plants.

Captiva Cruises tour the barrier and out islands off Fort Myers.

Clearwater Marine Aquarium allows visitors to view the rehabilitation and long-term care of dolphins and other sea creatures.

Conch Tour Train offers close-up views of historic Key West.

Coral Castle in Homestead was singlehandedly built over 30 years.

Deering Estate at Cutler is an unusual environmental, archaeological, historical, and architectural preserve in Miami.

Discovery Cove at Orlando is a reservations-only attraction featuring snorkeling and swims with the dolphins.

Discovery Cruise Line in Miami offers day cruises to the Bahamas from Miami.

Dow Museum of Historic Houses in St. Augustine puts 400-years of history in one city block.

Edison/Ford Winter Estates in Fort Myers feature tours of the neighboring homes and work areas of the two famous innovators and inventors.

Ernest Hemingway Home and Museum in Key West displays the long-term inspiration for the author.

Everglades Alligator Farm near Homestead is Florida's oldest alligator farm and features airboat rides into the wilderness.

Fairchild Tropical Gardens at Miami is an 83-acre botanical garden of palms, cycads, and colorful tropical plants.

Fantasy of Flight features flight

simulators and 30 historic vintage aircraft spanning the eras of aviation at Polk City.

Flamingo Gardens in Fort Lauderdale is a tram tour, or a walk through native hammocks and the Wray Botanical Gardens.

Florida Air Museum at Sun 'n Fun has added year-round and major additional aviation exhibits to its lineup in league with Lakeland's giant air show.

Florida Aquarium, Florida's newest, in Tampa, explores Florida's water story from its underground sources to the open sea.

Fruit & Spice Park in Homestead presents a dazzling array of tropical fruits, vegetables, herbs, spices, and nuts, including 150 varieties of mango.

Fun Spot of Florida is a modern amusement park complete with rides and arcades in Orlando.

Gatorland in Orlando is home to thousands of alligators, crocodiles, and wildlife birds.

Ghost Tours of St. Augustine guides visitors through the dark past of the nation's oldest city.

Historic Bok Sanctuary, at Lake Wales, is a serene landscaped garden from which rises a tower offering carillon music.

Historical Museum of Southern Florida in Miami offers a tour through south Florida's past at one of the largest private regional history museums in North America.

Homosassa Springs State Wildlife Park allows visitors to walk underwater in the natural spring and meet friendly manatees.

Imaginarium Hands On Museum, at Fort Myers, has more than 60 hands-on exhibits for children and adults.

Island Queen Cruises offer sightseeing tours of Miami.

Jungle Island is the successor to the venerable Parrot Jungle attraction now moved to Watson Island between Miami and Miami Beach.

Jungle Queen Riverboat at Fort Lauderdale provides a barbecue and dinner cruise up New River.

Kennedy Space Center offers tours of the space launch facility and tells the story of the U.S. space effort in three Imax theaters.

Key West Aquarium provides individual and guided tours.

Lightner Museum in St. Augustine is the legacy of one man's collection of antiques and mechanical musical instruments.

Lion Country Safari at West Palm Beach is a 500-acre drive-through wildlife preserve, North America's original "cageless zoo."

Marie Selby Botanical Gardens at Sarasota features a spectacular display greenhouse, replicating a rain forest and showcasing unusual tropical plants.

Marineland's Dolphin Conservatory on the upper east coast is at the tiny self-contained city of Marineland and the world's original marine attraction features dolphin and other water-themed shows.

Medieval Times in Kissimmee entertains with a feast, jousting, and sword fighting in an 11th-century castle.

Miami Children's Museum offers workshops, classes, and clubs on a variety of issues of interest to children.

Miami Metrozoo represents the finest in zoo design, providing visitors scenes of exotic animals in natural habitats.

Miami Science Museum & Planetarium explore the wonders of science and nature with hands-on activities.

Miami **Seaquarium** includes whale, dolphin, and shark feedings.

Miccosukee Indian Village offers airboat rides and a multifaceted look at the state's "other tribe" on the Miami end of the Tamiami Trail.

Monkey Jungle in Miami hosts a colony of wild monkeys in a tropical setting.

Morikami Museum and Japanese Gardens in Delray Beach provides a taste of Japan in a 200-acre park.

MOSH—the Museum of Science and History of Jacksonville examines, among other things, the history of man in northeast Florida.

MOSI—the Museum of Science & Industry in Tampa features hands-on exhibits and IMAX film presentations.

Mote Marine Laboratory and Aquarium at Sarasota takes visitors into serious marine science.

Museum of Arts and Sciences in Daytona Beach offers a self-guided tour through various art venues.

National Museum of Naval Aviation in Pensacola focuses on naval aviation past and present.

Old Florida Museum at St. Augustine is an appropriate living history attraction in the nation's oldest city.

Oldest Wooden School House in the U.S.A. has been preserved to show how it used to be in the oldest city, St. Augustine.

Old Town Trolley Tours hits the 100 high points of St. Augustine.

The Pier is downtown St. Petersburg's landmark attraction, jutting into Tampa Bay and drawing throngs of visitors day and night.

Pirate Adventures cruises Miami waterways including Biscayne Bay and the Venetian Islands.

Pirate's Dinner Adventure in Orlando offers swashbuckling family-oriented interactive dinners.

Ponce de Leon's Fountain of Youth National Archeological Park exhibits foundations and artifacts of the first St. Augustine mission and colony, and features Landmark Spring.

Potter's Wax Museum presents impressions of more than 150 American personalities in St. Augustine.

Ringling Museum of Art at Sarasota covers a 68-acre estate that includes the official state art museum, the circus museum, the Ringling home, and the Asolo Theatre.

Ripley's Believe It or Not! Museum of St. Augustine is the original featuring one-of-a-kind exhibits.

Ripley's Believe It or Not! Odditorium in Orlando displays the world's most unusual collection of oddities, curiosities, and art objects collected by the famous traveler.

Ripley's Sightseeing Trains in St. Augustine offer step-on step-off tours of the nation's oldest city.

St. Augustine Alligator Farm exhibits include all 23 species of crocodiles found around the world.

St. Augustine Lighthouse & Museum pays tribute to the state's first official and still operating light that in 1875 replaced the one erected in 1565.

St. Augustine Scenic Cruise is a conducted tour of the St. Augustine waterfront and Matanzas Bay.

St. Augustine Spanish Quarter Museum in St. Augustine is a living history museum in a restored colonial building.

Sarasota Jungle Gardens is a beauty spot with jungle trails, wild animals, birds of prey, and tropical flowers.

Sawgrass Recreation Park at Fort

Lauderdale has tours via airboat, an alligator and reptile exhibit, and an 18th-century Indian village.

Sea World of Florida in Orlando is a spectacle of shows and exhibits featuring killer whales, dolphins, penguins, sharks, seals, polar bears, and other creatures of the sea.

Shipwreck Island Waterpark at Adventure Landing on Jacksonville Beach is an interactive seasonal playground featuring slides and an endless array of surprise nozzles.

Silver Springs at Ocala is a 350-acre nature theme park famous for its glass-bottom boats.

Southwest Florida Museum of History presents the Ft. Myers area's colorful past and its connection with the Everglades.

Tampa's Lowry Park Zoo includes mammals, birds, and reptiles, many on the endangered list. Noted for its numerous special events.

Theater of the Sea at Islamorada features native fish and marine life in close encounters with visitors.

Universal Studios at Orlando is a spacious motion-picture and television lot with multiple theme parks, including the Wizarding World of Harry Potter.

Viscaya in Miami is a 70-room Italian Renaissance-style palace set in 10 acres of formal gardens along Biscayne Bay.

Walt Disney World Resort at Orlando is the nation's leading vacation destination with 28,000 acres featuring four theme parks—the Magic Kingdom, EPCOT Center, Disney-MGM Studios, and the Animal Kingdom.

Wannado City at Sunrise is the nation's first indoor role-playing theme park for children.

Weeki Wachee Springs at Weeki Wachee features daily live underwater productions featuring the "living mermaids."

Wet 'n Wild in Orlando is the nation's best-attended recreational water park.

World Golf Hall of Fame at St. Augustine offers an IMAX theater and an interactive appreciation of the game.

EVENTS

Specific dates for popular events vary from year to year, but may be obtained by contacting the area chambers of commerce.

January
Art Deco Weekend, Miami Beach
Beaux Arts Festival, Coral Gables
Billfish Invitational Tournament, Fort Pierce
Bonita Springs Festival of Arts
Brooksville Raid Festival
Broward Shell Show, Pompano Beach
Canada Fest, Fort Lauderdale
Cape Coral Festival of the Arts
Capital One Bowl, Orlando
Carillon Festival at Bok Tower Gardens, Lake Wales
Celebrity Golf Classic, New Port Richey
Deerfield Beach Festival of the Arts
Doral-Ryder PGA Golf, Miami
Epiphany Glendi, Tarpon Springs
Florida Citrus Festival, Winter Haven
Florida Keys Renaissance Faire, Key West
Florida Manatee Festival, Brooksville
Frog Leg Festival, Fellsmere
Gator Bowl, Jacksonville
Health South LPGA Classic, Orlando
International Miniature Arts Show, Dunedin
Key West Literary Seminar
Kumquat Festival, Dade City
Los Olas Art Fair, Ft. Lauderdale
Miniature Harness Racing, Ocala
Naples Invitational Art Fair
Orange Bowl, Miami
Oshogatsu Celebration, Delray Beach
Outback Bowl, Tampa
Punta Gorda Craft Festival
St. Armand's Circle Art Festival, Sarasota
South Florida Orchid Extravaganza, Miami
Space Coast Seashell Festival, Melbourne
Steven Foster Day, White Springs
Upper Keys Seafood Festival, Islamorada
Walt Disney World Marathon, Orlando
Winter Equestrian Festival, Palm Beach
Zora Neale Hurston Festival of the Arts, Eatonville

February
ArtiGras, Jupiter Beach
Bach Festival, Winter Park
Baseball Spring Training, pitchers & catchers, statewide
Battle of Olustee
Bok Tower Azalea Celebration, Lake Wales
Chautaugua Assembly, DeFuniak Springs
Daytona 500, Daytona Beach
Everglades Seafood Festival, Everglades City
Gasparilla Invasion and Parade, Tampa
Edison Festival of Light, Fort Myers
Farm Fest & Quilt Show, Dade City
Fiesta of Arts, Boca Raton
Finlandia Week—Midnight Sun Festival, Lake Worth
Florida Keys Paddling Festival, Key Largo
Florida State Fair, Tampa
Gasparilla Distance Classic, Tampa
Goody's 300, Daytona Beach
Grant Seafood Festival, Melbourne
Hoggetown Medieval Faire, Gainesville
International Folk Festival, St. Petersburg
Italian Feast & Festival, Venice

Kissimmee Slough Shootout,
Clewiston
Lions Club Shrimp Festival, Estero
Mardi Gras on the Island, Okaloosa
Island
Miami/Coconut Grove Art Festival
Miami International Film Festival
Miami International Map Fair
Mount Dora Art Festival
National Art Festival, Naples
National Offshore Sail Races, St.
Petersburg
PGA Senior Classic, Tampa
Port Charlotte Invitational College
Baseball Tournament
Royal Poinciana Festival, Miami
Sarasota International Film Festival
Sarasota Jazz Festival
Seafood Festival, Everglades City
Seminole Tribe Fair, Hollywood
Seven Days of Opening Nights,
Tallahassee
Silver Spurs Rodeo, Kissimmee
St. Petersburg Grand Prix
South Beach Wine and Food
Festival, Miami Beach
Swamp Cabbage Festival, LaBelle
Palm Beach Seafood Festival, West
Palm Beach
Winter Park Sidewalk Art Festival
Yankee Yacht Race, Key West
Ybor City Fiesta Day, Tampa

March
All-Florida Championship Rodeo,
Arcadia
America Cup Gymnastics, Orlando
Antiquarian Book Fair, St.
Petersburg
Baseball Spring Training, statewide
Battle of Natural Bridge, Woodville
BayHill Invitational PGA Golf, Orlando
Bike Week, Daytona Beach
Carnival Miami
Catfish Festival, Crescent City
Chasco Fiesta, New Port Richey
Chili Cookoff , Lake Wales
Chowder Cook-Off, Cocoa Beach

Destin Cobia Tournament
Festival of States, St. Petersburg
Gasparilla Sidewalk Art Festival,
Tampa
Gate River Run, Jacksonville
Gatornationals drag racing, Gainesville
International Fringe Festival, Orlando
Italian Renaissance Fair, Miami
Little Everglades Steeplechase,
Dade City
Kissimmee Blue Grass Festival
Manatee Heritage Week, Bradenton
Miami Grand Prix
Palm Beach International Film
Festival
President's Cup Regatta crew races,
Tampa
St. Petersburg Grand Prix
Seminole Indian Days,
Chokoloskee
Strawberry Festival, Plant City
The Players PGA Championship,
Ponte Verde Beach
12 Hours of Sebring
Winter Equestrian Festival, Tampa
World of Nations Celebration,
Jacksonville
Zora Fest, Fort Pierce

April
Bookfest of the Palm Beaches, West
Palm Beach
Cabbage and Potato Festival, Hastings
Conch Republic Celebration, Key
West
Crawfish Festival, Jacksonville Beach
Crescent City Catfish Festival
Easter Boogie skydiving,
Zephyrhills, Deland, Sebastian
Emerald Coast Volleyball Week,
Okaloosa Island
Florida Derby, Hallandale
Fort Lauderdale Seafood Festival
Fort Walton Beach Seafood Festival
Gulf Coast Offshore Power Boat
Races, Panama City Beach
Indian River Festival, Titusville
Jacksonville Blues Festival

Orange Cup Regatta, Lakeland
Pensacola Jazz Festival
PGA Senior Championship, Palm
    Beach Gardens
Ribfest & Hot Air Balloon Rally,
    Melbourne
Springing the Blues Music Festival,
    Jacksonville
Southernmost Purple Martin
    Festival, Homestead
St. Anthony World Cup Triathlon,
    St. Petersburg
Sugar Festival, Clewiston
Sun & Fun Fly-in, Lakeland
Title Holder LPGA Championship,
    Daytona Beach
Wild Beast Festival, Trenton

May
ArtsQuest Week, Sandestin
Clearwater to Key West Yacht Race
Five Freedoms Festival, Madison
Florida Folk Festival, White Springs
Great Dock Canoe Race, Naples
Isle of Eight Flags Shrimp Festival,
    Fernandina Beach
Jacksonville Film Festival
Miami International Film Festival
Old Spanish Trail Festival, Crestview
Pensacola Crawfish Festival
Roaring Twenties Days at Sebring
Sarasota Music Festival
Tarpon Rodeo, Sanibel Island
Week of Blessings, Destin
Zellwood Corn Festival

June
Drake's Raid, St. Augustine
Fiesta of Five Flags, Pensacola
Gospel Jubilee, Live Oak
International Food & Music
    Festival, Cocoa
Ladies Billfish Tournament,
    Panama City Beach
Lincolnville Music Festival, St.
    Augustine
Miracle Strip Open Spearfishing
    Tournament, Panama City Beach

Monticello Watermelon Festival
Palatka Blueberry Festival
Southernmost Seminole Golf
    Tournament, Key West
Summerfest Canoe Race, Fort Myers
Sunshine State Games, Tallahassee

July
Central Florida Soap Box Derby,
    Sanford
Destin Shark Fishing Tournament
Firecracker 400, Daytona Beach
Florida International Festival,
    Daytona Beach
Florida State Water Ski
    Championships, Mulberry
Hemingway Days Festival, Key West
Pensacola Beach Air Show
Silver Spurs Rodeo, Kissimmee
Taste of Soul Festival, Orlando

August
Boca Festival Days, Boca Raton
Caladium Festival, Lake Placid
Canterbury Dressage Horse Show,
    Newberry
Greater Jacksonville Offshore
    Grand Prix, Jacksonville Beach
Jacksonville Crawfish Festival
King Mackerel Tournament, Destin
Real McCoy International Rum and
    Music Festival, Daytona Beach
St. Petersburg Fishathon
Wausau Possum Festival

September
American Grand Prix, Miami
Days in Spain, St. Augustine
Labor Day Fish Fry, Punta Gorda
Melrose Grape Festival
New Smyrna Beach Jazz Festival
Osceola Art Festival, Kissimmee
Pensacola Lobster Festival
Pioneer Florida Days, Dade City
Scallop Day Festival, Port St. Joe
Springfield Jazz & Heritage Festival,
    Jacksonville
Tangerine Blues Festival, Gulfport

Union Garrison Weekend,
Fernandina Beach

October
Biketoberfest, Daytona Beach
Boggy Bayou Mullet Festival, Niceville
Broward Navy Days and Fleet Week,
Port Everglades
Caribbean Carnival, Miami
Cedar Key Seafood Festival
Clearwater Jazz Holiday
DeLand Original Music Festival
Destin Seafood Festival
Disney PGA Classic, Orlando
Dixie Sailing Regatta, Sanford
Fantasy Fest, Key West
Festival of Reading, St. Petersburg
Florida Forest Festival, Perry
Florida Skyfest, Daytona Beach
Fort Lauderdale International Boat
Show
Goat Day, Blountstown
Great Bowls of Fire Chili Cook-off,
DeLand
Guavaween, Tampa
Halifax Art Festival, Daytona Beach
Indian Summer Seafood Festival,
Panama City Beach
Jay Peanut Festival
Jeannie Auditions and Ball, White
Springs
Mayport Seafood Festival
Monarch Butterfly Festival, St. Marks
NSRA Southeast Street Rod
Nationals, Tampa
Oak Hill Mullet Festival
Octoberfest Music Festival,
Brooksville
Rattlesnake Festival, San Antonio
Ringling International Arts Festival,
Sarasota
Riverwalk Fall Art Show, Fort
Lauderdale
Seminole Indian and Florida
Pioneer Festival, Cocoa
Superboat Offshore National
Championship, Clearwater
Weeki Wachee River Raft Regatta
Williston Peanut Festival

November
Apalachicola Seafood Festival
Birthplace of Speed Celebration,
Ormond Beach
Country Fried Festival, Jacksonville
DeLand Festival of the Arts
Fall Country Jamboree, Barberville
Florida-Georgia Football Game,
Jacksonville
Florida Tastefest, Jacksonville
Grand National Auto Racing,
Homestead
Great Gulf Coast Arts Festival,
Pensacola
Hollywood Jazz Festival
Inglis-Yankeetown Seafood Festival
International Folk Festival, Eustis
Jazz Festival of South Walton, Seaside
Kahlua Club International Yacht
Races, Clearwater
Miami Book Fair
National Native American Festival,
Jacksonville
Riverwalk Blues Fest, Fort Lauderdale
Seafood & Arts Festival, Ruskin

December
Art Basel, Miami Beach
Beef 'O' Brady's Bowl, St. Petersburg
British Nightwatch, St. Augustine
Champs Sports Bowl, Orlando
Christmas Boogie, Zephyrhills
Christmas in the Park, Winter
Haven
Festival of Lights, Fanning Springs
Florida Senior Games
Championships, Fort Myers
Fort Pierce Raid
Gator Bowl Junior Tennis
Championships, Jacksonville
Great Florida Shootout, Kissimmee
Illuminated Boat Parade, St.
Petersburg
King Mango Strut, Coconut Grove
Selby Gardens Holiday, Sarasota
Ted Keller International Diving
Meet, Fort Lauderdale
Victorian Seaside Christmas,
Amelia Island

ARTS AND CULTURE

MUSEUMS AND ART CENTERS
(Members of the Florida Association of Museums)

Anna Maria
Anna Maria Island Historical Museum
Apalachicola
John Gorrie State Museum
Apopka
Apopka Historical Society and Museum of Apopkans
Avon Park
Avon Park Depot Museum
South Florida Community College Museum of Florida Art and Culture
Barberville
Pioneer Settlement for the Creative Arts
Bartow
Polk County Historical Museum
Blountstown
Panhandle Pioneer Settlement
Boca Raton
Boca Raton Historical Society
Boca Raton Museum of Art
Children's Science Explorium
University Galleries, Florida Atlantic University
Bokeelia
Useppa Island Historical Museum
Bowling Green
Paynes Creek State Historic Site
Boynton Beach
Schoolhouse Children's Museum
Bradenton
DeSoto National Memorial
Manatee Village Historical Park
Powel Crosley Museum of the Entrepreneur
South Florida Museum, Parker Marine Aquarium & Bishop Planetarium
Real Trail
Bristol
Torreya State Park/Gregory House

Brooksville
Hernando Historical Museum
Bunnell
Bulow Plantation Ruins State Historic Site
Bushnell
Dade Battlefield State Historic Site
Cantonment
Roy L. Hyatt Environmental Center
Cape Coral
Cape Coral Historical Museum
Carrabelle
Camp Gordon Johnson World War II Museum
Cedar Key
Cedar Key Historical Museum
Cedar Key State Museum
Charlotte Harbor
Charlotte County Historical Center
Chokoloskee
Historic Smallwood Store
Christmas
Fort Christmas Museum
Clearwater
Clearwater Marine Aquarium
Moccasin Lake Nature Park
Clewiston
Ah-Tha-Thi-Ki Museum
Clewiston Museum
Cocoa
BCC Planetarium and Observatory
Florida Solar Energy Center (University of Central Florida)
Coconut Grove
The Barnacle Historic State Park
Coral Gables
Coral Gables Museum
Fairchild Tropical Garden
Lowe Art Museum
Merrick House

Coral Springs
Coral Springs Museum of Art
Cross Creek
Marjorie Kinnan Rawlings
Historic State Park
Crystal River
Coastal Heritage Museum
Crystal River State Archeological
Site
Marine Science Station
Dade City
Pioneer Florida Museum
Dania Beach
International Game Fishing Hall
of Fame & Museum
Davie
Broward Community College
Gallery
Buehler Planetarium, Broward
Community College
Flamingo Gardens
Old Davie School Historical
Museum
Young at Art Children's Museum
Daytona Beach
The Art League of Daytona Beach
Halifax Historical Museum/
Archives
Museum of Arts and Sciences
Southeast Museum of Photography
DeBary
DeBary Hall Historic Site
Deerfield Beach
Old Deerfield School Museum
Butler House Museum
Deerfield Beach Historical
Society
Pioneer House (Kester Cottage)
South Florida Railway Museum
DeLand
DeLand House Museum/
Memorial Hospital Museum
Museum of Florida Art
DeLand Naval Air Station
Museum
Duncan Art Gallery, Stetson
Department of Art
Gillespie Museum of Minerals

Delray Beach
American Orchid Society &
Botanical Garden
Cason Cottage Museum
Cornell Museum of Art and
American History
Delray Beach Historical Society
Morikami Museum & Japanese
Gardens
Spady Cultural Heritage
Museum
Destin
Destin History and Fishing
Museum
Dunedin
Dunedin Fine Art Center
Dunedin Historical Society
Museum
Eatonville
Zora Neale Hurston National
Museum of Fine Arts (The
Hurston)
Eglin Air Force Base
Air Force Armament Museum
Ellenton
Gamble Plantation State Historic
Site
Estero
Koreshan State Historic and
Mound Key Archaeological State
Park
Eustis
Eustis Historical Museum &
Preservation Society, Inc.
Lake Eustis Museum of Art
Everglades City
Museum of the Everglades
Fernandina Beach
Amelia Island Museum of
History
Fort Clinch State Park
Fort Lauderdale
Ah-Tah-Thi-Ki Museum
Bonnet House and Gardens
Fort Lauderdale Antique Car
Museum
International Swimming Hall of
Fame

Museum of Art
Museum of Discovery & Science
My Jewish Discovery Place
Children's Museum
Old Dillard Museum
Old Fort Lauderdale Museum of
History
Palm Beach Museum of National
History
Stranahan House
Terramar Visitors Center
Fort Myers
Burroughs House
Calusa Nature Center &
Planetarium
Edison and Ford Winter Estates
Imaginarium Hands-On
Museum
Railroad Museum of South
Florida
Southwest Florida Museum of
History
Rauschenberg Gallery at Edison
College
Fort Myers Beach
The Mound House Cultural and
Environmental Learning Center
Fort Pierce
Harbor Branch Oceanographic
Museum
Heathcote Botanical Gardens
Navy UDT-Seal Museum
Fort Walton Beach
Fort Walton Beach Art Museum
Camp Walton Schoolhouse
Museum
City Heritage Park
Emerald Coast Science Center
Garner Post Office Museum
Indian Temple Mound Museum
Gainesville
Alachua County Historic Trust
Matheson Museum
Florida Museum of Natural
History
Harn Museum of Art
Kanapaha Botanical Gardens
Morningside Nature Center

Santa Fe Community College
Teaching Zoo
Thomas Center Galleries
University of Florida University
Galleries
Geneva
Museum of Geneva History
Gulf Breeze
Gulf Islands National Seashore
Hawthorne
Hawthorne Historical Museum
and Cultural Center
Hobe Sound
Trapper Nelson Interpretive Site
at Jonathan Dickinson State Park
Hollywood
Art and Culture Center of
Hollywood
Homeland
Homeland Heritage Park
Homestead
Florida Pioneer Museum
Historic Homestead Townhall
Museum
Immokalee
Immokalee Pioneer Museum at
Roberts Ranch
Inverness
Old Courthouse Heritage
Museum
Islamorada
Florida Keys Museum of Diving
History
Lignumvitae Key State Botanical
Site
Jacksonville
Beaches Area Historical Society
Cummer Museum of Art &
Gardens
Florida Community College
Kent Campus Museum/Gallery
Fort Caroline National Memorial
Jacksonville Maritime Museum
Society, Inc.
Jacksonville Historical Society
Jacksonville Museum of Modern
Art
Jacksonville Zoological Gardens

Karpeles Manuscript Library
Kingsley Plantation Timucuan
Preserve, NPS
Mandarin Museum & Historical
Society
Museum of Science and History
Museum of Southern History
Ritz Theatre and LaVilla
Museum
Sojourner Truth Library
Museum
Timucuan Ecological and
Historic Preserve/Ft Caroline Nat'l
Memorial
Tree Hill Jacksonville's Nature
Center
Wilson Center for the Arts
Jensen Beach
Maritime & Yachting Museum
Juno Beach
Loggerhead Marinelife Center
Jupiter
Burt Reynolds & Friends
Museum
Hibel Museum of Art
Lighthouse Art Center
Loxahatchee River History
Center & Museum, Jupiter Inlet
Light
Kennedy Space Center
Kennedy Space Center Visitors
Complex
Key Biscayne
Cape Florida Lighthouse Bill
Baggs State Recreation Area
Key Largo
John Pennekamp Coral Reef
State Park
Key West
Audubon House and Gardens
Donkey Milk House, c. 1866
Historic Home
Fort East Martello Museum
Fort Zachary Taylor State
Historic Site
Lighthouse Museum
Key West Museum of Art and
History

Mel Fisher Maritime Museum
The Oldest House Museum
San Carlos Institute
Kissimmee
Osceola Center for the Arts
Osceola County Historical
Museum and Pioneer Enrichment
Center
Veterans Tribute and Museum
Lake City
Columbia County Historical
Museum
Lakeland
Explorations V Children's
Museum
Florida Air Museum
Polk Museum of Art
Lake Monroe
Central Florida Zoological Park
Lake Wales
Bok Tower Gardens
Lake Wales Museum and
Cultural Center (The Depot)
Lake Worth
Museum of Polo and Hall of
Fame
Museum of the City of Lake
Worth
Largo
Armed Forces Military Museum
Heritage Village
Leesburg
Leesburg Heritage Museum
Live Oak
Suwannee County Historical
Museum
Longboat Key
Longboat Key Art Center
Madison
North Florida Community
College Art Gallery
Maitland
Maitland Art Center
Maitland Art and History Society
and Museums
Marathon
Museums and Nature Center of
Crane Point

Mayport
Marine Science Education Center
Melbourne
Brevard Art Museum
Brevard Zoo
Florida Institute of Technology Botanical Gardens
Liberty Bell Memorial Museum
Melbourne Beach
Sebastian Fishing Museum
Miami
Bay of Pigs Museum
Black Heritage Museum
Cuban Museum of the Americas
Deering Estate at Cutler
Frost Art Museum
Gallery North, Miami-Dade Community College, North Campus
Gold Coast Railroad
Haitian Heritage Museum
Historic Virginia Key Beach Park and Museum
Knight Foundation
Miami Art Central
Miami Art Museum
Miami Children's Museum
Miami-Dade Community College Kendall Campus Art Gallery
Miami-Dade Community College, Wolfson Galleries
Miami Fire Museum, Inc.
Miami Metrozoo
Miami Space Museum and Planetarium
Museum of Contemporary Art in Miami
Vizcaya Museum and Gardens
Wings over Miami
Miami Beach
Art Center/South Florida
Bass Museum of Art
Jewish Museum of Florida
The Wolfsonian at FIU
Miami Lakes
Jay I. Kislak Foundation, Inc.
Miami Springs

Miami Springs Historical Museum
Micanopy
Micanopy Historical Society Museum
Middleburg
Middleburg Historic Museum
Mount Dora
Antique Boat Museum
Mount Dora Center for the Arts
Royellou Museum
Mulberry
Mulberry Phosphate Museum
Naples
Golisano Children's Museum of Naples
Collier County Museum
Conservancy Naples Nature Center
Holocaust Museum of Southwest Florida
Naples Depot Museum
Naples Historical Society
Naples Botanical Garden
Naples Museum of Art
Rockery Bay National Estuarine Research Reserve
Von Liebig Art Center
New Port Richey
West Pasco Historical Society Museum and Library
New Smyrna Beach
Atlantic Center for the Arts
Black Heritage Festival/Museum
New Smyrna Museum of History
Niceville
Kelly Arts Center Galleries at Northwest Florida State College
North Miami
Museum of Contemporary Art in Miami
North Miami Beach
Ancient Spanish Monastery of St. Bernard De Clairvaux Cloisters
Holocaust Documentation and Education Center
North Palm Beach
Florida Power & Light Historical Museum

John D. MacArthur Beach State Park

Ocala
Appleton and Webber Galleries at Central Florida Community College
Discovery Science Center
Don Garlits Museum of Drag Racing
Marion County Museum of History
Silver River Museum and Environmental Education Center

Ocoee
Ocoee Hisorical Committee
Withers/Maguire House

Olustee
Olustee Battlefield Historic Site

Orlando
Harry P. Leu Gardens
Mennello Museum of American Folk Art
Museum of the Seminole Tribe
National Vietnam War Museum
Orange County Regional History Museum
Orlando Museum of Art
Orlando Science Center
University of Central Florida Art Gallery
Wooten Gallery at Valencia Community College

Osprey
Historic Spanish Point

Palatka
Putnam Historic Museum
Ravine State Gardens

Palm Beach
Henry Morrison Flagler Museum
Palm Beach Maritime Museum
Society of the Four Arts

Palm Coast
Florida Agricultural Museum

Palm Harbor
North Pinellas Historical Museum

Panama City
Gulf Coast Community College Art Gallery

John Hargrove Motor Car Museum
Junior Museum of Bay County
Visual Arts Center of Northwest Florida

Panama City Beach
Museum of Man in the Sea

Parrish
Florida Railroad Museum

Patrick AFB
Air Force Space and Missile Museum

Pensacola
Historic Pensacola Village and T.T. Wentworth, Jr. State Museum
National Museum of Naval Aviation
Pensacola Historical Museum
Pensacola Museum of Art
Switzer Center for the Visual Arts

Perry
Forest Capital State Museum

Pinellas Park
Tampa Bay Automobile Museum

Plantation
Plantation Historical Museum

Plant City
Pioneer Heritage Museum

Point Washington
Eden State Gardens

Polk City
Water Ski Hall of Fame

Pompano Beach
Pompano Beach Historical Society Museum
Sample-McDougald House

Ponce Inlet
Marine Science Center
Ponce De Leon Inlet Lighthouse

Port St. Joe
Constitution Convention State Museum

Punta Gorda
Military Heritage of Aviation Museum

Safety Harbor
Safety Harbor Museum of Regional History

St. Augustine
Castillo de San Marcos and Ft.
Matanzas National Monuments
Colonial Spanish Quarter
Lightner Museum
Pena-Peck House
St. Augustine Lighthouse &
Museum
St. Photios Greek Orthodox
National Shrine
World of Golf Hall of Fame
Ximenez-Fatio House
St. James City
Museum of the Islands
St. Petersburg
Boyd Hill Nature Center
Florida Holocaust Museum
Florida Sports Hall of Fame
Great Explorations-The Hands
On Museum
Morean Arts Center
Museum of Fine Arts
Pier Aquarium, Inc.
Ransom Art Center at Eckerd
College
St. Petersburg Museum of History
Salvador Dali Museum
Science Center of Pinellas
County
Weedeon Island Preserve
Cultural & Natural History Center
Dr. Carter G. Woodson African
American Museum
Sanford
Museum of Seminole County
History
Sanford Museum
Seminole County Student Museum
Sanibel
Bailey-Matthews Shell Museum
Sarasota
Arts Center Sarasota
Crowley Museum and Nature
Center
G WIZ Hand-on Science
Museum
Marie Selby Botanical Gardens
Mote Aquarium

Ringling Museum of Art
Selby Gallery Ringling School of
Art & Design
Sebring
Children's Museum of the
Highlands
Highlands Hammock State Park
Highlands Museum of the Arts
Seminole
Panama Canal Museum
Starke
Camp Blanding Museum and
Memorial Park
Stuart
Elliott Museum
Florida Oceanographic Coastal
Center
Gilbert's Bar House of Refuge
Museum
Stuart Heritage Museum
Tallahassee
Alfred B. Maclay State Gardens
Black Archives at Union Bank
Black Archives Research Center
& Museum
Florida Historic Capitol Museum
Foster-Tanner Fine Arts Gallery
Goodwood Museum and
Gardens
Knott House Museum
Lake Jackson Mounds State
Archaeological Site
LeMoyne Art Museum
Mary Brogan Museum of Arts
and Science
Mission San Luis
Museum of Fine Arts Florida
State University
Museum of Florida History
Riley House Museum of African-
American History and Culture
San Marcos de Apalache Historic
State Park
Tallahassee Museum of History
& Natural Science
Tampa
Cracker Country Florida State
Fairgrounds

Florida Aquarium
Florida Museum of
Photographic Arts
Henry B. Plant Museum
Lowry Park Zoological Garden
Glazer Children's Museum
MOSI (Museum of Science &
Industry)
Tampa Bay History Center
Tampa Firefighters Museum
Tampa Museum of Art
Tampa Police Museum
University of Tampa Scarfone/
Harley Galleries
USF Botanical Gardens
USF Contemporary Art Museum
Ybor City Museum State Park
Tarpon Springs
Leepa-Rattner Museum of Art
Tarpon Springs Area Historical
Society
Tarpon Springs Cultural
Treasures
Tavares
Lake County Historical Museum
Titusville
American Police Museum & Hall
of Fame
Valiant Air Command Aviation
Museum
Valparaiso
Heritage Museum of Northwest
Florida
Venice
Venice Art Center
Vero Beach
Environmental Learning Center
Indian River Citrus Museum
Laura Riding Jackson Home
McKee Botanical Garden
McLarty Treasure Museum
The Railroad Museum
Vero Beach Museum of Art
Weirsdale
Florida Carriage Museum and
Resort
West Palm Beach
Ann Norton Sculpture Garden

Armory Art Center
Imagination Station
Mounts Botanical Garden
Norton Museum of Art
Palm Beach History Museum
Palm Beach Photographic
Museum
Palm Beach Zoo at Dreher Park
South Florida Science Museum
White Springs
Stephen Foster State Folk
Culture Center State Park
Winter Garden
Central Florida Railroad
Museum
Winter Garden Heritage
Museum
Winter Haven
Polk Community College Art
Gallery
Winter Park
Albin Polesek Museum and
Sculpture Gardens
Cornell Fine Arts Museum
Crealde School of Art
Morse Museum of American Art
Winter Park Historical
Association and Museum
Zephyrhills
Zephyrhills Depot Museum
Zephyrhills World War II
Barricks Museum
Note: The Cayman Islands National
Museum at George Town, Grand
Cayman, is a member of the Florida
Association.

SYMPHONY ORCHESTRAS
(Chamber, Pops, Youth,
Community College, University)

Alachua County Youth Orchestra
(Gainesville)
Alhambra Community Orchestra
(Miami)
Ars Flores Symphony Orchestra
(Fort Lauderdale)

Atlantic Classical Orchestra
(Stuart)
The Bach Festival Chamber
Orchestra (Winter Park)
Big Bend Community Orchestra
(Tallahassee)
Brevard Symphony Orchestra
(Melbourne)
Brevard Symphony Youth
Orchestra (Melbourne)
Broward Community College Youth
Symphony (Pompano Beach)
Broward Symphony Orchestra
(Fort Lauderdale)
Central Florida Symphony (Ocala)
Charlotte Chamber Music Society
(Punta Gorda)
Concert Association of Greater
Miami (Miami Beach)
Daytona Beach Symphony Society
Emil Maestre Music Association (St.
Augustine)
Florida Orchestra (Tampa Bay)
Florida Space Coast Philharmonic
(Cocoa)
Florida State University Symphony
(Tallahassee)
Florida Symphonic Pops (Boca
Raton)
Florida Symphony Youth Orchestra
(Winter Park)
Florida West Coast Symphony
Orchestra (Sarasota)
Florida West Coast Symphony
Youth Orchestra (Sarasota)
Florida Young Artist Orchestra
(Orlando)
Florida Youth Orchestra
(Hollywood)
Gainesville Chamber Orchestra
Gainesville Symphony Orchestra
Greater Miami Youth Symphony
Greater Palm Beach Symphony
Greater Pensacola Symphony
Orchestra
Imperial Symphony Orchestra
(Lakeland)
Jacksonville Symphony Orchestra

Jacksonville Symphony Youth
Orchestra
Key West Symphony
The Naples Philharmonic
New World Symphony (Miami)
Northwest Florida Symphony
Orchestra (Niceville)
Northwest Florida Symphony Youth
Orchestra (Niceville)
Ocala Festival Orchestra
Okaloosa Symphony Orchestra
(Fort Walton Beach)
Orchestra of St. Andrew Bay
(Pensacola)
Orlando Philharmonic
Palm Beach Pops
Palm Beach Symphonette
Pensacola Symphony Orchestra
Pinellas Youth Symphony (St.
Petersburg)
St. Johns River City Band
(Jacksonville)
Sarasota-Manatee Community
Orchestra (Longboat Key)
Sinfonia (Destin)
South Florida Youth Symphony
(Miami)
Southwest Florida Symphony (Fort
Myers)
Suncoast Symphony (Clearwater)
The Tallahassee Symphony
Tampa Bay Chamber Orchestra
(Tampa)
Tampa Bay Community Symphony
(St. Petersburg)
Tampa Bay Symphony (Seminole)
Tampa Bay Youth Orchestras
(Tampa)
Treasure Coast Symphony (Fort
Pierce)
Venice Symphony

ARTISTS' HALL OF FAME

The Florida Artists' Hall of Fame
was created by the 1986 Legislature
to honor individuals who have made

significant contributions to the arts in Florida. The Hall of Fame is permanently installed on the Plaza level of the Capitol in Tallahassee, with additional information about each member displayed on the 22nd floor.

Members are
George Abbott, director, playwright
  Miami Beach
A. E. "Bean" Backus, painter
  Fort Pierce
Jimmy Buffett, singer, songwriter, author
  Key West
Fernando Bujones, dancer
  Miami
Clyde Butcher, photographer
  Ochopee
Ray Charles, musician
  Greenville
Harry Crews, author
  Gainesville
Earl Cunningham, folk artist
  St. Augustine
Bo Diddley, musician
  Archer
Marjory Stoneman Douglas, author
  Coconut Grove
George Firestone, patron
  Miami
Dr. William P. Foster, marching-band director
  Tallahassee
Alfred Hair and the Highwaymen, landscape painters
  Fort Pierce
Duane Hanson, sculptor
  Davie
Martin Johnson Heade, painter
  St. Augustine
Ernest Hemingway, author
  Key West
Zora Neale Hurston, author, folklorist
  Eatonville
Lou Jacobs, clown
  Sarasota

James Weldon Johnson, writer, composer
  Jacksonville
John Rosamond Johnson, composer, conductor, actor
  Jacksonville
Stetson Kennedy, folklorist, author
  Beluthahatchee
Elaine L. Konigsburg, author, illustrator
  Ponte Vedra Beach
Doris Leeper, sculptor, painter
  New Smyrna Beach
Hank Locklin, singer, songwriter
  McLellan
John D. MacDonald, author
  Sarasota
Will McLean, folk artist
  Chipley
Addison Mizner, architect
  Boca Raton
Ralph Hubbard Norton, patron, collector
  West Palm Beach
Victor Nunez, film director
  Tallahassee
Albin Polasek, sculptor
  Winter Park
W. Stanley "Sandy" Proctor, sculptor
  Tallahassee
Robert Rauschenberg, visual artist
  Captiva
Marjorie Kinnan Rawlings, author
  Cross Creek
Burt Reynolds, actor
  Jupiter
John N. Ringling, patron, collector
  Sarasota
Gamble Rogers, troubadour
  St. Augustine
James Rosenquist, visual artist
  Aripeka
Augusta Savage, sculptor
  Green Cove Springs
Patrick D. Smith, author
  Merritt Island
Christopher Still, painter
  Tarpon Springs

Mel Tillis, singer, songwriter
  Silver Springs
Jerry N. Uelsmann, photographer
  Gainesville
Edward Villela, choreographer,
  dancer
  Miami

Hiram D. Williams, painter
  Gainesville
Tennessee Williams, playwright
  Key West
Ellen Taaffe Zwilich, composer
  Miami

Post Office Murals

During the Great Depression the U.S. Department of Treasury commissioned artists to paint murals in all post office buildings erected during the 1930s. In all, 1,118 were done under this program, but few remain. Twelve in Florida have survived.

They are in post offices (and other government buildings that served as post offices in the 1930s) in the cities of West Palm Beach, Miami, Fort Pierce, Miami Beach, Palm Beach, Sebring, Lake Wales, Madison, Milton, Tallahassee, DeFuniak Springs, and Jasper.

A hanging in the Lake Worth post office was commissioned under a different federal program during the 1930s.

All the murals depict facets of Florida history or life. Some of them measure up to 10 by 14 feet.

The most famous murals are in the West Palm Beach post office and commemorate "The Barefoot Mailman." Enshrined in legend by having one of their number presumably fall prey to an alligator, the "barefoot" mailmen walked the mail along the beach from Palm Beach to Miami and back in the late 1880s and represented a communications revolution. The three-day trip cut seven weeks from the time it took to send a letter from Miami to New York.

Artists were paid an average of $700 to paint the giant canvases.

Today the Florida Department of State continues to hire artists for works in new state public buildings. The program requires that half a percent of the cost of a new public building be set aside to buy art from Florida artists for display in and around the buildings.

AUDITORIUMS—ARENAS—AMPHITHEATERS

City	Name	Seating
Boca Raton	Seabreeze Amphitheater	2,000
	Suncoast Cover Amphitheater	5,000
Bradenton	Municipal Auditorium	1,600
Clearwater	Ruth Eckerd Hall	2,182
	Capitol Theater	459
Coconut Creek	Omni Auditorium	1,960
Coral Springs	City Centre Theater	1,534
Davie	Davie Arena	7,500

Daytona Beach	Ocean Center	9,496
	Municipal Stadium	10,000
	Peabody Auditorium	2,552
	Bethune Performing Arts Center	2,600
DeLand	Municipal Stadium	6,000
Estero	TECO Center Arena	7,200
Eustis	Lake County Expo Hall	2,440
Fort Lauderdale	Omni Auditorium	2,007
	Amaturo Theater	595
	Bailey Hall	1,197
	Parker Playhouse	1,200
	War Memorial Auditorium	2,110
	Broward Performing Arts Center	2,700
	Office Depot Center	20,000
Fort Myers	Lee Civic Center	9,000
	Exhibition Hall	1,233
	Harborside Convention Center	3,134
	Performing Arts Hall	1,765
Fort Pierce	St. Lucie County Civic Center	4,000
Gainesville	Hippodrome Theater	266
	O'Connell Center	12,500
	Performing Arts Center	1,823
Jacksonville	Civic Auditorium	3,809
	Flag Pavilion	2,000
	Convention Center	7,000
	Florida Theatre Performing Arts	1,978
Kissimmee	Tupperware Center Theater	2,000
Lakeland	Civic Center Theater	2,282
	George Jenkins Arena	10,000
	Lakeland Auditorium	600
Melbourne	Arsht Center for the Performing Arts	2,400
	King Center for the Performing Arts	2,016
	Melbourne Auditorium Theater	1,336

Miami	Knight International Center	5,174
	County Auditorium-Theater	2,498
	Coconut Grove Exhibition Hall	10,600
	Bayfront Park Auditorium	19,000
	Expo Center	5,000
	Municipal Auditorium	10,400
	Metrozoo Amphitheater	1,500
	Gusman Performing Arts Center	1,739
	Marine Stadium	6,500
	American Airlines Arena	19,000
	Miami Arena	15,200
Miami Beach	Convention Center	12,000
	Jackie Gleason Theater	2,716
Naples	Philharmonic Center	1,221
Orlando	Orange County Convention Center	11,072
	Convention Center Chapin Theater	2,643
	Expo Centre	1,300
	Bob Carr Performing Arts Center	2,518
	Univ. of Central Fla. Arena	10,000
	Amway Arena	17,248
Palmetto	Manatee Civic Center	4,000
Panama City	Marina Civic Center	2,900
Pensacola	Civic Center	10,268
	Saenger Theater	1,778
	Univ. of West Fla. Main Theater	450
Punta Gorda	Charlotte County Memorial	1,416
Rockledge	Brevard County Fair Stadium	8,000
St. Petersburg	Bayfront Center Mahaffey Theater	2,000
	Tropicana Field	50,000
Sarasota	Asolo Center for Performing Arts	503
	Civic Center Exhibition Hall	1,200
	Opera House	1,033
	Van Wezel Performing Arts Hall	1,761
Sunrise	Sunrise Music Theater	4,088

Tallahassee	Civic Center	14,000
	Fla. A&M Gaither Athletic Center	3,500
	Florida State Conference Center	1,100
Tampa	Univ. of South Florida Sun Dome	10,895
	Florida State Fair and Expo Center	12,000
	Florida State Fair Music Hall	4,500
	Straz Performing Arts Center	3,600
	Convention Center	11,100
	St. Pete Times Forum	19,510
	Fairgrounds Amphitheater	19,500
West Palm Beach	WPB Auditorium	2,119
	Kravis Center for Performing Arts	2,200
	WPB Municipal Arena	7,056
	Cruzan Amphitheater	19,000

MISS FLORIDA WINNERS
(Miss America Contest)

The annual Miss Florida pageant dates back to the 1930s when it was held at Miami Beach and sponsored by the Miami Beach Jaycees. In later years the pageant, sponsored by the Florida Jaycees, was held in Orlando in 1947, in Marineland in 1948, and in Jacksonville from 1949 to 1953. In 1954 and 1955, sponsorship was taken over by the Florida Citrus Exposition and the pageant held in Winter Haven. Sarasota became the pageant site in 1956, where it remained through 1968, first under the sponsorship of Sunshine Springs and Gardens and then by the Sarasota County Chamber of Commerce. Beginning in 1969, it was staged in Orlando and sponsored by the Miss Florida Pageant of Orlando. It moved to St. Petersburg in 2003. The pageant is headquartered in Miami.

Following are the pageant winners and the city, county, or university they represented in the competition. Miss Florida 1992, Leanza Cornett, went on to win the 1993 Miss America Pageant. Miss Florida 2003, Ericka Dunlap, was Miss American 2004.

1935—Elizabeth Hull, Plant City
1936—Not held
1937—Not held
1938—Mary Joyce Walsh, Miami
1939—Rose Marie Magrill, Miami
1940—Not held
1941—Mitzi Strother, Miami
1942—Eileen Irma Knapp, Miami
1943—Muriel Elizabeth Smith, Miami
1944—Virginia Warlen, Miami
1945—Virginia Freeland, Miami
1946—Jacquelyn Jennings, Miami
1947—Eula Ann McGehee, St. Petersburg
1948—Rosemary Carpenter, Miami
1949—Shirley Ann Rhodes, Tampa
1950—Janet Ruth Crockett, St. Petersburg
1951—Mary Godwin, Gainesville
1952—Marcia Crane, Orlando

1953—Marjorie Simmons, Tampa
1954—Ann Gloria Daniel, Dade City
1955—Sandra Wirth, Miami
1956—Sally Fisher, Miami
1957—Dorothy Steiner, Boca Raton
1958—Dianne Tauscheer, Orlando
1959—Nancy Rae Purvis, Manatee County
1960—Kathy Magda, Fort Lauderdale
1961—Sherry Grimes, Sarasota
1962—Gloria Brody, Jacksonville
1963—Flora Jo Chandonnet, Miami
1964—Priscilla Schnarr, Hollywood
1965—Carol Blum, Fort Lauderdale
1966—Diane Colston, Sarasota (Christine Torgeson, Manatee County, named to title when Colston resigned)
1967—Dawn Cashwell, Pensacola
1968—Linda Fitts, Panama City
1969—Lynee Edea Topping, Dade County
1970—Lisa Louise Donovan, Sarasota
1971—Barbara Jo Ivey, Winter Park
1972—Suzanne Charles, Miami
1973—Ellen Meade, Manatee County
1974—Delta Burke, Orlando
1975—Ann Schmalzried, Univ. of Florida
1976—Nancy Stafford, Fort Lauderdale
1977—Cathy LaBelle, Tampa
1978—Caroline Cline, Tampa (resigned, title filled by runner-up Wendy Sue Cheatham, Lee County)
1979—Marti Sue Phillips, Manatee County
1980—Caroline Dungan, Manatee County
1981—Dean Herman, Jacksonville
1982—Deanne Pitman, Sanford
1983—Kimberly Boyce, Manatee County

1984—Lisa Valdez, Manatee County
1985—Monica Farrell, Jacksonville University
1986—Molly Pesce, Seminole County
1987—Jennifer Anne Sauder, Homestead
1988—Melissa Aggeles, Manatee County
1989—Sandra Frick, Coral Springs
1990—Dana Dalton, Orlando
1991—Mary Ann Olson, Manatee County
1992—Leanza Cornett, Winter Park (Melinda Miller, Altamonte Springs, named to title when Cornett became Miss America)
1993—Nicole Padgett, Tampa
1994—Magan Elizabeth Welch, Mt. Dora
1995—Kristen Alicia Beall Ludecke, Central Florida
1996—Jamie Bolding, Mount Dora
1997—Christy Neuman, University of North Florida
1998—Lissette Gonzalez, Miami
1999—Kelli Meierhenry, University of Central Florida
2000—Candace Rodatz, First Coast
2001—Kelly Gaudet, Largo
2002—Katherine Carson, Largo
2003—Ericka Dunlap, City Beautiful (Shauna Pender, St. Petersburg, named to title when Dunlap became Miss America)
2004—Jenna Edwards, Winter Park
2005—Candance Cragg, Jacksonville (Mari Wilensky, University of Florida, named to title when Cragg resigned)
2006—Allison Kreiger, Miami
2007—Kylie Williams, Tallahassee
2008—Sierra Minott, Palm Beach County
2009—Rachael Todd, Suncoast
2010—Jaclyn Raulerson, Largo

STATE OF THE ARTS

Florida has more than 300 museums and galleries, 80 dance companies, 250 theater companies, and scores of symphony orchestras. In all, the arts organizations in the state employ more than 88,000 and generate $3.1 billion in revenues annually.

ADULTHOOD

In 1973 Florida lowered the legal age from 21 to 18. As a result, 18-year-olds now are permitted to apply for jobs as policemen and firemen, drive city buses, and be notary publics and bondsmen; they can also gamble, purchase a shotgun or rifle, enter into contracts, obtain credit, purchase automobiles, and get married. An 18-year-old also can vote, be called for jury duty, run for city or county office, and be sued. A person still must be 21 years old, however, to purchase a handgun and to run for the legislature. Drinking age in Florida also is 21.

COMMON-LAW MARRIAGES

The legitimacy of new common-law marriages was abolished in Florida in 1968. Only those live-in arrangements or common-law marriages that began prior to 1968 are recognized and require a divorce to end.

MAIDEN NAME

Florida does not require a married woman to take her husband's name. A court in 1976 stated that although it is general custom for a woman to change her name upon marriage, law does not compel her to. Early records show husband and wife often were known by different names, according to the court. Mere recitation of marriage vows, stated the court, does not legally change a woman's name.

MILLIONAIRES

Florida has the second-largest number of millionaires in the nation, with 199,000. It trails only California. The state's millionaires are concentrated in the Vero Beach area on the east coast and from Bradenton through Naples on the west coast.

AGRICULTURE

Next to tourism, agriculture is Florida's primary economic resource. Each year, Florida is often the nation's top producer of citrus, sugarcane, tomatoes, foliage, honey, and strawberries. Other Florida commodities often in the top 10 nationally are eggs, peanuts, beef cattle, tobacco, potatoes, and broilers. Florida produces all of the nation's commercially grown limes and mangos.

CITRUS INDUSTRY

The citrus tree is a native of the Orient, from which it was carried by man ever westward, to India, to the Mediterranean, and then across the Atlantic Ocean. It is believed to have been first brought to the Americas by Columbus. He brought citrus seeds that were planted on the island of Haiti.

The first seeds planted on the mainland of the Americas were brought by the expedition of Juan de Grijalva when he landed in Central America in mid-July 1518. Exact date of the citrus tree's introduction into Florida is not known, but from a statement made by Pedro Menendez, dated April 2, 1579, it appears citrus fruits were growing in abundance around St. Augustine at that time. Early settlers in Florida some two centuries later found wild citrus trees scattered over the state. One of the oldest cultivated groves planted in Florida is thought to be the Don Phillipe grove in Pinellas County, planted in 1833. It is believed that Duncan grapefruit originated in this grove. The site now is Phillipe Park near Safety Harbor.

Citrus production in Florida had soared to an all-time high of more than five million boxes when the Great Freeze of 1894-95 almost totally wiped out the citrus industry. It was not until 1909-10 that this level was again reached. Since that time the volume steadily increased and by the mid-1940s Florida was producing more than half the nation's citrus fruit supply.

Florida surpassed all other states in bearing citrus acreage in 1932-33 with 265,400 acres, which accounted for 46 percent of the U.S. total bearing acreage. As the decade of the 1970s began, Florida's dominance of the nation's citrus production became even more apparent and in 1980-81 the Sunshine State was producing 61.9 percent of the nation's supply.

Severe freezes in 1983 and 1985 seriously hurt Florida's citrus industry. The effects showed up in a 15 percent reduction in the number of citrus farms to 8,121 in 1987, from 9,588 in 1982. Groves also were severely harmed in 1984 and 1985 when many growers were ordered to burn their trees because of an outbreak of citrus canker disease. Some large growers, economically hurt by the dual scourges, did not replant. Others, to avoid the freezes of north and central Florida, have replanted farther south in counties such as Hendry, Lee, and Collier. Despite the decade's adversities, Florida in the 1989-90 season produced 62.7 percent of the nation's citrus.

After the tree-killing freezes in the 1980s, growers replaced groves in central Florida with younger trees and planted more trees in south Florida, to take advantage of its warmer climate. But it was too late for lemons and limes. Although still bountiful in backyards, commercial production has ceased. With no comparable freezes since, production rates rose to record highs, but in this century citrus faced new catastrophes. Canker came to the groves, killing trees. An eradication program made headway until the 2004 and 2005 hurricane seasons. Those storms destroyed an average of 15 percent of the citrus and other crops. Hurricanes also spread canker throughout the groves, nullifying all eradication efforts. Groves not infected with canker were hit by "greening," a devastating insect-borne disease. Topping the list of woes, healthy groves faced a severe labor shortage stemming from Florida's booming economy and from uncertainty caused by the ongoing national immigration debate. Fruit was left on the trees.

The newest major problem for the citrus industry is a result of the economy. More than 10,000 acres of citrus have been abandoned in recent years by developers who bought up the properties during better times. The neglected groves are helping to spread disease and decline, especially those adjacent to tended groves.

Despite all the problems, Florida still produced 80 percent of the nation's crop, led the world in grapefruit production, and produced oranges second in volume only to Brazil. Ninety percent of Florida citrus goes into juice.

Significant Modern Freezes
December 12-13, 1957
December 11, 13-16, 1962
January 19-21, 1971
January 17-22, 1977
January 12-13, 1981
January 11-14, 1982
December 24-25, 1983
January 21-22, 1985
December 23-24, 1989

Major Citrus Varieties
AVON LEMON is a most popular lemon of all around use. It is of good quality in fresh fruit form, and of superior quality for processing.

DANCY TANGERINE is the smallest and best known of the Mandarin tangerine group. It has a high color, and peels and sections smoothly. Used for out-of-hand eating, fruit cups, salads, and concentrates, the Dancy is in season from November to March.

DUNCAN GRAPEFRUIT is considered superior in flavor to other grapefruits. It is generally large with a thick, pale yellow skin, contains some seeds, and its flesh is white. With a season from September to May, the Duncan is used for halves, sections, juice, fruit cups, salads, and concentrates.

HAMLIN ORANGE is an early season orange, maturing between October and December. It is medium size, oval shaped, has a slightly thin skin and few seeds, and is used primarily as fresh fruit. It is also excellent for juice and concentrate.

KEY LIME is grown principally in the Florida Keys and along the Gulf coast. It is a seedy, small-sized fruit colored light green to yellow and ripens year around. Use is limited mainly to Key Lime pies, a south Florida specialty.

KUMQUAT is a small, orange-like fruit three-quarters to an inch in size with a spicy sweet rind and tart flesh. It is used widely for decorative purposes, but is often eaten whole, and used in marmalade, jellies, and candies.

MARSH SEEDLESS GRAPEFRUIT is a medium to large fruit, usually flattened at each end. Its skin is thin, smooth, and yellow. The flesh is white and nearly seedless. Used for halves, juice, sections, fruit cups, salads, and concentrates, it ripens between October and June.

MEYER LEMON is rated the best looking of the lemon family. Not a true lemon, it is a hybrid of orange and grapefruit, has an oval grapefruit shape, and a slight grapefruit flavor with an orange texture. The skin is smooth and thin, with an orange tinge and a high juice content. The Meyer is popular with home gardeners because of its showiness and dependability.

PERSIAN LIME is larger than the Key lime. It is oval-shaped, seedless, has a smooth, dark green skin and pale green pulp, and yields abundant acid juice of excellent flavor. It accounts for most of the state's lime production. It also is called the Tahiti lime.

RUBY RED GRAPEFRUIT, a variation of the Marsh seedless with outstanding flavor, has become a consumer favorite and is the prevailing colored variety in Florida, accounting for 60 percent of all grapefruit production in the state. Its yellow rind distinguishes itself with a red blush. It has a deep-red flesh that fades to pink with maturity.

TANGELO is a tangerine-grapefruit hybrid. It resembles an orange in appearance and a tangerine in flavor. Its skin is generally thin and either smooth or slightly bumpy. It is best for fresh fruit or out-of-hand eating.

TEMPLE ORANGE is a mid-season hybrid of sweet orange and tangerine, placing it in the tangor family. It peels easily and is generally regarded as an excellent eating orange, but it also is used for concentrates, juice, salads, and fruit cups.

THOMPSON PINK GRAPEFRUIT is a mutation of Marsh seedless and has a similar taste. Used for halves, sections, fruit cups, and salads, it is in season October to May.

VALENCIA ORANGE, the "juice orange," is the most widely planted orange in the world. Medium to large size, the Valencia matures late, from February to June, but may be kept on the tree several months during which it grows sweeter. The Valencia accounts for roughly half of the Florida orange crop. It is difficult to peel and section, and best used for concentrates, juice, sections, fruit cups, and salads.

WASHINGTON NAVEL ORANGE is an early season orange known as an eating orange because it peels and sections easily, and is generally seedless. It is characterized by a distinctive "navel" on the blossom end.

Citrus Acreage by County, 2009

County	Acres	County	Acres
Brevard	3,622	Glades	9,040
Charlotte	12,098	Hardee	47,130
Citrus	139	Hendry	66,821
Collier	31,247	Hernando	971
DeSoto	62,304	Highlands	62,443

County	Acres	County	Acres
Hillsborough	10,946	Palm Beach	1,013
Indian River	38,377	Pasco	7,615
Lake	12,884	Polk	82,629
Lee	10,477	Putnam	203
Manatee	18,609	St. Lucie	45,800
Marion	1,183	Sarasota	1,411
Martin	18,999	Seminole	482
Okeechobee	7,930	Volusia	1,065
Orange	3,618	Other counties	44
Osceola	9,718	State Total	568,814

Citrus Acreage, 1966-2008

Census Year	Oranges	Grapefruit	Specialty Fruit	Total Acres
1966	673,086	103,224	81,772	858,082
1968	713,400	119,883	97,966	931,249
1970	715,806	124,050	101,615	941,471
1972	659,418	124,142	94,459	878,019
1974	642,431	130,326	91,341	864,098
1976	628,567	137,909	85,893	852,369
1978	616,020	136,342	78,873	831,235
1980	627,174	139,994	78,165	845,333
1982	636,864	139,939	71,053	847,856
1984	573,991	134,680	52,694	761,365
1986	466,252	117,845	40,395	624,492
1988	536,737	119,606	41,586	697,929
1990	564,809	125,300	42,658	732,767
1992	608,636	135,166	47,488	791,290
1994	653,370	146,915	54,407	854,692
1996	656,598	144,416	56,847	857,861
1998	658,529	132,817	54,053	845,260
2000	665,529	118,145	48,601	832,275
2002	648,806	105,488	43,009	797,303
2004	622,821	89,048	36,686	748,555
2006	529,241	63,419	28,713	621,373
2008	496,518	56,881	23,178	576,577

FLORIDA ORANGE PRODUCTION
(in millions of boxes)

2009-10	133.6
2008-09	162.4
2007-08	170.2
2006-07	129
2005-06	147.9
2004-05	169.1
2003-04	246
2002-03	204
2001-02	230
2000-01	223.3
1999-2000	233
1998-99	186
1997-98	244
1996-97	266.2
1995-96	203.3
1994-95	205.5
1993-94	174.4
1992-93	186.6
1991-92	139.8
1990-91	151.6
1989-90	110.2
1988-99	146.6

WHEN TO PICK FLORIDA CITRUS

In the land of backyard fruit trees, fruit often rots on the trees not from disinterest but from confusion about when it should be picked.

Grapefruit: white and pink, can be picked when it appears ripe anytime except July and August.

Red Navel Oranges: October, November, and December.

Ambersweet Oranges: September through January.

Hamlin Oranges: October, November, and December.

Navel Oranges: October through January.

Pineapple Oranges: October through February.

Valencia Oranges (the juice orange): February through June.

Temple Oranges: January, February, and March.

Sunburst and Fallglow Tangerines: October, November, and December.

Robinson Tangerines: September, October, and November.

Royal Lee Tangerines: November and December.

Dancy Tangerines: December and January.

Honey Tangerines: January through April.

Nova Tangelos: October and November.

Orlando Tangelos: November, December, and January.

Mineola Tangelos: January and February.

SELECTED FRUIT SPECIES

Besides a variety of citrus, Florida offers a delicious selection of other fruits not common to most of the U.S. Among them are

AVOCADO was a dinner treat for the explorer Cortez when he feasted with Montezuma II in the early 1500s. Indians in Central America have eaten avocados for centuries, but the fruit first came to this country in 1833 when Henry Perrine brought some trees from Mexico and planted them just south of Miami. By 1880 the fruit was being grown commercially. The avocado matures at different times in different sites in Florida, but is most plentiful between January and July. Those trees that bear well usually come from a seedling to which good varieties have been grafted. Avocados are loaded with calories, a tiny piece of just four ounces containing nearly 300. And, except for the ripe olive, an avocado has more oil than any other fruit. It also contains much protein, but little sugar. Avocados come round, oval, and elongated. Growers divide them into three "races"—the thin-skinned Mexican, the West Indian (Florida's commercial crop), and the hardy Guatemalan fruit.

BANANAS are not grown commercially in Florida to any extent. The varieties often seen in the state, usually in backyards, are the Lady Finger or Hart, which bears a small fruit four to six inches long weighing about two ounces; the Cavendish of Chinese origin, a dwarf-type tree that grows to about five to seven feet in height; and the Horse or Hog banana, often grown as an ornamental planting. It takes 12 to 18 months for a banana plant to bear fruit. A medium-sized banana has about 90 calories.

BARBADOS CHERRY is a soft, juicy fruit that grows to about one inch in diameter, is deep red in color, and usually sprouts in clusters of two or three. The plants are dense and spreading and can grow as tall as 12 feet when not trimmed. In south Florida the tiny cherry flowers, usually pale pink or rose, blossom in April; the fruit begins to ripen in early May. Barbadoes cherries can be tart or sweet, and are quite perishable. The cherries have a higher acid content than other fruits; just one berry provides a daily ration of Vitamin C.

CALAMONDIN is a relative of the citrus and looks like a tiny orange or tangerine. Because the fruit is so sour it often is used as a substitute for limes or lemons. The calamondin tree is relatively small but bears volumes of fruit, each usually less than an inch in diameter. Florida newcomers often confuse the kumquat with the calamondin because both are used mainly as ornamental trees. The calamondin tree blossoms most of the summer, with the green fruit turning to a ripening orange color in fall. The fruit is ready for picking in winter.

CARAMBOLA, an exotic-looking fruit introduced a century ago from Asia, is quite tropical and easily killed by freezing temperatures. The egg-shaped, slightly translucent fruit is yellow and is distinguished by its five definitive exterior ribs and its star-shaped interior. It has a shiny, waxy look when ripe. The flesh is crisp and juicy and may be sweet or acid. The carambola is best eaten fresh. It begins to ripen in September and continues to produce and ripen through March.

CARISSA, seen mainly as a hedge, actually produces a dark fruit that matures in the summer and grows to two inches in diameter. The skin is thin and the juice white and fairly gummy. With the seeds removed, carissa is used in salads and sauces or can be eaten off the bush. Carissa makes a tight hedge because its shrubs have strong, two-pointed thorns. Its small white flower is wonderfully fragrant.

CEYLON GOOSEBERRY is an attractive shrub that can be grown farther north in Florida than most tropical trees, and its fruit is excellent for salads, jellies, and preserves. The plants are easy to grow. Its fruit is round, about an inch in diameter, and turns to maroon-purple when ripe. The berry's flesh is acidic and juicy with soft, flat seeds.

CITRON is a tree that looks much like an overgrown lemon tree. The fruit's skin is quite thick and resembles a lemon. It is often preserved and used in candies or cakes. Citron pulp has only a tiny amount of juice.

COCONUTS, grown on trees primarily in south Florida, have been fighting a losing battle with blight for more than two decades. To the shopper, the best coconuts are heavy, with milk sloshing around inside. Without milk, the coconut is spoiled. Moldy eyes also are undesirable. Caution is advised in eating coconuts off trees in Florida because many of the trees, to save them from blight, are being injected with antibiotics and insecticides.

CUSTARD APPLE has never been popular for the dinner table, but deserves mention because it is grown so abundantly in south Florida. The fruit also is called the Jamaica Apple or Bullock's Heart. Almost smooth on the surface and reddish brown when ripe, the fruit grows to weigh a pound when mature. It tapers from a rather flat top side, where it is attached to the twig, to more of a point at the bottom. It is sometimes mistaken for the Cherimoya, well known in Cuba. The custard apple fruit has little dietary significance; its flavor may seem quite insipid and sweet.

FIG is a small brownish to yellow fruit grown in many backyards. From June until September, when a fig tree begins to shed leaves, its fruit is plentiful. Ripe figs are quite soft and perishable and when overripe give off a fermented smell. The fruit needs no flavoring and is best eaten when freshly picked. Beware, however, for figs are slightly laxative. The trees like warm weather best, but will grow in protected areas farther north.

GRAPES are grown in most areas of the state, regardless of the soil, the temperature, or the rainfall. In recent years they have been the basis for a growing wine industry in the state. Numerous varieties are grown. Muscadine hybrids are popular in central Florida. The Scuppernong, an old favorite, gives forth a bronze fruit with delicious, musky-flavored juice and pulp. Many growers rate its flavor unexcelled. The wild grape is usually black with thick skin and heavy flesh but little juice, and makes a popular wild grape jelly.

GUAVA trees are small and spreading, appearing more like shrubs. Native to the Caribbean, guava trees are related to the custard apple, but there the comparison ends, for unlike custard apple, the guava is desired and served in many ways. The flavor ranges from strawberry through lemon to tropical. And, when ripe, it is quite aromatic. Guava fruit varies from one to four inches in diameter, its flesh ranging from white to pink to light red. Once ripe, it should be refrigerated. The fruit is used as a paste, marmalade, or sauce and can be eaten directly off the tree. Guava is high in potassium and vitamins A and C. Ironically, while guava is a favorite with backyard gardeners and is grown commercially in Florida, the state also considers it an invasive pest. Nurseries follow a voluntary ban on the sale of guava trees.

JACKFRUIT is quite large, often weighing from 10 to 40 pounds.

Because the tree itself grows large, it is often used as an ornamental. Jackfruit is ripe in south Florida in July and August. The fruit is oblong and many grow to two feet in length. Its skin is rough to the touch. Inside, the flesh is soft, juicy, and yellow when ripe, and can be eaten fresh or preserved. The seeds are sometimes roasted and eaten.

JAMBOLAN PLUM ripens from May through July, its deep purple-maroon fruit making a delicious jelly. Its tartness demands plenty of sugar. The fruit is slightly curved and grows to about one inch in length.

LOQUAT is a garden-gate variety tree that reaches 20 feet in height. Its thick foliage springs white, fragrant flowers. Sometimes the tree is grown for the flower rather than the fruit. Loquat fruit is round or oval and one to three inches long. It is pale orange to yellow with large seeds. The rather acidic flavor reminds one of a cherry. Its skin is thin, the flesh firm and somewhat meaty. The fruit ripens early in the winter, but a second flowering may occur in spring. Loquats, like kumquats, can be preserved whole or can be made into jams and preserves.

LYCHEE NUT has an origin buried in antiquity. Even its name is spelled several different ways. In any case, a lychee nut, resembling a strawberry in its fresh form, is a taste treat. Some say its flavor is like a grape, others liken it to a raisin. The outside of the lychee nut is rough and scale-like, but peels easily. Lychee trees grow to 40 feet or more in height, with dense, shiny leaves.

MACADAMIA NUTS, also called the Queensland Nut, is grown in modest numbers in Florida. The tree often reaches 30 feet in height and produces shiny green leaves that look like holly. The fruit is a round brown seed that contains the edible white kernel or nut.

MANGO is the apple of the tropics and one of the world's finest fruits. It is an import from Asia that bears fruit from May to October. The tree itself grows quite large, with attractive green, leathery leaves. Mangoes may weigh up to four pounds. They can be apple-shaped, round or oblong, and the color may be green, yellow, or a subdued red. Some say mangoes have the scent of turpentine, and some mangoes do, but the Haden, the most popular variety, does not. Mangoes can be peeled and sliced, or eaten like peaches. For first-timers, however, caution is advised—some people break out in a rash after touching or eating this rich fruit.

MONSTERA DELICIOSA is a vine-like shrub, also called Ceriman, and has huge split leaves with aerial roots. Its flower looks like a calla lily and an ear of corn combined. From summer to early fall, at least a year after blooming, the fruit turns to soft pulp. The scaly peel comes off easily, and the fruit has a delicate pineapple-banana smell and taste. But beware, for the pulp can burn the mouth with its crystals.

PAPAYAS are a football-shaped fruit, green or yellow in color, and emit a pungent smell that is welcomed by some and rejected by others. Papaya's skin is smooth and thin; its fruit can be cubed, chilled and sweetened, or left unsweetened and eaten like a melon. Papaya has an enzyme called papain that breaks down protein; it is used to tenderize meats and is believed to aid digestion. The fruit mixes well in salads and, when green, makes an excellent pie. The juice is used in face creams, teas, and syrups. Do not confuse papayas with paw paws, which are grown in colder climates.

PECANS are a sizable commercial crop in Florida, mostly grown in north Florida. The nuts mature in the fall and are in much demand during the holiday season.

PINEAPPLE plantations used to be plentiful in the Keys generations ago, and today some remain in the Miami and Fort Pierce areas. Short-stemmed, the plants grow to only two or three feet in height. Leaves are long, thin, and sharp-pointed with rough edges. Purplish flowers grow separately at the plant's top but together near its base, where they form the fruit.

PERSIMMON comes in both a native variety common in Florida and also in a cultivated Japanese variety. The Japanese type is about three inches long, longer than the native variety, has a yellow skin that turns reddish as it ripens, and is best eaten fresh.

POMEGRANATE is found throughout Florida, grows on bushes 15 to 20 feet high, and produces a fruit the size of an orange. Its smooth leather skin is yellow or red. Inside, several "cells" contain small grains of juicy red pulp, but it is the sweet seeds that are generally eaten. It is used for drinks, jellies, and marmalades.

SAPODILLA is a handsome evergreen tree that yields a white latex from which chicle, the base of chewing gum, is made. The fruit grows to about four inches in diameter with a harsh, brown skin. When ripe, it can be used as a dessert fruit.

SAPOTE is not a well-known tree because it grows only in the southern sector of Florida, and because its fruit yield is sparse. The fruit ripens in May, is yellowish, grows up to four inches in diameter, is shaped like a top, has a thin skin, a soft flesh, and can be sweet or bitter. It can be eaten fresh, and is used in ices and jellies.

SEA GRAPE is used more as an ornamental shrub than as a fruit-bearer. It provides attractive foliage and does furnish purple grape-like clusters of fruit. It is most commonly used to make jelly, or juice for fruit punch.

SOURSOP is a small tree with leathery, shiny leaves that is grown as a "dooryard" tree in south Florida. The large, heart-shaped fruit weighs up to four pounds. The fruit flesh is aromatic but has a cottony texture. Soursop sherbet is delicious.

STRAWBERRY, a major Florida crop, is grown mostly in the central part of the state, primarily near Plant City. Harvesting begins as early as January if the weather has been warm, but March is the major month for harvest. Newspapers in the area often run classified ads inviting residents to come to the fields and pick their own berries at a bargain rate. One innovation in recent years is the black plastic planting strip through which baby plants are pulled, thereby keeping the berries free of sand and ground rot to increase the yield. Another is growing the berries outdoors hydroponicly, vastly increasing yields per acre.

SURINAM CHERRY plants make excellent hedges, growing from three feet upward. Leaves are reddish when small, then turn green as they grow larger. A white flower means a cherry soon will form. The main crop comes in spring, its fruit ribbed and bright red. The flesh is juicy and soft, and has an unusual resin-like odor, which is unpleasant to some. Cherries can be eaten off the plant or used in salads, jellies, and sherbets.

TAMARIND is used as a shade tree in south Florida but bears a fruit pod about six inches long. When young, the pod is green and acidic; it is used at this stage for seasoning of fish and meats. Inside the outer brown shell a mature pod contains the pulp from which tamarindade is made.

VARIETIES OF WATERMELON

Watermelon lovers have an increasing variety of the fruit from which to choose in Florida, the nation's leading producer of watermelons. And new types come out almost annually as researchers strive to create a sweeter, more disease-resistant melon with fewer seeds.

Years ago the biggest seller was the Cannonball. But it was too susceptible to various field wilt diseases, prompting researchers to search for a more hardy yet equally popular replacement. After years of crossbreeding, they came up with the now familiar Charleston Gray. Developed in 1954 in South Carolina, the Charleston Gray has wilt-resistant qualities as well as excellent flavor.

A Kansas grower, noting the Charleston Gray's popularity, began experimenting with the melon, crossing it with other types of existing melons. The result was that in 1963 another winner was introduced, the Crimson Sweet.

That same year University of Florida researcher J. M. Crall borrowed from the Charleston Gray's qualities to create still a third popular seller today, the Jubilee.

Currently, the Charleston Gray, Crimson Sweet, and Jubilee account for about 75 percent of all retail sales. Experts believe the Crimson Sweet and Jubilee sell so well partly because they are both striped and people expect watermelons to be striped. The Charleston Gray has no stripes but makes up for this shortcoming by satisfying another consumer prejudice about watermelons: size. It is an oblong, unusually large melon that persuades shoppers that it offers a lot for the money.

A watermelon similar in size and shape to the popular Charleston Gray called the Charlee is showing up on fruit stands. It is the result of matings of the Charleston Gray with such lesser-known varieties as the Calhoun Gray and the Smokylee.

Also a newcomer is a spinoff of the popular Jubilee, called the Jubilee II. On the fruit stand it is hard to differentiate from the original Jubilee, but watermelon experts say the Jubilee II has better texture, a sweeter flavor, and a more attractive interior color.

Today's smaller American families, averaging two adults and one child, are creating a demand for smaller watermelons. This trend is being met by "icebox melons." Among the earliest of this smaller type is the Georgia-born Sugar Baby, and the New Hampshire Midget. So far, both have had limited sales. The Midget suffers from a rind so thin that pickers must wear soft gloves or risk puncturing the fruit. As for the Sugar Baby, its problem is it fast loses its quality and flavor between harvesting and marketing.

In 1986 Florida growers got their own icebox melons when Crall developed the Minilee and Mickeylee. Each weighs an average of seven to nine pounds, compared to the larger variety of melons that often tip the scales at 20 pounds or more. Neither the Minilee nor the Mickeylee is striped, but both are rated to be internally more red than other melons, and have smaller and fewer seeds.

Researchers have been flirting with a watermelon variety that has the sweetness and flavor of the best sellers but none of the seeds. In recent years a "Seedless Watermelon" has appeared on shelves, but it has had few takers. The industry refers to this seedless variety as Tri-X 313 and Tri-X 317, both tracing back to an experimental grower in Indiana. Samplers say the seedless offers excellent quality but at a high price.

Floridians moving from other regions of the country also may be familiar with numerous other varieties that are seldom seen in the Sunshine State, namely the Allsweet, Peacock, Yellow Flesh, Graybelle, Early Canada, Dixielee, and the Petite Sweet.

These varieties still may have their supporters, but Florida watermelons continue to dominate the national market. The state produces nearly 38 percent of all watermelons consumed in the U.S.

Florida growers also are quick to point out that the state's watermelons are a nutritious food. A 10-inch slice about one-inch thick is only 152 calories but supplies 77 percent of the daily recommended Vitamin C, 35 percent of the daily recommended Vitamin B-6, 26 percent of the daily requirement of thiamine, and 560 milligrams of potassium.

PRINCIPAL VEGETABLES BY PRODUCING AREAS

1. **West**
   Escambia County: Potatoes.
   Holmes, Jackson, Washington counties: Butter beans, field peas, watermelons.
   Gadsden County: Pole beans, squash, sweet corn, tomatoes.
2. **North**
   Starke, Brooker, Lake Butler areas: Lima beans, snap beans, cucumbers, green peppers, squash, strawberries.
   Hastings area: Cabbage, potatoes.
   Gainesville, Alachua area: Bush beans, cucumbers, peppers, potatoes, squash.

Island Grove, Hawthorne areas: Cucumbers, peppers, sweet corn, squash, watermelons.
3. **North Central**
   Oxford, Pedro areas: Tomatoes, watermelons.
   Sanford, Oviedo, Zellwood areas: Cabbage, carrots, celery, sweet corn, cucumbers, escarole, greens, lettuce, peppers, radishes, spinach.
   Webster area: Cucumbers, eggplant, peppers.
4. **West Central**
   Plant City, Balm areas: Bush and pole beans, lima beans, cabbage, cucumbers, eggplant, field peas, greens, squash, strawberries, watermelons.

Palmetto, Ruskin areas:
Cabbage, cauliflower, potatoes, strawberries, tomatoes, watermelons.
Sarasota area: Cabbage, celery, sweet corn, escarole, lettuce, radishes.
Wauchula area: Cucumbers, eggplant, peppers, tomatoes, watermelons.

5. **East Central**
Fort Pierce area: Tomatoes, watermelons.

6. **Southwest**
Fort Myers, Immokalee areas: Sweet corn, cucumbers, eggplant, peppers, potatoes, squash, tomatoes, watermelons.

7. **Everglades**
Bush beans, cabbage, celery, Chinese cabbage, sweet corn, escarole, greens, lettuce, potatoes, radishes.

8. **Southeast**
Martin County: Cabbage, potatoes, tomatoes, watermelons.
Pompano Beach area: Bush beans, lima beans, sweet corn, cucumbers, eggplant, peppers, squash, tomatoes.
Homestead area: Bush and pole beans, cabbage, sweet corn, cucumbers, potatoes, squash, strawberries, tomatoes.

HOME VEGETABLE PLANTING GUIDE

Vegetable	North	Central	South
Beans, Snap	Mar-Apr, Aug-Sep	Feb-Mar	Sep-Mar
Beans, Pole	Mar-May	Feb-Apr	Jan-Feb September
Beans, Lima	Mar-Apr	Mar-May	Sep-Mar
Beets	Sep-Mar	Oct-Mar	Oct-Feb
Broccoli	Aug-Sep	Aug-Sep	Sep-Oct
	*Nov-Feb	*Nov-Feb	*Dec-Jan
Cabbage	Aug-Sep	Aug-Sep	Sep-Oct
	*Nov-Feb	*Nov-Feb	*Dec-Jan
Cabbage, Chinese	Oct-Feb	Oct-Feb	Nov-Jan
Carrots	Sep-Mar	Oct-Mar	Oct-Feb
Chard	Sep-Mar	Oct-Apr	Oct-Apr
Collards	Aug-Feb	Sep-Feb	Sep-Jan
Corn, sweet	Mar-Apr	Feb-Mar	Jan-Mar
Cowpeas	Mar-May	Mar-May	Feb-May
Eggplant	*March	*March	*Sep-Feb
Endive	Sep-Feb	Sep-Feb	Sep-Jan
Lettuce	Sep-Oct	Sep-Feb	Sep-Feb
	Feb-Mar		
Melon	Mar-Apr	Feb-Mar	Feb-Mar
Okra	Mar-June	Mar-Aug	Feb-Oct
Onions, green	*Aug-Apr	*Aug-Mar	*Sep-Mar

Peas	Jan-Mar	Sep-Feb	Sep-Feb
Pepper	*March	*Feb	*Oct-Feb
Radish	Oct-Mar	Oct-Mar	Oct-Mar
Spinach	Oct-Feb	Oct-Feb	Nov-Jan
Squash	Mar-Apr	Aug-Sep	Sep-Mar
	September	Feb-Mar	
Tomato	*Mar-Apr	*Jan-Feb	*Aug-Mar
	August	*Aug-Sep	
Turnip	Aug-May	Sep-Feb	Oct-Feb

Transplants or sets

RECORD-SIZED VEGETABLES
(Records kept by Institute of Food and Agricultural Sciences)

Vegetable (variety)	Size	County
Bean, lima (pod)	9.5 in.	St. Lucie
Beet (Detroit red)	8 lb. 1 oz.	Duval
Boniata	12 lb. 10 oz.	Seminole
Broccoli	5 lb. 4 oz.	Suwannee
Cabbage (early round Dutch)	20 lb. 9 oz.	St. Johns
Cantaloupe	35 lb. 3 oz.	Manatee
Carrot (Chantenay)	3 lb. 1 oz.	Pinellas
Cassava	15 lb. 4 oz.	Palm Beach
Cauliflower	15 lb. 6 oz.	Alachua
Chicory (Magdeburg)	1 lb. 3 oz.	Alachua
Collard (Georgia)	13 ft. 3 in.	Leon
Corn, sweet (Skyscraper)	3 lb.	Suwannee
Cucumber (weight) (Burpless)	4 lb. 7 oz.	Suwannee
Cucumber (length)	2 ft. 3 in.	Suwannee
Cucumber (Armenian Japanese)	2 ft. 6 in.	Escambia
Eggplant (Black beauty)	4 lb. 8 oz.	Palm Beach
Garlic (Elephant)	1 lb. 8 oz.	St. Johns
Gourd (Fields common)	3 lb. 7 oz.	Suwannee
Gourd (cucuzzi)	5 ft. 1.5 in.	Hernando
Honeydew (Tam-dew)	11 lb. 2 oz.	Escambia
Jicama	21 lb. 8 oz.	Palm Beach
Kohlrabi	19 lb. 8 oz.	Duval

Lettuce (Grand Rapids)	3 lb. 10 oz.	Suwannee
Malanga	29 lb. 15 oz.	Palm Beach
Melon, (winter)	80 lb. 13 oz.	Palm Beach
Mustard (Florida broadleaf)	20 lb. 4 oz.	Palm Beach
Okra (pod) (weight)	8 oz.	Suwannee
Okra (pod) (length)	22.25 in.	Suwannee
Okra plant stalk (La. Green Velvet)	19 ft. 10.5 in.	Flagler
Onion (Grano)	3 lb. 11 oz.	Manatee
Pepper (experimental)	1 lb. 3.8 oz.	Palm Beach
Potato (Frito 92)	2 lb. 13 oz.	St. Johns
Potato (sweet)	44 lb. 2 oz.	Palm Beach
Pumpkin (Atlantic giant)	610 lb.	Manatee
Radish, summer (red summer)	5 lb. 2 oz.	Palm Beach
Radish, winter	25 lb.	Hillsborough
Radish, daikon	23 lb. 5 oz.	Alachua
Rutabaga	34 lb. 3 oz.	Santa Rosa
Squash (banana)	47 lb.	Putnam
Squash (butternut)	23 lb. 12 oz.	Santa Rosa
Squash (calabaza LaPrima)	36 lb., 8 oz.	Seminole
Squash, Hubbard	131 lb. 12 oz.	Santa Rosa
Squash, (scal)	3 lb. 12 oz.	Nassau
Squash, (spaghetti)	47 lb. 9 oz.	Duval
Squash, (summer)	6 lb. 2 oz.	Escambia
Squash, zucchini (Parks black)	14 lb. 10 oz.	Nassau
Squash, zucchini hybrid	16 lb. 6 oz.	Marion
Taro	8 oz.	Palm Beach
Tomato (Brandywine Red)	3 lb. 4.3 oz.	Palm Beach
Turnip	21 lb. 11 oz.	Santa Rosa
Watermelon (Carolina cross)	205 lb.	Levy
Yam (True)	12 lb. 15 oz.	Palm Beach
Yard-long bean	52 in.	Orange

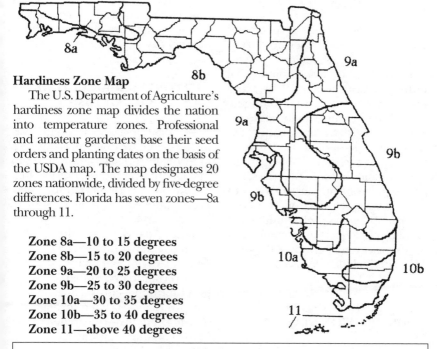

Hardiness Zone Map
    The U.S. Department of Agriculture's hardiness zone map divides the nation into temperature zones. Professional and amateur gardeners base their seed orders and planting dates on the basis of the USDA map. The map designates 20 zones nationwide, divided by five-degree differences. Florida has seven zones—8a through 11.

Zone 8a—10 to 15 degrees
Zone 8b—15 to 20 degrees
Zone 9a—20 to 25 degrees
Zone 9b—25 to 30 degrees
Zone 10a—30 to 35 degrees
Zone 10b—35 to 40 degrees
Zone 11—above 40 degrees

FERN CAPITAL

The leatherleaf fern is possibly the most important cut foliage crop in Florida. The ferns and leafy greens are used in floral arrangements, and no state produces more cut foliage. The industry of 600 growers is centered in Volusia County, primarily around the town of Pierson, but it has spread to nearby Lake, Orange, and Putnam counties. The area produces 83 percent of the world's ornamental ferns.

The plumosa fern was introduced into Volusia County in the late 1800s by a Massachusetts man named Pierson who had raised it in hothouses up north. He found that his indoor crop thrived outdoors in Florida. The plumosa fern was the exclusive fern crop in the area until the mid-1940s, when growers began to experiment with the leatherleaf fern. Today, leatherleaf accounts for approximately 95 percent of sales.

Leatherleaf and plumosa ferns are not to be confused with ferns such as Boston and maidenhair, which are used as potted plants or hanging baskets. Volusia County's products are used mostly as background material by florists.

Florida fern production has no defined peak season, the crop being grown and harvested year round. Harvesting is done by hand, and each field can be cut weekly with an average yield of 18 cases of cut, bunched ferns per acre. Because the plant is regenerative, each planting can last several years or more.

The greatest danger to the fern industry is development. The value of fern land has jumped from $3,000 to $30,000 per acre.

ADD FERTILIZER

Sandy Florida soils are poor and the wise gardener uses fertilizers. Organic fertilizers supply steady but slow nutrients. Commercial fertilizers are also available and provide a quicker boost of nitrogen, phosphorous, and potassium. In addition, gardens and landscapes need periodic applications of iron, zinc, magnesium, manganese, copper, and boron. Experts say a common problem, particularly with citrus trees, is a lack of iron. However, a growing number of counties are banning certain fertilizers completely or during certain periods of the year. The bans include sale and use.

AGRICULTURAL INSPECTION STATIONS

Florida has established 23 agricultural inspection stations along its many roads leading into and out of the state to help fight and control diseases and pests in vegetables and fruits. The inspection stations make an unbroken chain on every paved road across the Suwannee and St. Mary's rivers in north Florida. They are intended to make it impossible for a trucker or motorist to bring agricultural products into Florida, or to take them out, without the products being inspected. Numerous unpaved roads lead to both rivers that must be crossed when leaving the state, but none of the unpaved roads has a crossing bridge. The state, in concert with federal agricultural officials, in 1934 began building the Florida inspections stations to prevent inferior fruit, mainly citrus, from leaving the state for northern markets. All trucks and trailers are required to stop at the stations, which are open every hour of every day.

FLORIDA AGRICULTURE HALL OF FAME

In 1980 a Hall of Fame was established to recognize those individuals who have contributed to the agricultural industry of Florida. Nominees are submitted by their peers. Inductees have been

Alto Lee Adams, Jr.—cattle rancher, environmentalist
Tom Adams—Lieutenant Governor, dairy, timber
Karl Albritton—citrus leader
Richard Alger—farmer, leader
Cedric D. Atkins—researcher
Leroy Baldwin—cattleman
Richard Barber, Jr.—peanuts
Raymond B. Becker—researcher
Al Bellotto—cattle, citrus
Jack M. Berry—citrus
Faye and Victor Blackstone—rodeo, cattle
Bill Boardman—dariy, marketing
John B. Boy, Sr.—sugar cane industry leader
Irlo O. Bronson—cattleman
Neal Palmer ("Pal") Brooks— tropical fruit grower
Clarence L. Campbell, Jr.— veterinarian
Edward J. Campbell—agricultural innovator, conservationist
Bill and Trudy Carey—cattle, dairy
Doyle Carlton, Jr.—cattleman
Pete Clemons—cattle, Okeechobee Livestock Market
J. Francis Cooper—agricultural writer, broadcaster
William Pat Cockrell—educator, Farm Bureau executive

Tony J. Cunha, Jr.—educator
B. Edmund David, Jr.—cattle breeder, trade promoter
Dr. James M. Davidson—soil science
Roy Gene Davis—nursery
Snead Young Mathews Davis—cattle rancher
Paul B. Dickman—inventor grower
Paul J. DiMare—tomatoes
Andrew Duda, Jr.—marketing specialist
John Duda—farm and packing house machinery developer
Bernard A. Egan—citrus
Hugh English—citrus management, research
Willard M. Fifield—researcher, educator
Edwin H. Finlayson—farmer and county agent
John M. Fox—researcher
Henry Gatrell—swine rancher
William Graham—dairy cattle
J. R. "Rip" Graves—citrus
Albert Greenberg—Aquaculture founder
Barnette E. ("Barney") Greene, Jr.—cattle rancher, citrus grower
Ben Hill Griffin, Jr.—cattleman, processor
Ben Hill Griffin III—citrus
Dr. James Griffiths—citrus researcher, grower
Martin Copeland Griswold—cotton
Miles Edward Groover—4H and minority development
Peter S. Harlee—tomato industry leader
Robert H. Harms—poultry nutrition researcher
Bert J. Harris, Jr.—legislator
Wayne Hawkins—founder of modern agriculture cooperate exchange
Elton L. Hinton—educator
Rudy Hamrick—expert and county agent
Lena S. Hughes—researcher

Lillie "Belle" Jeffords—advocate
Ken F. Jorgensen—farmer
Arlen Jumper—citrus, turfgrass
Richard Kelly—education
William "Bill" H. Krome—tropical fruit grower
Julian B. Lane—dairyman
Louis E. Larson—dairyman
Thomas G. Lee—dairyman
Edna Pearce Lockett—cattle rancher, business and government leader
William Loften—educator
William D. "Billy" Long—harvesting
Buster Longino—cattle, citrus, forester, conservationist
Carl B. Loop, Jr.—nursery
Maxie D. Love, Jr.—farm finance
Charles P. Lykes—cattleman, meatpacking executive
Dr. Paul Lyrene—plant breeder, blueberry developer
Louis G. MacDowell—researcher
Elliott L. Maguire—forestry
Latimer "Latt" Maxey—citrus, cattle
Donald Fariss May—tobacco
Fountain H. May—nursery
Nathan Mayo—state Commissioner of Agriculture
James Neville McArthur—dairy
Dan McClure—tomato farmer, modernizer
Richard "Dick" Minton—citrus, fertilizer
Wayne Mixon, Governor—farmer
Fred Y. Montsdeoca—cattle, fertilizer
Edwin L. Moore—researcher
Robert N. "Bob" Morris—banker
John Mortensen—vegetable breeder
Julia Morton—botanist
Copeland Newbern—educator
Alan J. Norden—researcher
Joseph O'Farrell, Sr.—thoroughbred horse racing breeder
Raymond P. Oglesby—plant scientist

Joseph Orsenigo—research, plant pathology
Henry O. Partin—cattleman
J. O. Pearce, Jr.—cattle and livestock leader
Curtis Peterson—nurseryman, landscape architect
Robert G. Pitman, Jr.—agricultural tax expert
Hoyle Pounds—inventor
Edgar Price, Jr.—citrus executive
Dudley Adelbert Putnam—citrus, cattle
Egbert N. Reasoner—horticulturist
Pliny W. Reasoner—horticulturist
Herman J. Reitz—scientist, administrator, author
J. Wayne Reitz—educator
Kay Richardson—cattle
Martha Rhodes Roberts—food safety
Bert Edward Roper—citrus
Carl G. Rose—thoroughbred horse breeder
Anthony T. Rossi—inventor, citrus grower, marketer
Mabel Claprood Simmons—ornamental horticulture
Charles R. "Chuck" Smith—county agent, legislator
Jo Ann Doke Smith—management
George F. Sorn—labor expert
Mason Smoak—citrus, cattle manager
J. R. "Jack" Sprat—agriculture pioneer

Eric Stein—cattle, sugar
Don A. Storms, Sr.—educator
Dr. Alto Straughn—research, education, commercial farming
William H. Stuart, Sr.—cattle, citrus
Henry Swanson—horticulture
Kenneth D. Tefertiller—educator, researcher
Gilbert A. Tucker—cattleman
Raymon F. Tucker—horse breeder, cattle rancher
Latimer H. Turner—cattleman
Vance Vogel—tomato grower
Donald L. Wakeman—educator
John Powell Wallace—poultry farmer
Marshall Watkins—extension service director
James N. Watson—county agent, county fair co-founder
George H. Wedgeworth—vegetable and sugar producer
Ruth S. Wedgworth—agricultural innovator
James S. Wershow—educator, agricultural tax expert
Robert "Bob" Billingsley Whisenant—agriculture pioneer
Frank "Sonny" Williamson, Jr.—citrus, aquaculture
Ed and Imogene Yarborough—cattle, education
Stephen M. Yoder—farmer and rancher
E. T. York, Jr.—educator

CATTLE COUNTRY

Floridians are aware that their state is the fourth most populated in the nation, but few know that it is also the third largest cattle state east of the Mississippi River. Second only to the citrus and agricultural industry, ranching in Florida involves 1.7 million cattle.

The state's, and the nation's, largest cattle operation is the 300,000-acre Deseret Ranch, which spreads out over both Osceola and Brevard counties. It is owned by the Mormon church in Salt Lake City.

But large, privately owned spreads of pasture and rangeland are prevalent throughout the hinterland of central and south Florida. Places like Arcadia, Fort Meade, Kissimmee, Yeehaw Junction, and Okeechobee still are known to many residents as cow towns. In all, some 5 million acres of the state are devoted to raising cattle. Registered cattle brands in Florida number nearly 3,000.

The state's rangeland is largely grass and marshes, hammocks and brush. Thus, the acreage is best worked by cowboys on horseback, not by ranch-hands in four-wheel-drive vehicles as is done today in much of the West.

Historians say Florida got its start in cattle from the Spanish settlers, who brought with them a breed that today is called the Florida Cracker. For 400 years this scrawny but tough animal was the only breed that could survive the heat, bugs, and parasites of subtropical Florida.

Cousins to the Texas Longhorn, Florida Cracker cattle are now nearly extinct. But some ranchers, with the aid of the Florida Department of Agriculture and the Florida Cracker Cattle Association, are determined to revive the breed in large numbers.

Florida Crackers usually are small and lean. They come in every color and pattern, and sport long, threatening horns. Their supporters say the timing is excellent to revive the breed because Florida Crackers produce a lean type of beef, a desirable quality in today's fat-conscious society.

Most credited with saving the state's cattle industry, however, is an imported breed, the Brahma. Brought from India via Texas, Brahmas have proven most resistant to Florida's heat and disease. Since their introduction, they have been crossed with the Angus to produce the Brangus, with the Charolais to produce the Charbrays, and with the Herefords to produce the Brafords, all of which flourish on Florida's tough rangeland.

Because Florida lacks feed grain production, state ranchers sell and ship about three-quarters of a million calves each fall to western states such as Colorado, Texas, Oklahoma, and Arizona.

Rustling was, and still is, a problem in Florida. The Florida Department of Law Enforcement uses four undercover agents to chase down cattle thieves.

EXOTIC PEST PLANTS

An estimated one-third of the state's plants are intruders, referred to as exotic species. It is a cause of concern among state biologists. They see signs that the plant newcomers, breeding indiscriminately, are choking out the state's natives, estimated to number 3,448 species.

Native plants are part of a biological chain. If the chain is interrupted by exotic species, it affects every other insect, bird, or mammal that depends on the native plants.

Trying to stave off the introduction into Florida of new exotic species, and curtail those that already are entrenched, state officials are forbidding nurseries and growers to sell some exotic species familiar to Floridians. Among them are Brazilian pepper, punk trees, Australian pines, and the Chinese tallow tree. Biologists see such species as pollutants, and harmful to the state's ecology as hazardous wastes.

Some exotics were brought into Florida years ago to alleviate ecological problems. For example, the Australian pine and kudzu were planted to prevent soil erosion. The punk tree, formally known as the melaleuca, was imported to soak up water from the Everglades and thus make that region suitable for development.

Two exotic pest plant lists exist. One is the Department of Environmental Protection's list of prohibited aquatic weeds. The other list is a compilation by the Exotic Pest Plant Council; it contains more than 400 exotic plant species that either now threaten Florida's ecology or that will cause problems if left unchecked.

Some species on the council's list will surprise homeowners. One is schefflera. It is not a problem in northern Florida, but in south Florida it has proliferated so wildly that it is crowding out such native plants as oaks, saw palmetto, and scrub rosemary. Plant experts say that in the south schefflera is shading and thus killing out the native plants, ruining the region's natural ecosystem.

Seven of the most troublesome exotic plant species are:

1.) Melaleuca, sometimes called the punk tree or cajeput. It grows 80 to 100 feet tall, its trunk is layered with papery bark, and the tree's leaves have a medicinal odor. The tree flowers in summer and fall with white bottle-brush blooms. Brought to Florida in the early 1900s to dry up wetlands, the tree is considered a destroyer of natural habitat. One acre of melaleuca consumes 2,100 gallons of water per hour.

2.) Catclaw Mimosa, brought into Florida in 1953 from Central America. A shrub, it grows up to 10 feet tall. It has stems for fern-type fans composed of smaller leaflets. Blooms are fluffy pink balls. Also a threat to the state's wetlands, this plant obstructs water flow while increasing flooding and sedimentation. A mature plant is capable of producing 40,000 seeds.

3.) Australian pine, planted in Florida in the late 1800s to prevent soil erosion in coastal areas. It grows best in sandy soil and salty open areas. It can soar to 115 feet. Not a true pine, the tree's branches are covered by thin needles of dark green. Its small cones are round and prickly. The tree uproots easily in high winds because its roots are so shallow. Almost nothing grows under this tree because it sheds needles laced with a chemical that kills native species.

4.) Brazilian pepper, which reportedly came into Florida around Punta Gorda in the 1920s from Brazil. It reaches up to 40 feet, and bears small white flowers in early fall that are followed by hundreds of round berries. Birds eat the berries, spreading hundreds of seedlings. The tree's rapid growth often chokes out native plants.

5.) The Chinese tallow tree, sometimes called the popcorn tree. It originated in China and grows up to 30 feet tall. Its leaves have sharp, prickly edges. An attractive tree, it has been used to beautify highways and public areas in north Florida, but can grow anywhere in Florida. The tree has the potential of becoming the melaleuca of north Florida.

6.) Hydrilla, an aquatic plant from Africa, was discovered in Florida in

1960 in both a Miami canal on the east coast and in the Crystal Rier on the West Coast. Hydrilla has long, thin stems segmented into three or five-leafed whorls and it grows at the rate of one inch a day. It thrives in more than 50,000 acres of Florida lakes and waterways, and is hard on the state's fish population. Since 1980, Florida has spent more than $50 million to control this plant and in the same period it is estimated to have caused an adverse economic impact of a quarter-billion dollars.

7.) Kudzu, a supervine. Each shoot grows as much as 12 inches a day. It was introduced into the South by the U.S. government in the 1930s as a means of preventing soil erosion. In less than two decades, this species, which Southerners call "Wahoo," covered a half-million acres of farmland. It shades and crowds out native species. Asians use kudzu as food, a medicine to treat colds and diarrhea, a sobering agent, and to make a superb, acid-free paper, but to Americans it is a nuisance plant that is a place where, says a Southern folktale, naughty children are tossed to quickly disappear.

Other major exotic plants that state officials prefer would go away are: the Bishopwood tree, woman's tongue, earleaf acacia, Cuban laurel, lofty fig, banyan tree, air potato, climbing fern, cork tree, downy rose myrtle, Japanese honeysuckle, jasmine, Java plum, lather leaf, lead tree, Murray red gum, rose apple, shoebutton ardisia, strawberry guava, and tree hibiscus.

Aquatic weeds fouling Florida's water, and listed as prohibited, are alligator weed, African elodea, ambulia, Eurasian watermilfoil, exotic bur-reed, hippo grass, hygro, tropical pickerelweed, water-aloe, water chestnut, water fern, water lily, and water spinach.

NOT FOR SALE

Members of the Florida Nurserymen and Growers Association have stopped selling several plants considered invasive pest plants. Among them

Mother-in-law's tongue tree, *Albizia lebbck*
Orchid tree, *Bauhinia variegata*
Bishopwood tree, *Bischofia javanica*
Cat's claw vine, *Macfadyena unguis-cati*
Chinaberry tree, *Melia azedarach*
Erect sword fern, *Nephrolepis cordifolia*
Guava, *Psidium guajava*
Oyster plant, *Rhoeo spathacea*
Java plum tree or jambolan, *Syzygium cumini*
Seaside mahoe tree, *Thespesia populnea*

It became illegal in 2001 to sell or distribute the Carrotwood, *Cupaniopsis anacardioides.*

LEGAL RESIDENCY

To become a resident of Florida, a person must establish a home or a permanent dwelling place and demonstrate intent to make Florida the place of permanent legal residence. No fixed waiting period is required for a person to become a resident, but newcomers are urged to show their intent by filing a sworn statement with the clerk of circuit court in the county where the new home is situated. A small charge is made for recording the affidavit.

No residency requirements are necessary for employment with state or county government agencies, but preference may be given to Florida residents.

Once a resident, the Floridian is entitled to property tax exemptions of $25,000 on the assessed value of the homestead.

To vote in Florida, a person must be 18 years of age or older, a citizen of the U.S., and a permanent resident of Florida and of the county in which the resident wishes to vote. One must register to vote, of course, with the county supervisor of elections.

Jurors are selected from lists of Florida driver's license holders who are U.S. citizens.

Pupils in kindergarten through 12th grade whose parents or guardians are non-residents may be charged a tuition fee at the time the pupil is enrolled. Fees may be waived for certain categories such as military personnel. To qualify for in-state tuition fees at a state public university or community college, the student (or parent or guardian, if the student is a dependent) must have resided in Florida for 12 consecutive months prior to enrollment.

To obtain a divorce in Florida, one of the parties in the marriage must live in Florida for six months before filing the petition.

All candidates for public office must be U.S. citizens and registered voters in Florida. Candidates for governor, lieutenant governor, and the cabinet must be at least 30 years of age and have been a Florida resident the preceding seven years. A candidate for the state legislature must be at least 21 years old and live in the district he or she wishes to represent. Candidates for local offices must be residents of their appropriate districts.

To operate a motor vehicle in Florida, new residents are required to obtain a Florida driver's license within 30 days, and register their motor vehicles within 10 days of accepting gainful employment, entering children in public schools, registering to vote, or filing for homestead exemption. Full-time non-resident college students and non-resident military personnel on active duty in Florida are exempt from this requirement.

For a resident statewide non-commercial fishing license, an applicant must have resided for six continuous months in Florida, or filed a domicile certificate with the county clerk.

Establishing legal residence in Florida does not automatically make a person from another country a citizen of the United States. A foreign national, although having become a legal Florida resident, still must become a U.S. citizen to vote, serve on a jury, or hold elective office. Floridians without U.S. citizenship wishing to obtain it should seek information from the U.S. Immigration and Naturalization Service in Miami.

POPULATION

There are more than 18.8 million Floridians, according to the 2010 census, giving the state two more representatives in the U.S. Congress and thus 29 votes in the Electoral College.

The growth over the decade was enough to assuage fears that the state had stopped growing, which it did briefly for the first time in nearly half a century. Florida grew at a rate of just more than 17 percent, its lowest decennial growth rate in a century. Still it remained the nation's fourth largest state.

Whites who are not of Hispanic origin are the largest racial group in the state by a wide margin, comprising 59 percent of the state's population. Those of Hispanic origin account for more than 21 percent of the population, up from 16 percent a decade ago. Blacks increased to 16 percent.

Both the Hispanic and black populations are well above the national average. Asians account for more than 2 percent, well below the national average. Floridians who are foreign-born account for more than 15 percent of the population, a trend seen as growing stronger. Nearly a quarter of the population speaks a language other than English at home. Floridians live in nearly nine million homes.

Most immigrants come from South America, the Caribbean, and Eastern Europe. An estimated 6 percent of the state's population is in the state illegally. But Florida was the only state to see a decrease in its number of illegal immigrants.

Most Floridians are female by a slight margin, on a par with the national average. Despite the reputation as the nation's best place to retire, young people, those under age 18, outnumber old people, those 65 and older, by a margin of 22 to 17.

The median age is 40. Median household income dropped below $50,000 during the economic downtown starting in late 2008. Florida's unemployment rate at both the start of 2010 and at the end of that year stood at 12 percent. Still, according to the Census Bureau, the median monthly home mortgage payment was $1,565 while the median monthly rent was $952. But 15 percent of all Floridians were living below the poverty line.

Eighty-five percent of the adult population graduated from high school, 25 percent held college degrees. Seventy-nine percent of those with jobs drove alone to and from work and had an average commute of 25.4 minutes.

The Miami area remains the state's largest metropolitan area in population, but Jacksonville, which includes all of Duval County, is Florida's largest city.

The state's population center remained in south central Polk County, in Central Florida, where it's been for half a century.

For the decade, Florida's new population grew at the rate of 772 per day.

POPULATION OF THE STATE:
EARLIEST CENSUS TO 2010

1830	34,730		1930	1,468,211
1840	54,477		1940	1,897,414
1850	87,445		1950	2,771,305
1860	140,424		1960	4,951,580
1870	187,748		1970	6,791,418
1880	196,493		1980	9,739,992
1890	391,422		1990	12,937,926
1900	528,542		2000	15,982,378
1910	752,619		2010	18,801,310
1920	968,470			

COUNTY POPULATIONS AND DENSITIES
(2000 Census)

County	1980	1990	2000	Persons Per Square Mile
Alachua	151,369	181,596	217,955	226.8
Baker	15,289	18,486	22,259	37.9
Bay	97,740	126,994	148,217	172.1
Bradford	20,023	22,515	26,088	85.5
Brevard	272,959	398,978	476,230	363.5
Broward	1,018,257	1,255,488	1,623,018	1,330.30
Calhoun	9,294	11,011	13,017	23
Charlotte	58,460	110,975	141,627	170.2
Citrus	54,703	93,515	118,085	178.6
Clay	67,052	105,986	140,814	218.7
Collier	85,971	152,099	251,377	118.6
Columbia	35,399	42,613	56,513	71.6
De Soto	19,039	23,865	32,209	44.7
Dixie	7,751	10,585	13,827	19.5
Duval	571,003	672,971	778,879	927.3
Escambia	233,794	262,798	294,410	386.4
Flagler	10,913	28,701	49,832	98.9
Franklin	7,661	8,967	11,057	19.6
Gadsden	41,674	41,105	45,087	86.2

Gilchrist	5,767	9,667	14,437	41.5
Glades	5,992	7,591	10,576	11.8
Gulf	10,658	11,504	13,332	23.1
Hamilton	8,761	10,930	13,327	25.9
Hardee	20,357	19,499	26,938	42.8
Hendry	18,599	25,773	36,210	30.5
Hernando	44,469	101,115	130,802	257.5
Highlands	47,526	68,432	87,366	78.1
Hillsborough	646,939	834,054	998,948	940.6
Holmes	14,723	15,778	18,564	38.4
Indian River	59,896	90,208	112,947	205.7
Jackson	39,154	41,375	46,755	49.8
Jefferson	10,703	11,296	12,902	21.2
Lafayette	4,035	5,578	7,022	12.7
Lake	104,870	152,104	210,528	181
Lee	205,266	335,113	440,888	438.7
Leon	148,655	192,493	239,452	344
Levy	19,870	25,923	34,450	30.3
Liberty	4,260	5,569	7,021	8.3
Madison	14,894	16,569	18,733	26.5
Manatee	148,445	211,707	264,002	342
Marion	122,488	194,833	258,916	156.7
Martin	64,014	100,900	126,731	217.8
Miami-Dade	1,625,509	1,937,094	2,253,362	1,068.50
Monroe	63,188	78,024	79,589	56.1
Nassau	32,894	43,941	57,663	85.9
Okaloosa	109,920	143,776	170,498	170.8
Okeechobee	20,264	29,627	35,910	46
Orange	470,867	677,491	896,344	893.7
Osceola	49,287	107,728	172,493	117.6
Palm Beach	576,754	863,518	1,131,184	438.8
Pasco	193,661	281,131	344,765	446.6
Pinellas	728,531	851,659	921,482	2982.1
Polk	321,652	405,382	483,924	236.3
Putnam	50,549	65,070	70,423	80.1

St. Johns	51,303	83,829	123,135	186.6
St. Lucie	87,182	150,171	192,695	307.8
Santa Rosa	55,988	81,608	117,743	102.2
Sarasota	202,251	277,776	325,957	579
Seminole	179,752	287,529	365,196	1,037.50
Sumter	24,272	31,577	53,345	92.9
Suwannee	22,287	26,780	34,844	50.7
Taylor	16,532	17,111	19,256	18.3
Union	10,166	10,252	13,442	54.9
Volusia	258,762	370,712	443,343	367.3
Wakulla	10,887	14,202	22,863	36
Walton	21,300	27,760	40,601	35.8
Washington	14,509	16,919	20,973	34.3

According to the 2000 census, Pinellas County continues to have the highest population density, with 2,982 people per square mile; and Liberty County continues as the least densely populated with 8 persons per square mile.

POPULATION OF CITIES AND OTHER COMMUNITIES
(2000 Census)

Places	Counties	1980	1990	2000
Alachua	Alachua	3,866	4,529	6,098
Alford	Jackson	548	472	466
Altamonte Springs	Seminole	21,499	34,879	41,200
Altha	Calhoun	478	497	502
Anna Maria	Manatee	1,537	1,744	1,814
Apalachicola	Franklin	2,565	2,602	2,334
Apopka	Orange	6,019	13,512	26,642
Arcadia	De Soto	6,002	6,488	6,604
Archer	Alachua	1,230	1,372	1,289
Astatula	Lake	755	981	1,298
Atlantic Beach	Duval	1,471	1,636	13,368
Atlantis	Palm Beach	1,325	1,653	2,005
Auburndale	Polk	6,501	8,858	11,032
Aventura	Miami-Dade	—	—	25,267

Avon Park	Highlands	8,026	8,042	8,542
Baldwin	Duval	1,526	1,450	1,634
Bal Harbor	Miami-Dade	2,973	3,045	3,305
Bartow	Polk	14,780	14,716	15,340
Bascom	Jackson	134	90	106
Bay Harbor Islands	Miami-Dade	4,869	4,703	5,146
Bay Lake	Orange	—	—	23
Bell	Gilchrist	227	267	349
Belleair	Pinellas	3,673	3,968	4,067
Belleair Beach	Pinellas	1,643	2,070	1,632
Belleair Bluffs	Pinellas	2,522	2,128	2,243
Belleair Shore	Pinellas	80	60	75*
Belle Glade	Palm Beach	16,535	16,177	14,906
Belle Isle	Orange	2,848	5,272	5,531
Belleview	Marion	1,913	2,666	3,478
Beverly Beach	Flagler	217	312	547
Biscayne Park	Miami-Dade	3,088	3,068	3,269
Blountstown	Calhoun	2,632	2,404	2,444
Boca del Mar	Palm Beach	—	—	21,832
Boca Raton	Palm Beach	49,446	61,492	74,764
Bonifay	Holmes	2,534	2,612	4,078
Bonita Springs	Lee	—	—	32,797
Bowling Green	Hardee	2,310	1,836	2,892
Boynton Beach	Palm Beach	35,624	46,194	60,389
Bradenton	Manatee	30,227	43,779	49,504
Bradenton Beach	Manatee	1,603	1,657	1,482
Brandon	Hillsborough	—	—	77,895
Branford	Suwannee	622	670	695
Briny Breezes	Palm Beach	387	400	411
Bristol	Liberty	1,044	937	845
Bronson	Levy	853	875	964
Brooker	Bradford	429	312	352
Brooksville	Hernando	5,582	7,440	7,264
Bunnell	Flagler	1,816	1,873	2,122
Bushnell	Sumter	983	1,998	2,050

Callahan	Nassau	869	946	962
Callaway	Bay	7,486	12,253	14,233
Campbellton	Jackson	336	202	212
Cape Canaveral	Brevard	5,733	8,014	8,829
Cape Coral	Lee	32,103	74,991	102,286
Carol City	Miami-Dade	—	—	59,443
Carrabelle	Franklin	1,304	1,200	1,303
Caryville	Washington	633	631	218
Casselberry	Seminole	15,037	18,911	22,629
Cedar Grove	Bay	1,104	1,479	5,367
Cedar Key	Levy	700	668	790
Center Hill	Sumter	751	735	910
Century	Escambia	2,394	1,989	1,714
Chattahoochee	Gadsden	5,332	4,382	3,287
Chiefland	Levy	1,986	1,917	1,993
Chipley	Washington	3,330	3,866	3,592
Cinco Bayou	Okaloosa	202	322	377
Citrus Ridge	Palm Beach	—	—	12,015
Clearwater	Pinellas	86,212	98,784	108,787
Clermont	Lake	5,461	6,910	9,333
Clewiston	Hendry	5,219	6,085	6,460
Cloud Lake	Palm Beach	160	121	167
Cocoa	Brevard	16,096	17,722	16,412
Cocoa Beach	Brevard	10,926	12,123	12,482
Coconut Creek	Broward	8,174	17,485	43,566
Coleman	Sumter	1,022	857	647
Conway	Orange	—	—	14,394
Cooper City	Broward	10,140	20,791	27,939
Coral Gables	Miami-Dade	43,241	40,091	42,249
Coral Springs	Broward	37,349	79,443	117,549
Coral Terrace	Palm Beach	—	—	24,380
Cottondale	Jackson	1,056	900	869
Crescent City	Putnam	1,722	1,859	1,776
Crestview	Okaloosa	7,617	9,886	14,766
Cross City	Dixie	2,154	2,041	1,775

Crystal River	Citrus		2,873	4,044
Cutler	Miami-Dade	—	—	17,390
Cutler Ridge	Miami Dade	—	—	24,781
Dade City	Pasco	5,234	5,633	6,188
Dania Beach	Broward	11,796	13,024	20,061
Davenport	Polk	1,509	1,529	1,924
Davie	Broward	29,278	47,217	75,720
Daytona Beach	Volusia	54,553	61,921	64,112
Daytona Beach Shores	Volusia	1,324	2,335	4,299
De Bary	Volusia	—	—	15,559
Deerfield Beach	Broward	39,193	46,325	64,583
De Funiak Springs	Walton	5,563	5,120	5,089
DeLand	Volusia	15,571	16,491	20,904
Delray Beach	Palm Beach	34,475	47,181	60,020
Deltona	Volusia	—	—	69,543
Destin	Okaloosa	3,913	8,080	11,119
Doral	Miami-Dade	—	—	20,438
Dundee	Polk	2,227	2,335	2,912
Dunedin	Pinellas	30,203	34,012	35,691
Dunnellon	Marion	1,427	1,624	1,898
Eagle Lake	Polk	1,678	1,758	2,496
Eatonville	Orange	2,185	2,170	2,432
Ebro	Washington	233	255	250
Edgewater	Volusia	6,726	15,337	18,666
Edgewood	Orange	1,034	1,062	1,901
El Portal	Miami-Dade	2,055	2,457	2,505
Englewood	Orange	—	—	16,196
Ensley	Escambia	—	—	18,752
Estero	Lee	—	—	9,503
Esto	Holmes	304	253	356
Eustis	Lake	9,453	12,967	15,106
Everglades	Collier	524	321	479
Fanning Springs	Gilchrist/Levy	314	493	737
Fellsmere	Indian River	1,161	2,179	3,813
Fernandina Beach	Nassau	7,259	8,765	10,549

Ferry Pass	Escambia	—	—	27,176
Flagler Beach	Flagler	2,208	3,820	4,954
Florida City	Miami-Dade	6,174	5,806	7,843
Forest City	Orange	—	—	12,612
Fort Lauderdale	Broward	153,279	149,377	152,397
Fort Meade	Polk	5,546	4,976	5,691
Fort Myers	Lee	37,454	45,206	48,208
Fort Pierce	St. Lucie	33,802	36,830	37,516
Fort Walton Beach	Okaloosa	20,829	21,471	19,973
Fort White	Columbia	386	268	409
Freeport	Walton	669	843	1,190
Frostproof	Polk	2,995	2,808	2,975
Fruit Cove	St. Johns	—	—	16,077
Fruitland Park	Lake	2,259	2,754	3,186
Fruitville	Sarasota	—	—	12,741
Gainesville	Alachua	81,371	84,770	95,447
Glen Ridge	Palm Beach	235	207	276
Glen St. Mary	Baker	462	480	473
Glenvar Heights	Miami-Dade	—	—	16,243
Golden Beach	Miami-Dade	612	774	919
Golden Gate	Collier	—	—	20,951
Goldenrod	Orange	—	—	12,871
Golf	Palm Beach	110	234	230
Gonzalez	Escambia	—	—	11,365
Graceville	Jackson	2,918	2,675	2,402
Grand Ridge	Jackson	591	536	792
Greenacres City	Palm Beach	8,777	186,803	27,569
Green Cove Springs	Clay	4,154	4,497	5,378
Greensboro	Jackson	562	586	619
Greenville	Madison	1,096	950	837
Greenwood	Jackson	577	474	735
Gretna	Gadsden	1,557	1,981	1,709
Groveland	Lake	1,992	2,300	2,360
Gulf Breeze	Santa Rosa	5,478	5,530	5,665

Gulfport	Pinellas	11,180	11,727	12,527
Gulf Stream	Palm Beach	475	690	716
Haines City	Polk	10,799	11,683	13,174
Hallandale	Broward/ Miami-Dade	36,517	30,996	34,282
Hampton	Bradford	466	296	431
Hastings	St. Johns	636	595	521
Havana	Gadsden	2,782	1,654	1,713
Haverhill	Palm Beach	1,249	1,058	1,454
Hawthorne	Alachua	1,303	1,305	1,415
Hialeah	Miami-Dade	145,254	188,004	226,419
Hialeah Gardens	Miami-Dade	2,700	7,713	19,297
Highland Beach	Palm Beach	2,030	3,209	3,775
Highland Park	Polk	184	155	244
High Springs	Alachua	2,491	3,144	3,863
Hillcrest Heights	Polk	177	221	266
Hilliard	Nassau	1,869	1,751	2,702
Hillsboro Beach	Broward	1,554	1,748	2,163
Hobe Sound	Palm Beach	—	—	11,376
Holiday	Pasco	—	—	21,904
Holly Hill	Volusia	9,953	11,141	12,119
Hollywood	Broward	121,323	121,697	139,357
Holmes Beach	Manatee	4,018	4,810	4,966
Homestead	Miami-Dade	20,668	26,866	31,909
Homosassa Springs	Citrus	—	—	12,458
Horseshoe Beach	Dixie	304	252	206
Howey-in-the-Hills	Lake	626	724	956
Hudson	Pasco	—	—	12,765
Hypoluxo	Palm Beach	573	830	2,015
Immokalee	Collier	—	—	19,763
Indialantic	Brevard	2,883	2,844	2,944
Indian Creek	Miami-Dade	103	44	33
Indian Harbour Beach	Brevard	5,967	6,933	8,152
Indian River Shores	Indian River	1,254	2,278	3,448

Indian Rocks Beach	Pinellas	3,717	3,963	5,072
Indian Shores	Pinellas	984	1,405	1,705
Inglis	Levy	1,173	1,241	1,491
Interlachen	Putnam	848	1,160	1,475
Inverness	Citrus	4,095	5,797	6,789
Islandia	Miami-Dade	12	13	6
Jacksonville	Duval	540,920	672,971	735,617
Jacksonville Beach	Duval	15,462	17,839	20,990
Jacob City	Jackson	224	261	281
Jasper	Hamilton	2,093	2,099	1,780
Jay	Santa Rosa	633	666	579
Jennings	Hamilton	749	712	833
Jensen Beach	Palm Beach	—	—	11,100
Juno Beach	Palm Beach	1,142	2,121	3,262
Jupiter	Palm Beach	9,868	24,986	39,328
Jupiter Inlet Colony	Palm Beach	378	405	368
Jupiter Island	Martin	364	549	620
Kendall	Miami-Dade	—	—	75,226
Kenneth City	Pinellas	4,344	4,462	4,400
Key Biscayne	Miami-Dade	—	—	10,507
Key Colony Beach	Monroe	977	977	788
Key Largo	Monroe	—	—	11,886
Keystone Heights	Clay	1,056	1,315	1,349
Key West	Monroe	24,382	24,832	25,478
Kissimmee	Osceola	15,487	30,050	47,814
La Belle	Hendry	2,287	2,703	4,210
La Crosse	Alachua	170	122	143
Lady Lake	Lake	1,193	8,071	11,828
Lake Alfred	Polk	3,163	3,622	3,890
Lake Butler	Union	1,830	2,116	1,927
Lake City	Columbia	9,257	10,005	9,980
Lake Clarke Shores	Palm Beach	3,174	3,364	3,451
Lake Hamilton	Polk	1,552	1,128	1,304
Lake Helen	Volusia	2,047	2,344	2,743

Lakeland	Polk	54,422	70,576	78,752
Lake Mary	Seminole	2,853	5,929	11,458
Lake Park	Palm Beach	6,909	6,704	8,721
Lake Placid	Highlands	963	1,158	1,668
Lake Wales	Polk	8,466	9,670	10,194
Lakewood Park	St. Lucie	—	—	10,458
Lake Worth	Palm Beach	27,048	28,564	35,133
Land O' Lakes	Pasco	—	—	20,971
Lantana	Palm Beach	8,048	8,392	9,437
Largo	Pinellas	58,180	65,674	69,371
Lauderdale-by-the-Sea	Broward	2,639	2,990	2,563
Lauderdale Lakes	Broward	25,426	27,341	31,705
Lauderhill	Broward	37,271	49,708	57,585
Laurel Hill	Okaloosa	610	543	549
Lawtey	Bradford	692	676	656
Layton	Monroe	88	183	186
Lazy Lake	Broward	31	33	38
Lee	Madison	297	306	352
Leesburg	Lake	13,191	14,903	15,956
Lehigh Acres	Lee	—	—	33,430
Leisure City	Miami-Dade	—	—	22,152
Lighthouse Point	Broward	11,488	10,378	10,767
Live Oak	Suwannee	6,732	6,332	6,480
Lockhart	Orange	—	—	12,944
Longboat Key	Manatee/ Sarasota	4,843	5,937	7,603
Longwood	Seminole	10,029	13,316	13,745
Lutz	Hillsborough	—	—	17,081
Lynn Haven	Bay	6,239	9,298	12,451
Macclenny	Baker	3,851	3,966	4,459
McIntosh	Marion	404	411	453
Madeira Beach	Pinellas	4,520	4,225	4,511
Madison	Madison	3,487	3,345	3,061
Maitland	Orange	8,763	9,110	12,019
Malibar	Brevard	1,118	1,977	2,622

Malone	Jackson	897	765	2,007
Manalapan	Palm Beach	329	312	321
Mangonia Park	Palm Beach	1,419	1,453	1,283
Marathon	Monroe	—	—	10,255
Marco Island	Collier	—	—	14,879
Margate	Broward	35,891	42,985	53,909
Marianna	Jackson	7,006	6,292	6,230
Marineland	Flagler/St. Johns	31	21	6
Mary Esther	Okaloosa	3,530	4,139	4,005
Mascotte	Lake	1,112	1,761	2,687
Mayo	Lafayette	891	917	988
Medley	Miami-Dade	537	663	1,098
Melbourne	Brevard	46,536	59,646	71,382
Melbourne Beach	Brevard	2,713	3,021	3,335
Melbourne Village	Brevard	1,004	591	706
Mexico Beach	Bay	632	992	1,017
Miami	Miami-Dade	346,681	358,548	362,470
Miami Beach	Miami-Dade	96,298	92,639	87,933
Miami Lakes	Miami-Dade	—	—	22,676
Miami Shores	Miami-Dade	9,244	10,084	10,380
Miami Springs	Miami-Dade	12,350	13,268	13,712
Micanopy	Alachua	737	612	653
Middleburg	Clay	—	—	10,338
Midway	Gadsden	1,385	852	1,446
Milton	Santa Rosa	7,206	7,216	7,043
Minneola	Lake	851	1,515	5,435
Miramar	Broward	32,813	40,663	72,739
Monticello	Jefferson	2,994	2,573	2,533
Montverde	Lake	397	890	822
Moore Haven	Glades	1,250	1,432	1,635
Mount Dora	Lake	5,883	7,196	9,418
Mulberry	Polk	2,932	2,988	3,230
Naples	Collier	17,581	19,505	20,976

Neptune Beach	Duval	5,248	6,816	7,270
Newberry	Alachua	1,826	1,644	3,316
New Port Richey	Pasco	11,448	14,044	16,117
New Smyrna Beach	Volusia	13,557	16,543	20,048
Niceville	Okaloosa	8,624	10,507	11,684
Noma	Holmes	113	207	213
Norland	Miami-Dade	—	—	22,995
North Bay Village	Miami-Dade	4,920	5,383	6,733
North Fort Myers	Lee	—	—	40,214
North Lauderdale	Broward	18,661	26,506	32,264
North Miami	Miami-Dade	42,566	49,998	59,880
North Miami Beach	Miami-Dade	36,553	35,359	40,786
North Palm Beach	Palm Beach	11,344	11,343	12,064
North Port	Sarasota	6,205	11,973	22,797
North Redington Beach	Pinellas	1,156	1,135	1,474
Oak Hill	Volusia	938	917	1,378
Oakland	Orange	658	700	936
Oakland Park	Broward	22,944	26,326	30,966
Oakridge	Orange	—	—	22,349
Ocala	Marion	37,170	42,045	45,943
Ocean Breeze Park	Martin	466	519	463
Ocean Ridge	Palm Beach	1,355	1,570	1,636
Ocoee	Orange	7,803	12,778	24,391
Ojus	Miami-Dade	—	—	16,642
Okeechobee	Okeechobee	4,225	4,943	5,376
Oldsmar	Pinellas	2,626	8,361	11,910
Olympia Heights	Miami-Dade	—	—	13,452
Opa-locka	Miami-Dade	14,460	15,283	14,951
Orange City	Volusia	2,909	5,347	6,224
Orange Park	Clay	8,766	9,488	9,081
Orchid	Indian River	23	10	140
Orlando	Orange	128,291	164,693	185,951
Ormond Beach	Volusia	21,438	29,721	36,301
Otter Creek	Levy	167	136	121

Oviedo	Seminole	3,074	11,114	26,316
Pahokee	Palm Beach	6,346	6,822	5,985
Palatka	Putnam	10,175	10,201	10,033
Palm Bay	Brevard	18,560	62,632	79,413
Palm Beach	Palm Beach	9,729	9,814	10,468
Palm Beach Gardens	Palm Beach	14,407	22,965	35,058
Palm Beach Shores	Palm Beach	1,232	1,040	1,269
Palm Coast	Flagler	—	—	32,732
Palmetto	Manatee	8,637	9,268	12,571
Palm Harbor	Pinellas	—	—	59,248
Palm Shores	Brevard	77	210	794
Palm Springs	Palm Beach	8,166	9,763	11,699
Palm Valley	Duval	—	—	19,860
Panama City	Bay	33,346	34,378	36,417
Panama City Beach	Bay	2,148	4,051	7,671
Parker	Bay	4,298	4,598	4,623
Parkland	Broward	545	3,558	13,835
Paxton	Walton	659	600	656
Pembroke Park	Broward	5,306	4,933	6,299
Pembroke Pines	Broward	35,862	65,452	137,427
Penney Farms	Clay	630	609	580
Pensacola	Escambia	57,619	58,165	56,255
Perry	Taylor	825	7,151	6,847
Pierson	Volusia	1,085	2,988	2,596
Pine Hills	Orange	—	—	41,764
Pinellas Park	Pinellas	32,811	43,426	45,658
Pinewood	Miami-Dade	—	—	16,523
Plantation	Broward	48,653	66,692	82,934
Plant City	Hillsborough	17,064	22,754	29,915
Polk City	Polk	576	1,439	1,516
Pomona Park	Putnam	791	663	789
Pompano Beach	Broward	63,063	72,411	78,191
Ponce de Leon	Holmes	454	406	457
Ponce Inlet	Volusia	1,003	1,704	2,513

Port Charlotte	Charlotte	—	—	46,451
Port Orange	Volusia	18,756	35,317	45,823
Port Richey	Pasco	2,165	2,523	3,021
Port Salerno	Palm Beach	—	—	10,141
Port St. Joe	Gulf	4,027	4,044	3,644
Port St. Lucie	St. Lucie	14,690	55,866	88,769
Princeton	Miami-Dade	—	—	10,090
Punta Gorda	Charlotte	6,797	10,747	14,344
Quincy	Gadsden	8,591	7,444	6,982
Raiford	Union	259	198	187
Reddick	Marion	657	554	571
Redington Beach	Pinellas	1,708	1,626	1,593
Redington Shores	Pinellas	2,142	2,366	2,338
Riviera Beach	Palm Beach	26,489	27,639	29,884
Rockledge	Brevard	11,877	16,023	20,170
Royal Palm Beach	Palm Beach	3,423	14,589	21,523
Safety Harbor	Pinellas	6,461	15,124	17,203
St. Augustine	St. Johns	11,985	11,692	11,592
St. Augustine Beach	St. Johns	1,289	3,657	4,683
St. Cloud	Osceola	7,840	12,453	20,074
St. Leo	Pasco	917	1,009	595
St. Lucie	St. Lucie	593	584	604
St. Marks	Wakulla	286	307	272
St. Pete Beach	Pinellas	9,354	9,200	9,929
St. Petersburg	Pinellas	238,767	238,629	248,232
San Antonio	Pasco	529	776	655
San Carlos Park	Lee	—	—	16,317
Sandalfoot Cove	Palm Beach	—	—	16,582
Sanford	Seminole	23,176	32,387	38,291
Sanibel	Lee	3,363	5,468	6,064
Sarasota	Sarasota	48,868	50,961	52,715
Satellite Beach	Brevard	9,163	9,889	9,577
Sebastian	Indian River	2,861	10,205	16,181
Sebring	Highlands	8,736	8,900	9,667

Seminole	Pinellas	6,419	9,251	10,890
Sewall's Point	Martin	1,187	1,588	1,946
Shalimar	Okaloosa	390	341	718
Sneads	Jackson	1,690	1,746	1,919
Sopchoppy	Wakulla	444	367	426
South Bay	Palm Beach	3,886	3,558	3,859
South Daytona	Volusia	11,252	12,482	13,177
South Miami	Miami-Dade	10,895	10,404	10,741
South Miami Heights	Miami-Dade	—	—	33,522
South Palm Beach	Palm Beach	1,304	1,480	699
South Pasadena	Pinellas	4,188	5,644	5,778
Springfield	Bay	7,504	8,715	8,810
Starke	Bradford	5,306	5,226	5,593
Stuart	Martin	9,467	11,936	14,633
Sun City Center	Hillsborough	—	—	16,321
Sunny Isles Beach	Miami-Dade	—	—	15,315
Sunrise	Broward	39,681	64,407	85,779
Surfside	Miami-Dade	3,763	4,108	4,909
Sweetwater	Miami-Dade	8,067	13,909	14,226
Tallahassee	Leon	106,179	124,773	150,624
Tamarac	Broward	29,376	44,822	55,588
Tampa	Hillsborough	271,578	280,015	303,447
Tarpon Springs	Pinellas	13,251	17,906	21,803
Tavares	Lake	4,984	7,383	9,700
Temple Terrace	Hillsborough	11,278	16,444	20,918
Tequesta	Palm Beach	3,685	4,499	5,273
Titusville	Brevard	31,910	39,394	40,670
Treasure Island	Pinellas	6,316	7,266,	7,450
Trenton	Gilchrist	1,131	1,287	1,617
Umatilla	Lake	1,872	2,350	2,214
Valparaiso	Okaloosa	6,142	4,672	6,408
Venice	Sarasota	12,424	16,922	17,764
Vernon	Washington	885	778	743

Vero Beach	Indian River	16,176	17,350	17,705
Virginia Gardens	Miami-Dade	2,098	2,212	2,348
Waldo	Alachua	993	1,017	821
Warrington	Escambia	—	—	15,207
Wauchula	Hardee	3,296	3,253	4,368
Wausau	Washington	347	313	398
Webster	Sumter	856	746	805
Weeki Wachee	Hernando	8	53	12
Welaka	Putnam	492	533	586
Wellington	Palm Beach	—	—	38,216
West Melbourne	Brevard	5,078	8,399	9,824
West Miami	Miami-Dade	6,076	5,727	5,863
Weston	Broward	—	—	49,286
West Palm Beach	Palm Beach	63,305	67,643	82,103
Westville	Holmes	343	257	221
Westwood Lakes	Miami-Dade	—	—	12,005
Wewahitchka	Gulf	1,742	1,779	1,722
White Springs	Hamilton	781	704	819
Wildwood	Sumter	2,665	3,421	3,924
Williston	Levy	2,240	2,179	2,297
Windermere	Orange	1,302	1,371	1,897
Winter Garden	Orange	6,789	9,745	14,351
Winter Haven	Polk	21,119	24,725	26,487
Winter Park	Orange	22,339	22,242	24,090
Winter Springs	Seminole	10,475	22,151	31,666
Worthington Springs	Union	220	178	193
Yankeetown	Levy	600	635	629
Yeehaw Junction	Osceola	—	—	21,778
Zephyrhills	Pasco	6,137	8,220	10,833
Zolfo Springs	Hardee	1,495	1,219	1,641

Belleair Shore was one of a half-dozen American cities found by the 2000 Census to have zero population. The census, acting on a request of city fathers, recounted and found that the beach city in Pinellas County had 75 residents. They may ask for another. At the time of the recount, the city had 93 registered voters.

VITAL STATISTICS

LEADING CAUSES OF RESIDENT DEATHS
(Per 100,000 population)

Age Group	Cause of Death	Rank	Deaths	2008 Rates
Less than One	ALL CAUSES	—	1,667	728.2
	Perinatal Conditions	1	842	367.8
	Congenital Anomalies	2	312	136.3
	Accidents	3	126	55
	Sudden Infant Death	4	80	34.9
	Heart Diseases	5	32	14
1 to 4	ALL CAUSES	—	304	33.5
	Accidents	1	108	11
	Congenital Anomalies	2	38	4.2
	Homicide	3	23	2.5
	Cancer	3	23	2.5
	Heart Diseases	5	10	1.1
5 to 14	ALL CAUSES	—	273	11.8
	Accidents	1	77	3.3
	Cancer	2	44	1.9
	Congenital Anomalies	3	27	1.2
	Heart Diseases	4	10	0.4
	Homicide	5	10	0.4
15 to 24	ALL CAUSES	—	2,227	92
	Accidents	1	1,078	44.5
	Homicide	2	400	16.5
	Suicide	3	224	9.3
	Cancer	4	111	4.6
	Heart Diseases	5	58	2.4
25 to 34	ALL CAUSES	—	2,908	127.2
	Accidents	1	1,194	52.2
	Suicide	2	332	14.5
	Homicide	3	304	13.3
	Cancer	4	214	9.4
	Heart Diseases	5	188	8.2

35 to 44	ALL CAUSES	—	5,157	206.3
	Accidents	1	1,253	50.1
	Cancer	2	828	33.1
	Heart Diseases	3	629	25.2
	Suicide	4	467	18.7
	HIV	5	365	14.6
45 to 54	ALL CAUSES	—	1,247	469.7
	Cancer	1	3,394	127.8
	Heart Diseases	2	2,185	82.2
	Accidents	3	1,552	58.4
	Chronic Liver Disease, Cirrhosis	4	652	24.5
	Suicide	5	642	24.2
55 to 64	ALL CAUSES	—	19,112	856.2
	Cancer	1	6,827	305.9
	Heart Diseases	2	3,904	174.9
	Chronic Lower Respiratory Disease	3	909	40.7
	Accidents	4	898	40.2
	Diabetes	5	833	37.2
65 to 74	ALL CAUSES	—	27,441	1,721.70
	Cancer	1	10,069	631.8
	Heart Diseases	2	5,941	372.8
	Chronic Lower Respiratory Disease	3	2,220	139.3
	Diabetes	4	1,148	72
	Stroke	5	1,137	71.3
75 to 84	ALL CAUSES	—	48,064	3,930.00
	Cancer	1	12,138	1,035.60
	Heart Diseases	2	11,641	993.2
	Chronic Lower Respiratory Disease	3	3,680	314
	Stroke	4	2,674	228.1
	Alzheimer's	5	1,447	123.5

85 +	ALL CAUSES	—	52,822	10,553.20
	Heart Diseases	1	17,330	3,462.30
	Cancer	2	6,893	1,377.10
	Stroke	3	3,431	685.5
	Alzheimer's	4	3,022	603.8
	Chronic Lower Respiratory Disease	5	2,982	595.8

LIFE EXPECTANCY

A person born in Florida in 2008 could expect to live 79.2 years, down slightly from previous years. Life expectancy declined for men and women, white and nonwhite.

White Florida females born in 2008 had a life expectancy of 82.8 years, the highest of any group. White males could expect to live 76.8 years, a decline from 2007. Nonwhite males continued to have the shortest life expectancy at 73.6 years.

BIRTHS

Florida resident live births declined to 231,417 in 2008, and the birth rate declined to 12.3 per 1,000 population. Florida's birth rate continued to lag behind the national rate.

The birth rate among whites was 11.0, the lowest on record. The birthrate among nonwhites was 17.4 per 1,000, a slight decrease from the year before.

The percentage of births to mothers under the age of 18 decreased in 2008 to 6.3 and declined from both white and nonwhite mothers. Of live births to unwed mothers, 12.4 percent were to women 18 years and younger. Births to mothers 18 or younger declined to 6.3 percent of the total. Births to mothers age 35 and over accounted for 18.3 percent of all births. Of mothers aged 15 to 19 years, 18.3 percent had one or more previous live births.

In 2008, 46.9 percent of live births, was to an unwed mother. For blacks, seven of every ten live births, 70.1 percent, were to unwed mothers. The rate among white mothers was 40.9 percent.

Of the resident live births in 2008, 8.8 percent of births involved a birthweight of less than 2,500 grams (5 lbs., 8.2 oz.) while 1.7 percent had a birthweight of less than 1,500 grams (3 lbs., 4.9 oz.). At the other end of the scale, 6.4 percent of resident live births had birthweights of 4,000 grams (8 lbs., 13.1 oz.) or more.

Nearly 99 percent of all births occurred in hospitals in 2008, and 88.7 percent of those hospital births were attended by a physician, with 80 percent of all mothers receiving prenatal care in the first trimester.

More births occurred in September than in any other month.

DEATHS

Florida resident deaths increased to 170,473, a 1.6 percent increase from 2007.

Heart disease continued to be the leading cause of death followed, as it has been, by cancer, stroke, chronic lower respiratory disease, and accidents. Heart disease caused almost three in every ten deaths in the state.

Cancer was the cause in almost one in every four deaths, but the age-adjusted death rate for cancer continued to decline. Respiratory cancer was the most pervasive cause of cancer death.

Accidents were the leading cause of death among the population between the ages of 1 through 44, accounting for 34.1 percent of all deaths in that age group.

There were 114 fewer deaths associated with HIV in 2008 than in 2007, a 7.5 percent decrease, but it remained the fourth leading cause of death among nonwhites. The death rate among nonwhite males was greater than the rate for white males and females and nonwhite females combined. HIV was the fifth leading cause of death in persons 35 through 44, accounting for 14.6 percent of total deaths in that age group.

The homicide rate decreased for white and nonwhite males but increased for white females in 2008. Still, the rate for nonwhite males was five times the rate for white males. Including homicide, major external causes of death (accident, suicide, legal intervention) accounted for 7.6 percent of deaths in the state during 2008.

Diabetes was the sixth leading cause of death in the state, followed by Alzheimer's and influenza.

Both the number and the rate of neonatal (under 28 days) deaths decreased in 2008. Overall the neonatal death rate was 4.5 per 1,000 live births. There was an overall decrease in infant (under one year) deaths. The death rate fell to 6.90 per 1,000 births, a record low. The infant mortality rate has dropped 28.1 percent since 1990. But the infant mortality rate for nonwhites, 12.1. Of the total deaths occurring in the first year of life, 65.2 percent were less than 28 days old with 39.5 percent occurring among those less than one day old.

There were 81,918 abortions in Florida during 2009, 73,626 for personal choice. More than 75,000 early terminations were performed on mothers age 12 and under. There were only five among mothers 25 or older. Most abortions, more than 18,000, were performed in Miami-Dade County.

A total of 8,779 persons died in 2008 due to accidents, the fourth leading cause of death in Florida.

March recorded the highest number of deaths.

PAINKILLERS KILL

Oxycodone was the cause of death for 1,185 people in Florida in 2009. That represented a 26 percent increase over 2008 and a 240 percent increase over 2005.

Of the 24 medical examiner districts in the state, the St. Petersburg area reported the most oxycodone deaths with 197, followed by the Fort Lauderdale, West Palm Beach, and Tampa areas. The St. Petersburg office, which covers Pinellas and Pasco counties, also reported the

highest number of methadone (117) and hydrocodone (43) deaths.
Overall, prescription drug deaths in Florida totaled 2,488. Statewide, benodiazepines killed 1,099, methadone 720, ethyl alcohol including ethanol 530, cocaine 529, and morphine 302. More than 4,000 people had alcohol in their systems when they died.

DISPOSAL OF REMAINS

After its two-decade rise in popularity, cremation passed the incidence of burial for those who died in Florida in 1997 and has continued to gain popularity. In 2008, cremations outnumbered burials among whites, 58.6 percent. But blacks continued to favor burials over cremations 66 to 24 percent. Removal of remains from the state continued to decline, to 11.3 percent.

MARRIAGES AND DISSOLUTIONS

The marriage rate continued its decade-long decline to 7.9 in 2008. Meanwhile, the dissolution rate, including annulments, also declined to 4.2 per 1,000 population.

More than 90 percent of marriages involved couples of the same race. More than half of all dissolutions involved no minor children. The mean duration rate of dissolved marriages in 2008 was 7.9 years.

The number of marriages in 2008 decreased to 147,888 from 2007's 155,990. Dissolutions decreased to 79,868 from 84,386.

May was the most popular month in 2008 to be married, while September was the month in which the most dissolutions of marriage were granted.

The marriage rate is nearly twice the dissolution rate in Florida, and both are higher than the U.S. rate.

MARRIAGE LICENSES

Marriage license applications can be taken out in the clerk of circuit court's office in any county, regardless of where the parties live in Florida. Minimum legal age is 18 for both males and females. If the parties are not of legal age, both parents, if living, or a legal guardian, must sign their consent to the marriage. The license is valid for 60 days. The marriage may take place in any county, but the license must be returned within 10 days after the marriage to the county which issued it for there to be an official record of the union.

However, prospective newlyweds who are Floridians are required to take a 4-hour marriage course or wait three days for a license. Those who opt for the three-day waiting period will pay a high price, $93.50, for a marriage license. Those taking the course may obtain a marriage license for $61.00. The courses are given by churches and other nonprofit organizations. Non-residents do not have to meet the requirements. The law requiring either counseling or a cooling off period also mandates that Florida high-school students take a course on marriage although that curriculum may be included in another course.

LIVING WILL

Under Florida law, adults have the right to make certain decisions concerning medical treatment and to have that right and their wishes respected if they are too ill to make such decisions themselves at the time, codified as a living will.

Persons have the right, under certain conditions, to decide whether to accept or reject medical treatment, including whether to continue medical treatment and/or other procedures that would prolong their lives artificially. A living will contains a person's personal directions about life-prolonging treatment in the case of serious illness that could cause death.

A person may also designate another person, or surrogate, who may make decisions for them if he or she becomes mentally or physically unable to do so. This surrogate may function on the ill person's behalf for a brief time, or longer for a life threatening or a non-life threatening illness. Clear limits may be put on what a surrogate may do.

The 1999 legislature strengthened the law by adding "end-stage" condition to the situations that would trigger the provisions of a living will and specified feeding and hydration as "life prolonging procedures" that a living will could prevent.

ORGAN DONATIONS

Florida allows motorists to indicate on their driver's license or identification card that they wish to donate organs or tissues after their death.

CRIME

CRIMES AND RATES

Florida's crime rate declined to a 39-year low in 2009, dropping nearly 60,000 below the number of crimes reported the year before. The nearly 7 percent drop represented the lowest number of crimes committed in the state since 1971. Violent crimes dropped 10 percent from 2008 while non-violent crimes decline 6 percent.

Crime did rise by three percent in one statistical category, domestic battery, with 20 percent of the state's murders involving domestic disputes. Overall, however, the number of murders dropped 12.9 percent.

Declines in other crime categories included vehicle thefts by 20.9 percent, robberies 14.8 percent, aggravated assaults 8.4 percent; forcible sex offenses 5.5 percent and larcenies 5.3 percent. Preliminary reports indicated that crime, especially violent crime, continued to trend downward in 2010.

Florida's Department of Law Enforcement has compiled crime statistics from, county and municipal law enforcement agencies since 1930.

2009

Crime Volume	
Violent	113,415
Nonviolent	711,144
TOTAL	824,559
Property Value	
Total Stolen	$1,637,567,694
TOTAL RECOVERED	$353,139,358
Arrests	
Adult	944,113
Juvenile	105,816
Male	801,244
Female	248,685
TOTAL	1,049,929

Offense	2008	2009	Percentage Change
Murder	**1,168**	**1,017**	**-12.9**
Firearm	780	695	-10.9
Knife	163	136	-16.6
Barehanded	95	87	-8.4
Other	130	99	-23.8
Forcible sex offenses	**10,823**	**10,227**	**-5.5**
Rape	5,962	5,494	-7.5
Sodomy	1,301	1,306	0.4
Fondling	3,560	3,427	-3.7
Robbery	**36,232**	**30,881**	**-14.8**
Firearm	16,917	13,688	-19.2
Knife	2,268	1,938	-14.6
Barehanded	13,971	12,543	-10.2
Other	3,076	2,732	-11.2
Aggravated Assault	**77,849**	**71,290**	**-8.4**
Firearm	16,666	14,982	-10.1
Knife	14,565	13,420	-7.9
Barehanded	14,911	14,273	-4.3
Other	31,707	28,615	-9.8
Burglary	**188,159**	**181,658**	**-3.5**
Forced Entry	113,890	109,317	-4
No Forced Entry	60,665	58,289	-3.9
Attempted Entry	13,604	14,052	3.3
Larceny	**506,237**	**479,282**	**-5.3**
Pocket Picking	2,354	2,508	6.5
Purse Snatching	1,779	1,465	-17.7
Shoplifting	83,878	85,147	1.5
From Motor Vehicle	144,583	139,695	-3.4
Motor Vehicle Parts	52,000	47,321	-9
Bicycles	17,857	17,617	-1.3
From Buildings	44,017	40,280	-8.5
From Vending Machines	1,841	1,670	-9.3
All Other	157,928	143,579	-9.1
Auto Theft	**63,437**	**50,204**	**-20.9**
TOTAL	**883,905**	**824,559**	**-6.7**

CRIME TRENDS

Year	Total Crimes	Percentage Change	Violent Crimes	Percentage Change	Non-Violent Crimes	Percentage Change
1992	1,112,746	-1.5	161,137	1.87	951,609	-2.05
1993	1,116,567	0.34	161,789	0.4	954,778	0.33
1994	1,130,875	1.28	157,835	-2.44	973,040	1.91
1995	1,078,619	-4.62	150,208	-4.83	928,411	-4.59
1996	1,079,642	0.09	151,369	0.76	928,273	-0.01
1997	1,073,757	-0.5	150,801	-0.5	922,956	-0.6
1998	1,025,100	-4.5	139,673	-7.4	885,427	-4.1
1999	934,349	-8.9	128,859	-7.7	805,490	-9
2000	895,708	-4.1	128,041	-0.6	767,667	-4.7
2001	911,292	1.7	130,323	1.8	780,969	1.7
2002	900,155	-1.2	127,905	-1.9	722,250	-1.1
2003	881,615	-2.1	124,236	-2.9	757,379	-1.9
2004	850.49	-3.5	123,697	-0.4	726,793	-4
2005	838,063	-1.5	125,825	1.7	712,238	-2
2006	849,926	1.4	129,501	2.9	720,425	1.1
2007	876,981	3.2	131,781	1.8	745,200	3.4
2008	883,905	0.8	126,072	-4.3	757,833	1.7
2009	824,559	-6.7	113,415	-10	711,144	-6.2

Domestic Violence

Primary Offense	2008	2009	Percentage Change
Murder	180	208	15.6
Manslaughter	14	24	71.4
Rape	931	958	2.9
Sodomy	290	334	15.2
Fondling	744	850	14.2
Aggrav. Assault	20,462	20,115	-1.7
Aggrav. Stalking	193	254	31.6
Simple Assault	87,303	90,525	3.7
Threat/Intimid.	2,655	2,822	6.3
Simple Stalking	351	417	18.8
TOTAL	133,123	116,547	-3

Domestic Violence
Victim's Relationship to Offender

2009	
Spouse	25,137
Parent	12,249
Child	8,135
Sibling	9,571
Other Family	6,349
Cohabitant	34,304
Other	20,802
Total Arrests	67,928

Value of Stolen Property—2009

Type	Stolen Value	Recovered Value
Currency, Notes, etc.	$124,724,041	$2,483,823
Jewelry, Prec. Metals	$245,858,108	$11,219,228
Clothing, Furs	$87,095,116	$4,827,111
Motor Vehicles	$438,021,081	$263,102,045
Office Equipment	$122,858,523	$4,827,111
TVs, Stereos, etc.	$91,911,002	$5,043,546
Firearms	$10,437,730	$1,197,955
Household Goods	$35,980,439	$1,163,070
Consumable Goods	$17,216,315	$1,499,482
Livestock	$994,747	$78,174
Miscellaneous	$462,520,592	$57,325,938
TOTALS	**$1,637,567,694**	**$352,139,358**

Vehicle Recovery—2009

Stolen and Recovered Locally	54,125
Stolen Locally and Recovered by Other Jurisdictions	53,224
Stolen in Other Jurisdictions and Recovered Locally	15,767

Arson—2009

Structure	Inhabited	Abandoned	Attempted
Single Residence	464	184	52
Other Residence	178	41	23
Storage	12	8	0
Ind./Manufacturing	11	5	1
Commercial	100	29	6
Community/Public	139	23	11
All Other Structures	50	27	4
Motor Vehicles	306	216	21
Other Mobile	7	7	0
Other	286	130	16
TOTAL	**1,553**	**670**	**134**

FDLE CRIME LABORATORIES

The Florida Department of Law Enforcement operates seven crime laboratories throughout the state. The labs perform crime scene analysis, forensic investigations, chemical and DNA analysis and drug detection, document investigations, and firearms and latent fingerprint tests for police agencies. The crime labs are located in Pensacola, Jacksonville, Orlando, Tallahassee, Tampa, Fort Myers, and Daytona Beach. The FDLE also operates two Computer Crime Centers, located in Tallahassee and Tampa as well as mobile computer crime platform.

CORRECTIONAL INSTITUTIONS

Florida prisons in 2009 held more than 100,000 prisoners with men held in 128 facilities including 56 prisons while women are in 18 facilities including six prisons. Other facilities include work camps, boot camps, stand alone work and forestry camps, a treatment center, work release centers and road prisons. Some institutions operate multiple facilities under one umbrella. Six prisons are privately operated.

Florida law requires persons convicted of a crime to serve at least 85 percent of their sentences. The requirement is a major reason the population of correctional institutions has increased to its historic level. The requirement is also credited with the record-setting decline in crime.

It costs $55 a day to maintain a prisoner.

The largest group incarcerated, nearly 30 percent, committed drug crimes.

Facility	City	Max. Inmate Capacity	Inmates (July 2009)
Apalachee West	Sneads	915	874
Apalachee East	Sneads	1,322	1,268
Avon Park Correctional	Avon Park	956	998
Baker Correctional	Sanderson	1,165	1,153
Bay Correctional**	Panama City	985	974
Blackwater Correctional	Milton	2,000	#
Brevard Correctional	Cocoa	1,032	1,020
Broward Correctional*	Ft. Lauderdale	753	731
Calhoun Correctional	Blountstown	1,354	1,421
Central Fla. Recp. Ctr	Orlando	1,659	1,436
CFRC East	Orlando	1,088	658
CFRC South	Orlando	150	102
Century	Century	1,345	1,382
Charlotte Correctional	Punta Gorda	1,289	1,097
Columbia Correctional	Lake City	1,344	1,254
Columbia Annex	Lake City	1,073	890
Cross City Correctional	Cross City	1,022	1,024
Dade Correctional	Florida City	1,659	1,604
DeMilly Correctional	Polk City	372	#
DeSoto Correctional	Arcadia		##
DeSoto Annex	Arcadia	1,453	1,543
Everglades Correctional	Miami	1,788	1,725
Florida State Prison West	Raiford	802	774
Florida State Prison	Raiford	1,460	501
Franklin Correctional	Carrabelle	1,492	1,438
Gadsden Correctional* ***	Quincy	1,520	1,497
Gainesville Correctional	Gainesville	378	545
Glades Correctional	Belle Glade	1,045	962
Graceville Correctional ***	Graceville	1,500	1,487
Gulf Correctional	Wewahitchka	1,486	1,601
Gulf Annex	Wewahitchka	1,396	1,460
Hamilton Correctional	Jasper	1,177	1,281
Hamilton Annex	Jasper	1,408	1,407
Hardee Correctional	Bowling Green	1,541	1,589
Hendry Correctional	Immokalee	1,229	947

Hernando Correctional*	Brooksville	431	405
Hillsborough Correctional*	Riverview	486	290
Holmes Correctional	Bonifay	1,185	1,143
Homestead Correctional*	Florida City	668	671
Indian River Correctional	Vero Beach	484	492
Jackson Correctional	Malone	1,386	1,285
Jefferson Correctional	Monticello	1,179	1,180
Lake City Correctional***	Lake City	894	803
Lake Correctional	Clermont	1,093	1,193
Lancaster Correctional	Trenton	570	622
Lawtey Correctional	Lawtey	832	837
Liberty Correctional	Bristol	1,330	1,292
Lowell Correctional*	Ocala	1,244	1,245
Lowell Annex*	Ocala	1,272	1,229
Madison Correctional	Madison	1,189	1,271
Marion Correctional	Lowell	1,282	1,416
Martin Correctional	Indiantown	1,509	1,301
Mayo Correctional	Mayo	1,641	1,324
Moore Haven Correctional***	Moore Haven	985	972
New River Correctional	Raiford	1,071	852
New River O-Unit	Raiford	567	501
Okaloosa Correctional	Crestview	894	952
Okeechobee Correctional	Okeechobee	1,632	1,652
Polk Correctional	Polk City	1,200	1,193
Putnam Correctional	East Palatka	458	469
Quincy Annex	Quincy	408	393
Reception & Medical Center	Lake Butler	1,503	1,480
RMC West	Lake Butler	1,148	886
Santa Rosa Correctional	Milton	1,614	1,352
Santa Rosa Annex	Milton	1,272	1,159
South Bay Correctional***	South Bay	1,862	1,851
South Florida Recp Ctr.	Miami	1,315	564
South Fla. Recp. Ctr-South	Doral	889	975
Sumter Correctional	Bushnell	1,502	1,680
Taylor Correctional	Perry	1,228	1,353

Taylor Annex	Perry	1,326	1,296
Tomoka Correctional	Daytona Beach	1,263	1,318
Union Correctional	Raiford	2,172	2,046
Wakulla Annex	Crawfordville	1,532	936
Wakulla Correctional	Crawfordville	1,326	1,314
Walton Correctional	DeFuniak Springs	1,199	1,299
Washington Correctional	Chipley	1,156	1,264
Zephyrhills Correctional	Zephyrhills	758	643

*Women's institution
** Men's and Women's units
***Privately operated facility
#Under development
##Closed for renovation

Florida law allows correctional facilities to operate at 150 percent of capacity. Although statistically some prisons appear overcrowded, most operate auxiliary facilities with sliding capacities.

In addition to those in such facilities, more than 12,000 inmates are in vocational camps, hospitals, community correction centers (work release), and drug treatment facilities. An additional 195,000 were under community control at the end of June 2005.

There were 371 prisoners on death row.

"FAITH-BASED PRISONS"

Florida now operates four correctional facilities as faith and character-based institutions, popularly called "faith-based prisons." The four are Lawtey, Hillsborough (for women), Glades, and Wakulla.

Prisoners volunteer to enter these institutions and must meet eligibility requirements, including not being under maximum security. The facilities can accommodate all of the world's major religions. Prisoners who profess no religion participate in the institutions' secular "character" activities, programs, and classes.

The program also is offered at seven other prisons with "faith-based/self-improvement" dormitories.

FOR SENIORS ONLY

River Junction Work Camp at Chattahoochee was refurbished and reopened in 2000 as Florida's first prison facility for the "elderly offender," defined as prisoners over the age of 50. In addition to age, an inmate must be in both good health and have a medium, minimum, or community custody rating to qualify for assignment to River Junction. The camp, with an inmate population of 334, is administered by Apalachee Correctional Institute, and workers are assigned to maintain the Florida State Hospital on the grounds shared by the two facilities.

INCARCERATION BY OFFENSE—2009

Offense	Number of Inmates (as of July 2009)
Homicide, first degree	103
Homicide, second degree	167
Homicide, third degree	9
Homicide, other	21
Manslaughter	145
DUI, manslaughter	104
DUI, cause injury	186
DUI, no injury	1,756
Sexual battery, capital	153
Sexual battery, life	70
Sexual battery, 1st degree	102
Sexual battery, 2nd degree	196
Sexual battery, other	10
Lewd, lascivious	1,003
Robbery, armed	1,216
Robbery, unarmed	1,558
Home invasion, robbery	101
Home invasion, other	2
Carjacking	129
Aggravated assault	1,719
Aggravated battery	1,524
Assault and battery on officer	1,608
Battery, other	692
Aggravated stalking	242
Resisting arrest, violence	1,029
Kidnapping	417
Arson	187
Child abuse	1,507
Leaving scene	415
Other violent offenses	3,874
Burglary, structure	5,183
Burglary, dwelling	2,717
Burglary, armed	313
Burglary, assault	341
Burglary, other	1,302
Grand theft	11,041
Grand theft, auto	1,621

Stolen property	2,652
Forgery, uttering, counterfeiting	3,282
Worthless checks	679
Fraud	4,491
Other theft	1,982
Drugs, trafficking	1,219
Drugs, possession	22,390
Drugs, sale, manufacturing, purchase	7,975
Escape	2,045
Weapon, discharging	300
Weapon, illegal possession	2,284
Weapon, other	17
Racketeering	86
Traffic, other	5,355
Pollution, hazardous materials	105
Justice Sustem Process Violations	1,834
Other offenses	1,119
N/A	36
TOTAL	**100,619**

PRISONER PROFILE—2009

More than half of inmates in Florida prisons in 2009 were 34 years old or younger, and the largest segment of the population was between 24 and 34 years of age. Of the 100,619 inmates, 71 percent were men. Both white males and white females outnumbered their black counterparts by nearly two-to-one.

Inmates from Broward County made up the largest contingent with 9,567, 9.5 percent of the prison population. For nearly 60 percent of the prison population, it is their first stay in a Florida correctional facility. A majority of inmates were sentenced to less than two years with six years probation.

Most prisoners function at the sixth-grade level. But nearly 2,000 earned high school diplomas in 2009.

Florida held 5,744 confirmed alien inmates, and nearly 60 percent of that group was serving time for violent crimes. Cuban nationals (1,952), Mexicans (1,211), and Jamaicans (460) lead the number of incarcerated aliens.

Prisoners under the age of 18 number 418, 1,137 were over 70.

A DEATH SENTENCE'S LONG JOURNEY THROUGH THE COURTS

The time between the day a murderer is caught and the day he or she is executed can be years, often more than a decade. Appeals, new trials, new hearings, court reviews, and clemency pleadings—all grind slowly through the judicial system.

• **Step One**—Trial. If guilty and sentenced to death, the case moves to . . .

• **Step Two**—Automatic review by the Florida Supreme Court. If that court upholds the sentence, defense attorneys move to . . .

• **Step Three**—An appeal to the U.S. Supreme Court which, if it refuses to reconsider the case, may prod the case on to . . .

• **Step Four**—A hearing before the cabinet acting in its role as clemency board, which if denied, moves the case to . . .

• **Step Five**—the first death warrant signed by the governor, which prompts defense attorneys to . . .

• **Step Six**—Petition the Florida Supreme Court a second time with briefs stating new evidence is available, which if denied, takes lawyers back to . . .

• **Step Seven**—The trial court, which is advised the defendant did not get a fair first trial or that new evidence is now available, and if the trial court adheres to its original decision, the defense lawyers move to . . .

• **Step Eight**—the Florida Supreme Court a third time and if that court refuses to stay the execution, defense attorneys file to . . .

• **Step Nine**—the Federal District Court, which is told the defendant deserves a stay of execution or that the sentence is unfair and if the Federal District Court refuses to change the sentence, defense lawyers move to . . .

• **Step Ten**—the U.S. Eleventh Court of Appeals in Atlanta with an appeal to stop the execution and if that court is not swayed, the defense moves to . . .

• **Step Eleven**—a final appeal to the U.S. Supreme Court, which if unmoved, leaves only one last walk . . . to execution.

DEATH ROW

Prior to the introduction of the electric chair in 1924, Florida counties hanged prisoners who were sentenced to death. With the introduction of the state's famous execution device, "Ol' Sparky," the legislature mandated executions be held at Starke, which was the main state prison. There it established "death row."

Over the next forty years, Florida electrocuted 196 prisoners convicted of capital crimes.

Florida's death penalty was suspended in 1964, pending

litigation. In 1972, the United States Supreme Court held that capital punishment was unconstitutional. Florida commuted the death sentences of the 95 men and one woman on death row to life in prison.

Four years later, the U.S. high court reversed its decision. In the interim, 89 prisoners, including one woman, had been sentenced to death in Florida under new statutes and in anticipation of an eventual Supreme Court reversal.

Governor Reubin Askew signed the first death warrant under the new rules in 1997, and executions resumed under the new rules in 1979. John Spenkelink was the first to die.

Since the resumption of the death penalty, 69 prisoners were executed as of the year 2010.

1995	3
1996	2
1997	1
1998	4
1999	1
2000	6
2001	1
2002	3
2003	3
2004	2
2005	1
2006	4
2007	0
2008	2
2009	2
2010	1

Executions Since the Reinstatement of the Death Penalty

1979	1
1980	0
1981	0
1982	0
1983	1
1984	8
1985	3
1986	3
1987	1
1988	2
1989	2
1990	4
1991	2
1992	2
1993	3
1994	1

Despite the Supreme Court ruling, both the death penalty and the electric chair continued to be challenged as "cruel and unusual punishment." Anticipating the possibility that the electric chair might be deemed as such, in the Florida special session in January 2000 the legislature voted to give condemned prisoners the choice of death in the electric chair or by lethal injection. All since chose lethal injection, with Terry M. Sims, 58, being the first. The electric chair, last used to execute Allen Lee Davis in 1999, has been placed in a small storage room behind the execution chamber.

The Florida legislature has banned the execution of the mentally disabled.

Men on death row are housed at Florida State Prison at Union Correctional Institution in Raiford. The one women on death row is housed at Lowell Correctional Institution Annex in Ocala.

Executions are conducted at Starke. The official executioner is an anonymous private citizen who is paid $150 per execution.

Death-row inmates are distinguished by their orange T-shirts and by being among the few Florida prisoners housed individually in cells. Almost all other inmates in Florida are held in open-bay dormitories. When the governor signs a death warrant, the named prisoner is transferred to a "death watch" cell, closer to the execution site.

Inmates sentenced to die spend an average of nearly 12 years on death row. Their daily routine includes being accounted for at least once an hour, and being given three meals a day for which they receive utensils. They spend almost all of their time in their respective cells. They are escorted in handcuffs at all times except when in their cells, in the shower—which they may take every other day—and in the exercise yard. They are allowed pre-approved visitors and may participate in media interviews but have no common room privileges. They may receive mail on weekdays and are allowed cigarettes, snacks, radios, and black-and-white television in their cells. If transferred to a death watch cell, they receive limited phone privileges but the radio and television are moved outside the cell. Death row is not air-conditioned.

It costs the state $74 per day to incarcerate a prisoner on death row, $19 more than other inmates.

SHERIFFS

County	Sheriff
Alachua	Sadie Darnell
Baker	Joey Dobson
Bay	Frank McKeithen
Bradford	Gordon Smith
Brevard	Jack Parker
Broward	Al Lamberti
Calhoun	David L. Tatum
Charlotte	Bill Cameron
Citrus	Jeff Dawsy
Clay	Rick Beseler
Collier	Kevin Rambosk
Columbia	Mark Hunter
DeSoto	Will Wise
Dixie	Dewey H. Hatcher
Duval	John H. Rutherford
Escambia	David Morgan
Flagler	Donald Fleming
Franklin	Skip Shiver, Jr.
Gadsden	Morris A. Young
Gilchrist	Daniel Slaughter
Glades	Stuart Whidden
Gulf	Joe Nugent
Hamilton	J. Harrell Reid
Hardee	Arnold Lanier
Hendry	Steve Whidden
Hernando	Al Nienhuis
Highlands	Susan Benton
Hillsborough	David A. Gee
Holmes	Tim Brown
Indian River	Deryl B. Loar
Jackson	Lou Roberts III
Jefferson	David C. Hobbs
Lafayette	Brian Lamb
Lake	Gary Borders

Lee	Mike Scott
Leon	Larry Campbell
Levy	Johnny M. Smith
Liberty	Donny Conyers
Madison	Benjamin Stewart
Manatee	Brad Steube
Marion	Ed Dean
Martin	Bob Crowder
Miami-Dade	James K. Loftus*
Monroe	Bob Peryham
Nassau	Tommy Seagraves, Jr.
Okaloosa	Larry R. Ashley
Okeechobee	Paul C. May
Orange	Jerry L. Demings
Osceola	Robert E. Hansell
Palm Beach	Ric L. Bradshaw
Pasco	Bob White
Pinellas	Jim Coats
Polk	Grady Judd
Putnam	Jeff Hardy
St. Johns	David B. Shoar
St. Lucie	Ken J. Mascara
Santa Rosa	O. Wendell Hall
Sarasota	Tom Knight
Seminole	Donald Eslinger
Sumter	Bill Farmer, Jr.
Suwannee	Tony Cameron.
Taylor	L. E. "Bummy" Williams
Union	Jerry Whitehead
Volusia	Ben F. Johnson
Wakulla	David F. Harvey
Walton	Michael A. Adkinson, Jr.
Washington	Bobby Haddock

appointed, director, Miami-Dade Police Dept.

YOUTH RANCHES

The Florida Sheriffs Youth Ranches began when two sheriffs traveled to Texas to bring back two teenage armed robbery suspects and learned of a ranch established for needy and neglected boys. They brought the idea home with them and soon their colleagues in the Florida Sheriffs Association joined them in a private effort to help kids, one that today is recognized as one of the nation's finest residential child-care programs.

When the sheriffs sought to buy land on the Suwannee River to establish such a ranch, a Live Oak civic club and a local business leader combined to donate 140 acres to the project. The sheriffs took out bank loans to purchase 410 additional acres. They were down to $2,000 when word of the project finally went public beyond Live Oak and donations began pouring in, enabling the sheriffs to build their first ranch cottage in time for staff and the first residents to arrive in 1959.

Today, there are six Youth Ranches, including Girls Villa, two camps and numerous other child-care programs serving the children of Florida. They are still sponsored by the Florida Sheriffs Association and still funded by private donations.

NOTABLE UNSOLVED FLORIDA CRIMES

Florida has had its share of unsolved murders and disappearances. Some have received national attention, while others are notorious only to Floridians. Following are some of the most talked-about to this day.

1915—Trenton physician Henry Owens is gunned down and dragged through town streets by an angry mob. Only motive ever considered was that Owens, separated from his wife, was romancing another woman. No arrests were ever made.

1957—Wealthy Parrish grocer Gettis Lee and his wife disappear. Muriel Lee's body is found two days later in a ditch along a rural road near Parrish. Her husband's skeleton is not discovered until 1963, in a scrub field also near town. A possible link to illegal gambling was rumored.

1959—University of Florida student Chandler Steffens is murdered while on break in his Sarasota home. He had been bound, slashed, and his face covered in an adhesive mask. More than 400 persons were questioned and 48 given polygraph tests, but the murderer was never found.

1959—Ranch hand Clifford Walker, his wife, and two children are found shot to death in their Christmas-decorated Osprey home. No motive or leads have been uncovered. The case earned national attention when mentioned by writer Truman Capote in his best-selling classic, *In Cold Blood.*

1966—Nancy Leichner, 21, and Pamela Nater, 20, vanish while walking near Alexander Springs in the Ocala National Forest. The women left their camp site without their purses, shoes, and other belongings. Investigators found the day's park sign-in sheet had been torn out. Despite 10 days of searching, the two women never were found.

1966—Nationally renowned computer expert Robert Sims, 42, his wife, and 12-year-old daughter are shot to death in their Tallahassee home. No motive was established, although police reported finding "enough evidence to fill five file drawers."

1974—Athalia Lindsley, a 52-year-old former model said to have connections to the Kennedy family, was hacked to death on the front steps of her St. Augustine home. St. Johns County Manager Alan Stanford, a neighbor, was arrested but a jury found him innocent. No other suspect has ever surfaced.

1976—Bones identified as those of 21-year-old Douglas Sumner of Tampa are found by hunters in rural Dixie County. An investigation reveals Sumner was padlocked to a pine tree during the previous year and left to starve. Objects at the scene included a Bible, a wallet, keys, a belt, clothing fragments, and the novel *A Man Called Peter.* Theories about Sumner's slow death ranged from suicide to a religious ritual to drug-related.

1980—Tampa pediatrician Juan Dumois, his two sons, and an unrelated man are killed by a gunman at a Holmes Beach boat ramp. Police theorize the kills may have been the work of a psychopath. Witnesses reported the gunman ran to a waiting getaway car.

1991—A series of home invasions leaves a couple in Port Charlotte shot to death and a man and three of his stepchildren (ages 9, 11, and 13) shot to death in North Port. One child, 8, is shot but survives. No suspects have been charged despite a $10,000 reward.

1993—Jennifer Renee Odom, a 13-year-old Pasco County student, disappears after getting off her school bus approximately 150 yards from her front door. Her body was found six days later in another county. Her schoolbooks, backpack, clarinet, and purse, with her when she disappeared, have never been found, nor has her killer or killers.

1997—Sabrina Aisenberg was kidnapped from her crib in her parents' upscale Brandon home by an abductor who passed through unlocked doors in the pre-dawn hours without disturbing the family dog. A nationwide search has produced no clues toward the infant's fate. Her well-respected parents declined to cooperate with police after they found themselves prime suspects. In 1999, her parents were indicted by a federal grand jury and charged, not with murder or kidnapping, but with conspiracy and lying to a grand jury. But in 2001 the indictment was dismissed and an investigation of the investigators began.

1999—Sonphet "Tim" Chanthavong, a young St. Petersburg mortgage loan officer, loved his super sharp car, a red 1994 Acura NSX. After leaving a music store, Chanthavong and his car were approached by a black male teen who shot and killed him, then stole the car and went for a joyride until he crashed the car. Although there were witnesses to the crime, the joyride, and the crash, no one has come forward to identify the killer. The case has become a textbook example of a growing and disturbing trend.

EVERYDAY NOISE BANNED

Martin County has banned every sound from its quiet streets. An ordinance caps noise levels for homes at 60 decibels, businesses at 65 decibels, and the maximum noise level on industrial or agricultural sites at 70 decibels. Nighttime levels are lower still. Violation carries a $500 fine. A normal speaking voice is in the range of 60 decibels.

WOMEN'S HALL OF FAME

The Florida Women's Hall of Fame began in 1982 under the aegis of the Governor's Commission on the Status of Women, to recognize and honor those women who, through their works and lives, have made significant improvement of life for women and for all citizens of Florida. The Women's Hall of Fame is located in the state capitol.

Annie Ackerman—political leader

Caridad Asensio—migrant worker advocate

Rosemary Barkett—judge

Alicia Baro—political leader

Nikki Beare—feminist

Mary McLeod Bethune—educator, civil rights leader

Sarah Ann Blocker—educator, founder of Florida Memorial College

Roxcy O'Neal Bolton—feminist leader

Marjorie Harris Carr—environmentalist

Betty Castor—Commissioner of Education

Gwendolyn Sawyer Cherry—legislator

Eugenia Clark—marine biologist

Jacqueline Cochran—aviator

Helene S. Coleman—civic leader

Shirley D. Coletti—community mental health leader

Carita Doggett Corse—author, historian, feminist

Louise Courtelis—businesswoman, philanthropist

Evelyn Stocking Crosslin—physician

Helen Gordon Davis—legislator

Mattie Belle Davis—judge

Dorothy Dodd—journalist, author, state librarian

Marjory Stoneman Douglas—journalist, author

Jessie Ball duPont—philanthropist

Victoria Joyce Ely, R.N.—first nurse

Gloria Estevan—singer-songwriter, philanthropist

Chris Evert—athlete

Tillie Kidd Fowler—member of Congress

Betty Skelton Frankman—aviator, auto racer

Barbara Landstreet Frye—journalist

Christine Fulwylie-Bankston—poet

Althea Gibson—athlete

Elaine Gordon—legislator

Mary R. Grizzle—legislator

Marion P. Hammer—second amendment advocate

Elsie Jones Hare—educator

Wilhelmina Celeste Goehring Harvey—first woman mayor of Key West

Paula Hawkins—U.S. Senator

Lena B. Smithers Hughes—citrus scientist

Zora Neale Hurston—author

Toni Jennings—legislator, Lt. Gov.

Elizabeth McCullough Johnson—first woman state senator

Betty Mae Tiger Jumper—Seminole Chief

Lynda Keever—publisher

Judith Kersey—scientist

Frances Bartlett Kinne—educator, college president

Gwen Margolis—state senator

Marianne Mathewson-Chapman, Ph.D.—Major General

Carrie P. Meek—member of Congress

Gladys D. Milton—midwife

Paula Mae Milton—educator, dramatist

Sybil Collins Mobley—educator
JoAnn Hardin Morgan—
engineer
Lucy W. Morgan—journalist
Helen Lennehan Muir—
journalist, author
Lenore Carrero Nesbit—judge
Sister Jeanne O'Loughlin, OP,
Ph.D—university president
Ruth Bryan Owen—Member of
Congress
Barbara Jo Palmer—athletic
director
Barbara Pariente—state
Supreme Court Justice
Arva Jeane Moore Parks—author
Palava Patel, MD—pediatrician,
philanthropist
Maryly VanLeer Peck, Ph.D.—
scientist, educator
Paulina Pedroso—Cuban
independence leader
Dessie Smith Prescott—pioneer
Sarah "Aunt Frances" Brooks
Pryor—postmaster
Peggy A. Quince—state Supreme
Court Justice

M. Athalie Range—Secretary of
Community Affairs
Marjorie Kinnan Rawlings—
author
Janet Reno—U.S. Attorney
General
Ileana Ros Lentinen—member
of Congress
Claudia Ryce—child advocate
Florence Barbara Seibert—
biochemist
Betty Schlesinger Sembler—
ambassador, drug-free advocate
Marilyn K. Smith—volunteer
Gladys Pumariega Soler—
pediatrician
Ivy Julia Cromartie Stranahan—
Seminole mentor
Francis Langford Stuart—
entertainer
Dara Torres—Olympian
Julia DeForest Sturtevant
Tuttle—Miami pioneer
Eartha Mary Magdalene White—
educator, publisher

LIBRARIES

DOCUMENT LIBRARIES

State documents are distributed to the following depository libraries and are available to Florida citizens for use either in the libraries or on interlibrary loan:

Boca Raton
Florida Atlantic University Library
Chiefland
Levy County Public Library
Cocoa
Mid-Brevard Library and Reference Center
Coral Gables
University of Miami Richter Library
Daytona Beach
Volusia County Library Center
DeLand
Stetson University DuPont-Ball Library
Fort Lauderdale
Broward County Division of Libraries
Fort Myers
Lee County Library System
Gainesville
University of Florida Library
Jacksonville
Jacksonville Public Library
Jacksonville University Swisher Library
University of North Florida Library
Miami
Florida International University Library
Miami-Dade Public Library
North Miami
Florida International University Library, Biscayne Bay Campus
Orlando
Orange County Library

University of Central Florida Library
Pensacola
University of West Florida Pace Library
St. Petersburg
St. Petersburg Public Library
Tallahassee
Florida State University Strozier Library
State Library of Florida
Tampa
Tampa-Hillsborough County Libraries
University of South Florida Library

U.S. documents are distributed to the following depository libraries:

Boca Raton
Florida Atlantic University Wimberly Library
Bradenton
Manatee County Public Library
Clearwater
Clearwater Public Library
Coral Gables
University of Miami Richter Library
Daytona Beach
Volusia County Public Library
DeLand
Stetson University DuPont-Ball Library
Fort Lauderdale
Broward County Library
Nova Southeastern University Law Library
Fort Pierce
Indian River State College Miley Resource Center
Gainesville
University of Florida Lawton Chiles Legal Information Center
University of Florida Map & Imaging Center

University of Florida Smathers Library

Gulfport
Stetson University College of Law Library

Jacksonville
Jacksonville Public Library
Jacksonville University Swisher Library
University of North Florida Carpenter Library

Lakeland
Lakeland Public Library

Leesburg
Lake-Sumter State College Library

Melbourne
Florida Institute of Technology Evans Library

Miami
Florida International University Green Library
Miami-Dade Public Library
St. Thomas University Library

Naples
Hodges University Information Resource Center

North Miami
Florida International University Biscayne Bay Library

Orlando
University of Central Florida Library

Pensacola
University of West Florida Pace Library

St. Petersburg
St. Petersburg Public Library

Sarasota
New College Cook Library
Selby Public Library

Tallahassee
Florida A&M University Coleman Library
Florida State University Law Library
Florida State University Strozier Library
Florida Supreme Court Library
State Library of Florida

Tampa
Tampa-Hillsborough Germany Library
University of South Florida Library
University of Tampa Kelce Library

Winter Park
Rollins College Olin Library

LIBRARY SERVICE

Numerous Florida library systems have formed regional consortiums under which patrons of one system may use the services of another as if they were local cardholders.

EDUCATION

Public education in Florida began in 1822 when the region became a territory. At that time every sixteenth section of land in each township was reserved for primary schools. In practice, however, the only actual teaching was done at a few Spanish missions.

Until 1845 the only true public schools in the territory were in Franklin and Monroe counties. The few who were educated attended private academies. With statehood, interest in a public school system grew, and in 1851 counties were authorized to levy taxes for the support of common schools, up to $4 per child. The legislature also provided that if income from a permanent state school fund did not reach at least $2 per child, other state funds could be used to make up the difference.

Each Florida county is a unified school district. Schools are financed by county ad valorum taxes. The state supplements those revenues with direct funding to each county based on a formula designed to ensure equitable funding for every school district regardless of its location, economy, or the property tax base available to support it.

ADMISSION REQUIREMENTS

All children who have attained the age of 6 or who will have attained that age by Feb. 1 of any school year, or who are between the ages of 6 and 16, are required to attend school regularly during the entire school term.

Any child who has attained the age of 6 on or before Sept. 1 of the school year and who has been enrolled in a public school, or has satisfactorily completed the requirements for kindergarten in a nonpublic school from which the district school board accepts transfer of academic credit, shall be enrolled.

Children who have attained the age of 5 on or before Sept. 1 of the school year shall be eligible for admission to public kindergartens during the school year. Kindergarten is a mandatory grade. Voluntary prekindergarten for 4-year-olds is available in all Florida school districts.

A child who attained the age of 16 during the school year shall not be required to attend school beyond his birthday.

A legal birth certificate or other authentic proof of a child's age, as required by law, must be submitted prior to a student's initial entry into kindergarten. A full measure of inoculations is also required for admission.

For other than the first grade, a transcript or last report card is required. By legislative mandate the school term may not begin sooner than 14 days prior to Labor Day and must end in May with 180 school days on the calendar.

All public schools are directed and controlled at the county level by a county school board. The chief officer is the superintendent of schools, who may be elected or appointed. Textbooks are provided free. School bus service is available to all rural and suburban pupils residing two miles or more from school. Some variation may occur in some of the larger cities where city bus service is operating. A pupil whose parents or guardian are nonresidents must pay a tuition fee at enrollment. No fee is charged if the parent or guardian is in military service, a migratory agricultural worker, or a federal civilian employee where the federal government provides an educational subsidy.

REQUIRED IMMUNIZATIONS

The following student immunizations are required for admission to Florida's schools:

Grades K-2
• Diphtheria-tetanus-pertussis—four or five doses.
• Polio—three or four doses.
• Measles-mumps-rubella—two doses.
• Hepatitis B series—three doses over a six-month period.
• Varicella—two doses are now required for kindergarten and first

and second grades or a history of chickenpox documented by a health provider.

Grades 3-6
The above but one dose of varicella vaccine or a documented history.

Grade 7
The above plus:
• Tetanus-diphtheria-pertussis booster —one dose. (A tetanus booster alone is not acceptable.)

Grades 8-12
The above but
• Chickenpox vaccine or history, not required for grades 10-12
• Tetanus-diphtheria booster dose required for grades 9-12.

All immunization dates must be on a Florida Certificate of Immunization.

PUBLIC-SCHOOL ENROLLMENT
Pre-kindergarten—Grade 12
(2009-2010)

County	Pupils
Alachua	27,757
Baker	5,050
Bay	25,893
Bradford	3,275
Brevard	72,402
Broward	256,175
Calhoun	2,233
Charlotte	16,935
Citrus	16,083
Clay	35,998
Collier	42,714
Columbia	10,096
DeSoto	4,989

County	Pupils
Dixie	2,110
Duval	122,649
Escambia	40,610
Flagler	13,138
Franklin	1,295
Gadsden	6,331
Gilchrist	2,737
Glades	1,429
Gulf	2,031
Hamilton	1,818
Hardee	5,032
Hendry	6,902
Hernando	22,893
Highlands	12,141

Hillsborough	193,239		Palm Beach	173,025
Holmes	3,382		Pasco	67,143
Indian River	17,750		Pinellas	105,176
Jackson	7,337		Polk	94,577
Jefferson	1,192		Putnam	11,418
Lafayette	1,163		St. Johns	29,822
Lake	41,099		St. Lucie	38,930
Lee	80,470		Santa Rosa	25,667
Leon	32,708		Sarasota	41,281
Levy	5,929		Seminole	64,460
Liberty	1,497		Sumter	7,554
Madison	2,736		Suwannee	6,129
Manatee	42,922		Taylor	3,179
Marion	42,040		Union	2,339
Martin	18,024		Volusia	62,329
Miami-Dade	345,766		Wakulla	5,244
Monroe	8,278		Walton	7,114
Nassau	11,116		Washington	3,486
Okaloosa	28,887		State Special Schools	981
Okeechobee	6,963		University Laboratory Schools	6,150
Orange	173,021			
Osceola	52,142		**TOTAL**	**2,634,382**

VIRTUAL SCHOOL

In addition to its county-based school systems, Florida has another school district: Florida Virtual School. Because of its scope, the state no longer includes it in its count of public school students. The internet-based school serves students with a vigorous curriculum in grades K through 12. The distance-learning district opened as a pilot program in 1997 and established itself as an independent education entity with its own governor-appointed governing board in 2002. It opened as a high school but has since added middle and elementary schools. The school is free to Floridians and serves public, private, and homeschooled students. Floridians have a right to enroll in Florida Virtual School for all or part of their education. Out-of-state and foreign students also may enroll on a tuition basis. More than 200,000 students are enrolled full and part-time.

PRIVATE SCHOOLS

More than 10 percent of Florida's

schoolchildren, 313,291, in grades pre-K-12 for the 2009-2010 school year, attended Florida's more than 2,000 nonpublic schools. These schools are required to meet public health and safety standards and attendance requirements but the state generally has declined to codify or apply additional strictures on them. The state recognizes the standards of various nonpublic school accrediting agencies and it can and does provide special services to children in nonpublic schools when appropriate.

There are private schools open in every county. Jefferson County has the highest percentage of private school students, nearly 25 percent. Nine other counties have private school enrollment above 10 percent. Miami-Dade County has the largest private-school enrollment, nearly 61,000 in more than 350 schools.

HOMESCHOOLING

The "homeschooling" education movement is developing in Florida and in 2009 involved more than 60,000 students. There are homeschoolers in every Florida county, with Palm Beach having the largest homeschooled population.

As with private schools, the state regulates education at home only lightly. Parents must register their children with their local school district, may not teach the children of others, must maintain records and materials, and must provide the district with an annual evaluation of their children's progress although they have a wide variety of options on how to do that.

Local school districts in turn must provide homeschoolers with special needs with special services and some districts are providing homeschoolers with extra curricula opportunities, including varsity sports. School districts do not give diplomas to homeschoolers but the state will provide a homeschooler with a General Equivalency Diploma (GED) to those who qualify for and seek it.

STATE UNIVERSITY SYSTEM

Florida's university system was established in 1905 when the legislature passed the Buckman Act, which consolidated the state's various post-high school institutions into three institutions under a Board of Control. After consolidation, the system consisted of the University of the State of Florida in Gainesville, the Florida A&M University in Tallahassee, and the Florida State College for Women in Tallahassee.

As the state's population grew, urban areas started to compete for degree granting institutions. By 1963, the University of South Florida in Tampa was operating. In addition, Florida Atlantic University in Boca Raton was on the drawing board, and two more institutions, one in Pensacola and one in Orlando, were authorized.

To coordinate the growing system, the legislature created the Board of Regents as the single governing body of the state-supported universities. Education reforms of 2001 eliminated the Board of Regents and established the Board of Education to replace it and to oversee all education in the state, but giving each of the universities its own board of trustees. Proponents of the Regents, however, put a successful initiative on the ballot in 2002, creating a Board of Governors to oversee college education. That new board was duly established but, appointed by the governor, it in turn has fully supported the reforms of 2001, including the Board of Education's oversight over the state university system. Today, the system consists of 11 institutions of higher learning placed throughout the state.

University of Florida

UF is the oldest and foremost of the state's public universities. It is a residential land-grant comprehensive institution noted for both its teaching and its research at the undergraduate and graduate level. It operates 16 colleges and offers professional degrees in medicine, dentistry, pharmacy, veterinary, and law. Its Agriculture College is the basis for the state's extension services. Founded in 1853, its nearly 2,000-acre main campus in Gainesville hosts the state's largest library resource.

Florida State University

FSU is a comprehensive and graduate research university. It offers professional degrees in medicine and law. Established in 1857, its more than a thousand-acre campus is located near the capitol in Tallahassee. It hosts 41,000 students, including 30,251 full-time undergrads. Its College of Medicine is building a branch at Daytona Beach.

Florida A&M University

FAMU was founded in 1887 as a land-grant university for black Floridians. It remains a predominantly black institution. Originally a teachers college, and while today it offers numerous graduate programs and degrees, its student body is primarily undergraduates who make up 86 percent of a 13,100 student body. It has a higher percentage of full-time students (88 percent) than any other full state university. Although its main campus is half the size of nearby FSU, it enjoys similar proximity to the capitol in Tallahassee. Its law school is in Orlando.

University of South Florida

USF is a metropolitan graduate and undergraduate university with its main campus on a 1,900-acre site in Tampa. It has major branches in St. Petersburg and Lakeland and an upper-level and graduate branch in Sarasota, hosting 45,000 students. Founded in 1956, it was the first of the state's universities established in the 20th century. It offers numerous doctoral programs and is an important research center in a wide variety of fields. Its medical school at Tampa is highly rated and is a major medical research center. Seventy-six percent of its students are undergraduates, but only half of its student body are full-time, the lowest percentage among the state universities.

Florida Atlantic University

FAU was founded in 1962 as an upper-division and graduate university, the nation's first. It added a lower division and offered a full undergraduate program in 1984. Today, it serves 27,000 students on seven campuses in and around Boca Raton.

University of Central Florida

Central Florida is the state's

largest university. Founded as Florida Technical University in 1963 at Orlando, its first class entered in 1968. A decade later, the legislature changed its name to reflect the area it served and to avoid confusion with Florida Institute of Technology, a private institute. UCF is an urban, research-oriented university serving graduates and undergraduates. Although established on 1,400 acres with room to grow, it is now well within the Orlando metropolitan area. With a total enrollment of more than 48,000, it hosts 28,500 full-time undergraduates. Its first medical school class received free tuition.

University of West Florida

UWF was established in 1963 and opened in 1967 with an upper-division and graduate-level programs, on a 1,600-acre nature preserve just north of Pensacola. It added a lower level in 1983. With a student body of 12,000 students, its main campus is a 1,600-acre nature preserve located 10 miles north of downtown Pensacola. It also has a campus in Fort Walton and a center at Eglin Air Force Base.

New College of Florida

New College of Florida in Sarasota is unique among state universities in that its entire student body of 785 is made up of full-time undergraduates. Founded in 1964 as an academically elite, private liberal arts college, its freewheeling, open education for gifted students quickly gained it national stature but not support, and after a decade of operation, it was in danger of closing. Considered a valued if unusual asset, the state took control of the college, giving its administration

to the University of South Florida and leaving its criteria, design, and curriculum intact. In 2001, the legislature "set it free," making it the 11th state university although it remains a liberal arts college with a very limited enrollment and a 10-1 student-teacher ratio, half that of the university system's average institution. Its campus is a 110-acre portion of the historic Ringling family compound on Sarasota Bay.

Florida International University

FIU in Miami was created in 1965 and welcomed its first classes in 1972 as an upper-division and graduate institution. Its main campus is small compared to other universities, 539 acres, but full degree programs are offered on two campuses in the Greater Miami area and at two Fort Lauderdale academic centers. The FIU law school welcomed its first students in 2002, and a medical school opened in 2009. The university has more than 40,000 students, 75 percent are undergraduates, nearly half are full-time.

University of North Florida

UNF opened in Jacksonville as an upper-division school but now offers full programs at both the undergraduate and the graduate level. Seventy percent of its more than 16,000 students are full-time undergraduates.

Florida Gulf Coast University

Gulf Coast was authorized in 1991 and welcomed its first students in 1997. Despite being the newcomer, the university is already nationally noted for its advocacy of distance learning and for its "no tenure" faculty policy. It has the smallest student body of the state's full universities, 10,200. The campus is on 760 acres of restored and preserved wetlands outside Fort Myers.

STATE UNIVERSITY SYSTEM ENROLLMENT
(2009-2010)

	Full-Time Undergraduates	Total Enrollment
Florida A&M University, Tallahassee	8,832	11,848
Florida Atlantic University, Boca Raton	13,511	29,335
Florida Gulf Coast University, Fort Myers	7,032	10,221
Florida International University, North Miami	19,166	40,455
Florida State University, Tallahassee	24,065	40,255
New College of Florida	825	825
University of Central Florida, Orlando	41,580	56,235
University of Florida, Gainesville	34,612	49,693
University of North Florida, Jacksonville	11,228	16,719
University of South Florida, Tampa	22,801	31,126
University of West Florida, Pensacola	8,707	11,191
Total University System Enrollment	**192,359**	**297,903**

The state university system does not have a standard tuition. Tuitions, fees, and other costs vary from one university to another and, at multi-campus universities, from one campus to another.

FLORIDA PRE-PAID COLLEGE PLAN

The Florida Pre-Paid College Plan is the largest such plan in the nation, with more than one million contracts taken by Floridians interested in paying today's costs for tomorrow's college education. The plan, a qualified "529" plan, is guaranteed by the state of Florida. It has assets of more than $6.5 billion and actuarial reserves of $530 million. It pays tuition, fees, and dorm plans when a child gets to college at the rates in force when the plan is purchased. Plan prices start at $33 per month for a two-year community college plan and $95 a month for the four-year university plan. Prices vary based on the plan and the age of the child enrolled in the plan. Once set, the price never increases. To qualify, the child or the child's parents or guardians must be residents of Florida, but anyone can purchase the plan on behalf of a qualifying minor. When a child is ready for college, the program covers the actual cost at any Florida public university or community college. The value of the plan may be transferred to most private colleges in Florida, select technical schools, and most out-of-state colleges. Enrollment in the plan is open for two and a half months at the end of the year.

AVERAGE UNIVERSITY TUITIONS AND FEES (2010)
Per Credit Hour Per Semester

State Resident Students

Undergraduates	$164.53
Graduate Students	$350.81

Out-of-State Students

Undergraduates	$691.91
Graduate Students	$990.92

For the purposes of tuition, after one year a non-resident student may become a resident of Florida by meeting the residency requirements of any other new resident.

UNIVERSITY FEES PER YEAR FOR MEDICAL PROGRAMS (2010)

Medical

State Resident Students	$26,371
Out-of-State Students	$55,981

Dentistry

State Resident Students	$30,879
Out-of-State Students	$51,359

Veterinary

State Resident Students	$24,710
Out-of-State Students	$45,685

LAW SCHOOL TUITIONS
Average Per Credit Hour Per Semester (2010)

State Resident Students	$483.57
Out-of-State Students	$1,083.35

BOARD OF EDUCATION

The State Board of Education oversees all education in Florida. Its members appointed by the governor are:

T. Willard Fair, Chair
Mark Kaplan
Roberto Martinez
John R. Padgett
Kathleen Shanahan
Eric J. Smith, Commissioner of Education

BOARD OF GOVERNORS

The Board of Governors oversees the state university system. Appointed by the governor, its members are:

Ava A. Parker, Chair
Richard A. Beard
Dean Colson
Ann W. Duncan
Charlie Edwards
Gallop Franklin II
Patricia Frost
Morteza Hosseini
J. Stanley Marshall
Frank Martin
Tico Perez
John Rood
Eric J. Smith, Commissioner of Education
Gus Stavros
John W. Temple
Norman D. Trip
Richard A. Yost

STATE COLLEGE SYSTEM

Florida's community colleges make up a public two-year college program dating back to 1947 with the creation of Palm Beach Junior College. But the system did not take on statewide significance until 1955 when the legislature established the Community College Council, which set up a master plan for public community colleges throughout Florida. The legislature in 2009, recognizing the authorizations it had made to numerous community colleges to bestow four-year bachelor degrees, renamed the system the Florida College System. Some of the 28 institutions continue as traditional two-year institutions.

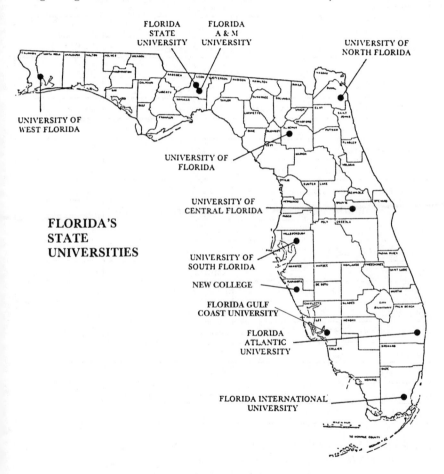

FLORIDA
STATE
UNIVERSITY

FLORIDA
A & M
UNIVERSITY

UNIVERSITY OF
NORTH FLORIDA

UNIVERSITY OF
WEST FLORIDA

UNIVERSITY OF
FLORIDA

UNIVERSITY OF
CENTRAL FLORIDA

**FLORIDA'S
STATE
UNIVERSITIES**

UNIVERSITY OF
SOUTH FLORIDA

NEW COLLEGE

FLORIDA GULF
COAST UNIVERSITY

FLORIDA
ATLANTIC
UNIVERSITY

FLORIDA INTERNATIONAL
UNIVERSITY

STATE COLLEGES
2010 FTE

College	City	Enrollment
Brevard	Cocoa	13,831
Broward College	Fort Lauderdale	30,801
College of Central Florida	Ocala	6,840
Chipola College	Marianna	1,707

Daytona State College	Daytona Beach	17,034
Edison State College	Fort Myers	12,447
Florida State College	Jacksonville	25,861
Florida Keys	Key West	1,044
Gulf Coast	Panama City	5,145
Hillsborough	Tampa	21,935
Indian River State College	Fort Pierce	14,900
Florida Gateway College	Lake City	2,322
Lake-Sumter	Leesburg	3,361
State College of Florida, Manatee	Bradenton	9,129
Miami-Dade College	Miami	60,660
North Florida	Madison	1,036
Northwest FloridaState College	Niceville	6,072
Palm Beach State College	Lake Worth	21,461
Pasco-Hernando	Dade City	7,844
Pensacola State College	Pensacola	9,481
Polk State College	Winter Haven	7,347
St. Johns River	Palatka	5,358
St. Petersburg College	St. Petersburg	22,573
Santa Fe College	Gainesville	12,777
Seminole State College of Florida	Sanford	15,795
South Florida	Avon Park	2,824
Tallahassee	Tallahassee	12,157
Valencia	Orlando/Kissimmee	31,846
TOTAL		**384,408**

PRIVATE COLLEGES AND UNIVERSITIES

Florida's private upper-level schools far outnumber those in the state university system, but many have small enrollments or only part-time enrollments, and are specialized, teaching art or Bible studies and other theological subjects. Some are large and prestigious institutions, however, and the following list is of those institutions accredited by the Southern Association of Colleges and Schools.

Ave Maria University, Ave Maria
Barry University, Miami Shores
Bethune-Cookman College, Daytona Beach
Clearwater Christian College, Clearwater
Eckerd College, St. Petersburg
Edward Waters College, Jacksonville

Embry-Riddle Aeronautical
University, Daytona Beach
Flagler College, St. Augustine
Florida College, Temple Terrace
Florida Hospital College of Health
Sciences, Orlando
Florida Institute of Technology,
Melbourne
Florida Memorial College, Miami
Florida Southern College, Lakeland
International College, Naples
Jacksonville University, Jacksonville
Lynn University, Boca Raton
Nova Southeastern University, Fort
Lauderdale

Palm Beach Atlantic College, West
Palm Beach
Ringling School of Art and Design,
Sarasota
Rollins College, Winter Park
St. Leo University, St. Leo
Saint Thomas University, Miami
Southeastern College, Lakeland
Stetson University, DeLand
University of Miami, Coral Gables
University of Sarasota, Sarasota
University of Tampa, Tampa
Warner Southern College, Lake Wales
Webber International University,
Babson Park

OLD RIVALRY

In the never ending rivalry between the University of Florida and Florida State University, FSU president Talbot D'Alemberte proclaimed 1851, rather than 1857 as the school's founding date. The claim was based on legislation passed in 1851 authorizing the opening of two "seminaries," one east of the Suwannee River (UF) and one west of the river (FSU). East Florida Seminary opened in 1853 in Ocala and moved up the road to Gainesville in 1866. Florida carries the 1853 date on its seal. The West Florida Seminary opened in Tallahassee in 1857, the date on its seal until D'Alemberte's assertion. In 1905 the legislature combined six state-supported academies into three, the University of Florida, the Florida Female College (which became FSU and went co-ed after World War II), and the State Normal College for Colored Students (which became Florida A & M University). It named 1905 as the founding year of each institution. But in 1935, the Board of Control, predecessor to the state Board of Regents, declared the University of Florida to have been founded in 1853 and FSU in 1857. Prior to making his declaration, FSU President D'Alemberte wrote to University of Florida Pres. Charles Young suggesting they get together on a common date. Young, in a one-paragraph note, referred him to the work of University of Florida history professor emeritus, Samuel Proctor. According to Proctor, the University of Florida was authorized by act of Congress in 1836, nine years before Florida became a state.

BANKS

HISTORY OF BANKING IN FLORIDA

The development of commerce and banking in Florida often is at odds with the popular history of the state as perceived both then and now.

The history of Florida banking began with what today would be called a private/public partnership. That deal forged in 1565 was made personally between Philip II of Spain and St. Augustine founder Pedro Menendez de Aviles. Under its terms, Menendez would conquer Florida and establish a colony all at his own expense. In return, Menendez received a large land grant and an exclusive on maritime trade. It was a proprietary arrangement, not dissimilar to other Spanish colonial empire systems and those used by other European nations.

But after nine relatively successful years, Menendez died. His influence was such that Spain was left to either abandon the Florida project or convert it to being a directly controlled military outpost, the option the crown exercised for strategic reasons. Florida languished for nearly two centuries, introducing only one item of eventual benefit: citrus.

Florida became English in 1763, a spoil of the Seven Years' War, and private enterprise made its first appearance since Menendez. English trading companies, based in Georgia, began operations in Florida. Most important among them was Panton, Leslie and Co., which worked diligently to increase Florida trade, most involving its customer, the Indians. Under British administration, shipping rose dramatically, as did exports. Indigo was Florida's first cash crop with exports rising from 3 tons in 1770 to more than 60 tons just 12 years later. Citrus exports went from 21 barrels in 1764 to 65,000 barrels in 1776.

The Spanish returned in 1783 but not all the British left. Panton, Leslie and Co. remained, encouraged to do so by the Spanish administration primarily because of its position relative to the Indians.

Most of the major Southeastern tribes included Florida in their trading markets and while they had other priorities, they were noted for their business acumen and innovation including the hiring of commercial managers to run their enterprises, a practice that continues today. Their relationship with the Panton firm also was modern: the company served as banker and factor for the tribes. The hand-in-glove relationship between the Panton partners and the Creek, Cherokee, Choctaw, and Chickasaw nations, as well as the breakaway Seminoles, was a major factor in the decision to break the barrier they represented with Andrew Jackson's march into Florida.

John Forbes and Co., the successor to the Panton firm, provided what early 19th-century banking services were available to the fewer than 15,000 residents of the new U.S. territory. In the first year as military governor, Jackson wrote to then Secretary of State John Quincy Adams requesting a branch of the Bank of the United States for Pensacola. Nothing happened, however, and private banking such as it was continued. With a quickly growing population, the need for a consistent medium of exchange (something Florida had never experienced) and broader access to credit became apparent. Although fought for several years by civilian governor William Duval who feared Florida falling victim to the "bank frenzie" rampant in the states, the territory chartered its first bank, the Bank of Florida at Tallahassee, in 1828 with a capitalization of a half-million dollars. It, too, was a private/public partnership with half its directors chosen from investors, the other half appointed by the governor and the legislative council. It became the depository for state funds.

The Bank of West Florida at Marianna was chartered in 1829, followed by the Bank of St. Augustine and the Bank of Pensacola two years later. The competition arrived in 1832 with the chartering of the Central Bank of Tallahassee with $1 million in authorized capital.

Banking in Florida during its territorial period was a typical mixture of politics and economics, battered by the Indian wars. A great benefit of territorial banking was the issuance of species that traded at par and was accepted in all channels of internal trade. But that ended with the panic of 1837 and the suspension of specie throughout the United States. As local money became valueless, Floridians came to depend on bank bills of exchange, most issued by Georgia institutions. All of the territorial banks eventually closed.

The St. Joseph Constitution put severe restrictions on banking and the first years of statehood saw the return of private banking, primarily through agents from out of state institutions. Economic conditions improved with statehood and in 1853, the legislature, now representing more than 100,000 residents, began chartering banks again, but only a half dozen operating banks prior to the outbreak of the War Between the States. In January 1861, Florida seceded from the Union and the following month joined in the formation of the Confederacy.

From the start of the Civil War, however, Florida was broke. Tax collections were negligible. The state issued war bonds and sold federal lands it had seized. Florida banks made loans to the state and "railroad notes" filled the currency gap when silver coinage became too scarce for everyday transactions. When Confederate currency entered Florida, residents hoarded Florida notes and bills, issued by the state, but soon both declined in value. The economy also suffered from the federal blockade although many subsequent leading Florida families earned their fortunes and their reputations as blockade runners. Inflation caused by scarcity further weakened the medium of exchange. Even the state dabbled in what would today be called the "black market" to bring in revenue. Florida's primary task in the war was to serve as a gateway for goods and as the Confederacy's breadbasket. By the end of the war, it could do neither and most Floridians were bankrupt.

Private banking returned after the war with more than a half dozen domestic operations a decade after the war. The economy began to recover rather quickly during Reconstruction with Northern capital entering the state for legitimate investment and with a vast upswing in something the state would soon get used to: immigration from other states.

Reconstruction established the Freedmen's Bank under federal regulation with branches in Tallahassee and Jacksonville opening in 1866. Corruption took its toll, however, and the Florida bank was closed in 1874, paying 62 cents on the dollar to its depositors.

The National Bank Act, passed to bring order out of chaos during the Civil War, came to Florida in 1874 with the chartering of the First National Bank of Florida at Jacksonville in 1874. It thrived without competition until 1880 but went into receivership in 1903, when its phosphate investments collapsed. The year 1886 was a banner one for the opening of national banks, and all flourished for a while but of the group that came into being, only one survives in a straight line from that time, now part of an interstate holding company.

Although banks opened and closed regularly at the end of the 19th century and the beginning of the 20th, by comparison to banking in the rest of the nation, Florida's compared favorably, ebbing and flowing with booms and panics and adjusting to the establishment of the Federal Reserve System.

But in 1925 came disaster, the bust of the Florida Boom. Rampant real estate and other business speculation were reflected at Florida banks. That year there were 271 banks in Florida. Deposits were $875 million, up from $180 million just three years before, and rising at a rate of $32 million a month.

Then the bottom fell out, real estate values crashed, and banks began to fail at a rate of more than one a month. The state was further buffeted by the economic impact of horrific hurricanes in 1926 and 1928. Finally, the stock market crashed in 1929 and the rest of the nation joined Florida in the Great Depression. By 1934, the number of state banks fell to 105 and deposits from their 1920s peak of $269.1 million to just $38.5 million. National banks survived the federal bank holiday of 1933 and only one went into receivership.

Modern banking in Florida matches that of the rest of the nation except that it has had to contend with ever expanding growth, fueled primarily by its vast increase in population. Bank "merger-mania" has hurt Florida more than any other state. Florida has lost most of its banking assets to out-of-state banks since 1992. Most of Florida's losses went into gains for North Carolina and Alabama.

In 2004, there were 191 bank companies in the state with assets of $52.1 billion. But in 2009 and 2010, more than 40 of those banks failed.

FLORIDA TOP 20 BANK HOLDING COMPANIES—2010
(Total Florida Deposits)

Bank	Headquarters	Deposits (in billions)
1. Bank of America	Charlotte NC	$72.80
2. Wachovia/Wells Fargo	San Francisco CA	64.3
3. Sun Trust Banks	Atlanta GA	39.9

4. Regions Financial	Birmingham AL	17.5
5. Colonial Bank/BB&T	Winston-Salem NC	16.3
6. JP Morgan Chase	New York NY	10.7
7. Citibank	New York NY	8.9
8. Fifth Third Bank	Cincinnati OH	7.6
9. PNC Financial	Pittsburgh PA	6
10. Northern Trust	Chicago IL	5.1
11. Ocean Bankshares	Miami	4
12. Mercantil Commerce	Miami	3.8
13. Synovus Financial	Columbus GA	3.4
14. HSBC Bank USA	New York NY	3.3
15. Mercantile Bank	Greenville SC	3.1
16. Riverside Banking	Fort Pierce	2.8
17. City National Bank	Miami	2.7
18. Royal Bank of Canada	Raleigh NC	2.6
19. Iberia Bank	Naples	2.1
20. Compass Bankshares	Birmingham AL	2

FLORIDA TOP 20 FEDERAL CREDIT UNIONS—2010
(Total Assets)

Credit Union	City	Total Assets (in thousands)
1. Suncoast Schools	Tampa	$5,438,741
2. Vystar	Jacksonville	3,991,124
3. Southeast Corporate	Tallahassee	3,334,855
4. Space Coast	Melbourne	3,188,985
5. MacDill	Tampa	1,733,149
6. GTE	Tampa	1,658,946
7. Fairwinds	Orlando	1,554,023
8. Mid-Florida	Lakeland	1,364,719
9. Eglin	Ft. Walton Beach	1,221,819
10. Central Florida Educators	Orlando	1,165,474
11. Community First of Florida	Jacksonville	1,103,832

12. Campus USA	Gainesville	1,088,626
13.Tyndall	Panama City	1,006,922
14. Pen Air	Pensacola	1,004,784
15. Achieva	Largo	878,707
16. IBM Southeast Employees	Boca Raton	828,316
17. South Florida Educational	Miami	687,893
18. Tropical Financial	Miami	677,145
19. Publix Employees	Lakeland	554,182
20. Dade County	Miami	512,128

CASH AND CARRY

More homes, nearly 60 percent, are purchased for cash at Sun City Center, south of Tampa, then anywhere else in the United States. Palm Beach is second, with 57 percent of homes purchased for cash. Ocala is fourth in the nation, with 52 percent of home sales being all-cash transactions. Florida leads the nation in cash sales of homes, with more than 21 percent.

UTILITIES

PUBLIC SERVICE COMMISSION

Regulation of utilities companies is the responsibility of the Public Service Commission. The commission was established by the legislature in 1887 as the Florida Railroad Commission. At that time, its primary purpose was regulating railroads. But regulatory authority was added over the years to include telephone companies (in 1911) and electric utilities (in 1951). Today, the commission, renamed in 1965, also regulates the water and sewer and natural gas industries.

All five commission members are appointed by the governor to four-year terms. Present commissioners are Art Graham (chair), Eduardo Balbis, Lisa Polak Edgar, Ronald A. Brisé, and Julie Imanuel Brown.

TELEPHONE COMPANIES
2010

Name/Headquarters	Number of Exchanges	Access Lines
AT&T		
Miami	102	3,551,609
Fairpoint		
Florala AL	17	39,547
Embarq Florida		
Tallahassee	104	1,387,568
Frontier Communications Company of the South		
Atmore AL	2	3,371
ITS		
Indiantown	1	3,131
Northeast Florida Telephone Company		
MacClenny	2	7,911
Quincy Telephone Company		
Quincy	3	11,009
Smart City Telecommunications		
Lake Buena Vista	2	14,130
Verizon		
Tampa	24	1,190.19
Windstream Florida		
Live Oak	27	83,040
TOTAL	**284**	**6,291,559**

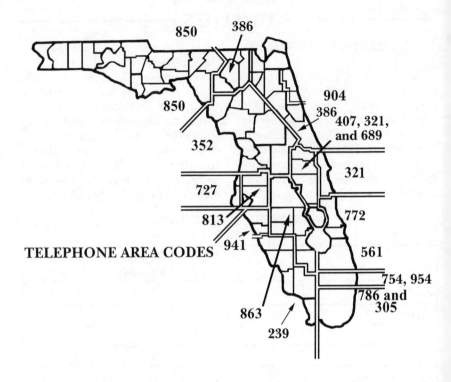

TELEPHONE AREA CODES

Thirteen Telephone Area Codes

Florida grew from three area codes in 1990, to 18 in 2006.

The state's area codes are

239: Ft. Myers and Naples areas and the mainland portion of Monroe County

305: Old numbers in Miami-Dade County and the Keys portion of Monroe County

321: Brevard County and some numbers in the metropolitan Orlando area

352: West Central Florida including Gainesville and a portion of Pasco County

386: Old north Florida inland to Daytona Beach

407: Old numbers in the metropolitan Orlando area

561: Palm Beach

689: New numbers in the Greater Orlando area

727: Pinellas County and a portion of Pasco County

754: New numbers in the Ft. Lauderdale area

772: The middle Atlantic coast

786: New numbers in Miami-Dade County and the Florida Keys

813: Hillsborough County and a portion of Pasco County

850: The Florida Panhandle including Pensacola and Tallahassee

863: Inland south central Florida including Lakeland

904: The Greater Jacksonville area

941: The Sarasota-Bradenton area

954: Ft. Lauderdale's Broward County

ELECTRIC UTILITIES

The state is served by three types of electric utilities. They are rural cooperatives, investor-owned, and municipal utilities.

Rural Electric Cooperatives

Florida's 16 electric rural distribution cooperatives serve power to more than 1.4 million residents. Other utilities, the municipal and investor-owned, also serve within the cooperative areas but their services are either to towns or cities or along major highways. By far, the majority of land area in the state, 65 percent, is served by the 16 cooperatives, which provide power in 59 of the state's 67 counties. That vast area requires 46,000 miles of electric lines for cooperatives to serve less than 10 percent of the state's population. By contrast, to service the other 90 percent, municipal and investor-owned utilities have strung 70,000 miles of lines. Florida's first electric cooperative was organized in 1936. At that time, only 7.8 percent of Florida farms had electricity. Today, more than 99 percent of rural residents receive power.

The cooperatives, and the counties or parts of counties they serve, are

Cooperative	Headquarters	Counties Serviced
Tri-County	Madison	Jefferson, Madison, Taylor
Escambia River	Jay	Escambia, Santa Rosa
Choctawhatchee	DeFuniak Springs	Santa Rosa, Walton, Holmes, Okaloosa
Gulf Coast	Wewahitchka	Washington, Gulf, Calhoun, Bay
Suwannee Valley	Live Oak	Hamilton, Columbia, Suwannee, Lafayette
Okefenokee	Nahunta GA	Nassau, Duval, Baker
West Florida	Graceville	Washington, Holmes, Calhoun, Jackson
Talquin	Quincy	Gadsden, Leon, Liberty, Wakulla, Franklin
Central Florida	Chiefland	Dixie, Gilchrist, Levy, Alachua
Sumter	Sumterville	Marion, Sumter, Levy, Hernando, Citrus, Pasco, Lake
Clay	Keystone Heights	Duval, Clay, Levy, Putnam, Columbia, Baker, Bradford, Union, Alachua, Volusia, Lake, Marion
Withlacoochee	Dade City	Citrus, Hernando, Hillsborough, Pasco, Pinellas, Polk
Peace River	Wauchula	Hardee, De Soto, Polk, Indian River, Manatee, Highlands, Sarasota, Brevard, Hillsborough, Osceola
Lee County	North Fort Myers	Lee, Charlotte, Collier, Hendry, Broward
Glades	Moore Haven	Glades, Highlands, Okeechobee, Hendry
Florida Keys	Tavernier	Monroe

COOPERATIVE UTILITIES
TYPICAL ELECTRICAL BILL COMPARISONS
Residential Service (2010)

Cooperative	Minimum Bill or Customer Charge	—KWH— 500	1000
Central Florida	$15.00	$110.00	$205.00
Choctawhatchee	$24.00	$76.88	$129.77
Clay	$11.00	$61.75	$112.50
Escambia River	$25.00	$85.50	$146.00
Florida Keys	$10.00	$68.00	$126.00
Glades	$15.50	$70.80	$126.10
Gulf Coast	$19.45	$67.89	$116.33
Lee County	$15.00	$67.18	$119.36
Okefenokee	$10.00	$65.50	$121.00
Peace River	$12.25	$72.10	$131.95
Sumter	$14.50	$70.18	$125.85
Suwannee Valley	$12.00	$66.60	$121.20
Talquin	$10.00	$67.45	$124.90
Tri-County	$17.50	$58.14	$98.79
West Florida	$20.00	$81.90	$143.90
Withlachoochee	$15.00	$66.66	$118.31

Above figures exclude local taxes and franchise fees. Fuel and Purchased Power Costs are included.

INVESTOR-OWNED UTILITIES
TYPICAL ELECTRIC BILL COMPARISONS
Residential Service (2010)

Utility	Minimum Bill or Customer Charge	—KWH— 500	1000
Florida Power & Light Company	$5.69	$56.84	$107.95
Progress Energy	$8.84	$66.81	$124.76
Gulf Power Company	$10.00	$64.23	$118.83
Tampa Electric Company	$10.50	$61.17	$111.80
Florida Public Utilities Company			
Marianna Division	$12.00	$72.65	$133.29
Fernandina Beach Division	$12.00	$89.37	$126.74

Above figures exclude local taxes and franchise fees but include 1.5 percent gross receipt tax. Fuel Rates are included

MUNICIPAL UTILITIES
TYPICAL ELECTRIC BILL COMPARISONS
Residential Service (2010)

Municipal Utilities	Minimum Bill or Customer Charge	—KWH—	
		500	1000
Alachua	$8.00	$62.40	$116.80
Bartow	$6.70	$69.68	$132.65
Blountstown	$3.59	$69.53	$135.53
Bushnell	$7.40	$77.73	$148.05
Chattahoochee	$6.50	$67.85	$129.20
Clewiston	$6.50	$67.03	$127.55
Fort Meade	$12.96	$92.26	$171.56
Fort Pierce	$6.01	$75.62	$147.84
Gainesville	$8.45	$60.20	$130.45
Green Cove Springs	$6.00	$66.94	$130.38
Havana	$6.00	$69.32	$132.63
Homestead	$5.60	$62.08	$118.55
Jacksonville	$5.50	$65.51	$125.52
Jacksonville Beach	$4.50	$71.21	$137.91
Key West	$6.75	$79.65	$152.55
Kissimmee	$10.17	$71.12	$132.06
Lakeland	$8.00	$59.94	$111.87
Lake Worth	$8.50	$74.70	$140.90
Leesburg	$10.41	$73.50	$136.58
Moore Haven	$8.50	$59.75	$111.00
Mount Dora	$8.44	$72.44	$136.43
Newberry	$7.50	$74.25	$141.00
New Smyrna Beach	$5.65	$64.73	$123.80
Ocala	$9.33	$74.59	$139.84
Orlando	$8.00	$63.92	$119.82
Quincy	$6.00	$58.83	$111.66
Reedy Creek	$2.85	$61.35	$119.84
St. Cloud	$8.32	$66.47	$124.61
Starke	$6.45	$71.84	$138.62
Tallahassee	$6.32	$67.91	$129.50
Vero Beach	$7.21	$74.11	$141.01

Wauchula	$8.62	$69.07	$129.52
Williston	$8.00	$73.57	$139.41
Winter Park	$9.35	$66.19	$123.01

Above figures exclude local taxes, franchise fees, and gross receipt taxes. Fuel and Purchased Power Costs are included.

INVESTOR-OWNED NATURAL GAS UTILITIES
TYPICAL GAS BILL COMPARISONS
Residential Service (2010)

Utility	Minimum Bill or Customer Charge	—Therms—	
		50	100
Chesapeake Utilities Corp*	$15.00	$44.35	$73.69
Florida City Gas	$8.00	$111.00	$211.53
Florida Public Utilities	$11.00	$119.57	$228.13
Indiantown Gas Co.*	$9.00	$27.92	$46.84
Peoples Gas System Inc.	$12.00	$102.32	$192.65
St. Joe Natural Gas Co.	$20.00	$107.44	$194.87
Sebring Gas System Inc*	$9.00	$37.57	$66.14

*These companies no longer purchase gas for their customers; they deliver gas that the end use customers purchase. The rates do not include the cost of gas.

NUCLEAR PLANTS IN FLORIDA

Florida has five nuclear power plants that provide about 17 percent of the state's electricity. The Crystal River plant is owned by Progress Energy Florida of St. Petersburg. The other four plants are owned by Florida Power & Light Co. of Miami.

Plant Name	Location	Year Service Began
Turkey Point 3	Miami-Dade County	1972
Turkey Point 4	Miami-Dade County	1973
St. Lucie 1	St. Lucie County	1976
St. Lucie 2	St. Lucie County	1983
Crystal River	Citrus County	1977

GOVERNMENT

Florida has two United States senators and 25 representatives in Congress, having received two additional representatives in 2002. The 2010 census awarded two more representatives to the state. The following are the current Florida members in Congress.

U.S. SENATORS
Bill Nelson (D)
Born—Miami, FL. Sept. 29, 1942
Education—BA, Yale University; JD, University of Virginia.
Prior occupation—Treasurer of Florida, astronaut
Elected to U.S. House 1978; to U.S. Senate 2000
Address—716 Hart Building, Washington, DC 20510
Phone—(202) 224-5274

Marco Rubio (R)
Born—Miami, FL, May 28, 1971
Education—BS, University of Florida; JD, University of Miami
Prior Occupation—attorney, speaker of the Florida House
Elected in 2010
Address—B40A Dirksen Building, Washington, DC 20510
Phone—(202) 224-3041

U.S. REPRESENTATIVES
1st District
Jeff Miller (R)
Born—St. Petersburg, FL, June 27, 1959
Education—BA, University of Florida
Prior occupation—law enforcement
Elected in 2001
Address—2416 Rayburn Building, Washington, DC 20515
Phone—(202) 225-4136
District offices: Pensacola, Fort Walton Beach

2nd District
Steve Sutherland (R)
Born—Panama City, FL, Oct. 10, 1965
Education—BS, Troy State University
Prior occupation—funeral director
Elected in 2010
Address—1229 Longworth Building, Washington, DC 20515
Phone—(202) 225-5235
District offices: Panama City

3rd District
Corrine Browne (D)
Born—Jacksonville, FL, Nov. 11, 1946
Education—BS, MS, Florida A&M University; Ed.S, University of Florida
Prior occupation—educator
Elected in 1982
Address—2336 Rayburn Building, Washington, DC 20515
Phone—(202) 225-0123
District offices: Jacksonville, Orlando

4th District
Ander Crenshaw (R)
Born—Jacksonville, FL, Sept. 1, 1944
Education—BA, University of Georgia; JD, University of Florida Law School
Prior occupation—investment banker
Elected in 2000
Address—440 Cannon Building, Washington, DC 20515
Phone—(202) 225-2501
District offices: Jacksonville, Lake City

5th District
Richard Nugent(R)
Born—Evergreen Park, IL, May 26, 1951
Education—BS, St. Leo College; MPA, Troy State University
Prior occupation—sheriff
Military service—Air National Guard
Elected in 2010
Address—1517 Cannon Longworth Building, Washington, DC 20515
Phone—(202) 225-1002
District offices: Brooksville

6th District
Clifford B. Stearns (R)
Born—Washington, DC, April 16, 1941
Education—BS, George Washington University
Prior occupation—motel management
Military service—U.S. Air Force
Elected in 1988
Address—2370 Rayburn Building, Washington, DC 20515
Phone—(202) 225-5744
District offices: Orange Park, Gainesville, Ocala

7th District
John L. Mica (R)
Born—Binghamton, NY, Jan. 27, 1943
Education—BA, University of Florida
Prior occupation—business
Elected in 1992
Address—2187 Rayburn Building, Washington, DC 20515
Phone—(202) 225-4035
District offices: Deltona, Maitland, Ormand Beach, Palm Coast, Palatka, St. Augustine

8th District
Daniel Webster (R)
Born—Charleston, WV, April 27, 1949
Education—BS, Georgia Tech
Prior occupation—business, legislator
Elected in 2010
Address—1039 Longworth Building, Washington, DC 20515
Phone—(202) 225-2176
District offices: Orlando, Eustis, Ocala

9th District
Gus Bilirakis (R)
Born—Gainesville, FL, Feb. 8, 1963
Education—BA, University of Florida; JD Stetson College
Prior occupation—attorney, state legislator
Elected in 2006
Address—407 Cannon Building, Washington, DC 20515
Phone—(202) 225-5755
District offices: Palm Harbor, Plant City

10th District
C. W. "Bill" Young (R)
Born—Harmarville, PA, Dec. 16, 1930
Education—Pinellas County public schools
Prior occupation—Insurance executive
Military service—National Guard
Elected in 1970
Address—2407 Rayburn Building, Washington, DC 20515
Phone—(202) 225-5961
District offices: St. Petersburg, Largo

11th District
Kathy Castor (D)
Born—Miami, FL, Aug. 20, 1966
Education—BA, Emory University; JD, Florida State University
Prior occupation—attorney, county commissioner
Elected in 2006
Address—137 Cannon Building, Washington, DC 20515
Phone—(202) 225-3376
District office: Tampa

12th District
Dennis Ross (R)
Born—Lakeland, FL, Oct. 18, 1959
Education—BS, Auburn University; JD, Cumberland School of Law
Prior occupation—attorney
Elected in 2010
Address—404 Cannon Building, Washington, DC 20515
Phone—(202) 225-1252
District office: Bartow

13th District
Vern Buchanan (R)
Born—Detroit, MI, May 8, 1951
Education—BBA, Cleary University; MBA, University of Detroit
Prior occupation—business
Military service—Air National Guard
Elected in 2006
Address—221 Cannon Building, Washington, DC 20515
Phone—(202) 225-5015
District offices: Bradenton, Sarasota

14th District
Connie Mack (R)
Born—Fort Myers, FL, Aug. 12, 1967
Education—BS, University of Florida
Prior occupation—business, state legislator
Elected in 2004
Address—115 Cannon Building, Washington, DC 20515

Phone—(202) 225-2536
District offices: Cape Coral, Naples

15th District
Bill Posey (R)
Born—Washington, DC, December 18, 1947
Education—AA, Brevard Community College
Prior occupation—realtor
Military service—U.S. Army
Elected in 2008
Address—120 Cannon Building, Washington, DC 20515
Phone—(202) 225-3670
District office: Melbourne

16th District
Tom Rooney (R)
Born—Philadelphia, PA, Nov. 21, 1970
Education—BA, Washington Jefferson College; MA, University of Florida; JD, University of Miami
Military service—U.S. Army
Prior occupation—attorney
Elected in 2008
Address—1529 Longworth Building, Washington, DC 20515
Phone—(202) 225-5792
District offices: Stuart, Punta Gorda, Fort Pierce

17th District
Frederica S. Wilson (D)
Born—Miami, FL, Nov. 15, 1942
Education—BS, Fisk University; MA, University of Miami
Prior occupation—educator
Elected in 2010
Address—208 Cannon Longworth Building, Washington, DC 20515
Phone—(202) 225-4506
District offices: Miami Gardens

18th District
Ileana Ros-Lehtinen (R)
Born—Havana, Cuba, July 15, 1952
Education—BS, MS, Florida
International University
Prior occupation—educator
Elected in 1988
Address—2206 Rayburn Building,
Washington, DC 20515
Phone—(202) 225-3931
District office: Miami, Miami
Beach, Key West

19th District
Ted Deutch (D)
Born—Bethlehem, PA, May 7, 1966
Education—BA, JD, University of
Michigan
Prior occupation—attorney
Elected in 2010
Address—2241 Rayburn Building,
Washington, DC 20515
Phone—(202) 225-3001
District offices: Boca Raton,
Margate, Lake Worth, Tamarac

20th District
Debbie Wasserman Schultz (D)
Born—Queens, NY, Sept. 27, 1966
Education—BS, MS, University of
Florida
Prior occupation—state legislator
Elected in 2004
Address—118 Cannon Building,
Washington, DC 20515
Phone—(202) 225-7931
District offices: Pembroke Pines,
Aventura

21st District
Mario Diaz-Balart (R)
Born—Fort Lauderdale, FL, Sept.
25, 1961
Education—attended University of
South Florida
Prior occupation—U.S.
Representative
Elected in 2010

Address—328 Cannon Building,
Washington, DC 20515
Phone—(202) 225-2778
District office: Miami, Naples

22nd District
Allen West (R)
Born—Atlanta, GA, Feb. 7, 1961
Education—BA, University of
Tennessee; MA, Kansas State
University
Prior occupation—defense
contractor
Military service—U.S. Army
Elected in 2010
Address—1708 Longworth
Building,
Washington, DC 20515
Phone—(202) 225-3026
District offices: Fort Lauderdale

23rd District
Alcee L. Hastings (D)
Born—Altamonte Springs, FL,
Sept. 5, 1936
Education—BA, Fisk University; JD,
Florida A&M University
Prior occupation—attorney
Elected in 1992
Address—2353 Rayburn Building,
Washington, DC 20515
Phone—(202) 225-1313
District offices: Fort Lauderdale,
West Palm Beach

24th District
Sandra Adams (R)
Born—Wyandotte, MI, Dec. 14, 1956
Education—BA, Columbia College
Prior occupation—law enforcement
Military service—U.S. Air Force
Elected in 2010
Address—216 Cannon Building,
Washington, DC 20515
Phone—(202) 225-2706
District offices: Orlando, Port
Orange, Titusville

25th District
David Rivera (R)
Born—New York, NY, 1965
Education—BA, Florida
International University
Prior occupation—legislator

Elected in 2010
Address—417 Cannon Building,
Washington DC 20515
Phone—(202) 225-2778
District offices: Miami

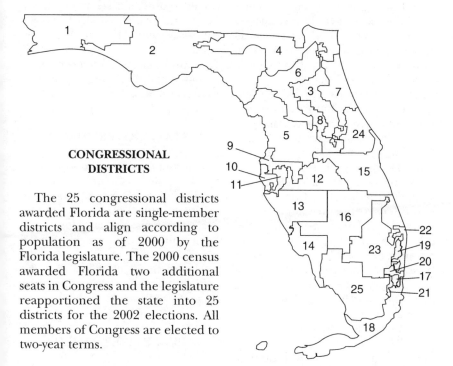

CONGRESSIONAL DISTRICTS

The 25 congressional districts awarded Florida are single-member districts and align according to population as of 2000 by the Florida legislature. The 2000 census awarded Florida two additional seats in Congress and the legislature reapportioned the state into 25 districts for the 2002 elections. All members of Congress are elected to two-year terms.

STATE CONSTITUTION

Acquisition of Florida by the U.S. from Spain in 1819 ended a 300-year period during which Florida was an international pawn among nations striving for control of the Gulf of Mexico and Atlantic sea-lanes. Under U.S. rule the territory developed rapidly, and by 1837 its legislative council authorized an election to determine popular opinion on statehood. The idea was approved and the historic Constitutional Convention of 1838 was called to meet in St. Joseph.

Major features of the document limited the vote to white males over 21 years of age who were enrolled in the state militia, and the decision to elect, by popular vote, 17 senators and 41 representatives, with the governor the only state executive officer to be elected by the people.

Congress admitted Florida to the Union in 1845. To keep a balance between slave and free states, Iowa, a free state, was admitted at the same time as Florida, a slave state.

In 1861, Florida seceded from the Union, the third southern state to do so after the outbreak of the War

Between the States. When the war ended, President Andrew Johnson set up a provisional government in Florida. Its appointed governor, William Marvin, called for a constitutional convention in 1865. The 1865 constitution promptly annulled the state's secession ordinance but contained provisions that still harbored discrimination against Negroes. As a result, Congress refused to seat the Florida congressional delegation and reinstituted military rule in Florida and several other southern states whose constitutions were not acceptable.

To free the state from such rule, Floridians called another constitutional convention for 1868. This constitution, sometimes referred to as the Carpetbagger's Constitution, extended voting privileges to all males 21 and older, including Negroes. This proviso, along with others more acceptable to politicians in Washington, earned Congressional approval; Florida was once again in the Union and had its civil government restored.

By the mid-1880s, economic and political factional disputes developed within the state and another constitution, the 1885 Constitution, was drafted and enacted. It represented a compromise between the necessities of the times and the political philosophy of the Old South. But, with most of the state's population in the northern counties, the document was conceived primarily with the problems of the north Florida agricultural area in mind.

Amended over the years, the 1885 Constitution got its last thorough revision in 1968. This revision was brought about in part by Florida's tremendous urban growth in middle and south Florida following World War II, making necessary reapportionment of the state legislature. The 1968 Constitution requires that reapportionment take place after each 10-year federal census, it allows the governor to succeed himself if he has not served more than six years, and it keeps the state's unique elected cabinet system. The state continues to operate under this revised 1885 Constitution as amended over more recent years, including a provision diminishing the cabinet system.

STATE GOVERNMENT

The state constitution declares that the powers of state government be divided into three separate and relatively independent branches—executive, legislative, and judicial. It is basically the same governmental system found at the national level and in all 50 states. But the application of this basic system is in some ways unique in Florida.

EXECUTIVE BRANCH

Florida is unique among the states by having its executive branch of government administered by a governor and an elected cabinet. Although the size of the cabinet was drastically cut by voters beginning in 2003, it still functions with its own specific duties, and each cabinet member has basic powers and duties independent of the governor.

Each cabinet member has one vote. Although not a member, the governor serves in practice as chairman of the cabinet and also has one vote.

Beginning in 2003, the cabinet was reduced in number from six to three, each elected statewide in the same year as the governor in even-numbered years between presidential elections. The cabinet members are the attorney general, the commissioner of agriculture, and the chief financial officer.

Offices eliminated from the cabinet were those of secretary of state and commissioner of education, which are now filled by appointments by the governor. Voters combined the cabinet offices of the comptroller and the treasurer-insurance commissioner into the one elected office of chief financial officer.

The new system is still feeling its way. At the very first meeting of the new cabinet, for instance, members found they could do nothing because the cabinet was no longer large enough to meet its old quorum requirement, an oversight quickly remedied by the legislature.

On issues germane to the cabinet, the governor may be outvoted, except when meeting as the state pardon board, in which case the governor's vote is the only one that counts.

The governor and cabinet members may serve two successive four-year terms.

THE GOVERNOR

The governor is responsible for the day-to-day operations of the state and is its chief law-enforcement officer. Heads of those departments for which the governor is responsible are appointed by the governor. The governor also appoints heads of those departments who are under both the governor and cabinet, with the approval of that panel. The governor also appoints individual members of many regulatory boards and commissions.

By executive order, the governor may suspend from office any state or county elected official who is not subject to impeachment. Grounds for such suspension include malfeasance, misfeasance, neglect of duty, drunkenness, incompetence, permanent inability to perform duties, and commission of a felony. The governor cannot suspend the lieutenant governor, cabinet members, or judges of the supreme court, appeals courts, or circuit courts; they can be removed only by impeachment by the legislature.

The governor also has authority to fill vacancies in county or state elected offices that may occur between elections.

LIEUTENANT GOVERNOR

The 1968 revision of the constitution authorized the new position of lieutenant governor. Duties were left to the discretion of the governor and legislature, with the only constitutional chore being to assume the office of governor should the office become vacant due to death, impeachment trial, incapacity, absence or resignation.

The lieutenant governor is elected on the same ticket as the governor; they run as a team.

DEPARTMENTS DIRECTLY UNDER GOVERNOR'S CONTROL

Departments that are the direct responsibility of the governor include

DEPARTMENT OF STATE: Headed by the appointed secretary of state, and responsible for elections throughout the state, for maintaining an archives of state documents and actions, and for issuing charters to corporations.

DEPARTMENT OF BUSINESS AND PROFESSIONAL REGULATION: Licenses, examines, and investigates complaints that have to do with establishing qualifications and skills for various occupations and professions; regulates alcohol and tobacco, land sales, condominium and mobile-home sales, hotels and restaurants, pari-mutuel wagering, and boxing. It is financed not by taxes but by fees charged for testing and licenses.

DEPARTMENT OF CHILDREN AND FAMILIES: Handles child-abuse investigations, economic-assistance programs, and mental-health and substance-abuse counseling.

DEPARTMENT OF ELDER AFFAIRS: Oversees the needs of and provides services to the state's older population.

DEPARTMENT OF ENVIRONMENTAL PROTECTION: Regulates and monitors the state's environment, concerning itself with prevention of air, water, and land pollution, and enforcing adopted rules and regulations.

DEPARTMENT OF HEALTH: Heads the state's public-health efforts and regulates the health-care profession.

DEPARTMENT OF TRANSPORTATION: Concerns itself with the state's primary roads, interstate highway system, secondary road network, mass transportation, licensing of airports, and the operation of toll roads.

DEPARTMENT OF CITRUS: Establishes grading criteria and standards for all types of citrus fruits, as well as researching new uses for citrus and conducting advertising campaigns promoting Florida's production. Funded by taxes and levies on growers, the department is commonly called the Citrus Commission.

AGENCY FOR WORKFORCE INNOVATION: The old Department of Labor, charged with labor and employment security of employees in Florida, and operates unemployment offices.

DEPARTMENT OF MANAGEMENT SERVICES: Administers the state employees merit system, prepares a state budget, and drafts long-range comprehensive plans for development of the state.

DEPARTMENT OF CORRECTIONS: Operates and oversees prisons; responsible for the rehabilitation of adult offenders.

DEPARTMENT OF JUVENILE JUSTICE: Responsible for detention of juvenile offenders and for victim services.

DEPARTMENT OF COMMUNITY AFFAIRS: Serves as a liaison between local, state, and federal governmental units in connection with public housing, planning grants, and emergency management.

DEPARTMENT OF THE LOTTERY: Conducts and manages the state lottery games.

DEPARTMENT OF MILITARY AFFAIRS: Heading this department, which is authorized to provide a state militia, is the state adjutant general. But the governor is the commander-in-chief of all state military forces while not in federal service, and appoints officers in the state's national guard.

FISH AND WILDLIFE CONSERVATION COMMISSION: Responsible for establishing and enforcing rules and regulations governing hunting and freshwater fishing in the state.

DEPARTMENTS UNDER BOTH GOVERNOR AND CABINET

DEPARTMENT OF LAW ENFORCEMENT: Leads the state government's war on crime. Department agents may investigate reports and complaints of wrongdoing in all sectors, including suspected lawbreaking charges against appointed or elected officials.

DEPARTMENT OF HIGHWAY SAFETY AND MOTOR VEHICLES: Enforces the state's traffic laws, tests drivers and issues licenses, oversees sale of vehicle tags and mobile-home and motor-carrier compliance.

DEPARTMENT OF REVENUE: Administers and enforces state laws that produce revenue for the state. It collects funds from all sources and turns them over to the state treasurer for deposit.

DEPARTMENT OF VETERANS AFFAIRS: Focuses exclusively on the needs of Florida's two million veterans.

PAROLE COMMISSION: Determines which prisoners in the state's penal system shall be paroled, fixes the conditions of parole, and supervises the parole. It also supervises persons placed on probation by courts.

DEPARTMENTS DIRECTLY UNDER CABINET CONTROL

DEPARTMENT OF LEGAL AFFAIRS: Headed by the attorney general, this department serves as legal advisor to state officials, and issues legal opinions upon request from public officials.

DEPARTMENT OF FINANCIAL SERVICES: Headed by the chief financial officer, it keeps records of all state revenues collected and disbursed, publishes annual reports on the financial status of each county, and supervises banks and other financial institutions. Newly reorganized, it also absorbs the state fire marshal's office and entire former Department of Insurance.

DEPARTMENT OF AGRICULTURE AND CONSUMER SERVICES: Headed by the commissioner of agriculture, it provides state services to agricultural interests in Florida. It also operates the state's farmer's markets and inspects weighing and measuring devices such as gasoline pumps and market scales. It oversees consumer protection, food quality and safety, and forest and resource protection.

OTHER DEPARTMENTS

DEPARTMENT OF EDUCATION: Headed by the appointed commissioner of education, this department allocates state educational funds to local school boards and is charged with overseeing matters in the state's primary and secondary public schools, community colleges, and public universities.

PUBLIC SERVICE COMMISSION: This commission crosses the traditional lines that separate the executive, legislative, and judicial branches of state government. The commission has control of rates and services provided by transportation businesses and privately owned utilities and telephone companies operating in Florida. It has subpoena powers and can levy fines. Members of the five-person commission are appointed by the governor.

BOARD OF ADMINISTRATION: This board, composed of the governor, the chief financial officer, and the attorney general, administers debt service for county road and bridge bonds and county or state school bonds. It must approve bonds of all state agencies before issuance. It also manages the assets of the state's various trust funds.

THE CABINET
Governor
Rick Scott (R)
Born—Bloomington, IL, Dec. 1, 1952
Education—BS, University of Missouri; JD, Southern Methodist University
Prior occupation—business
Military service—U.S. Navy
Elected in 2010
Term ends—January 2014

Lieutenant Governor*
Jennifer Carroll (R)
Born—Port of Spain, Trinidad & Tobago, Aug. 27, 1959
Education—BA, University of New Mexico; MBA, St. Leo College
Prior Occupation—legislator
Military service—U.S. Navy
Elected in 2010
Term ends—January 2014

Attorney General
Pam Bondi (R)
Born—Tampa, FL, Nov. 17, 1965
Education—BA, University of Florida; JD, Stetson Law School
Prior occupation—prosecutor

Elected in 2010
Term ends—January 2014

Chief Financial Officer
Jeff Atwater (R)
Born—St. Louis, MO, April 8, 1958
Education—BA, MBA, University of Florida
Prior occupation—legislator
Elected in 2010
Term ends—January 2014

Agriculture Commissioner
Adam Putnam (R)
Born—Bartow, FL, July 31, 1974
Education—BS, University of Florida
Prior occupation—U.S. Congressman
Elected in 2010
Term ends 2014

Member of the cabinet only when serving as acting governor.

GOVERNORS OF FLORIDA

Provisional/Military
Andrew Jackson—1821-22

Territorial
William DuVal—1822-34
John H. Eaton—1834-35
Richard K. Call—1835-40
Robert R. Reid—1840-41
Richard K. Call—1841-44
John Branch—1844-45

State
William D. Moseley—1845-49
Thomas Brown—1849-53
James E. Broome—1853-57
Madison S. Perry—1857-61
John Milton—1861-65
A. K. Allison—1865*
William Marvin—1865*
David S. Walker—1865-68
Harrison Reed—1868-72

Ossian B. Hart—1873-74 (Died in office)
Marcellus L. Stearns—1874-77
George F. Drew—1877-81
William D. Bloxham—1881-85
Edward A. Perry—1885-89
Francis P. Fleming—1889-93
Henry L. Mitchell—1893-97
William D. Bloxham—1897-1901
W. S. Jennings—1901-05
Napoleon B. Broward—1905-09
Albert W. Gilchrist—1909-13
Park Trammell—1913-17
Sidney J. Catts—1917-21
Cary A. Hardee—1921-25
John W. Martin—1925-29
Doyle E. Carlton—1929-33
David Scholtz—1933-37
Fred P. Cone—1937-41
Spessard L. Holland—1941-45
Millard F. Caldwell—1945-49
Fuller Warren—1949-53
Dan T. McCarty—1953 (Died in office)

Charley E. Johns—1953-55*
LeRoy Collins—1955-61
Farris Bryant—1961-65
Haydon Burns—1965-67**
Claude Kirk, Jr.—1967-71
Reubin Askew—1971-79
Robert Graham—1979-87
Wayne Mixson—1987
Bob Martinez—1987-91
Lawton Chiles—1991-98 (Died in office)
Buddy MacKay—1998-99***
Jeb Bush—1999-2006
Charlie Crist—2007-2010
Rick Scott—2011-

*Not elected governor but served in the position by appointment, in most cases because of death of elected governor.
**Burns in 1965 served only two years, as the election cycle was ordered changed.
***Succeeded to office upon the death of Lawton Chiles.

SHORTEST TERM

The shortest term as governor was the three-day tenure of Wayne Mixson from Jan. 3 to Jan. 6, 1987. As lieutenant governor under Governor Graham, Mixson was sworn in as governor when Graham, newly elected to the U.S. Senate, had to be in Washington, D.C., three days before his gubernatorial term expired. With the newly elected Governor Martinez not scheduled to be sworn in until Jan. 6, Mixson became governor for three days.

LEGISLATIVE BRANCH

The Florida Legislature consists of two bodies, the state senate and the house of representatives. Legislation on any subject may be introduced into either house. Regular sessions of the legislature are each year, for 60 days, beginning in March. Any number of special sessions, for up to 20 days, may be called by the governor.

The senate and house exercise tremendous influence on the daily lives of Florida residents. They do so both through enacting state laws and through passing laws applying to specific cities, counties, or regions. Because of its control over the affairs of cities and counties, plus its control over the appointments of the governor, and its investigative and budgetary control over all phases of state government and state agencies, the legislature is considered by many to be the most powerful of the three branches of state government.

senate districts, some senators find themselves representing only one county or part of one, while others may represent several counties.

SENATORS AND HOUSE MEMBERS AND DISTRICTS

SENATE

The senate has 40 members, each elected to a four-year term. One-half the senate is elected every two years, providing for staggered terms. Representation is based on population. Based on the 2000 census, each senator represents approximately 399,500 residents. Because population is the key factor in designating various

HOUSE OF REPRESENTATIVES

House representation also is based solely on population. The house has 120 members, or one for approximately every 133,000 residents. All members are elected every two years, during general elections held in even-numbered years. As is true in the senate, the house has some members who represent only a portion of a county, others representing an entire county or more.

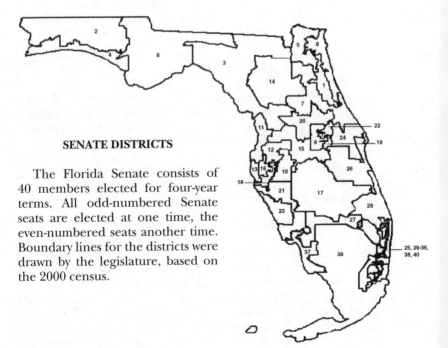

SENATE DISTRICTS

The Florida Senate consists of 40 members elected for four-year terms. All odd-numbered Senate seats are elected at one time, the even-numbered seats another time. Boundary lines for the districts were drawn by the legislature, based on the 2000 census.

STATE SENATE DISTRICTS
(Counties within Districts)

1. Portions of Duval, Flagler, Putnam, St. Johns, and Volusia
2. Holmes, Washington, and portions of Escambia, Bay, Holmes, Okaloosa, Santa Rosa, Walton, and Washington
3. Baker, Dixie, Hamilton, Lafayette, Suwannee, Taylor, and portions of Citrus, Columbia, Jefferson Leon, Levy, Madison, and Marion
4. Portions of Bay, Escambia, Okaloosa, Santa Rosa, and Walton
5. Portions of Clay, Duval, Nassau, and St. Johns
6. Calhoun, Franklin, Gadsden, Gulf, Jackson, Liberty, Wakulla, and portions of Bay, Jefferson, Leon, and Madison
7. Portions of Clay, Marion, Putnam, and Volusia
8. Portions of Duval, Flagler, Nassau, St. Johns, and Volusia
9. Portions of Orange, Osceola, and Seminole
10. Portions of Hillsborough, Pasco, and Polk
11. Portions of Citrus, Hernando, Pasco, and Pinellas
12. Portions of Hillsborough and Pasco
13. Portion of Pinellas
14. Alachua, Bradford, Gilcrest, Union, and portions of Columbia, Levy, Marion, and Putnam
15. Portions of Hernando, Lake, Osceola, Polk, and Sumter
16. Portions of Hillsborough and Pinellas
17. Hardee, Highlands, and portions of Desoto, Glades, Okeechobee, Polk, and St. Lucie
18. Portions of Hillsborough, Manatee, and Pinellas
19. Portions of Orange and Osceola
20. Portions of Lake, Marion, Seminole, Sumter, and Volusia
21. Portions of Charlotte, De Soto, Lee, Manatee, and Sarasota
22. Portions of Orange and Seminole
23. Portions of Charlotte, Manatee, and Sarasota
24. Portions of Brevard, Orange, and Seminole
25. Portions of Broward and Palm Beach
26. Portions of Brevard, Indian River, Osceola, and St. Lucie
27. Portions of Charlotte, Glades, Hendry, Lee, and Palm Beach
28. Martin and portions of Indian River, Okeechobee, Palm Beach, and St. Lucie
29. Portions of Broward and Palm Beach
30. Portions of Broward and Palm Beach
31. Portion of Broward
32. Portion of Broward
33. Portion of Miami-Dade
34. Portions of Broward and Miami-Dade
35. Portions of Broward and Miami-Dade
36. Portion of Miami-Dade
37. Portions of Collier and Lee
38. Portion of Miami-Dade
39. Hendry, Monroe, and portions of Broward, Collier, Hendry, Miami-Dade, and Palm Beach
40. Portion of Miami-Dade

STATE HOUSE DISTRICTS
(Counties Within Districts)

1. Portions of Escambia, Okaloosa, and Santa Rose

2. Portion of Escambia
3. Portion of Escambia
4. Portions of Okaloosa and Santa Rose
5. Holmes, Washington, and portions of Jackson, Okaloosa, and Walton
6. Gulf and portions of Bay and Franklin
7. Calhoun, Liberty, and portions of Gadsden, Jackson, Leon, Okaloosa, Wakulla, and Walton
8. Portions of Gadsden and Leon
9. Portions of Leon, Jefferson, and Gadsden
10. Hamilton, Madison, Taylor, and portions of Alachua, Columbia, Dixie, Franklin, Jefferson, Levy, and Wakulla
11. Gilcrest, Lafayette, Suwannee, and portions of Alachua, Columbia, and Dixie
12. Baker, Nassau, Union, and portions of Bradford, Clay, and Duval
13. Portions of Clay and Duval
14. Portion of Duval
15. Portion of Duval
16. Portion of Duval
17. Portion of Duval
18. Portions of Duval and St. Johns
19. Portions of Clay, Duval, and St. Johns
20. Portions of Clay, Flagler, and St. Johns
21. Putnam and portions of Bradford, Clay, Lake, Marion, and Volusia
22. Portions of Alachua, Levy, and Marion
23. Portions of Levy and Marion
24. Portion of Marion
25. Portions of Lake, Seminole, and Volusia
26. Portions of Flagler and Volusia
27. Portion of Volusia
28. Portion of Volusia
29. Portions of Brevard and Indian River
30. Portion of Brevard
31. Portion of Brevard
32. Portions of Brevard and Orange
33. Portions of Orange, Seminole, and Volusia
34. Portions of Orange and Seminole
35. Portion of Orange
36. Portion of Orange
37. Portions of Orange and Seminole
38. Portion of Orange
39. Portion of Orange
40. Portion of Orange
41. Portions of Lake, Orange, and Osceola
42. Portions of Lake, Marion, and Sumter
43. Citrus and portions of Hernando and Levy
44. Portions of Hernando, Pasco, and Sumter
45. Portions of Pasco and Pinellas
46. Portion of Pasco
47. Portion of Hillsborough
48. Portions of Pasco and Pinellas
49. Portions of Orange and Osceola
50. Portion of Pinellas
51. Portion of Pinellas
52. Portion of Pinellas
53. Portion of Pinellas
54. Portion of Pinellas
55. Portions of Hillsborough, Manatee, Pinellas, and Sarasota
56. Portion of Hillsborough
57. Portion of Hillsborough
58. Portion of Hillsborough
59. Portion of Hillsborough
60. Portions of Hillsborough and Pasco
61. Portions of Hillsborough and Pasco
62. Portions of Hillsborough and Pasco

63. Portions of Hillsborough and Polk
64. Portion of Polk
65. Portion of Polk
66. Portions of Hardee, Highlands, and Polk
67. Portions of Hillsborough, Manatee, and Sarasota
68. Portions of Hillsborough and Manatee
69. Portions of Manatee and Sarasota
70. Portion of Sarasota
71. Portions of Charlotte, Lee, and Sarasota
72. De Soto and portions of Charlotte and Lee
73. Portion of Lee
74. Portions of Charlotte and Lee
75. Portions of Collier and Lee
76. Portion of Collier
77. Glades, Hendry, and portions of Collier and Highlands
78. Portions of Martin, Okeechobee, Palm Beach, and St. Lucie
79. Portions of Okeechobee, Orange, Osceola, and Polk.
80. Portions of Brevard, Indian River, and St. Lucie
81. Portions of Martin and St. Lucie
82. Portions of Martin, Palm Beach, and St. Lucie
83. Portion of Palm Beach
84. Portion of Palm Beach
85. Portion of Palm Beach
86. Portion of Palm Beach
87. Portions of Broward and Palm Beach
88. Portion of Palm Beach
89. Portion of Palm Beach
90. Portions of Broward and Palm Beach
91. Portions of Broward and Palm Beach
92. Portion of Broward
93. Portion of Broward
94. Portion of Broward
95. Portion of Broward
96. Portion of Broward
97. Portion of Broward
98. Portion of Broward
99. Portion of Broward
100. Portion of Broward
101. Portions of Broward and Collier
102. Portions of Broward and Miami-Dade
103. Portions of Broward and Miami-Dade
104. Portion of Miami-Dade
105. Portion of Miami-Dade
106. Portion of Miami-Dade
107. Portion of Miami-Dade
108. Portion of Miami-Dade
109. Portion of Miami-Dade
110. Portion of Miami-Dade
111. Portion of Miami-Dade
112. Portions of Broward, Collier, and Miami-Dade
113. Portion of Miami-Dade
114. Portion of Miami-Dade
115. Portion of Miami-Dade
116. Portion of Miami-Dade
117. Portion of Miami-Dade
118. Portion of Miami-Dade
119. Portion of Miami-Dade
120. Monroe and portion of Miami-Dade

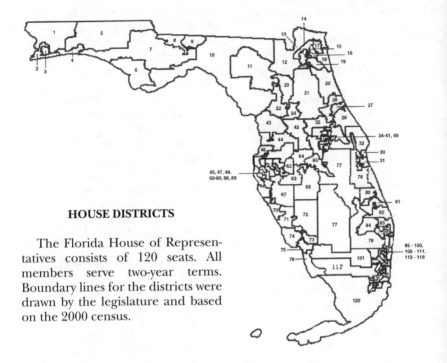

HOUSE DISTRICTS

The Florida House of Representatives consists of 120 seats. All members serve two-year terms. Boundary lines for the districts were drawn by the legislature and based on the 2000 census.

LEGISLATORS
STATE SENATORS

Alexander, J. D.—Lake Wales
District 17—(R)
Altman, Thad—Rockledge
District 24—(R)
Bagdanoff, Ellyn—Palm Beach
District 25—(R)
Benacquisto, Lizbeth—Greenacres
District 27—(D)
Bennett, Mike—Bradenton
District 21—(R)
Bullard, Larcenia J.—Miami
District 39—(D)
Dean, Charlie—Lecanto
District 3—(R)
Detert, Nancy C.—Venice
District 23—(R)
Diaz de la Portilla, Miguel—Miami
District 36—(R)
Evers, Greg—Crestview
District 2—(R)

Fasano, Mike—New Port Richey
District 11—(R)
Flores, Anitere—Miami
District 38—(R)
Gaetz, Don—Destin
District 4—(R)
Garcia, Rene—Hialiah
District 40—(R)
Gardinier, Andy—Orlando
District 9—(R)
Geller, Steve—Fort Lauderdale
District 31—(D)
Haridopolos, Mike—Melbourne
District 26—(R)
Hays, Alan—Leesburg
District 20—(R)
Hill, Tony—Jacksonville
District 1—(D)
Jones, Dennis—Miami
District 13—(R)
Joyner, Arthenia L.—Tampa
District 18—(D)

Latvala, Jack—St. Petersburg
District16—(R)
Margolis, Gwen—Miami Beach
District 35—(D)
Monford, Bill—Tallahassee
District 6—(D)
Norman, Jim—Tampa
District 12—(R)
Negron, Joe—Palm City
District 28—(R)
Oelrich, Steve—Gainesville
District 14—(R)
Rich, Nan H.—Sunrise
District 34—(D)
Richter, Garretts—Naples
District 37—(R)
Ring, Jeremy—Tamarac
District 32—(D)
Sachs, Maria Lorts—Boca Raton
District 30—(R)
Simmons, David—Orlando
District 22—(R)
Siplin, Gary—Orlando
District 19—(D)
Smith, Chris—Oakland Park
District 29—(D)
Sobel, Eleanor—Hollywood
District 15—(R)
Storms, Ronda—Brandon
District 10—(R)
Thrasher, John—Jacksonville
District 8—(R)
Wilson, Frederica S.—Miami
District 33—(D)
Wise, Stephen R.—Jacksonville
District 5—(R)

STATE REPRESENTATIVES

Abruzzo, Joseph—Wellington
District 85—(D)
Ahern, Larry—St. Petersburg
District 51—(R)
Albritton, Ben—Winter Haven
District 66—(R)
Allen, Bob—Merritt Island
District 32—(R)

Artilis, Frank—Miami
District 119—(R)
Aubuchon, Gary—Cape Coral
District 74—(R)
Baxley, Dennis K.—Ocala
District 24—(R)
Bembrey, Leonard L.—Carabelle
District 10—(D)
Berman, Lori—Delray Beach
District 86—(D)
Bernard, Mack—West Palm Beach
District 84—(D)
Bileca, Michael—Miami
District 117—(R)
Bovo, Esteban Jr.—Hialeah
District 110—(R)
Boyd, Jim—Bradenton
District 68—(R)
Brandes, Jim –St. Petersburg
District 52—(R)
Branynon, Oscar II—Miami
District 103—(D)
Brodeur, Jason—Oveido
District 33—(R)
Bronson, Doug—Milton
District 1—(R)
Bullard, Dwight M.—Miami
District 118—(D)
Burgin, Rachel—Tampa
District 56—(R)
Caldwell, Matthew H.—Fort Myers
District 73—(R)
Campbell, Daphne D.—Miami
Shores
District 108—(D)
Cannon, Dean—Winter Park
District 35—(R)
Chessnut, Chuck—Gainesville
District 23—(D)
Clark-Reed, Gwyn—Wilton Manors
District 92—(D)
Clemons, Jeff—Palm Beach
District 89—(D)
Coldey, Marti—Marianna
District 7—(R)
Corcoran, Richard—New Port
Richey
District 45—(R)

Costello, Fred—DeLand
District 26—(R)
Cruz, Janet—Tampa
District 58—(D)
Davis, Daniel J.—Jacksonville
District 13—(R)
Diaz, Jose Felix—Miami
District 115—(R)
Dorworth, Chris—Lake Mary
District 34—(R)
Drake, Brad—DeFuniak Springs
District 5—(R)
Eisenauglo, Eric—Orlando
District 40—(R)
Ford, Clay—Pensacola
District 3—(R)
Fresen, Eric—Coral Gables
District 111—(R)
Frishe, Jim—Seminole
District 54—(R)
Fullwood, Reggie—Jacksonville
District 15—(D)
Gaetz, Matt—Fort Walton Beach
District 4—(R)
Garcia, Luis—Miami
District 107—(R)
Gibbons, Joe—Hollywood
District 105—(D)
Glorioso, Richard—Plant City
District 62—(R)
Gonzalez, Eddie—Hialiah
District 102—(R)
Goodson, Tom—Titusville
District 29—(R)
Grant, James—Tampa
District 47—(R)
Grimsley, Denise—Coral Springs
District 77—(R)
Haiger, Bill—Delray Beach
District 87—(R)
Harrell, Gayle B.—Stuart
District 81—(R)
Harrison, Shawn—Tampa
District 60—(R)
Holder, Doug—Orlando
District 70—(R)
Hooper, Ed—Clearwater
District 50—(R)

Horner, Mike—Kissimmee
District 79—(R)
Hudson, Mike—Naples
District 101—(R)
Hukill, Dorothy—New Smyrna Beach
District 28—(R)
Ingram, Chris—Pensacola
District 2—(R)
Jenne, Evan—Dania Beach
District 100-(D)
Jones, Mia L.—Jacksonville
District 14—(D)
Julien, John Patrick—North Miami
District 104—(D)
Kiar, Martin David—Weston
District 97—(D)
Kreegel, Paige—Punta Gorda
District 72—(R)
Kriseman, Rick—St. Petersburg
District 53—(D)
Legg, John—Port Richey
District 46—(R)
Logan, Ana Rivas—Miami
District 114—(R)
Lopez-Cantera, Carlos—Miami
District 113—(R)
Mayfield, Debbie—Vero Beach
District 80—(R)
McBurney, Charles—Jacksonville
District 16—(R)
McKeel, Seth—Lakeland
District 63—(R)
Metz, Larry—Mt. Dora
District 25—(R)
Moraitis, George—Fort Lauderdale
District 91—(R)
Nehr, Peter—Palm Harbor
District 48—(R)
Nelson, Bryan—Apopka
District 38—(R)
Nunez Jeanette—Fernandina Beach
District 12—(R)
O'Toole, H. Marlene—Lady Lake
District 42—(R)
Pafford, Mark S.—Lantana
District 88—(D)
Passidemo, Kathleen C.—Naples
District 76—(R)

Patronis, Jimmy—Panama City
District 6—(R)
Perman, Steve—Delray Beach
District 78—(D)
Perry, Keith—Ocala
District 22—(R)
Pilon, Ray—Sarasota
District 69—(R)
Plakon, Scott—Longwood
District 37—(R)
Porter, Elizabeth—Lake City
District 11—(D)
Porth, Ari Abraham—Coral Springs
District 96—(D)
Precourt, Steve—Celebration
District 41—(R)
Proctor, Bill—St. Augustine
District 20—(D)
Randolph, Scott—Orlando
District 36—(D)
Ray, Lake—Jacksonville
District 17—(R)
Reed, Betty—Tampa
District 59—(D)
Renwart, Ronald—Jacksonville
District 18—(R)
Roberson, Ken—Englewood
District 71—(R)
Rogers, Hazelle P.—Lauderhill
District 94—(D)
Rooney, Pat—Palm Beach Gardens
District 83—(R)
Rouson, Darryl E.—St. Petersburg
District 55—(D)
Sanders, Ron—Key West
District 120—(D)
Sands, Franklin—Plantation
District 98—(D)
Schneck, Robert—Brooksville
District 44—(R)
Schwartz, Elaine J.—Hollywood
District 99—(D)
Slosberg, Irv—Boca Raton
District 90—(D)
Smith, Jimmie T.—Lecanto
District 43—(R)
Snyder, William—Stuart
District 82—(R)

Soto, Darren—Orlando
District 49—(D)
Stafford, Cynthia—Miami
District 109—(D)
Stargel, Kelli—Lakeland
District 64—(R)
Steinberg, Richard L.—Miami
Beach
District 106—(D)
Steube, Greg—Sarasota
District 67—(R)
Taylor, Dwayne L.—DeLand
District 27—(D)
Thompson, Geraldine—Orlando
District 39—(D)
Thurston, Perry E.—Fort Lauderdale
District 93—(D)
Tobia, John—Melbourne
District 31—(R)
Trujillo, Carlos—Miami
District 116—(R)
Van Zant, Charles E.—Palatka
District 21—(R)
Vasilinda, Michelle Rehwinkle—
Tallahassee
District 9—(D)
Waldman, Jim—Coconut Creek
District 95—(D)
Weatherford, Will—Dade City
District 61—(R)
Weistein, Mike—Jacksonville
District 19—(R)
Williams, Alan B.—Tallahassee
District 8—(D)
Williams, Trudi K.—Fort Myers
District 75—(R)
Wood, John—Haines City
District 65—(R)
Workman , Ritch—Melbourne
District 30—(R)
Young, Dana—Tampa
District 57—(R)

HOW LAWS ARE MADE

All state laws must be enacted
by the legislature, and each law is

restricted to a single subject plus such details that are connected with that subject. A bill may originate in either the house or senate.

To be introduced by a house member, a bill must be prepared in proper form and delivered to the clerk of the house. The clerk assigns it a number, and it is then read on the house floor by its title only. After the title reading, it is referred by the house speaker to the appropriate committee for discussion.

The committee studies the bill, hearing witnesses for or against it. If the committee votes to recommend the bill not be passed, it will not be considered by the full house. (A two-thirds vote of the house, however, can bring the measure to the house floor.) If the committee recommends passage of the bill, the bill is placed on the house calendar for a second reading.

At this reading house members may vote their approval of the bill, in which case it is revised (engrossed) with amendments, if any, that house members want included. The bill is then placed on the house calendar for a third and final reading, during which it often is debated before the final vote on its fate.

Should the house vote for passage, the bill is sent to the senate where it undergoes the same treatment, that is, first reading, committee hearing, second reading, engrossment, third reading, and final vote.

Often the house and senate versions of the same bill will differ as a result of amendments and changes made after a committee hearing or floor debate. When this occurs, the differences in the bill are settled in a special conference committee whose members come from both the house and senate.

Once the differences are ironed out, the final version is sent back to both the house and senate where it is again voted on for final passage.

Bills that pass both the house and senate are called "acts," and they are sent on to the governor for signature. The governor has three choices—sign the act and make it law, hold it for seven days and permit it to become law without signature, or veto it.

Vetoed "acts" are returned to the legislature where both the house and senate can override the governor's veto. To override, each body must again pass the bill or "act" by a two-thirds majority.

JUDICIAL BRANCH

Florida's judicial branch of state government consists of a series of courts with differing levels of authority and jurisdictions. Judicial power is vested in a Supreme Court, District Courts of Appeal, circuit courts, and county courts.

Supreme Court

This highest of state courts consists of seven members. Each is appointed by the governor, but must submit to a statewide merit retention vote in the general election that occurs after the justice has served at least 12 months. The election provides a six-year term. Justices then select one of their number to be chief justice for a two-year term. Five justices constitute a quorum, but before decisions are reached, four members must concur, regardless of the number present.

The Supreme Court hears appeals directly from trial courts in criminal cases when the death penalty has been imposed; in civil cases when the trial court's decision passes on the validity of a state or federal law, a treaty, or on a provision of the state or federal constitutions, or in cases concerning the validity of revenue or general obligations bonds. All other appeals must be processed through a District Court of Appeals.

District Court of Appeals

The state is divided into five appellate districts, each with a court of appeals. Each court has 9 to 13 judges elected to six-year staggered terms. Four judges may constitute a quorum but a majority of the total court members is required for it to reach a decision. The appeals courts have jurisdiction of all appeals not directly appealable to the Supreme Court or a circuit court. An appeals court also may issue writs of mandamus, certiorari, prohibition, quo warranto, and habeas corpus.

Circuit Court

This court is the state's highest trial court, and the one with the most general jurisdiction. The state is divided into 20 judicial circuits, and circuit judges are elected to six-year terms. In each circuit the judges choose from among them a chief judge who is responsible for administrative supervision of the circuit and county courts in each circuit.

Circuit courts have exclusive original jurisdiction in all actions of law not vested in county courts. That includes all civil actions involving amounts in excess of $2,500. Circuit courts also cover proceedings relating to settlement of estates; competency and involuntary hospitalization; all cases in equity including all cases relating to juveniles except certain traffic cases; all cases involving legality of tax assessments or tolls; actions of ejectment; actions involving titles or boundaries or rights of possession of real property; all felonies or misdemeanors arising out of same circumstances as a felony; and jurisdiction over all appeals from county courts.

County Court

At least one county court judge is specified for each county, and is elected to a four-year term. Vested in county courts is jurisdiction over all misdemeanor cases that the circuit court does not have authority to try, all violations of municipal ordinances, and all civil actions in which the amount involved is less than $2,500.

SUPREME COURT JUSTICES
(Six-year Terms)

Charles Canady	(To January 2016)
Jorge LaBarga	(To January 2016)
Peggy Ann Quince	(To January 2012)
R. Fred Lewis	(To January 2012)
Barbara Joan Pariente	(To January 2012)
James E. C. Perry	(To January 2016)
Ricky L. Polston	(To January 2016)

DISTRICT COURTS OF APPEALS

First Appellate District, Counties: Escambia, Okaloosa, Santa Rosa, Walton, Franklin, Gadsden, Jefferson, Leon, Liberty, Wakulla, Columbia, Dixie, Hamilton, Lafayette, Madison, Suwannee, Taylor, Clay, Duval, Nassau, Alachua, Baker, Bradford, Gilchrist, Levy, Union, Bay, Calhoun, Gulf, Holmes, Jackson, and Washington.

Second Appellate District, Counties: Pasco, Pinellas, Hardee, Highlands, Polk, De Soto, Manatee, Sarasota, Hillsborough, Charlotte, Collier, Glades, Hendry, and Lee.

Third Appellate District, Counties: Miami-Dade and Monroe.

Fourth Appellate District, Counties: Palm Beach, Broward, Indian River, Martin, Okeechobee, and St. Lucie.

Fifth Appellate District, Counties: Citrus, Hernando, Lake, Marion, Sumter, Flagler, Putnam, St. Johns, Volusia, Orange, Osceola, Brevard, and Seminole.

JUDICIAL CIRCUITS

First: Escambia, Okaloosa, Santa Rosa, and Walton counties.
Second: Franklin, Gadsden, Jefferson, Leon, Liberty, and Wakulla counties.
Third: Columbia, Dixie, Hamilton, Lafayette, Madison, Suwannee, and Taylor counties.
Fourth: Clay, Duval, and Nassau counties.
Fifth: Citrus, Hernando, Lake, Marion, and Sumter counties.
Sixth: Pasco and Pinellas counties.

Seventh: Flagler, Putnam, St. Johns, and Volusia counties.
Eighth: Alachua, Baker, Bradford, Gilchrist, Levy, and Union counties.
Ninth: Orange and Osceola counties.
Tenth: Hardee, Highlands, and Polk counties.
Eleventh: Miami-Dade County
Twelfth: De Soto, Manatee, and Sarasota counties.
Thirteenth: Hillsborough County.
Fourteenth: Bay, Calhoun, Gulf, Holmes, Jackson, and Washington counties.
Fifteenth: Palm Beach County.
Sixteenth: Monroe County.
Seventeenth: Broward County.
Eighteenth: Brevard and Seminole counties.
Nineteenth: Indian River, Martin, Okeechobee, and St. Lucie counties.
Twentieth: Charlotte, Collier, Glades, Hendry, and Lee counties.

STATE AGENCIES

Administration, Board of
1801 Hermitage Blvd.
Tallahassee 32317
Agriculture and Consumer Services, Department of
The Capitol
Tallahassee 32399
Attorney General
The Capitol
Tallahassee 32399
Auditor General
111 W. Madison St.
Tallahassee 32399
Bar Examiners, Board of
1891 Elder Court
Tallahassee 32399
Business and Professional Regulation, Department of
1940 N. Monroe Street
Tallahassee 32399

Children and Families, Department of
1317 Winewood Blvd.
Tallahassee 32399
Citrus, Department of
1115 E. Memorial Blvd.
Lakeland 33802
Community Affairs, Department of
2555 Shumard Oak Blvd.
Tallahassee 32399
Corrections, Department of
2601 Blair Stone Road
Tallahassee 32399
Education, Department of
325 W. Gaines St.
Tallahassee 32399
Elder Affairs, Department of
4040 Esplanade Way
Tallahassee 32399
Environmental Protection, Department of
3900 Commonwealth Blvd.
Tallahassee 32399
Ethics Commission
3600 Maclay Blvd.
Tallahassee 32312
Financial Regulation, Office of
200 E. Gaines Street
Tallahassee 32399
Fish and Wildlife Conservation Commission
620 S. Meridian St.
Tallahassee 32399
Governor
The Capitol
Tallahassee 32399
Health, Department of
2585 Merchants Row Blvd.
Tallahassee 32399
Health Care Administration, Agency of
2727 Mahan Dr.
Tallahassee 32308
Highway Safety and Motor Vehicles, Department of
2900 Apalachee Pkwy.
Tallahassee 32399
Juvenile Justice, Department of

2737 Centerview Drive
Tallahassee 32399
Law Enforcement, Department of
2331 Phillips Rd.
Tallahassee 32308
Legal Affairs, Department of
The Capitol
Tallahassee 32399
Lottery, Department of the
250 Marriott Dr.
Tallahassee 32301
Management Services, Department of
4050 Esplanade Way
Tallahassee 32399
Military Affairs, Department of
St. Francis Barracks
82 Marine St.
St. Augustine 32084
Parole Commission and Office of Executive Clemency
2601 Blairstone Road
Tallahassee 32399
Prosecution Coordination Office
The Capitol
Tallahassee 32399
Public Counsel, Office of
111 West Madison Street
Tallahassee 32399
Public Service Commission
2540 Shumard Oak Blvd.
Tallahassee 32399
Revenue, Department of
5050 W. Tennessee St.
Tallahassee 32399
State, Department of
500 S. Bronough
Tallahassee 32399
Transportation, Department of
605 Suwannee St.
Tallahassee 32399
Veterans Affairs, Department of
11351 Ulmerton Rd.
Largo 33778
Workforce Innovation, Agency for
107 E. Madison St.
Tallahassee 32399

THE RIGHT TO WORK

"The right of persons to work shall not be denied or abridged on account of membership or non-membership in any labor union or labor organization. The right of employees, by and through a labor organization, to bargain collectively shall not be denied or abridged. Public employees shall not have the right to strike."

Florida's constitutional Right to Work provision means that, except for persons employed on federal enclaves, employees cannot be required to be members of a labor organization as a condition of employment or continued employment. This, however, does not limit companies and labor organizations (or unions) from constructing arrangements whereby the parties agree that the union will exclusively provide labor for a particular job site. If the union has an exclusive hiring hall agreement with the company, then all persons hired into the specified labor positions covered by the agreement must be registered with the union's hiring hall in order to be referred, consistent with the terms of the parties' agreement. If the union has a nonexclusive hiring-hall agreement with a company, then persons seeking to be hired into one of the specified labor positions may do so either through the union's hiring hall or directly through the company, consistent with the terms of the parties' agreement. Companies are not obligated to enter into agreements with unions as a source of labor; alternatively, companies may wish to utilize other means of pooling qualified candidates from which to hire its labor.

STATE SYMBOLS

STATE FLAG

The present state flag, which features the state seal garnished with diagonal red bars, was proposed in a constitutional amendment by the 1889 Legislature. Voters in 1900 approved the amendment and the existing state flag was officially adopted.

STATE MOTTO

"In God We Trust" was declared to be the state motto in 1970 but was not enacted by the Legislature until 2006. Identical to the motto of the United States, it was put on the state seal in 1868 and is a variation on the state's first motto, "In God is our Trust."

STATE FRUIT

To no one's surprise, the Orange was declared the official state fruit by the 2005 Legislature.

STATE TREE

Designated by the 1953 Legislature, the Sabal Palm (Sabal Palmetto) possesses a majesty that sets it apart from other trees. It is tolerant of a wide variety of soil types and grows throughout the state. The Sabal Palm played an important part in the early history of Florida, providing both food and shelter for the settlers. The young buds were eaten, the trunks were cut into logs for the walls of forts and homes, and leaves made weather-resistant roof thatching.

STATE NICKNAME

The state nickname, "Sunshine State," was adopted by the 1970 Legislature.

STATE SONG

A legend has arisen surrounding composer Stephen Foster's famous song, "Old Folks at Home". The story goes that Foster needed the name of a river containing two syllables. He looked at a map of the southern part of the United States and his eyes fell on a Florida river, the "Suwannee," which had three syllables. He shortened it to "Swanee" and used it in the song, "Old Folks at Home," which was adopted as Florida's official song by the 1935 Legislature.

STATE ANTHEM

Because some found Steven Foster's "Old Folks at Home" objectionable and controversial, a movement began to replace it as the official state song. A contest was held by the state's Music Educators Association, and the winner, in 2007, was music teacher Jan Hinton's "Florida, Where the Sawgrass Meets the Sky." The legislature approved it in 2008, but since many saw "Old Folks at Home" as neither objectionable nor controversial, it approved the new tune as the state anthem, leaving the state song in place.

POET LAUREATE

Edmund Skellings of Dania was appointed Florida's poet laureate in 1980.

STATE THEATER

The 1965 Legislature established the Asolo Theater, at the Ringling Museum complex in Sarasota, as the official "State Theater of Florida." Three other theaters in Florida are designated state theaters—the Hippodrome in Gainesville, the Caldwell Theatre Co. in Boca Raton, and the Coconut Grove Playhouse in Miami.

STATE PLAY

"Cross and Sword" was designated the official state play by the 1973 Legislature. It is a dramatization of the story of the Spanish establishment of the nation's oldest city, St. Augustine, and was presented there annually from 1965 to 1996.

STATE ART MUSEUM

Sarasota's John and Mabel Ringling Museum of Art was designated by the 1980 Legislature as Florida's official art museum.

STATE REPTILE

The alligator was named state reptile by the 1987 Legislature.

STATE MARINE MAMMALS

The manatee, or sea cow, was chosen the state marine mammal by the 1975 Legislature. At the same time, the Legislature designated the dolphin as the state saltwater mammal.

STATE BIRD

The 1927 Legislature chose the mockingbird to be the official state bird. A year-round Florida resident, this gray songster is an expert imitator of other birds' calls. Its Latin name means "mimic of many tongues."

STATE BUTTERFLY

The 1996 Legislature designated the Zebra Longwing as the state butterfly.

STATE BEVERAGE

The 1967 Legislature declared "the juice obtained from mature oranges of the species citrus sinensus and hybrids is hereby adopted as the official beverage of the State of Florida."

STATE LITTER CONTROL

The litter control symbol and official litter control trademark of the Florida Federation of Garden Clubs—"Glenn Glitter"—was adopted by the 1978 Legislature as the Florida litter control symbol.

STATE ANIMAL

The Florida panther, a cousin of the mountain lion and an endangered species, was named state animal by the 1982 Legislature.

STATE FISH

Two fish were adopted by the 1975 Legislature to be the official fish symbols for the state—the largemouth bass as the freshwater fish, and the Atlantic sailfish as the saltwater. No other state has two state fish.

STATE FLOWER

As a tribute to the role of citrus in the state's economy, the 1909 Legislature proclaimed the orange blossom as the state flower.

STATE WILDFLOWER

The coreopsis, a tall, yellow flower found in every county, was designated the state wildflower by the 1991 Legislature. The coreopsis is a perennial wildflower resembling the black-eyed Susan. It has a long blooming season and reseeds itself. The flower is a food source for seed-eating birds, and is neither toxic nor invasive.

STATE SOIL

Mayakka Fine Sand, a deep sandy soil that covers 800,000 acres southward from St. Augustine on the east coast and Cedar Key on the west coast, was named the state's official soil by the 1989 Legislature.

STATE GEM AND STATE STONE

The 1970 Legislature named the moonstone as Florida's state gem on the occasion of the second moon landing, which originated from Cape Canaveral. In 1979, the Legislature added the agatized coral as the state stone.

STATE SHELL

In 1969, the horse conch or giant band shell, known for its vibrant pinkish-orange coloring, was selected the state shell.

STATE ROCK

Ocala Limestone was recognized by the 2006 Legislature as the official state rock. It underlies most of Florida and is considered unusual in that it is composed of almost pure calcium carbonate.

STATE MINERAL

Calcite was designated the state's official mineral in 2006. It is composed of calcium carbonate. The basic component of Ocala limestone, it is also the principal mineral in seashells.

STATE BAND

The St. Johns River City Band is the official band of the state of Florida, under legislation passed by the 2000 legislature. It is also the official band of the city of Jacksonville.

STATE DAY

April 2 is the official state day, as declared by the 1953 legislature. Although not a holiday, it commemorates Ponce de Leon's sighting of Florida in 1513.

FLAGS OVER FLORIDA

The flags of five nations have flown over Florida: Spain, France, Great Britain, the United States, and the Confederate States of America.

Some historians say Florida's first state flag was designed by the "governor first elected," William D. Moseley, and flew for the first, and last, time at his inaugural ceremonies on June 25, 1845. It had five horizontal bars in blue, orange, red, white, and green, with the printed legend "Let Us Alone." It was never officially adopted as the state flag.

Prior to the War Between the States, various unofficial "secession" flags were being flown throughout the state, but at the 1868 Constitutional Convention an official state flag finally was designed. It bore the state's seal on a field of white.

The design was altered in 1900 when the state's voters okayed the addition of diagonal red bars. A minor change occurred in 1966 when voters voted to change the flag's dimensions so it would conform to the flag industry's rectangular standard.

STATE SEAL

Before becoming a state, Florida, as a territory, had a seal. It was described as follows: "An American eagle with outspread wings, resting on a bed of clouds, occupies the center of a circular field. In the right talon of the eagle are three arrows, in the left an olive branch. Above the eagle is a semi-circle of 13 stars. Around the outer circle is the legend, 'The Territory of Florida.' The diameter of the seal is two inches."

When the territorial constitution of 1838 was adopted, seven years prior to Florida joining the Union, the framers stated the seal designed for the territory shall become the official seal for Florida when it becomes a state ". . . with such devices as the governor first elected may direct . . ."

It turned out the first-elected governor, William D. Moseley, did indeed have some "devices" for the seal that he wished to direct and he ordered a new seal. It was to be the first Great Seal of the State of Florida. Delivered to the secretary of state in December 1846, a year after statehood, it was ordered to replace the territory seal.

Records do not indicate who designed the new seal, nor is there a description of it. But from impressions on early official documents, it has been described as follows:

"An outline map of Florida occupies the top and right of a circular field. On an island in the lower left are one large and three small palm trees and an oak tree, under which sits a female figure with one hand outstretched to the Gulf of Mexico and the other holding a pike upon which rests a liberty cap. About her are casks and boxes and a variety of flowering shrubs. On the water are four ships—a three-masted square-rigger under full sail, another under jibs and topsails, a schooner, and a fishing shack. The legend around the outer rim is 'State of Florida—In God is Our Trust.' The diameter of the seal is two and three-fourths inches."

Gov. Moseley's seal was used during the War Between the States. And the 1865 constitution, which had the effect of taking Florida out of the Confederacy following the war, stated, "The state seal last heretofore used shall continue to be the Great Seal of the State." But in the 1868 constitution, which readmitted Florida to the Union, state officials ordered the legislature to "adopt a seal for the state, and such a seal shall be the size of the American silver dollar, but said seal shall not again be changed after its adoption by the legislature."

Following these orders, the 1868 Legislature adopted a joint resolution that was approved by Gov. Harrison Reed that year. The resolution stated: "That a seal the size of the American silver dollar having in the center thereof a view of the sun's rays over a highland in the distance, a cocoa tree, a steamboat on water, and an Indian

Present Seal   *1868 Seal*

female scattering flowers in the foreground, encircled by the words, 'Great Seal of the State of Florida: In God We Trust,' be and the same is hereby adopted as the Great Seal of the State of Florida."

The 1885 constitution, under which the state operated until 1968, retained that seal. In the 1968 constitution revision, the design of the seal was formally made the legislature's responsibility. It since has chosen not to redesign it, but merely to refine it (in 1985).

STATE TAXES

Florida is prohibited by its constitution from levying a personal income tax. The state also has no inheritance tax. Among its major taxes are those listed below.

Ad Valorem Tax

Statutes provide for the annual assessment and collection of ad valorem taxes on real and personal property. These taxes are assessed and collected at the county level as revenue for counties, municipalities, school districts, and special taxing districts.

Each year the county property appraiser is to determine the "just value" of all real property in the county as of Jan. 1. Factors determining "just value" include present cash value, use, location, quantity and size, cost or replacement value, and condition. On the basis of "just value," less exemptions and immunities, the tax due is computed by applying the millage rates established by the taxing authorities in that county. Counties are required to provide property owners with a TRIM (Truth in Millage) notice, which details past, present, and proposed taxation based on assessments.

The tax bill is mailed to the taxpayer usually no later than Nov. 1 and payment must be made to the tax collector by March 31 of the following year. Discounts are allowed for early payment. Payment on an installment plan is also usually offered.

The Save Our Homes amendment to the Florida Constitution limits annual property-assessment increases on homesteaded property to 3 percent or to a figure equal to the increase in the consumer price index, whichever is less.

Homestead and Personal Exemptions

The state's constitution provides a series of exemptions from taxation on an owner-occupied home,

GOVERNMENT

461

condominium, or cooperative apartment.

Every person who has legal or equitable title to real property in the state and who resides thereon, and in good faith makes it his or her permanent home, is eligible for $25,000 homestead exemption. If a homestead is valued at more than $75,000 an additional $25,000 exemption applies. This second $25,000 exemption does not apply to school taxes.

Applicants must reside on their property on Jan. 1 of the current taxable year and apply for the exemption by March 1. Annual renewal of the exemption is automatic unless the status of the property changes.

An extra $500 exemption may be claimed by widows and by widowers, by non-veteran homeowners totally and permanently disabled, and by veteran homeowners with a 10 percent or greater disability if that disability is military service connected.

Some counties provide an additional exemption for the elderly. Deployed military can receive a property tax credit.

Certain others are eligible for complete exemption from property taxes. They include quadriplegics; totally and permanently disabled veterans; totally disabled persons confined to a wheelchair; totally and permanently disabled persons who are blind, or who are partially blind but cannot meet an income test; and paraplegics and hemiplegics if their total household income does not exceed $14,500 annually.

Beverage Tax

Type of Beverage	Alcohol by Volume	Excise Tax Per Gallon
Beer	—	$0.48
Hard Cider	not more than 7%	$0.89
Wine	less than 17.2%	$2.25
Wine	17.2% or more	$3.00
Sparkling Wine	all	$3.50
Wine Coolers	all	$2.25
Liquor	under 17.2%	$2.25
Liquor	17.2% to 55.7%	$6.50
Liquor	55.7% or more	$9.53

Cigarette Tax

Cigarettes of common size are taxed at $1.34 a package. For larger sizes and non-standard packs, the rate is $1.43 a package. All non-cigarettes tobacco products other than cigars are taxed at the rate of 25 percent of the wholesale sales price.

Citrus Tax

A tax of 35 cents per box is

imposed on grapefruit; 25 cents on oranges; 11 cents on other varieties, primarily tangerines; and 18 cents on specialty fruits. For processed fruit the tax is 22 cents. Revenues are used to promote Florida citrus products and fight diseases, primarily canker and greening. The tax, paid by growers and processors, has been collected for 70 years but is only now facing legal challenges.

Documentary Stamp Tax

On promissory notes, mortgages, trust deeds, security agreements, and other written promises to pay money, the tax imposed is 35 cents per $100; on documents that convey an interest in realty, the tax imposed is 70 cents per $100.

Driver's Licenses

(A schedule of fees is listed in the Motoring section.)

Estate Taxes

Florida has no inheritance tax; however, any estate with a value requiring the filing of a federal estate tax return and involving Florida property must file a copy of the federal estate tax return with Florida and pay any Florida estate tax due, the amount of state tax credit on the federal return.

Hunting and Fishing Licenses

(A schedule of licenses for various types of hunting and fishing, for residents and nonresidents, is in the Hunting and Fishing section.)

Local Option Taxes

Transit Surtax: Eligible counties may impose, if approved by referendum, a 1 percent sales surtax on a transit system's transactions.

Convention Development: Eligible counties may impose a 1 to 3 percent tax on transient rentals.

Gasoline: Any county may levy up to six cents per gallon upon majority vote of the county commission. An additional one-cent per gallon may be imposed upon approval in a countywide referendum.

Tourist Development: A county, upon referendum approval, may impose a 1 to 5 percent tax on rental charges in the county. In addition, the county may charge another 1 percent tourist impact tax on referendum approval.

Motorboat Licenses

(Cost of licenses for varying size boats is in the Boating section.)

Motor Fuel Tax

The tax rates on gasoline include 18.4 cents federal, 14.5 cents state, and average of 14.6 cents county, and 2 cents state pollution tax.

Motor Vehicle Licenses

(Rates differ for all types and weights of vehicles. See Motoring section for specific rates.)

Pari-mutuel Tax

Tax on the handle (total amount) for a regular season of racing is as follows: horse and harness racing, 0.5 percent of handle; jai alai, 2 percent of handle; and greyhounds, 5.5 percent of handle. In addition, the state imposes a $100 license fee per horserace, $40 per jai-alai game, and $80 per greyhound race. An admissions tax of 15 percent also is charged patrons at pari-mutuel facilities.

Sales Tax

The greatest amount of state

revenue is derived from a 6 percent tax on retail sales. Sixty counties have voted an additional sales tax of from .5 to 1.5 percent.

Corporate Income Tax

A tax based on net income is imposed on all domestic and foreign corporations, associations, financial institutions, and other artificial entities, as declared on federal tax returns. The rate is 5.5 percent. Individuals, partnerships, estates, and private trusts are not subject to the tax.

COUNTY TAX COMPARISON

The following chart ranks Florida counties highest to lowest by average millage rates assessed. Millage is the rate at which property is taxed for ad valorem purposes. One mill equals $1 of tax per $1,000 of assessed property value.

The columns at right indicate taxable property values within each county and rank of county according to revenue. Homeowners receive as much as $50,000 "homestead" exemption.

2008

Rank by Rate	County	Average Millage	Taxable Property Value (thousands)	Rank by Revenue
1	Alachua	19.085	5,392,850	(25)
2	Union	18.782	75,227	(64)
3	Hamilton	18.500	62,528	(61)
4	Columbia	18.363	1,695,92	(41)
5	Dixie	18.350	66,328	(57)
6	Hendry	17.887	1,420,230	(42)
7	Gilchrist	17.807	164,488	(60)
8	Liberty	17.738	31,418	(65)
9	St. Lucie	176,406	5,985,303	(16)
10	Hardee	17.422	162,520	(46)
11	Glades	17.413	107.854	(55)
12	Madison	17.329	108,545	(59)
13	Calhoun	17.291	74,783	(63)
14	Lafayette	16.933	54,509	(66)
15	Gadsden	16.931	392,751	(50)
16	Bradford	16.864	239,104	(55)
17	Wakulla	16.638	436,036	(51)
18	Washington	16.445	147,762	(54)
19	Putnam	16.390	711,234	(40)
20	Suwannee	16.241	391,740	(47)

21	Baker	16.145	297,865	(56)
22	Okeechobee	16.144	434,553	(44)
23	Jefferson	16.119	155,386	(67)
24	Holmes	15.831	94,541	(62)
25	Leon	15.642	5,583,769	(24)
26	Citrus	15.541	3,894,192	(33)
27	DeSoto	15.235	323,328	(45)
28	Taylor	15.199	177,817	(52)
29	Levy	15.173	547,130	(43)
30	Palm Beach	15.038	62,511,273	(3)
31	Escambia	14.881	3,964,054	(27)
32	Highlands	14.787	1,408,947	(39)
33	Pinellas	147,296	25,514,419	(7)
34	Manatee	14.637	13,035,798	(14)
35	Volusia	14.630	11,732,253	(11)
36	Hillsborough	14.574	28,781,639	(5)
37	Osceola	14.460	5,156,943	(17)
38	Polk	14.453	8,745,746	(13)
39	Miami-Dade	14.276	79,034,291	(1)
40	Hernando	14.209	3,672,865	(32)
41	Pasco	14.093	10,455,165	(18)
42	St. Johns	13.958	9,936,506	(20)
43	Broward	13.903	58,527,287	(2)
44	Nassau	13.825	2,473,542	(36)
45	Santa Rosa	13.715	3,423,456	(37)
46	Jackson	13.495	311,756	(53)
47	Flagler	13.466	3,332,901	(34)
48	Sumter	13.46	3,021,076	(38)
49	Charlotte	13.306	5,555,169	(22)
50	Seminole	13.184	12,830,492	(15)
51	Martin	13.161	8,115,855	(23)
52	Clay	12.910	4,401,402	(31)
53	Lake	12.506	9,325,712	(19)
54	Gulf	12.461	261,253	(48)

55	Sarasota	12.426	19,863,418	(9)
56	Lee	123,497	23,675,699	(6)
57	Orange	12.108	29,016,117	(4)
58	Brevard	12.055	14,143,923	(12)
59	Marion	11.378	6,430,028	(21)
60	Bay	11.318	3,171,831	(30)
61	Indian River	11.073	7,341,502	(26)
62	Okaloosa	10.974	4,718,237	(28)
63	Collier	9.564	25,144,552	(10)
64	Franklin	8.270	376,592	(49)
65	Walton	8.107	1,905,392	(35)
66	Duval	8.032	19,750,929	(8)
67	Monroe	6.897	6,522,343	(29)

FINANCE

What has come to be called the Great Recession had a major impact on the finances of the State of Florida, which is but one of the states required by its constitution to operate on a balanced budget and allowing deficits only within the confines of long-term bonded indebtedness. The state went from record employment to record unemployment, worse than the national average. The state's economy, especially housing and tourism, plummeted, and sales tax collections, the state's primary source of income, went with it. While Florida has joined in the national economy's slight and slow upturn, the effects of the downturn are projected to linger for one to two decades.

Faced with hard times, the Florida Legislature began cutting expenditures to match revenues in 2009 but, with the continued battering of the economy, entered 2011 still facing a $3 billion shortfall, which called for new rounds of budget cutting.

The state's greatest source of revenue is its 6 percent sales tax collected on the sale of all goods except unprepared foods, prescription medicines, and some services. But a tax based solely on consumer spending leaves the state budget very much at the mercy of the general economy.

Florida does not have an income tax; it is specifically banned by the state constitution. The state has numerous other taxes and fees, but many are required by law for funding specific purposes.

Florida's finances are operated through "funds." The state's major funds are the General Fund, used for most normal government functions; the Special Revenue Funds, which handle revenues that are legally restricted to expenditures for specific purposes; Capital Projects Funds, Debt Service Funds, and Fiduciary Funds, in which the state acts as trustee or agent for both governmental and private organizations.

Florida government also operates Enterprise Funds, of which the largest is the Florida Lottery. As "enterprise" implies, these are funds that function as would private-sector businesses. The net assets of state enterprises declined $1.1 billion to $7.5 billion.

In all, Florida operates 170 component units. These are legally separate units for which the state is financially accountable, including joint ventures, non-profit organizations, and public-private partnerships. Primarily dealing with education, their financial operations are part of the public record. They are all on the books primarily to keep the state budget from being misleading or incomplete in the eyes of officials, legislators, or the public.

Ad valorem taxes are reserved to the counties, which also get a share of the sales tax and have the option of adding up to an additional 1.5 percent within their confines. The counties are also the major recipients in the state's spending, primarily through their school systems.

Generally, Health and Human Services has the state's largest expenditures, nearly one-third of the budget while ostensibly education accounts for slightly less. But on a net basis, education spending dwarfs all other government activities.

Sales and use taxes accounted for slightly more than 60 percent of the state's governmental revenues in 2009. State sales-tax collection fell during the fiscal year to $14.4 billion. After taxes, the second largest revenue generator was grants and donations, which provided

another $22 billion to the state's operating revenues.

Florida's state government spending for 2009 was $60.7 billion. Its revenues were $55.2 billion.

The governmental funds, the General Fund, had a balance of $6.9 billion in 2009. The Lawton Chiles Endowment Fund, a Republican memorial to the late Democratic Governor and used to fund children's and other health programs and research related to tobacco use, was transferred to the General Fund in 2008. Two emergency funds, the Budget Stabilization Fund and the Hurricane Catastrophe Fund, made major contributions to the General Fund in the budget crunch. The Budget fund still contained $274 million while the Hurricane funds retained assets of $1.7 billion in 2009.

Surplus, reserve, and trust revenues don't remain idle. The State Treasurer invests the money of the state, counties, and other units in certificates of deposit in Florida banks, direct obligations of the U.S. Treasury, commercial paper and banker's acceptances, medium-term corporate notes, and commingled and mutual funds. In 2009 Florida had $18.5 billion working.

Florida maintained its top-rated bond rating from the three major investor services, but the credibility of those institutions took a beating during the recession. Many of the state's investment vehicles had lower ratings.

Most Florida bonds reach maturity after the year 2020.

The state does not count as assets those it considers priceless and irreplaceable, such as its vast collections of everything from art to artifacts.

Controversial and risky investments by the State Board of Administration in 2007 did serious damage to the state's pension fund, which fell from 107 percent funded to 88 percent funded in 2010. In 2011, the state was still $3.7 billion short. It has more than a quarter-million pensioners.

Florida self-insures its general liability, its real capital assets, its employee health care, and its medical professional exposure with commercial insurance backup. Florida operates hospitals and medical centers through its universities including medical, dental, and veterinary schools. As of July 2009, it had a total exposure of $649 million. The state's catastrophic exposure is believed to be more than $2 trillion.

Florida had a per capita full faith and credit debt of $671.86 at the end of the fiscal year.

2009 FLORIDA REVENUES
(in thousands)

Taxes	$27,693,512
Licenses and permits	1,261,366
Fees and charges	3,521,215
Grants and donations	22,075,028
Investment earnings	-164,294
Fines, forfeitures, judgments	764,021
Other	58,257
TOTAL	**$55,209,715**

2009 SPENDING BY FUNCTION
(in thousands)

General Government	$6,878,903
Human Services	23,988,006
Criminal Justice and Corrections	4,037,197
State Courts	426,639
Education	18,722,159
Natural resources & environmental management	2,614,491
Transportation	3,850,791
Capital outlay	143,712
Debt service	1,612,320
TOTAL	**$60,669,218**

TAX REVENUES BY SOURCE
(in thousands)
2009

Sales Tax	17,415,648
Motor Fuel Tax	21,313,437
Communications Service Tax	1,541,548
Corporate Income Tax	1,698,356
Intangible Personal Property Tax	197,391
Documentary Stamp Tax	1,104,758
Alcohol Beverage Tax	616,812
Gross Receipts Utility Tax	662,059
Cigarette Tax	418.127
Estate Tax	4,650
Insurance Premium Tax	846,851
Hospital Public Assistance Tax	482,510
Pollutant Tax	2,131,437
Pari-mutuel Wagering Tax	127,772
Citrus Excise Tax	49,048
Solid Materials Severance Tax	69,710
Aviation Fuel Tax	52,147
Smokeless Tobacco Tax	28,554
Oil & Gas Production Tax	6,010
Other	4,157
TOTAL	**$27,693,512**

LOW TAX

Fifteen counties in Florida collect the 6 percent state sales tax without an additional local option added to it. The counties are Alachua, Brevard, Broward, Citrus, Collier, Franklin, Lee, Marion, Orange, Palm Beach, Pasco, Polk, Putnam, St. Johns, and Volusia.

CITY GOVERNMENT

Cities or municipalities are "creatures of the legislature," explains the Supreme Court. It refers to the fact that the constitution states, "Municipalities may be established or abolished . . . their charters amended" by the legislature. The legislature has the power by "general or specific law" to control the operation of a city, to abolish it, to change its charter, to incorporate in it any restrictions it desires, even to enact a law concerning a city.

Use of this power is, of course,

tempered by a city's voter control over their members of the legislature at election time.

There are two ways to establish a municipality in Florida. One is for the legislature to grant a specific charter under state law, usually a special law applying to only one city. The other method is for freeholders (property owners) in an area to establish a city under a general charter, as provided for under a general law of the state.

The first method calls for the legislature, after having advertised its intention of passing a law to create a city, or after having provided for a referendum among affected citizens, to pass a law giving the new city its charter. Most such laws encompass a referendum seeking approval of residents affected.

The second method permits "free-holders and registered voters of any hamlet, village or town not less than 1,000 in number . . . to establish for themselves a municipal government." In most cases, cities are established in Florida by the first, rather than the second, method. That is because the incorporation requirements under the second method are cumbersome.

Florida has many communities that have features of a city but not the legal status of one. Some of these "cities" even boast populations greater than established municipalities. Usually, residents of these large communities prefer to remain unincorporated for tax purposes. To live in an incorporated area or city means to be subject to additional taxes, that is, a city resident must pay not only county and school board taxes but also the city's taxes.

Increasingly, residents of unincorporated areas rely heavily on the county government for services often afforded by a city government, and a growing number of counties levy additional taxes on residents of areas that receive city-type services.

Three types of municipal government are prevalent in Florida—council/manager, council/mayor, and the commission.

Most popular is the council/manager type, particularly in larger cities. Day-to-day operation of the government is assigned to the full-time city manager, who is appointed by the elected council members. He or she does not make policy, but implements it as it comes from the council. The manager often is a professional, someone trained and educated in municipal government operations. A council/manager type may have a mayor, but his or her duties often are limited to presiding at meetings and representing the city at ceremonial functions. He or she does not have any more power, nor a greater vote, than any council member. The mayor's selection often is made by the council members, and the position often is rotated among the members.

In the council/mayor type of government, the mayor is the chief administrative officer. Elected separately from the council, he or she is responsible only to the voters. Under this form the mayor usually has veto powers over the council, but that veto can be overridden.

The commission type is generally found in smaller cities. Commission members are elected by voters and not only set city policy but administer it as well. One commissioner may be responsible for roads, another for parks, and so on. Charters of most cities incorporate features from all three types of government.

LEGAL HOLIDAYS

The following holidays, provided by Florida statutes, are observed as paid holidays by state agencies:

New Year's Day—Jan. 1
Martin Luther King, Jr.'s birthday—third Monday in January
Memorial Day—observed last Monday in May
Independence Day—July 4
Labor Day—observed on first Monday in September
Veterans Day—Nov. 11
Thanksgiving—observed the Friday after Thanksgiving Day
Christmas—Dec. 25
(If any of these holidays fall on Saturday, the proceeding Friday is observed as the holiday. If any fall on Sunday, the following Monday is observed as the holiday.)

Florida statutes also prescribe other "legal" holidays, days that institutions and individuals may or may not choose to observe. They are

Robert E. Lee's birthday—Jan. 19
Lincoln's birthday—Feb. 12
Susan B. Anthony's birthday—Feb. 15
Washington's birthday (Presidents' Day)—observed third Monday in February
Good Friday
Confederate Memorial Day—April 26
Jefferson Davis' birthday—June 3
Flag Day—June 14
Columbus Day—second Monday in October
General Elections Day—first Tuesday after first Monday in November

THE PORTS OF FLORIDA

With its huge coastline, Florida has more than a dozen deep-water ports, both natural and man-made, which account for billions of dollars in international and domestic trade.

2009				
Port	City	Cargo (tons)	Containers	Passengers (cruise)
Port Canaveral	Port Canaveral	2,300,926	7,611	1,189,000
Port Everglades	Fort Lauderdale	20,058,993	4,721,162	1,277,000

Port of Fernandina	Fernandina Beach	900,000	114,385	5,000
Port of Fort Pierce	Fort Pierce	360,000	13,800	0
Port of Jacksonville	Jacksonville	17,686,279	3,533,177	188,000
Port of Key West	Key West	0	0	930,000*
Port Manatee	Palmetto	2,897,599	123,037	0
Port of Miami	Miami	6,771,535	6,197,533	2,032,000
Port of Palm Beach	Riviera Beach	2,341,642	823,308	750,000
Port of Panama City	Panama City	2,461,497	209,687	0
Port of Pensacola	Pensacola	710,180	800	0
Port of St. Petersburg	St. Petersburg	0	0	0**
Port of Tampa	Tampa	34,888,052	360,111	386,000
Port St. Joe	Port St. Joe	0	0	0***

port of call
** *inactive*
*** *under development*

TRADE

Florida exported $58.9 billion in goods in 2009 while imports totaled $55.9 billion.

FLORIDA'S TOP TRADING PARTNERS

1. Brazil
2. Japan
3. Germany
4. Venezuela
5. China
6. Columbia
7. Chile
8. Dominican Republic
9. Costa Rica
10. Honduras

FLORIDA'S TOP EXPORT DESTINATIONS

1. Brazil
2. Venezuela
3. Columbia
4. Germany
5. Dominican Republic
6. Costa Rica
7. Argentina
8. Chile
9. Honduras
10. Mexico

FLORIDA'S TOP SOURCES OF IMPORTS

1. Japan
2. China
3. Brazil
4. Germany
5. Chile
6. France
7. United Kingdom
8. Columbia
9. Mexico
10. Dominican Republic

FLORIDA'S TOP IMPORTED PRODUCTS

1. Vehicles
2. Mineral fuel, oil, etc.
3. Apparel
4. Machinery
5. Electrical machinery
6. Copper
7. Aircraft, spacecraft
8. Woven apparel
9. Precious materials
10. Special, others

FLORIDA'S TOP EXPORT PRODUCTS

1. Machinery
2. Electrical machinery
3. Vehicles
4. Optical, medical instruments
5. Aircraft, spacecraft
6. Fertilizer
7. Plastics
8. Pharmaceutical products
9. Precious materials
10. Woven apparel

ELECTIONS

VOTER REGULATIONS

Any U.S. citizen who is at least 18 years old, or who will turn 18 before an election and who is a permanent Florida resident and resides in the county where he or she wishes to register, is eligible to vote in Florida. If any questions arise at registration time regarding the person's eligibility, the supervisor of elections may require proof of qualification. A voter at the polls with questionable qualification can be issued a provisional ballot, which will be counted if review establishes the voter's qualification.

Persons not entitled to vote are those not registered, those judged mentally incompetent, and those convicted of a felony who have not had their civil rights restored.

ELECTIONS 2012
General Election: Nov. 6

VOTING TERMS
"Primary election" means the election preceding the general election, and is held to select a party nominee. The primary is "open" if the winner of the election is determined by the primary result. If not, the primary is "closed," allowing only registered party members to vote for their party's nominee.

"General election" means an election held on the first Tuesday after the first Monday in November in the even-numbered years for the purpose of elective offices and voting on constitutional amendments.

"Elector" is synonymous with the word voter.

A "freeholder" is a person who owns taxable property in the state.

"Absentee voter" is a voter who votes by absentee ballot prior to Election Day. An absentee voter no longer needs a reason to cast such a ballot.

"Early voting" allows voters to cast ballots at select locations in a period prior to election day.

A person who moves out of the county in which he or she is registered into another Florida county, after registration books are closed, may cast an absentee ballot in the old county in national and state races.

A person moving to another state after registration books are closed may cast an absentee ballot in Florida for national races if the person's new state deems he or she is not yet eligible there as a voter.

REGISTERED VOTERS
(Nov. 1, 2010)

County	Republican	Democrat	Other Parties	No Party Affiliation	Total
Alachua	42,370	78,080	4,238	27,320	152,008
Baker	5,443	7,349	214	907	13,913
Bay	52,548	37,050	3,004	1,547	108,910
Bradford	5,998	7,979	309	16,168	15,833
Brevard	154,057	130,214	13,728	59,821	357,820
Broward	246,714	548,658	30,527	229,347	1,041,641
Calhoun	1,548	6,233	79	591	8,487

Charlotte	49,906	37,699	5,163	23,787	116,481
Citrus	41,355	34,504	3,446	18,712	98,018
Clay	67,662	31,088	3,952	18,314	122,016
Collier	91,992	46,251	6,824	35,507	180,674
Columbia	14,852	19,203	1,443	4,483	39,981
DeSoto	4,451	8,843	366	2,433	16,093
Dixie	2,315	6,778	303	888	10,264
Duval	194,998	233,750	18,249	80,082	527,079
Escambia	86,565	77,786	6,035	29,146	199,532
Flagler	23,450	24,088	2,090	15,393	65,021
Franklin	1,590	5,462	138	534	7,724
Gadsden	3,881	23,375	420	1,762	29,444
Gilchrist	4,317	5,019	357	1,148	10,840
Glades	1,904	3,694	174	780	6,552
Gulf	3,138	5,436	152	606	9,332
Hamilton	1,597	5,569	193	556	7,920
Hardee	4,115	6,474	234	1,280	12,112
Hendry	5,334	8,531	431	1,860	16,156
Hernando	48,567	46,976	5,219	22,320	123,082
Highlands	27,517	24,767	2,272	8,708	63,266
Hillsborough	226,907	286,406	23,284	140,743	677,340
Holmes	3,361	6,948	155	784	11,248
Indian River	43,692	27,505	3,524	16,177	90,898
Jackson	7,445	18,209	398	1,933	27,935
Jefferson	2,190	6,676	243	604	9,713
Lafayette	1,069	3,097	54	188	4,413
Lake	86,477	67,449	8,491	32,607	195,024
Lee	155,397	106,311	12,342	73,416	347,466
Leon	46,812	94,512	4,558	22,446	168,328
Levy	8,225	12,693	1,233	2,749	24,900
Liberty	425	3,645	27	160	4,257
Madison	2,169	8,315	240	737	11,461
Manatee	87,187	67,400	6,913	41,210	202,710
Marion	89,506	83,324	12,841	28.743	214,414
Martin	49,760	28,776	6,164	16,562	101,262
Miami-Dade	368,221	532,095	17,072	288,382	1,205,770
Monroe	19,030	18,021	1,866	12,344	51,261
Nassau	26,345	15,399	2,068	5,803	49,615
Okaloosa	74,314	29.719	291	22,330	126,654

Okeechobee	6,009	9,674	557	2,259	18,499
Orange	192,334	274,039	17,836	140,491	624,700
Osceola	41,703	65,192	4,799	35,327	147,021
Palmetto	238,879	374,469	31,656	176,846	821,850
Pasco	115,727	108,689	17,237	56,340	297,993
Pinellas	221,120	231,511	27,043	125,238	604,912
Polk	123,010	134,727	11,079	56,749	325,565
Putnam	13,910	23,295	1,178	5,618	44,001
Santa Rosa	63,540	28,204	3,699	16,928	112,371
Sarasota	117,268	86,030	8,335	52,749	264,382
Seminole	108,170	92,240	8,674	57,095	266,116
St. Johns	73,556	37,674	5,327	23,218	139,775
St. Lucie	53,602	72,860	6,527	32,827	165,816
Sumter	31,128	22,127	3,032	9.062	65,349
Suwanee	8,329	13,520	1,247	1,838	24,934
Taylor	3,172	8,686	279	710	12,847
Union	2,103	4,422	111	396	7,032
Volusia	108,922	127,566	10,939	71,346	318,773
Wakulla	5,342	10,178	599	1,603	17,722
Walton	19,783	11,003	923	5,249	36,958
Washington	4,900	7,606	252	1,136	13,897
Total	**4,039,259**	**4,631,068**	**360,811**	**2,186,246**	**11,214,384**

MAJOR ELECTIVE OFFICES

Office	Term	Salary	Requirements
U.S. Senate	Six years	$170,000	Must be at least 30 years old, a U.S. citizen for nine years, and a Florida resident.
U.S. House	Two years	$170,000	Must be at least 25 years old, a U.S. citizen for seven years, and a Florida resident.
Governor	Four years	$130,273	Must be at least 30 years old and a Florida resident for seven years.
Lt. Governor	Four years	$124,851	Must be at least 30 years old and a Florida resident for seven years.
State Cabinet	Four years	$128,972	Must be at least 30 years old and a Florida resident for seven years.

Attorney General	—	—	Must also be a member of the Florida Bar for five years.
Public Service Commissioner	Four years	$129,000	May not hold any interest in a railroad or utility.
Florida Supreme Court Justice	Six years	$157,976	Must be a member of the Florida Bar for 10 years.
District Court of Appeals Judge	Six years	$153,140	Must be a member of the Florida Bar for 10 years.
Circuit Court Judge	Six years	$145,080	Must be a member of the Florida Bar for 10 years.
State Senate	Four years	$29,697	Must be at least 21 years old and a state resident for two years.
State House of Representatives	Two years	$29,697	Must be at least 21 years old and a state resident for two years.
County Commissioner	Four years	*	Must be a resident of the district at least six months.
School Board	Four years	*	Must be a resident of the district at least six months.
Tax Collector	Four years	*	Must be a registered voter.
Tax Assessor	Four years	*	Must be a registered voter.
Supervisor of Elections	Four years	*	Must be a registered voter.
County Judge	Four years	*	Must be a member of the Florida Bar.
State Attorney	Four years	**	Must be a member of the Florida Bar for five years.
Clerk of Court	Four years	*	Must be a registered voter.
Sheriff	Four years	*	Must be a registered voter.
Superintendent of Schools	Four years	*	Must be a registered voter.***

*Determined in part by population of district.
**Determined in part by population of Judicial Circuit.
***Does not apply to appointed superintendents.

STATE PRESIDENTIAL VOTE, 1848 TO PRESENT
(Major Party Popular Vote in Florida)

1848:	Zachary Taylor (Whig)	4,117
	Lewis Cass (Dem.)	3,083
1852:	Franklin Pierce (Dem.)	4,318
	Winfield Scott (Whig)	2,875
1856:	James Buchanan (Dem.)	6,358
	Millard Fillmore (American)	4,833
1860:	John C. Breckinridge (Dem.)	8,155
	John Bell (Constitutional Union)	4,731
	Stephen Douglas (Ind. Dem.)	221
1864:	(No election)	
1868:	Republican electors chosen by Legislature	
1872:	Ulysses S. Grant (Rep.)	17,765
	Horace Greeley (Dem.)	15,428
1876:	Rutherford B. Hayes (Rep.)	23,849
	Samuel J. Tilden (Dem.)	22,923
1880:	Winfield S. Hancock(Dem.)	27,925
	James A. Garfield (Rep.)	23,686
1884:	Grover Cleveland (Dem.)	31,766
	James G. Blaine (Rep.)	28,031
1888:	Grover Cleveland (Dem.)	39,561
	Benjamin Harrison (Rep.)	26,659
1892:	Grover Cleveland (Dem.)	30,143
	James Weaver (People's)	4,843
1896:	William J. Bryan (Dem.)	30,683
	William McKinley (Rep.)	11,288
	William J. Bryan (People's)	2,053
	John M. Palmer (National Dem.)	1,778
1900:	William J. Bryan (Dem.)	28,625
	William McKinley (Rep.)	7,314
	William J. Bryan (People's)	1,070
	John G. Woolley (Prohibition)	2,234
1904:	Alton B. Parker (Dem.)	27,046
	Theodore Roosevelt (Rep.)	8,314
	Thomas E. Watson (People's)	1,605
	Eugene Debs (Socialist)	2,337
1908:	William J. Bryan (Dem.)	31,104
	William H. Taft (Rep.)	10,654
	Eugene Debs (Socialist)	3,747
	Eugene Chafin (Prohibition)	1,356
1912:	Woodrow Wilson (Dem.)	36,417
	William H. Taft (Rep.)	4,279
	Eugene Debs (Socialist)	4,806
	Eugene Chafin (Prohibition)	1,854
	Theodore Roosevelt (Progressive)	4,535
1916:	Woodrow Wilson (Dem.)	55,984

	Charles Evans Hughes (Rep.)	14,611
	A. L. Benson (Socialist)	7,814
	J. Frank Hanly (Prohibition)	4,855
1920:	James M. Cox (Dem.)	90,515
	Warren G. Harding (Rep.)	44,853
	Warren G. Harding (Rep. White)	10,118
	Eugene Debs (Socialist)	5,189
	Aaron Sherman (Prohibition)	5,124
1924:	John W. Davis (Dem.)	62,083
	Calvin Coolidge (Rep.)	30,633
	Herman Faris (Prohibition)	5,498
	Robert M. La Follette (Progressive)	8,625
	Gilbert Nations (American)	2,315
1928:	Herbert Hoover (Rep.)	144,168
	Alfred E. Smith (Dem.)	101,764
	Norman Thomas (Socialist)	4,036
	William Foster (Communist)	3,704
1932:	Franklin D. Roosevelt (Dem.)	206,307
	Herbert Hoover (Rep.)	69,170
1936:	Franklin D. Roosevelt (Dem.)	249,117
	Alfred Landon (Rep.)	78,248
1940:	Franklin D. Roosevelt (Dem.)	359,334
	Wendell Willkie (Rep.)	126,158
1944:	Franklin D. Roosevelt (Dem.)	339,377
	Thomas E. Dewey (Rep.)	143,215
1948:	Harry S. Truman (Dem.)	281,988
	Thomas E. Dewey (Rep.)	194,280
	Strom Thurmond (States Rights)	89,750
	Henry A. Wallace (Progressive)	11,620
1952:	Dwight D. Eisenhower (Rep.)	544,036
	Adlai E. Stevenson (Dem.)	444,036
1956:	Dwight D. Eisenhower (Rep.)	643,849
	Adlai E. Stevenson (Dem.)	480,371
1960:	Richard M. Nixon (Rep.)	795,476
	John F. Kennedy (Dem.)	748,700
1964:	Lyndon B. Johnson (Dem.)	948,540
	Barry M. Goldwater (Rep.)	905,941
1968:	Richard M. Nixon (Rep.)	886,804
	Hubert H. Humphrey (Dem.)	676,794
	George C. Wallace (Am. Ind.)	624,207
1972:	Richard M. Nixon (Rep.)	1,857,759
	George S. McGovern (Dem.)	718,117
1976:	Jimmy Carter (Dem.)	1,636,000
	Gerald R. Ford (Rep.)	1,469,531
1980:	Ronald Reagan (Rep.)	2,046,951
	Jimmy Carter (Dem.)	1,419,475
1984:	Ronald Reagan (Rep.)	2,730,350
	Walter F. Mondale (Dem.)	1,448,816

1988:	George Bush (Rep.)	2,618,885
	Michael S. Dukakis (Dem.)	1,656,701
1992:	George Bush (Rep.)	2,137,752
	Bill Clinton (Dem.)	2,051,845
	H. Ross Perot (Ind.)	1,041,607
1996:	Bill Clinton (Dem.)	2,545,968
	Bob Dole (Rep.)	2,243,324
	H. Ross Perot (Ref.)	483,776
2000:	George W. Bush (Rep.)	2,912,790
	Al Gore (Dem.)	2,912,253
	Ralph Nader (Green)	97,488
2004:	George W. Bush (Rep.)	3,964,522
	John Kerry (Dem.)	3,583,544
2008:	Barrack Obama (Dem.)	4,282,074
	John McCain (Rep.)	4,045,624

RECENT GENERAL ELECTION RESULTS
2006 General Election

U.S. Senate

| Bill Nelson (Dem.) | 2,890,548 |
| Katherine Harris (Rep.) | 1,826,127 |

2010 General Election

U.S. Senate

Mario Rubio (Rep.)	2,644,539
Charlie Crist (NPA)	1,606,726
Kendrick Meek (Dem.)	1,092,059
Alexander Sankter (Lib.)	24,831
Sue Askeland (NPA)	15,336

U.S. House of Representatives

Dist. 1:	Jeff Miller (Rep.)	170,760
	Joe Cantrell (NPA.)	23,243
Dist. 2:	Ken Sutherland (Rep.)	136,271
	Allen Boyd (Dem.)	105,169
Dist. 3:	Corrine Browne (Dem.)	94,706
	Michael Yost (Rep.)	50,914
Dist. 4:	Andrew Crenshaw (Rep.)	176,145
	Troy Stanley (NPA)	52,508
Dist. 5:	Richard B. Nugent (Rep.)	208,791
	James Piccillo (Dem.)	100,852
Dist. 6:	Clifford Sterns (Rep.)	179,318
	Steve Schonberg (NPA.)	71,626

Dist. 7:	John L. Mica (Rep.) Heather Beaven (Dem.)	185,437 83,177
Dist. 8:	Daniel Webster (Rep.) Alan Grayson (Dem.)	125,571 84,148
Dist. 9:	Gus Bilirakis (Rep.) Anita de Palma (Dem.)	165,455 66,186
Dist. 10:	C. W. Bill Young (Rep.) Charlie Justice (Dem.)	137,916 71,291
Dist. 11:	Kathy Castor (Dem.) Mike Prendergast (Rep.)	91,280 61,787
Dist. 12:	Dennis Ross (Rep.) Lori Edwards (Dem.) Randy Wilkinson (Tea)	102,736 87,791 22,865
Dist. 13:	Vern Buchanan (Rep.) James T. Golden (Dem.)	183,796 83,102
Dist. 14:	Connie Mack (Rep.) James L. Roach (Dem.)	188,332 74,515
Dist. 15:	Bill Posey (Rep.) Shannon Roberts (Dem.)	162,214 85,532
Dist. 16:	om Rooney (Rep.) Jim Horn (Dem.)	162,214 80,306
Dist. 17:	Frederica S. Wilson (Dem.) Roderick D. Vereen (NPA)	106,336 17,007
Dist. 18:	Ileana Ros-Lehtinen (Rep.) Roland A. Banciella (Dem.)	102,355 46,222
Dist. 19:	Ted Deutch (Dem.) Joe Budd (Rep.)	131,750 78,503
Dist. 20:	Debbie Wasserman Schultz (Dem.) Karen Harrington (Rep.)	100,699 63,770
Dist. 21:	Mario Diaz-Balart (Rep.)	Unopposed
Dist. 22:	Allen West (Rep.) Ron Klein (Dem.)	118,539 99,591

Dist. 23:	Alcee L. Hastings (Dem.)	99,730
	Bernard Sansaricq (Rep.)	26,365
Dist. 24:	Sadra Adams (Rep.)	146,051
	Suzanne Kosmas (Dem.)	98,708
Dist. 25:	David Rivera (Rep.)	74,855
	Joe Garcia (Dem.)	61,133

2010 GENERAL ELECTION
State Cabinet

Governor

Rick Scott (Rep.)	2,618.419
Alex Sink (Dem.)	2,556,453

Attorney General

Pam Bondi (Rep.)	2,881,877
Dan Gelber (Dem.)	2,180,129

Chief Financial Officer

Jeff Atwater (Rep.)	2,967,052
Loranne Ausley (Dem.)	2,151,232

Commissioner of Agriculture

Adam Putnam (Rep.)	2,907,095
Scott Maddox (Dem.)	1,982,107

2008 CONSTITUTIONAL AMENDMENTS
(60 percent required for Adoption)

1. A Declaration of Rights
   Yes 3,564,090   **No** 3,871,704 (Failed)
2. Marriage Protection
   Yes 4,890,883   **No** 3,008,026 (Passed)
3. Housecleaning Not Affecting Assessed Value of Residential Real Property
   Yes 4,351,975   **No** 2,839,825 (Passed)
4. Property Tax Exemption for Perpetually Conserved Land
   Yes 4,875,162   **No** 2,235,969 (Passed)
5. Assessment of Working Waterfront Property Based on Current Use
   Yes 4,983,313   **No** 2,072,041 (Passed)
6. Local Option Community College Funding
   Yes 3,210,481   **No** 4,161,731 (Failed)

2010 CONSTITUTIONAL AMENDMENTS
(60 percent required for Adoption)

1. Repeal of Political Public Financing of Elections
   Yes 2,587,543   **No** 2,342,137 (Failed)

2.Homestead Ad Volorum Tax Credit for Deployed Military
   Yes 3,936,526   No 1,122,053
3. Requiring Referenda for Local Land Use Plan
   Yes 1,682,177   No 3,424,204(Failed)
4. Standards for Legislative Redistricting
   Yes 3,155,149   No 1,885,860
5. Standards for Congressional Redistricting
   Yes 3,153,199   No 1,857.748
6. Revision of Public School Class Size Amendment
   Yes 2,751,878   No 2,298,001(Failed)

NON-BINDING REFERENDUM
7. Balance the Federal Budget
   Yes 3,524,629   No 1,377,352

PRESIDENT AND VICE PRESIDENT
(2008—By County)

County	McCain/Palin (Rep.)	Obama/Biden (Dem.)	Others
Alachua	48.513	75,565	1,441
Baker	8,672	2,326	60
Bay	56.683	23,653	790
Bradford	8,135	3,430	110
Brevard	157,536	127,561	2,648
Broward	237,724	492,633	3,529
Calhoun	4,345	1,821	98
Charlotte	45,205	39,031	922
Citrus	43,706	31,460	992
Clay	67,203	26,697	676
Collier	86,379	54,450	881
Columbia	18,668	9,171	287
DeSoto	5,625	4,378	116
Dixie	5,184	1,925	145
Duval	210,537	202,618	2,606
Escambia	91,411	61,572	1,464
Flagler	23,951	24,726	354
Franklin	3,818	2,133	77

Gadsden	6,805	15,566	117
Gilchrist	5,656	1,996	131
Glades	2,533	1,674	33
Gulf	4,980	2,149	76
Hamilton	3,179	2,360	44
Hardee	4,763	2,568	81
Hendry	5,780	4,998	101
Hernando	45,020	41,883	994
Highlands	26,221	18,135	747
Hillsborough	236,355	272,963	3,587
Holmes	7,033	1,446	110
Indian River	40,176	29,710	705
Jackson	13,717	7,671	177
Jefferson	3,784	4,082	72
Lafayette	2,677	640	70
Lake	82,802	62.948	1,176
Lee	147,608	119,701	1,957
Leon	55,805	91,747	1,156
Levy	11,764	6,711	260
Liberty	2,339	895	44
Madison	4,544	4,270	93
Manatee	80,721	70,034	1,239
Marion	89,608	70,815	1,555
Martin	44,143	33,508	643
Miami-Dade	360,551	499,831	3,104
Monroe	18,933	20,907	432
Nassau	27,403	10,618	278
Okaloosa	68,789	25,872	868
Okeechobee	7,561	5,108	117
Orange	186,832	273,009	2,870
Osceola	40,086	59,902	622
Palm Beach	226,000	361,206	3,190
Pasco	110,104	102,417	2,345
Pinellas	209,978	248,138	4,015

Polk	128,878	113,865	2,090
Putnam	19,637	13,236	298
Santa Rosa	55,972	19,470	743
Sarasota	102,897	102,686	1,770
Seminole	105,070	99,335	1,490
St. Johns	69,223	35,786	831
St. Lucie	52,512	67,125	942
Sumter	30,866	17.655	347
Suwannee	12,534	4,916	212
Taylor	6,457	2.803	106
Union	3,933	1,299	53
Volusia	113,938	127,795	2,091
Wakula	8,873	5,312	143
Walton	17,561	7,174	311
Washington	8,177	2,863	90
Totals	**4,045,624**	**4,282.07**	**62,746**

State total is official. County totals include official and unofficial, audited and unaudited returns.

The **Others** and their statewide results include:

Nader/Gonzalez (ECO)	28,124
Barr/Root (LIB)	17,218
Baldwin/Castle (CPF)	7,815
McKinney/Clemente (GRE)	2,887
Keyes/Rorhbough (AIP)	2,550
LaRiva/Puryear (PSL)	1,516
Jay/Smith (BTP)	795
Harris/Kennedy (SWP)	533
Stevens/Link (OBJ)	419
Moore/Alexander (SPF)	405
Nettles/Krones (WRI)	391
Amondson/Platten (PRO)	203

GUBERNATORIAL VOTE, 1845 TO PRESENT
(Election Results)

1845: William D. Mosely (Dem.)   3,292
       Richard K. Call (Whig)   2,679
1848: Thomas Brown (Whig)   3,801
       William Bailey (Dem.)   3,354

1852:	James E. Broome (Dem.)	4,628
	George T. Ward (Whig)	4,336
1856:	Madison S. Perry (Dem.)	6,214
	David S. Walker (American)	5,894
1860:	John Milton (Dem.)	6,994
	Edward Hopkins (Constitutional Union)	5,284
1865:	David S. Walker (Conservative Dem.—no opposition)	5,873
1868:	Harrison Reed (Rep.)	14,421
	George W. Scott (Dem.)	7,731
	Samuel Walker (Radical Rep.)	2,251
1872:	Ossian B. Hart (Rep.)	17,603
	William D. Bloxham (Dem.)	16,004
1876:	George F. Drew (Dem.)	24,179
	Marcellus L. Stearns (Rep.)	23,984
1880:	William D. Bloxham (Dem.)	28,378
	Simon D. Conover (Rep.)	23,297
1884:	Edward A. Perry (Dem.)	32,087
	Frank W. Pope (Rep.)	27,845
1888:	Francis P. Fleming (Dem.)	40,255
	V. J. Shipman (Rep.)	26,485
1892:	Henry L. Mitchell (Dem.)	32,064
	Alonzo P. Baskin (People's)	8,309
	N. J. Hawley (Prohibition)	297
1896:	William D. Bloxham (Dem.)	27,172
	Edward R. Gunby (Rep.)	8,290
	William A. Weeks (People's)	5,270
1900:	William S. Jennings (Dem.)	29,251
	Matthew B. MacFarlane (Rep.)	6,238
	A. M. Morton (People's)	631
1904:	Napoleon B. Broward (Dem.)	28,971
	Matthew B. MacFarlane (Rep.)	6,357
	W. R. Healey	1,270
1908:	Albert W. Gilchrist (Dem.)	33,036
	John M. Cheney (Rep.)	6,453
	A. J. Pettigrew (Socialist)	2,427
1912:	Park Trammel (Dem.)	38,977
	Thomas W. Cox (Socialist)	3,647
	William R. O'Neal (Rep.)	2,646
	William C. Hodges (Progressive)	2,314
	J. W. Bingham (Prohibition)	1,061
1916:	Sidney J. Catts (Dem.)	39,546
	William V. Knott (Dem.)	30,343
	George W. Allen (Rep.)	10,333
	C. C. Allen (Socialist)	2,470
	Noel A. Mitchell	193
1920:	Gary A. Hardee (Dem.)	103,407
	George E. Gay (Rep.)	23,788
	W. L. VanDuzer (Rep. White)	2,654
	F. C. Whitaker (Socialist)	2,823

1924:	John W. Martin (Dem.)	84,181
	William R. O'Neal (Rep.)	17,499
1928:	Doyle E. Carlton (Dem.)	148,455
	W. J. Howey (Rep.)	95,018
1932:	Dave Sholtz (Dem.)	186,270
	W. J. Howey (Rep.)	93,353
1936:	Fred P. Cone (Dem.)	253,638
	E. E. Callaway (Rep.)	59,832
1940:	Spessard Holland (Dem.—no opposition)	334,152
1944:	Millard F. Caldwell (Dem.)	361,007
	Bert L. Acker (Rep.)	96,321
1948:	Fuller Warren (Dem.)	381,459
	Bert L. Acker (Rep.)	76,153
1952:	Dan McCarty (Dem.)	624,463
	Harry S. Swan (Rep.)	210,009
1954:	LeRoy Collins (Dem.)	287,769
	J. Tom Watson (Rep.)	69,852
1956:	LeRoy Collins (Dem.)	747,753
	William A. Washburne (Rep.)	266,980
1960:	Farris Bryant (Dem.)	849,407
	George C. Petersen (Rep.)	569,936
1964:	Haydon Burns (Dem.)	933,554
	Charles Holley (Rep.)	686,297
1966:	Claude Kirk (Rep.)	821,190
	Robert King High (Dem.)	668,233
1970:	Reubin Askew (Dem.)	984,305
	Claude Kirk (Rep.)	746,243
1974:	Reubin Askew (Dem.)	1,118,954
	Jerry Thomas (Rep.)	709,438
1978:	Robert Graham (Dem.)	1,406,580
	Jack Eckerd (Rep.)	1,123,888
1982:	Robert Graham (Dem.)	1,739,553
	L. A. Bafalis (Rep.)	949,023
1986:	Bob Martinez (Rep.)	1,847,525
	Steve Pajcic (Dem.)	1,538,620
1990:	Lawton Chiles (Dem.)	1,995,206
	Bob Martinez (Rep.)	1,535,068
1994:	Lawton Chiles (Dem.)	2,135,008
	Jeb Bush (Rep.)	2,071,068
1998:	Jeb Bush (Rep.)	2,186,283
	Buddy MacKay (Dem.)	1,771,269
2002:	Jeb Bush (Rep.)	2,856,845
	Bill McBride (Dem.)	2,201,427
2006:	Charlie Crist (Rep.)	2,519,845
	Jim Davis (Dem.)	2,178,289
2010:	Rick Scott (Rep.)	2,619,335
	Alex Sink (Dem.)	2,557,785
	Peter Allen (Ind.)	123,832

FIRST AND SECOND

Beth Johnson was the first woman elected to the Florida Senate. The second woman elected to the Florida Senate was Beth Johnson. The first was from Orlando, the second from Cocoa.

ISLANDS

Florida has the second highest number of islands among the states, with Alaska having the most. Florida's number of islands of 10-acre size or greater is estimated to be 4,510.

MIAMI MOST FOREIGN

More than half the residents of Miami-Dade County were born in other countries, the highest percentage of any county in the country. More than 60 percent of the residents of the city of Miami were foreign-born, the highest percentage among U.S. major cities. Nearly 1.2 million foreign-born residents live in Miami-Dade.

LINGUA HIALEAH

Hialeah has the highest percentage of residents who speak a foreign language of any large city in the country. Ninety-three percent of its 228,000 residents speak a language other than English. The city of Miami ranks eighth with 75 percent of its residents speaking a foreign language.

FOREIGN CONSULS

Florida has the nation's fourth largest Foreign Consular Corps. Below is a list of those countries and the cities where offices are situated. (For specific addresses and phone numbers call directory assistance for those cities.)

Antigua & Barbuda—Miami
Argentina—Miami
Australia—Key Biscayne
Austria—Miami
Bahamas—Miami
Barbados—Coral Gables
Belgium—Miami
Belize—Coconut Grove
Bolivia—Miami
Brazil—Miami
Bulgaria—Boca Raton
Canada—Miami
Chile—Miami
Colombia—Coral Gables
Costa Rica—Miami
Czech Republic—Fort Lauderdale
Denmark—Ft. Lauderdale
Dominican Republic—Miami
Ecuador—Miami
El Salvador—Miami
Equatorial Guinea—Miami
Finland—Coral Gables, Lake Worth
France—Miami, Clearwater,
Gambia—North Miami
Germany—Miami, Naples
Greece—Tampa
Grenada—Miami
Guatemala—Miami
Guinea—Ft. Lauderdale
Guyana—Miami
Haiti—Miami
Honduras—Coral Gables
Hungary—Coral Gables
Iceland—Hollywood
Ireland—Naples
Israel—Miami
Italy—Miami
Jamaica—Miami

Japan—Miami
Korea—Miami
Latvia—Fort Lauderdale
Lebanon—Miami
Liberia—Tampa
Lithuania—Palm Beach
Mali—Fort Lauderdale
Malta—Delray Beach
Mexico—Miami
Monaco—Miami
Netherlands—Miami
Nicaragua—Miami
Norway—Miami
Panama—Tampa, Coral Gables
Paraguay—Miami
Peru—Miami
Philippines—Fort Lauderdale
Poland—Miami
Portugal—Coral Gables
Romania—Key Biscayne
Russia—Clearwater
Santa Lucia—Miami
Senegal/Togo—Miami
Singapore—Coconut Grove
Slovakia—Lauderhill
Slovenia—Palm Beach
Spain—Coral Gables
Surinam—Miami
Sweden—Fort Lauderdale
Switzerland—Miami
Taiwan—Coral Gables
Tanzania—Delray Beach
Thailand—Coral Gables
Trinidad & Tobago—Miami
Tunisia—Miami
United Kingdom—Miami
Uruguay—Coral Gables
Venezuela—Miami

MILITARY

During World War II Florida was one of the major training areas of the nation, particularly for the training of pilots. Municipal airports in every part of the state were taken over by the Army Air Corps, predecessor of the present U.S. Air Force. Men from around the nation and foreign countries made their temporary homes in Florida while instructors taught them to fly fighters, bombers, and other types of aircraft.

Gen. Jimmy Doolittle and his flight crews received special training in launching B-25s from the decks of an aircraft carrier at what is now part of Eglin Air Force Base near Fort Walton Beach. After completing their training, they flew their planes to the nation's West Coast, loaded them aboard the carrier, and in April 1942 conducted the first air raid on Tokyo. A monument to this event is situated along U.S. 90 between Crestview and DeFuniak Springs, just north of Eglin.

The state also was an important site for naval bases during the war. With the state's vast coastline on both the Atlantic Ocean and the Gulf of Mexico, Florida's ports were strategically located in the Navy's fight against German U-Boats.

Many of the jungle fighters of the U.S. Army were trained in the semitropical regions of Florida before they went into battle in the South Pacific. The state's shores and beaches were the scene of many soldiers' and marines' first taste of amphibious training.

INSTALLATIONS

Florida has major military installations throughout the state. Bases play a vital role in local economies by providing substantial payrolls for large numbers of people who, in turn, buy local goods and services. Each base also allocates a percentage of its procurement activity to small or disadvantaged businesses. Counties and schools impacted by the military receive additional federal education funds. Bases in the state include:

Air National Guard, 125th Fighter Group	Jacksonville
Army Air Reserve Station	Clearwater
Avon Park Bombing Range	Highlands and Polk Counties
Cape Canaveral Air Force Station	Cape Canaveral
Coast Guard Air Station	Clearwater
Coast Guard Air Station	Miami
Duke Field	Okaloosa County
Eglin Air Force Base	Valparaiso
Homestead Air Force Reserve Base	Homestead
Hurlburt Field	Fort Walton Beach
Jacksonville Naval Air Station	Jacksonville
Key West Naval Air Station	Key West
MacDill Air Force Base	Tampa
Mayport Naval Station	Mayport
National Guard Adjutant General	St. Augustine
National Guard Maintenance Office	Camp Blanding

Panama City Naval Coastal Systems Center	Panama City
Patrick Air Force Base	Cocoa Beach
Pensacola Naval Training Center	Pensacola
Tyndall Air Force Base	Panama City
U.S. Coast Guard Integrated Support Command	Miami
Whiting Field Naval Air Station	Milton

UNIFIED COMMANDS

Florida is home to three of the nation's nine unified military commands: Central Command and Special Operations Command, both headquartered at Tampa, and Southern Command, headquartered at Doral.

CONGRESSIONAL MEDAL OF HONOR WINNERS
(place of residence in parentheses)
Army/Air Force

Bennett, Emory L., Pfc. (Cocoa)*
Bolton, Cecil H. (Crawfordville)
Bowen, Hammett L., Jr., S/Sgt. (Jacksonville)*
Condon, Clarence M., Sgt. (St. Augustine)
Cutinha Nicholas J., Spec. 4 (Fernandina Beach)*
Femoyer, Robert E., 2nd Lt. (Jackson)*
McGuire, Thomas B., Jr., Maj. (MacDill Field)
Mills, James H., Pvt. (Fort Meade)
Nininger, Alexander R., Jr., 2nd Lt. (Fort Lauderdale)*
Paine, Adam, Pvt., Indian Scouts (Floridian)
Sims, Clifford C., S/Sgt (Port St. Joe)*
Smith, Paul R., Sgt 1st (Tampa)*
Varnum, Charles A., Capt. (Pensacola)
Navy/Marine Corps
Carter, Bruce W., Pfc. (Jacksonville)*
Corry, William M., Lt. Cmdr. (Quincy)*

Ingram, Robert R. Corpsman 3 (Clearwater)
Jenkins, Robert H., Pfc. (Interlachen)*
Lassen, Clyde E., Lt. j.g. (Fort Myers)
Lopez, Baldomero, 1st Lt. (Tampa)*
McCampbell, David, Cmdr. (Pensacola)
McTureous, Robert M., Jr., Pvt. (Altoona)*
Norris, Thomas, Lt. (Jacksonville)
Ormsbee, Francis E., Jr., CMM (Pensacola)*
Smedley, Larry E., Cpl. (Orlando)*
Posthumous award

NATIONAL CEMETERIES

Florida has seven national cemeteries around the state although one, **St. Augustine National Cemetery,** is closed while another, **Bay Pines National Cemetery,** is closed to all but cremated remains. But **Barrancas National Cemetery** in Pensacola and the recently expanded **Florida National Cemetery** at Bushnell are fully operational. In addition, three new national cemeteries have recently opened: **Sarasota National Cemetery, Jacksonville National Cemetery,** and **South Florida National Cemetery** at Lake Worth.

An estimated 1.7 million veterans live in Florida.

Veterans with discharges, not dishonorable, their spouses and dependent children are eligible for burial in a national cemetery.

VETERANS HOSPITALS

There are six Veterans Hospitals in Florida: at Gainesville, Lake City, Miami, St. Petersburg, Tampa, and West Palm Beach. The Department of Veterans Affairs also operates outpatient clinics in Florida's major cities and offers community outpatient centers throughout the state, along with Veterans Readjustment Counseling Centers.

THE C.S.S. *FLORIDA*

Damage done by Confederate cruisers to U.S. merchant marine commerce during the Civil War is estimated at more than $15 million. The C.S.S. Florida was one of the most successful Confederate cruisers. During two years of operation she is credited with destroying more than $4 million worth of shipping commerce, including the taking of 60 prizes in two voyages. Built in England, the C.S.S. Florida put to sea in 1862. She weighed 700 tons, had a length of 192 feet, a beam of just over 27 feet, and a maximum cruising speed of 12 knots. In November 1864, after a still-controversial Federal capture at the neutral Brazilian port of Bahia, the C.S.S. Florida collided with a U.S. transport vessel and sank off the Virginia coast. The C.S.S. Florida was the first iron-hulled vessel to make a transatlantic crossing.

CIVIL WAR BLOCKADE

In order to cut off the delivery of useful goods to the South during the Civil War, President Abraham Lincoln established a shipping blockade that surrounded the entire Florida peninsula westward to the Mexican border. Steamships continued to run the blockade, but success favored a long, low, swift silhouette and a shallow draft. Smokeless coal was the fuel of choice.

SPACE EXPLORATION

CAPE CANAVERAL— SPACE CENTER

Midway between Jacksonville and Miami, on Florida's east coast, the National Aeronautics and Space Administration operates the huge Spaceport. The sprawling launch installation, with its gargantuan engineering creations that send off manned and unmanned space flights, contrasts sharply with the surrounding natural setting and early history of this area.

Cape Canaveral on the Atlantic Ocean buffers Merritt Island to its west, which lies between the cape and the mainland. The area is a rich deposit for archaeologists, who have uncovered traces of human activity on the island predating the Christian era. They have found burial mounds and refuse piles left by Indians, and relics from Spanish and French forays into the area during 16th-century explorations. Some experts believe the Kennedy Space Center built on Merritt Island rests over sites where Western civilization first came to the New World.

Today, astronauts train and lift off into space within the view of duck hunters and fishermen along the adjacent Banana River. Much of the area, in fact, despite its technological development, still remains in a natural state as a national wildlife refuge.

The cape and Merritt Island were chosen for the U.S. space program shortly after World War II. In the program's early years, Redstone and Jupiter rockets were launched from the cape from blockhouses protecting 50-man firing teams from the unexpected. Launch crews of the later 1950s multiplied many times into an organization that, at its peak in September 1968, employed 26,500 administrators, engineers, and technicians. This upsurge in activity occurred during the manned flights of Mercury, Gemini, and Apollo missions.

In 1960, seven years after exploratory rockets began lifting off the cape and manned flights were being readied, the space agency began expanding its modest land holdings on the cape and Merritt Island. In 1962 it bought 84,000 upland acres and leased from the state of Florida another 56,000 submerged acres, most of which lie within Mosquito Lagoon. The cost of the expansion was $72 million.

Today, the southern boundary of the space center runs east/west along the Barge Canal that connects Port Canaveral with the Banana and Indian rivers, and parallels the southern tip of Cape Canaveral. From that point the tract extends northward some 30 miles, almost as far as New Smyrna Beach. The spread is bounded on the east by the Atlantic Ocean, and on the west by the Indian River.

From the beginning, NASA, the National Aeronautic and Space Administration, has maintained a good neighbor policy and left unchanged some vital features of Merritt Island's ecology and economy. The agency, in the course of its acquisitions, took over 3,300 acres containing 185,000 citrus trees; the groves were then leased to the former owner so he could care for and harvest the fruit. Beekeepers were paid by NASA to maintain hives for pollination of the citrus groves.

NASA also fenced off three private burial grounds containing 19 graves on its newly acquired property and permits relatives to visit them as they wish.

Meanwhile, wildlife continues to inhabit the area, apparently oblivious or inured to rocket blastoffs, the daily presence of thousands of space workers, and heavy vehicular traffic. Raccoons, bobcats, alligators, and wild pigs still roam the scrub palmetto on Merritt Island. And the Audubon Society still conducts, successfully, an annual bird census in the area, usually identifying more than 200 species.

On the cape, across the Banana River from Merritt Island, a rocket museum marks the site from which, on Jan. 31, 1958, the U.S. launched its first Earth satellite, *Explorer I,* and from which the first U.S. astronaut, Alan Shepard, was sent into suborbital flight on May 5, 1961.

The name of the cape—Canaveral—dates back for centuries. It was renamed Cape Kennedy upon the death of President John F. Kennedy, but in 1973 its original name was restored. The facilities on the cape remain known as the Kennedy Space Center.

MANNED LAUNCHES
PROJECT MERCURY RECORD

Spacecraft	Date	Astronauts	Highlights
Freedom 7	May 5, 1961	Alan Shepard	Suborbital
Liberty Bell 7	July 21, 1961	Virgil Grissom	Suborbital
Friendship 7	Feb. 20, 1962	John Glenn	3 orbits
Aurora 7	May 24, 1962	Scott Carpenter	3 orbits
Sigma 7	Oct. 3, 1962	Walter Schirra	6 orbits
Faith 7	May 15, 1963	Gordon Cooper	22 orbits

PROJECT GEMINI RECORD

Gemini 3	May 23, 1965	Virgil Grissom John Young	3 orbits
Gemini 4	June 3, 1965	James McDivitt Edward White	62 orbits/spacewalk
Gemini 5	Aug. 21, 1965	Gordon Cooper Charles Conrad	120 orbits
Gemini 7	Dec. 4, 1965	Frank Borman James Lovell	206 orbits
Gemini 6	Dec. 15, 1965	Walter Schirra Thomas Stafford	163 orbits
Gemini 8	Mar. 16, 1966	Neil Armstrong David Scott	Docking in space

Gemini 9	June 3, 1966	Thomas Stafford Eugene Cernan	Rendezvous space- walk
Gemini 10	July 18, 1966	John Young Michael Collins	Rendezvous spacewalk
Gemini 11	Sept. 12, 1966	Charles Conrad Richard Gordon	Docking
Gemini 12	Nov. 11, 1966	James Lovell Edwin Aldrin	Spacewalks

PROJECT APOLLO RECORD

Apollo 7	Oct. 11, 1968	Walter Schirra Donn Eisele Walter Cunningham	163 orbits
Apollo 8	Dec. 21, 1968	Frank Borman James Lovell William Anders	Voyage around moon
Apollo 9	Mar. 3, 1969	James McDivitt Russell Schweickart David Scott	151 orbits
Apollo 10	May 18, 1969	Thomas Stafford Eugene Cernan John Young	Descent to 9 miles of moon surface
Apollo 11	July 16, 1969	Neil Armstrong Edwin Aldrin Michael Collins	Landing on moon
Apollo 12	Nov. 14, 1969	Charles Conrad Alan Bean Richard Gordon	Second moon landing
Apollo 13	Apr. 13, 1970	James Lovell John Schwigert Fred Haise	Aborted after 87 hours
Apollo 14	Jan. 30, 1971	Alan Shepard Edgar Mitchell Stuart Roosa	Lunar rocks collected
Apollo 15	July 26, 1971	David Scott James Irwin Alfred Worden	Geological probe on moon
Apollo 16	Apr. 16, 1972	John Young Thomas Mattingly Charles Duke	Fifth lunar moon probe

Apollo 17	Dec. 7, 1972	Eugene Cernan Harrison Schmidt Ronald Evans	Geological probe on moon

SKYLAB PROGRAM RECORD

Skylab	May 14, 1973	Unmanned	Launch of a space station
Skylab I	May 26, 1973	Charles Conrad Joseph Kerwin Paul Weitz	Shakedown cruise
Skylab II	July 28, 1973	Alan Bean Owen Garriott Jack Lousma	80,000 photos taken
Skylab III	Nov. 16, 1973	Gerald Carr Edward Gibson William Pogue	85 day mission

APOLLO FINALE

Apollo-Soyuz	July 16, 1975	Thomas Stafford Vance Brand Donald Slayton	Linkup with Soviet spacecraft

Space Shuttle Flight Program

On April 12, 1981, shuttle flights into space with reusable spacecraft were inaugurated. Launched from Cape Canaveral, these craft are sent into orbit with regularity, carrying large crews that conduct experiments and launch both military and commerical satellites. Flights were halted temporarily in early 1986 when the spacecraft Challenger exploded after liftoff on Jan. 28, killing the seven astronauts aboard. Shuttle flights resumed in 1988.

The shuttle program received a boost with the building and supplying of the international space station but was again devastated by another tragedy, the disintegration of the oldest space shuttle, Columbia, over Texas on February 1, 2003, just 16 minutes from its scheduled touchdown at Cape Canaveral. All aboard perished and the program again suspended pending investigation. The tragedy was the first in which a foreign astronaut, Ilan Ramon of Israel, perished.

The space shuttle program ended in 2011. Its duties, primarily resupplying the International Space Station, will go to private space programs, rockets, and vehicles.

ASTRONAUTS MEMORIAL

In January 1987, NASA and directors of the Astronauts

Memorial Foundation agreed on a six-acre tract on which to build a monument to fallen astronauts. It is situated near the Visitors Center at Spaceport USA and features a 50-foot wide by 40-foot high mirror-finished granite surface that tracks the sky and names the astronauts who perished in the space program.

Killed While Training
1964—Theodore Freeman
1966—Charles Bassett
      Elliot See
1967—Clifton Williams
1991—Manley Lenier Carter

Killed in Fire Aboard *Apollo I*
January 27, 1967
Roger B. Chaffee
Virgil I. Grissom
Edward H. White

Killed in Shuttle *Challenger* Explosion
January 28, 1986
Greg Jarvis
Christa McAuliffe
Ron McNair
Ellison Onizuka
Judy Resnick
Dick Scobee
Mike Smith

Killed in Shuttle *Columbia* Disintegration
February 1, 2003
Michael Anderson
David Brown
Kalpana Chawla
Laurel Clark
Rick Husband
William McCool
Ilan Ramon

FIRST COMMERCIAL FLIGHT
The world's first regularly scheduled airline was inaugurated by Tony Jannus and his Benoist plane on January 1, 1914, when he flew across Tampa Bay from St. Petersburg to Tampa.

HIGHEST LAND
Florida's highest sections are (1) from Orlando south to Sebring, with elevations varying from less than 40 feet above sea level to 325 feet at the summit of Iron Mountain near Lake Wales, and (2) an area near DeFuniak Springs in the northwest with an elevation of 345 feet at Lakewood.

GAMING

Once upon a time, while illegal gambling flourished, Floridians believed legalized bingo offering small cash rewards was the road to perdition. Today, Florida is the nation's fourth largest legal gambling state.

The 2010 finalization of the Seminole Gambling Compact brought legal full-casino operation to the state. It had been inching in for years as the Seminole Tribe of Florida, treading lightly in their home state where they had spent years building a reputation as good corporate citizens, slowly tested Florida's resolve on the issue. In contrast, the tribe is credited with spreading Indian casino gambling throughout the nation, using precedents and procedures they set in Florida and, as consultants, encouraging other tribes to act, often less prudently, in their own states.

The state itself helped smooth the way to gambling's giant expansion by having long ago approved pari-mutuel events and more recently going into high-stakes gaming itself with the 1988 introduction of the Florida Lottery and enhancing it in 2009 when the Powerball national lottery moved to Florida and became part of the state's package.

The compact provides that the state keeps the $250 million already paid by the tribe based on the original 2007 compact thrown out by the courts. The tribe will pay the state a guaranteed minimum of $1 billion over five years. An alternative plan based on percentages could net the state more. Much of the financial arrangements are based on the tribe maintaining exclusivity in the casino arena. But even in this area, the state and the tribe have given each other room to move.

The state already takes in more than $2 billion annually from its lottery operations. Other legal gaming brings $150 million into the state's coffers annually. The weak link in the state's field is the pari-mutuels: the horse tracks, dog tracks and jai-alai frontons. They have been in decline in both customers and handles for the past 20 years, ever since the Seminoles opened their first bingo halls. To keep them viable, the state has allowed them to operate season and off-season local-option slots, distance wagering, and poker rooms, including the 2010 legalization of no-limit poker. As long as the issue has been viability rather than competitiveness, the tribe has not objected. The pari-mutuels, of course, are expected to continue pushing their envelope toward greater casino-like operations.

CASINOS

There are seven casinos operating in the state, six run by the Seminoles at Clewiston, Coconut Creek, Hollywood, Immokalee, Okeechobee, and Tampa. Their cousins operated the Miccosukee Resort and Gaming Center in Miami. Most have been relatively small operations, but the Seminole Hard Rock Hotels and Casinos at Hollywood and Tampa are already in the major leagues of casino operations. The Seminoles own the international Hard Rock franchise and have opened their famous Hard Rock Cafes in both casino resorts. Meanwhile, another tribe from the Creek Nation, the Poarch of southern Alabama, already a Florida pari-mutuel investor, has announced it will open Florida's first quarter horse pari-mutuel track and poker room at Gretna in Gadsden County.

PARI-MUTUELS

The state's pari-mutuel sites, with other gaming, are listed in the Sports chapter.

LOTTO

The Florida Lottery offers a wide variety of drawing and scratch-off games available through 13,000 dealers throughout the state.

The drawing games include Lotto, a six-ball game; Mega Money, a four-plus-one ball game; and Powerball, a five-plus-one ball national lottery. There are also lower-paying drawing games, Fantasy 5, Play 4, and Cash 3. The latter two are drawn twice a day. Fantasy 5, played daily, pays down the line if no one has all five winning numbers. Tickets for the games are $1, although enhanced prizes can be gained with additional dollars.

The odds of winning the jackpot in Lotto are 23 million to 1; in Powerball, 195 million to 1.

Scratch-off games number more than 50 at any given time with cards selling in a range from $1 to $20. Many of the games feature a limited number of very large payoffs in addition to minor ones. Information on how many large payouts remain in any scratch-off game is readily available. Some games are pari-mutuels, the prize depending on the amount played.

WINNERS AND LOSERS

The largest jackpot in the history of the Florida Lottery came with the Lotto win of $106.5 million in September of 1990. The winnings were split among six lucky ticket holders. The largest jackpot to go to just one winner was $81.6 million in March of 2000. The largest Powerball jackpot to be won by a Floridian awarded $189 million in October 2009. The biggest loser was the one person with the Lotto winning ticket who never claimed the $53.7 million prize in March 2003. Winners have 180 days to claim the prize.

HOW-TO FOR LOTTERY WINNERS

A Florida Lottery Department pamphlet advises Lotto winners about getting financial advice, dealing with the press, and paying taxes. Among the words of wisdom: "Consider using professional financial and legal advisors." And when talking to the media, "try to relax, be friendly, and enjoy the experience." The booklet also suggests changing the winner's telephone number.

ANTIQUES OK
Slot machines have to have been manufactured at least 20 years ago in order for their ownership by an individual to be legal in Florida.

TOLL-FREE NUMBERS

Following are toll-free phone numbers established by various agencies or private organizations to assist Floridians. Dial 1-800 before the listed numbers.

Abuse Hotline	962-2873
AIDS Hotline	342-2437
Alligators (nuisance/dangerous)	dial toll-free: 1-866-392-4286
Alzheimer's & related disorders information	621-0379
American Red Cross (information)	dial toll-free: 1-866-438-4636
Automobile complaints (Lemon Law)	321-5366
Automobile Safety hotline	424-9393
Banking complaints (Comptroller)	848-3792
Blind services	342-1828
Cancer Information	422-6237
Child abuse	342-9152
Child support collection	622-5437
Clean Air Act complaints	337-3742
Condominium Bureau	226-6028
Consumer information	435-7352
Customs violations	232-5378
D.C. Capitol Switchboard	284-2915
Department of Insurance, consumer service	342-2762
Department of Transportation	dial toll-free: 1-866-374-3368
Disability, comprehensive information	dial toll-free: 1-888-838-2253
Discrimination in housing and employment	342-8170
Domestic Abuse	500-1119
Elder Helpline (service information)	963-5337
Emergency (information)	342-3557
Emergency (reporting)	320-0519
Enviro-Line	828-9338
FEMA	621-3362
Fire and Arson	342-5869
Fish and Wildlife Conservation Commission, Wildlife Alert Emergency:	342-5367 or 1-888-404-3922
Fish Kills	636-0511
Marine Patrol	342-5367

Fishing Licenses (to order)	dial toll-free: 1-888-347-4356
Food Stamp fraud	342-9274
Funeral complaints	323-2627
Free credit report	dial toll-free: 1-877-322-8228
Hazardous/toxic materials information	367-4378
Health Cost Containment and Complaints	dial toll-free: 1-888-419-3456
Hepatitis C hotline	dial toll-free: 1-866-352-4372
Hunting Licenses (to order)	dial toll-free: 1-888-486-8356
Identity Theft hotline	dial toll-free: 1-866-966-7226
Internal Revenue Service	829-1040
Internal Revenue Service (TDD)	829-4059
Legislation, status	342-1827
Lemon Law (new car problems)	321-5366
Long-term Care Ombudsman	dial toll-free: 1-888-831-0404
Medicare claims and information	333-7586
Mildew hotline	543-8279
Missing and Exploited Children, National	843-5678
Oil and chemical spills, terrorism (national number)	424-8802
Park reservations	326-3521
Poison Control Center	282-3171
Professional regulation complaints	342-7940
Public Service Commission	342-3552
Radon Gas Hotline	543-8279
Restaurant complaints	880-7753
Senior Legal Helpline	dial toll-free: 1-888-895-7873
Sex Offender/Preditor Unit, FDLE	dial toll-free: 1-888-357-7332
Social Security	772-1213
Sport Fishing information	275-3474
State Bar Association (legal information)	342-8011
Telemarketing Opt-out	567-8688
Unemployment fraud	342-9909
Veterans (to report fraud and waste)	488-8244
Veterans Affairs	827-1000
Whistleblowers hotline	543-5353
Workers compensation claims	342-1741

ZIP CODES

32615	Alachua		33154	Bal Harbour
32616	Alafaya		34667	Bayonet Point
32420	Alfred		34207	Bayshore Gardens
32123	Allandale		33756	Bellaire
32346	Alligator Point		33430	Belle Glade
32702	Aloma		32809	Belle Isle
32714	Altamonte Springs		34420	Belleview
32421	Altha		34464	Beverly Hills
32702	Altoona		33043	Big Pine Key
33820	Alturas		33161	Biscayne Park
33920	Alva		32424	Blountstown
32461	Alys Beach		33921	Boca Grande
32034	Amelia Island		33431	Boca Raton
32080	Anastasia Island		34135	Bonita Springs
34216	Anna Maria		33436	Boynton Beach
32617	Anthony		34206	Bradenton
32320	Apalachicola		34217	Bradenton Beach
33572	Apollo Beach		33511	Brandon
32712	Apopka		32008	Branford
34266	Arcadia		33231	Brickell
32618	Archer		32621	Bronson
34679	Aripeka		34603	Brooksville
32033	Armstrong		33438	Bryant
34705	Astatula		32110	Bunnell
32102	Astor		33513	Bushnell
32233	Atlantic Beach		32404	Callaway
33462	Atlantis		32920	Cape Canavaral
33823	Auburndale		33904	Cape Coral
34142	Ave Maria		33946	Cape Haze
33160	Aventura		33924	Captiva
33825	Avon Park		33055	Carol City
33827	Babson Park		32425	Caryville
33830	Bartow		32707	Casselberry

32625	Cedar Key		32724	DeLand
32308	Centerville		32130	DeLeon Springs
32324	Chattahoochee		33446	Delray Beach
32626	Chiefland		32738	Deltona
32428	Chipley		32541	Destin
32709	Christmas		33122	Doral
32966	Citrus Ridge		32060	Dowling Park
34433	Citrus Springs		34698	Dunedin
33758	Clearwater		34432	Dunnellon
33767	Clearwater Beach		32751	Eatonville
34711	Clermont		32934	Eau Gallie
33440	Clewiston		32132	Edgewater
32922	Cocoa		32809	Edgewood
32931	Cocoa Beach		34222	Ellenton
33063	Coconut Creek		34295	Englewood
33133	Coconut Grove		33928	Estero
33001	Conch Key		32726	Eustis
33158	Coral Gables		34139	Everglades City
33065	Coral Springs		32693	Fanning Springs
32327	Crawfordville		32034	Fernandina Beach
34242	Crescent Beach		33310	Fort Lauderdale
32112	Crescent City		32136	Flagler Beach
32531	Crestview		34436	Floral City
32628	Cfross City		33034	Florida City
34429	Crystal River		33907	Fort Myers
33157	Cutler Ridge		33931	Fort Myers Beach
33525	Dade City		34981	Fort Pierce
33312	Dania		32548	Fort Walton Beach
33837	Davenport		33843	Frostproof
33024	Davie		32602	Gainesville
32114	Daytona Beach		33050	Grassy Key
32713	De Bary		32043	Green Cove Springs
33441	Deerfield Beach		32331	Greenville
32433	DeFuniak Springs		34736	Groveland

32561	Gulf Breeze	32159	Lady Lake
33707	Gulfport	32055	Lake City
33844	Haines City	33805	Lakeland
33009	Hallandale	32746	Lake Mary
32333	Havana	33852	Lake Placid
33409	Haverhill	33853	Lake Wales
34607	Hernando Beach	34202	Lakewood Ranch
33010	Hialeah	33461	Lake Worth
32643	High Springs	34637	Land O Lakes
33455	Hobe Sound	33460	Lantana
34690	Holiday	33770	Largo
33022	Hollywood	33062	Lauderdale by the Sea
33030	Homestead	33311	Lauderhill
34487	Homosassa	34461	Lecanto
34667	Hudson	34748	Leesburg
34142	Immokalee	33936	Lehigh Acres
32903	Indialantic	32064	Live Oak
33785	Indian Rocks Beach	32750	Longwood
32148	Interlachen	33549	Lutz
34450	Inverness	33708	Madeira Beach
33036	Islamorada	32340	Madison
32565	Jay	32751	Maitland
32203	Jacksonville	33050	Marathon
32250	Jacksonville Beach	34145	Marco Island
34957	Jensen Beach	33063	Margate
33458	Jupiter	32446	Marianna
33156	Kendall	34604	Masaryktown
33037	Key Largo	32066	Mayo
33040	Key West	32227	Mayport
34741	Kissimmee	32901	Melbourne
33935	La Belle	32953	Merritt Island
33859	Lake Alfred	33110	Miami
32630	Lake Buena Vista	33119	Miami Beach
32054	Lake Butler	33166	Miami Springs

32667	Micanopy	32137	Palm Coast
32068	Middleburg	34220	Palmetto
32570	Milton	34683	Palm Harbor
33023	Miramar	32401	Panama City
32344	Monticello	33019	Pembroke Pines
33471	Moore Haven	32501	Pensacola
32757	Mount Dora	33157	Perrine
34251	Myakka City	32348	Perry
34102	Naples	32808	Pine Hills
34653	New Port Richey	33156	Pinecrest
32168	New Smyrna Beach	33781	Pinellas Park
32578	Niceville	33563	Plant City
34275	Nokomis	33311	Plantation
33918	North Fort Myers	33060	Pompano Beach
34287	North Port	32082	Ponte Vedra Beach
33304	OaklandPark	33952	Port Charlotte
34478	Ocala	32123	Port Orange
32183	Ocklawaha	34668	Port Richey
34761	Ocoee	32456	Port St. Joe
34972	Okeechobee	34952	Port St. Lucie
34677	Oldsmar	33950	Punta Gorda
32680	Old Town	32351	Quincy
33165	Olympia Heights	33170	Quail Heights
33054	Opa-Locka	32026	Raiford
32763	Orange City	33156	Richmond Heights
32003	Orange Park	33523	Ridge Manor
32801	Orlando	33569	Riverview
32174	Ormond Beach	33403	Riviera Beach
32765	Oviedo	32955	Rockledge
32177	Palatka	33411	Royal Palm Beach
32905	Palm Bay	32084	St. Augustine
33480	Palm Beach	34769	St. Cloud
33403	Palm Beach Gardens	33706	St. Pete Beach
34990	Palm City	33730	St. Petersburg

34695	Safety Harbor		33617	Temple Terrace
33576	San Antonio		32780	Titusville
32771	Sanford		32784	Umatilla
34230	Sarasota		33594	Valrico
32958	Sebastian		34285	Venice
33870	Sebring		32960	Vero Beach
33584	Seffner		32162	Villages, The
33772	Seminole		32327	Wakulla Springs
34489	Silver Springs		34606	Weeki Wachee
32460	Sneads		33411	Wellington
32358	Sopchoppy		33416	West Palm Beach
34604	Spring Hill		34785	Wilwood
32091	Starke		34787	Winter Garden
34994	Stuart		33880	Winter Haven
34492	Summerfield		32789	Winter Park
33573	Sun City Center		32707	Winter Springs
33304	Sunrise		32096	White Springs
32692	Suwanee		34972	Yeehaw Junction
32301	Tallahassee		32097	Yulee
33309	Tamarac		32798	Zellwood
33601	Tampa		33540	Zephyrhills
34689	Tarpon Springs		33890	Zolfo Springs

STORM SURGE RISKS

Florida's Division of Emergency Management estimates that about 25 percent of the state's population resides in areas that would be seriously affected by a Category 3 or stronger hurricane storm surge. Regions of the central-southern Gulf Coast south of St. Petersburg are considered to be at the most risk because some 90 percent of residents live on land that would be submerged by swollen tides.

MILEAGES

	BARTOW	BELLE GLADE	BOYNTON BEACH	BRADENTON	CLEARWATER	COCOA	CORAL GABLES	DAYTONA BEACH	FORT LAUDERDALE	FORT MYERS	FORT PIERCE	FORT WALTON BEACH	GAINESVILLE	HIALEAH	HOLLYWOOD	JACKSONVILLE	KEY WEST
Apalachicola	312	449	480	324	287	342	518	293	507	407	411	122	196	512	510	234	662
Arcadia	50	104	139	53	94	144	174	161	162	46	100	465	183	168	166	241	317
Bartow		140	171	64	61	94	208	113	198	96	108	415	133	203	201	184	353
Bradenton	64	157	192		41	164	222	172	215	83	153	427	168	221	219	236	358
Brooksville	64	204	234	85	55	111	276	110	262	160	173	351	85	267	265	151	417
Bushnell	60	200	226	94	76	95	271	89	261	159	164	354	78	263	265	140	412
Clearwater	61	198	230	41		152	263	160	256	124	170	390	132	261	259	195	399
Crestview	413	547	577	422	385	440	616	387	605	505	508	33	294	610	608	318	760
Cross City	162	299	330	174	137	192	368	148	357	257	261	255	51	362	360	111	512
Dade City	42	181	211	72	60	107	250	109	239	138	150	373	100	245	243	161	394
DeFuniak Springs	382	519	549	394	357	412	588	359	577	477	480	47	265	582	580	290	732
DeLand	94	192	209	153	141	71	269	23	239	188	140	386	98	263	246	100	413
Fort Lauderdale	198	67	30	215	256	167	31	232		139	98	610	321	27	8	323	183
Fort Myers	96	81	132	83	124	193	139	208	139		126	510	229	145	143	287	275
Fort Pierce	108	72	69	153	170	69	130	134	98	126		515	225	125	106	220	281
Gainesville	133	263	293	168	132	156	332	97	321	229	225	301		326	324	71	476
Jacksonville	184	292	293	236	195	156	354	91	323	287	220	327	71	350	331		505
Jasper	204	334	362	232	195	224	402	160	392	304	293	247	74	397	395	89	547
Key West	353	222	212	358	399	350	156	416	183	275	281	765	476	161	175	505	
Kissimmee	46	140	167	110	97	50	217	71	197	141	102	415	126	212	205	152	361
Lake City	175	305	332	205	169	194	374	129	361	273	263	267	46	368	366	60	518
Live Oak	195	325	355	215	179	217	393	152	383	291	286	244	65	388	386	84	537
Madison	224	354	384	240	204	246	423	182	412	320	315	217	94	417	415	111	567
Marianna	326	463	493	338	301	356	531	303	521	421	424	103	209	526	524	234	675
Miami	211	80	54	229	270	192	7	257	24	146	123	626	334	8	17	347	158
Moore Haven	104	35	85	122	163	144	104	197	93	55	76	516	228	99	97	278	248
Naples	132	117	164	119	160	232	103	248	134	36	162	549	268	109	126	325	236
Ocala	97	226	253	134	103	119	295	80	284	193	185	326	37	289	291	99	438
Okeechobee	94	48	75	117	153	105	126	163	105	90	36	505	217	120	113	244	270
Orlando	59	157	184	121	106	47	234	55	214	154	116	398	109	229	222	133	378
Palatka	142	249	256	188	157	118	316	53	285	234	187	343	44	312	293	53	468
Panama City	353	490	520	364	328	382	558	334	548	448	451	66	237	553	551	265	702
Pensacola	459	592	623	467	433	485	661	436	650	550	554	40	339	655	653	368	805
Perry	208	344	375	219	183	237	413	188	402	302	306	210	91	408	406	130	557
Punta Gorda	75	105	155	59	100	169	163	187	163	24	126	486	208	168	166	267	299
St. Augustine	157	254	256	216	185	118	316	53	285	251	187	363	72	312	293	38	468
Sarasota	76	154	189	12	52	176	211	184	211	71	150	438	180	216	214	248	344
Sebring	48	94	123	79	109	124	162	140	152	86	85	460	171	157	155	221	304
Tallahassee	260	397	427	271	235	289	465	237	455	355	358	159	143	460	458	168	606
Tampa	39	178	209	40	20	130	247	138	237	123	148	394	130	242	241	196	391
Titusville	99	160	157	158	146	19	217	46	186	194	88	431	142	213	194	135	369
Vero Beach	94	87	83	155	153	55	144	120	113	141	14	499	210	140	121	210	295
West Palm Beach	158	40	10	181	217	127	71	192	40	121	59	569	278	70	48	279	223

	LAKELAND	LEESBURG	MIAMI	MIAMI BEACH	OCALA	ORLANDO	PANAMA CITY	PENSACOLA	PLANT CITY	POMPANO BEACH	ST. AUGUSTINE	ST. PETERSBURG	SARASOTA	TALLAHASSEE	TAMPA	WEST PALM BEACH	WINTER HAVEN
Apalachicola	299	254	520	522	223	295	60	168	295	500	263	301	335	76	291	469	312
Arcadia	62	121	176	180	147	107	402	505	73	160	205	79	80	309	89	129	60
Bartow	13	73	211	216	97	59	353	458	23	192	157	59	76	260	39	158	12
Bradenton	66	115	229	233	134	121	364	467	56	213	216	26	12	271	40	181	76
Brooksville	52	43	275	282	53	65	288	391	47	255	135	63	97	195	45	224	69
Bushnell	47	22	271	277	41	49	292	394	46	251	123	78	105	199	60	220	62
Clearwater	54	97	270	274	103	106	328	433	44	250	185	21	52	235	20	217	67
Crestview	397	352	618	619	321	393	86	53	393	598	352	403	436	150	389	567	410
Cross City	150	105	371	372	73	145	189	295	145	350	123	151	186	96	142	320	162
Dade City	29	43	253	257	63	61	311	413	25	232	145	57	83	218	38	201	44
DeFuniak Springs	369	324	590	591	293	365	67	81	365	570	324	371	405	122	361	539	382
DeLand	89	45	263	268	61	35	324	427	98	230	63	138	165	231	119	199	82
Fort Lauderdale	210	253	24	29	284	214	548	650	221	9	285	241	211	455	237	40	198
Fort Myers	109	167	146	151	193	154	448	550	119	152	251	109	71	355	123	121	106
Fort Pierce	121	157	123	128	185	116	451	554	132	90	187	167	150	358	148	59	108
Gainesville	121	68	334	336	37	109	237	339	124	314	72	145	180	143	130	278	126
Jacksonville	181	128	347	348	99	133	265	368	186	314	38	217	248	168	196	279	181
Jasper	191	139	405	406	108	180	182	287	194	383	124	211	243	85	196	352	203
Key West	365	407	158	164	438	378	702	805	376	191	468	381	344	606	391	223	353
Kissimmee	45	59	220	224	89	17	353	455	56	188	115	94	121	257	78	155	34
Lake City	162	110	376	378	79	151	204	310	165	353	94	185	217	108	167	321	174
Live Oak	182	130	396	397	99	171	181	284	187	376	117	195	227	85	183	345	188
Madison	216	159	425	426	128	200	152	255	212	405	146	220	252	55	208	374	224
Marianna	313	268	534	535	237	309	53	137	309	514	268	317	349	66	305	483	326
Miami	224	266		5	297	237	561	663	234	33	310	255	217	468	251	67	212
Moore Haven	117	159	107	111	191	143	454	557	128	106	240	148	119	361	143	77	105
Naples	145	202	110	115	229	194	483	589	155	143	292	146	107	391	159	160	144
Ocala	84	31	297	299		72	264	366	87	277	82	116	146	171	98	242	92
Okeechobee	107	148	129	130	180	108	443	546	117	96	206	145	114	348	133	65	94
Orlando	54	42	237	242	72		336	438	63	205	98	104	130	243	84	171	47
Palatka	130	78	310	314	54	92	281	387	139	276	28	173	200	184	152	245	127
Panama City	340	295	561	562	264	336		107	336	541	298	344	376	97	332	507	353
Pensacola	442	397	663	665	366	438	107		442	643	404	448	481	199	434	609	455
Perry	195	150	416	417	118	191	145	248	191	396	158	196	231	52	187	365	208
Punta Gorda	88	146	169	175	172	133	424	526	99	176	230	85	48	331	99	145	87
St. Augustine	152	106	310	314	82	98	298	404	168	277		198	230	201	180	243	145
Sarasota	78	126	217	223	146	130	376	481	68	210	230	39		283	51	179	88
Sebring	63	102	165	169	134	86	397	500	74	144	183	106	92	304	90	113	51
Tallahassee	247	202	468	469	171	243	97	199	243	448	201	248	283		239	412	260
Tampa	33	81	251	255	98	84	332	434	22	230	180	19	51	239		199	49
Titusville	94	75	211	215	105	41	369	471	103	177	99	143	170	276	124	146	87
Vero Beach	107	143	137	142	173	101	437	542	117	104	173	153	165	343	133	73	84
West Palm Beach	173	216	67	71	242	171	507	609	184	31	243	208	179	412	199		158

INDEX